Studies in the History of Medieval Religion

ISSN 0955–2480

General Editor
Christopher Harper-Bill

Previously published volumes in the series
are listed at the back of this volume

To Melanie, Steven, Samuel &
Leon - An

love,
Martin

Studies in the History of Medieval Religion

VOLUME XXII

THE DEPENDENT PRIORIES OF
MEDIEVAL ENGLISH MONASTERIES

Although hundreds of dependent priories were founded across medieval Europe, they remain little studied and much misunderstood. Usually dismissed as mere administrative units, many were in fact genuine religious houses set up for spiritual reasons. This study charts for the first time the history of the 140 or so daughter houses of English monasteries, which have always been overshadowed by the French cells in England, the so-called alien priories. The first part of the book examines the reasons for the foundation of these monasteries and the relations between dependent priories and their mother houses, bishops and patrons. The second part investigates everyday life in cells, the priories' interaction with their neighbours and their economic viability. The unusual pattern of dissolution of these houses is also revealed. Because of the tremendous bulk of material to survive for English dependencies, this is the most detailed account of a group of small monasteries yet written. Although daughter houses are in many ways unrepresentative of other lesser monasteries, their experience sheds a great deal of light on the world of the small religious house, and suggests that these shadowy institutions were far more central to medieval religion and society than has been appreciated.

Dr MARTIN HEALE is Lecturer in Late Medieval History at the University of Liverpool.

THE
DEPENDENT PRIORIES OF
MEDIEVAL ENGLISH MONASTERIES

MARTIN HEALE

THE BOYDELL PRESS

First published 2004
The Boydell Press, Woodbridge

ISBN 1 84383 054 X

The Boydell Press is an imprint of Boydell & Brewer Ltd
PO Box 9, Woodbridge, Suffolk IP12 3DF, UK
and of Boydell & Brewer Inc.
668 Mt Hope Avenue, Rochester, NY 14620, USA
website: www.boydellandbrewer.com

A catalogue record for this book is available
from the British Library

Library of Congress Cataloging-in-Publication Data
Heale, Martin, 1974–
   The dependent priories of medieval English monasteries / Martin
Heale.
      p.   cm. – (Studies in the history of medieval religion, ISSN
0955–2480 ; v. 22)
   Includes bibliographical references and index.
   ISBN 1–84383–054–X (alk. paper)
   1. Monasticism and religious orders – England – History – Middle
Ages, 600–1500.   2. Priories – England – History.   3. England –
Church history – 1066–1485.   I. Title.   II. Series.
BX2592.H43   2004
271'.00942'0902 – dc22   2003020726

This publication is printed on acid-free paper

Printed in Great Britain by
Antony Rowe Ltd, Chippenham, Wiltshire

Contents

The publication of this book has been assisted by
a grant from The Scouloudi Foundation
in association with the Institute of Historical Research

Figures and Tables

FOR MEL

Acknowledgements

One incurs many debts in writing a book, and I have been particularly fortunate in the help I have received over the past six years; indeed, many of those named below are habitués of acknowledgements pages, renowned for their generosity to fellow labourers in the field. I am especially indebted to Professor Barrie Dobson and Dr Roger Lovatt, who supervised the Cambridge dissertation on which this book is based. Professor Dobson guided me through the first two years of my research with tremendous encouragement and care, and since his retirement has continued to offer advice and help well beyond the call of duty. Dr Lovatt provided invaluable assistance during the drafting of the dissertation, and saved me from many errors, infelicities and overblown conclusions. Since leaving Cambridge, I consider it my great good fortune to have come to work in close proximity to Professor David Smith. He has aided me on matters large and small with the greatest generosity, and has read the entire manuscript in various drafts. Professor Nicholas Orme has been a wise mentor and friend, and a source of unceasing kindness, over the years. To all of the above, I am more grateful than I can say.

Several others have read parts of this work at various stages of production. Professor Christopher Brooke and Dr Marjorie Chibnall kindly read my first chapter, and their criticisms have improved it enormously; I am only sorry that I have been unable to take fuller advantage of assistance of this calibre. Chapter Six owes a great deal to the advice and expertise of Dr Chris Briggs and Dr John Lee. Professor Joan Greatrex read an entire draft of this work in an earlier version, and I am very grateful to her for her comments and for the interest she has taken in my work. The examiners of my Ph.D., Professor Jonathan Riley-Smith and Professor Christopher Harper-Bill, also offered much helpful advice and encouragement. Indeed, without their willingness to examine me at very short notice to ensure I met a critical academic deadline, this book would probably never have been written. Professor Harper-Bill has since proved a generous, and even talismanic, patron in all my endeavours. My thanks also go to Dr James Clark, Dr Peter Cunich, Dr James Davis, Dr Joseph Gribbin, Dr Julian Luxford, Dr Edward Meek, Kaele Stokes, Dr Benjamin Thompson and Dr Ted Westervelt for the help they have offered along the way. I am equally grateful to my colleagues at the Centre for Medieval Studies and the Borthwick Institute in York, who have provided such a congenial environment for my work over the past two years. And Dr Claire Noble deserves special thanks for first suggesting this topic to me as a worthy subject of research.

I am obliged to all those institutions which provided permission to consult manuscripts in their care. To the many archivists and librarians who have facilitated my studies I also offer warm thanks, and in particular to Alan Piper whose unflagging assistance enabled me to extract more information from a short visit to Durham than I would have believed possible and who very generously lent me his unpublished transcripts of the Durham visitation material. I am greatly indebted to the Arts and Humanities Research Board and the British Academy for the postgraduate and postdoctoral funding that has made this work possible, and to the Scouloudi Foundation and the Institute of Historical Research for a six-month fellowship to enable me to finish my dissertation. The Richard III Society, the Dean's Fund of the Faculty of Arts at Liverpool and the Sir John Plumb Charitable Trust have also given much-appreciated financial help. I would also like to thank Caroline Palmer and Pru Harrison of Boydell & Brewer for their hard work, expertise and above all their patience in the publication of this book.

My greatest debts are, of course, to my family. My parents have always supported and encouraged me in everything I have done, and I am happy to be able to offer them something tangible in return, with much love. I cannot say that Jonathan and Beth have assisted in the writing of this book, but the distractions that they have provided have always been welcome and great fun – at least in the hours of daylight. Most of all, I wish to thank my wife, Mel. I started work on dependent priories only weeks after we were married and she has lived with them ever since. Her support and tolerance has never wavered, even when I have withdrawn from the world to write for weeks at a time. The maps and figures below could not have been produced without her skill and extraordinary patience, and her proofreading abilities are greatly valued. This book is for her.

Leeds, July 2003
Martin Heale

Abbreviations

Amundesham	*Chronica Monasterii Sancti Albani: Annales Mon. S. Alb. a Johanne Amundesham, monacho (1421–1440)*, ed. H. T. Riley, 2 vols, RS, xxviii(v) (1870–1)
ANS	*Anglo-Norman Studies*
BL	British Library
C&Y Soc.	Canterbury and York Society
CBM	*Documents Illustrating the Activities of the General and Provincial Chapters of the English Black Monks 1215–1540*, ed. W. A. Pantin, 3 vols, Camden Society, 3rd series, xlv, xlvii, liv (1931–7)
CClR	*Calendar of Close Rolls* (HMSO, 1892–1963)
CFR	*Calendar of Fine Rolls* (HMSO, 1911–63)
Cowley, *Monastic Order*	F. G. Cowley, *The Monastic Order in South Wales 1066–1349* (Cardiff, 1977)
CPL	*Calendar of Entries in the Papal Registers relating to Great Britain and Ireland: Papal Letters, 1198–1492*, 19 vols (London, 1893–1998)
CPR	*Calendar of Patent Rolls* (HMSO, 1891–1916)
CUL	Cambridge University Library
DCM	Durham Cathedral Muniments
Dobson, *Durham Priory*	R. B. Dobson, *Durham Priory 1400–1450* (Cambridge, 1973)
EcHR	*Economic History Review*
EETS	Early English Text Society
EHR	*English Historical Review*
GASA	*Chronica Monasterii Sancti Albani: Gesta Abbatum Mon. S. Alb.*, ed. H. T. Riley, 3 vols, RS, xxviii(iv) (1867–9)
Greatrex, BRECP	J. G. Greatrex (ed.), *Biographical Register of the English Cathedral Priories of the Province of Canterbury, c.1066–1540* (Oxford, 1997)
Hist. et Cart. Gloucestriae	*Historia et Cartularium Monasterii Sancti Petri Gloucestriae*, ed. W. H. Hart, 3 vols, RS, xxxiii (1863–7)
HRH	*Heads of Religious Houses, England and Wales, I, 940–1216*, ed. D. Knowles, C. N. L. Brooke and V. C. M. London, 2nd edn (Cambridge, 2001); *II, 1216–1377*, ed. D. M. Smith and V. C. M. London (Cambridge, 2001)

JBAA	Journal of the British Archaeological Association
JEH	Journal of Ecclesiastical History
Knowles and Hadcock	D. Knowles and R. N. Hadcock (eds), Medieval Religious Houses: England and Wales, 2nd edn (London, 1971)
Knowles, MO	D. Knowles, The Monastic Order in England: A History of its Development from the Times of St Dunstan to the Fourth Lateran Council, 940–1216, 2nd edn (Cambridge, 1963)
Knowles, RO	D. Knowles, The Religious Orders in England, 3 vols, Cambridge (1948–59)
L&P	Calendar of the Letters and Papers, foreign and domestic, of the Reign of Henry VIII, ed. J. Brewer, J. Gairdner and R. H. Brodie, 22 vols (HMSO, 1864–1932)
Matthew, Norman Monasteries	D. Matthew, The Norman Monasteries and their English Possessions (Oxford, 1962)
Mon. Ang.	W. Dugdale, Monasticon Anglicanum, ed. J. Caley, H. Ellis and B. Bandinel, 6 vols (London, 1817–30)
Morgan, Bec	M. Morgan (Chibnall), The English Lands of the Abbey of Bec (Oxford, 1946)
NRO	Norfolk Record Office, Norwich
OHS	Oxford Historical Society
Piper, Jarrow	A. J. Piper, The Durham Monks at Jarrow, Jarrow Lecture (1986)
Piper, 'Stamford'	A. J. Piper, 'St Leonard's Priory, Stamford', The Stamford Historian, 2 parts, v (1980), pp. 5–25, vi (1982), pp. 1–23
Piper, 'Wearmouth'	A. J. Piper, 'The Durham Monks at Wearmouth', Wearmouth Historical Pamphlet, no. 9 (1973)
PRO	Public Record Office
PRS	Pipe Roll Society
PUE	Papsturkunden in England, ed. W. Holtzmann, 3 vols (Berlin, 1930–52)
Raine, Jarrow and Monk-Wearmouth	The Inventories and Account Rolls of the Benedictine Houses or Cells of Jarrow and Monk-Wearmouth in the County of Durham, ed. Rev. J. Raine, SS, xxix (1854)
Raine, Priory of Finchale	The Charters of Endowment, Inventories, and Account Rolls of the Priory of Finchale, ed. J. Raine, SS, vi (1837)
Registra	Chronica Monasterii Sancti Albani: Registra quorundam Abbatum Mon. S. Alb., qui saeculo xvᵐᵉ floruere, ed. H. T. Riley, 2 vols, RS, xxviii(vi) (1872–3)
RS	Rolls Series
St Mary's Chronicle	The Chronicle of St Mary's Abbey, York, ed. H. H. E. Craster and M. E. Thornton, SS, cxlviii (1934)
SCH	Studies in Church History

Sharpe, *Shorter Catalogues*	*English Benedictine Libraries: The Shorter Catalogues*, ed. R. Sharpe, J. P. Carley, R. M. Thomson and A. G. Watson, Corpus of British Medieval Library Catalogues, IV (1996)
SROI	Suffolk Record Office, Ipswich Branch
SS	Surtees Society
TBGAS	*Transactions of the Bristol and Gloucestershire Archaeological Society*
TRHS	*Transactions of the Royal Historical Society*
Valor	*Valor Ecclesiasticus temp. Henrici VIII auctoritate regia institutus*, ed. J. Caley and J. Hunter, 6 vols (HMSO, 1810–34)
VCH	*Victoria History of the Counties of England*, ed. W. H. Page (Oxford and London, 1900–)
Wilkins, *Concilia*	*Concilia Magnae Brittaniae et Hiberniae, AD 446–1716*, ed. D. Wilkins, 4 vols (London, 1737)
YAJ	*Yorkshire Archaeological Journal*

Map 1: The Dependent Priories of the Benedictine Monasteries of Medieval England (England and Wales)

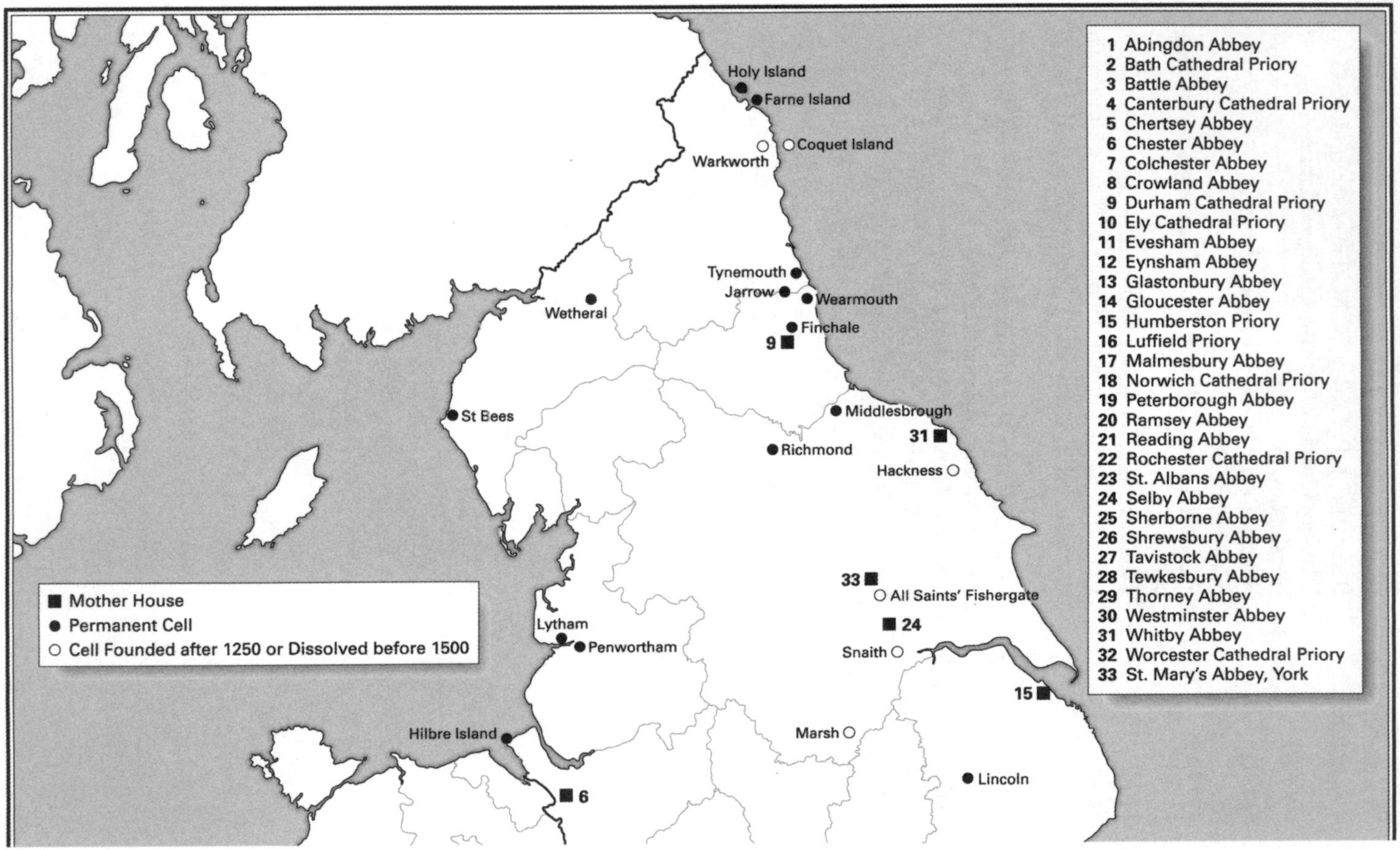

1 Abingdon Abbey
2 Bath Cathedral Priory
3 Battle Abbey
4 Canterbury Cathedral Priory
5 Chertsey Abbey
6 Chester Abbey
7 Colchester Abbey
8 Crowland Abbey
9 Durham Cathedral Priory
10 Ely Cathedral Priory
11 Evesham Abbey
12 Eynsham Abbey
13 Glastonbury Abbey
14 Gloucester Abbey
15 Humberston Priory
16 Luffield Priory
17 Malmesbury Abbey
18 Norwich Cathedral Priory
19 Peterborough Abbey
20 Ramsey Abbey
21 Reading Abbey
22 Rochester Cathedral Priory
23 St. Albans Abbey
24 Selby Abbey
25 Sherborne Abbey
26 Shrewsbury Abbey
27 Tavistock Abbey
28 Tewkesbury Abbey
29 Thorney Abbey
30 Westminster Abbey
31 Whitby Abbey
32 Worcester Cathedral Priory
33 St. Mary's Abbey, York

Holy Island
Farne Island
Coquet Island
Warkworth
Tynemouth
Jarrow
Wearmouth
Finchale
9
Wetheral
St Bees
Richmond
Middlesbrough
Hackness
31
All Saints' Fishergate
24
33
Snaith
15
Lincoln
Marsh
Lytham
Penwortham
Hilbre Island
6

Mother House
Permanent Cell
Cell Founded after 1250 or Dissolved before 1500

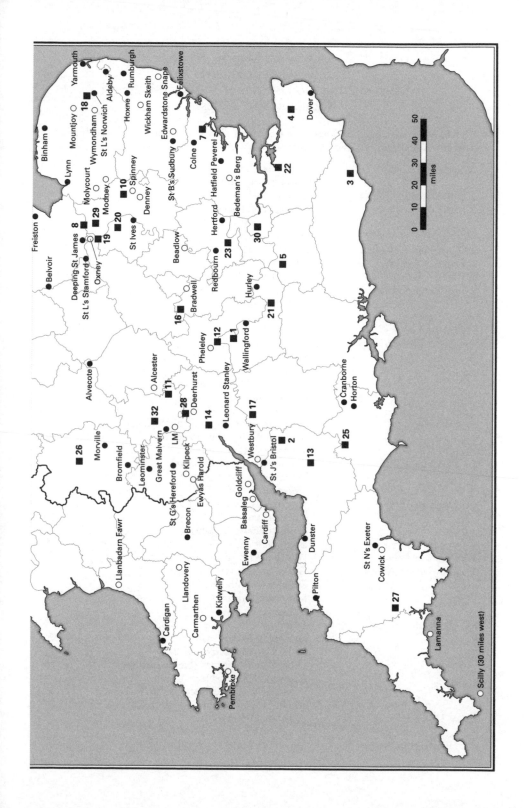

Yarmouth

Binham

Mountjoy ○

Rumburgh

18 ■

Wymondham ○

Aldeby ●

Lynn ●

Molycourt ○

St L's Norwich ○

Hoxne ●

Wickham Skeith ●

Edwardstone ●

Snape

Felixstowe ●

29 ■

Modney ○

10 ■

St B's Sudbury ●

Colne ●

7 ■

4 ■

Dover

Freiston ●

Spinney ○

Hatfield Peverel

Belvoir ●

Denney ○

Hertford ●

Bedeman's Berg ○

22 ■

Deeping St James ○

8 ■

20 ■

St Ives ●

Redbourn ●

23 ■

3 ■

St L's Stamford ○

19 ■

Oxney ○

Beadlow ○

30 ■

Bradwell ●

5 ■

Alvecote ●

16 ■

Hurley ●

Alcester ○

21 ■

Pheleley ○

12 ■

1 ■

32 ○

11 ■

Deerhurst ○

Wallingford

Cranborne ●

Morville ●

28 ■

Leonard Stanley ●

Horton ●

26 ■

Great Malvern ○

14 ■

17 ■

Bromfield ●

LM ○

Leominster ●

Westbury ○

25 ■

St G's Hereford ●

Kilpeck ○

2 ■

St J's Bristol ●

Brecon ●

Ewyas Harold ○

13 ■

Llanbadarn Fawr ○

Goldcliff ○

Bassaleg ○

Dunster ●

Llandovery ●

Ewenny ●

Cardiff ●

Pilton ●

Cardigan ●

Carmarthen ●

Kidwelly ●

St N's Exeter ●

Cowick ○

27 ■

Pembroke ○

Lamanna ○

Scilly (30 miles west) ○

0   10   20   30   40   50

miles

Key for Map 1:
The Dependent Priories of
the Benedictine Monasteries of Medieval England
(England and Wales)

NB On both maps, mother houses not numbered are shown in the maps as cells. Italicised entries indicate cells outside England and Wales, not displayed on the maps.

1. Abingdon Abbey	Colne (Essex)
	Edwardstone (Suffolk)
2. Bath Cathedral Priory	Dunster (Somerset)
3. Battle Abbey	Brecon (Brecknock)
	Carmarthen (Carmarthenshire)
	St Nicholas' Exeter (Devon)
4. Canterbury Cathedral Priory	Dover (Kent)
5. Chertsey Abbey	Cardigan (Cardiganshire)
6. Chester Abbey	Hilbre Island (Cheshire)
7. Colchester Abbey	Bedeman's Berg (Essex)
	Snape (Suffolk)
	Wickham Skeith (Suffolk)
8. Crowland Abbey	Freiston (Lincolnshire)
9. Durham Cathedral Priory	*Coldingham (Scotland)*
	Farne Island (Northumberland)
	Finchale (Durham)
	Holy Island (Northumberland)
	Jarrow (Durham)
	Lytham (Lancashire)
	St Leonard's Stamford (Lincolnshire)
	Warkworth (Northumberland)
	Wearmouth (Durham)
10. Ely Cathedral Priory	Denney (Cambridgeshire)
	Spinney (Cambridgeshire)
	Molycourt (Norfolk)
11. Evesham Abbey	Alcester (Warwickshire)
	Odense (Denmark)
	Penwortham (Lancashire)
St Nicholas' Priory Exeter	*Begerin (Ireland)*
12. Eynsham Abbey	Pheleley (Oxfordshire)
13. Glastonbury Abbey	*Ardaneer (Ireland)*
	Bassaleg (Monmouthshire)
	Kilcommon (Ireland)
	Lamanna (Cornwall)
14. Gloucester Abbey	Bromfield (Shropshire)
	Ewenny (Glamorgan)
	Ewyas Harold (Herefordshire)
	St Guthlac's Hereford (Herefordshire)
	Kilpeck (Herefordshire)
	Leonard Stanley (Gloucestershire)
	Llanbadarn-Fawr (Cardiganshire)
Great Malvern Priory	Alvecote (Warwickshire)
	Llandovery (Carmarthenshire)
15. Humberston Priory	Marsh (Tickhill) (Nottinghamshire)

Little Malvern Priory   *Castleknock (Ireland)*
16. Luffield Priory   Bradwell (Buckinghamshire)
17. Malmesbury Abbey   Pilton (Devon)
18. Norwich Cathedral Priory   Aldeby (Norfolk)
                                           Hoxne (Suffolk)
                                           Lynn (Norfolk)
                                           St Leonard's Norwich (Norfolk)
                                           Yarmouth (Norfolk)
19. Peterborough Abbey   Oxney (Northamptonshire)
20. Ramsey Abbey   Modney (Norfolk)
                                           St Ives (Huntingdonshire)
21. Reading Abbey   Leominster (Herefordshire)
                                           May (Scotland)
                                           Rhynd (Scotland)
22. Rochester Cathedral Priory   Felixstowe (Suffolk)
23. St Albans Abbey   Beadlow (Bedfordshire)
                                           Belvoir (Lincolnshire)
                                           Binham (Norfolk)
                                           Hatfield Peverel (Essex)
                                           Hertford (Hertfordshire)
                                           Pembroke (Pembrokeshire)
                                           Redbourn (Hertfordshire)
                                           Tynemouth (Northumberland)
                                           Wallingford (Berkshire)
                                           Wymondham (Norfolk)
St Bees Priory   *Nendrum (Ireland)*
24. Selby Abbey   Snaith (West Yorkshire)
25. Sherborne Abbey   Horton (Dorset)
                                           Kidwelly (Carmarthenshire)
26. Shrewsbury Abbey   Morville (Shropshire)
27. Tavistock Abbey   Cowick (Devon)
                                           Scilly (Cornwall)
28. Tewkesbury Abbey   St James' Bristol (Gloucestershire)
                                           Cardiff (Glamorgan)
                                           Cranborne (Dorset)
                                           Deerhurst (Gloucestershire)
                                           Goldcliff (Monmouthshire)
29. Thorney Abbey   Deeping St James (Lincolnshire)
                                           Trokenholt (Cambridgeshire)
Tynemouth Priory   Coquet Island (Northumberland)
30. Westminster Abbey   Great Malvern (Worcestershire)
                                           Hurley (Berkshire)
                                           St Bartholomew's Sudbury (Suffolk)
31. Whitby Abbey   Hackness (North Yorkshire)
                                           Middlesbrough (North Yorkshire)
                                           All Saints' Fishergate, York (Yorkshire)
32. Worcester Cathedral Priory   Little Malvern (LM) (Worcestershire)
                                           Westbury upon Trym (Gloucestershire)
Wymondham Priory   Mountjoy (Norfolk)
33. St Mary's Abbey, York   Lincoln (Lincolnshire)
                                           Richmond (North Yorkshire)
                                           Rumburgh (Suffolk)
                                           St Bees (Cumberland)
                                           Wetheral (Cumberland)

Map 2: The Dependent Priories of the Augustinian Monasteries of Medieval England (England and Wales)

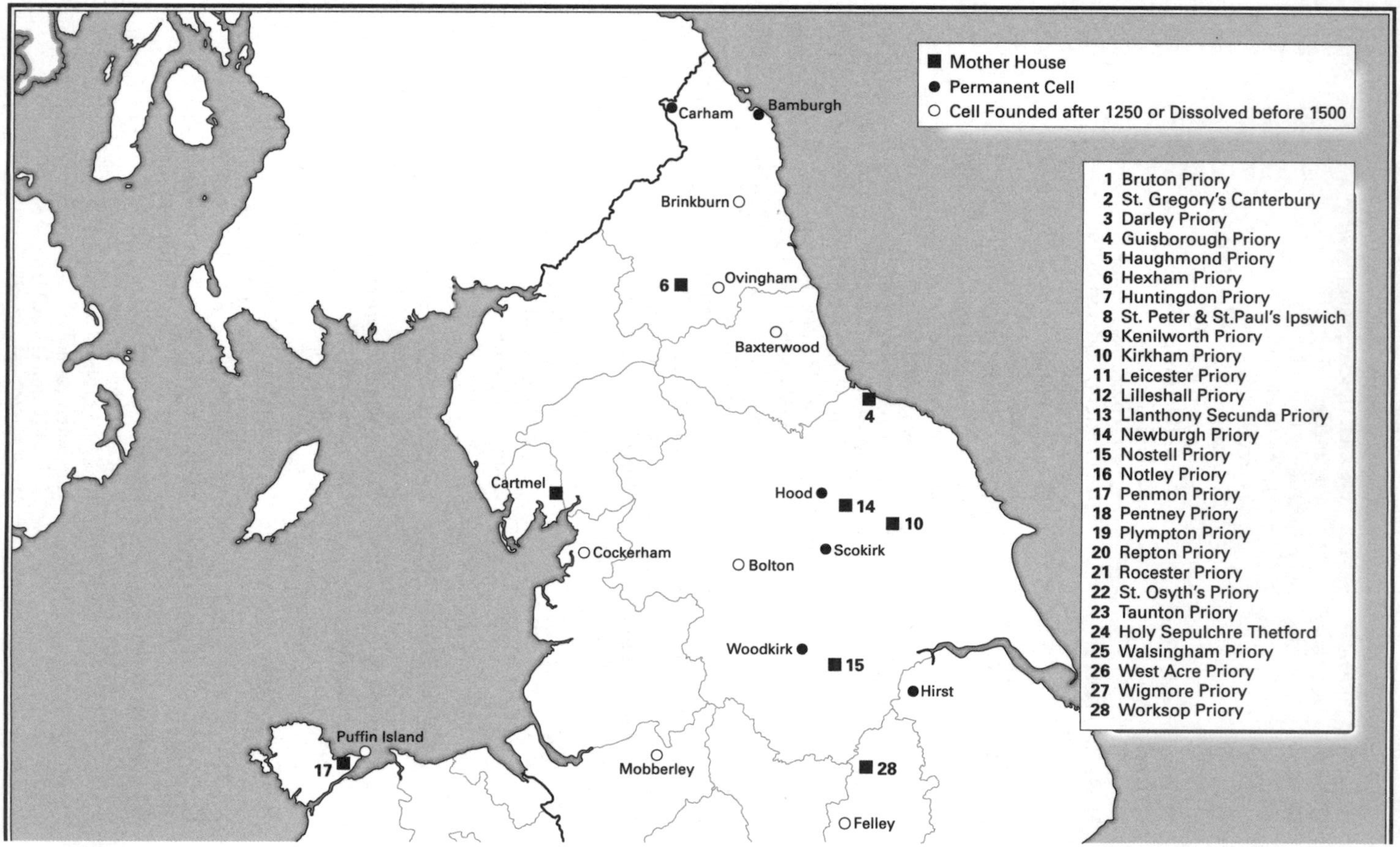
■ Mother House
● Permanent Cell
○ Cell Founded after 1250 or Dissolved before 1500
1 Bruton Priory
2 St. Gregory's Canterbury
3 Darley Priory
4 Guisborough Priory
5 Haughmond Priory
6 Hexham Priory
7 Huntingdon Priory
8 St. Peter & St.Paul's Ipswich
9 Kenilworth Priory
10 Kirkham Priory
11 Leicester Priory
12 Lilleshall Priory
13 Llanthony Secunda Priory
14 Newburgh Priory
15 Nostell Priory
16 Notley Priory
17 Penmon Priory
18 Pentney Priory
19 Plympton Priory
20 Repton Priory
21 Rocester Priory
22 St. Osyth's Priory
23 Taunton Priory
24 Holy Sepulchre Thetford
25 Walsingham Priory
26 West Acre Priory
27 Wigmore Priory
28 Worksop Priory
Carham
Bamburgh
Brinkburn
6
Ovingham
Baxterwood
4
Cartmel
Hood
14
10
Scokirk
Cockerham
Bolton
Woodkirk
15
Hirst
Puffin Island
17
Mobberley
28
Felley

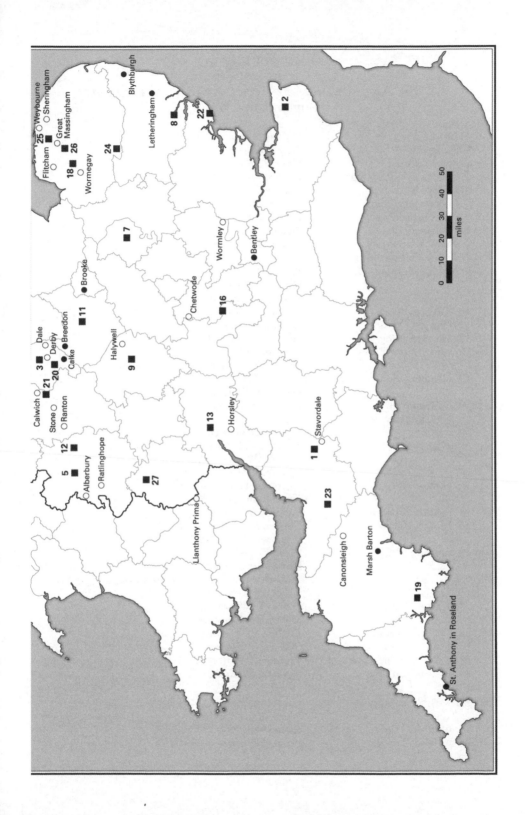

Weybourne ○
Sheringham ○
Blythburgh ●
Great
Massingham ○
25 ■
26 ■
Flitcham ○
18 ■
24 ■
Wormegay ○
Letheringham ●
8 ■
22 ■
2 ■

7 ■
Wormley ○
Bentley ●
Brooke ●
Chetwode ○
16 ■
11 ■
Dale ○
Derby ○
Breedon ●
Calke ■
Halywell
3 ■
21 ■ 20 ■
9 ■
Calwich ○
Stone ○
Ranton ○
Horsley ○
13 ■
12 ■
Stavordale ○
Alberbury ○
Rattlinghope ○
1 ■
5 ■
27 ■
23 ■
Llanthony Prima ○
Canonsleigh ○
Marsh Barton ●
19 ■
St. Anthony in Roseland ●

0   10   20   30   40   50
                     miles

Key For Map 2:
The Dependent Priories of
the Augustinian Monasteries of Medieval England
(England and Wales)

1. Bruton Priory
Calke Priory
Cartmel Priory
2. St Gregory's Canterbury
3. Darley Priory
4. Guisborough Priory
5. Haughmond Priory
6. Hexham Priory
7. Huntingdon Priory
8. St Peter & St Paul's Ipswich
9. Kenilworth Priory

10. Kirkham Priory
11. Leicester Priory
12. Lilleshall Priory
Llanthony Prima Priory

13. Llanthony Secunda Priory

14. Newburgh Priory
15. Nostell Priory

16. Notley Priory

17. Penmon Priory
18. Pentney Priory

19. Plympton Priory

20. Repton Priory
21. Rocester Priory

22. St Osyth's Priory
23. Taunton Priory
24. Holy Sepulchre, Thetford
25. Walsingham Priory

26. West Acre Priory

27. Wigmore Priory
28. Worksop Priory

Horsley (Gloucestershire)
Dale (Derbyshire)
Kilrush (Ireland)
Bentley (Middlesex)
St Helen's Derby (Derbyshire)
Baxterwood (Durham)
Ranton (Staffordshire)
Ovingham (Northumberland)
Bolton (West Yorkshire)
Letheringham (Suffolk)
Brooke (Rutland)
Calwich (Staffordshire)
Stone (Staffordshire)
Carham (Northumberland)
Cockerham (Lancashire)
Alberbury (Shropshire)
Colp (Ireland)
Llanthony Secunda (Gloucestershire)
Duleek (Ireland)
Llanthony Prima (Monmouth)
Hood (North Yorkshire)
Bamburgh (Northumberland)
Breedon (Leicestershire)
Hirst (Lincolnshire)
Scokirk (West Yorkshire)
Woodkirk (West Yorkshire)
Chetwode (Buckinghamshire)
Sheringham (Norfolk)
Puffin Island (Anglesey)
Brinkburn (Northumberland)
Wormegay (Norfolk)
Canonsleigh (Devon)
Marsh Barton (Devon)
St Anthony in Roseland (Cornwall)
Calke (Derbyshire)
Halywell (Warwickshire)
Mobberley (Cheshire)
Blythburgh (Suffolk)
Stavordale (Somerset)
Wormley (Hertfordshire)
Flitcham (Norfolk)

Great Massingham (Norfolk)
Weybourne (Norfolk)
Ratlinghope (Shropshire)
Felley (Nottinghamshire

Introduction

Of all the groups of religious houses in medieval England and Wales, the dependent priories of English monasteries are the least studied. This neglect can largely be attributed to the widespread belief that small daughter houses were unimportant appendages to their parent abbeys with no independent history of their own and often mere instruments of estate management. The more exotic 'alien priories', the satellites of French abbeys founded in England after the Conquest, have been able to attract considerable attention, primarily because of their dramatic suppression over a century before the general Dissolution;[1] but English dependencies have been much less fortunate. Yet a glance at the statistics compiled by Professor David Knowles and R. Neville Hadcock reveals that the cells of English abbeys and priories were an important part of the monastic landscape of medieval England and Wales.[2] About eighty Benedictine and thirty-four Augustinian daughter houses were established between the Conquest and 1250 in Britain, together with eight small cells in Ireland and Evesham Abbey's dependency of Odense in Denmark. Although thirty-one or so of these houses had lapsed, or had ceased to be cells, by the end of the thirteenth century, another nineteen were later founded or acquired as satellites by English abbeys.[3] Put another way, of about 130 denizen Benedictine houses in fifteenth-century England and Wales, thirty-two possessed at least one dependency and a further seventy-one were themselves satellites.

Another reason for studying English dependencies is the enormous quantity of documentation pertaining to them that survives collectively in the archives of their mother houses. Some of these parent houses, in particular the Benedictine cathedral priories, are among the best-recorded institutions of medieval England and as a result a wide range of source material survives for their cells. For many houses, numerous charters can be found in abbey

---

1 For the alien priories see Matthew, *Norman Monasteries*; Morgan, *Bec*; and more recently the work of Dr Benjamin Thompson, and in particular 'The Statute of Carlisle, 1307, and the Alien Priories', *JEH*, xli (1990), pp. 543–83; '*Habendum et Tenendum*: Lay and Ecclesiastical Attitudes to the Property of the Church', in *Religious Belief and Ecclesiastical Careers in Late Medieval England*, ed. C. Harper-Bill (Woodbridge, 1991), pp. 197–238; and 'The Laity, the Alien Priories, and the Redistribution of Ecclesiastical Property', in *England in the Fifteenth Century*, ed. N. Rogers (Stamford, 1994), pp. 19–41.
2 Knowles and Hadcock, pp. 52–82, 137–80. The information provided in this volume has been modified slightly in the appendices and the revised statistics given here are taken from that latter source.
3 See Appendices One, Two and Five.

cartularies to illuminate their early history whereas the affairs of others, in particular the priories of St Albans, can be followed in mother-house chronicles.[4] For sixteen Benedictine mother houses, abbots' or priors' registers survive which also contain information about their satellites.[5] The cells of Durham and Norwich Cathedral Priories are especially well recorded, most notably through their long runs of accounts. Although the large families of St Albans, Durham and Norwich are by far the best documented, and therefore form the basis of this study, there are also numerous survivals from other Benedictine daughter houses. Considerably less material remains from the Augustinian cells, but even these priories are often illuminated by mother-house cartularies and, for the later middle ages, by the records generated by the Crown or the Church. This harvest far exceeds anything available for independent monasteries of a similar size and indeed most medium-sized abbeys too, and it is deserving of much closer attention than it has to date received.

Historiography

It would be wrong, however, to imply that this store of material has been totally ignored. Local historians have often noted the bulk of documentation surviving for cells and numerous studies of individual dependencies have been produced. A good many of these are antiquarian works, several compiled by parish priests serving the former monastic churches, and though containing much useful information they lack critical perspective.[6] Even more helpfully, some amateur historians – most notably James Raine father and son – undertook, with variable success, to edit original records pertaining to their local dependencies.[7] More recently, scholarly editions of the surviving charters from Blythburgh, Ewyas Harold and St Bartholomew's, Sudbury, have been published.[8] Valuable modern articles have also been written on the Welsh priories of Brecon and Kidwelly and the work of Mr

---

[4] G. R. C. Davis, *Medieval Cartularies of Great Britain* (London, 1958); GASA; *Amundesham*.

[5] W. A. Pantin, 'English Monastic Letter-Books', in *Historical Essays in Honour of James Tait*, ed. J. G. Edwards, V. H. Galbraith and E. F. Jacob (Manchester, 1933), pp. 201–22.

[6] Many of the entries for dependencies in the *Victoria County History* exhibit a similar failing.

[7] E.g. Raine, *Priory of Finchale*; *The Correspondence, Inventories, Account Rolls and Law Proceedings of the Priory of Coldingham*, ed. J. Raine, SS, xii (1841); Raine, *Jarrow and Monk-Wearmouth*; *Documents relating to the Priory of Penwortham, and other Possessions in Lancashire of the Abbey of Evesham*, ed. W. A. Hulton, Chetham Society, xxx (1853); *St Mary's, Hurley, in the Middle Ages*, ed. F. T. Wethered (London, 1898).

[8] *Blythburgh Priory Cartulary*, ed. C. Harper-Bill, 2 parts, Suffolk Records Society, Suffolk Charters, II–III (1980–1); *A Register of the Churches of the Monastery of St Peter's Gloucester*, ed. D. Walker, in *An Ecclesiastical Miscellany*, Publications of the Bristol and Gloucestershire Archaeological Society, Record Section, XI (1976), pp. 3–61; *Charters of St Bartholomew's Priory, Sudbury*, ed. R. Mortimer, Suffolk Records Society, Suffolk Charters, XV (1996).

Alan Piper has greatly illuminated the affairs of the Durham dependencies.[9] Moreover, several archaeological and architectural studies of daughter houses have been produced, including amongst others notable studies of the material remains at Felixstowe (Walton), Finchale and St Leonard's Stamford.[10] However, very few attempts have been made to examine English cells as a group in the way that the alien priories have been studied.[11] As a result, although we know a good deal about several individual dependencies, the significance of this category of monastery remains largely unexplored.

As has been implied above, this oversight must be attributed to the view that most daughter houses were not genuine monasteries. This attitude can be seen in several of the *Victoria County History* entries for cells which justify a cursory treatment of a priory by dismissing its history as 'derivative'. But its most influential adumbration is found in the work of Professor Dom David Knowles, who remains the dominant authority on English monasticism more than forty years after the completion of his classic three-volume work, *The Religious Orders in England*. Knowles regarded cells as 'the most considerable of all the elements of spiritual decay in the monastic life of the country', and considered them to be abuses which went against the spirit and the letter of the Benedictine Rule.[12] Nevertheless, it is difficult to escape the conclusion that his implacable hostility towards dependent priories was to some extent the product of controversies within modern Benedictinism in which his own community of Downside played a major part.[13] His views on 'Benedictine monachism' were influenced by his first superior in religion, Abbot Cuthbert

9   D. Walker, 'Brecon Priory in the Middle Ages', in *Links with the Past: Swansea and Brecon Historical Essays*, ed. O. W. Jones and D. Walker (Llandybie, 1974), pp. 37–66; G. Williams, 'Kidwelly Priory', in *Sir Gâr: Studies in Carmarthenshire History*, ed. H. James, Carmarthenshire Antiquarian Society Monograph Series, IV (1991), pp. 189–204; Piper, 'Wearmouth'; Piper, 'Stamford'; Piper, *Jarrow*.

10 S. E. West, 'The Excavation of Walton Priory', *Proceedings of the Suffolk Institute of Archaeology*, xxxiii (1975), pp. 131–52; C. R. Peers, 'Finchale Priory', *Archaeologia Aeliana*, 4th series, iv (1927), pp. 193–220; C. M. Mahany, 'St Leonard's Priory, Stamford', *South Lincolnshire Archaeology*, i (1977), pp. 17–22.

11 The only collective studies of English daughter houses to date have been Professor Barrie Dobson's chapter on the Durham dependencies in the first half of the fifteenth century and Dr F. G. Cowley's monograph on the monasteries of south Wales, many of which were cells, between the Conquest and the Black Death: Dobson, *Durham Priory*, pp. 297–341; Cowley, *Monastic Order*.

12 Knowles, MO, p. 136. In particular, Knowles saw small dependencies as violating the central Benedictine concept of the religious community as a family: cf. D. Knowles, *From Pachomius to Ignatius. A Study in the Constitutional History of the Religious Orders* (Oxford, 1966), p. 6.

13 A. Clark, 'The Return to the Monasteries', in *Monks of England. The Benedictines in England from Augustine to the Present Day*, ed. D. Rees (London, 1997), pp. 213–34; D. Knowles, 'Edward Cuthbert Butler: 1858–1934', in *The Historian and Character and Other Essays* (Cambridge, 1964), pp. 264–362; C. Butler, *Benedictine Monachism. Studies in Benedictine Life and Rule* (London, 1919); A. Morey, *David Knowles. A Memoir* (London, 1979); C. N. L. Brooke, R. Lovatt, D. Luscombe and A. Sillem, *David Knowles Remembered* (Cambridge, 1991).

Butler, whose career was dominated by the struggle to free Downside from the central control of the English Congregation and from many of the demands of parochial ministry. Knowles shared Butler's belief that permanent ties of dependence were un-Benedictine;[14] and he also followed his first abbot in considering the placement of individual monks to serve parishes harmful to their own spiritual development and to the welfare of the monastery as a whole. It is therefore unsurprising that Knowles found the medieval practice of sending monks in twos and threes to man small dependencies so uncongenial. These are not unreasonable views, although they are not shared by every Benedictine monk.[15] But Knowles' refusal to see anything good in small daughter houses must be regarded as something of a blind spot and should not be accepted uncritically.

Definition of 'cell'

For Knowles and for many writers in his stead, the majority of daughter houses were administrative tools, with 'little that was specifically monastic or even ecclesiastical about them'.[16] Indeed, the word 'cell' is commonly employed to denote a small religious house established by a larger abbey or priory in order to manage its distant property. This usage has proved particularly popular among historians of the alien priories, who have needed a term to distinguish the tiny depots established by French houses solely to collect and dispatch the revenues from their English estates across the Channel from those daughter houses with genuinely monastic characteristics. This distinction was adopted by C. W. New in 1916 and more recently by such scholars as Janet Burton and Benjamin Thompson.[17] Nor is it simply a modern typology. A similar distinction was utilised by the government and the Commons as a guiding principle for the suppression of the alien priories.[18] We should be wary, however, of accepting fifteenth-century categorisations entirely at face value, since it was in the interests of the lay elites to maximise the number of French dependencies which were said to be performing no spiritual function and were therefore deserving of suppression.

---

[14] Daughter houses lacked 'the final perfection of autonomy', and 'such houses, however regular, lacked a fully responsible spiritual head, and so could never fully realise the life of the Rule': Knowles, MO, pp. 134, 687.

[15] For instance, see Morey, David Knowles, p. 130.

[16] Knowles, RO, II, p. 164.

[17] C. W. New, History of the Alien Priories in England to the Confiscation of Henry V (Chicago, 1916), p. 47; J. Burton, Monastic and Religious Orders in Britain 1000–1300 (Cambridge, 1994), pp. 29–30, which differentiates between dependent priories and 'the monastic cells, which were little more than economic units designed to administer the British estates of foreign houses'; Thompson, 'Redistribution of Ecclesiastical Property', pp. 21–3.

[18] Thompson, 'Redistribution of Ecclesiastical Property'; Matthew, Norman Monasteries, pp. 120–3. The principle being that houses whose main purpose was to send revenues back to France should not be allowed to survive.

As a result, the government's definition of what constituted a 'conventual' priory was altered in the early fifteenth century to allow a greater number of houses to be dissolved; and throughout the long process of confiscation the French mother houses argued loudly but ineffectually for a recognition of the spiritual services many of these satellites were said to be performing. Yet the dichotomy between the administrative 'cell' and the genuine religious house remains useful, and probably essential, for an analysis of the alien priories.

It is, however, a central contention of this study that only a small minority of the dependencies of English monasteries existed primarily for administrative purposes (see Chapter One). From this it follows that the distinction generally made between alien 'priories' and 'cells' is of little utility for an understanding of the English dependencies. Consequently, I have chosen to use the term 'dependent priories' in the title of this work to denote all English daughter houses. In the light of this usage, there remains the semantic problem of how we should employ the term 'cell'. Should it be avoided altogether, because of its unhelpful administrative connotation? To reserve 'cell' for smaller dependencies, as is sometimes done, certainly does not appear to be a satisfactory solution.[19] Apart from its arbitrariness (did a 'cell' transform into a 'priory' when a fourth or fifth member of the community was found?), this usage tends to reinforce the questionable connection between small dependencies and an administrative rationale. As a result of these problems of terminology, I have employed the term 'cell' throughout according to the medieval usage of the word *cella*: that is, as a synonym for daughter house, regardless of its size and function.

This usage of 'cell' is not to deny the importance of the distinction between conventual and non-conventual dependencies, which was crucial to the everyday operation of a daughter house. Rather it shifts attention to the dividing line between the small dependent priory, which retained many of the characteristics and functions of a religious house, and the administrative unit, or bailiwick, which just happened to be populated by monks or canons. This line is by no means easy to discern. Where a monastery sent out a solitary monk for a limited time to manage an estate, such as the monk-wardens of Christ Church Canterbury who were administering groups of priory manors in the late thirteenth century, it is clear that this does not constitute a cell.[20] But when a succession of individual monk-wardens were posted at a site, as was done at St Mary's York's properties of Sandtoft and Henes in Lincolnshire, the boundary between 'cell' and bailiwick or grange begins to blur.[21] Similarly, the numerous cases where houses of Augustinian canons sent out members of their community to serve as parish priests in cures some

---

19 Knowles and Hadcock draw a tenuous distinction between 'priories' with at least four religious, 'priory cells' with fewer than four and 'cells' with fewer than three religious: Knowles and Hadcock, p. 48.
20 Knowles, *RO*, I, pp. 38–9.
21 *St Mary's Chronicle*, pp. 4, 24, 80. Matters are further complicated by the designation of the monk who administered these properties as 'the prior of Sandtoft and Henes'.

distance from the monastery cannot be considered to comprise cells. Yet as reforming injunctions required the posting of more than one canon in such instances to dwell out of the monastery, such a settlement if regularly occupied might begin to resemble a daughter house.[22] These difficulties do not exist only for the historian; they were equally baffling to contemporaries. Therefore we find occasional references to the 'prior' of Caversham to denote the canon from Notley who was sent (with or without companions) to supervise the chapel of St Mary there and to safeguard the profits from the miraculous image of the Virgin it housed.[23] Similarly, a dispute arose in 1387 between the 'prior' of Duleek and the archbishop of Armagh over whether Duleek should be considered, as it was reputed to be, a priory and therefore subject to the metropolitan's visitation. In response, the canons of Duleek claimed that their house was 'not a priory nor a priory cell but a mere depot or grange' ('non prioratus seu sella prioratus set nudum receptaculum domus seu grangia'), for the sending of Irish revenues and produce to its mother house, the priory of Llanthony Secunda.[24] The canons were able to prove their case, and the archbishop declared them free from his visitation.

Despite these ambiguities, there does therefore seem to have been a discernible difference between the dependent priory and the bailiwick, to which the canons of Duleek could appeal. It is important to seek to understand this distinction, since our evaluation of this category of religious house will hang largely on our definition of what can be called a 'cell'. In his valuable Oxford D.Phil. thesis, Dr Edward Impey includes under the heading 'non-conventual cells' numerous monastic settlements which would in fact be better categorised as granges or bailiwicks. As a result, he naturally concludes that economic factors were paramount in the organisation of monastic dependencies.[25] How, then, might one define a cell so as to exclude bailiwicks and similar settlements? The essential feature of a *cella* between the eleventh and sixteenth centuries was its status as a (dependent) religious house; to denude the term 'cell' of this central characteristic would be to alter drastically its original meaning. For a monastic settlement to be considered a religious house, it may be argued that two basic criteria must be met: firstly the continuous presence of at least two monks or canons at the site (for either religious or economic purposes), and secondly the presumption

---

[22] For regulation against religious dwelling alone outside their monasteries, see for example *Councils and Synods with other Documents Relating to the English Church, II: 1205–1313*, ed. F. M. Powicke and C. R. Cheney, 2 parts (Oxford, 1964), I, pp. 92–3, 464, II, p. 786; CBM, I, nos 3, 13, 135, pp. 17, 38, 234.

[23] C. Haigh and D. Loades, 'The Fortunes of the Shrine of St Mary of Caversham', *Oxoniensia*, xlvi (1981), pp. 62–72.

[24] *The Irish Cartularies of Llanthony Prima and Secunda*, ed. E. St John Brooks, Irish Manuscripts Commission (Dublin, 1953), no. 92, pp. 281–6.

[25] E. Impey, 'The Origins and Development of Non-Conventual Monastic Dependencies in England and Normandy, 1000–1350', 2 vols, unpublished Oxford D.Phil. thesis (1991).

that the settlement was long-term.[26] Such a definition rules out the short-term posting of one or more monks to administer a grange or a distant estate, or even the dispatch of successive but solitary monk-wardens to fulfil a similar role. Similarly, it excludes pairs of canons sent out to serve a parish church, unless there is evidence that this was considered to be a long-standing arrangement. It does not, however, rule out short-lived dependencies for which there is good evidence of an intention or aspiration to maintain monks or canons in perpetuity, but which subsequently lapsed. One final element in the definition of a cell employed in this study must be taken into account. Only those houses staffed by professed members of the parent community or at least by religious of the same order who recognised the overlordship of another house are considered here to have been true dependencies. As a result, neither those nunneries with ties of affiliation to male monasteries, nor hospitals staffed by secular priests under the aegis of a monastic community are included below.[27]

Yet it remains the case that this definition leaves much room for uncertainty. We cannot always judge whether a monastic settlement was intended to be long-standing, and the numbers at a cell at any one time are often unknown. Assessing which houses meet these criteria is therefore problematic, as the example of the two Mowbray 'dependencies' established on the isle of Axholme illustrates. In the 1120s, Nigel d'Aubigny provided certain small gifts of land and food rents to 'the *monasterio* of Hirst and Ralph the canon living there, and after that Ralph the canons serving God there always in the hand of the priory of St Oswald [Nostell], for the love of God and for the salvation of my soul'.[28] D'Aubigny may have intended his foundation to be a hermitage, although he called it a *monasterium*, and it is usually said that only one canon at a time was ever stationed here.[29] However, between 1138 and 1148, the Hirst food rents were doubled by Nigel's son, Roger de Mowbray, in order that two Nostell canons should occupy the site; and some of his subsequent charters refer to the 'canons at Hirst'.[30] Although there are signs that a single canon was again dwelling at Hirst in the later middle ages,[31] the presence of two canons there for a time and de Mowbray's intention that

---

26 Dr J. C. Dickinson offered a similar, though slightly narrower definition of a 'cell', reserving the term for 'institutions with at least a handful of brethren where some degree of common life could be maintained', in contrast to short-lived settlements for the management of property or the service of parish churches: J. C. Dickinson, *The Origins of the Austin Canons and their Introduction into England* (London, 1950), p. 158.

27 Equally, the Augustinian priory of Burtle, dependent on Glastonbury but not staffed by its monks, is not considered a true dependency for the purposes of this study.

28 *Charters of the Honour of Mowbray 1107–1191*, ed. D. E. Greenway, British Academy Records of Social and Economic History, new series, I (London, 1972), no. 15, pp. 17–18.

29 E.g. D. M. Robinson, *The Geography of Augustinian Settlement in Medieval England and Wales*, British Archaeological Reports, British Series, LXXX (1980), p. 361.

30 *Mowbray Charters*, nos 215, 219, 221, pp. 151–2, 154–7.

31 VCH, *Yorkshire*, III, p. 233; Leeds, West Yorkshire Archives, NP/C1, p. 158.

this number should be maintained at the site means that Hirst can be considered a true cell according to the above definition. Around the same time as his grant to Hirst, however, Roger de Mowbray established a very similar settlement at Sandtoft, which he granted to St Mary's Abbey, York. But rather than arranging for two religious to occupy the site as at Hirst, Roger instead provided 'the monk of Sandtoft' with a canine companion, a mastiff who was 'to guard his house and his croft from strange animals'. There is no evidence that an extra monk was ever assigned to Sandtoft and by the end of the thirteenth century the settlement had been evacuated and its endowment amalgamated with that of St Mary's cell at Lincoln.[32] Although Hirst and Sandtoft are in many ways comparable, and were no doubt conceived by Roger de Mowbray as sister foundations, they fall on opposite sides of our dividing line: one man and his dog cannot easily be considered to make up a true religious house.

Although this distinction might appear arbitrary, it is nevertheless clear that many of the settlements sometimes designated cells were no such thing. Numerous attributions have their root in the researches of antiquarians, such as Tanner and Dugdale, who tended to accept a single reference to the 'prior' or 'priory' of any location as sufficient to demonstrate the existence of a cell. Inevitably this approach suffers from the imprecise vocabulary often used by contemporaries when referring to settlements like Caversham or Sandtoft. Therefore, where we are reliant on the unreferenced statement of an antiquary for the presence of a notional cell, it seems reasonable to exclude such sites from our enquiry. In other instances, it is reasonably clear that a projected dependency was nothing more than a monastic bailiwick or manor house, occupied by a single religious or by several only intermittently; such locations have also been passed by. In making one's way through this minefield, the historian of English monasticism is highly fortunate to have Knowles and Hadcock's *Medieval Religious Houses: England and Wales* as a guide. In numerous cases, the authors have located the source of dubious claims for the existence of a small dependency, and have demonstrated the lack of supporting evidence. In doing so, they have sought to distinguish between genuine cells and spurious ones; and in most cases, though not quite all, their judgement accords with the above definition of a dependent priory. It is always possible that additional evidence might arise that demonstrates that a shadowy and therefore excluded cell in fact enjoyed a long, if obscure, existence. But it is unlikely that the houses identified as genuine dependent priories by Knowles and Hadcock, and amended only slightly in the appendices below, will ever need substantial revision.

Scope and aims of study

This study sets out to examine the history of the 143 Benedictine and Augustinian dependencies of English monasteries, which seem to fit the

---

[32] *Mowbray Charters*, no. 317, pp. 205–6; *Mon. Ang.*, III, p. 617.

definition of 'cell' given above. The daughter houses of federated orders, like the Cluniacs, Cistercians and Premonstratensians, have been excluded, since filiation was built into the constitution of these orders and therefore almost every house could be considered a dependency. A number of small Cluniac and Premonstratensian houses, such as Mendham or Hornby, were dependent on English monasteries and bear some resemblance to Benedictine and Augustinian cells. However, it would be a distortion of these priories' history to study them apart from the affairs of their orders, and they have therefore been omitted. Moreover, it has not been thought necessary to include the very few examples of female dependencies in medieval England. Nunnery cells were considered undesirable for the obvious reason that small communities of two or three women might find themselves dangerously isolated. And although a handful of female houses which may be considered genuine dependencies were established in the twelfth century, the little that can be recovered about this subject has already been carefully analysed by historians of nunneries.[33] Finally, the university cells, which were *sui generis* and alone among English dependencies have already received considerable attention, do not feature below.[34]

Even within these guidelines, the sheer weight of documentation surviving for Benedictine and Augustinan cells means that much remains uninvestigated. Although covering the entire period between the Conquest and the Dissolution, the main emphasis of this work after the first chapter lies on the later middle ages (1300–1540). Moreover, the voluminous archive of Durham Cathedral Priory has not been examined with any thoroughness and I have relied heavily though not exclusively on printed material for the history of that house's cells.[35] No doubt much material concerning the English dependencies remains to be discovered in unpublished bishops' registers and public records. Perhaps most frustratingly –

---

[33] There is evidence that Nun Cotham and Catesby Priories were initially daughter houses of Swine, and that Langley Priory was founded as a dependency of Farewell. In the fourteenth century Seton is described as a cell of Nunburnholme and the prioress of Oldbury as removable at the will of the abbess of Polesworth. A few abortive efforts to establish nunnery cells or ties of dependence between existing nunneries are also recorded: see S. Thompson, *Women Religious. The Founding of English Nunneries after the Norman Conquest* (Oxford, 1991), pp. 70, 175, 195, 215–16; S. K. Elkins, *Holy Women of Twelfth-Century England* (North Carolina, 1988), pp. 53, 71–3, 185–6; HRH, II, p. 597. See also R. Gilchrist, *Gender and Material Culture. The Archaeology of Religious Women* (London, 1994), pp. 38–9; and B. Kerr, *Religious Life for Women c.1100–c.1350: Fontevraud in England* (Oxford, 1999).

[34] E.g. *Canterbury College Oxford, Documents and History*, ed. W. A. Pantin, 4 vols, OHS, new series, vi–viii, xxx (1947–85); Dobson, *Durham Priory*, pp. 343–59; R. B. Dobson, 'The Religious Orders 1370–1540', in *The History of the University of Oxford, II, Late Medieval Oxford*, ed. J. I. Catto and R. Evans (Oxford, 1992), pp. 539–80; M. R. Foster, 'Durham Monks at Oxford c.1286–1381: a House of Studies and its Inmates', *Oxoniensia*, lv (1990), pp. 99–114.

[35] This includes transcripts of unpublished Durham visitation material very generously supplied by Mr Alan Piper.

though inevitably in a study of this nature – it has been necessary to truncate discussion of numerous points of interest in order to prevent this from becoming an excessively long and unwieldy work. It is also in many ways regrettable that a Continental dimension cannot be included here, since the dependent priory was an extremely prominent feature of the monastic scene in many parts of Europe. It is hoped, however, that the conclusions of this study may not be entirely irrelevant to the cells of France, Spain and the rest of Europe.

But despite these caveats, I have attempted to provide a complete over-view of the dependent priories of English monasteries. Although it would be possible to write the history of the cells of Durham, Norwich or St Albans alone, the advantages of producing such an overview have seemed more pressing. Firstly, one of the most important characteristics of English dependencies was their diversity. The varied circumstances of their founda-tion or the different methods employed by mother houses in the manage-ment of their satellites could not be fully seen from the study of an individual family. Secondly, the kinds of sources surviving from different groups of dependency – principally accounts and inventories from Durham and Norwich and mother-house ordinances and chronicles from St Albans – complement each other well and allow a much more rounded picture of the satellite priory than would otherwise emerge. And thirdly, it would be impossible to appreciate the overall significance of numerous features of daughter houses, such as the role and motivations of laymen in their founda-tion, the sharing of their churches with parishes or the appeal of their saint cults, by concentrating on a single family of dependencies. Although an examination of the Durham or St Albans cells would be extremely valuable and would allow a much fuller treatment of the development of these prio-ries than is possible here, this study will take a broader approach.

It is divided into two parts. The first seeks to explore the relationship between mother and daughter houses. Chapter One examines the circum-stances in which English Benedictine and Augustinian monasteries acquired daughter houses. These are shown to be varied, but it is argued that a spiri-tual rather than economic rationale lay behind the majority of foundations, and that most were considered to be genuine if diminutive monasteries whose primary function was intercessory prayer. Chapter Two considers the constitutional position of different groups of satellites and traces the complex and shifting relations between mother and daughter house, bishop and patron. Chapter Three questions Knowles' dictum that cells should be considered 'a source of weakness to the house that owned them',[36] assessing the quality of discipline at dependencies and investigating the ways in which abbeys made use of their daughter houses.

If the majority of English cells were indeed intended to serve a similar

---

[36] Knowles, MO, p. 136.

function to independent religious houses, then it follows that they deserve to be studied as monasteries in their own right and not dismissed as mere appendages of their parents, or even as an 'abuse'. The second part of the book, therefore, uses the wealth of evidence for the English dependencies to try to shed some light on the obscure and little-studied world of the small religious house. Chapter Four examines what can be learned about the everyday life of these priories, including the range of activities and the standard of living available to the many monks and canons who spent time at a daughter house in the later middle ages. Chapter Five considers the relations of cells with their localities outside the monastery, arguing that their impact on the religious lives of their neighbours was often far more important than has been allowed. Chapter Six surveys the economy of English dependencies, utilising their numerous surviving accounts to reveal the financial pressures they encountered in the later middle ages, but also the resilience with which many small houses seem to have faced up to difficult economic conditions. And finally, the Epilogue provides an account of the unique path taken in the dissolution of English daughter houses, a process which tells us much about the ways in which contemporaries viewed these small cells. The extent to which dependent priories are representative of lesser monasteries in general remains difficult to judge, not least because of the paucity of research on the many smaller religious houses of medieval England. But it is likely that in some areas at least, the experience of cells can be used to offer insights into the problems and opportunities faced by all lesser monasteries. Nevertheless, the significance of dependent priories does not reside solely in their possible resemblance to other small religious houses. They are an important facet of the monastic life of medieval England in their own right, and the weight of information surviving about these houses is much too important to be cast aside lightly.[37]

---

[37] Cf. Knowles, *RO*, II, p. 363.

PART I

The Dependent Priory as Daughter House

1

The Foundation of English Cells

Origins

The daughter house is as old as cenobitic monasticism itself. The first communal Christian monastery, established at Tabennisi in Egypt by Pachomius (286–346), soon became the head of a small but tightly-knit group of houses founded as its offshoots.[1] Yet although this structure held together after Pachomius' death, it does not seem to have greatly influenced the development of Eastern monasticism. In the West, too, independent monasteries predominated. The first Frankish Council at Orléans in 511 and subsequent councils forbade the grouping together of monasteries under a single abbot, and the Rule of St Benedict (c.530×540) made no mention of monastic affiliation.[2] However, in societies characterised by overlordship, the principle of the mother church held considerable appeal. Where a single founder of sanctity established a number of monasteries, it was natural for each house to acknowledge the headship of the saint's own abbey. Monastic federations of this kind were particularly common in Irish monasticism and were spread widely by St Columbanus and other missionaries. Very little evidence survives about the strength and endurance of the ties that bound Irish houses together and it is quite possible that many affiliations were loose and fleeting. Rather more is known about the Ionan federation of houses, largely from Adomnán's *Life of St Columba*.[3] Iona possessed several daughter

[1] The 'Pachomian system' exhibited a remarkable degree of centralisation. The heads of all its houses were appointed by the superior-general, who regulated and supervised each monastery by regular visitation and through biannual gatherings at the mother house: P. Ladeuze, *Etude sur le cénobitisme Pakhomien pendant le ive siècle et la première moitié du ve* (Louvain, 1898); W. H. Mackean, *Christian Monasticism in Egypt to the Close of the Fourth Century* (London, 1920), pp. 91–110; D. Knowles, *From Pachomius to Ignatius. A Study in the Constitutional History of the Religious Orders* (Oxford, 1966), pp. 3–5.

[2] J. Ryan, *Irish Monasticism. Origins and Early Development* (Dublin, 1931), p. 272; *The Rule of St Benedict in Latin and English*, ed. J. McCann (London, 1952). St Benedict himself established twelve monasteries at Subiaco, before departing to Monte Cassino, but each was ruled by its own abbot: C. Butler, *Benedictine Monachism. Studies in Benedictine Life and Rule* (London, 1919), pp. 8–9.

[3] *Adomnán of Iona, Life of St Columba*, ed. R. Sharpe (London, 1995).

houses, all of St Columba's foundation, on both sides of the Irish Sea. The saint is shown appointing and recalling heads of these satellites, and there is some evidence to suggest that St Columba and his successors as abbots of Iona made visitations of their daughter houses.[4] Although much about the organisation of the Ionan *familia* remains unclear, it retained sufficient cohesion to persist into the twelfth century.

It may be that the dependent monastery was introduced into Anglo-Saxon England from Iona. The relations between Iona and Lindisfarne are entirely obscure, and there is no indication that there were enduring ties between the two houses. However, Lindisfarne seems to have inherited the Irish practice of exerting some level of authority over other monasteries and to have passed it on to other north-eastern houses. Abbot Aethelwulf's *De Abbatibus* is set in a *cella* of Lindisfarne, founded in the early eighth century, and Whitby Abbey possessed at least three dependencies, male and female, in the late 600s.[5] Indeed, Mr Eric Cambridge has argued from material evidence that dependencies were an integral feature of north-eastern monasticism at this date, although the precise relationship between these mother and daughter houses remains vague. Professor Stenton drew attention to another contemporary grouping of monasteries belonging to the abbey of Medeshamstede (later Peterborough).[6] In the late seventh century the abbey was granted land in 'Bredun' for the foundation of a monastery, and a monk of Medeshamstede, Hedda, was appointed abbot there 'on condition that he should acknowledge himself to be one of their fraternity'. Stenton argued that the preservation of records pertaining to the monasteries of Hoo, Bermondsey and Woking at Peterborough (the latter two of which were named in the twelfth century as daughter houses of Medeshamstede) indicates a significant level of dependence on that abbey. However, in the early eighth-century papal privilege granted to Abbot Hedda of Bermondsey and Woking it is specified that on his death a successor was to be chosen by the congregation of both houses from among their

---

4   Ibid., pp. 29–30, 43; M. Herbert, *Iona, Kells and Derry. The History and Hagiography of the Monastic Familia of Columba* (Oxford, 1988), p. 45.

5   *Aethelwulf, De Abbatibus*, ed. A. Campbell (Oxford, 1967); E. Cambridge, 'The Early Church in County Durham: A Reassessment', *JBAA*, cxxxvii (1984), pp. 65–85. Dr Sarah Foot, however, has argued that *cella* was often used as a synonym of *monasterium* at this date, and has thus cast doubt on the subject status of the monastery in *De Abbatibus*: S. Foot, 'Anglo-Saxon Minsters: a review of terminology', in *Pastoral Care before the Parish*, ed. J. Blair and R. Sharpe (Leicester, 1992), p. 220.

6   F. M. Stenton, 'Medeshamstede and its Colonies', in *Historical Essays in Honour of James Tait*, ed. J. G. Edwards, V. H. Galbraith and E. F. Jacob (Manchester, 1933), pp. 313–26; F. M. Stenton, *Anglo-Saxon England*, 3rd edn (Oxford, 1971), p. 160. The monastery of Brixworth was also said in the twelfth century to have been founded by Medeshamstede, although no other evidence survives to support this statement: *The Peterborough Chronicle of Hugh Candidus*, ed. C. Mellows and W. T. Mellows (Peterborough, 1941), p. 8.

own number, with no mention of the rights of Medeshamstede.[7] Whatever links existed between Medeshamstede and its offshoots, then, were evidently much less restrictive than later became commonplace.

There survives a little more evidence for the establishment of daughter houses in Anglo-Saxon England after the tenth-century monastic revival. No lasting affiliations resulted from the leadership of Glastonbury, Abingdon and Westbury in the restoration of Anglo-Saxon monasticism and it was not until the early eleventh century that signs of more binding ties of dependence can be seen. Perhaps in c.1017, a cell of Ramsey Abbey was founded at St Ives on the site where the body of St Ivo had been discovered a few years before. Similarly, between 1047 and 1064, a monk of St Benet Holme was permitted to dwell in a 'certain cell called Rumburgh', which was to be subject to Holme.[8] There might also have been pre-Conquest dependencies of some kind at Alkborough, Tewkesbury and Thetford.[9] The precise nature of the dependence of pre-1066 daughter houses to their parent abbeys is obscured by the fact that much of the evidence for these relationships comes from the post-Conquest period, when clear motives for the exaggeration of old connections had sometimes arisen. This is particularly true for the priories of St Neots and Spalding, said to have been cells of Ely and Crowland respectively. Dr Chibnall has cast serious doubt on Ely's twelfth-century claims that St Neots Priory had been their closely-controlled satellite before its re-foundation as a cell of Bec in the 1080s. The *Liber Eliensis* claimed that three Ely monks were expelled from the priory by Gilbert, count of Eu, whose son, Richard fitz Gilbert de Clare, gave the house to Bec. However, Domesday evidence shows that the original endowment of St Neots had been scattered by 1086, suggesting that the priory had lapsed before the Conquest, probably as the result of Danish raids.[10] The later Crowland account of how Ivo Taillebois drove out three of the abbey's monks from their cell at Spalding to replace them with brethren from St Nicholas' Angers, at around the same time, is also highly dubious.[11] Although Professor Knowles and Dr Burton are wrong to state that no

---

[7] Stenton, 'Medeshamstede', pp. 320–1.

[8] *The Register of St Benet Holme, 1020–1210*, ed. J. R. West, 2 vols, Norfolk Record Society, ii–iii (1932), I, no. 159, pp. 89–90. There were twelve monks at 'Wisseta' in 1086 (Rumburgh lay in the parish of Wisset): *Domesday Book*, ed. A. Farley and H. Ellis, 4 vols (HMSO, 1783–1816), II, p. 293a.

[9] Knowles and Hadcock, pp. 58–9, 77–8. The 'cell' of Bury St Edmunds at Thetford, however, does not seem to have been occupied by monks of the abbey: *Mon. Ang.*, III, pp. 477–8, no. 1.

[10] *Liber Eliensis*, ed. E. O. Blake, Camden Society, 3rd series, xcii (1962), pp. 102–4, 188–9; M. Chibnall, 'History of the Priory of St Neots', *Proceedings of the Cambridgeshire Antiquarian Society*, lix (1966), pp. 67–74.

[11] Pseudo-Ingulph is the earliest source for the story that a cell of Crowland was founded at Spalding by Thorold de Bukenhale in 1052, in an obviously forged charter: *VCH, Lincolnshire*, II, p. 106; F. M. Page, *The Estates of Crowland Abbey: A Study in Manorial Organisation* (Cambridge, 1934), p. 6n.

dependencies were to be found in England at the Norman Conquest, the precise relations between the few mother and daughter houses that did exist at that date are far from clear.[12] The origins of the great expansion of the satellite priory must be sought on the Continent.

Cluny and its Imitators

Although their history is obscure, some small dependencies certainly existed in Carolingian Europe. The 817 decrees of Benedict of Aniane permitted abbeys to possess *cellae* provided no fewer than six monks dwelt therein.[13] Indeed, as the numbers of monks at Aniane became unmanageable, Benedict himself was said to have 'built cells in suitable places, in which he placed monks with masters set over them.'[14] But it was the development of the Cluniac order that transformed the dependent priory from an occasional anomaly into a central feature of the monastic landscape.[15] This change was gradual and far from inevitable. As her reputation grew, Cluny's abbots were much in demand as agents of reform in the monasteries of tenth-century France. In the majority of reformed houses, Cluniac customs were adopted but no permanent links with the abbey were established; although occasionally during the course of the tenth century, lay patrons gave monasteries to Cluny on a permanent basis in order that they should share in that abbey's practices and privileges. Estimates vary, but at least a dozen Cluniac dependencies had been acquired by the death of Abbot Maiolus in 994. Under Abbot Odilo (994–1048), the absorption of reformed monasteries into the Cluniac family began in earnest, with the abbey having accumulated over fifty daughter houses at his death. It is not entirely clear what caused this critical development. The abbey of Gorze, which was as influential in reforming monasteries in tenth-century Germany as Cluny was in France, never took the step of subjecting abbeys to its jurisdiction. But it may well

---

12 Knowles, MO, p. 100; J. Burton, *The Monastic Order in Yorkshire, 1069–1215* (Cambridge, 1999), p. 4.

13 Two different versions of this edict survive. Two mid-ninth-century copies of the legislation specify six as the minimum number allowed in a cell, whereas the twelfth-century manuscript used by Hallinger as the main authority for Benedict's decrees specified a minimum of two monks. This discrepancy may well represent a later liberalisation as the small dependency became more common: *Corpus Consuetudinum Monasticarum*, ed. K. Hallinger, I (Siegburg, 1963), pp. 474, 550, 559.

14 W. Williams, 'St Benedict of Aniane', *Downside Review*, new series, xxxv (1936), p. 365.

15 No systematic account of the formation of the Cluniac order and the relations between the mother house and its daughters has yet been written. The outlines of the expansion can be followed in a number of works, most notably: J. Evans, *Monastic Life at Cluny 910–1157* (Oxford, 1931); Knowles, MO, pp. 145–50; N. Hunt, *Cluny under Saint Hugh 1049–1109* (London, 1967); H. E. J. Cowdrey, *The Cluniacs and the Gregorian Reform* (Oxford, 1970); and G. Constable, *Cluniac Studies* (London, 1980).

be, as Professor Cowdrey has suggested, that the growing body of Cluny's papal privileges and their extension to all the abbey's dependencies in the early eleventh century provided the impetus for this expansion.[16] In any case, it was the abbacy of St Hugh (1049–1109) that witnessed the tremendous explosion in daughter houses that marks out the Cluniac order as radically different from any grouping of monasteries that had preceded it: by the end of Hugh's rule perhaps a thousand houses, spread across western Europe, acknowledged their dependence on Cluny.

This remarkable expansion proceeded in a haphazard manner and the Cluniac body remained relatively decentralised under St Hugh. A number of houses subject to Cluny retained the status of abbeys and in practice enjoyed considerable independence. Many others were essentially economic units, established to manage outlying estates, rather than priories. But although the Cluniacs had not by this time established a 'highly organised, strictly centralised system' by later monastic standards,[17] the ties binding its many daughter houses to Cluny by the end of the eleventh century were far stronger than those linking the much looser confederations of houses that had come before. As Noreen Hunt has demonstrated, Cluny's authority over its daughter houses was based on charters of gift, which provided a clear juridical link between abbey and dependency and implied a permanence for this relationship that had previously been lacking. Although the status of Cluny's daughter houses varied, certain fundamental marks of dependence were almost everywhere in evidence by the time of Hugh's abbacy. All monks of Cluniac houses were considered inmates of the mother house and received their profession from the abbot of Cluny alone; the priors of daughter houses were appointed by the abbot as his deputies and were subject to his visitation; and modest tributes, as a mark of subjection, were owed to Cluny from all its satellites. Although further measures of centralisation, such as annual general chapters, did not develop at Cluny until the thirteenth century, already by the time of Abbot Hugh the essential characteristics of the permanent daughter house had been established.

In Cluny's stead, a number of aggrandising Continental houses, mostly French abbeys, set about acquiring their own congregations of dependencies which were tightly controlled in the Cluniac manner.[18] By the middle of the eleventh century, abbeys like Charroux, Marmoutier and St-Florent-les-Saumur had begun to accumulate daughter houses on a considerable scale. Dependencies were therefore being founded all over northern France,

---

[16] In 1024, Pope John XIX declared that all Cluniac monks, 'wherever they may be placed', were exempt from episcopal jurisdiction: Cowdrey, *Cluniacs and Gregorian Reform*, pp. 70–1.

[17] Hunt, *Cluny under Saint Hugh*, p. 184.

[18] For an outline of all the families of daughter houses in medieval Europe, see P.-R. Gaussin, *L'Europe des ordres et des congrégations*, CERCOM (Saint-Etienne, 1984). This volume provides only rough statistics and does not take into account differing levels of dependence, and so must be used cautiously.

including Normandy, at the time of the Norman invasion and this process was naturally imported into England after 1066.[19] It is against the backdrop of the massive expansion of the great French houses' families that the far more modest groupings of daughter houses established in England must be seen. From the very first, the Conqueror's newly enriched companions lavished English lands and churches on their favoured home monasteries, resulting in a network of French dependencies across the Channel: the so-called 'alien priories'.[20] By 1086, lands to the value of well over £1,000 had passed to foreign houses and up to 130 'priories' eventually sprang from these grants in England and Wales. These French dependencies have been well studied by historians. Much less familiar, though hardly less important, are the daughter houses of English monasteries founded at the same time.

English Foundations

The only study to date to focus on the foundation of English dependencies is Dr Marjorie Chibnall's 'Le problème des réseaux monastiques en Angleterre', which deals primarily with the satellites of St Albans, but also discusses those of Durham and Gloucester.[21] In the light of the large number of such foundations in Anglo-Norman England, not to mention the wealth of research on twelfth-century monasticism, this neglect is surprising. In all, about eighty Benedictine and thirty-four Augustinian priories dependent on English abbeys were founded in Britain between the Conquest and c.1250, along with eight Irish cells and the priory of Odense in Denmark (see Appendix One).[22] This figure of about 123 English dependencies compares with the foundation of up to 130 alien priories, twenty-three independent Benedictine foundations, about 183 independent Augustinian houses,

---

19 M. Chibnall, 'Monastic Foundations in England and Normandy, 1066–1189', in *England and Normandy in the Middle Ages*, ed. D. Bates and A. Curry (London, 1994), pp. 37–49.

20 For the foundation of the alien priories, see in particular Matthew, *Norman Monasteries*, pp. 27–71; Morgan, *Bec*, pp. 9–25; and R. Graham, 'Four Alien Priories in Monmouthshire', *JBAA*, new series, xxxv (1929), pp. 102–21.

21 M. Chibnall, 'Le problème des réseaux monastiques en Angleterre', in *Naissance et fonctionnement des réseaux monastiques et canoniaux*, CERCOM (Saint-Etienne, 1991), pp. 341–52, reprinted in M. Chibnall, *Piety, Power and History in Medieval England and Normandy* (Aldershot, 2000). The foundation of English cells also receives occasional notice in E. Cownie, *Religious Patronage in Anglo-Norman England 1066–1135* (London, 1998).

22 Twelve Evesham monks were sent to colonise the newly founded cathedral priory of Odense in 1095 or 1096, on the request of the Danish king, Eric the Good. Evesham's hold over the priory was always limited, however, and Odense was effectively an independent house after the twelfth century: Knowles, MO, pp. 163–4; C. A. J. France, 'English Influence on Danish Monasticism', *Downside Review*, lxxviii (1960), pp. 181–91.

seventy-one Cistercian abbeys and around 137 nunneries between the same dates.[23]

The first post-Conquest English cell was probably Belvoir Priory, a satellite of St Albans, established some time between 1076 and 1088 by Robert de Tosny. By the end of the eleventh century, at least a further eleven Benedictine dependencies had been set up. But it was during the reigns of Henry I and Stephen that the foundation of English cells was most fashionable, and when about half of the total number were established at a rate of one per year. New dependencies continued to be founded regularly throughout the remainder of the twelfth century, before becoming increasingly rare in the first half of the thirteenth. A relatively high proportion of these later foundations were Augustinian cells, reflecting the patterns of the establishment of independent houses of the order; indeed, more than half of all Augustinian daughter houses were set up after 1150. The Irish dependencies were also prominent among the later foundations, with every one established in the generation following the Anglo-Norman invasion of 1169.

The geographical distribution of daughter houses is also of interest. Every region controlled by the Norman conquerors saw the establishment of at least one dependency, although satellite priories were far more common in some areas than others (see Maps). But the most obvious conclusion to draw from these maps is the way in which the location of Benedictine and Augustinian cells mirrors that of the independent houses of their orders.[24] Those areas where Benedictine abbeys were most prominent, in particular East Anglia, the fenlands and the Severn valley, saw the greatest concentration of black monk dependencies. In contrast, very few Benedictine cells were established in the Midlands and the north of England where independent abbeys of this order were scarce. Similarly, the greatest number of Augustinian cells can be found in the Midlands, a region in which the black canons were very well represented, no doubt at least partly to fill the void left by the Benedictines. Indeed it is only for south Wales, an area where independent Benedictine houses were unknown but black monk cells not uncommon, that this pattern breaks down.

The distribution of cells among mother houses appears at first glance to be rather more perplexing (see the keys to the Maps for a list of cells arranged according to mother house). Although no English abbey possessed a large family of daughter houses on the Continental scale,[25] thirty-six Benedictine monasteries acquired at least one cell. Augustinian dependencies were less common, but twenty-seven houses nevertheless obtained a satellite of one kind or another. But it is striking that while a small group of English abbeys and cathedral priories – Durham, St Albans, Gloucester, Norwich, Nostell

---

[23] These figures are taken from Knowles and Hadcock.

[24] For the distribution of monasteries according to their order, see the maps at the end of Knowles and Hadcock.

[25] Chibnall, 'Problème des réseaux monastiques', p. 341.

and St Mary's York – headed small families of five to nine daughter houses, several other great houses, including Bury St Edmunds, St Augustine's Canterbury, Cirencester, Merton, Peterborough and the two Winchester houses, remained barren. A close investigation of the circumstances surrounding the establishment of English cells is evidently needed to shed light on this apparently haphazard allocation.

Typologies

It requires little investigation, however, to appreciate that the main obstacle to understanding the foundation of dependent priories is the great diversity of this genre of monastery. Writing about the alien priories, Dr Chibnall opined that this class of monastery 'lacks any true unity and is less encouraging to the historian than any of the great monastic orders'.[26] This judgement applies equally well to the dependencies of English monasteries. These priories ranged from large and important centres of religion like Tynemouth and Coldingham to tiny establishments of only two monks or canons with arguably few monastic characteristics, such as Carham or Bedeman's Berg. Furthermore, it is clear that English cells were founded in very different circumstances and for very different reasons. As a result, the majority of commentators on daughter houses have quickly appreciated the necessity of distinguishing between different types of dependency. Such typologies have ranged from the simple distinction between genuine 'priories' and administrative 'cells',[27] to highly sophisticated attempts to differentiate between categories of houses. In his interesting though dated study of the alien priories, C. W. New divided these dependencies (including Cluniac houses) into three classes, which he believed to be roughly equal in size: conventual houses, dative houses (by which he meant small cells with no independence of action from their mother houses) and mere bailiwicks.[28] This classification is, however, more apposite for a later period when the difference between 'conventual' and 'dative' houses had become more clearly defined. With more regard to the circumstances of foundation, Professor Knowles also asserted that three main categories of dependency, both alien and denizen, could be discerned.[29] The first included a small number of originally independent houses, which having fallen into decline were absorbed as cells by more thriving abbeys for reasons of tradition and, according to Knowles, administrative convenience. A second, slightly larger body of dependencies comprised 'houses professedly founded as monasteries in miniature', which

26 Morgan, *Bec*, p. 2.
27 See above, pp. 4–8.
28 C. W. New, *The History of the Alien Priories in England to the Confiscation of Henry V* (Chicago, 1916), pp. 18–20, 37–44.
29 Knowles, MO, pp. 134–5.

failed to develop as their founders had probably intended. Knowles thought his third category of cell to be by far the most common, containing over five-sixths of all small satellites. This was the administrative cell, planted by abbeys in order to guard and manage their more distant estates.

Knowles' classification of cells is of much value, although his weighting of the three categories of daughter house is questionable. It does, however, omit another potential explanation for the foundation of dependent priories: that is, parochial service. The possibility that a significant number of alien priories were established primarily to serve castle chapels and parochial altars was first suggested by Donald Matthew in the early 1960s.[30] This thesis generated a heated debate, and a considerable amount of criticism.[31] However, in subsequent years Matthew's contentions have gradually met with increasing acceptance, particularly as the work of Dr John Blair and others has begun to transform our understanding of parochial service before the Gregorian reform.[32] As a result, the most recent account of the foundation of daughter houses, by Dr Edward Impey, a student of Blair, has laid considerable stress on the performance and supervision of parochial work as a reason for the establishment of alien and English cells alike.

To date, therefore, four main reasons have been identified for the establishment of the 123 or so dependent priories of English monasteries set up between 1066 and c.1250: to administer mother house estates; to serve traditionally cenobitic sites; to carry out parochial work; and to perform the functions of an ordinary religious house (i.e. primarily intercessory prayer). Yet in seeking to understand the foundation of English cells, it is inadvisable to construct too rigid a typology. It may well be that more than one factor contributed to the foundation of a priory, and for this reason it is better to talk of varying reasons for the establishment of cells rather than categories of foundation. Secondary motivations should also be considered, such as the concern of both mother house and lay founder for prestige. Nevertheless, it is crucial for any understanding and evaluation of English cells that we seek to weigh up the relative importance of each of these factors in their establishment. Knowles' belief that the large majority of satellite houses were set up for administrative reasons underpinned his dismissal of these priories as essentially an abuse which 'served no religious purpose whatever'.[33] But equally if one concludes that the majority of English cells were in fact set up to perform some religious function, this category of monastery would appear to merit a more sympathetic treatment than it has often received in the past.

---

[30] Matthew, *Norman Monasteries*, p. 58.
[31] See below, pp. 35–6.
[32] In particular, see the several contributions in Blair and Sharpe (eds), *Pastoral Care before the Parish*; and J. Blair, 'Introduction: from Minster to Parish Church', in *Minsters and Parish Churches. The Local Church in Transition 950–1200*, ed. Blair, Oxford University Committee for Archaeology, Monograph no. XVII (1988), pp. 1–19.
[33] Knowles, MO, pp. 135–6.

In seeking to understand the main reasons for the foundation of dependent priories, one further distinction needs to be made: that is, between those
motivations that caused mother houses to establish a cell and those that animated lay founders. Although there may well have been much common
ground between abbey and benefactor, it does appear that each of the different reasons given above applied to one side more than the other. Therefore,
whereas mother houses are most likely to have been motivated by administrative convenience, historical sensibility or the glory of their abbey, lay
benefactors – although not necessarily indifferent to these factors – would
presumably have been more concerned with intercession, pastoral work and
their own status. To identify the driving force behind the establishment of a
dependency, we are reliant on foundation charters and mother-house chronicles. The paucity of such evidence for the alien priories creates a certain
haze around these houses, but for English cells numerous cartularies and
chronicles are available. In many instances, therefore, it is possible to judge
with some confidence who was primarily responsible for the priory, which is
a vital first step in assessing the likely reasons for the foundation.

Economic Reasons

In the eyes of many historians, the daughter house was first and foremost an
administrative tool. As we have seen, this was overwhelmingly the view of
Professor Knowles, whose judgements remain highly influential today in
writings on medieval monasticism. More recently, the predominance of
economic motivations in the foundation of dependencies has been
emphasised by writers such as Janet Burton and Edward Impey, although the
latter in particular has drawn attention to numerous other important factors
in their establishment.[34] All these writers couple together alien and English
dependencies in their analyses without considering whether the two were
necessarily alike. But in fact there is good reason to believe that French
abbeys had a much greater need to dispatch monks to oversee the property
granted to them by the Anglo-Norman baronage than did their English
counterparts. The distances dividing French mother houses from their cells
were much more daunting than those faced by most English abbeys. Closer
examination of Maps One and Two reveals that rather more than half of
English dependencies were situated less than fifty miles from their mother
houses, a surprising statistic which explains the observed confluence in the
siting of mother and daughter houses. In contrast the French abbeys
concerned were separated from their properties by the Channel and in many

---

[34] E.g. J. Burton, *Monastic and Religious Orders in Britain 1000–1300* (Cambridge, 1994),
p. 30; E. Impey, 'The Origins and Development of Non-Conventual Monastic
Dependencies in England and Normandy 1000–1350', 2 vols, unpublished Oxford
D.Phil. thesis (1991), I, pp. 37–79, esp. pp. 65, 67.

cases over two hundred miles, as well as by the borders of another kingdom. In such cases, it was imperative to send out monks just to protect and preserve their holdings, regardless of the need to administer them directly. The experience of English and French parent abbeys was, therefore, not as closely analogous as has usually been assumed.

This contention can be illustrated by considering the foundation of two English cells in Northumberland, Bamburgh and Carham. The Yorkshire priories of Nostell and Kirkham were both granted valuable property near the Scottish border during the reign of Henry I, based on the wealthy parishes of Bamburgh and Carham respectively.[35] Since the far north was not yet fully integrated into the English kingdom, these two mother houses faced similar difficulties in ensuring the receipt of their revenues to many French abbeys with English estates. Moreover, for both mother houses, matters were further complicated by alternative claims to the property. Despite the earlier grant to Nostell, Bamburgh was given to Hugh Murdac by Henry II and then successively to Peter des Roches and Cardinal Stephen de Fossa Nova by King John; in consequence, the church did not come into Nostell's hands until the 1220s. Carham, meanwhile, had been granted to the monks of Durham by Queen Matilda before 1118, and the cathedral priory does not seem to have given up its claims until the mid-thirteenth century.[36] Since no stipulation was made for the sending of canons to either church in the charters which granted the property to Nostell and Kirkham, it seems safe to conclude that these two cells were set up by their mother houses to preserve their valuable Northumberland properties from the dual insecurity of Scottish raiders and alternative claimants. In later years, Bamburgh and Carham can both be seen sending most of their house's revenues back to their parents, and there is therefore no reason to doubt that their rationale was overwhelmingly administrative. In this, however, these two priories were highly unusual among English cells, which in general disbursed the bulk of their revenues on their own needs.[37] This contrast between the majority of English dependencies and the very cells which were established in circumstances most similar to the alien priories suggests that we should exercise

---

35 Henry I granted the church of Bamburgh to Nostell Priory in 1121, and Kirkham's Northumberland property was given by the priory's founder Walter Espec about ten years later. It has been suggested that both gifts were intended to help absorb the far north more securely into England: *A History of Northumberland*, ed. H. H. E. Craster, 15 vols (Newcastle, 1893–1940), I, pp. 73–94; ibid., XI, pp. 12–17. In 1291, the church of Bamburgh was valued at £230 9s. 4d., whereas the Kirkham cartulary contains a tax assessment of the priory's property in Durham diocese, under the heading 'Carham', with a valuation of £219 4s. 6½d.: ibid.

36 Ibid., I, pp. 74–82, XI, pp. 12–13. Carham was said to have been granted to St Cuthbert by King Ecgfrid in c.674: E. Craster, 'The Patrimony of St Cuthbert', *EHR*, lxix (1954), pp. 183–4.

37 See Chapter Six, pp. 229–76.

considerable caution before assuming that foreign and denizen cells were essentially interchangeable.[38]

The underlying supposition that grants of more distant estates to English abbeys inevitably provoked the sending out of monks to manage them directly also requires some reconsideration. Confronted with the problem of outlying estates, four main alternatives presented themselves to monasteries of which only one involved the monk-bailiff. They could also administer manors directly using lay stewards, whom they would have to pay but who might prove better administrators than the monks themselves. Alternatively, for the twenty-four English Benedictine houses burdened with knight service, distant manors could be shed through subinfeudation. Studies of patterns of subtenancies suggest that the size of the manor rather than its location dictated which were kept in demesne; but some faraway manors were dealt with in this way and Westminster, for example, subinfeudated most of its demesne in Worcestershire and Gloucestershire.[39] Finally, remote estates could be farmed for a fixed term of years. This last option has sometimes been seen as uneconomical and dangerous, most notably by Professor Postan who emphasised those farmers 'who proved themselves inefficient, extortionist, or otherwise dishonest'. However, despite the hazards involved, this method of estate management was by far the most common in twelfth-century England, and possibly in the late eleventh century too, when economic conditions did not favour demesne agriculture.[40] These three methods, then, were quite acceptable alternatives to the monk-bailiff and all were utilised by abbeys. It was far from the case that every grant of a profitable distant estate was followed up with the establishment of a monastic bailiwick or administrative cell. It is significant that canons of Leicester were sent to dwell at the abbey's Lancashire church of Cockerham only when this was demanded by lay benefactors fifty years after the initial grant of the manor, whereas a great abbey like Bury St Edmunds with its lands

---

[38] Alien and English cells also seem to have differed in the layout of their buildings. Whereas a good number of alien priories are known to have resembled manor houses, most English dependencies appear instead to have followed a standard monastic plan. See below, pp. 185–7.

[39] R. V. Lennard, *Rural England 1086–1135: A Study of Social and Agrarian Conditions* (Oxford, 1959), pp. 49–51; E. King, *Peterborough Abbey 1086–1310: A Study in the Land Market* (Cambridge, 1973), pp. 13–18; B. F. Harvey, *Westminster Abbey and its Estates in the Middle Ages* (Oxford, 1977), pp. 71–6.

[40] M. M. Postan, 'A Note on the Farming Out of Manors', *EcHR*, 2nd series, xxxi (1978), p. 524; Lennard, *Rural England*, pp. 105–212; E. Miller, 'England in the Twelfth and Thirteenth Centuries: An Economic Contrast', *EcHR*, 2nd series, xxiv (1971), pp. 1–14; S. P. J. Harvey, 'The Extent and Profitability of Demesne Agriculture in England in the Later Eleventh Century', in *Social Relations and Ideas: Essays in Honour of R. H. Hilton*, ed. T. H. Aston et al. (Cambridge, 1983), pp. 45–72. A. L. Bridbury, 'The Farming Out of Manors' *EcHR*, 2nd series, xxxi (1978), pp. 503–20, contends that leasing was often a highly efficient practice.

scattered across several counties was able to manage without any dependen-cies at all.[41]

If not ubiquitous, the practice of sending out monks to administer manors was not unusual among English abbeys in the Anglo-Norman period. This method of estate management is particularly associated with the Cluniacs, but was also relatively common among the mainstream black monks. Profes-sor Lennard collected together several examples from the eleventh century of individual Benedictines entrusted with the management of an estate, and Dr Gabrielle Lambrick drew attention to the employment of seven monk-bailiffs by Abingdon Abbey on important north Berkshire manors in the same period.[42] However, as has been argued above, the presence of such individual monk-administrators should not be considered to constitute a cell.[43] In the face of disapproval from the ecclesiastical authorities, monaster-ies may often have sent out a second inmate as a companion at such sites.[44] However, it would seem that in a number of cases the bailiff and his fellow monk or canon were withdrawn from the estate after a time and not replaced. Dr Chibnall has suggested that in the twelfth century the abbey of Bec placed monks at several of its manors, before rationalising its estate management by reducing its 'cells' to a minimum.[45] Indeed, one explanation for many of the alleged dependencies listed by Knowles and Hadcock for which little or no concrete evidence survives is that they were short-lived administrative settlements of this kind.

However, there is also evidence that a number of permanent or semi-permanent dependencies grew out of bailiwicks in this way. Mr Piper has suggested with some plausibility that the Durham cell of St Leonard's Stamford might have replaced a monk-bailiff at Normanton on Soar (Nottinghamshire) as Durham's instrument for managing its East Midlands properties.[46] It has also been argued convincingly that the far more substan-tial dependencies at Coldingham (Durham) and Leominster (Reading) began as bailiwicks since at both there are signs at first of a single religious administering extensive lands there, with a convent of monks apparently

---

41 *Final Concords of the County of Lancaster, 1196–1307*, ed. W. Farrer, Lancashire and Cheshire Record Society, xxxix (1899), no. 44, pp. 25–6.
42 Knowles, *MO*, pp. 432–3; V. H. Galbraith, 'Osbert, Dean of Lewes', *EHR*, lxix (1954), pp. 289–302; Lennard, *Rural England*, pp. 157–8; G. Lambrick, 'Abingdon Abbey Administration', *JEH*, xvii (1966), pp. 159–83.
43 See above, pp. 5–6.
44 See above, pp. 5–6.
45 Morgan, *Bec*, pp. 20–1. Soon after the 1170s, Lewes Priory decided to discontinue its practice of maintaining a monk in Norfolk to manage its estates there: Galbraith, 'Osbert, Dean of Lewes', pp. 294–5.
46 Piper, 'Stamford', part i, p. 7. The existence of a Durham monk at Normanton during the reign of Stephen is attested to in a miracle story of Reginald of Durham: *Reginaldi Monachi Dunelmensis Libellus de Admirandis Beati Cuthberti*, ed. J. Raine, SS, i (1835), chap. 67, pp. 134–7.

sent only decades after the initial grants.[47] The process by which a daughter
house could grow out of considerations of property management is most
clearly illustrated in the Battle chronicle's detailed description of the foundation of that abbey's satellite of St Nicholas' Exeter in the last years of the
Conqueror's reign.[48] If this late twelfth-century account can be trusted, it
appears that on receipt of property in Devon, Battle immediately dispatched
monks to administer its holdings in both Cullompton and Exeter. At first a
single monk, Gunter, 'an enterprising man', was sent to Exeter but his
replacement, Cono, was given an assistant. Cono 'put his mind straightaway
to enlarging and building up the place committed to him', and through a
combination of energetic management and the propagation of the cult of St
Olaf he was able to attract sufficient benefactions to initiate the foundation
of a sizeable cell, for which a new church dedicated to St Nicholas was built.
According to the Battle chronicle, the abbey's priory at Brecon also
stemmed from the endeavours of a Battle monk, one Roger, in the administration of lands granted by Bernard of Newmarch and not at Bernard's own
demand.[49] It may be therefore that several dependencies started out as
bailiwicks, gradually developing into formal, perpetual monastic settlements
as this came to appear to abbeys to be a better way of managing properties, or
as reforming attitudes frowned increasingly on the isolation of individual
monk-bailiffs. But as the examples of Coldingham, Leominster, St Nicholas'
Exeter and Brecon show, the cells that may have originated in this way did
not necessarily retain an administrative flavour and might develop into sizeable priories.

Although we cannot always judge whether economic motivations were
prevalent in the establishment of a cell, the surviving charter evidence often
provides hints of when an administrative rationale was behind a foundation
rather than a patron's desire to establish a religious house. Firstly, it is
reasonable to assume that where a benefactor granted property to an abbey
with no mention in his charter of gift that a monastic settlement of some
kind should be, or already had been, begun in return, he probably did not
intend to found a religious house. The tangible benefits accruing to a
founder of a monastery render it unlikely that a donor wanting to establish
his own house would endanger the project by omitting reference to it in his
charter. The Battle version of the foundation of Brecon, although containing several errors of detail, looks to be validated by the fact that neither of
the charters of Bernard of Newmarch preserved in the Brecon cartulary,
making the grants which would form the core of the priory's endowment,

[47] G. W. S. Barrow, 'Scottish Rulers and the Religious Orders 1070–1153', *TRHS*, 5th
series, iii (1953), pp. 77–100; B. R. Kemp, 'The Monastic Dean of Leominster', *EHR*,
lxxxiii (1968), pp. 505–15.

[48] *The Chronicle of Battle Abbey*, ed. E. Searle, Oxford Medieval Texts (Oxford, 1980),
pp. 80–5.

[49] Ibid., pp. 86–9.

contain any mention of the formation of a Battle dependency there.[50] Such
an omission also occurs in the donation charters for Aldeby, Blythburgh,
Lynn, Kidwelly and possibly Dunster, where the 'founder' William de
Mohun vaguely requested that the bishop and monks of Bath 'build and
exalt' the church of St George, Dunster.[51]

A second indication that a dependency might have been established at
the initiative of the mother house for administrative purposes is given where
there appears to have been a very long delay after the making of a grant
before any signs of a monastic settlement are found, or when the original
grant itself cannot be traced. These *ex silentio* arguments are clearly hazardous, especially since very little evidence survives for a number of satellites;
indeed it may be that the number of alien priories established primarily for
economic reasons has been exaggerated because of assumptions based on a
lack of evidence. Moreover, it is sometimes very difficult to pin down exactly
when a cell was set up. When a royal, papal or episcopal confirmation
charter calls one of an abbey's churches a *cella*, it is fairly certain that a
formal dependency had been established. But such confirmations are far
from precise or consistent in their terminology and it cannot be assumed that
where a possession is described as an *ecclesia*, no dependency yet existed. The
first definite evidence of a cell of Norwich at Yarmouth comes from the confirmation charter of Bishop Walter Suffield of 1253, despite the fullness of
the mother house archive; but the twelfth-century Norwich confirmations
did not distinguish between cells and churches.[52] Matters are made clearer
when a dependency can be seen to have been founded on land already
belonging to the mother house. This was the case at St Nicholas' Exeter and
quite possibly at another Devon dependency, Pilton. The manor and church
of Pilton were apparently given to Malmesbury by King Athelstan, yet no
religious house was recorded there in 1086 and the cell was presumably set
up by its mother house some time in the twelfth century.[53]

In a few cases, later information provides strong evidence that a dependency was not established at the behest of any individual founder. In the fifteenth century, Prior Wessington of Durham asserted that St Leonard's
Stamford had been founded by William I and Bishop William of St Calais;

---

50 *Cartularium Prioratus S. Johannis Evangeliste de Brecon*, ed. R. W. Banks, *Archaeologia
   Cambrensis*, 4th series, xiii–xiv (1882–3), esp. xiv, pp. 141–3; *Mon. Ang.*, III, p. 264,
   no. 2.
51 *The Charters of Norwich Cathedral Priory*, ed. B. Dodwell, 2 vols, PRS, new series, xl,
   xlvi (1965–80), I, no. 20, pp. 13–14 (Aldeby), I, no. 107, pp. 57–8 (Lynn); *Blythburgh
   Priory Cartulary*, ed. C. Harper-Bill, 2 vols, Suffolk Records Society, Suffolk Charters,
   II–III (1980–1), I, pp. 34, 55–6, nos 7, 62; F. Wormald, 'The Sherborne "Chartulary"',
   in *Fritz Saxl 1890–1948: A Volume of Memorial Essays from his Friends in England*, ed.
   D. J. Gordon (London, 1957), nos 13–14, p. 113; *Two Chartularies of the Priory of St
   Peter at Bath*, ed. W. Hunt, Somerset Record Society, vii (1893), I, no. 34, p. 38.
52 *Norwich Charters*, I, no. 215, p.126. See also ibid., I, nos 35, 117, 278, pp. 21–2, 65–6,
   176–8.
53 *Mon. Ang.*, IV, p. 443; Knowles and Hadcock, p. 73.

but as Piper has shrewdly demonstrated this was not believed to be the case at late twelfth-century Durham, since forgeries produced at this time purporting to be charters of the aforementioned king and bishop made no mention of a priory or of any property at Stamford.[54] That the priory was founded by Durham on lands previously donated by the king and the bishop would seem to be the best explanation for these contradictory messages. The circumstances surrounding the foundation of St Mary's York's cell at Lincoln were also outlined in a dispute over the temporary withdrawal of the York monks from the house around Michaelmas 1392. After initial claims to the contrary, it was eventually judged in October 1406 that the abbey was not bound to keep any monks at Lincoln since the donor of the property on which the cell was founded, one Rumfarus, had not stipulated that services should be maintained on the site for his soul.[55] This information implies that the cell at Lincoln was erected on land given by a lay benefactor but at the initiative of the mother house at some later date. By their very nature, tiny cells founded mainly for administrative purposes are difficult to identify. But as far as can be seen, only a minority of English cells can be confidently stated to fall into this category, and certainly nothing like the proportion identified by Knowles. Moreover, there is plentiful evidence of the importance of religious reasons in the foundation of a large number of dependencies, which must now be examined.

Serving Holy Places

Knowles considered his first category of dependency, 'houses, originally independent, which had decayed and been subsequently absorbed by others [as daughter houses]', to be numerically insignificant.[56] However, there are signs that cells established for historical reasons, or to occupy and mark sites hallowed in some other way, were rather more common that he believed. It is likely too that Knowles' contention that such satellites were established partly as a means of managing mother house estates is mistaken: in general these cells held little property and several were situated in the immediate vicinity of their parent abbey. There was, of course, an economic rationale behind the absorption of another monastery. In such cases, part of the endowment of the assimilated abbey or priory was diverted to its new mother house, and poverty was stated to be the cause of more than one merger. Henry I's charter to Sherborne confirming its union with the abbey of Horton declared his agreement with Bishop Roger of Salisbury that 'it was well to make out of two small and needy foundations one substantially larger and more securely founded'; whereas Simeon of Durham wrote that Bishop

---

[54] Piper, 'Stamford', part i, p. 6.
[55] CCIR, 1396–1399, p. 156; CPR, 1405–1408, p. 249.
[56] Knowles, MO, p. 134.

William of St Calais incorporated Jarrow and Wearmouth into his new foundation at Durham 'because the small bishopric was not sufficient for three houses (*coenobia*) of monks'.[57] However, it was apparently for reasons of tradition alone that the abbeys concerned chose to keep up some monastic presence at these locations, rather than simply evacuating the site and taking all the revenues.

The desire to preserve the monastic character of a traditionally cenobitic site was therefore the decisive factor in the foundation of this type of dependency. Several of these satellites were intended to form a remnant of monastic observance after the religious had moved, for whatever reason, to another location. Some presence was probably maintained at Jarrow and Wearmouth after their communities were transferred to Durham in 1083, and similar provision was made at Cranborne when Robert fitz Hamo moved its monks to Tewkesbury in 1102, and at Calke after Matilda, countess of Chester, relocated that community to Repton in 1172.[58] Interestingly, even a short sojourn at another site might engender a cell of this kind. The settlement at St Leonard's Norwich originated as Bishop Herbert de Losinga's

---

57 J. Fowler, *Mediaeval Sherborne* (Dorchester, 1951), p. 111; *Symeonis Monachi Opera Omnia*, ed. T. Arnold, 2 vols, RS, lxxv (1882–5), I, p. 10: '*quia episcopatus parvitas ad tria monachorum coenobia non sufficeret*'.

58 *Symeonis Opera*, I, p. 10; *Mon. Ang.*, II, pp. 59–60, no. 1; *Descriptive Catalogue of Derbyshire Charters*, ed. I. H. Jeayes (London, 1906), nos 531, 1939, pp. 68, 242–3. Mr Piper has argued that Simeon's description of the union of Jarrow and Wearmouth with Durham (see n. 57) indicates that no community was left behind at the two former sites in 1083: Piper, 'Wearmouth', p. 2; Piper, *Jarrow*, pp. 4–5. However, the similar language used for Horton, where there is no doubt that a monastic presence was preserved, casts some doubt on this interpretation. *Coenobium*, like *monasterium*, was generally used at this date to indicate a fully-fledged, independent monastery as opposed to a cell. Simeon's statement therefore does not preclude the possibility that a small community remained at Jarrow and Wearmouth after the main body of monks had moved to Durham. There is no evidence of a formalised monastic presence at either site until the early thirteenth century, although Piper suggested that both might have been served by isolated monk-chaplains before this time. Whatever form the settlement took, it is very likely that one or more Durham monks remained at Jarrow and Wearmouth throughout the twelfth century. Durham's service of Tynemouth Priory before that house was lost to St Albans in c.1089 provides an interesting parallel. This was described in 1121 in support of Durham's appeal against St Albans' possession of Tynemouth, narrated by Simeon in his *Historia Regum*. Before 1083, individual monks from nearby Jarrow were said to have been sent regularly to Tynemouth to say the offices there. After the move to Durham, one of that priory's community, Turketil, was sent to Tynemouth on a more permanent basis, 'who, having repaired the roof of this church, lived there for a long time', until he was driven out by Robert de Mowbray: *Symeonis Opera*, II, pp. 260–1. It is not clear from this account whether Turketil dwelt alone or with one or more companions at Tynemouth, but a similar arrangement might well have obtained at Jarrow and Wearmouth. Even if this was not the case, it seems quite probable that the unexpected and deeply resented loss of Tynemouth would have stimulated the monks of Durham to safeguard their possession of Jarrow and Wearmouth by ensuring that these important sites were not left unattended.

temporary solution to accommodation difficulties during the construction of Norwich Cathedral Priory in the 1090s, but developed into a satellite priory when it was decided not to evacuate the site on the completion of the cathedral buildings.[59] The Augustinian cell of Hood came into being in similar circumstances. From c.1142 the temporary home of the Bridlington canons who were to form the first community of Newburgh Priory, Hood was not abandoned after the transfer to Newburgh in 1145 but was maintained as a cell of that priory.[60] A cell might also have been established for a few years at Hackness, the brief home of the monks of Whitby; and a dependency at St Helen's Derby was maintained for a short time after that priory's canons moved to Darley.[61]

Little material advantage proceeded from such foundations and they were kept as small as possible so as not to burden the parent abbey. But it was clearly thought appropriate that sites of this kind should not be abandoned wherever possible. In some instances, it may be that another party was partially responsible for the decision to maintain a monastic presence at a site. The foundation of a cell at Hood may be connected with the stipulation of the monks of Byland in releasing their former home to the Bridlington community 'that there should be founded there an abbey of their canons to remain there perpetually with a full convent'. Equally, Countess Matilda's grant of Repton church 'on the condition that a convent should remain there as the head, to which Calke should be subjected', may have been responsible for the continuation of monastic life at Calke.[62] Nevertheless, this attitude was apparently shared by the religious themselves. A later Tewkesbury chronicler tells how Abbot Gerald ensured that a prior and two monks should be perpetually maintained at Cranborne 'for the sake of the memory of the founders of that place'.[63] And a similar argument was included in a late twelfth-century Durham forgery, which ordered that

---

59 *The First Register of Norwich Cathedral Priory*, ed. H. W. Saunders, Norfolk Record Society, xi (1939), pp. 30–1.

60 Burton, *Monastic Order in Yorkshire*, pp. 86–7; *Early Yorkshire Charters*, ed. W. Farrer and C. T. Clay, 12 vols in 10, Yorkshire Archaeological Society, Record Series, Extra Series, I–X (1914–65), IX, p. 209, no. 122. It is not clear how long canons remained at Hood, however.

61 The early history of the Whitby community is remarkably complicated. The monks spent some years at Hackness, probably to avoid robbers and pirates, under Priors Reinfrid and Serlo, before returning to Whitby in c.1091–2. Professor Hamilton Thompson doubted that any monastic presence was retained at Hackness thereafter, but there is some evidence to suggest that a few Whitby monks continued to dwell there for a time after the main community had returned to Whitby: A. H. Thompson, 'The Monastic Settlement at Hackness and its relation to the Abbey of Whitby', *YAJ*, xxvii (1924), pp. 388–405; J. Burton, 'The Monastic Revival in Yorkshire: Whitby and St Mary's York', in *Anglo-Norman Durham 1093–1193*, ed. D. Rollason, M. Harvey and M. Prestwich (Woodbridge, 1994), pp. 41–52. For St Helen's Derby, see *The Cartulary of Darley Abbey*, ed. R. R. Darlington, 2 vols (Kendal, 1945).

62 *Early Yorkshire Charters*, IX, p. 207, no. 120; *Derbyshire Charters*, no. 1939, pp. 242–3.

63 *Mon. Ang.*, II, p. 60, no. 1.

monastic services should be continued at Jarrow, Wearmouth and Holy Island 'for the reverence and ancient dignity of the places'.[64] Horton provides a slight variant on these reverential foundations. A small abbey, with estates to the value of only twelve pounds or so in 1086, it was appropriated to Sherborne for financial reasons despite the lack of any previous connection between the two houses. Here too, for the sake of propriety, a presence of the smallest acceptable size was maintained as a cell of Sherborne. It is possible that the appearance of shadowy cells at eremitical sites such as Coquet Island, Hilbre Island, Lamanna, Scilly and Trokenholt resulted from similar attitudes towards the occupation of sacred sites; but in none of these cases are the circumstances of foundation clear.

Another small group of dependencies was established for very similar reasons on the site of lapsed monastic communities, or at locations with historical links to the mother house. Bishop Wulfstan re-founded St Oswald's monastery at Westbury Upon Trym in c.1093 as a cell of Worcester Cathedral Priory; and small tributaries were set up at Holy Island (probably during the third quarter of the twelfth century) and Farne Island (c.1193) by Durham and at Puffin Island by the canons of Penmon, commemorating the life of St Cuthbert and St Seiriol respectively at these locations. Popular veneration at Holy Island and Farne Island provided further impetus for the planting of monastic communities there. Reginald of Durham's collection of the miracles of St Cuthbert shows that both islands were important twelfth-century centres for the cult of Durham's patron. Edward the monk was said to be supervising the 'tumba' of St Cuthbert on Holy Island in the 1120s and catering for the many pilgrims who visited the island on the saint's feast day; and in her fine study of Reginald's *Libellus*, Dr Victoria Tudor has suggested that Farne was initially a more popular pilgrimage site than Durham itself for those living north of the Tyne.[65]

Indeed it appears that the hope of either harnessing a thriving saint cult or propagating a potential one was the driving force behind the establishment of a number of English dependencies. The cells at St Ives and Redbourn originated with the discoveries, nearly two centuries apart, of the bodies of St Ivo and St Amphibalus. The saints were translated to Ramsey and St Albans respectively, but it was deemed appropriate to mark the former resting place of both with a permanent religious community. At both, miracles soon followed and St Ives in particular remained an important pilgrimage site throughout the twelfth century and beyond.[66] Similar

---

64 *Durham Episcopal Charters 1071–1152*, ed. H. S. Offler, SS, clxxix (1968), no. 7, pp. 53–8.

65 *Lib. de Admirandis B. Cuthberti*, chap. 22, pp. 47–50; V. Tudor, 'The Cult of St Cuthbert in the Twelfth Century: The Evidence of Reginald of Durham', in *St Cuthbert, His Cult and His Community to AD 1200*, ed. G. Bonner, D. Rollason and C. Stancliffe (Woodbridge, 1989), p. 69.

66 A miraculous healing spring appeared at the site where St Ivo had been discovered and thereafter formed the basis of the cult at St Ives: see below, pp. 218–21. St Albans

motives were prominent in the foundation of Finchale Priory, Durham's vehicle for arrogating the cult of St Godric. The establishment of the cell at Finchale was perhaps one of the more disreputable incidents of twelfth-century monastic history. Durham first laid claim to the site through a forged charter of Bishop Flambard. The bulk of Finchale's endowment was then obtained through a campaign of harassment waged against Guisborough Priory's cell at Baxterwood, a few miles from Durham, founded by Henry du Puiset, son of the bishop of Durham. Having succeeded in hounding the Guisborough canons from the neighbourhood, Durham persuaded Henry to transfer Baxterwood's possessions to a new priory at Finchale, dependent on Durham and in honour of St Godric, whose cult the monks of the cathedral priory wished to control.[67] But although the appearance of cells of this kind could represent the self-interest of the mother house, it would seem that the main reason for their establishment was a concern that certain hallowed sites were fittingly served by a small body of monks or canons. That so many foundations can be explained in this way suggests that this attitude was widely held and was more prominent in the foundation of dependent priories than Knowles and others have allowed.

Pastoral Reasons

The first two reasons for the foundation of English cells discussed above applied mainly, though not exclusively, to the mother houses themselves. It can be seen that a significant number of dependencies were established without discernible external influence, and that administrative convenience was only one factor in foundations of this kind. It is now necessary to turn our attention to lay motivations for the establishment of cells. The attitudes and intentions of lay benefactors are indeed crucial for an understanding of the foundation of English dependencies, since there is good evidence to believe that well over half of these priories were established primarily at the behest of laymen (see Appendix One). This fact in itself suggests strongly that we should not overemphasise the importance of economic factors in the foundation of cells, since these were of little interest to lay founders. But precisely what drove so many lords to establish daughter houses between 1066 and 1250 remains a difficult and controversial question to answer.

---

even established a religious house, the hospital of St Mary de Pré, at the site where St Amphibalus' relics, in the process of being translated to St Albans, met the shrine of St Alban, brought out to welcome his evangeliser: GASA, I, pp. 199–204.

67 *Durham Episcopal Charters*, no. 10, pp. 68–72; *English Episcopal Acta XXIV: Durham 1153–1195*, ed. M. G. Snape (Oxford, 2002), nos 5, 65, pp. 5–6, 59–60; Raine, *Priory of Finchale*, pp. x–xii; *Historiae Dunelmensis Scriptores Tres*, ed. J. Raine, SS, ix (1839), p. 18. That the cult of St Godric was regarded as a rival to that of St Cuthbert is indicated by a number of Durham miracle stories probably from the 1170s in which sick pilgrims were healed by Cuthbert having first appealed to Godric without effect: Tudor, 'Cult of St Cuthbert', p. 459.

The central problem to address is why so many barons chose to found dependent houses, rather than fully-fledged independent monasteries. Daughter houses were set up by great magnates and relatively humble sub-tenants alike, and were founded with some regularity throughout the entire twelfth century and beyond. Should we attribute all these foundations to one or two fundamental causes, or was a multiplicity of factors involved? Perhaps the most important question is whether lay founders expected the small dependencies they were establishing to perform similar functions to larger monasteries, or whether they intended them to fulfil some other purpose. In particular, it has been questioned whether the motivations for these founda-tions were essentially private – that is, focused on the spiritual well-being of the founder, his relations and overlords – or whether they were more out-ward-looking. The possibility that a significant number of dependent prio-ries, both alien and denizen, were set up primarily to perform a pastoral function was first aired by Professor Donald Matthew in 1962. In examining the foundation of the satellites of Norman monasteries in eleventh- and twelfth-century England, Matthew perceived that a significant number of priories did not appear to have been established for administrative purposes. In contrast to the alien bailiwicks which administered large tracts of land on behalf of their mother house, these small priories grew out of the grant of one or more churches and perhaps a little land to a French abbey. The location of many dependencies outside their founders' castles and the prominence of churches in their endowments drew Matthew to conclude that these houses were founded by Norman barons because they wanted trustworthy French monks to serve their castle chapels and parish churches.[68] As well as drawing attention to a number of potential examples of monks serving as parish priests, Matthew also pointed to the foundation of numerous alien cells in parish churches to bolster his case.

This thesis provoked a lively debate over the prevalence of the monk-priest in Anglo-Norman England. Knowles drew attention to the paucity of concrete examples of monks serving parish churches, whereas Pro-fessor Christopher Brooke argued that the monk-priest was rather 'a deliber-ate part of the economy of the old monasticism' which became incongruous only with the victory of the Gregorian reform movement in England several decades into the twelfth century. Dr Chibnall in turn pointed out that the functions of a priest were relatively undefined before the time of Gratian and that monks might have contributed to 'priestly' tasks, even if they did not regularly serve parish churches as Matthew suggested.[69] In more recent years, however, there has been gathering support for the contention that monks

---

68 Matthew, *Norman Monasteries*, pp. 51–65.
69 D. Knowles, Review of Matthew, *Norman Monasteries*, in *JEH*, xiv (1963), pp. 93–4, and see Knowles, *RO*, II, p. 289; A. Morey and C. N. L. Brooke, *Gilbert Foliot and his Letters* (Cambridge, 1965), pp. 84–5; M. Chibnall, 'Monks and Pastoral Work: A Problem in Anglo-Norman History', *JEH*, xviii (1967), pp. 165–72.

did regularly serve as parish priests before the Norman Conquest and beyond. Professor Giles Constable has also argued for a close connection between grants of churches to religious houses and the service of those churches by monks, whereas John Blair, Gervase Rosser, Alan Thacker and others have argued that early *monasteria* invariably fulfilled a pastoral function, which continued up to the Gregorian reform.[70] Moreover, Blair has argued for the importance of public motives in the building of minster churches in Anglo-Saxon England; that is, that the lords who established these churches were as concerned in so doing about the religious needs of their tenants as they were in the concomitant private benefits of status and proprietorship.[71]

This historiographical shift has recently engendered a skilful refining of Matthew's thesis by Dr Edward Impey. Like Matthew, Impey argues that a desire to improve pastoral service was one of the main incentives for the foundation of non-conventual cells in eleventh- and twelfth-century England and Normandy. However, he contends that the actual service of parochial altars by the religious was only part of their role; rather 'it was in their capacity as supervisors of the extension and maintenance of pastoral service that their contribution in this respect was most important'.[72] This may indeed be so, but it is difficult to believe that this was a dominant factor in the foundation of many English daughter houses. Since many English cells were not sited at a great distance from their parents, the supervision of parochial service could often have been directed from the mother house without great difficulty. To make a convincing case for the importance of pastoral motivations in the foundation of English dependencies, it is necessary to retain the projected role of the religious in serving parish churches themselves as an explanation for the posting of monks to these locations.

In fact, Impey himself contends that 'the performance of pastoral work by monks in Normandy and England in the period before about 1150, in spite of the dearth of absolutely specific evidence, was probably fairly widespread'.[73]

---

[70] G. Constable, 'Monasteries, Rural Churches and the *Cura Animarum* in the Early Middle Ages', *Settimane di studio del centro Italiano di studi sull'alto medioevo*, xxviii (1982), pp. 349–89; Blair, 'From Minster to Parish Church'; A. Thacker, 'Monks, Preaching and Pastoral Care in early Anglo-Saxon England', in Blair and Sharpe (eds), *Pastoral Care before the Parish*, pp. 137–70; G. Rosser, 'The Cure of Souls in English Towns before 1000', in ibid., pp. 267–84. For an alternative view, see D. Rollason, 'Monasteries and Society in Early Medieval Northumbria', in *Monasteries and Society in Medieval Britain*, ed. B. Thompson (Stamford, 1999), pp. 59–74. Important discussions of the twelfth-century evidence can also be found in B. Kemp, 'Monastic Possession of Parish Churches in England in the Twelfth Century', *JEH*, xxxi (1980), pp. 133–60; and J. Burton, 'Monasteries and Parish Churches in Eleventh- and Twelfth-Century Yorkshire', *Northern History*, xxiii (1987), pp. 39–50.
[71] Blair, 'From Minster to Parish Church', p. 8. See also the contrasting views expressed in R. Morris, *Churches in the Landscape* (London, 1989), p. 133.
[72] Impey, 'Origins and Development', I, pp. 52–61.
[73] Ibid., I, p. 57.

It remains true, however, that disconcertingly few concrete examples of monks serving parish churches before the mid-twelfth century can be adduced. The only two foundation charters said to request the service of the parish by the monks cited by Matthew, those of Ellingham and Minster Lovell, in fact request only the service of an altar for the souls of the founder and his family (*'facient celebrare in prenominata ecclesia de Elingeham unam missam pro animabus patris matrisque mee omniumque fidelium defunctorum'*) or divine service (*'semper unus vel duo monachi de supradicto cenobio ibidem Deo deservire valeant'*).[74] It must also be noted that the evidence from English dependencies adds little to the store of unambiguous examples. For only three cells was the service of a parish church by the monks of the new foundation clearly indicated. Firstly, in notifying the men of Lynn that he had given the church of St Margaret to the monks of Norwich, Bishop de Losinga added that 'to the monk who has been in that church, I give licence to enjoin penances of all sins and to carry out all the service of a priest'. Secondly, in c.1155 Robert de Haseley, a monk of Gloucester, was instituted as both parson and prior of Bromfield. And thirdly, when a final concord of 13 May 1207 between Leicester Abbey and Heloise of Lancaster and her husband Gilbert, son of Roger fitz Reinfred arranged for the placement of Leicester canons at Cockerham, the abbot and convent undertook to place three religious in the church and to add a fourth on the death of the secular chaplain who had been serving the parochial altar there.[75] It is, however, quite possible that the monastic presence at Lynn at this date comprised only a monk-priest and not a formalised cell, whereas the late date of the Bromfield and Cockerham examples sits uncomfortably with the arguments of Matthew and Impey.

This absence of clear evidence, of course, does not indicate that the religious did not serve parish churches in this period. A similar paucity of material survives to support the opposite case.[76] Rather, it is necessary to infer arrangements from other sources. The case for the prevalence of the monk-priest, laid out by Matthew, Impey and others, points to three main

---

74 Matthew, *Norman Monasteries*, p. 58. Impey also cites these instances, although both he and Matthew acknowledge that a secular priest had been installed in each church within twenty years of the foundation: Impey, 'Origins and Development', I, p. 54.

75 *Norwich Charters*, I, no. 107, pp. 57–8; *English Episcopal Acta VII: Hereford 1079–1234*, ed. J. Barrow (Oxford, 1993), no. 75, p. 59; *The Letters and Charters of Gilbert Foliot*, ed. A. Morey and C. N. L. Brooke (Cambridge, 1967), no. 303, p. 368; *Lancaster Final Concords*, no. 44, pp. 25–6. The priory of Colne, meanwhile, was granted on its foundation the parish church of St Andrew and the land of Ranulf the Priest, which may suggest that the monks usurped his role: *Mon. Ang.*, IV, p. 99, no. 1.

76 Indeed only one straightforward counter-example survives for English cells: in his foundation charter for Penwortham (1104×1122), Warin Bussel stated as a condition of his benefaction 'that three brethren with one chaplain should serve God there': *The Lancashire Pipe Rolls and Early Lancashire Charters*, ed. W. Farrer (Liverpool, 1902), series V, no. 3, pp. 320–2. Farrer misdated Bussel's charter owing to the confusion surrounding the dates of Abbot Robert of Evesham: Knowles and Hadcock, p. 73.

indicators: the frequency with which cells were endowed with parish churches and tithes; the foundation of numerous priories actually within parish and minster churches (sometimes accompanied by the transfer of the priest's property to the religious); and later evidence for the service of churches by the religious. All three of these factors clearly apply to English cells as well as alien ones. The prevalence of spiritualities in the initial endowments of these priories is particularly striking. Maurice of London's re-foundation of Ewenny in 1141 was based on the grant of eight churches and a chapel, whereas Freiston Priory was given six churches by its founder, Alan de Craon. Even more remarkable is Harold of Ewyas' provision for his priory of Ewyas Harold, which consisted entirely of churches and tithes.[77] Similarly, as Appendix Four indicates, more than half of English dependencies were placed in parish churches on their foundation. Finally, it is not uncommon to find monks and canons themselves serving parochial altars, particularly of these shared churches, in the later middle ages.[78] The specific grant of the property of an existing secular priest at the foundation of a priory, as occurred at Bamburgh and Colne, might also suggest that parochial service by the religious was intended. Moreover, Impey has argued that when a secular vicar is later found being fed at the religious' table, as was the case at Breedon, we can infer that he has replaced a regular as priest.[79]

For a significant number of English cells, therefore, it is possible to point to potential evidence for the service of parish churches by the religious themselves. For the cells of Augustinian canons, moreover, there is an even stronger case for stressing pastoral motives in their foundation, because of the well-documented role played by that order in parochial ministry. Nevertheless, it cannot be ignored that alternative explanations for every possible indicator of parish work by the religious can be found. The gift of spiritualities was a convenient and relatively economical way to endow a religious house. A grant of tithes to a monastery affected the income of a priest rather than the donor or his heirs, whereas the value of a church given *in proprius usus* would be multiplied since through appropriation the monastery could draw a far greater income from the church than could a layman.[80] Moreover, that there was necessarily a close connection between the foundation of a monastery in a parish church and how that church was intended

---

[77] J. Conway Davies, 'Ewenny Priory: some recently-found records', *National Library of Wales Journal*, iii (1943–4), pp. 135–6; *Mon. Ang.*, IV, p. 125, no. 1; *A Register of the Churches of the Monastery of St Peter's, Gloucester*, ed. D. Walker, in *An Ecclesiastical Miscellany*, Publications of the Bristol and Gloucestershire Archaeological Society, Record Section, XI (1976), no. 98, p. 39.

[78] See below, pp. 216–17.

[79] Impey, 'Origins and Development', I, p. 57; R. McKinley, 'The Cartulary of Breedon Priory', unpublished Manchester MA thesis (1950), no. 13, pp. 14–15.

[80] R. A. R. Hartridge, *A History of Vicarages in the Middle Ages* (Cambridge, 1930), pp. 4–5; Chibnall, 'Monks and Pastoral Work', pp. 168–9; Kemp, 'Monastic Possession of Parish Churches', pp. 134–5; Burton, 'Monasteries and Parish Churches', pp. 42–4.

to be served is thrown into some doubt by the insertion of numerous convents of nuns into such churches in twelfth-century England.[81] And although religious can be found serving their own churches with some regularity in the later middle ages, in many cases this appears to have been done intermittently, and often in response to particular financial needs.[82] It would be hazardous, therefore, to assume that these instances necessarily reflect twelfth-century practice. As for the donation of the property of the current priest and later evidence of vicars dining at the monks' table, neither precludes the possibility that the priory employed secular chaplains to serve the parish in the twelfth century. Even for cells established in minster churches, another explanation for the foundation is sometimes apparent: for example, when Bishop Robert de Béthune established Shrewsbury monks at Morville in 1138 the rationale of the cell was said to be 'to make hospitality there according to the means of the place'.[83]

The case for the prevalence of the monk-priest in twelfth-century England, although growing in force in recent years, therefore remains very difficult to prove. Nevertheless, to contend that the monks and canons of several English cells were involved in parochial service of some kind does not seem particularly problematic. But even if it could be demonstrated without doubt that the monk-priest was a common figure in the Anglo-Norman parish, this would not in itself establish the contention that the service of parish churches and castle chapelries was the principal reason for the foundation of many small cells and not just a by-product. It is therefore worth considering whether any other explanation for the foundation of the dependent priories of English monasteries by laymen presents itself. In particular, the grounds for believing that these small cells were very often conceived, in Knowles' phrase, as 'monasteries in miniature' with essentially the same functions as independent houses must be examined.

Prayer

Wherever the foundation charters of dependent priories survive, it is striking that they emphasise again and again the founder's private motivations in establishing the cell, that is the provision of prayer for the good of his and his family's souls, while very rarely mentioning the public. It may be, as Impey has argued, that this reflects convention more than genuine motivation.[84]

---

81 See R. Gilchrist, *Gender and Material Culture. The Archaeology of Religious Women* (London, 1994), pp. 99–105; Chibnall, 'Monks and Pastoral Work', p. 169.
82 See below, pp. 216–17.
83 *The Cartulary of Shrewsbury Abbey*, ed. U. Rees, 2 vols (Aberystwyth, 1975), II, no. 334, pp. 303–5. See also the cases of Bromfield and Dover below, p. 52, which appear to have had little pastoral motivation.
84 Impey, 'Origins and Development', I, p. 41. For a more positive view of these clauses, see Burton, *Monastic Order in Yorkshire*, pp. 193–5.

But foundation charters, or other sources, sometimes provide more particular indications of a founder's thinking than these standardised clauses. In studying English dependencies (or at least the Benedictine cells) we are fortunate to have an unusually large number of such charters available, as well as mother-house chronicles, and are therefore less reliant on informed speculation than is inevitably the case with the alien priories. And in numerous instances the overwhelming implication of this evidence is that the priory was indeed set up primarily to provide intercessory prayer for its benefactors.

Where a cell was clearly intended to be conventual, we can assume without much difficulty that its founder considered himself to be establishing a fully-fledged monastery, which just happened to be dependent on another house. In such cases, there is little reason to doubt that the priory's primary function was to be, along with most independent houses, the performance of the *opus dei* for the glory of God and the well-being of its benefactors' souls. Indeed, Matthew and Impey sought to apply their theses only to small, non-conventual cells, thereby implicitly accepting this distinction. In several instances, the intention of the founder to establish a fully-fledged, conventual priory can be inferred from the size of the cell's endowment. The scale of Robert de Mowbray's ambition for his foundation at Tynemouth is clearly indicated by his provision of the manors of Tynemouth, Preston and Amble with Hauxley, together with Tynemouth and Woodham churches and various tithes.[85] Less impressive, but nonetheless sizeable donations of property were also made by, amongst others, the founders of Binham (including the manor and church of Binham), Freiston (six churches), Snape (the manors of Snape and Aldeburgh) and Wetheral (the manor of Wetheral and two valuable churches).[86]

Another indication that a founder considered himself to be establishing a fully-fledged priory can be seen where he sought to circumscribe significantly the mother house's authority over the cell. Clauses designed to delimit the powers of their parents were inserted in the foundation charters of Binham, Snape and Wymondham, suggesting that their founders were not entirely comfortable with their priories' status as dependencies.[87] For another small group of foundations, there is good evidence that a monastery's subjection was entirely the result of mother-house pressure and may even have been against the will of the founder (see below). That Robert II of Stafford hoped to establish an independent priory at Stone, for example, is implied by the omission of any reference to Kenilworth in any of his

---

[85] *History of Northumberland*, VIII, pp. 47–50.

[86] *Mon. Ang.*, II, pp. 345–6, no. 1; ibid., IV, p. 125, no. 1; *Cartularium Monasterii Sancti Johannis Baptiste de Colecestria*, ed. S. A. Moore, Roxburghe Club, 2 vols (1897), I, pp. 168–70; *The Register of the Priory of Wetherhal*, ed. J. E. Prescott, Cumberland and Westmorland Antiquarian and Archaeological Society, Extra Series, I (1897), nos 1–3, pp. 1–12.

[87] For a fuller discussion of these founders' intentions, see below, pp. 65–7.

charters to his foundation.[88] Equally, it is possible to view a founder's desire to be buried in his priory as a sign that the house was designed primarily for intercession and commemoration. Robert II of Stafford expressed such a wish for Stone Priory, where his father had also been buried, and Robert of Gloucester chose to be interred at his priory of St James' Bristol. The founders of Belvoir and Hertford in their charters, meanwhile, requested burial either in these priories or at their mother house (in both cases St Albans).[89]

But fortunately it is not always necessary to infer a founder's desire to establish a fully-fledged priory from other evidence. In several cases, the intended conventuality of a cell is explicitly recorded in its foundation charter or a chronicle. Geoffrey I de Mandeville's charter for the foundation of Hurley Priory states that his generous endowment, which included the church and vill of Hurley, the church of Little Waltham and the island and fishery of 'Hely', was made 'solely for the support of a convent of monks serving God in perpetuity in the same church'. Similarly, the annals of Colchester Abbey record under 1155 the foundation of that house's dependency, the 'conventual church' of Snape.[90] Even more specifically, in re-founding Rumburgh Priory as a satellite of St Mary's York in 1136, Alan the first earl of Richmond stipulated that twelve York monks should comprise the community; and the same demand was made of Gloucester by Maurice of London for his re-foundation of Ewenny and of Tewkesbury by Robert of Gloucester for St James' Bristol. Equally helpfully, the Abingdon *Gesta Abbatum* relates how Abbot Faritius acquired the church of Colne 'in which he placed six monks, and afterwards enlarged it up to twelve'.[91]

It would, however, be a mistake to employ too rigid a notion of 'conventuality' when judging a founder's intentions in establishing a cell. The ideal of the reformed orders that a genuine monastery required a convent of at least a dozen religious was not shared by all. Numerous independent priories of under twelve religious, which were unquestionably designed to be authentic if diminutive monasteries, were established for pragmatic reasons in eleventh- and twelfth-century England. Therefore, where evidence survives that a cell's founder required several religious to occupy his priory, it is reasonable to assume that his intentions were little

---

88 'The Staffordshire Chartulary, series I–II', ed. G. Wrottesley, *Staffordshire Historical Collections*, ii(i) (1881), pp. 210–14, 233–8.
89 'Staffordshire Chartulary', ii(i), pp. 210–11; *Mon. Ang.*, II, p. 61, no.1, III, pp. 288–9, no. 1, pp. 299–300, no. 1.
90 *Mon. Ang.*, III, p. 433, no. 1; *Annales Colecestrenses*, in *Ungedruckte Anglo-Normannische Geschichtesquellen*, ed. F. Liebermann (Strasbourg, 1879), p. 163.
91 Oxford, Bodleian Library, MS Top. Suffolk, d.15, fols 35r–35v: this charter resolves the long-standing confusion over the identity of the founder of St Mary's York's cell at Rumburgh in favour of Alan III of Richmond; *Mon. Ang.*, II, p. 61; *The Original Acta of St Peter's Abbey, Gloucester, c.1122 to 1263*, ed. R. B. Patterson, Publications of the Bristol and Gloucestershire Archaeological Society, Gloucestershire Record Series, XI (1998), no. 25, pp. 22–3; *Chronicon Monasterii de Abingdon*, ed. J. Stevenson, 2 vols, RS, ii (1858), p. 288.

different from those of Alan of Richmond or Robert of Gloucester. We learn from the foundation charter of Binham Priory that Peter de Valognes required 'eight brethren and no less' from St Albans to be maintained at his priory. Meanwhile, Ralph de Limesy and William le Meschin, the founders of Hertford and St Bees Priories, were content at least initially with just six monks.[92] But most revealing of all is Robert de Tosny's foundation of Belvoir, probably the earliest denizen dependency in post-Conquest England. As the founder's unusually informative charter explains, Robert set out to establish an independent house outside his castle at Belvoir, evidently designed to be his family monastery and mausoleum, but quickly ran out of funds. He therefore turned to Abbot Paul of St Albans to take over and bring to completion the project. In return, it was agreed that Belvoir should become a cell of St Albans and that Abbot Paul 'should place there four monks from [his] convent, who .. should pray for the souls of Earl Robert [of Mortain] and King William, and for both the same Robert [de Tosny] and his wife, Adela, and his children and parents'.[93]

That Robert de Tosny, with his initially elevated expectations for Belvoir Priory, was willing to settle for such a small body of monks suggests that it was not only the founders of larger cells who had ambitious plans for their priories. It is also true that the provision of an initially modest endowment does not necessarily indicate that a founder did not aspire towards the foundation of a conventual priory. This endowment after all was not limited to the founder's original grant. William d'Aubigny considerably augmented Wymondham Priory's resources in the 1120s when its monks buried his wife, granting the manor and church of Happisburgh; and the foundation charters of Robert de Tosny and Peter de Valognes both arranged for property to pass to their priories at their decease.[94] Founders also expected their heirs to continue the endowment process they had initiated and in most cases these expectations were realised, although certain founders' sons chose to establish their own independent houses and thus diverted patronage away from their fathers' foundations.[95]

Equally, it was not only their patrons' families who made important benefactions to cells. Several lords succeeded in significantly augmenting their priory's revenues by involving their homagers in the foundation: at Colne, St

---

[92] Mon. Ang., III, pp. 345–6, no. 1, pp. 299–300, no. 1; The Register of the Priory of St Bees, ed. J. Wilson, SS, cxxvi (1915), no. 2, pp. 28–30.

[93] Mon. Ang., III, pp. 288–9, no. 1.

[94] Ibid., III, pp. 330–1, no. 3; C. Harper-Bill, 'The Struggle for Benefices in Twelfth-Century East Anglia', ANS, xi (1988), p. 114; Mon. Ang., III, pp. 288–9, no. 1, pp. 345–6, no. 1.

[95] The eldest sons of William le Meschin (Calder Abbey), Geoffrey I de Mandeville (Walden Abbey), Robert of Gloucester (Keynsham Abbey), William I de Mohun (Bruton Priory), Robert I de Ferrers (Merevale Abbey) and Harold of Ewyas (Abbey Dore) all founded their own independent houses, although each also made grants, some very generous, to their fathers' priories.

Bees and Wetheral in particular the role of the honorial barons in the cell's endowment is most noticeable.[96] Geoffrey the Chamberlain's initial endowment of Wallingford Priory, meanwhile, was considerably enlarged by Nigel d'Aubigny's grant of ten hides and the church in West Hendred and a little land in Wallingford itself. Such grants might even result in an enlargement of the community. Both Simon of Ropsley and Oliver Deincourt made grants to Belvoir in the mid-twelfth century on the condition that its monks should maintain an extra inmate with the proceeds.[97] The optimism with which a founder might regard the prospects of his small cell is particularly well illustrated in Ralph de Limesy's foundation charter for Hertford Priory. Having outlined his relatively modest endowment of the cell, Ralph went on to stipulate that St Albans was to add to the priory's population of six monks if more lands were received, and that Ralph and Hadewise his wife were to be buried at St Albans 'unless their aforesaid church should attain to such honour that they would rather lie there'.[98] In the event, this ambition was in part fulfilled by the de Limesys themselves when Hadewise granted land from her dower to the priory to provide for an additional monk, who was to pray specifically for her and her husband's souls after their deaths.[99]

It can be seen, therefore, that even small priories of four or six monks, like Belvoir or Hertford, could be considered by their founders to constitute 'monasteries in miniature', designed to fulfil all the basic functions of an independent house. But it is the large number of tiny dependencies, of two or three monks or canons, established by lay founders, that best fit Matthew's thesis. This category of satellite may be illustrated by the foundation charter of Hoxne Priory, a tributary of Norwich, issued by Maurice of Windsor and his wife Edith on 25 May 1130. To the monks of Norwich, they granted

> the church of St Edmund of Hoxne freely and peacefully for our souls and those of all our ancestors and successors and for the soul of Ralph the steward who began that church from its first foundations. Bishop Everard and the monks [of Norwich] should place there monks according to the possibility of the place, on condition that if the place with it should happen to be improved, the number of monks staying there should similarly be increased.

The bishop and monks of Norwich also agreed to grant their land in Yaxley to the new priory, and Maurice and Edith were granted fraternity with the

---

96 *Cartularium Prioratus de Colne*, ed. J. L. Fisher, Essex Archaeological Society, Occasional Publications, I (1946), esp. nos 58–70, pp. 31–7; *Register of St Bees*, esp. nos 1–4, pp. 27–33; *Register of Wetherhal*, nos 1–2, 5, pp. 1–9, 14–19.

97 *Mon. Ang.*, III, pp. 279–30, no. 2; J. Nichols, *The History and Antiquities of the County of Leicester*, 4 vols (London, 1795–1811), II(i), Appendix II, nos 9, 14, pp. 4–5.

98 *Mon. Ang.*, III, pp. 299–300, no. 1.

99 Ibid., III, p. 300, no. 2.

Norwich community and permission to dwell in the cathedral precinct or receive a corrody of two monks if they preferred.[100]

The language of this charter implies that the cell was founded at the initiative of the Windsors, although Hoxne was undoubtedly an attractive site to the monks of Norwich for the establishment of a daughter house because of its connections with St Edmund.[101] Moreover, any administrative rationale is surely excluded by Hoxne's closeness to its mother house (only twenty miles), the smallness of its landed endowment and the stipulation that any increase in its possessions was to be used to augment the size of the community and, by implication, not to be diverted to the mother house. But neither is there an obvious pastoral motive to this foundation: the church of Hoxne was not parochial and no tithes were granted to the cell by the founders. On the contrary, however, the expressed hope that the priory would grow in endowment and numbers suggests that Maurice and his wife at least hoped that they were establishing what would develop into a full religious house.

In fact, several other similarly optimistic clauses were inserted by lay founders in their charters of gift for what were extremely small foundations. In 1159, William Burdet agreed with Great Malvern that his foundation at Alvecote would initially be manned by two Malvern monks with two more sent the following Michaelmas and, on the completion of the monastic buildings, '[further] monks should be added to serve God there in perpetuity, according to the means of the place'. On granting to the abbey of Reading the church of Rhynd in Perthshire with a small endowment some time between 1143 and 1147, King David I of Scotland also ordered that if this grant was sufficiently enlarged Reading should send there a convent of monks.[102] Nor were these ambitions entirely unrealistic. David's plans for Rhynd were fulfilled (although its endowment was soon transferred to another Reading dependency of David's foundation at May) and William of London's small foundation at Ewenny in Glamorgan was later re-endowed as a 'conventual' house by his son, Maurice.[103]

100 B. Dodwell (ed.), 'Some Charters Relating to the Honour of Bacton', in A Medieval Miscellany for Doris Mary Stenton, ed. P. M. Barnes and C. F. Slade, PRS, new series, xxxvi (1960), no. 6, pp. 161–2.

101 M. Carey Evans, 'The Contribution of Hoxne to the Cult of St Edmund King and Martyr in the Middle Ages and Later', Proceedings of the Suffolk Institute of Archaeology, xxxvi (1987), pp. 182–95. The cells at Lamanna and St Bees were also established by lay founders on sites of sanctity, and Jane Herbert has argued that such foundations carried some social cachet: J. Herbert, 'The Transformation of Hermitages into Augustinian Priories in Twelfth-Century England', in Monks, Hermits and the Ascetic Tradition, ed. W. J. Sheils, SCH, XXII (1985), p. 144.

102 Mon. Ang., III, pp. 455–6, no. 1; Calendar of Documents relating to Scotland preserved in Her Majesty's Public Record Office, ed. J. Bain, 4 vols (HMSO, 1881–8), II, no. 1985(i).

103 'Documents relating to the Priory of the Isle of May, c.1140–1313', ed. A. Duncan, Proceedings of the Antiquaries of Scotland, xc (1956–7), pp. 52–80; Cowley, Monastic Order, pp. 15–16.

The elevated ambitions of the founder of a small cell can also be seen in a handful of cases where the dependency was quickly re-founded as a larger dependency or an independent house. Having constructed and endowed a priory at Alberbury in the 1220s, Fulk fitz Warin approached the Augustinian abbey of Lilleshall to receive his house as a dependency. The abbey consented, but it soon became apparent to Lilleshall that, because of the inadequacy of its endowment, the cell 'was not as useful and desirable as it had seemed to us, but rather a heavy and expensive thing to our own house'. When Fulk nevertheless demanded that Lilleshall send a convent of canons to Alberbury, Abbot William opted instead to relinquish the daughter house. Fulk's evident intention to establish a fully-fledged monastery was soon fulfilled, however, with the re-foundation of Alberbury as a Grandmontine house, some time before 1232.[104] Equally, the generous endowment subsequently provided for the conventual Finchale Priory suggests that Henry du Puiset was planning a sizeable foundation at Baxterwood before he was headed off by the monks of Durham. And it may well be that the conversion of William de Gynes' small priory of Mountjoy from a cell of Wymondham to an independent house of Augustinian canons resulted from de Gynes' dissatisfaction with the dependent status of his foundation.[105] At Mobberley, meanwhile, the opposite scenario took place when Patrick of Mobberley's independent foundation was converted into a cell of Rocester in c.1130 by Patrick's great-nephew, Sir Gilbert de Barton.[106] Barton's action was presumably motivated by the financial weakness of the priory and there is no reason to think that any change in Mobberley's function accompanied its change in status.

There is evidence, therefore, that at least some tiny dependencies were conceived as larger monasteries which just never developed as their founders had hoped, or in Knowles' more colourful language remained 'arrested and undeveloped, like some biological species left behind in the gradual evolution'.[107] But even if no such ambitions were kindled, and the cell was always intended by its founder to remain minute, it does not rule out the possibility that intercessory prayer was conceived as the house's main function. Indeed, some of the smallest of these lesser dependencies seem to have been considered what might be described as free-standing chantries, set up with the sole

---

[104] R. Graham and A. Clapham, 'Alberbury Priory', *Transactions of the Shropshire Archaeological Society*, 4th series, xi (1927–8), pp. 257–303, esp. the documents printed in Appendix III.

[105] See above, p. 34; *VCH, Norfolk*, II, p. 387.

[106] F. I. Dunn, 'The Priory of Mobberley and its Charters', *Cheshire History*, viii (1981), pp. 73–88.

[107] Knowles, MO, p. 135.

aim of praying for their founders.[108] The Whitby Abbey 'Memorial' certainly viewed its tiny satellites at All Saints' Fishergate in York and Middlesbrough in these terms, stating that monks had been sent to both places at the founder's wishes 'pro eo orarent'.[109] The cell at Fishergate was established by William II to intercede for him and his heirs and a second royal chantry was set up at Writtle (later known as Bedeman's Berg) as a dependency of Colchester. During Stephen's reign, Robert de Sakeville, on founding a cell of Colchester at Wickham Skeith, became a monk of that abbey and was granted a hermitage in the royal forest of Writtle by the king. On Robert's death, the hermitage was given to Colchester by Henry II on the condition that 'two monks who are priests, staying perpetually in the same hermitage should always beseech the mercy of God for the salvation of the living king and for the souls of deceased kings'.[110] Nothing was to distract the Colchester monks from their supplication; instead of a landed endowment they were to receive 4d. per day of the king's alms and were even to be provided with two men to collect nuts for them in the forest.[111]

The resemblance to chantries of the small Suffolk dependencies of Edwardstone and Wickham Skeith is equally striking.[112] Established as cells of Abingdon and Colchester respectively by their founders on becoming monks of those abbeys, both were discontinued only a generation later with the assent of their sons. In each case, however, the suffrages to be said for the souls of the fathers were carefully safeguarded. In c.1160, Hugh de Montchesney agreed that the two monks stationed at Edwardstone 'for the soul of my father Hubert' were to be replaced by two extra religious at Abingdon's larger cell at Colne; whereas Jordan de Sakeville arranged about four years later for 'the four monks who were sustained in the said manor [Wickham Skeith] for the soul of Robert should serve God perennially in the monastery of Colchester'.[113] The wording of both sons' charters indicates that they considered the suffrages for their fathers' souls to be the central purpose of these foundations, which were henceforward to be performed as more conventional chantries in a larger monastic community. It may be questioned why, if Edwardstone and Wickham Skeith were established simply for prayer, their founders did not instead make provision for their commemoration in the abbeys they themselves were entering.[114] But that

---

108 For some examples of early chantries, see K. Wood-Legh, Perpetual Chantries in Britain (Cambridge, 1965), pp. 8–11.
109 Cartularium Abbathiae de Whiteby, ed. J. C. Atkinson, 2 vols, SS, lxix, lxxii (1878–9), I, pp. 55–7.
110 Cart. Mon. Colecestria, II, pp. 529–30, I, pp. 38–9.
111 By the time of Richard I's confirmation of the hermitage to Colchester in 1198, however, the abbey possessed twenty-four acres of assarts in Writtle: ibid., I, pp. 42–7.
112 Professor Harper-Bill has also likened Edwardstone Priory to a chantry: Harper-Bill, 'Struggle for Benefices', p. 114.
113 Mon. Ang., IV, p. 101, no. 12; Cart. Mon. Colecestria, I, pp. 131–3.
114 Matthew's principal reason for looking beyond prayers alone as the motivating factor for the establishment of many small alien priories was that intercession could have

this latter option was clearly considered second best is indicated by the substantial compensation of forty silver marks, a messuage and scattered lands comprising over thirty-four acres granted by Colchester to Jordan de Sakeville after he agreed to the closure of Wickham Skeith, even though four extra monks were to be admitted at Colchester to fulfil the abbey's obligation of prayer to his father in full.[115]

It remains true however, as Matthew and Impey have noted, that the grants forming the basis of numerous small cell foundations were largely composed of spiritualities. That this was also the case for several conventual or semi-conventual cells, such as Ewenny and Freiston, however, indicates that an endowment based on churches and tithes does not necessarily imply that parochial service was the central ingredient in the foundation. Closer inspection of the endowments of many small dependencies, moreover, shows that a significant number of these cells, including Beadlow, Hoxne, Richmond, St Bartholomew's Sudbury, Hirst, Marsh Barton and Scokirk, were not established in parish churches and in several cases were not even provided with a single advowson in their endowment. This surely precludes any pastoral rationale, whereas these priories' lack of temporal property makes an administrative role equally implausible. How then might we explain the numerous small foundations of this kind in twelfth-century England?

In the light of the evidence considered above, the best interpretation available seems to be that these houses were established primarily to pray for their lay founders. Indeed, it may well make more sense to consider cells of this kind less as a contravention of Gregorian reforming ideals than as a product of them. This movement provoked a massive transfer of spiritual property from laymen to the Church and in particular to religious houses. Pressurised by reformers into handing over valuable assets, it may be that some landholders sought a more concrete return from this transaction, the foundation of their own religious house. The spiritual benefits accorded to the founder of even a small monastery were considerable, and would obviously increase if the priory expanded at a later date as several founders expressly hoped. Moreover, as the Hoxne foundation charter shows, the founder of a cell would also be remembered in the mother house's prayers.[116]

been provided for the founders at the mother house: Matthew, *Norman Monasteries*, p. 29n.

[115] The later foundation of Halywell, a cell of Rocester, some time in the mid-thirteenth century provides another example of a small dependency closely resembling a chantry. Indeed Halywell, established by Robert de Cotes and Richard Fiton at the church of St Giles there, was described as a 'chantry' in 1325 when the Rocester canons were given permission to withdraw because of the dangers of its location on Watling Street. As with Edwardstone and Wickham Skeyth, the prayers for the founder were to be performed at the mother house instead: *CPR, 1324–1327*, p. 202.

[116] The St Albans *Liber Benefactorum* gives the founders of the abbey's dependencies a position of some prominence, whereas the Belvoir Priory martyrology includes the founders of that cell's sister houses among those commemorated there: BL, Cotton MS Nero D.vii, fols 91v–92r; Cambridge, Trinity College, MS O.9.25, fols 155v–166r.

When one adds the secular advantages accompanying the establishment of a monastery (see below), it is not difficult to see why several lesser barons preferred to found a small cell with the modest endowment they had to hand, rather than simply making a benefaction to the mother house. This desire for a *quid pro quo* from what must have sometimes seemed a mandatory grant, therefore, may well lie behind the foundation of many of the tiny religious houses founded during the twelfth century.

It might also be added that the chronology of the foundation of small English dependencies by laymen fits more closely with this interpretation than the view that pastoral motivations predominated. It can be seen from Appendix One that, of all lay foundations, the larger daughter houses tended to be founded earliest, and that relatively few small priories were set up by laymen before the end of Henry I's reign. This pattern is easily explicable if most lesser cells were established to be monasteries in miniature or free-standing chantries, devoted primarily to prayer: it is, after all, well known that the foundation of religious houses by lesser men became increasingly common over the twelfth century.[117] However, this chronology presents problems for the view that pastoral work was the main function of these houses, since by the 1140s and 1150s hardening attitudes towards the monk-priest would have discouraged foundations of this kind. It must be acknowledged that a very different chronology operated for the alien priories, which formed the entirety of Matthew's sample of cells and the majority of Impey's: their theses may, therefore, hold good for foreign dependencies. But there is every reason to believe that intercessory prayer was a much more important lay motivation for the foundation of English cells than the service of parish churches ever was.

Additional Benefits to Lay Founders

This is not to deny that pastoral motivations played a part in the thinking of some lay founders when they decided to establish a daughter house. But it is likely that such motivations were largely a secondary factor, and parochial work by the religious more commonly a by-product of these foundations than the driving force behind them. In considering this balance between private and public motivations, however, it should not be forgotten that prayers were not the only return a founder might receive from his monastery. Any religious house, no matter how small, would confer on the founder certain secular benefits which must have played a significant part in his thinking. To found a monastery demonstrated one's status and conferred considerable prestige. Equally, where a religious house was planted at or near the head of

---

117 See, for example, B. Thompson, 'Monasteries and their Patrons at Foundation and Dissolution', *TRHS*, 6th series, iv (1994), pp. 103–26; J. C. Dickinson, *The Origins of the Austin Canons and their Introduction into England* (London, 1950), pp. 140–2.

one's lordship, as were numerous cells including Brecon, Cardiff, Dunster, Kilpeck and Richmond, it provided a spiritual focus for the honour. Wherever it was located, a lord's monastery could bind together his baronage in a common spiritual endeavour, as the examples of Colne, St Bees and Wetheral given above show. And of course, founders were accorded special privileges over their communities, including rights of custody and hospitality and a voice in monastic elections, which could prove to be profitable.[118]

There were, moreover, certain advantages that accompanied the particular foundation of a daughter house. Most obviously, a dependency could be considerably cheaper and more convenient to set up than an independent monastery, as the example of Belvoir discussed above shows. To found a daughter house also ensured that the monks of the new foundation would be of high quality and it established enduring ties with a monastery of renown. That these factors could appeal to men of the highest rank is illustrated by the list of men who founded English cells, which included Earls Robert of Gloucester, Robert de Mowbray of Northumberland and Alan of Richmond, as well as the first Geoffrey de Mandeville, Aubrey de Vere and Roger Bigod. And, although Dr Chibnall has argued that dependent houses were often considered inferior in pre-1066 Normandy, there are few signs that the foundation of a dependent priory carried any great stigma in twelfth-century England.[119]

A founder might also find it advantageous to associate a powerful monastic corporation with his project. This was particularly true for those laymen seeking to establish a religious house on disputed or insecure territory. The foundation of a daughter house might commend itself to the holder of a contested estate as a means of strengthening his claims to that land and winning powerful allies to his cause. We learn that a cell of St Benet Holme at South Walsham had to be aborted when its founder, Ralph de Criketot, was adjudged not to be the rightful owner of the priory's endowment.[120] Such considerations were particularly pressing in newly conquered territory, since not only would a dependent priory bolster a founder's hold on the land, but it would also provide him with a body of trustworthy monks to circumnavigate the need for local recruitment. Consequently the first two monasteries founded in Cumberland after its absorption into England by William Rufus, the le Meschin priories of Wetheral and St Bees, were both made cells of St Mary's York. A similar explanation can be given for the popularity of

---

[118] S. Wood, English Monasteries and their Patrons in the Thirteenth Century (Oxford, 1955), pp. 40–121.

[119] Chibnall, 'Monastic Foundations', p. 38. It may be, though, that the spread of the Cluniac order in England helped to confer respectability on the daughter house among the Anglo-Norman baronage. Such a conclusion may perhaps be inferred from Peter de Valognes' citation of Earl William of Warenne's foundation of Lewes Priory as a dependency of Cluny as his model for Binham Priory: Mon. Ang., III, pp. 345–6, no. 1; see below, p. 65.

[120] Register of St Benet Holme, I, nos 145, 156, pp. 83, 88.

dependent priories in Anglo-Norman Wales and Ireland. Just as the Norman Conquest of England was followed by the foundation of many French dependencies, so the occupation of south Wales in the early twelfth century and of Ireland after 1169 saw the establishment of numerous daughter houses of English monasteries. Every Benedictine house established in south Wales in the twelfth century was a dependency, whereas eight new Irish cells were given to English abbeys and priories in the thirty years or so after the Anglo-Norman invasion.[121]

On encountering the very different character of the Welsh and Irish churches, the conquerors might also have required monks or canons from England for their personal religious needs. Matthew highlighted the desire of the founders of the alien priories to have French monks to serve their castle chapels and to minister to their families, and a similar concern probably animated the Anglo-Norman barons settling in Wales and Ireland. Indeed in a number of instances, we hear of English regulars accompanying the conquerors before a daughter house was established. The Battle account of the foundation of Brecon Priory describes how a monk of that abbey, Roger, perhaps acting as Bernard of Newmarch's chaplain, advised that magnate to establish a cell of Battle there. Similarly, the charters effectively establishing the Irish priories of Ardaneer and Begerin as cells of Glastonbury and St Nicholas' Exeter respectively, both mention individual monks of those houses already in Ireland.[122] Perhaps more than anything else, however, these priories served as instruments of conquest in themselves, symbolising the success of the Anglo-Norman invasion and contributing to the assimilation of the new subject populations. Situated at the heart of the conquerors' baronies, priories like Brecon, Cardiff, Ewenny and Kidwelly were as important a part of the colonisation of south Wales as the castles that overlooked them.[123]

121 C. N. L. Brooke, 'St Peter of Gloucester and St Cadog of Llancafarn', in Brooke, The Church and the Welsh Border in the Central Middle Ages (Bury St Edmunds, 1986), pp. 50–94; Cowley, Monastic Order, pp. 9–39; Chibnall, 'Problème des réseaux monastiques', pp. 347–9; A. Gwynn and R. N. Hadcock (eds), Medieval Religious Houses: Ireland (London, 1970), pp. 104–8, 153–200; 'Unpublished Charters relating to Ireland, 1177–82, from the Archives of the City of Exeter', ed. E. St John Brooks, Proceedings of the Royal Irish Academy, xliii (1936), pp. 313–66; E. St John Brooks, 'Irish Daughter Houses of Glastonbury', Proceedings of the Royal Irish Academy, lvi (1953–4), pp. 287–95; W. T. McIntire, 'A Note on Grey Abbey and other Religious Foundations on Strangford Lough affiliated to the Abbeys of Cumberland', Transactions of the Cumberland and Westmorland Antiquarian and Archaeological Society, new series, xli (1941), pp. 161–73.
122 Battle Chronicle, pp. 86–9; St John Brooks, 'Irish Daughter Houses', p. 291; St John Brooks (ed.), 'Unpublished Charters', no. 1, pp. 316–19.
123 Cf. M. W. Thompson, 'Associated Monasteries and Castles in the Middle Ages: a tentative list', Archaeological Journal, cxliii (1986), pp. 305–21.

Mother-house Prestige

If the various lay benefits, both spiritual and secular, for establishing small cells are reasonably clear, it is also important to ask why mother houses were willing to accept dependencies set up primarily at the behest of lay benefactors. In general, it would appear that most abbeys were extremely glad to take on a conventual or semi-conventual priory. Abbeys were quick to obtain episcopal, royal and, from the 1130s, papal confirmations of the grants of priories 'in cellam', but the most striking testament to the attitudes of mother houses to their larger dependencies are the attempts of Gloucester and Durham to recover lost cells. The monks of Gloucester were deprived of their satellite priory at Llanbadarn Fawr by the Welsh re-conquest of Ceredigion in 1136, but did not lightly relinquish their claims: they appealed unsuccessfully to Pope Alexander III in 1175, and were still seeking redress as late as 1251.[124] Similarly, after they were dispossessed of Tynemouth by Robert de Mowbray, the monks of Durham continued to dispute its subjection to St Albans for nearly a century, producing a number of forgeries to bolster their cause.[125] Another illustration, quite literally, of how great a value an abbey placed on the acquisition of a substantial dependency is found in the late twelfth-century Guthlac Roll.[126] In one of the roundels therein, a group of Crowland Abbey benefactors are depicted crowding around St Guthlac to offer him grants of lands, in what constitutes a hall of fame of the leading Crowland patrons. The only post-Conquest donation represented is Alan de Craon's grant of Freiston Priory.

No doubt a number of factors contributed to this enthusiasm. A sizeable dependency could be taxed by the mother house in the form of an annual pension.[127] Abbeys might also have considered the receipt of daughter houses as an effective means of attracting more widespread patronage to themselves. But the most likely reason for their willingness to take on dependencies was the prestige of fostering a family of satellites. By accepting tributary houses, abbeys were able to show themselves fecund and to spread their influence and the honour of their patron saint further afield. Since large daughter houses were so desirable, it is not surprising to find hints that mother houses often played some part in persuading lay founders to establish their dependent priories. The negotiations behind foundations are usually hidden from us, but Robert de Tosny's agreement with Abbot Paul of St Albans for the joint establishment of Belvoir Priory is described in his charter; and William Burdet's charter for the establishment of Alvecote as a

---

[124] Hist. et Cart. Gloucestriae, II, pp. 76–7, 79.
[125] Durham Episcopal Charters, nos 4–5b, 7, pp. 26–47, 53–8.
[126] G. Warner (ed.), The Guthlac Roll, Roxburghe Club (1928), plate 18.
[127] See below, pp. 138–41.

cell of Great Malvern is also presented as a *conventio* with the mother house rather than a straightforward donation.[128]

Mother-house lobbying was probably only a secondary factor in the creation of most dependencies, but for a handful of cells there are even signs that a monastery's desire for prestige was the single most important determinant in their foundation as daughter houses. Each of these instances involved the takeover of a long-existing or newly founded religious community, where an endowment had already been provided and so where lay involvement was less important. The annexations of Dover by Christ Church Canterbury and of Bromfield and Leonard Stanley by Gloucester, illustrate this process well. In 1130, Henry I granted the royal free chapel of St Martin, Dover, to Archbishop Corbeil and 'the church of Christ, Canterbury', for the substitution of Augustinian canons for the secular canons whose service of the church had apparently proved unsatisfactory. However, on the archbishop's death in 1136, the monks of the cathedral priory forcibly took possession of the church of Dover claiming that the reference to 'the church of Christ' in the royal charter in fact referred to their monastery. Though temporarily ejected by the legate, Henry of Blois, the cathedral priory succeeded in winning the support of the new archbishop, Theobald, himself a Benedictine, who reinstated twelve Canterbury monks to Dover in January 1139.[129]

Gloucester Abbey's acquisition of Bromfield, another royal free chapel, seems also to have depended largely on the mother house's initiative. Bromfield became a satellite of Gloucester in 1155 when, according to the abbey *Historia*, 'the canons . . . gave their church and themselves to become monks of the church of St Peter's, Gloucester'. Eleven years later, however, it was complained to Archbishop Becket that 'the canons of Bromfield were made monks in the monastery of Gloucester by certain defrauding and trickery, and the possessions and goods of the church by this opportunity directed to the aforesaid monastery'.[130] Similar tactics were quite possibly employed in Gloucester's appropriation of Leonard Stanley in 1146, a house of Augustinian canons. Not long after this event, Hugh de Cotes, a former canon of Leonard Stanley, appealed to the pope that he had been violently ejected from the priory by the monks of Gloucester.[131] For takeovers of this kind, episcopal support was crucial, and it is probably no coincidence that at the time of the Bromfield assimilation the bishop of Hereford was Gilbert Foliot, former abbot of Gloucester. The Gloucester monks, moreover, must also have won the support of Leonard Stanley's patron, Roger III of Berkeley, for their annexation of that priory. But nevertheless, it would seem that it was

128 *Mon. Ang.*, III, pp. 288–9, no. 1, pp. 455–6, no. 1.
129 Ibid., IV, p. 538, no. 7; *The Historical Works of Gervase of Canterbury*, ed. W. Stubbs, 2 vols, RS, lxxiii (1879–80), I, pp. 96–101, 109.
130 *Hist. et Cart. Gloucestriae*, I, pp. 19–20, 66; *Materials for the History of Thomas Becket, Archbishop of Canterbury*, ed. J. C. Robertson and J. B. Sheppard, 7 vols, RS, lxvii (1875–85), V, no. 202, pp. 401–2.
131 *Letters and Charters of Gilbert Foliot*, no. 91, pp. 125–6.

the proactive and even aggressive stance taken by the monks of Canterbury and Gloucester that was instrumental in the establishment of these cells.

The Anglo-Norman period also witnessed numerous attempts by monasteries to assert jurisdiction over an otherwise independent priory of the same order. Any monastery founded with monks from another institution might find its sovereignty impugned. Battle Abbey, for example, faced forty years of intermittent claims for its subjection to Marmoutier, whose monks had provided the first colony of Battle inmates.[132] Worcester Cathedral Priory also claimed lordship over Alcester Abbey on the (possibly spurious) grounds that its convent had provided Alcester's first abbot in 1140, and it took Archbishop Theobald's intervention to free the smaller house from Worcester's pretensions.[133] Similar problems arose after William, the charismatic first prior of Luffield (d.1164), was persuaded by the founders of Walden and Bradwell to take charge of their new foundations too. Geoffrey de Mandeville, first earl of Essex, succeeded in ensuring that this arrangement would not prejudice the independence of his foundation at Walden, but the founder of Bradwell, Meinfelin lord of Wolverton, was less influential. Consequently, it was not until the early 1180s that the monks of Bradwell were able to establish their house's independence from Luffield, and only then at the price of their church of Thornborough.[134]

Similar claims to monastic overlordship might arise when one monastery had a prior claim to the property used to endow another house. Indeed, this seems to be the best explanation for a small group of Augustinian foundations which, most unusually, remained subject to the house that provided its initial community of canons.[135] There is no evidence that the lay founders of the priories of Bolton, Brinkburn, Canonsleigh, Felley and Stone set out to establish daughter houses. But the monasteries of Huntingdon, Pentney, Plympton, Worksop and Kenilworth respectively nevertheless succeeded in asserting their authority as mother houses over these priories. As Hamilton Thompson argued, Huntingdon's case for the subjection of Embsay/Bolton seems to have rested on William le Meschin's earlier grant to a Huntingdon canon of the church of Skipton; and the claims of Pentney over Brinkburn may well have

---

[132] *Battle Chronicle*, pp. 46–7, 68–77, 116–17.

[133] *The Cartulary of Worcester Priory*, ed. R. R. Darlington, PRS, new series, xxxviii (1962–3), no. 77, pp. 46–8; A. Saltman, *Theobald Archbishop of Canterbury* (London, 1956), no. 1, pp. 232–3; D. Styles, 'The Early History of Alcester Abbey', *Transactions of the Birmingham Archaeological Society*, lxiv (1941–2), pp. 20–38; HRH, I, p. 26.

[134] *Luffield Priory Charters*, ed. G. R. Elvey, 2 vols, Northamptonshire Record Society, xxii, xxvi (1968–73), II, pp. xiv–xviii.

[135] For the marked independent-mindedness of the Augustinian canons, see Dickinson, *Origins of Austin Canons*, pp. 158–9.

had similar origins.[136] More explicitly, Walter de Clavile, the founder of Canonsleigh, had previously given much of that priory's property to Plympton Priory, whereas Ralph Brito of Annesley granted the church of Felley to Worksop in 1151 five years before establishing a priory there. Finally, the basis for the endowment of Stone Priory had been acquired by Geoffrey de Clinton for his foundation of Kenilworth, several years before Robert II of Stafford established his house there.[137] In all these cases, the authority of the mother house was circumscribed and eventually challenged and completely overturned.[138] Nevertheless, they exemplify the ways in which a monastery might, by defending its perceived rights, enhance its prestige and secure the subjection of another priory largely as the result of its own efforts.

If the enthusiasm of abbeys for substantial dependencies is easily explicable, it is rather more difficult to understand the attraction of very small cells, such as Ewyas Harold and Scokirk, to mother houses. Most satellites of this kind cannot have brought much material benefit to their parents, whereas the disciplinary risks of sending two or three inmates to dwell out of the monastery were obvious. There can be little doubt that such cells represented the interests of lay benefactors much more than the mother houses which populated and preserved them. Yet only one clear example of an English monastery turning down the offer of a dependency, as Abbot Hugh of Cluny was known to have done on several occasions, is recorded: Abbot William of Lilleshall's renunciation of Alberbury.[139] In addition, one or two instances of benefactors requesting the establishment of a cell apparently without effect can be found, quite possibly because of mother-house reluctance. In the mid-twelfth century Hugh fitz Pinceon fruitlessly granted various possessions in Lincolnshire, including the church of Kirkby-on-Bain, to Durham for the foundation of a religious house there. And a few years earlier, Hugh son of Ivo of Claxton, on confirming the grants of his father and brother to Belvoir Priory, released the abbot and convent of St Albans from 'his claim to place monks at Claxton'.[140] Such evasion, however, seems to have been rare, and mother houses were apparently willing to accept almost any dependency offered to them.

That this attitude could prove problematic for a mother house is indicated by the premature withdrawal of religious from the cells of Wickham Skeith

---

136 A. H. Thompson, *History and Architectural Description of the Priory of St Mary, Bolton-in-Wharfedale*, Thoresby Society, xxx (1928), pp. 51–2; *The Cartulary of Brinkburn Priory*, ed. W. Page, SS, xc (1893), no. 1, pp. 1–2.

137 *The Cartulary of Canonsleigh Abbey. A Calendar*, ed. V. C. M. London, Devon and Cornwall Record Society, new series, viii (1965), pp. ix–x; *VCH, Nottinghamshire*, II, p. 109; 'Staffordshire Chartulary', ii(i), pp. 199–206. London suggested that Canonsleigh was formed after a breakaway of Plympton canons.

138 For a discussion of this process, see below, pp. 104–7.

139 See above, p. 45; Hunt, *Cluny under Saint Hugh*, pp. 151–2.

140 Piper, 'Stamford', part i, p. 7; *Historical Manuscripts Commission: The Duke of Rutland*, IV (1905), pp. 129–30.

and Edwardstone described above.[141] The potential clash of interests between founder and abbey over the smallest dependencies is equally well illustrated by the dispute between Robert II of Ewyas and the monks of Gloucester over their minute religious house of Ewyas Harold. No doubt owing to the cell's poverty, Gloucester had discontinued its presence at Ewyas some time before 1196. This had been strongly opposed by Robert as patron and in February that year an agreement was made to end the dispute. Gloucester agreed to send back a prior and one monk to Ewyas Harold by the following Michaelmas and that a convent of monks should be established there from additional revenues provided for the cell from one or more of its parish churches on their next vacancy. Monks soon returned to Ewyas, but predictably this second requirement was never fulfilled and Ewyas Harold remained a tiny, indigent cell until Gloucester eventually managed to disband it in the mid-fourteenth century.[142] With hindsight, the facility with which mother houses were prepared to take on small cells might appear fool-hardy, even to them. It may be that abbeys like Gloucester shared the opti-mism of the founders of small cells that these priories would grow into something more substantial. But the best explanation for the proliferation of tiny dependencies in Anglo-Norman England may well be that even small cells were considered to bring prestige to their mother houses.

Patterns of Foundation

Now that we have discussed the varying circumstances behind and reasons for different foundations, we are in a position to identify some general trends and to answer some general questions about the establishment of English dependencies. When were these cells founded and by whom? What does this tell us about the religious attitudes of the Anglo-Norman aristocracy? And how can the seemingly haphazard distribution of cells to English mother houses be explained? Significant in their own right as a conspicuous monastic development, the English dependencies are equally important for what they reveal about their founders and their parent abbeys. The majority of these daughter houses came into being through the benefactions of a lay patron and therefore serve as an indication of the piety and religious tastes of the Anglo-Norman aristocracy. It used to be thought that the Norman barons favoured the monasteries of their duchy over English houses well into the second quarter of the twelfth century.[143] However, Emma Cownie has now demonstrated that 'many of the English religious houses benefited from

141 See pp. 46–7.
142 *Hist. et Cart. Gloucestriae*, I, pp. 76–7, 287–8. Gloucester's failure to increase the size of the Ewyas community aroused further discontent from the priory's new patron in 1222: ibid., I, pp. 210–11.
143 'This process of losing touch with Normandy is hardly noticeable before the death of Henry I': Matthew, *Norman Monasteries*, p. 28.

the generosity of the continental newcomers, and in a few cases this happened quite soon after 1066'.[144] Benefactions are clearly essential signposts for tracing the religious predilections of the donors, but they often point in more than one direction since patrons could and did give to more than one institution. Brian Golding has argued for the choice of burial site as a sure indicator of religious preference, since it required a definite choice of religious house.[145] The same might be said for monastic foundations. The fact that a group of Anglo-Norman barons chose an English abbey to preside over their personal foundation is highly significant, as is their particular choice of mother house.

The most reliable statistics available for the foundation of English dependencies are those assembled in the *Medieval Religious Houses* volumes.[146] The figures gleaned from this source by Professor Barlow remain widely quoted today by historians using monastic foundations to try to locate the moment when English abbeys superseded Norman and other French houses in the affections of the Anglo-Norman ruling class: from 1066 to 1100, according to Barlow, thirty priories subordinate to Norman abbeys and about fourteen to neighbouring French houses were established in England and Wales, compared to only eighteen subject to English abbeys. Between 1100 and 1135, there were over eighty new foundations, of which over forty were dependent on English houses, and only half that number on French houses.[147]

Although helpful, these figures provide only a rough guide to patterns of foundation. Indeed it is clear from our discussion of the different reasons for the establishment of English dependencies that Barlow's figures must be pruned before they can be made to tell us anything about the religious preferences of the Anglo-Norman nobility. Where there are reasonable grounds for thinking that a satellite priory was established by the mother house alone, with little or no part played by a secular benefactor, then this house must be removed from any statistics purporting to be indicators of lay religious sentiment. As we have seen, it is often difficult to be sure whether a lay founder was involved or not. In those cases where a religious settlement quickly followed a grant, even when there are doubts over whether this was the benefactor's intention, the house can be included in our statistics: such donors

---

[144] E. Cownie, 'The Normans as Patrons of English Religious Houses, 1066–1135', ANS, xviii (1995), p. 48.

[145] B. Golding, 'Anglo-Norman Knightly Burials', in *The Ideals and Practice of Medieval Knighthood*, ed. C. Harper-Bill and R. Harvey (Woodbridge, 1986), pp. 35–48.

[146] Knowles and Hadcock, pp. 52–82, 137–80. The volumes for Scotland and Ireland, where fewer foundations existed, were able to give much fuller coverage of each house's history: I. B. Cowan and D. E. Easson (eds), *Medieval Religious Houses: Scotland*, 2nd edn (London, 1976); Gwynn and Hadcock, *MRH: Ireland*. But see Appendix One for amendments to the dates of foundation provided by these volumes.

[147] F. M. Barlow, *The English Church 1066–1154* (London, 1979), pp. 184, 193.

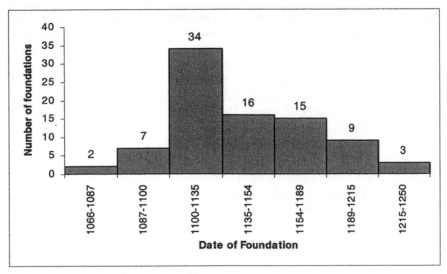

Figure 1.1: The Foundation of English Cells, 1066–1250

were always regarded as the house's founder and in a real sense so they were. The following statistics cannot be regarded as exact, but despite the difficulties involved they are much more useful than the untreated figures.

The 124 cells of English abbeys founded before c.1250 (including St Ives) are laid out in Appendix One. Of these 124, I have isolated thirty-eight as foundations where significant lay involvement is in serious doubt, for one of the reasons outlined above.[148] The chronological distribution of the remaining eighty-six lay or partially lay foundations is shown in Figure 1.1.[149] It emerges clearly from this figure that the peak period for the establishment of English dependencies by lay benefactors was the reign of Henry I, when about 40 per cent of such foundations were made. Foundations then continued at a similar rate of about one per year until the 1150s, before gradually tailing off thereafter. It is also significant that only nine houses were founded by laymen before 1100, and of these only two were established before the Conqueror's death. Cownie has argued for the division of England and Normandy after the Conqueror's death as the point when Norman patronage of English religious houses became wholly acceptable and normal, and the evidence for the foundations of the English dependencies suggests a similar conclusion.[150] Although relatively few, these early foundations are important indicators of a change in Norman attitudes to English monasteries. To make

---

148 See entries marked 'Mother' or with episcopal founders in Appendix One.
149 Where a dependency was re-founded, as at St Guthlac's Hereford and Ewenny, the date of its first foundation has been used. For Tynemouth, however, the date utilised is that of its granting to St Albans, since it is unlikely that this was ever a formal cell of Durham. Cf. Appendix One.
150 Cownie, 'Normans as Patrons', p. 60; Cownie, *Religious Patronage*, pp. 193–4.

benefactions to these houses showed an acceptance of their spiritual creden-
tials. But the moment when Norman barons were prepared to entrust their
personal foundation to an English abbey was the moment when they felt able
to place complete faith in the merits of at least some English monasteries.
This point had been reached by the 1090s, but not much before.

The sort of men who established English dependencies changed over
time. Up to the middle of Henry I's reign, the majority of founders were
wealthy tenants-in-chief. A few very great men set up cells, such as Robert of
Gloucester (St James' Bristol), Robert de Mowbray (Tynemouth), Alan III
of Richmond (Rumburgh), Roger Bigod (Felixstowe), Robert fitz Hamo
(Cardiff) and Gilbert fitz Richard (Llanbadarn-Fawr), although these houses
were sometimes their second or third foundations, intended to be the spiritual focus of a particular grouping of estates. But the majority of early founders were important tenants-in-chief, barons of the second rank. A handful of
the earlier dependencies were established by relatively humble men, such as
Geoffrey the Chamberlain (Wallingford), Ralph de Lisle (Woodkirk) or
Wymar the Steward (Richmond). But by the end of Henry I's reign, when
great men were beginning to turn to the Cistercians, honorial barons like
Maurice of Windsor (Hoxne), William Burdet (Alvecote), Warin Bussel
(Penwortham), Hugh of Kilpeck (Kilpeck) or Ralph Brito of Annesley
(Felley) became the typical founders of daughter houses. The vast majority
of founders had no strong connections to Normandy nor to French abbeys
and very few planted alien priories as well. One cell, Ewyas Harold, was
founded by an Englishman, Harold of Ewyas, the son of the unfortunate earl
of Hereford, Ralph the Timid. In contrast to the independent houses of
Augustinian canons, only a small number of cells were episcopal foundations
and nearly all of these may be considered self-foundations since the bishops
in question (Wulfstan and Simon of Worcester, Herbert de Losinga and
Roger of Salisbury) were heads of the communities concerned (Worcester,
Norwich and Sherborne).[151]

With the self-founded dependencies put to one side, moreover, the seemingly haphazard distribution of cells, with some great abbeys receiving
several and others none, begins to take on a more explicable form. Historians
have never proposed a satisfactory answer for why some great houses, such as
St Albans or Durham, received several satellites and others just as powerful,
like Bury St Edmunds or St Augustine's Canterbury, obtained none. Dr
Chibnall has been the only scholar to address this question in any detail,
suggesting that the rule of vigorous abbots was the principal factor in the
accumulation of dependencies.[152] Energetic superiors like Abbots Paul of St

---

[151] The only episcopal foundations of English dependencies that cannot be attributed to
the mother house are Bishop Robert de Béthune of Hereford's establishment of a cell
of Shrewsbury at Morville and perhaps the foundation of Bentley by an archbishop of
Canterbury.

[152] Chibnall, 'Monastic Foundations', p. 43.

Albans and Faricius of Abingdon were evidently fundamental to their houses' success in attracting patronage. But this explanation alone does not explain how the resolute and popular Abbot Baldwin of Bury St Edmunds attracted no daughter houses to his abbey, nor why only one of the seven cells accumulated by Gloucester was established during the rule of Serlo (1072–1104), by far the house's most dynamic abbot. A more complex solution is required.

After those thirty-eight cells established without significant lay participation have been removed from the statistics, the remaining eighty-six were granted to forty-eight different monasteries. The most popular recipients were St Albans with eight, Gloucester with six and St Mary's York, Nostell and Glastonbury with four each, and only thirteen other abbeys were granted more than one dependency. It is not, therefore, so much the failure of a Bury St Edmunds or St Augustine's Canterbury to attract daughter houses that needs to be explained as the phenomenal popularity as a mother house of St Albans, and to a lesser extent of Gloucester, St Mary's York, Nostell and Glastonbury. The towering predominance of St Albans can be best accounted for by a happy combination of a saint of the very first rank, the abbey's reputation as a monastery of strict observance, two particularly energetic abbots, family connections and the sponsorship of the most eminent churchman of late eleventh-century England. As Pamela Taylor has recently stressed, St Alban was no ordinary saint.[153] As England's proto-martyr and a Roman saint rather than an Anglo-Saxon, St Alban was accepted and venerated by the Norman conquerors as one from the highest echelons of sainthood and much of his abbey's post-Conquest popularity can be attributed to this recognition. St Albans was also fortunate in being ruled by two abbots, Paul (1077–1094) and Richard d'Aubigny (1097–1119) capable of capitalising on the opportunities provided by their powerful patron saint. Under Paul, St Albans gained a reputation, preserved by Richard, as a house of the highest observance and thus a particularly worthy recipient of patronage. D'Aubigny family ties were also of importance in the foundation and endowment of the cells of Beadlow, Wallingford and Wymondham. The role of Lanfranc in the abbey's accumulation of dependencies also appears to have been significant. A close relative of Abbot Paul, Lanfranc seems to have widely recommended St Albans as a worthy mother house. Robert de Tosny stated in his foundation charter that he handed over Belvoir to St Albans 'with the advice of Lord Archbishop Lanfranc', whereas Matthew Paris accorded a similar role to the archbishop in the receipt of Wallingford and Tynemouth Priories.[154]

---

153 P. Taylor, 'The Early St Albans Endowment and its Chroniclers', *Historical Research*, lxviii (1995), pp. 129–30.
154 *Mon. Ang.*, III, pp. 288–9, no. 1; GASA, I, pp. 56–7. For similar conclusions, see Chibnall, 'Problème des réseaux monastiques', pp. 344–5.

No other monastery in Anglo-Norman England enjoyed such a potent combination of qualities. Nevertheless, the success of St Mary's York and Nostell in attracting cells can be put down to similar, if less pronounced, strengths. As a royal foundation, St Mary's Abbey attracted patronage from almost every baron with Yorkshire connections, but appears most notable for its dynamism. Not only did its monks receive three large dependencies, but they also colonised the independent abbey of Colchester and two or three small cells, as well as inadvertently spawning Fountains Abbey.[155] Nostell Priory appears equally energetic, attracting very widespread grants of land and providing the community for the first Augustinian priory in Scotland, the royal foundation of Scone.[156] That Archbishop Thurstan also played an important part in attracting patronage to both St Mary's York and Nostell is occasionally intimated in surviving records. William le Meschin's foundation charter for St Bees notes that his foundation was placed under the obedience of St Mary's York 'by your advice, Archbishop Thurstan', whereas the grant of Woodkirk to Nostell by William earl of Warenne, Ralph de Lisle and his son William was said to have been made 'by the hand of Archbishop Thurstan'.[157] Gloucester's popularity as a recipient of dependencies, meanwhile, seems to have resulted primarily from its use by the barons who conquered Wales as a means for reforming the Celtic church;[158] and Glastonbury seems to have performed a similar role, since three of its four daughter houses were situated in Ireland or Wales.

An abbey might also be selected as a mother house because of its reputation in a particular region. Evesham was selected to colonise the new monastic cathedral at Odense, for example, owing to its reputation in Scandinavia, preserved after the Conquest by Abbot Aethelwig.[159] But in many cases, the choice of mother house probably arose from the accidents of feudal geography or simply the appearance of a benefactor wishing to found a cell within a monastery's sphere of influence. Peter de Valognes' grant of Binham Priory to St Albans can be partly explained by the location of his principal manor of Bennington in Hertfordshire, not far from that great abbey.[160] Similarly, houses from western England were usually chosen to preside over Irish foundations because of the provenance of many of the Anglo-Norman conquer-

155 A. Dawtry, 'The Last Bulwark of Anglo-Saxon Monasticism', in *Religion and National Identity*, ed. S. Mews, SCH, XVIII (1982), pp. 92–3; D. Bethell, 'The Foundation of Fountains Abbey and the State of St Mary's York in 1132', *JEH*, xvii (1966), pp. 11–27.
156 T. Burrows, 'The Geography of Monastic Property in Medieval England: a case study of Nostell and Bridlington Priories (Yorks)', *YAJ*, lvii (1985), pp. 79–86; J. Wilson, 'The Foundation of the Austin Priories of Nostell and Scone', *Scottish Historical Review*, vii (1910), pp. 141–59.
157 *Register of St Bees*, no. 2, pp. 28–30; *Early Yorkshire Charters*, III, no. 1616, pp. 278–9.
158 Brooke, 'St Peter of Gloucester', pp. 50–94; Chibnall, 'Problème des réseaux monastiques', pp. 346–7.
159 France, 'English Influence on Danish Monasticism', pp. 181–91.
160 J. A. Green, *The Aristocracy of Norman England* (Cambridge, 1997), p. 397.

ors.[161] Equally there might be a feudal connection between the founders of a cell and its mother house: the choice of Kenilworth as the mother house of Calwich, for instance, was presumably connected with the fact that Margery, the wife of its founder, Nicholas of Gresley, had been a ward of Geoffrey de Clinton.[162] Personal contacts between abbots and founders also played their part, and Abingdon's acquisition of Colne stemmed from Abbot Faricius' medical services to the family of Aubrey de Vere. When seeking to explain the haphazard distribution among cells, the importance of individual relations and coincidence must therefore be taken into account. The acquisition of one or two daughter houses by a large number of monasteries was the natural result of such circumstances.

But since the acquisition of at least one dependency was so common it must still be asked why great abbeys like Bury St Edmunds, Peterborough, St Augustine's Canterbury and the two Winchester houses received none. Part of the elusive answer to this question, apart from the element of contingency involved, probably lies in the patterns of lay benefactions to English abbeys traced by Emma Cownie. Several of the abbeys which were granted no cells were those which received relatively little lay patronage in general in the century after the Conquest, such as Peterborough and the two Winchester houses. But for abbeys such as Bury St Edmunds or St Augustine's Canterbury which quickly attracted considerable Norman support, these benefactions seem to have come too early to result in dependencies. Cownie has highlighted how grants tailed off at St Augustine's following the disastrous internal feud of 1089 and at Bury after the death of the inspirational Abbot Baldwin in 1098.[163] Their period of popularity arrived before the foundation of cells was common or fashionable and so they missed out on this particular form of patronage, for better or for worse.

The other reason why some abbeys possessed dependencies and others did not was of course their willingness or need to establish their own cells. Those abbeys with the necessary religious or antiquarian stimuli or with outlying estates they preferred to administer in this way acquired satellites, whereas others did not. It is striking that so many dependencies – about thirty-six in all (excluding two cells which were set up by episcopal founders who were not also *ex offico* heads of the mother houses concerned) – seem to have been established primarily at the mother house's own initiative; twenty-five monasteries apparently set up their own cells. But with the exception of the monasteries whose satellites were founded by their episcopal heads, only two – Durham and Battle – seem to have established more

161 For example, see McIntire, 'A Note on Grey Abbey', pp. 161–73.
162 M. Fortescue, *The History of Calwich Abbey* (London, 1914), p. 5.
163 Cownie, 'Normans as Patrons', p. 55; Cownie, *Religious Patronage*, pp. 66–79, 97–108. Bury St Edmunds possessed a daughter house at Thetford, which was converted into a nunnery in c.1160. Although not a true cell, since it was staffed by canons and not by Bury monks, the experience of presiding over the penurious Thetford might have dissuaded the abbey from acquiring other dependencies.

than one dependency themselves. Although not uncommon, therefore, the foundation of one's own daughter houses was not, it seems, undertaken lightly. Durham alone, which established a remarkable seven satellites, was prepared to set up a family of cells itself. Nevertheless, a surprising number of abbeys seem to have established a single dependency either for religious or economic reasons. For the great houses of Anglo-Norman England, it would appear that the possession of a cell or two was for a time a fashionable appendage.

Conclusion

The circumstances surrounding the foundation of dependent priories are worth studying in some detail, both for the light they throw on lay religion and because of the prevalence of cells in Anglo-Norman England, Wales and Ireland. The sheer variety of motivations for the establishment of English dependencies emerges clearly from this survey, and indicates that simple explanations for the appearance of this kind of monastery in England between 1066 and 1250 are unsatisfactory. Nevertheless, it is important to try to identify which of the several identifiable factors in the foundation of English cells were most influential. Previous assessments of this question, all of which have focused primarily on the alien priories (though usually including the less well-studied English cells in their calculations), have pointed to economic and pastoral considerations. However, it is the central contention of this chapter that, in common with most independent monasteries, satellite priories were most often established to intercede for the souls of their founders. It is also contended that cells set up to serve sites hallowed by their eremitic or saintly connections were more common than is usually believed. These conclusions, if accepted, have important ramifications for the evaluation of English dependencies. With so many apparently founded to fulfil a genuinely religious purpose, these cells certainly cannot be dismissed as mere tools of estate management with little or no spiritual value. Aided by hindsight, the historian might well decry the insistence of dependencies' founders in receiving a concrete return for their benefactions, the irresponsibility of great abbeys in accepting their proposals and the ossifying force of custom which made these sites thenceforward inalienably monastic; but he must also acknowledge that the intentions behind the majority of foundations were pious and honourable.

The circumstances of foundation for any monastery were also of great importance for that house's later history. In the case of daughter houses, this was especially true. An existence of tutelage was determined for these priories owing to their establishment by abbeys themselves or by their lay founders' lack of ability or desire, for whatever reason, to ensure the independent status of their foundation. The subsequent relations between mother and daughter house were strongly influenced by the manner in which the latter came into being. Those dependencies established by the abbeys themselves generally remained tightly bound to their parents. For houses set up by lay founders, a succession of patrons followed whose interests influenced and complicated the dealings between monastery and cell. And in the few cases where a pre-existing community was taken over somewhat ambiguously, as at Dover or Stone, the acquisitive and standardising instincts of powerful mother houses predestined a future of conflict and dispute. Equally, the size of the dependency's early endowment largely determined its fortunes thereafter: in general, those houses founded poor remained poor and their later existence was characterised by a long struggle for solvency. And finally, the purpose for which a dependency was established must have had a significant effect on the nature of its subsequent history. Cells founded as bailiwicks sometimes preserved their largely administrative role, whereas those set up in remote places for religious reasons often retained an eremitical character; for the monks of Durham, staying at the priory's cells at Stamford and Farne Island must have been very different experiences. In these ways and in others the origins of a dependency were pivotal to its future development. How they and their parent abbeys strove to cope with and escape from their destinies must now be examined.

2

The Constitutional Affairs of English Cells

The recorded history of English dependencies is littered with disputes. The many altercations involving cells, including some of the most interminable litigations known to medieval England, arose largely because daughter houses fell awkwardly between competing jurisdictions. The mother house, the cell itself, its patron and the ordinary (and to a lesser extent king and pope) all competed first to establish and then to defend the rights they believed were justly theirs. The normal relations between a monastery, its patron and its ecclesiastical overseer were thrown into confusion by the insertion of an additional jurisdiction, a mother house, whose jealous control of its daughter threatened to deprive its rivals of their accustomed powers. It was to take many decades, sometimes centuries, before workable compromises between abbey, patron and bishop were found. Relations between mother houses and their daughters were no less complicated. Some satellites were extremely tightly controlled by their parents; others were allowed a considerable measure of freedom in practice. Occasionally, serious disputes arose between abbeys and their dependencies and a number of cells even succeeded in extricating themselves to some extent from the grip of their parents. It is easy to exaggerate the storminess of these various relationships, since the surviving sources tend to emphasise discord rather than harmony. Nevertheless, a detailed examination of the ways in which the interests and expectations of the different parties clashed is necessary to make sense of the catalogue of disputes which dominate the recorded histories of so many dependent priories.

Founders' expectations

The precise relations between monastery and dependency were rarely defined at the moment of the cell's foundation, and most founders were content simply to signal their house's subjection to the larger house. It has sometimes been said that both abbeys and founders had only vague ideas about the status of the houses they were establishing. Dr Chibnall suggested that the cells of Bec were set up by men with unclear intentions and doubted that the early heads of Bec 'visualised any kind of constitutional bond to maintain the abbot's authority in the subject priories'.[1] In some cases this might have been so and it is likely that not all founders had the same expectations. But it is noticeable that several founders of larger dependencies used the word '*cella*' in their original charters of gift, and this word can also be found in many royal confirmations of daughter houses from an early date. What meaning did *cella* carry in these documents? By the time of the first foundations of satellite priories in medieval England, the fundamental characteristics of the daughter house had been well established by the Cluniacs and their imitators. These cells were at least partially subjected to the jurisdiction of their mother house and, where an external benefactor was involved, the issuing of a charter provided a juridical link between the two houses and implied an enduring union. The profession of all monks at the mother house, the appointment of priors by the abbot, an annual tribute as a mark of subjection and the abbot's right to visit and correct his satellites were all common features of existing networks of daughter houses.[2] It is therefore reasonable to assume that when Anglo-Norman benefactors donated a priory to a great abbey as a *cella*, their understanding of the term was based, however loosely, on these characteristics. This conclusion is supported by the stipulations made by founders who sought a greater degree of independence for their houses than was customary.

Although few founders of English dependencies specified the powers that the mother house was to enjoy over its new priory, those that did sought to limit the abbey's rights. Such attempts were not unprecedented. Many Cluniac houses on the Continent retained a good measure of independence and several English founders also succeeded in circumscribing Cluny's authority over their priories.[3] The compositions made between founders of English dependencies and their mother houses provide some indication of the norm from which they were seeking to depart. For his foundation at Binham, Peter de Valognes required in a charter of the early twelfth century that the priory 'should be subjected to the church of St Albans *in cella* in the same way that the church of St Pancras of Lewes is subject to the church of St Peter of Cluny'.[4] De Valognes added that Binham should pay an annual

1 Morgan, *Bec*, pp. 11–13.
2 See above, pp. 18–19.
3 Knowles, *MO*, pp. 151–8.
4 *Mon. Ang.*, III, pp. 345–6, no. 1. The meaning of this reference is not entirely clear. According to the forged foundation charter of Lewes Priory, William de Warenne had secured important privileges for the house: namely that its priors should be chosen from the most talented monks available to the abbot of Cluny (excepting the priors of Cluny and La Charité); that once installed those priors should be irremovable unless for a just cause; and that the mother house would interfere in domestic affairs only when issuing regulations for the entire order: ibid., V, pp. 12–13, no. 2. Professor Barlow, however, has suggested that all the constitutional clauses in this charter were later fabrications made in order to bolster Lewes' case in late twelfth-century disputes with Cluny. But de Valognes' reference loses all meaning if no provision for Lewes' relations with Cluny had been made at the priory's foundation. The 1181 and 1201

pension of one silver mark to St Albans and no more and that the abbot should stay at his cell just once each year, for a maximum of eight days and with only thirty men. Finally, it was stipulated that anyone admitted to the priory should be returned to Binham after they had been received, blessed, professed and if necessary (but only with the prior's permission) educated at St Albans.

At about the same time, the founder of Binham's sister house in Norfolk, Wymondham, also laid down certain regulations tending to restrict the authority of St Albans over his priory. William d'Aubigny enjoined that the monks of his foundation should elect their own priors, with the rights of the mother house reduced to an honourable reception at Wymondham when in the neighbourhood and a yearly payment of one silver mark as a recognition of the priory's subjection. A final, pregnant, clause was inserted, allowing the king or the patron to elevate Wymondham to the status of an abbey if they so wished, 'and then the abbey will be free and absolved from the silver mark'.[5] The initial charters of the considerably later foundations of Snape (c.1155) and Finchale (c.1193) also sought to limit the powers of the mother house. William Martel contented himself with restricting the pension and visiting rights of Colchester Abbey over Snape; but Henry du Puiset, founder of Finchale, was more ambitious, reserving to himself and his successors certain rights over the appointment of the house's prior, although he was soon persuaded by Durham to quitclaim these powers.[6]

From these few, limited attempts to restrict mother-house autonomy – less inhibiting than the privileges acquired by the founders of many Cluniac priories – some impression emerges of the rights parent abbeys were expected to enjoy. Attempts to limit the sums extracted from daughter houses and the length of visitations indicate that abbeys customarily levied an annual census from their cells and visited them regularly. Equally, the clauses inserted by the founders of Wymondham and Finchale restricting the mother house's ability to select the heads of these satellites suggest that St Albans and Durham would otherwise have automatically assumed such powers, as does Durham's reaction to du Puiset's demand. Peter de Valognes'

agreements between Lewes' patron and mother house suggest that the main issue at stake now was the method of appointment of the heads of the priory. Although both documents lay down that the prior of Lewes should be irremovable unless by a just cause, neither strongly emphasise this point and it may well be that these clauses represent the reassertion of an important principle rather than the negotiation of a new settlement. It is certainly not inconceivable that Lewes should have been granted the right to perpetual priors from the outset; the foundation charter of Lewes' daughter house of Farley stipulates that the latter house's prior could only be removed for a reasonable cause: F. Barlow, 'William I's Relations with Cluny', *JEH*, xxxii (1981), pp. 131–41; *Early Yorkshire Charters*, ed. W. Farrer and C. T. Clay, 12 vols in 10, Yorkshire Archaeological Society, Record Series, Extra Series, I–X (1914–65), VIII, pp. 59–62, nos 78–9, pp. 119–23; Knowles, MO, pp. 155–6.

5   *Mon. Ang.*, III, p. 330, no. 2.
6   Ibid., IV, p. 558, no. 1; Raine, *Priory of Finchale*, nos 22–3, pp. 23–5.

stipulation about new recruits may also imply that the right of a parent abbey to receive profession of its daughter's inmates was commonplace. In other words, the basic powers exercised by Cluny over its dependencies seem ordinarily to have been extended to the mother houses of English cells. Although no foundation charter specified that an abbey should enjoy these fundamental rights over its cells, the best explanation for this omission therefore is not that founders and abbeys did not know what they were committing themselves to, but rather that such powers were implicit in the grant of a *cella*.

In two cases, however, specific rights were accorded to the mother house in foundation charters, which may in turn suggest that they were not automatically received. Alan III of Richmond stated in his charter for Rumburgh of c.1136 that 'the monks of York will have the power to place and replace the priors and monks there at their will'.[7] Similarly, Richard fitz Roger's foundation charter for Lytham, issued much later (1191×1194), permitted the prior of Durham to appoint and remove the cell's monks at pleasure.[8] The ability to exercise complete control over the personnel of a daughter house represented a rather fuller dependence than was imposed on many contemporary Cluniac priories, whose communities were not constantly circulated. It may be that, like Peter de Valognes, some founders expected the priors of their houses, once appointed by the mother house, to be perpetual – that is, to remain in office until death or retirement, unless some reasonable cause necessitated their removal – and also that their monks would be recruited locally and, after profession and perhaps training in the parent abbey, would spend the rest of their careers in the daughter house. There was therefore more than one form that the relations between mother and daughter houses could take and it is quite feasible that many founders envisaged a rather looser dependence for their priories than later evolved. What limited material survives about the level of subjection of the English dependencies in the twelfth and thirteenth centuries, however, suggests that mother houses soon took advantage of the open-ended nature of most foundation charters to assert the fullest measure of control over their satellites.

By the fourteenth century, when good evidence can be found for the operation of several networks of cells, it is clear that the majority of mother houses exercised the right of appointing and removing at will both the priors and the monks of their dependencies.[9] At what point they assumed this power is not always clear. St Mary's York and Durham unquestionably enjoyed this privilege from the start over Rumburgh and Lytham. A later St Albans account of the foundation of Tynemouth asserted that Robert de

---

7 Oxford, Bodleian Library, MS Top. Suffolk d. 15, fols 35r–35v. This privilege was almost immediately confirmed by Bishop Everard of Norwich, hinting that it might have been vulnerable and therefore unusual: *English Episcopal Acta VI: Norwich 1070–1214*, ed. C. Harper-Bill (Oxford, 1990), no. 51, pp. 46–8.

8 *Mon. Ang.*, IV, p. 282, no. 1.

9 See below, pp. 115–28.

Mowbray granted to the abbots of St Albans 'the free disposition of the priors and monks [there], in both placing them and removing them, as they consider necessary'; unfortunately de Mowbray's foundation charter does not survive to confirm or refute this statement, which may well be anachronistic or untrustworthy.[10] In 1163, Pope Alexander III confirmed to Abbot Laurence of Westminster the three cells of his abbey, adding that 'absolutely no clerk or layman should set themselves against the placing or removing of the priors of the monks or the monks [in the abbey's dependencies], but the abbot of the time should have free faculty to place and remove them, where suitable, without any contradiction'.[11] Reading Abbey acquired a similar confirmation of these rights from the Holy See in the early thirteenth century, whereas St Osyth's approached the patron of its cell at Blythburgh, Henry II, for recognition of its powers. Between 1163 and 1170, the king granted to the abbot and canons of St Osyth's 'that they should have the free ability to place the prior they want in their church of Blythburgh . . . and to remove him from there according to their will'.[12] But since other mother houses contented themselves with obtaining royal, episcopal and papal confirmations of the mere fact of the possession of their cells, the precise powers they initially exercised remain difficult to recover.

Nevertheless, the manoeuvres employed by the abbey of St Albans to overcome the restrictive stipulations of its cells' founders illustrate well how mother houses might set out to maximise their influence over dependencies. By the time of Abbot Robert de Gorron (1151–66), St Albans had begun to appoint the priors of Wymondham itself, despite William d'Aubigny's explicit wish to the contrary.[13] When the founder's son, the first earl of Arundel, argued that the mother house's power over its cell consisted only of an annual tribute and two nights' hospitality when visiting neighbouring Binham, the abbot claimed his appointment of the current prior itself conveyed substantial rights: 'if the prior has the name and the office of prior from me, mine is whatever he possesses . . . [and] mine is to make good the failing of the prior in all things'.[14] Although the earl challenged this interpretation, he did not apparently dispute further the abbey's right to appoint and depose priors of Wymondham. There is also evidence that the privileges of Lewes – if they were genuine – demanded for Binham were not long if ever respected by St Albans. The claim to non-interference was in practice overridden by the abbot of St Albans' accustomed right of regular visitation,

10 *Matthaei Parisiensis, Monachi Sancti Albani, Chronica Majora*, ed. H. R. Luard, 7 vols, RS, lvii (1872–83), II, p. 31.
11 *PUE*, II, no. 101, pp. 364–6.
12 *Reading Abbey Cartularies*, ed. B. R. Kemp, 2 vols, Camden Society, 4th series, xxxi, xxxiii (1986–7), I, nos 361–2, pp. 293–4; *Blythburgh Priory Cartulary*, ed. C. Harper-Bill, 2 parts, Suffolk Records Society, Suffolk Charters, II–III (1980–1), I, no. 63, p. 56.
13 GASA, I, p. 171.
14 For Matthew Paris' account of this dispute, see ibid., I, pp. 166–75.

which was being exercised in Abbot Robert's time; and Abbot John de Cella (1195–1214), asserting that he was acting 'according to power not long ago granted to him by the Roman Pontiff', recalled and replaced Prior Thomas of Binham.[15] In other words, subsequent privileges, acquired either by precedent or papal grant, were claimed to have superseded the founders' original decrees for their cells. In the thirteenth century and beyond, Wymondham and Binham were controlled as tightly as the other St Albans dependencies.

That the abbots of St Albans should attempt to augment their power over their daughter houses is not surprising. More difficult to explain perhaps is the apparent lack of resistance to this endeavour from the priories' patrons. The dispute between Abbot de Gorron and the earl of Arundel did not stem from St Albans contravening the priory's foundation charter, but because the abbot had followed up complaints from priory tenants that the prior and the earl's men had molested them; only then did the quarrel spread to wider questions of jurisdiction. Thereafter, rather than defending their priory's autonomy, Wymondham's patrons concentrated their efforts on acquiring for themselves a voice in the selection of the house's prior (see below). Binham provides a similar story. The infamous siege of the priory by its patron Robert fitz Walter, relieved by King John himself, ended a dispute with St Albans over the aforementioned removal of Prior Thomas, a favourite of the patron.[16] However, rather than defend the cell's claim to perpetual priors which seems to have been implicit in its foundation charter (about which he was probably ignorant), fitz Walter procured a forged charter from a rogue monk of St Albans, which stated that the abbot could not remove Binham's prior without the consent of the house's patron. St Albans naturally opposed this deceit and after his suit failed in the *curia regis*, fitz Walter resorted to violence. Only after his death was the spurious charter recovered and no later attempts to enforce the spirit of Binham's foundation charter are recorded. These examples suggest that determined mother houses would have had little difficulty in maximising their rights over cells whose founders had made no such stipulations about the extent of the parent abbey's authority.

Disputes with Patrons

Although patrons do not seem to have striven to ensure maximum independence for their cells in the twelfth and thirteenth centuries, there was still considerable scope for conflict with mother houses. The majority of

---

[15] Ibid., I, pp. 169–70, 226. Perhaps a reference to Alexander III's 1170 bull, *Cum vos et*, which, among other things, gave the prior and convent of St Albans the power to institute and remove priors and monks in the abbey cells without contradiction, in times of an abbatial vacancy: *PUE*, III, no. 170, pp. 307–8.

[16] GASA, I, pp. 225–9.

problems arose, as Dr Wood has demonstrated, because parent abbeys claimed rights which would normally have belonged to patrons: namely, a voice in the election of priors and custody during vacancies.[17] Although the free election of monastic superiors was upheld by the early thirteenth century by both secular and canon law,[18] a lay patron might still seek to exert some influence on the choice of a prior. Such interference usually remained informal, but a small number of patrons succeeded in acquiring a more official role in the election of the heads of dependent priories in the late twelfth or thirteenth centuries. On demonstrating his right to the advowson of Stone Priory, after a dispute with its mother house Kenilworth, Robert III of Stafford was accorded between c.1184 and c.1194 certain limited powers concerning the priors of the house. It was agreed that 'if any canon should be found in the house of Kenilworth or in the church of Stone whom the said Lord Robert should specially love above the others, the prior of Kenilworth should take heed of the said Lord Robert for that canon', providing he was considered worthy in the mother house. Moreover, any absentee prior or canon at Stone, 'unless he mend his ways', should be removed at Stafford's petition. This settlement seems to have endured for only half a century, though, since at Easter 1243, Robert IV of Stafford quitclaimed the advowson of Stone, and presumably his rights over its priors, to Kenilworth in the *curia regis*.[19]

The part played in the choice of the priors of Wymondham and Breedon by the patrons of these cells in the thirteenth century was considerably more intrusive. Although the earl of Arundel was said to have influenced the appointment of two priors of Wymondham in the time of Abbot William of Trumpington of St Albans (1214–35),[20] in September 1264 'a startlingly uncanonical settlement' was made between Abbot Roger of St Albans and Isabella d'Aubigny, countess of Arundel: namely, that on the next vacancy the countess would nominate three worthy monks of St Albans from whom the abbot would choose a prior.[21] A similar agreement concerning the election of the priors of Breedon, a cell of Nostell, was brokered in the late twelfth or early thirteenth century.[22] The priory's patron Walter de Tateshall came to an agreement with Nostell that on a vacancy at its dependency, the mother house would present two Breedon canons to him from whom Walter

[17] S. Wood, *English Monasteries and their Patrons in the Thirteenth Century* (Oxford, 1955), esp. pp. 40–100.

[18] For a discussion of this development, see ibid., pp. 40–3.

[19] BL, Add. MS 47677, fols 110r–111r.

[20] GASA, I, pp. 260, 274–5.

[21] Ibid., I, pp. 407–9; Wood, *English Monasteries*, p. 61. The quotation is Dr Wood's.

[22] Nichols and Dugdale both dated this agreement to the early fourteenth century, but Walter de Tateshall died in 1199 or 1200: GEC, *The Complete Peerage*, ed. V. Gibbs et al., 12 vols in 13 (London, 1910–59), XII(i), p. 648; J. Nichols, *The History and Antiquities of the County of Leicester*, 4 vols (London, 1795–1811), III(ii), p. 694; *Mon. Ang.*, VI(i), p. 97.

would select a prior. If no suitable candidates could be found at the cell, two canons from Nostell would be presented to the patron instead. Not only was the mother house's right to appoint the priors of Breedon to be forfeited, but a further clause provided that the head of the cell 'will remain there in stability for all his life, as long as he behaves himself canonically, saving his profession and subjection to the church of St Oswald of Nostell'.[23] That this arrangement took root and endured is indicated by the findings of an episcopal inquiry held in March 1293, on the presentation of William de Willeys as prior of Breedon, that such a procedure was customary. Similarly, we learn from the St Albans chronicle that Prior Adam Pulleyn of Wymondham was appointed in this way, probably between c.1274 and 1282.[24]

Not surprisingly, the patronal exercise of powers usually held by the mother house was unpopular at both St Albans and Nostell, and both monasteries succeeded in reasserting full control over the selection of their cells' priors in the early fourteenth century. At Wymondham, the problems experienced during the lengthy rule of Prior Pulleyn, who was thought at the mother house 'to bend more to the patron's will than the abbot's', motivated St Albans to action.[25] The opportunity presented itself on the death of Prior Pulleyn in December 1303, during the minority of the cell's patron (who coincidentally, as at Breedon, was a de Tateshall). The following January, therefore, a successor, John of Stevenage, was selected at St Albans and presented to the king's escheator. The rather dramatic account of the abbey chronicler describes how the prior-elect entered Wymondham 'without any perturbation from the Escheator or anyone else', before being 'installed peacefully, without any secular presence' as head of the house.[26] Thereafter, it would seem that the priors of Wymondham were appointed without reference to the house's patron.

Though this was undoubtedly a bold move, Nostell's response to patronal interference at Breedon was even more audacious. In this case, the spur to action was the death of the last of Breedon's de Tateshall patrons in 1306. On the next vacancy at the priory, in 1314, a single canon, Robert of Pontefract, was presented to the patron. Even more daringly, this presentation was made not to the new lord of Breedon, John de Orreby, but to Thomas of Lancaster, who was asserted to be the heir of the earls of Derby, the founders of the priory. Lancaster was able to frustrate de Orreby's

23 R. McKinley (ed.), 'The Cartulary of Breedon Priory', unpublished Manchester MA thesis (1950), pp. 181–2.
24 *The Rolls and Register of Bishop Oliver Sutton 1280–1299*, ed. R. M. T. Hill, 8 vols, Lincoln Record Society, xxxix, xliii, xlviii, lii, lx, lxiv, lxix, lxxvi (1948–86), VIII, p. 53; GASA, II, pp. 82–3. Pulleyn is said here to have been appointed 'with the assent of the Lady [Isabella] Countess of Arundel', who died before November 1282. The latest known reference to preceding priors of Wymondham is to Prior Roger in c.1274: GEC, *Complete Peerage*, I, p. 239; HRH, II, p. 136.
25 GASA, II, p. 82.
26 Ibid., II, pp. 87–8.

attempts to recover the priory's advowson, which remained thereafter (apart from a brief period with the king following the earl's forfeiture) in Lancastrian hands.[27] Moreover, future priors of Breedon were chosen at Nostell, with just the assent of the patron, as was customary elsewhere, although many do seem to have remained in the post until their promotion or death.[28]

The replacement of an unsatisfactory patron with a more amenable advocate was a particularly radical response to irregular patronal demands. Disputes over vacancy rights, though not uncommon, proved easier to resolve.[29] In 1199, the seneschal of the earl of Richmond held an inquisition to learn whether his lord should have the custody of Rumburgh Priory during vacancies at the cell, and willingly accepted the verdict when it was concluded that the earl had no such right.[30] At Breedon and Ewyas Harold, meanwhile, it was agreed that the patron would send a representative to the priory during vacancies, but not take any proceeds thereof.[31] Indeed the most common instigator of custody disputes seems to have been the king, either as patron or via his escheator during minorities. St Albans, for example, faced royal claims to the custody of Wymondham Priory in 1303 by the Crown when a vacancy at the cell coincided with the minority of its patron. The abbey reacted with considerable alarm to this threat, not least because the regular rotation of the priory's heads would make this a particularly expensive precedent, but was able to ward off the escheator successfully.[32]

The fate of a cell during voidances of the mother house might also become a matter of dispute. In the 1320s, Thorney and Crowland Abbeys were forced to contest the king's attempts to take their dependencies of Deeping St James and Freiston into his custody during vacancies at the mother house.[33] Matters were further complicated when voidances at an abbey and its cell occurred at the same time, and in 1290 St Albans had to resist attempts to take Binham into the Crown's custody after its sick prior was recalled to the mother house during a vacancy there.[34] In each of these cases, the king withdrew his claims under challenge (though at Binham only

[27] Leeds, West Yorkshire Archives, NP/C1, pp. 98–9; McKinley, 'Cartulary of Breedon', no. 16, pp. 18–19.
[28] McKinley, 'Cartulary of Breedon', nos 15–17, 20, pp. 18–22; CPR, 1321–1324, p. 415. For lists of the priors of Breedon, see McKinley, 'Cartulary of Breedon', pp. xxxi–xxxiii, and HRH, II, pp. 344–5.
[29] For a discussion of the issues surrounding custody over cells, see Wood, English Monasteries, pp. 80–3.
[30] Mon. Ang., III, pp. 612–13, no. 4.
[31] McKinley, 'Cartulary of Breedon', no. 18, pp. 20–1; CClR, 1323–1327, p. 203; Calendar of Inquisitions Post Mortem (HMSO, 1904–), III, p. 455.
[32] GASA, II, pp. 83–7.
[33] CClR, 1323–1327, pp. 66–7; Mon. Ang., IV, pp. 170–1, no. 7 (Deeping St James, 1324); Calendar of Inquisitions Miscellaneous, 7 vols (HMSO, 1916–69), II, no. 844, p. 211; CClR, 1327–1330, p. 7 (Freiston, 1327).
[34] GASA, II, p. 16.

after the former prior was hastily restored), but there are signs that mother houses were not always able to rebuff patronal claims for custody of their cells. Edward III is found presenting to a church belonging to St Albans' cell of Hertford in 1375, during a vacancy of that priory, whereas in 1282 a dispute broke out between Edward I and Gilbert de Clare, earl of Gloucester and Hertford, over which of them as patrons of St James' Priory Bristol and its mother house (Tewkesbury) respectively should have custody of the cell during voidances at Tewkesbury.[35]

Another area of potential dispute concerned the supplementary advantages that accompanied the patronage of a monastery, such as hospitality. Once again, the main example of this kind of controversy comes from the St Albans chronicles: the clash in c.1299 between Robert V de Tateshall, patron of Wymondham, and the abbey over a dole of bread and ale allegedly owed by the cell to its patron.[36] But if there were several reasons why patrons and mother houses might clash over dependent priories, it remains difficult to assess how common such disputes were: it is noticeable that most of our examples of disharmony come from the chronicles of St Albans whose cells were unusual in their size and supposed liberties. It seems likely, therefore, that most patrons were content with the powers they were allowed to exercise over their priories. Yet for mother houses the danger remained that a dissatisfied patron might conclude that the best way to increase his authority over a daughter house was to secure its autonomy. As a result, the incentive to stay on good terms with the patrons of one's dependencies, wherever possible, was always strong.

Disputes with Bishops

It was not only with their daughter houses' patrons that abbeys might clash. Similar jurisdictional conflicts could arise with the ecclesiastical authorities. There were occasional disputes with rival religious institutions, such as the unsuccessful attempts of the dean and chapters of Exeter and Hereford to exert some dominion over the priories of St Nicholas and St Guthlac in their cities; and problems with the Holy See were not unknown.[37] But it was the

---

35 CPR, 1374–1377, p. 132, 1281–1292, pp. 21–2.
36 De Tateshall twice refused Abbot John de Berkhamsted (1290–1301) entry to the priory for his visitation because of the withdrawal of this dole. However, the abbot's successor, John de Maryns (1302–9), thought it prudent to settle the dispute and agreed to pay de Tateshall four loaves and four flagons of ale, worth £8, whenever he came to his manor of Wymondham: GASA, II, pp. 23, 63–4, 82–3. The next patroness of the priory remitted her claim to this allowance.
37 R. Graham, 'The Benedictine Priory of St Nicholas, at Exeter', JBAA, new series, xxxiii (1927), pp. 62–4; Oxford, Balliol College MS 271, fols 113r–113v. Monks were provided by the pope to the headships of the cells of Wetheral in 1310 and Penwortham in 1399, on the first occasion to the severe detriment of the priory, and ineffectually to Cardigan in 1368; and there were papal efforts to exercise some

diocesan who, like lay patrons, was most likely to find that rights which he ordinarily took for granted were questioned when he tried to assert them over dependencies. The presentation of priors to the bishop for institution and induction; the swearing of canonical obedience and the submission to his powers of correction and visitation; payment of the normal dues and attendance at his synod; and the bishop's discretion in appointing collectors for clerical taxation: all these episcopal rights over non-exempt monasteries, clearly established by the thirteenth century, were at one time or other brought into question by mother houses. The collision between two great ecclesiastical institutions, both jealous of their privileges and their churches' honour, was often dramatic. The origins of most of these conflicts can be traced to three main areas of uncertainty: the bishop's rights to visit dependencies; episcopal jurisdiction over the appointment and removal of dative priors (those removable at the will of the mother house); and the bishop's authority over the daughter houses of exempt abbeys.

Of these three kinds of dispute, disagreements over the visitation of daughter houses seem to have generated the least controversy. Where the dependency was situated in the same diocese as its parent, as was very often the case, the diocesan tended to examine both mother and daughter houses together.[38] But matters might be less straightforward for cells situated in a different diocese from their parent abbey. In such cases it was often accepted that the cell's diocesan should have the right to visit that priory separately; and late medieval visitation records survive from several dependencies in this situation, including Blythburgh, Breedon, St Leonard's Stamford and Leominster.[39] But several small satellites, such as Hirst, Kilpeck and Lincoln, seem to have escaped separate visitation even though they lay outside the diocese of their mother house. Presumably these priories avoided inspection on account of their small size and their resemblance to bailiwicks; the prior of Llanthony Secunda, as we have seen, succeeded in warding off episcopal visitation of its 'cell' at Duleek in the late fourteenth century by claiming

control over Tynemouth Priory during vacancies in the 1340s: *St Mary's Chronicle*, p. 47; *The Register of John de Halton, Bishop of Carlisle, AD 1292–1324*, ed. W. N. Thompson, 2 vols, C&Y Soc., xii–xiii (1913), II, pp. 11–12, 87–8 (Wetheral); *CPL*, V, p. 190 (Penwortham); *Accounts Rendered by Papal Collectors in England 1317–1378*, ed. W. E. Lunt and E. B. Graves (Philadelphia, 1968), pp. 355–6, 397 (Cardigan); *GASA*, II, pp. 390–4; J. E. Sayers, 'Papal Privileges for St Albans Abbey and its Dependencies', in *The Study of Medieval Records: Essays in Honour of Kathleen Major*, ed. D. A. Bullough and R. L. Storey (Oxford, 1971), p. 74 (Tynemouth).

38 See below, pp. 131–4.

39 *Visitations of the Diocese of Norwich AD 1492–1532*, ed. A. Jessopp, Camden Society, new series, xliii (1888), pp. 177, 216, 284–5; *Visitations of Religious Houses in the Diocese of Lincoln, 1420–1449*, ed. A. H. Thompson, 3 vols, Lincoln Record Society, vii, xiv, xxi (1914–29), II, pp. 40–3, III, pp. 346–7; *Registrum Thome de Cantilupo, Episcopi Herefordensis, AD 1275–1282*, ed. R. G. Griffiths, C&Y Soc., ii (1907), pp. 265–7; *Registrum Ricardi de Swinfield, Episcopi Herefordensis, AD 1283–1317*, ed. W. W. Capes, C&Y Soc., vi (1909), pp. 149–50.

that the house was a depot rather than a religious house.[40] Those distant cells that could not avoid the attention of their diocesan, however, might find themselves subject to dual visitation: the inmates of the cells of Durham, Kenilworth and Nostell, for example, were all summoned to mother-house visitations regardless of the fact that the priories of Lytham, St Leonard's Stamford, Brooke and Breedon were also inspected by their own diocesans.[41]

Episcopal rights of visitation and correction, however, might prove discomfiting in that the bishop thereby assumed the authority to dismiss unsuitable priors. This principle could hardly have been challenged by mother houses who tolerated the visitation in the first place, but in practice abbeys were sometimes reluctant to accept episcopal interference of this kind. On a visitation of St Guthlac's Hereford in 1321 Bishop Orleton deposed Prior William Ireby for dissolute living, without consulting Gloucester. The abbey might have accepted this decision had not Orleton appointed a successor himself. A fierce quarrel ensued, which ended with St Guthlac's in serious financial straits and with Ireby imprisoned by Orleton as the result of a bitter vendetta between the two.[42] Archbishop Pecham met with similar truculence during his metropolitan visitation of Wales in 1284, when he deposed the priors of the cells of Kidwelly and Brecon. In each case, an incredulous Pecham discovered that the offending prior had been restored almost immediately by the mother house;[43] and a disinclination to accept the archbishop's jurisdiction in this regard seems a more plausible explanation for their actions than disregard for the well-being of their daughter houses.

Disputes over the institution of dative priors, however, often proved even harder to resolve. Since only the headship of a perpetual priory constituted a benefice, the priors of most cells, being dative, did not in theory need to be presented to their ordinary. But the right to confirm and install the new heads of the religious houses in their dioceses was not lightly relinquished by bishops and many mother houses were unable to free themselves from this unwelcome procedure. Indeed the presentation of the priors of their cells for institution could prove highly damaging to a parent abbey wishing to maintain tight control over its satellites. The rite of institution implied security of tenure for the new incumbent, while most mother houses were determined to appoint and remove their subject priors at will. A rebellious prior could

---

40 See above, p. 6.
41 DCM, Register II, fols 67v, 85v, 142r; Dobson, *Durham Priory*, p. 232; VCH, *Warwickshire*, II, p. 88; *Visitations in the Diocese of Lincoln, 1517–31*, ed. A. H. Thompson, 3 vols, Lincoln Record Society, xxxiii, xxxv, xxxvii (1940–7), II, p. 86; VCH, *Yorkshire*, III, p. 233.
42 The story of Prior William Ireby is told in A. T. Bannister, 'A Note on an Obscure Episode in the History of St Guthlac's Priory, Hereford', *Transactions of the Woolhope Naturalists' Field Club*, xx (1908), pp. 20–4.
43 *Registrum Epistolarum fratris Johannis Peckham, Archiepiscopi Cantuariensis*, ed. C. T. Martin, 3 vols, RS, lxxvii (1882–5), III, no. 588, pp. 810–11; *The Register of John Pecham Archbishop of Canterbury 1279–1292*, ed. F. N. Davis and D. C. Douie, 2 vols, C&Y Soc., lxiv–lxv (1908–69), I, pp. 198–9.

point to his institution as evidence of his status as a perpetual prior, as did William Partrike at Lytham in the 1440s.[44] In 1433 or 1434, the abbot and convent of Chertsey wrote to Bishop Rudborne of St David's to request a remedy for unspecified problems that had arisen at their cell of Cardigan as a result of the institution of its heads to both the priory and the rectory there. According to the petitioners, the priors of Cardigan had not always been instituted in the past and this change, apparently made at the initiative of the abbey, had caused many disputes; and it may well be that their institution had made some of the heads of Cardigan more independently minded.[45]

The heads of many of the smallest cells, probably because they so little resembled perpetual priors, seem to have avoided this imposition in the same way that they remained clear of episcopal visitation. Moreover, a few mother houses successfully asserted the exemption of at least some of their satellites from the need to have their priors presented to and instituted by the diocesan. It would appear that the most effective way to achieve this end was to argue that the bishop's right of presentation and institution compromised the mother house's freedom to appoint and remove the heads of its cells at will. Indeed, episcopal confirmation of an abbey's right to place and replace the heads of its dependencies at pleasure was generally taken to acknowledge this position. 'Le Convenit' between the priory and bishop of Durham in 1229 admitted the former's complete freedom to appoint and remove all its monastic officials at will; thereafter, the heads of Durham's five cells within its own diocese were never presented to their ordinary.[46] Durham obtained no such confirmation from the bishops of Lincoln or the archdeacons of Richmond, and the priors of Stamford and Lytham continued to be presented to those dignitaries down to the Dissolution.

A similar arrangement obtained at Leominster Priory, a cell of Reading. In 1281 a dispute erupted between Bishop Cantilupe of Hereford and Reading Abbey after the latter omitted to present the new prior of Leominster, William of Kinton, to the former. Apart from arguing that Leominster was not a true priory and therefore not a benefice that could be instituted to, the abbey was able to point to Bishop Hugh Foliot's charter which acknowledged the abbey's rights to appoint and remove freely the

[44] Dobson, Durham Priory, pp. 327–41. See below, p. 95.

[45] Chertsey Abbey Cartularies, ed. M. S. Giuseppe and H. Jenkinson, 2 vols, Surrey Record Society, xii (1933–63), I, no. 104, pp. 104–5. Although the precise nature of the trouble is not clear from this incomplete document, Malden was certainly wrong in thinking that the problems referred to here concerned a clash with Gloucester Abbey over the very possession of Cardigan Priory: H. E. Malden, 'The Possession of Cardigan Priory by Chertsey Abbey (a study in some medieval forgeries)', TRHS, 3rd series, v (1911), pp. 141–56. See also C. N. L. Brooke, 'St Peter of Gloucester and St Cadog of Llancafarn', in Brooke, The Church and the Welsh Border in the Central Middle Ages (Bury St Edmunds, 1986), p. 56n.

[46] Feodarium Prioratus Dunelmensis, ed. W. Greenwell, SS, lviii (1872), p. 213. The five priories thus exempted were Farne Island, Finchale, Holy Island, Jarrow and Wearmouth.

heads of Leominster. In 1283 and again in 1285 Bishop Swinfield, Cantilupe's successor, confirmed these rights to Reading and the abbey's claims were thereby admitted: no future prior of Leominster was presented to the ordinary.[47] In this case, as at Durham, it was the existence of an earlier episcopal confirmation of Reading's powers that proved decisive. St Albans' *papal* confirmations of its freedom to place and replace the priors of its cells, however, were insufficient to earn their priors exemption from presentation to and institution by the diocesan (see below).

But although it might be argued that episcopal institution compromised a mother house's freedom to replace the heads of its cells as it wished, in reality few obstacles to the removal of instituted priors seem to have been raised. Only a handful of prelates are known to have challenged an abbey's liberty to change its subject priors at will on these grounds. Most prominent among these was Bishop Oliver Sutton of Lincoln (1280–99), whose insistence that evidence of a prior's resignation should be provided by the mother house before he would institute his successor led to a heated dispute with Kenilworth Priory in 1298–9 over its cell of Brooke. Sutton refused to accept the resignation of the prior of Brooke, Richard of Bromsgrove, on the grounds that it was made without his licence, and would not institute a successor until this was remedied. When his demand was ignored, the bishop deposed Bromsgrove and a new prior was installed. No further trouble over this matter is known at Brooke, and it is likely that Sutton's successors did not pursue his claims.[48] In 1334, Kenilworth faced another challenge to its right to recall freely the priors of its cells, this time from Bishop Northburgh of Coventry and Lichfield in relation to Calwich Priory; but the complaint was dropped after an inquisition found in favour of the priory.[49] Indeed, recorded instances of bishops successfully establishing the right to confirm the removal of the prior of an English cell are very rare. An agreement made in February 1267 between St Mary's York and Bishop de Chaury of Carlisle stipulated, amongst other things, that if the abbey wished to recall a prior of Wetheral, 'for any cause which the said abbot believed to be sufficient', they should send letters patent to the bishop informing him of their reasons for the dismissal, which was to be approved without difficulty.[50] The only other known instances of a bishop exercising any control over the removal of a

---

[47] *Reg. Swinfield*, pp. 28–32, 38–41 64, 100. The charter of Bishop Foliot that Swinfield confirmed was actually itself a confirmation of the acknowledgement of his predecessor, Hugh de Mapenore, of Reading's rights over its cell: *Reading Abbey Cartularies*, I, nos 361–3, pp. 293–5.

[48] *Sutton Rolls and Register*, II, pp. 157–9. For Sutton's record in this area, see R. Hill, 'Bishop Sutton and the Institution of Heads of Religious Houses in the Diocese of Lincoln', *EHR*, lviii (1943), pp. 201–9.

[49] *HRH*, II, p. 356; M. T. Fortescue, *The History of Calwich Abbey* (London, 1914), p. 22. For Northburgh's similar querying of Evesham's rights over its cell at Penwortham, see below, pp. 79–80.

[50] *The Register of the Priory of Wetherhal*, ed. J. E. Prescott, Cumberland and Westmorland Antiquarian and Archaeological Society, Extra Series, I (1897), no. 34, pp. 73–7.

dative prior relate to cathedral priories, where the bishop was titular abbot of the mother house.

As we have seen, Durham Priory succeeded from an early date in freeing itself from the interference of its bishop in monastic affairs, but other cathedral priories were less fortunate. The authority of the priors and convents of Canterbury and Worcester over Dover and Little Malvern respectively was seriously limited by their diocesans, who saw themselves rather than their chapters as the true masters of these cells.[51] The bishops of Norwich, whose predecessor, Herbert de Losinga, had been largely responsible for the foundation and endowment of four of their cathedral priory's five dependencies, also considered themselves to be entitled to a voice in these cells' affairs. Their right to institute the priors of Lynn, Yarmouth and Aldeby was established by the mid-thirteenth century, and the Norwich registers of the first half of the fourteenth century show the priory requesting episcopal permission to recall two priors of Hoxne.[52] In 1347, Bishop Bateman attempted to extend his powers over the Norwich dependencies by requiring the cathedral priory to send him the cells' yearly accounts for inspection; but this measure seems to have met with some resistance.[53] A far more serious dispute between the bishop and the cathedral priory broke out in 1386, which was not fully resolved until the mid-fifteenth century. Several areas of discord arose, but central to the quarrel was Bishop Despenser's claim to the power to appoint and remove several mother house obedientiaries and the priors of Lynn, Yarmouth, Aldeby and Hoxne. A judgement in favour of the bishop by Archbishop Walden and an appeal by both sides to the pope proved inconclusive, and in 1411 Archbishop Arundel devised a compromise which formed the basis of the eventual settlement. The bishop's claim to nominate and remove any of the priory's obedientiaries was found to be groundless, and the former arrangement whereby episcopal confirmation only was required for both the appointment and dismissal of the priors of Norwich's cells was ratified.[54]

The Norwich dispute and several of the other controversies mentioned above were drawn-out and acrimonious affairs. But the fiercest disputes between mother houses and bishops stemmed from the efforts of the exempt abbeys to extend their immunities to their satellites. It was by no means an established principle that daughter houses should enjoy the same privileges as their parents. Cluny's exemption from episcopal jurisdiction was granted

---

51 See below, pp. 102–4.

52 *The Charters of Norwich Cathedral Priory*, ed. B. Dodwell, 2 vols, PRS, new series, xl, xlvi (1965–80), I, no. 215, p. 126; NRO, DCN 40/10, fols 2v, 38r.

53 Of the two surviving copies of Bateman's injunctions, one has this ordinance deleted and the other omits it altogether: C. R. Cheney, 'Norwich Cathedral Priory in the Fourteenth Century', *Bulletin of the John Rylands Library*, xx (1936), p. 109.

54 CPL, V, pp. 11–12, 526–7. The Arundel ordinance is printed in E. H. Carter (ed.), *Studies in Norwich Cathedral History* (Norwich, 1935), pp. 46–59. This volume also contains a useful discussion of the dispute as a whole.

to her daughter houses in a bull of Pope Benedict VIII in 1016 and eight years later John XIX declared that all Cluniac monks should be freed from the authority of their diocesan.[55] However, the right to exemption of monasteries tied only loosely to Cluny was rarely accepted, and bishops often succeeded in modifying the liberties of a new dependency on the occasion of its foundation. As a result there grew up a patchwork of Cluniac immunities, with some houses enjoying full exemption from episcopal jurisdiction and others only partial freedom or none at all. There was, therefore, considerable scope for conflict when both rights of exemption and the satellite priory took root in English monasticism.

By the early thirteenth century, six English abbeys with cells had established their right to exemption.[56] These mother houses – Battle, Evesham, Glastonbury, Malmesbury, St Albans and Westminster – all needed to find a *modus vivendi* not only with their own bishops but also with the diocesans of their cells. The full extension of an abbey's right of exemption to its daughters would have conferred several valuable immunities: from the need to present new priors to the diocesan for their institution and induction; from the prior's oath of obedience to the bishop; from episcopal visitation; from the bishop's excommunication and general interdicts; and from attendance at and submission to the diocesan synod. It is often not clear precisely to what extent, if at all, the exempt abbeys' dependencies were released from episcopal jurisdiction. Both of Glastonbury's cells in England and Wales had been closed down by the mid-thirteenth century and consequently nothing is known about their relations with their diocesans. There seems to be no record of any dispute or composition between mother house and bishop over the cells of Battle either, but the earliest available records show the bishops of Exeter and St David's visiting Battle's dependencies in Exeter and Brecon and instituting their priors.[57] The bishops of Exeter reached a similar settlement with Malmesbury over Pilton Priory in April 1261. Despite Malmesbury's exemption, the right of the ordinary to visit Pilton and to institute its priors was confirmed, with a limit of 20s. placed on the procurations charged by the bishop on his visitation the only concession to the mother house.[58] Evesham, however, appears to have successfully asserted the exemption of Penwortham. Soon after his provision to the see of Coventry and Lichfield in 1321, Bishop Northburgh questioned Evesham's right to

[55] N. Hunt, *Cluny under Saint Hugh 1049–1109* (London, 1967), p. 157; H. E. J. Cowdrey, *The Cluniacs and the Gregorian Reform* (Oxford, 1970), p. 71.

[56] For the origins and growth of exemption in England, see Knowles, MO, pp. 575–91, and Knowles, RO, I, pp. 277–9.

[57] *The Register of Walter Bronescombe Bishop of Exeter 1258–1280*, ed. O. F. Robinson, vol. I, C&Y Soc., lxxxii (1995), nos 125, 152, pp. 38, 152; BL, Harley MS 3586, fol. 21v; *The Episcopal Registers of the Diocese of St Davids, 1397 to 1518*, ed. R. F. Isaacson, 3 vols, Cymmrodorion Record Series, vi (1917–20), I, pp. 224, 230–4.

[58] *Registrum Malmesburiense*, ed. J. S. Brewer and C. T. Martin, 2 vols, RS, lxxii (1879–80), II, chap. 222, pp. 78–9.

recall priors of Penwortham at pleasure. Stressing its immediate subjection to the Holy See and the dative status of their *custodes*, the abbey replied that the heads of its cell were never presented to or instituted by their diocesan and could therefore be removed without contradiction, and the bishop accepted this claim.[59] Equally, there is no record of the bishops of Coventry and Lichfield ever visiting Penwortham.

The reasons for these starkly differing settlements are not easy to find. Only for St Albans has the documentation survived for a reasonably full discussion of the issues faced by mother houses and diocesans concerning exemption. Controversy over the extent of its cells' freedom from episcopal jurisdiction continued well into the fifteenth century, despite many earlier efforts to resolve the issue. Of all the exempt abbeys, St Albans alone seems to have secured specific papal privileges concerning the exemption of its dependencies. In May 1170, Alexander III granted to St Albans that no prelate should excommunicate any of the monks staying in their cells nor impose on them any interdict, and that these monks 'should thus be free and immune from subjection to bishops, just as if they were staying in the body of your monastery'.[60] Despite this bull and subsequent confirmations, St Albans could not obtain the complete freedom of its cells from episcopal jurisdiction. Instead, after some decades of uncertainty and conflict, three separate agreements between the abbey and its satellites' diocesans were formulated by papal judges delegate.[61]

These were similar in content, though not identical, and each was based on the principle that the monks should come under episcopal jurisdiction only for the spiritual property they held in the diocese. It was conceded that the priors of St Albans' cells should be presented to and instituted by their ordinaries. Priors, however, should swear canonical obedience to the bishop only for their appropriated churches and not as heads of their cells, and they were to remain free from episcopal visitation and correction. The Norwich settlement bound the priors of Wymondham and Binham to attend the diocesan synod and to pay procurations to the bishops for the visitation of the parish churches which the monks shared; whereas the Durham *conventio* freed the priors of Tynemouth from attendance at all synods and chapters. Each composition, however, safeguarded the rights of the abbots of St Albans, in the words of the Norwich agreement, 'to correct the excess of the monks [in its cells], and remove and substitute priors, according to what

59 BL, Harley MS 3763, fols 183r–185v; *Documents relating to the Priory of Penwortham and other Possessions in Lancashire of the Abbey of Evesham*, ed. W. A. Hulton, Chetham Society, xxx (1853), no. 62, pp. 97–105. However, when Evesham appropriated Alcester Abbey as a cell in 1466, Bishop Carpenter of Worcester reserved the right to exercise jurisdiction over the new dependency: Worcestershire Record Office, b716.093–BA.2648/6(ii), fols 198v–200v.

60 *PUE*, III, no. 170, pp. 307–8; Sayers, 'Papal Privileges', pp. 57–84, esp. pp. 62–3.

61 Settlements were made with the bishop of Lincoln in 1219, the bishop of Norwich in 1228 and the bishop of Durham in 1247: GASA, I, pp. 275–7, 278–9, 390–1.

appears necessary, and according to the Rule of St Benedict and the rite of their institution'. In this way, the essential interests of both parties were preserved: the bishops secured recognition of their nominal authority over the cells but the abbey's ability to rotate its daughter houses' personnel was protected.

It was not long, however, before both sides tried to modify these agree-ments in their favour. Matthew Paris tells of how the bishop of Durham con-tinued to attack Tynemouth's privileges despite the 1247 agreement, moving the king to write to him on behalf of the monks the following year, and conflict over the extent of the bishop's jurisdiction over the priory raged for another thirty years.[62] Similarly, judgment in the papal court was given in favour of the archdeacon of Norfolk in 1249, after the priors of Wymondham and Binham had tried to prevent him from visiting the paro-chial parts of their churches. And eight years later, St Albans acquired a papal indult stating that the obedience due from the incumbents of the appropriated churches of the abbey and its cells should be made to the monks and not the diocesan.[63] Even when the agreed rights of each side were respected, relations between abbey and bishop were often tense. Bishop Sutton eight times refused to install priors of St Albans' cells in his diocese because of irregularities in the form or manner of presentation.[64] This posture of hostility continued into the fifteenth century, when the contro-versy centred around the exemption of St Albans' cells from collecting cleri-cal subsidies. Following the severe hardship endured by Wymondham arising from the tax-collecting duties of its priors, St Albans claimed in 1380 that its cells should be free from this duty owing to their exemption.[65] Despite the bitter resistance of Bishop Despenser of Norwich, the king eventually conceded this right. This privilege, however, was strongly resisted by Bishop Alnwick of Norwich in 1432–3, and then unsuccessfully challenged by an assembly of bishops, arguing that the king could not grant liberties from episcopal power.[66] Even in the mid-fifteenth century, therefore, the limits of

[62] *Chronica Majora*, V, pp. 9–13; R. Hill, *Ecclesiastical Letter-Books of the Thirteenth Century* (privately printed, no date), pp. 28–9.

[63] GASA, I, pp. 355–61; Sayers, 'Papal Privileges', pp. 67–8. The exemption of Wallingford also came under threat when, in April 1302, the official of Bishop Simon of Ghent of Salisbury attempted to visit the priory, a move vociferously resisted by Abbot de Maryns: BL, Cotton MS Tib. E.vi, fols 191v–192r.

[64] *Sutton Rolls and Register*, I, pp. 97–8, 203–4, 218–19, VI, pp. 7–8, VIII, pp. 95, 100–1, 120–1, 124–5. Bishop Sutton's determination to enforce the letter of the law, however, was not confined to the cells of St Albans, since he refused to accept fifty-three of the 105 elections brought before him during his pontificate: Hill, 'Bishop Sutton and Institution of Heads', pp. 201–9.

[65] GASA, III, pp. 122–34. In 1346–7, the prior of Wymondham was imprisoned and his priory greatly indebted owing to the arrears from a clerical subsidy he had collected in the 1340s: CClR, *1346–1349*, pp. 140, 164; CPR, *1345–1348*, p. 404.

[66] *Amundesham*, I, pp. 300–69. The southern Convocation issued several injunctions against collectors being exempted by royal privileges in the early fifteenth century, so

exemption remained questionable and this issue maintained its potential for endless disagreement.

However, the fiercest dispute between bishop and mother house over the exemption of a cell was undoubtedly the battle over the priory of Great Malvern between Bishop Giffard of Worcester, Archbishop Pecham and Westminster Abbey in 1282–3. The story of this altercation, described by one commentator as 'one of the most bitter ecclesiastical quarrels recorded in English history', has been told adequately more than once before, and it is unnecessary to rehearse again all its intricacies here.[67] The bishops of Worcester appear to have exerted full jurisdiction over Great Malvern before 1282, including the right to visit the priory, receive canonical obedience from its priors and institute them, albeit with periodical protests from Westminster. However, when Bishop Giffard visited Great Malvern in September 1282 and deposed the deeply unsuitable Prior William of Ledbury, apparently at the behest of some of the priory's monks, before taking the vacant priory into his custody, a terrible uproar ensued. Giffard excommunicated several monks and presided over the election of a new prior. In response, Westminster denied the bishop's jurisdiction over its dependency and threw the new prior, a nephew of Cardinal Hugh of Evesham, and his companions into jail. The king supported the abbey and asserted its cells' exemption from their diocesans, but Giffard, pointing to precedent, refused to yield and a flurry of denunciations and excommunications followed, particularly when Archbishop Pecham entered the fray in support of his bishop. Despite a successful appeal to Rome by Giffard, royal support proved decisive and in November 1283 the bishop was brought to recognise the exemption of the abbey and its cells, in return for the manor of Knightwick (a settlement Pecham thought might have been simoniacal). This resounding victory for Westminster was not accepted entirely willingly by future bishops of Worcester, but was never effectively challenged thereafter.[68]

The startlingly variable degrees of immunity secured by the cells of the exempt English abbeys well exemplify the tremendous scope for confusion and conflict that this issue generated. As the above account has indicated,

this case clearly touched a nerve: A. K. McHardy, 'Clerical Taxation in Fifteenth-Century England: the Clergy as Agents of the Crown', in *The Church, Politics and Patronage in the Fifteenth Century*, ed. R. B. Dobson (Gloucester, 1984), pp. 176–8.

67 The best account of the dispute is by M. M. C. Calthrop in *VCH, Worcestershire*, II, pp. 137–41. The materials for the conflict can be found in *Episcopal Registers, Diocese of Worcester: Register of Bishop Godfrey Giffard, 1268–1301*, ed. J. W. Willis Bund, 2 vols, Worcestershire Historical Society, xv (1898–1902), II, pp. 164ff.; *Registrum Epistolarum Peckham*, II, pp. 423–4, 676–8, 749; Westminster Abbey Muniments (WAM), Mun. book xi, Westminster Domesday, fols 307v–311v, WAM 32633–43.

68 In June 1333, papal letters were issued on the king's request requiring the bishop of Worcester to appropriate the church of Longdon in his diocese to Westminster, which he had refused to do unless the abbot conceded jurisdiction over the priory of Great Malvern to him: *CPL*, II, p. 393.

the threat to the authority of abbeys over their daughter houses from bishop, patron and, at times, king was potentially serious. Many mother houses suffered challenges to accustomed and cherished rights. In some cases, this might jeopardise a vital plank in the control structure employed by abbeys, such as their power to appoint and remove priors and monks without interference. However, much more damaging than the need to defer at times to other jurisdictions was the possibility that daughter houses might play off their parent against patron or bishop, or even win external support for a bid to throw off their subjection altogether. The later middle ages saw several attempts by satellite priories to loosen their ties of dependence, a number of which were successful. In the face of these centrifugal pressures, mother houses sought out new techniques for the preservation of their networks of cells. The remainder of this chapter will consider the ways in which abbeys tried to exercise control over their dependencies and examine the strain under which their families of satellites increasingly came.

Degrees of Dependence

The degree of leeway accorded to daughter houses by their parents varied considerably. Some cells were controlled extremely tightly and enjoyed little genuine freedom of action; others were allowed effectively to manage their own affairs, under the distant oversight of their abbot. A number of factors determined the level of independence conceded to a subject priory. Those cells established and largely endowed by the mother house itself tended to be the most rigidly governed, since no patrons existed to make their own claims on the priory. In general, the smaller the house, the more easily it could be subordinated to its parent, since such cells barely resembled priories and could more easily be portrayed as mere obediences outside the jurisdiction of patron or bishop. Distance from the mother house might also play a part in the degree of freedom enjoyed by a dependency. But despite the numerous grades of liberty accorded to them, very few English cells were allowed any real independence from their mother houses. The vast majority of priors remained dative, chosen by and removable at the will of their superiors; and the right to recruit and train their own monks, or even to enjoy a settled population and thereby engender some community feeling, was denied to most cells most of the time. This settled grip of parent abbeys over their priories' personnel prevented cells from controlling their own destinies, and dictated that they must continually feed on their mother house for inspiration and renewal. It was not a state of affairs that every prior or patron would accept willingly.

Although the majority of cells were very closely bound to their parents, some larger satellites were accorded several of the rights associated with 'conventual' houses, as defined by the fourteenth- and fifteenth-century commissioners employed to decide which of the alien priories should have

their endowments confiscated during the French wars.[69] These cells possessed a common seal, could present priests to benefices themselves and
often pleaded at law in their own name. But the defining characteristic of a
fully conventual house according to the commissioners, was the perpetuity of
its prior, and very few English cells can be seen to have enjoyed this right.
Walter de Tateshall's agreement with Nostell over the priors of Breedon
required that they should not be removed without reasonable cause, and it
may be that the perpetuity of Breedon's heads continued to be recognised
after the quashing of this settlement.[70] The priors of Horsley and
Letheringham, moreover, are also said to have been irremovable by their
mother houses, Bruton and St Peter and St Paul's Ipswich respectively; and a
handful of large dependencies succeeded in winning this right from their
parent abbeys at some point in their history.[71] However, in the light of the
dative status of the heads of most of those dependencies which were
accorded their own common seals and associated legal rights, these priories
can most accurately be described as 'semi-conventual'.[72]

Several English dependencies can be shown to have possessed a common
seal.[73] Some of these priories, like Ewenny and Pilton, were very small, containing only two or three monks by the sixteenth century, but preserved the
seals they had merited in more populous days. But in general those priories

---

69 See above, pp. 4–5; C. W. New, *History of the Alien Priories in England to the
Confiscation of Henry V* (Chicago, 1916), pp. 18–44.

70 See above, pp. 70–1.

71 *Two Cartularies of the Augustinian Priory of Bruton and the Cluniac Priory of Montacute
in the Co. of Somerset*, ed. T. S. Holmes et al., Somerset Record Society, viii (1894),
no. 366, p. 95; CPR, *1354–1358*, p. 266; VCH, *Suffolk*, II, p. 108. It would appear that
the priors of Letheringham were also elected by their own canons: NRO, Reg/2/4, fol.
104v. For the freedoms won by certain larger cells, see below, pp. 98–103.

72 Since there has been some disagreement about what constituted a 'conventual' house,
the use of this title might need some justification. The term is usually applied loosely
to those religious houses with 'a full compliment' of a superior and twelve inmates, or
at least a community of sufficient size to ensure 'an orderly and dignified performance
of the liturgical prayers' (Du Cange). This usage has its roots in medieval times, but a
more precise definition of conventuality would hang on the existence within the
monastery of a distinct body with established rights à propos the superior: as in 'prior
and convent'. With their common seal and associated rights, these larger
dependencies met this basic requirement.

73 Namely, the St Albans cells of Belvoir, Binham, Hatfield Peverel (and perhaps
Hertford), Tynemouth, Wallingford and Wymondham; Colne (Abingdon); Brecon
and St Nicholas' Exeter (Battle); Dover (Canterbury Cathedral Priory); Snape
(Colchester); Finchale (Durham); Ewenny and St Guthlac's Hereford (Gloucester);
Pilton (Malmesbury); Great Malvern and Hurley (Westminster); Little Malvern
(Worcester); and the Augustinian cells of Blythburgh (St Osyth's), Letheringham (St
Peter and St Paul's Ipswich) and perhaps Brooke (Kenilworth). This is probably not
an exhaustive list. Several of these seals are known from documentary references, but
conventual seals from Binham, Blythburgh, Brecon, Colne, St Nicholas' Exeter,
Finchale, St Guthlac's Hereford, Hurley, Letheringham, Pilton, Tynemouth,
Wallingford and Wymondham all survive.

with common seals were the largest English dependencies, even if few housed as many as a dozen inmates. Several cells can also be seen in episcopal institution lists to have presented priests to the churches they held, a group overlapping substantially with those priories possessing conventual seals.[74] Interestingly, the priors of the small cells of Cardigan, Kidwelly and Rumburgh presented to at least some of their churches in the later middle ages, apparently an instance of the devolution of rights to distant cells.[75] We cannot always be sure, however, that a prior presented to a church in his own right and not as the abbot's proctor. Equally, it is not clear how much discretion was accorded to a dependency in this regard and it may be that mother houses exerted influence on their cell's choice of incumbent. The priors of St Albans' cells were forbidden from presenting any priest without the consent of their abbot.[76] Lytham, meanwhile, was recognised as the patron of Appleby church in Leicestershire, but by a formal arrangement Durham nominated a clerk whom the prior would present to the bishop of Lincoln.[77]

A third indication of a priory's conventuality was its position before the law. Dative priors could not hold property in their own right and therefore could not plead or be impleaded in their own name in the secular courts.[78] However, the possession of a common seal and the right to present priests to its churches both implied that a priory did hold its property itself and not merely as a proctor on behalf of its mother house. In practice, several semi-conventual dependencies were involved in law suits in their own right, with no mention of their mother house made in the proceedings or final concord. Their ability to do so was occasionally challenged; but when in March 1430 a defendant in a case initiated by the prior of Pilton argued that the latter could not bring charges on his own account since he was 'an obedientiary of the abbot [of Malmesbury] . . . and was dative and removable

---

74 All the daughter houses of St Albans, including Hertford and Beadlow (although not the abbey's fifteenth-century acquisition, Pembroke), presented to their own churches. The abbot of Gloucester, however, presented to the churches of each of his dependencies, including Ewenny and St Guthlac's Hereford.

75 *Episcopal Registers of St Davids*, II, pp. 738, 770 (Cardigan), I, p. 388, II, pp. 454, 614 (Kidwelly). It was asserted after the dissolution of Rumburgh that its priors presented priests to the churches of St Andrew Wissett, St Michael South Elmham and Rumburgh itself: *Mon. Ang.*, III, pp. 615–16, no. 9.

76 See the internal constitutions of Abbots de Maryns and de la Mare: GASA, II, p. 96, 444.

77 E.g. DCM, Registrum III, fol. 1r.

78 *Bracton, De Legibus et Consuetudinibus Angliae*, ed. G. E. Woodbine, 4 vols (New Haven, 1915–42), II, p. 53, IV, pp. 69, 330. The position of dative priors in the church courts appears to have been less restrictive. Bracton notes that 'there are, however, some who are removable and may answer and bring a matter to judgement in spiritual places ('*in locis spiritualibus*'), as at St Albans'; and the dative prior of Lytham is found suing the abbot of Vale Royal over Kirkham church in 1428–9: ibid., II, p. 53; York, Borthwick Institute of Historical Research, CP F.167. I am grateful to Professor David Smith for drawing my attention to the latter document.

at the will of that abbot', the prior responded spuriously that he was in fact perpetual since he was instituted by his diocesan, and obtained the support of Bishop Lacy of Exeter in his claim.[79] Attempts to define the status of a semi-conventual cell might, therefore, prove problematic. Dr Chibnall has aptly characterised the priors of Bec's cells as 'amphibious beings, making the best of two worlds',[80] and the same evidently applies to the larger English cells which fell between contemporary definitions of conventual and non-conventual priories.

Although mother houses were generally unwilling to surrender genuine power to their daughters, semi-conventual cells were allowed more discretion in the management of their affairs than lesser dependencies. Numerous surviving leases show these priories demising at farm their properties in their own names and under their own common seals, often without the recorded consent of their mother houses. The priors of Hurley and Belvoir issued internal injunctions, assigned revenues to obedientiaries or for anniversaries, granted corrodies and demised lands, in Hurley's case apparently without Westminster's consent.[81] Fourteenth-century priors of St Nicholas' Exeter enfeoffed tenants and made agreements with their convents, again ostensibly without reference to the abbots of Battle.[82] Moreover, the heads of semi-conventual cells tended to enjoy longer priorates than their equivalents in smaller dependencies: the priors of Hurley, for example, were very rarely recalled to Westminster in the later middle ages.[83] The room for manoeuvre given to the priors of St Albans' cells was certainly sufficient for the most outstanding to make a name for themselves. Richard de Parco, prior of Binham (c.1227–44) was lauded by Matthew Paris for acquiring considerable tracts of property and rebuilding the church and parts of the priory in sumptuous style; and Prior William II of Belvoir was warmly remembered for clearing the house of debt, building two chapels and apparently adorning the priory precinct with a thousand trees.[84]

[79] The Register of Edmund Lacy Bishop of Exeter, 1420–1455: Registrum Commune, ed. G. R. Dunstan, 5 vols, C&Y Soc., lx–lxiii, lxvi (1963–72), I, pp. 227–9.

[80] Morgan, Bec, p. 32. Any effort to place dependent priories in neat categories is bound to encounter serious difficulties: e.g. New, History of Alien Priories, pp. 18–44.

[81] E.g., WAM 2088, 2199, 2219, 2259, 2294, 3571, 3595, 3665, 3742, 3744, 5399 (Hurley); Cambridge, Trinity College MS O.9.25, fols 9v, 12r; Nichols, History and Antiquities of Leicester, II(i), Appendix II, nos 45, 49, 55, 61, pp. 13–17; Historical Manuscripts Commission: The Duke of Rutland, IV (1905), pp. 117, 122 (Belvoir).

[82] BL, Cotton MS Vit. D.ix, fols 121r–122r, 128v–129r, 142v.

[83] See E. H. Pearce, The Monks of Westminster (Cambridge, 1916); HRH, II, pp. 113–14. There is no evidence that the priors of Hurley were considered to be perpetual, however.

[84] Chronica Majora, VI, pp. 85–91; Cambridge, Trinity College MS O.9.25, fol. 167r. Prior de Parco's west front at Binham was one of the earliest examples of bar tracery in medieval England: M. Thurlby, 'The West Front of Binham Priory, Norfolk, and the Beginnings of Bar Tracery in England', in England in the Thirteenth Century, ed. W. M. Ormrod (Stamford, 1991), pp. 155–65; E. Fernie, 'Binham Priory', Archaeological Journal, cxxxvii (1980), p. 329. Prior William of Colne was similarly celebrated for his

Most of our knowledge about the powers of the priors of St Albans' network of cells, however, comes from the abbey's attempts to limit them. In 1241, the abbey secured an indult from Pope Celestine IV that no prior or obedientiary should borrow money without the licence of the abbot.[85] More importantly, several sets of internal constitutions issued by the abbots of St Albans at their general chapter have been preserved, which seek to define and delineate the authority allowed to the priors of the abbey's cells. The constitutions of Abbot John de Maryns (1302–9) are the first to survive and contain several injunctions for St Albans' daughter houses, including one relating to the authority of their priors. In short, these heads were to consider themselves proctors rather than lords of their properties and do nothing without abbatial consent: no possessions should be alienated; no customary lands sold or demised to freemen; vacant churches should not be presented to without consultation; no titles, corrodies nor pensions granted in perpetuity, nor anything else done to burden their priory; and finally no manor, mill, tithes or rents should be sold or demised for more than three years, without having first obtained the abbot of St Albans' permission.[86]

The next recorded legislation pertaining to the priors of its cells was issued by Abbot de la Mare in 1351. De la Mare ordered that no deed should be sealed without his advice and special licence, 'unless for urgent necessity and manifest utility'. Priors should not 'sell corrodies, make recognizances or presume to present to vacant churches, nor at farm manors or churches, or sell or destroy woods, give surety for anyone else nor manumit anyone' without abbatial permission, on pain of excommunication. Moreover, to ensure these injunctions were kept, the abbot required that incoming priors and subpriors should swear an oath that they would comply with them and with the constitutions of the abbey more generally.[87] A year later, however, a new injunction relaxing the abbot's grip was published. De la Mare now recognised the inconvenience of a system requiring abbatial consent for every small act of estate management and permitted priors to demise at farm, with the consent of their convents alone, any possessions which had customarily been leased out, for a period of up to thirty years or two lives. This concession was made, however, only with the proviso that properties should not be demised to relatives or anyone else through affection, but only for the good of the church, and that rents should not be received in advance, but paid yearly; and no prior was to demise or hand over a serf.[88]

By the mid-fourteenth century, then, the priors of the semi-conventual cells of St Albans were permitted to proceed unmolested with the routine

programme of property acquisition, building and liturgical reform in the late twelfth or early thirteenth century: *Chronicon Monasterii de Abingdon*, ed. J. Stevenson, 2 vols, RS, ii (1858), II, Appendix II, pp. 294–5.

85 BL, Cotton MS Claud. D.xiii, fol. 25r.
86 GASA, II, p. 96.
87 Ibid., II, pp. 443–6. For oaths imposed on the priors of cells, see below, pp. 92–4.
88 Ibid., II, pp. 447–8.

management of their endowment. The collection of Wallingford Priory charters in the Bodleian Library shows its late medieval priors in more or less total control of their house's short- and medium-term financial strategy.[89] However, all St Albans' priors were expected to seek permission before undertaking any act which might have had a serious impact on the priory's financial security. What evidence survives suggests that the abbey's injunctions on this point were effectively enforced. The fifteenth-century abbey registers contain numerous instances of priors seeking and receiving abbatial approval for the granting of corrodies or annuities, demising property, presenting to churches or manumitting serfs;[90] and the majority of surviving late medieval leases among the Wallingford charters accord with de la Mare's regulations.[91] How restrictive the need to obtain mother-house consent for any major acts of policy was in practice cannot be said, and probably depended on the centralising tendencies of particular abbots. But it is clear that St Albans maintained overall control over the affairs of its semi-conventual dependencies in the later middle ages.

The smaller semi-conventual priories dependent on Malmesbury and Gloucester, however, seem to have been even more closely directed. The property of Pilton was managed largely from Malmesbury.[92] The same was true at Ewenny where the presentation to churches, the appointment of priory officials and all leases were apparently made by the abbot and convent of Gloucester and not the cell's prior.[93] Despite its common seal, Ewenny was controlled every bit as firmly as the other smaller cells of Gloucester whose complete subjection to their parent was openly acknowledged. The priors of the large number of non-conventual dependencies were considered mere obedientiaries, with none of the de facto powers enjoyed by the heads of semi-conventual cells. Indeed the inferior status of these superiors was often denoted by the withholding of the title of 'prior' by their mother houses. The heads of many small dependencies were instead styled *custos* or *magister* to highlight their role as proctors of their abbeys and not true priors with the rights that title implied.[94] The degree of freedom permitted to these heads

89 *Calendar of Charters and Rolls preserved in the Bodleian Library*, ed. W. H. Turner and H. O. Coxe (Oxford, 1878), pp. 4–23.
90 E.g., *Registra*, II, pp. 79–80, 104–6, 114–15; Cambridge, Trinity College MS O.9.25, fols 1v, 8v, 18v, 121v.
91 By the late 1490s, however, a few unlicensed leases for forty or sixty years are recorded at Wallingford; and Belvoir was doing much the same in the sixteenth century: PRO, E303/8/11–18. The lengthening of leases at this time is a phenomenon familiar to economic historians, and this trend was probably the result of economic considerations rather than a slackening of discipline at St Albans.
92 E.g. *Registrum Malmesburiense*, II, chap. 172–5, pp. 32–5.
93 BL, Add. Chs 1340, 1347; 'Early Deeds relating to St Peter's Abbey, Gloucester', ed. W. St Clair Baddeley, *TBGAS*, 2 parts, xxxvii–xxxviii (1914–15), I, no. 29, p. 233, II, nos 122, 145, pp. 40, 44–5; Gloucester, Dean and Chapter Library, Register C, fol. 135r.
94 In 1235, the heads of Durham's cells of Farne Island and Wearmouth were actually called 'procurators'. The styling of the prior of Leominster as dean had similar

was heavily restricted; their administrative role was circumscribed and they did not issue legislation for their houses. Some mother houses, however, ran a tighter ship than others and some variation in the powers allotted to heads can be seen.

The most strictly controlled cells were permitted almost no discretion at all in the management of their endowments. Bath Priory exercised a firm hold over its cell at Dunster, demising the satellite's possessions, appointing its servants, granting corrodies and even founding a chantry in the priory church and selecting chaplains to serve it.[95] Some priors might not even have held their own personal seals for the enactment of the most routine business: Archbishop Hubert Walter's constitutions for Ramsey (February 1205?), subsequently re-issued by the abbey, decreed that the prior of St Ives was not to have his own seal for farming lands or churches; and the 'chequer seal', needed for making leases or other basic tasks for the management of Leominster Priory, was apparently kept at Reading.[96] The priors of Cowick, moreover, were not permitted control over the everyday revenues of their house after its subjugation to Tavistock in 1462; instead a receiver took in the cell's proceeds, some of which were then assigned to the prior.[97]

Other dependencies, however, were granted a little more freedom. Most priors were allowed their own seals so that, as Abbot William Walle of Kenilworth put it in relation to the cell at Brooke, 'they need not have occasion to run for every grant to the masters of this house'.[98] The daughter houses of Norwich, Rochester and St Mary's York were allowed to lease their own property, usually (though not always) with mother-house consent, and therefore seem to have had some say in the management of their endowments.[99] We should not, therefore, exaggerate the uniformity of mother-house management: even within families of cells, some houses were permitted more freedom than others, whereas individual cells might enjoy differing

connotations: B. R. Kemp, 'The Monastic Dean of Leominster', *EHR*, lxxxiii (1968), pp. 505–15.

95 *Two Chartularies of the Priory of St Peter at Bath*, ed. W. Hunt, Somerset Record Society, vii (1893), part ii, nos 70, 245, 349, 368, 463, 560, 565, pp. 16, 55, 75, 79, 93, 109–10, for example.

96 *Cartularium Monasterii de Rameseia*, ed. W. H. Hart and P. A. Lyons, 3 vols, RS, lxxix (1884–93), II, nos 328, 331, pp. 204–7, 212–14; *English Episcopal Acta III: Canterbury 1193–1205*, ed. C. R. Cheney and E. John (Oxford, 1986), no. 582, pp. 235–6; *L&P*, VII, no. 1678, p. 622; BL, Cotton MS Domit. A.iii, fols 53r–53v.

97 Devon Record Office, W1258M/G4/53/1–5. It is probably true to say that the cells newly acquired in the fifteenth century were the most tightly controlled of all: see also *A Calendar of the Registers of the Priory of Llanthony by Gloucester 1457–1466, 1501–1525*, ed. J. Rhodes, Bristol and Gloucestershire Archaeological Society, Gloucestershire Record Series, XV (2002), nos 133, 251, 269, pp. 64, 103, 108–9.

98 *L&P*, VIII, no. 749, p. 280.

99 E.g., NRO, DCN 44/1/17 (Aldeby), 44/42/19, 46/76/37 (Lynn); BL, Cotton MS Faust. C.v, fols 118v–119r (Felixstowe); *The Register of the Priory of St Bees*, ed. J. Wilson, SS, cxxvi (1915), nos 23–5, pp. 50–3 (St Bees); SROI, HD1538/335/1, nos 20, 36–9 (Rumburgh).

amounts of responsibility over time.[100] This state of affairs might lead to confusion or attempted evasion. A lease made by a late medieval prior of Kidwelly was subsequently rendered void, when it was ruled that he 'had none authorite to make any leasse longer then his awne tyme yn somuch hit is a cell to the monasteri of Shirborn'; and one lessee of Bentley Priory sought to evade paying his rent on the grounds that the transaction had taken place without the permission of Bentley's mother house, St Gregory's Canterbury.[101] Nevertheless, at many small cells, the administrative role of the prior was effectively confined to the protection and preservation of their houses' possessions and privileges from encroachment, and directing the disbursement of whatever revenues were at his disposal, in the manner of an ordinary mother house obedientiary.

Regulation of Cells

In order to enforce this control, particularly in more distant cells, all mother houses required some system of regulation. Most abbeys relied on three main instruments: the annual audit of their cells' accounts, general chapters and abbatial visitation. The requirement that priors present yearly reckonings of their administration was universally recognised as the best way to prevent the dilapidation of a satellite's properties and the building-up of debt. As early as 1235, Prior Melsonby of Durham ordained that the heads of the cathedral priory's cells should record their receipts and expenses each year, keeping one copy themselves and sending another to Durham, and that they should visit the mother house once a year for the auditing of these accounts.[102] In May 1287, the York province of the Benedictine chapter required that 'all priors and wardens of cells should visit their mother house every year within fifteen days after the feast of St Michael or before . . . to display the state of their house purely, simply and faithfully to their superior and [his] convent with the laudable testimony of the brothers staying with them'; and the 1336 Benedictine constitutions of Benedict XII assumed that this practice was common to all abbeys with dependencies.[103]

These injunctions were clearly very widely observed and today account rolls from twenty-eight different cells survive.[104] The stipulation that priors personally visit their mother houses each year to render account gave rise to the internal general chapter, where the whole community of a monastery

---

100 Several mother houses, including Durham, Nostell, Sherborne, Tewkesbury, Thorney and Westminster are found demising at some times but not others properties belonging to their cells.

101 PRO, E135/2/53; *Registrum Roberti Winchelsey, Cantuariensis Archiepiscopi AD 1294–1313*, ed. R. Graham, C&Y Soc., 2 vols, li–lii (1952–6), II, p. 748.

102 *Historiae Dunelmensis Scriptores Tres*, ed. J. Raine, SS, ix (1839), p. xl.

103 CBM, I, no. 143, p. 255; Wilkins, *Concilia*, II, pp. 591–3, chap. 4.

104 See below, pp. 230–2.

would assemble to answer for their charges and to legislate for the administration and observance of the house and its offshoots. Such chapters might well have taken place at Durham from 1235, and the general chapter of St Albans and its cells was already functioning soon after 1264. Chapter ordinances from Norwich, meanwhile, survive from the early fourteenth century.[105] As the sets of ordinances from St Albans indicate, the general chapter could prove a useful tool for the regulation of daughter houses. It also provided an occasion for the disciplining of profligate or disobedient priors: the wasteful Prior Matthew of St Bees was deposed at the general chapter of St Mary's York, held on St Calixtus' day (14 October) in 1533.[106]

Perhaps the most effective way to monitor a daughter house was an internal system of visitation, and most abbeys seem to have exercised this power. Notifications of visitations by the abbot of Gloucester in 1378 and 1439 are recorded in the cartulary of St Guthlac's Hereford and others survive for St Nicholas' Exeter, Middlesbrough and Great Malvern.[107] But these fragments of information give no impression of the frequency of internal visitations. The foundation charter of Snape allowed the abbot of Colchester the right to visit his dependency twice a year and more often if necessary, whereas the 1217 *conventio* between Westminster and Great Malvern provided for yearly visitations (see below). Although the chronicle of St Mary's York mentions three occasions when abbots inspected their Cumberland cells, they were also reprimanded by Archbishop Melton in 1319 for not visiting their dependencies often enough.[108] Very few references to internal visitations appear in the voluminous archives of Durham and Norwich Cathedral Priories, suggesting that this practice was not especially common at either. Most evidence of such visitations survives for St Albans, but even here their regularity cannot be established. The *Gesta Abbatum* describes several perambulations of its dependencies by abbots and notes that recently elected superiors customarily visited the cells. The abbey registers also record numerous daughter-house visitations, but no two of the same priory within several years of one other.[109] Even allowing for the deficiencies of the evidence, there is therefore no sign that daughter houses were visited by their parents as often as once a year.

Although they provided for a regular check on the activities of their cells' priors, these three methods of regulation were not infallible instruments for the imposition of an abbey's will on its satellites. From time to time, priors

[105] Hill, *Ecclesiastical Letter-Books*, pp. 84–5; Cheney, 'Norwich Cathedral Priory', pp. 117–20.
[106] *L&P*, VI, no. 1359, p. 542. Matthew, however, was made prior of Richmond instead, at Cromwell's instance.
[107] Oxford, Balliol College MS 271, fols 6r, 8r; BL, Harley MS 3586, fol. 22v; *VCH, Yorkshire*, III, pp. 105–6; WAM 32659; BL, Cotton MS Faust. A.iii, fols 354v–355r.
[108] *Mon. Ang.*, IV, p. 558, no. 2, III, p. 449, no. 5; *St Mary's Chronicle*, pp. 8–9, 38–9, 73, 127.
[109] GASA, III, pp. 494–5; *Registra*, esp. vol. II.

flouted the rules in an attempt to secure a greater measure of freedom from their parents or even total independence. A number of mother houses, particularly after they had encountered resistance, sought new ways to ensure circumspection and loyalty. Abbot Roger of Norton of St Albans tried to encourage priors to rule carefully and obediently by a kind of performance-related pay. In an ordinance of July 1275, he decreed that the annuity to be received by retired priors in the mother house should be assessed according to the way they had discharged their duties: 'he who has laboured more strongly and usefully will receive greater honour and reward, according to the discretion of the abbot of the time; and he [who has laboured] less, less. And he who has neither lived honestly, nor administered the temporalities usefully to the manifest good of the house, should receive nothing.'[110]

A more common tactic for the promotion of loyalty was to impose an oath on the prior or monks of a cell. The earliest known declaration of allegiance was extracted by Abbot de Maryns of St Albans from Prior Pulleyn and the convent of Wymondham in August 1303. More a statement of submission than an oath, this consisted of a long recital of all the abbey's accustomed rights over their cell, to which the prior and convent bound themselves. This innovation no doubt stemmed from Pulleyn's dangerously close relations with his priory's patrons, and although the same submission was demanded from Prior John of Stevenage, Pulleyn's successor at Wymondham, there is no indication that the practice was extended to any of the abbey's other cells at this time.[111] However, the rebellion of William of Somerton (see below) led the next abbot of St Albans, Hugh of Eversden, to introduce at the abbey's 1319 general chapter another novelty: an oath of loyalty to be sworn by every incoming prior and monk of the abbey's satellites. They were henceforth to vow, touching the Holy Gospels and in the presence of the abbot, that they would acknowledge no jurisdiction other than the Holy See and St Albans.[112] The daughter-house oath thereafter became a settled institution at St Albans, although it took a number of different forms. Eversden's somewhat vague oath was reworked by Abbot de la Mare in 1351, when all priors and subpriors were required to swear not only to uphold their houses' privileges but also to rule according to the abbey's detailed constitutions of that year, which defined the limits of their authority. In 1424, Abbot Whethamstede in turn revised this oath, adding a clause specifically requiring each prior to swear that he 'will render a plain, full and faithful account every year before you [the abbot] or your commissary . . . of all receipts and expenses', and another requiring him to

---

[110] GASA, I, pp. 451–2.
[111] Ibid., II, pp. 145–8. For Pulleyn's relations with the patrons of St Albans, see above, p. 71.
[112] Ibid., II, p. 148.

promise to pay faithfully the annual census imposed on his priory by the mother house.[113]

This method of maintaining the loyalty of the priors of their dependencies was adopted by at least five other English mother houses.[114] It appears that oaths of this kind were most commonly employed in an attempt to bolster a monastery's authority over its cells during or after an act of rebellion, just as Abbot Eversden's oath was imposed in the wake of William of Somerton's revolt. In July 1376, it was enacted that the priors of Horsley should swear at their institution that they would return to Bruton if recalled, following the apparent refusal of the previous prior to do so; and Colchester Abbey sought to impose an oath of obedience on Prior John Mersey of Snape some time before November 1398, requiring the prior to act only under his abbot's orders.[115] Durham adopted a similar measure following William Partrike's insurrection at Lytham (see below). At the appointment of the first two priors of Lytham following Partrike's deposition, it was explicitly stated that they could be removed at will by Durham and that they were bound to render an annual account of their administration to the mother house. However, in August 1456 the new prior of Lytham, William Dalton, was required to swear an oath of fidelity, defining the limits of his powers as prior and committing him to observe, and not resist, Durham's rights over Lytham.[116] Subsequent heads of Lytham took the same vow and by 1462 Durham had thought it prudent to extend this practice to the priors of their other remote cell in Stamford.[117]

The effectiveness of this measure in preventing further resistance to mother-house authority, however, is questionable. Colchester's efforts to impose what was considered to be an unreasonable oath on the prior of Snape only served to add fuel to that conflagration. The oath imposed by Gloucester Abbey on the priors of St Guthlac's Hereford was no more successful. In the late fourteenth or early fifteenth century, Prior Walter Eton swore to be faithful to the mother house, to return willingly to the abbey when recalled and not to alienate, grant or sell any possessions, nor manumit any villeins, without mother-house consent. However, only a few years later, Prior Wynslade of St Guthlac's acquired a bull making him irremovable in

---

113 Ibid., II, pp. 443–6; *Amundesham*, I, pp. 210–11. For the controversy over the annual census at St Albans, see below, p. 140. Whethamstede's oath was first sworn by Michael Cheyne, who was instituted prior of Binham in July 1424: *Amundesham*, I, pp. 7–8; NRO, Reg/4/8, fol. 87v.

114 The priors of Bec's dependencies also apparently took an oath of obedience at the abbey's general chapter: Morgan, *Bec*, p. 17.

115 *A Calendar of the Register of Henry Wakefield Bishop of Worcester 1375–95*, ed. W. P. Marett, Worcestershire Historical Society, new series, vii (1972), no. 43, p. 7; PRO, E135/19/67. See below, pp. 108–9, for Mersey's rebellion against Colchester.

116 DCM, Register IV, fols 27r, 31v, 100r–100v.

117 Ibid., fols 103v, 145r, 153r–153v, 154r, 215v.

direct contravention of the priory's oath.[118] Similarly, Prior John Lose's resistance to Battle Abbey at Brecon in the 1360s was not hampered by the oath of fidelity and obedience to the mother house that was being sworn by the priors of Brecon in the time of Abbot Alan de Retlyng (1324–51).[119] Nevertheless, despite its obvious limitations, the oath of loyalty to the mother house was still considered by later abbots of Battle to be a valuable means of maintaining control over their distant cell. In the early fifteenth century, the priors of Brecon were required to swear on their appointment an extremely lengthy and specific oath, which may well indeed have been formulated as a direct response to Lose's disobedience.[120]

Resistance to Mother-house Authority

The adoption of oaths as a means of ensuring loyalty therefore seems to have been a response to the greater insecurity many mother houses experienced from the early fourteenth century, when their hold on their daughter houses was increasingly challenged. Resistance to mother-house authority might take a number of different forms, ranging from modest attempts to acquire short-term freedoms to full-scale revolts designed to throw off all marks of subjection. In the light of the restricted powers granted to many heads of cells, it is perhaps not surprising that some sought to extend their competence. While he remained removable at his abbot's will, no prior could freely act outside the boundaries erected by the mother house. Consequently, during the later middle ages, a number of ambitious priors claimed to be perpetual and managed to acquire papal privileges to that effect. The earliest known example of an individual prior obtaining a papal grant preventing his removal 'without reasonable cause' was Prior Robert of Kelloe of Lytham's acquisition in 1361 of a bull of perpetuity.[121] Kelloe was quickly forced to

---

[118] Oxford, Balliol College MS 271, fol. 6v. For Wynslade's manoeuvres, see below, p. 95. Eton's oath is undated, and the precise dates of his rule are at present unclear. However, the priory cartulary also includes a lease made by Prior Eton in the third year of a King Henry (a tear in the manuscript conceals the number): ibid., fol. 132r. Since William Wynslade was already prior of the cell in 1424, Eton probably ruled St Guthlac's in the early years of either Henry IV or Henry V.

[119] BL, Harley MS 3586, fol. 22r. For Prior Lose see below, p. 95n.

[120] By this oath, the priors of Brecon were bound to maintain the rights and possessions of the priory; to alienate no property without Battle's consent; to provide adequate transport for monks returning from the cell; to recognise the mother house's right to rotate Brecon's personnel; to return freely to Battle to discuss business whenever summoned; to submit to the visitation of the abbot or his commissaries; to pay due pensions; not to aid the opponents of Battle; and if contravening any of the above to renounce their institution and induction to their office and return willingly to the mother house: *Cartularium Prioratus S. Johannis Evangeliste de Brecon*, ed. R. W. Banks, *Archaeologia Cambrensis*, 4th series, xiii–xiv (1882–3), xiv, pp. 302–3.

[121] VCH, *Lancashire*, II, p. 108.

renounce the grant by Durham, but a handful of similar grants to priors were made in the first half of the fifteenth century: to William Wynslade, prior of St Guthlac's Hereford in 1424, to Michael Vynt (or Colchester) of Bedeman's Berg in 1430, to William Partrike of Lytham (again) in 1443 and to Richard Hall of Belvoir the following year.[122]

In each of these cases, the priors concerned had been appointed several years before and had grown comfortable in their posts. Wynslade, 'a sexagenarian or thereabouts', had ruled St Guthlac's for six years, during which time he had 'repaired its buildings and augmented divine worship therein'. And Hall was driven to action 'lest he be removed and recalled by the said abbot [of St Albans] on frivolous and perhaps unlawful grounds' from the priory that he had 'for some time laudably ruled'. These rather ingenuous petitions seem harmless enough, but to mother houses they represented a dangerous precedent. More seriously, papal grants of perpetuity might be interpreted as releasing the prior altogether from mother-house jurisdiction; Partrike claimed himself to be 'exemptt utterly fro the prior' of Durham after acquiring his bull.[123] There are also signs that at least some of these priors were backed by lay supporters. Partrike was able to resist the might of Durham for any length of time only through the support of the Stanley family and other local gentlemen; in his papal petition Hall alludes to 'the help of my friends' in his future rule at Belvoir; and Vynt is said elsewhere to have been 'of noble race'.[124]

These challenges to their authority could therefore not be taken lightly by the mother houses concerned. At Durham, Prior Wessington and his convent pursued every possible avenue to nullify their rebellious prior's privilege, seeking redress from the pope, the archbishop of York and the king. Eventually, they procured Partrike's excommunication and in early 1446 the surrender of his bull, although back at Durham he continued to intrigue for further papal preferment. It is not clear whether the other rebellious priors went so far as to claim that their bulls of perpetuity brought them total freedom from mother-house jurisdiction. In any case, the abbot and convent of Gloucester were unwilling to acknowledge Wynslade's new privileges. The first suggestion of mother-house opposition comes only in July 1441, when Wynslade was moved to obtain a royal pardon for seeking papal grants in defiance of the Statutes of Provisors. Ten months later, Abbot Reginald persuaded Pope Eugenius IV to revoke the prior's indult, which had

---

122 *CPL*, VII, p. 368, VIII, p. 163, IX, pp. 355, 453. For a definitive account of the Partrike case, see Dobson, *Durham Priory*, pp. 327–41.

123 Dobson, *Durham Priory*, p. 331. In a similar case, Prior John Lose of Brecon obtained a papal chaplaincy in 1363 and then proceeded to claim four years later that this freed him from the abbot of Battle's authority. After failing to bring Lose round with stern words, Battle managed to acquire a papal confirmation that this grant did not release the prior from the jurisdiction of the abbot and his successors: BL, Harley MS 3586, fols 26v–29r; *CPL*, IV, pp. 31, 75.

124 *CPL*, VIII, p. 150.

'emanated without consent of the then abbot and is greatly prejudicial to St Peter's [Gloucester]'.[125]

The reactions of Colchester and St Albans to their priors' acquisitions are not recorded. These two indults might not even have been executed: Hall had not yet acted on his privilege when he sought royal pardon for having obtained it in March 1449.[126] However, in contrast to the response of Durham and Gloucester, the attitude at St Albans to perpetual priors in the second half of the fifteenth century was remarkably relaxed. Between 1472 and 1484, the heads of nearly every remaining abbey cell were granted their office for life.[127] The first of these grants was made by Abbot Albon (1465–76) to William Dixwell, prior of Binham, but the remainder were all issued in the early years of the abbacy of William Wallingford (1476–92), who seems to have been rather careless with his monastery's rights.[128] At least two of these concessions were made at the request of external forces. Shortly before 1478, Abbot Wallingford granted the right to present Nicholas Boston to Tynemouth for life to Richard, earl of Gloucester and Sir John Say; and the perpetuity of Richard Lamplew of Hertford in 1484 was permitted on the request of Bishop Russell of Lincoln, Thomas Bryan, the Chief Justice of the King's Bench, and four members of the royal household.[129] The mother house did not suspend all its authority, however. Abbot Wallingford's grants to the priors of Pembroke and Wallingford made the proviso that they 'should be of good conversation and honest fame . . . and repair and sustain the aforesaid priory well and sufficiently, and keep it from indebtedness'; whereas Boston was forced to resign the priorate of Tynemouth by his abbot in 1480 despite having received his life-grant only two years earlier.[130] Nevertheless, this series of grants represents an extraordinary devolution of authority.

No other mother house is known to have pursued such a liberal course with its dependencies. Indeed, only two further cases of an abbey ceding the right of perpetuity to one of their priors voluntarily and on its own initiative are known. In 1499, Thomas Flete, an elderly monk of Westminster, was granted the cell of St Bartholomew's Sudbury for life, and in March 1510, Abbot Thornton and the convent of St Mary's York made Edmund Whalley prior of St Bees for the rest of his life as a reward for his good and faithful service. This grant, however, was made dependent on Whalley observing three *substancialia*: that he should submit to the abbot's visitation, render

---

125 CPR, 1436–1441, p. 550; CPL, IX, p. 272.
126 CPR, 1446–1452, p. 247.
127 Registra, II, pp. 111 (Binham), 184–5, 254 (Tynemouth), 211–12 (Pembroke), 235–6 (Wallingford), 268–9 (Hertford). Even the prioress of St Mary de Pré was granted this privilege in 1480: ibid., II, pp. 222–3. Wymondham Priory had broken away from St Albans in 1449 (see below).
128 For Abbot Wallingford, see D. Knowles, 'The Case of St Albans Abbey in 1490', JEH, iii (1952), pp. 144–58.
129 Registra, II, pp. 165–6, 268–9.
130 Ibid., II, pp. 214–16.

account of his administration each year and that he should not demise any of the cell's property without mother-house consent for a term longer than nine years.[131] St Mary's was also determined that this grant should not serve as a precedent. When Cromwell sought the headship of St Bees for life for Prior John Matthew in 1533, his request was resisted by St Mary's on the grounds of Matthew's unsuitability.[132]

If the majority of mother houses were not prepared to countenance the relatively small surrender of authority implicit in the grant of perpetuity to an individual prior, any more serious challenges to their position naturally provoked the fiercest response. In the early fourteenth century, Prior Stephen of Ketton and his two companions at Brooke were thrown into prison, deprived of their profession and required to vow perpetual silence by the prior of Kenilworth, because Ketton had made some unspecified appeal (perhaps resisting his recall) to the Apostolic See and the archbishop of Canterbury against the mother house.[133] An even more serious uprising took place at Breedon Priory in the mid-thirteenth century, when Prior Gervase of Breedon sought, with lay support, to sever ties with Nostell Priory altogether. Having been considered by papal judges delegate, the dispute was eventually referred to Bishop Grosseteste who ruled that Breedon's dependence should remain, and Gervase resign with an annual pension of twenty marks from the proceeds of his cell.[134]

The dispute which broke out in 1318 between Binham Priory and its mother house, St Albans, was yet more spectacular. The trouble originated when the house's prior, William of Somerton decided to resist Abbot Hugh of Eversden's crushing exactions from the abbey's cells.[135] Quickly this stance developed into a full-scale rebellion, as Somerton refused to allow the abbot to visit his priory. The prior was said to have been supported in his defiance by 'a band of noblemen of the area whom he had gathered together', including Binham's patron, Robert Walkefare, to whom Somerton granted an annual pension of £10 for life. Partly because of his kinship to Walkefare and partly because of Edward II's energetic support of St Albans, Thomas of Lancaster and his faction also took Somerton's side; and the prior carried his entire convent with him too.[136] Having pleaded his case with some success in

131 *Charters of St Bartholomew's Priory, Sudbury*, ed. R. Mortimer, Suffolk Records Society, Suffolk Charters, XV (1996), no. 131, pp. 89–90; York Minster Library, M2/6a, fols 16r–17r.
132 *L&P*, VI, nos 746, 1359, pp. 335, 542, VII, no. 295, p. 127.
133 *Regestum Clementis Papae V*, 9 vols in 7 (Rome, 1885–7), V, no. 6268, pp. 376–8; *CPL, 1305–1342*, p. 77.
134 *CClR, 1237–1242*, p. 449; *Rotuli Roberti Grosseteste, episcopi Lincolniensis, 1235–1253*, ed. F. N. Davis, C&Y Soc., x (1913), pp. 440–2.
135 See below, p. 138. The Somerton episode is vividly described in *GASA*, II, pp. 130–45, although the abbey chronicles give an extremely one-sided account of events and motivations.
136 The king ordered the arrest of Somerton and all thirteen of his monks in October 1320: *CClR, 1318–1323*, p. 271.

Rome by drawing attention to the clause in Peter de Valognes' foundation charter reducing the annual tribute to be paid by Binham to one silver mark, Somerton was nevertheless arrested on his return to England and handed over to his abbot. He was restored to Binham at the intercession of the queen, until, having accumulated enormous debts, he apostatised. The St Albans account is vague about precisely what Somerton sought, though it records that the prior wished 'to obtain exemption from the Supreme Pontiff'. It may be, however, that he wanted nothing more than exemption from the abbot's taxation or a life grant of his office.[137] Nevertheless, his was a serious challenge to St Albans and could have resulted in some permanent loss of authority had not the king supported Abbot Eversden, a personal friend, so strongly. In each of these three cases, therefore, the mother house succeeded in utterly defeating its daughter house's rebellion. Not every abbey, however, was able to win such an unequivocal victory in the face of concerted and determined resistance from its cells.

Breaking the Ties of Dependence

Effective independence

Outright rebellion against a mother house was relatively rare. Yet despite the implacable hostility with which any attempt to resist its authority was met, an abbey might sometimes be forced to concede that the only way to maintain the essential dependence of a cell was to surrender a large degree of control over its everyday affairs. This was particularly true where a daughter house was itself large and wealthy, and unwilling to accept excessive interference, as the example of Tynemouth Priory illustrates. Over time, this sizeable cell of St Albans gradually succeeded in obtaining effective self-government. Concessions were won by the monks of Tynemouth as early as the abbacy of Richard d'Aubigny of St Albans (1097–1119), who agreed to limit the length and size of mother-house visitations to the cell. Soon afterwards, taking advantage of the quarrel between St Albans and Durham over its subjection, the priory acquired in 1122 a charter from Henry I forbidding both these great houses from interfering in Tynemouth's affairs and allowing it to choose its own priors.[138] This charter was soon disregarded, but not, it seems, forgotten by the monks of Tynemouth, who later elected Prior Akarius themselves with the support of Henry II.[139] But an even more serious attack on St Albans' authority over Tynemouth was

---

[137] GASA, II, p. 130.
[138] Ibid., I, p. 69; *Regesta Regum Anglo Normannorum, 1066–1154*, ed. H. W. C. Davis, C. Johnson, H. A. Cronne and R. H. C. Davis, 4 vols (Oxford, 1913–69), II, no. 1331, p. 173.
[139] *Select Cases in the Court of King's Bench*, ed. G. O. Sayles, 3 vols, Selden Society, lv, lvii–lviii (1936–9), II, pp. 137–41.

launched in 1291–2 by Prior Adam of Tewing.[140] Tewing now invited
Edward I to claim the priory's advowson, which it was said should have
passed to the Crown on the forfeiture of Tynemouth's founder, Robert de
Mowbray. When the king's agents investigated this claim in 1293, the
monks of the cell produced Henry I's charter in support of their bid for independence from St Albans, and the precedent of Prior Akarius was also
invoked. Edward I duly ordered the abbey to surrender the advowson of
Tynemouth to him, but 'led by piety and encouraged by the pleading of his
nobles', the king was persuaded to withdraw his claims by Abbot
Berkhamsted.[141] Prior Tewing was then arrested by the abbot in a midnight
raid on the priory and brought back to the mother house in chains.

    Although St Albans succeeded in frustrating these moves for independ-
ence, the absence of any further serious uprisings against St Albans at
Tynemouth can probably be attributed to the way the mother house reduced
its demands on its cell thereafter. It would appear from the names of the priory's inmates, where they are known, that there was much local recruitment
at Tynemouth in the later middle ages. Moreover, in April 1465, Prior
Langton was permitted to receive the profession of the priory's recruits
himself because of 'the many and arduous occupations' which prevented
Abbot Albon from doing it himself; and two years later the prior was granted
this power apparently for the remainder of his rule. Langton was also given
licence to present to vacant churches, demise properties, sell tithes and
profits from his churches, appoint and remove the priory's monastic and lay
officers without abbatial consent and to hear his brethren's confessions and
absolve faults in cases customarily reserved to the abbot.[142] The late medieval priors of Tynemouth seem also to have enjoyed considerable security of
tenure and when Abbot Wallingford recalled Prior Langton in 1478 he felt
obliged to justify his decision, blaming the prior's 'contumacies and
disobediences'.[143] Moreover, the ceding of the nomination of Langton's
successor to Gloucester and Say in c.1477 seems to have established a precedent, and both Wolsey and Cromwell interfered in the running of the cell.[144]
The former as legate released Tynemouth from the jurisdiction of its mother
house during the lifetime of Prior John Stonywell, with Abbot Ramrygge's
consent, in 1519; and the latter secured a life grant of his office for Prior

---

[140] Craster questioned whether the St Albans *Gesta* was correct in naming Adam of
    Tewing as the prior responsible for this rebellion, since the assize roll of Edward I
    names Simon of Walden as prior of Tynemouth during the dispute: GASA, II, pp.
    19–23; *A History of Northumberland*, ed. H. H. E. Craster, 15 vols (Newcastle,
    1893–1940), VIII, pp. 80–2, esp. p. 82n. However, since Walden held office for
    several years after the dispute, it is much more likely that Tewing was the offending
    prior: HRH, II, p. 132.
[141] *Select Cases in King's Bench*, II, pp. 137–41; CPR, *1292–1301*, p. 11.
[142] *Registra*, II, pp. 44–6, 68–9.
[143] Ibid., II, pp. 186–7.
[144] *L&P*, IV(ii), no. 3478, p. 1574, XII(i), no. 822, p. 363.

Thomas Gardener in 1533.[145] It would appear, then, that the abbots of St Albans exerted very little practical authority over their distant cell in the last seventy-five years or so of its existence.

The monks of Westminster also found it necessary to make concessions from an early date in order to maintain any kind of authority over their size-able dependency of Great Malvern. During the rule of Abbot Herbert (1121–c.1136), the abbey farmed their manor of Powick (Worcestershire) to the priory, adding that 'they should hold [the manor] for as long as they are obedient and subject to their mother house'. By the mid-twelfth century, however, the cell was resisting Westminster's authority, and acquired an unspecified papal privilege threatening the abbey's position. When Abbot Gervase protested, the case was referred to Archbishop Theobald who ruled in favour of Westminster; and soon after, in 1157, the abbey's jurisdiction over Great Malvern received papal confirmation.[146] The 1163 confirmation of the abbot of Westminster's right to remove freely the priors and monks at its cells, if it took effect, implies that Malvern experienced a full measure of dependence in the second half of the twelfth century, but in c.1217 a *conventio* was made between Abbot William du Hommet of Westminster and Prior Thomas de Wichio of Great Malvern which severely curtailed the mother house's authority over its cell.[147] The priory's right to elect its heads from among its own number and recruit its own monks was now recognised. Great Malvern was to remain subject to Westminster, but the abbey's rights were restricted to confirming its daughter house's elections and receiving canonical obedience from the priors-elect, and taking the profession of the priory's inmates 'according to the old custom' after which they were to return to Malvern. The abbot also retained the powers of correction and visitation over Great Malvern, but he was not to remove its priors 'maliciously' (i.e. without canonical cause) nor 'to remove a monk from Malvern or to send there another from Westminster without our [the Malvern community's] consent'. From the early thirteenth century, therefore, Great Malvern enjoyed a considerable degree of independence from Westminster, whose role thereafter amounted to overseeing rather than managing the priory's affairs.[148]

---

[145] Ibid., III(i), no. 510, p. 176, VI, no. 754, pp. 337–8.

[146] *Westminster Abbey Charters 1066–c.1214*, ed. E. Mason, London Record Society, xxv (1988), nos 243, 164, pp. 112–13, 83; E. Mason, *Westminster Abbey and its People, c.1050–c.1216* (Woodbridge, 1996), pp. 238–9; *The Letters of John of Salisbury*, ed. W. J. Millor, H. E. Butler and C. N. L. Brooke, 2 vols (London and Oxford, 1955–79), I, no. 45, pp. 80–1.

[147] *Mon. Ang.*, III, p. 448, no. 5.

[148] Late medieval abbots of Westminster can be seen making visitations of and exercising powers of correction over the monks of Great Malvern, confirming the priory's elections and receiving profession of its monks; but they do not seem to have enjoyed any other rights over Great Malvern except by invitation: *Documents Illustrating the Rule of Walter de Wenlock, Abbot of Westminster, 1283–1307*, ed. B. F. Harvey, Camden Society, 4th series, ii (1965), pp. 34–45; WAM 22949, 32645–7, 32661–3.

The freedom obtained from its mother house by another sizeable cell, the priory of Colne, was of a similar nature to that of Great Malvern, although a great deal more information survives concerning the build-up to the final settlement. The founder of Colne, the first Aubrey de Vere, does not seem to have sought any special liberties for the priory when making it subject to Abingdon Abbey. Very little evidence for Abingdon's handling of its daughter house survives until the start of the fourteenth century, but the abbey seems to have enjoyed the usual powers over the personnel of its cell. However, between 1303 and 1311 Abingdon's customary rights were systematically dismantled, leaving Colne largely free from mother-house interference. The catalyst for this development was the abbey's use of its cell as a dumping ground for difficult monks and the force behind it was the priory's patron, Robert de Vere, sixth earl of Oxford. As the de Vere mausoleum, Colne was of great interest to its patrons, and it seems that Earl Robert was displeased with the quality of monks being sent to pray for him and his ancestors. In July 1303, following his visitation of the cell, Archbishop Winchelsey convened a meeting between the abbot of Abingdon, the prior of Colne, the earl of Oxford and the bishop of London at the latter's manor of Stepney. Here he promulgated an ordinance castigating the mother house for sending Abingdon monks who were 'absolutely useless and ignorant and not instructed in their service' to Colne and for using the priory as a prison. More significantly, it was decreed that in future the abbot should not move monks between Abingdon and Colne 'unless from a sure and reasonable cause'.[149]

This curtailing of their right to circulate their cell's personnel at will was a serious blow to Abingdon's control of Colne, but worse was to follow. In 1309, Bishop Baldock of London wrote to Abingdon, recommending a further abridgement of their powers. He claimed that Colne was in a depressed state and could only be reformed if the prior was allowed to recruit some honest men of the neighbourhood to make up the deficiency in numbers there. This action would, it was added, win 'the good will of the honest men of these parts' – no doubt a reference to Robert de Vere.[150] This was a bold request, since to concede to Colne local recruitment would be to surrender some authority over the composition of their daughter convent. However, two years later, Abingdon made an agreement with Colne, at the instance of de Vere, giving up their rights to select and remove not only the monks of their cell but also its priors.[151] The priory was given licence to

---

149 *Registrum Radulphi Baldock, Gilberti Segrave, Ricardi Newport, et Stephani Gravesend, Episcoporum Londoniensium, AD 1304–1338*, ed. R. C. Fowler, C&Y Soc., vii (1911), pp. 77–9.

150 *Reg. Baldock*, pp. 95–6. Baldock's strong disapproval of the rotation of monks in dependent priories is illustrated by his opposition towards this practice at the abbeys of St Osyth's and Colchester too: ibid., pp. 59, 131–3.

151 This composition is known only from its confirmation by Edward II in 1321: CPR, *1321–1324*, p. 25. The full text of this document is printed in *Mon. Ang.*, IV, p. 103, no. 20.

recruit any personnel it chose, who could not be transferred to Abingdon, and nor could any mother-house monks be sent to Colne. In addition, the priory was henceforth to elect its heads from among its own number. As at Great Malvern, to the mother house remained only the rights to visit Colne, to receive the profession of new recruits and to confirm and then present to patron and bishop the priors-elect of the cell without delay, unless 'evidently unworthy'. Although Colne remained a cell of Abingdon, from 1311 it was effectively master of its own affairs.[152]

Dover Priory also succeeded in securing considerable freedom from the authority of Christ Church Canterbury, but only after many decades of heated conflict.[153] The extent of Dover's subjection to Christ Church was questionable from the start. In particular, the controversy surrounding the foundation of the priory and the vague wording of Henry I's charter created uncertainty over the respective rights of the monks and the archbishop of Canterbury. Archbishop Theobald bolstered his authority over Dover with a papal confirmation from Adrian IV in 1155 denying the prior of Christ Church any right over Dover in vacancies of the see unless by archiepiscopal consent, and a charter from Henry II declaring the church of Dover to be 'in the hand and lordship' of the archbishop.[154] However, Theobald also recognised the rights of Christ Church in an ordinance of 1155×1161, which laid down that Dover was a cell of the cathedral priory, whose monks were to make profession at the mother house and whose priors must be professed Canterbury monks. The appointment and removal of those priors, however, was to be the archbishop's prerogative.[155] This concordat was quickly confirmed by Alexander III, although subsequent bulls issued by that pope in 1174–5 confirming Theobald's provision for vacancies and anathematising anyone in the churches of Dover or Canterbury who might seek to institute a prior to the cell suggest that Christ Church remained unsatisfied with its limited rights as mother house.[156]

---

[152] One mark of Colne's continued dependence on Abingdon was the latter's successful objection to its prior attending the Benedictine General Chapter in his own right in 1423. According to the statutes of Benedict XII establishing the chapter, the citation only of '*priorum, abbates propriores non habentium*' was allowed: CBM, II, no. 171, p. 138; Wilkins, *Concilia*, II, pp. 589–91, chap. 2.

[153] C. R. Haines devoted a chapter of his monograph on Dover Priory to the contentions between the priory and its mother house, but his account is imperfect in many respects, not least in its highly partisan stance: C. R. Haines, *Dover Priory* (Cambridge, 1930), pp. 59–110. For a briefer, but much more reliable discussion, see J. H. Denton, *English Royal Free Chapels 1100–1300. A Constitutional Study* (Manchester, 1970), pp. 57–66.

[154] PUE, II, no. 89, p. 269; *Mon. Ang.*, IV, pp. 538–9, no. 9.

[155] A. Saltman, *Theobald Archbishop of Canterbury* (London, 1956), no. 83, pp. 306–7. Saltman dated this *acta* to 1157×1161, and I am grateful to Dr Joseph Gribbin for information regarding the alternative dating.

[156] PUE, II, nos 110, 136, 145, pp. 298–9, 328–9, 335–6.

Throughout the thirteenth century, the monks of the cathedral priory endeavoured to augment their powers over Dover, with intermittent success. During the pontificate of St Edmund of Canterbury (1234–40), Christ Church won the archbishop's support for a composition which gave the monks a greater say over recruits to Dover and a strong voice in the election of the cell's subpriors; but this ordinance was overturned by St Edmund's successor.[157] The situation was considerably complicated by Dover's status as a royal free chapel, which ensured that the king retained a close interest in its affairs. Royal concerns to ensure that the priors of Dover were of a suitable standard led to Edward I challenging the rights of Christ Church Canterbury over its cell in the courts. In 1287, Theobald's ordinance was declared invalid, since it was made without the king's assent, and the sole right of the archbishop over Dover upheld according to the charter of Henry II. Nevertheless, Christ Church refused to abandon their claims to their cell's subjection and the conflict and litigation continued throughout the first half of the fourteenth century. Finally in May 1356, following a failed attempt to resolve the dispute six years earlier, Archbishop Islip acknowledged the rights of the monks of Canterbury over Dover and acquired a licence in mortmain to unite the two priories.[158] Haines was quite wrong however, to state that this union brought Dover under the full control of Christ Church. The archbishops of Canterbury continued to appoint and depose priors of Dover after 1356 and may even have received the profession of its novices. Moreover, after the mid-fifteenth century the priors of Dover were apparently no longer chosen from the Canterbury convent, as had usually been the case before this date.[159] Despite centuries of struggle, Christ Church was unable to exercise anything more than a nominal authority over its cell in the later middle ages.[160]

---

157 Haines, *Dover Priory*, pp. 82–4.
158 *CPR, 1348–1350*, pp. 508–9, *1354–1358*, pp. 379, 382–3. The archbishop is said to have acted thus because Dover 'is so wasted in its possessions and fallen away in its faculties that there is no relief for it but in ordering otherwise for it'.
159 *CPR, 1354–1358*, pp. 379, 382–3; *The Register of Henry Chichele, Archbishop of Canterbury, 1414–1443*, ed. E. F. Jacob and H. C. Johnson, 4 vols, C&Y Soc., xlv, xlii, xlvi–xlvii (1938–47), I, pp. 151–2, 163–4, 292–3, IV, p. 54; Greatrex, BRECP, p. 54. For relations between the two houses in the middle decades of the fifteenth century, see *The Chronicle of John Stone monk of Christ Church 1415–1471*, ed. W. G. Searle, Cambridge Antiquarian Society, Octavo Series, XXXIV (1902), esp. pp. 10, 33, 38.
160 A mark of the relatively tenuous links between the two houses is the fact that when Dover was suppressed in November 1535, only two of its brethren were received into the community of Christ Church Canterbury, and these only at the request of Cromwell: *L&P*, X, no. 13, p. 3.

Complete Independence

Not only did several cells succeed in winning a large degree of independence
of action, but a further eleven English dependencies managed to release
themselves entirely from the authority of their mother houses. Of these
eleven priories, however, seven (Bolton, Brinkburn, Little Malvern, Felley,
Weybourne, Llanthony Secunda and Ranton) never seem to have been fully
dependent in the first place. As Christ Church Canterbury found, to resist a
daughter house's bid for independence was particularly difficult where the
cell's subjection was already in some doubt. There is good reason to suspect
that the dependence of the priories of Bolton to Huntingdon and Brinkburn
to Pentney was never fully established. The only evidence we have for ties
between Bolton and Huntingdon comes from the latter priory's unsuccessful
attempts to press its case for authority over the former in the late twelfth
century. Similarly, no firm connections between Brinkburn and Pentney can
be discerned prior to Pentney's renunciation of its claims to the subjection of
Brinkburn in c.1188.[161] The independence achieved by Bolton and
Brinkburn in the late twelfth century may therefore have been nothing more
than a recognition of the status quo.

The extent to which Little Malvern was ever a dependency of Worcester
Cathedral Priory is also uncertain. Although its foundation charter stated
that the prior of Little Malvern should be elected in the Worcester chapter
and that no one should be admitted to the monastic habit at the priory
'without the consultation of the bishop and prior in the chapter of Worcester', and profession there, by the late thirteenth century the bishop alone was
claiming this authority over Little Malvern.[162] There is, moreover, no sign of
the Worcester monks enjoying any powers over this 'cell' in the voluminous
records of the cathedral priory (other than during vacancies of the see of
Worcester): if it ever had any substance, Little Malvern's dependence on
Worcester can have been short-lived at best. The subjection of Felley to
Worksop and Weybourne to West Acre was more tangible, but seems to
have been strictly limited and thus relatively easy to overthrow. Following
numerous 'cases and controversies' arising from Worksop's claims over
Felley, the latter house was granted freedom from all subjection in a docu-
ment confirmed by Archbishop Godfrey Ludham of York in March 1261.
From the instrument renouncing all its claims over Felley, however, it

---

[161] A. H. Thompson, *History and Architectural Description of the Priory of St Mary,
Bolton-in-Wharfedale*, Thoresby Society, xxx (1928), pp. 51–5; *The Cartulary of
Brinkburn Priory*, ed. W. Page, SS, xc (1893), no. 232, p. 184. For the circumstances
of the foundation of these two cells which engendered the claims to their subjection,
see above, pp. 53–4.

[162] *The Cartulary of Worcester Cathedral Priory*, ed. R. R. Darlington, PRS, new series,
xxxviii (1962–3), no. 61a, p. 37; *CPR, 1292–1301*, p. 370; *Register of Godfrey Giffard*,
II, pp. 372, 499, 503–5.

appears that the only specific powers Worksop had enjoyed were a tribute of 10s. and a voice in Felley elections.[163] Equally, it would seem from the 1314 settlement securing Weybourne's independence that the sole authority exercised by the canons of West Acre was the requirement that the priors of Weybourne be chosen from the 'mother house' convent. With the recognition that Weybourne could elect its heads internally, the links with West Acre seem to have been completely severed.[164]

The dependence of Llanthony Secunda in Gloucester to Llanthony Prima was equally tenuous. Prima found itself in the unique and impossible position of acquiring a daughter house larger and wealthier than itself. On the Welsh uprising following the death of Henry I, the canons were forced to flee their secluded home in Monmouthshire and were rehoused in Gloucester in 1136. Llanthony Secunda, as the new priory was named, was intended to be a daughter house of Prima, and in 1146 Eugenius III's bull confirming the property of Secunda also laid down that the priory 'should always remain subjected as a cell, just as it has been thus far'. However, the preference of the canons for Secunda and the lavish endowment and forceful backing of that house by its founder, Milo of Gloucester, made it impossible for the Monmouthshire priory to exercise its supposed authority. Instead Prima was itself subordinated to the needs of Secunda, and the eventual separation of the two houses in 1205 was in fact engineered by the patron of the former house, Walter Lacy, in order to abrogate its effective subjection to its Gloucester offshoot.[165]

Finally, it is likely that Ranton's successful breakaway from Haughmond Abbey in 1247 can also be best attributed to the questionable hold of the mother house over its dependency. Robert fitz Noel's foundation charter for Ranton, issued some time before 1166, records that the canons there were living 'under the rule and subjection of Haughmond'.[166] The precise nature of this subjection is, however, difficult to ascertain, and Ranton may well have resisted its dependence; the priory's confirmation charter from Archbishop Baldwin between 1185 and 1190 omits the word 'subjection' from the formula used in its foundation charter.[167] Perhaps because of

---

163 BL, Add. MS 36872, fols 130v–133v. In return for quitclaiming their rights over Felley, the prior and convent of Worksop were granted an annual pension of 20s. from their former daughter house.

164 F. H. Fairweather, 'The Augustinian Priory of Weybourne, Norfolk', *Norfolk Archaeology*, xxiv (1932), p. 203; F. Blomefield, *An Essay towards a Topographical History of the County of Norfolk*, 11 vols (London, 1805–10), IX, pp. 450–1.

165 *PUE*, I, no. 35, pp. 266–70; J. N. Langston, 'Priors of Lanthony by Gloucester', *TBGAS*, lxiii (1942), pp. 1–144, esp. pp. 2–36.

166 'The Chartulary of Ronton Priory', ed. G. Wrottesley, *Staffordshire Historical Collections*, iv(i) (1883), p. 267.

167 *English Episcopal Acta II: Canterbury 1162–90*, ed. C. R. Cheney and B. A. R. Jones (Oxford, 1986), no. 301, p. 256. The word 'subjection' was re-inserted in Archbishop Hubert Walter's confirmation charter a few years later, however, perhaps at Haughmond's insistence: *English Episcopal Acta III*, no. 583, pp. 236–7.

Ranton's reluctance to acknowledge Haughmond's authority, an agreement was made between the two houses, probably early in the thirteenth century, to define relations more clearly. The powers conceded to the abbot of Haughmond now were quite considerable. Not only might he visit Ranton once every year, but on vacancies of the latter house the canons of Ranton were to present one of their own number and one from the Haughmond convent to the abbot who was to select the new prior from them. And although Ranton was to be permitted to admit its own canons, they were to be professed at Haughmond.[168] Ranton, however, does not seem to have accepted this settlement, and further dissension over its status soon arose. In February 1247, having previously been taken to papal judges delegate, the matter came before Bishop Weseham of Coventry and Lichfield, who ruled that henceforth Ranton was to be completely independent, save for the annual payment of a pension of 100s. to Haughmond.[169]

In each of these seven instances, the ability of the cell to achieve independence, in almost every case within a century of its foundation, can be directly related to the tenuous authority exercised by its mother house. Where the subjection of a priory was fully established, however, it was considerably more difficult to contest one's dependence. In fact, only four English cells (Stone, Calwich, Snape and Wymondham) were ever able to overturn completely their full subjection to another monastery. Although Dr Dickinson questioned whether Stone was ever fully dependent on Kenilworth, the priory does seem to have enjoyed little independence of action before 1260. The Stone cartulary indicates that Kenilworth enjoyed considerable power over its cell's endowment prior to this date, with several leases and final concords made in the name of the mother house alone or together with Stone. Moreover, the agreement between Kenilworth and Robert III of Stafford over the advowson of Stone states that its priors would be chosen by Kenilworth from among its own convent; and the clause concerning the patron's power to demand the withdrawal of absentee priors may indicate their dative status. Finally, the specification in the 1260 agreement between the two priories that during his visitation of Stone, the prior of Kenilworth should not remove any canon of Stone nor send any other canon there from Kenilworth implies that this power had previously been exercised by the mother house.[170]

Before the mid-thirteenth century, the only recorded trouble Kenilworth encountered with its daughter house concerned the rights of its Stafford patrons.[171] However, by that time the question of Stone's dependence had

---

[168] *The Cartulary of Haughmond Abbey*, ed. U. Rees (Cardiff, 1985), no. 944, p. 184; *Mon. Ang.*, VI (ii), p. 750, no. 12.

[169] *Haughmond Cartulary*, nos 946–7, p. 184; *Magnum Registrum Album Lichfield*, ed. H. E. Savage, *Staffordshire Historical Collections* (1924), no. 107, p. 50.

[170] G. Wrottesley (ed.), 'The Stone Chartulary', *Staffordshire Historical Collections*, vi(i) (1885), pp. 1–28; BL, Add. MS 47677, fols 110r–112r.

[171] See above, p. 70.

become disputed, and in 1260 both sides submitted the matter to Bishop
Roger Longespee of Coventry and Lichfield for judgment. On consideration,
the bishop ordained that Stone should be 'free and exempt from all subjection, jurisdiction and power' of Kenilworth. Prior Roger of Worcester of
Stone and his convent were accordingly given the authority to receive and
profess their own canons (none of whom were ever to be sent to or from
Kenilworth) and to dispose of the priory's possessions without interference.
Kenilworth, however, was to retain the powers of a patron over Stone: that
is, hospitality during visits to the priory (to be restricted to one visit of two
days' duration with ten horses per year), custody in vacancies and giving
licence for the election of new priors. It was also laid down that when those
elections took place, two canons of Kenilworth were to be present.[172]

It may be that the patrons of Stone played an important part in this
episode, since the later *Historia* of Stone states that Robert IV of Stafford 'for
great love he had to Saint Wolfade, this church and the cannons from
Killingworth free he made'. In any case, Kenilworth was not prepared to
abandon its claims to Stone so easily, and sought to overturn the bishop's
decision. After further conflict, Prior Robert de Salle and the convent of
Kenilworth, in a document probably of 1292, agreed to desist in future from
the litigation they had been pursuing in an attempt to preserve Stone's
dependence. Instead they acknowledged without reservation the terms of
the 1260 ordinance, and agreed to accept and ratify the election of John
Tiney, Roger of Worcester's successor, as prior of Stone.[173] At about the
same time, a settlement was made concerning the division of the two priories' property, which seems to have been a matter of enduring dispute. In
return for its quitclaim of any rights over Stone's endowment, Kenilworth
was to receive from the Staffordshire priory an annual pension of twelve and
a half marks. Both these agreements were confirmed by the authorities and
accompanied with provisions for severe ramifications should either party
renege on their commitments.[174] That Kenilworth continued to exercise the
rights of patron over Stone is shown by the insertion of several documents
relating to the Stone election of 1524 in the Kenilworth cartulary.[175] Nevertheless, Stone can no longer be considered a true dependency after 1260 (or
perhaps 1292), and its priors were summoned to the Augustinian general
chapter in their own right during the later middle ages.[176]

Although it has recently been questioned, there can be little doubt that
Calwich Priory too was fully dependent on Kenilworth before its break-

---

172 BL, Add. MS 47677, fols 111r–112r.
173 Ibid., fols 114v–117r.
174 Ibid., fols 112r–114v.
175 Ibid., fols 117v–120r.
176 *Chapters of the Augustinian Canons*, ed. H. E. Salter, C&Y Soc., xxix (1922), pp.
103–4, 187, 272.

away.[177] Both the heads and the canons of Calwich were not only appointed by the mother house, but could also be removed according to its free will. Moreover, the canon selected to administer the priory was not even accorded the title of prior, but was instead styled 'keeper of Calwich'.[178] Yet in 1349 this dependence on Kenilworth was brought to an abrupt end by an instrument of Bishop Roger Northburgh of Coventry and Lichfield. This document explains that the bishop had been drawn to action by the ceaseless importuning of the priory's patron, Nicholas of Longford. Longford had complained that the constant rotation of the canons of Calwich by Kenilworth, and the uncertainty this produced, had resulted in 'tepid and remiss divine office and many bad and costly things for both places'. In response to these complaints, and the many quarrels reported to have raged between the parties, Bishop Northburgh declared the full independence of Calwich, with the payment of an annual pension of 60s. to Kenilworth in recompense.[179] No further connections between the two priories are recorded, and thereafter the heads of Calwich, now with the title of prior, were elected by their own community.

The successful resistance of Snape to Colchester Abbey about a century later encountered considerably more resistance than that of Calwich seems to have done. The first stage of this conflict centred around Prior John Mersey of Snape and the cell's patron, Isabella de Ufford, countess of Suffolk. Mersey and the abbot of Colchester were at loggerheads by November 1398, when the prior obtained papal support against an uncanonical oath and constitution imposed on him from Colchester.[180] In January 1400, after Mersey had secured absolution from both, Isabella de Ufford obtained a bull freeing Snape from the authority of its mother house, on the grounds that Colchester was breaking the conditions of the founder's charter; a claim based on extremely flimsy foundations.[181] In response, the abbey appealed to its patron, the king, who issued two commissions for Mersey's arrest in May

---

[177] *English Episcopal Acta XIV: Coventry and Lichfield 1072–1159*, ed. M. J. Franklin (Oxford, 1997), no. 48A, pp. 47–8.

[178] BL, Add. MS 47677, fol. 121v; *HRH*, II, pp. 355–6.

[179] BL, Add. MS. 47677, fols 121v–124r.

[180] See above, p. 93. According to Mersey, the abbot of Colchester had unreasonably made him swear to act only on abbatial orders and had then issued a constitution forbidding the monks of Snape to obey him: PRO, E135/19/67.

[181] *Mon. Ang.*, IV, p. 559, no. 4. In his foundation charter, William Martel had stipulated that monks should be maintained at Snape according to the priory's faculties and that the abbot of Colchester should visit twice a year or more often if necessary. The countess of Suffolk asserted in her petition that the first of these requirements was not being met, since only the prior resided at Snape permanently, with other monks sent only on a temporary basis. Her argument that this continual movement of monks diminished divine service in the priory might have had some substance, but Colchester's practice can hardly be deemed to have been breaking the terms of their cell's foundation: *Cartularium Monasterii Sancti Johannis Baptiste de Colecestria*, ed. S. A. Moore, 2 vols, Roxburghe Club (1897), I, pp. 168–70.

and July 1400 for obtaining papal privileges prejudicial to Colchester, which were subsequently judged to be in contravention of the Statute of Provisors.[182] Despite this defeat, the prior and his patron continued to press their claim, finally arguing spuriously in June 1409 that at the cell's foundation William Martel had ordained that the priors of Snape should be elected by their own convent and then presented by the house's patron to the bishop, as Mersey was said to have been.[183] The dispute outlived its protagonists and it is not until January 1444 that a final settlement is recorded. Now the abbot of Colchester granted to the prior of Snape and its new patron, William de la Pole, earl of Suffolk, and their successors the right to nominate the priors of their house whom the abbot would present to the bishops of Norwich. Even more significantly, however, the abbot and convent granted that 'they will not visit the priory hereafter nor have any spiritual jurisdiction or anything else therein, except a yearly pension of 6s. 8d., which they have had hitherto'.[184] Only the merest trace of subjection remained, therefore, and Snape can be considered an independent priory from this date.

The fourth and final English dependency to achieve independence from its parent abbey was Wymondham Priory, a cell of St Albans. Although the priory's patrons continually threatened to weaken St Albans' hold on Wymondham, the priors and monks of the cell seem to have caused little concern to their mother house, save for a few heads considered to be too intimate with their patrons. This was to change dramatically with the appointment by Abbot Stoke of the abbey archdeacon, Dr Stephen London, as prior of Wymondham in March 1447.[185] Stoke took this action to free himself from London's criticisms, but after a year or so decided to recall the prior. London refused to return, apparently at the behest of the priory's patron, Sir Andrew Ogard, who then petitioned the Holy See for the conversion of Wymondham into an independent abbey. Such exalted claims were feasible only because William d'Aubigny's foundation charter contained a clause allowing him to convert Wymondham into an independent abbey at some later date. Moreover, St Albans was clearly breaking the terms of the priory's foundation by appointing the cell's priors itself; although Ogard stretched the founder's meaning to state that Wymondham's priors

---

182 CPR, 1399–1401, pp. 271–2, 347; R. L. Storey (ed.), 'Clergy and Common Law in the reign of Henry IV' in Medieval Legal Records, ed. R. F. Hunnisett and J. B. Post (London, 1978), no. 15, pp. 390–1.

183 Cal. Inq. Misc., VII, no. 265, p. 138; PRO, E135/15/16. It may be that forgeries had been produced at Snape, since the cell's foundation charter made no such stipulation and John Mersey had been presented to the bishop of Norwich in November 1394 by the abbot and convent of Colchester, like all his fourteenth-century predecessors: NRO, Reg/5/9, fols 196r–196v.

184 CPR, 1441–1446, pp. 448–9. Small payments for the nomination of the new prior of Snape by the countess of Suffolk and for his presentation by the abbot of Colchester are found in the surviving priory account of 1515: PRO, SC6/HenVIII/3402.

185 NRO, Reg/6/11, fol. 48r. The Wymondham case is related in Registra, I, pp. 148–55.

should be perpetual.[186] London and his patron had a strong case therefore, and in October 1448 Pope Nicholas V issued a bull freeing Wymondham from the jurisdiction of its mother house and elevating the cell into an abbey.[187] In stark contrast to the Somerton incident, the king recognised the bull and added his protection to that of the pope, leaving St Albans with no means of reversing the decision. To add insult to injury, several of the abbey's monks were released from obedience to their abbot and allowed to join the renegade community, and London was formally installed as the first abbot of Wymondham in November 1449.[188] To crown his triumph, London sent a mocking letter to his former superior, glorying in the fact that 'never with his free will will you have Stephen as your subject'.[189]

Conclusions

The several instances where English cells succeeded in winning a substantial measure of independence from their mother houses have been described in some detail, partly because no wholly satisfactory account is currently available for most of them, and partly because they reveal so much about the relations between monastery, cell, patron, diocesan, king and pope. A number of conclusions emerge from these case studies. Firstly, and most obviously, the ability of mother houses to maintain their authority was considerably weakened where the subjection of a priory was not fully established. Several Augustinian cells were able to throw off their dependence altogether because the limited nature of their mother house's powers seems to have made these rights questionable in the eyes of the ecclesiastical authorities. Equally the existence of a foundation charter imposing some restriction on mother-house authority greatly assisted a cell's bid for freedom. These charters were often interpreted in ways which the founder could never have anticipated, and the tenuous attempts of the prior and patron of Snape to highlight stipulations in William Martel's charter that were arguably not being observed to the letter seem to have convinced no one. Nevertheless, it was unquestionably William d'Aubigny's provision for possible independence that enabled Wymondham to break free from St Albans so cleanly three hundred and fifty or so years later.

   Secondly, the importance of the patron in these resistance movements is abundantly clear. Dr Thompson has demonstrated how the denization of alien priories depended almost entirely on the support of influential lay patrons, and English cells seem to have been equally reliant on assistance of this kind. The successful campaigns of Colne, Stone, Calwich, Snape and

---

186 *Mon. Ang.*, III, pp. 330, 337–9, nos 2, 21; *CPR, 1446–1452*, p. 154.
187 *CPL*, X, pp. 19–20.
188 *Mon. Ang.*, III, p. 339, no. 21; *CPL*, X, p. 46; *Registra*, I, pp. 152–3.
189 *Amundesham*, II, Appendix I, pp. 366–9.

Wymondham were all instigated and carried through by their patrons, whereas it was only the backing of Walter Lacy that preserved Llanthony Prima from dwindling at the hands of its Gloucester offshoot. The status and resources of a powerful lay advocate were vital in the struggle against a richer and more powerful foe, not least since it might prove necessary, as the monks of Binham found, to resist forcibly mother-house moves to restore obedience. It is not difficult to see why the patron of a daughter house might support a bid for its independence. His or her influence would increase considerably with the weakening of the mother house's jurisdiction, as did the rights of the earls of Suffolk in 1444 with their newly acquired voice in the election of the priors of Snape. Patrons might also be motivated by concerns about the quality of the suffrages performed for them in a daughter house. The dissatisfaction of Robert de Vere and Nicholas of Longford with the manning of their priories with inmates who were either sent there for punishment or circulated too regularly seems to have been largely responsible for the breakaways of Colne and Calwich.[190]

Thirdly, the support of the diocesan was also crucial for any successful resistance to mother-house authority. This seems to have been especially true for the Augustinian canons. The independence of the Augustinian priories of Stone, Ranton and Calwich was won merely through a ruling in their favour by the bishop of Coventry and Lichfield after the mother house and cell had submitted their quarrel to his judgment; whereas the Breedon rebellion was defeated by the decision of Bishop Grosseteste of Lincoln that Nostell should retain authority over its cell. The role of Bishop Baldock of London in Robert de Vere's campaign for the freedom of Colne Priory was also of some importance. It would appear that these prelates shared to some extent the distaste of the priories' patrons for the way the mother houses concerned were managing their cells, even sometimes questioning whether their inmates' vows of stability were thereby being infringed. It is also clear that it was the opposition of their diocesans that prevented Christ Church Canterbury and Worcester from securing a significant level of control over the priories of Dover and Little Malvern.

Yet as William Partrike, William of Somerton and John Mersey discovered, no degree of local support could withstand a mother house determinedly assisted by the king. Royal assistance was particularly valuable in resisting a daughter house which had taken its case to Rome. Several cells trying to reduce or overturn their abbey's authority sought papal privileges, which, after 1351, any king could nullify by invoking the first Statute of Provisors. Indeed, there was considerable hostility from both the Crown and Parliament towards papal interference in the affairs of English monasteries, and individual religious risked the wrath of the secular authorities by appeal-

---

[190] Cf. B. Thompson, 'The Statute of Carlisle, 1307, and the Alien Priories', *JEH*, xli (1990), pp. 543–83, and its account of patronal hostility to the exploitation of alien cells by their mother houses.

ing to Rome in this way.[191] Acting as patrons of St Albans and Colchester, Edward II and Henry IV warded off the serious threats posed by Somerton and Mersey; and it is probably significant that the successful campaigns of Wymondham and Snape took place during the reign of the supine Henry VI. Similarly, St Albans was able to maintain its possession of Tynemouth in the 1290s only because Edward I voluntarily withdrew his claims to the priory's advowson.

It would be wrong, however, to conclude from these examples that mother houses were continually afflicted by acts of disobedience and rebellion from their cells. By and large, it was only the largest dependencies, and those whose subjection was questionable, which proved unwilling to accept the authority of their mother houses. At the mass of smaller cells, whose inmates were too closely regulated, too few and too frequently circulated to foster any community spirit, very little sign of resistance is discernible. Most mother houses preserved full control over their cells throughout the middle ages and it is striking that only four fully dependent English daughter houses were ever able to achieve untrammelled autonomy from their parents. We should not forget that there were certain advantages in dependence that might have dissuaded priors from seeking to break free from their parents. Some cells received a share in their mother house's privileges, such as exemption from episcopal jurisdiction, and it may well be that the sizeable cell of Great Malvern only tolerated subjection to Westminster Abbey in order to keep the bishop of Worcester at bay. Equally, the protection of a powerful abbey in times of need must have been greatly appreciated.[192] Moreover, the dative status of a prior might be useful in avoiding unwelcome impositions, and more than one cell secured exemption from tax collection by arguing that its head was a mere proctor of the mother house.[193] The priors of semi-conventual dependencies can also sometimes be seen exploiting their ambiguous position before the law, pleading in their own names when it suited them but claiming that they could not be sued by others because they were only mother-house obedientiaries.[194]

It should also be noted that none of Calwich, Snape or Wymondham found life easy after they had shaken off their mother houses' yoke. By the end of the fourteenth century, it was stated that only a prior and two canons were customarily maintained at Calwich, and serious financial problems were being experienced. The priory was eventually suppressed in 1532 by its

---

191 See R. L. Storey, 'Papal Provisions to English Monasteries', *Nottingham Medieval Studies*, xxxv (1991), pp. 77–91, including the notorious case of Edmund Bramfield, monk of Bury St Edmunds.

192 See below, p. 138, for mother-house protection of their cells at law.

193 E.g. NRO, Hare MS 2, fols 121r–122r (St Ives); *CPR, 1381–1385*, pp. 414–15; *CClR, 1381–1385*, p. 593, *1402–1405*, pp. 350–1 (Leominster).

194 E.g. PRO, E315/2/49; Morgan, *Bec*, pp. 32–3; cf. *VCH, Cambridgeshire and the Isle of Ely*, II, p. 253.

patron Sir Ralph Longford, in a move of dubious legality.[195] Snape, mean-while, narrowly avoided annexation to Butley Priory in the early years of the sixteenth century and held only two monks at the time of its premature suppression by Wolsey in 1526.[196] And Wymondham, although it avoided the running-down and early closure of Calwich and Snape, was shown to be far from flourishing in a series of visitations between 1492 and 1532.[197] In all, disputes with patrons or bishops over the position of dependencies seem to have been rather more common than those between mother and daughter houses themselves. Equally, in some of the instances where cells did resist their parent's authority, it is difficult to avoid the impression that the patron rather than prior was the driving force behind the insurrection. Most of the time, relations between mother houses and their cells were relatively harmonious, and far from providing endless trouble to their parents, satellite priories had the potential to be of some use and profit.

[195] VCH, Staffordshire, III, p. 239.
[196] Mon. Ang., IV, p. 560, no. 6; PRO, C142/76/37, 44.
[197] Norwich Visitations, pp. 20–3, 95–101, 161–4, 247–8.

3

'A Source of Weakness'?
Mother Houses and Their Daughters

To modern eyes, the possession of a family of cells has usually seemed a considerable burden to a monastery. The financial strain of preserving the fragile existence of a small dependency, the unrelenting contentions with bishop, patron or the cell itself, and above all the enormous potential for disciplinary problems at tiny isolated daughter houses; these disadvantages, it has always been thought, must surely have outweighed any benefits the ownership of a cell could have conferred. Professor Knowles' judgement that the vast majority of dependencies were inevitably 'a source of weakness to the house that owned them' has rarely if ever been questioned.[1] The spiritual dangers faced by monks with no eremitical calling, required to leave the supportive communal atmosphere of the mother house and to dwell in often remote cells with only one or two companions are indeed obvious. Any practical advantages a dependency might have brought to a mother house would have seemed hollow if service in its cells systematically corrupted the community. The question of discipline is therefore paramount in any assessment of the value of daughter houses to their parents.

Little favourable has been written about the standard of observance in small monasteries since the preamble to the 1536 Act of Dissolution denounced the 'manifest sin, vicious, carnal, and abominable living . . . daily used and committed amongst the little and small abbeys, priories, and other religious houses of monks, canons, and nuns, where the congregation of such religious persons is under the number of twelve persons';[2] and because they were the smallest houses of all, dependencies have usually been considered the worst. Knowles adjudged them 'the most considerable of all the elements of spiritual decay in the monastic life of the country', shown by visitation records to be 'almost without exception lax in discipline, if not positively

---

1 Knowles, MO, p. 136. This conclusion was echoed by Dr Chibnall, who believed that 'the existence of small and remote granges whose *raison d'être* was temporal administration could not fail to be a source of weakness to any monastery': Morgan, Bec, p. 37.
2 *Statutes of the Realm*, 10 vols (HMSO, 1810–24), III, p. 575.

corrupt'.[3] The small dependency attracted equally stern medieval critics, in particular Gerald of Wales, who claimed that it was a truth universally acknowledged that 'God granted abbeys, but cells and their occupants the Devil gave'.[4]

In assessing to what extent these implacably hostile judgements are justified, one must also consider the attitudes of mother houses towards their daughters. Other than the occasional remark in pursuance of tax relief, there are certainly few signs that the abbeys themselves regarded their dependencies as 'a source of weakness'. Not only might considerable practical benefits proceed from the possession of sizeable or strategically sited cells, but mother houses also had access to a number of methods to try to preserve a respectable standard of observance at their satellites. The tenacious commitment of almost every mother house to preserve its satellites at any cost must also be acknowledged. This has usually been attributed to unthinking inertia, or more plausibly a burning desire to keep the patrimony of their patron saint intact.[5] Yet the willingness of a number of houses to acquire new cells in the later middle ages suggests that owning dependent priories could be an attractive prospect. It is therefore worth examining in more detail the problems and advantages that might have arisen from the possession of cells, in order to judge the accuracy of Knowles' dictum.

The Operation of Dependencies: Monks and Canons

Before the disciplinary problems of owning cells can be evaluated, it is first necessary to ascertain how mother houses ran their networks of priories. No judgements can be made about the levels of observance at a dependency until such fundamental details as the type of monks sent to dwell in and rule cells or the duration of their stay have been established. As we have seen, most mother houses enjoyed two basic rights over their dependencies: the power to receive the profession of all the brethren dwelling there; and the right to appoint and remove the cell's personnel at pleasure.[6] The exercising of these privileges, stemming from the abbeys' desire to control their satellites closely, dictated the character of life in dependent priories. It is often difficult, however, to discern to what extent and in what ways they were applied, and it is in fact only for the best-recorded families of satellites that some sense of how cells were operated can be retrieved. As a result, the

---

3   Knowles, MO, p. 136; Knowles, RO, I, p. 112.
4   *Giraldi Cambrensis Opera*, ed. J. S. Brewer, J. F. Dimock and G. P. Warner, 8 vols, RS, xxi (1861–9), IV, p. 238.
5   J. C. Dickinson, 'Early Suppression of English Houses of Austin Canons', in *Medieval Studies Presented to Rose Graham*, ed. V. Ruffer and A. J. Taylor (Oxford, 1950), pp. 54–77; Dobson, *Durham Priory*, pp. 297–8.
6   See above, pp. 64–113.

following account relies heavily on the evidence from Durham and Norwich Cathedral Priories.

The requirement that every monk in a satellite priory be professed in his mother house could be met in two ways. Inmates recruited by a cell might be sent to the abbey for their profession before returning to the dependency to commence their noviciate, as took place at Great Malvern Priory from the early thirteenth century; or monks could be received and professed at the mother house and sent out to a cell only in subsequent years, as was the policy at Durham.[7] Evidence for local recruitment into cells is, in fact, slender. Most of the known instances resulted from benefactors making their reception into the priory, or that of a relative, a condition of their grant. Almost all these benefactions date from the twelfth century and belong to an era when wealthy donors regularly sought to take the monastic habit.[8] Occasionally, a patron was able to acquire the right to present monks to a cell and in these circumstances local recruitment also took place. Reginald fitz Peter presented two monks to Brecon Priory some time before 1283, and reacted violently when Archbishop Pecham removed them to Battle.[9] Such cases were clearly anomalous and local recruitment into daughter houses was probably common only in semi-independent houses like Great Malvern and Tynemouth.[10]

At many smaller cells, the absence of facilities for the training of monks would have made recruiting their own brethren impracticable. A few of the largest daughter houses may have instructed their own brethren, and there is some evidence that the more sizeable of St Albans' cells were allowed to train monks. The St Albans registers record that in June 1470 Andrew Derloue and Thomas Binham, 'monks of the priory of Binham in Norfolk were professed in the chapel of William, the Lord Abbot'. Whether this entry implies local recruitment at Binham, as its founder Peter de Valognes had intended, is not entirely clear. We also learn from the St Albans *Gesta Abbatum* that Thomas de la Mare, having been admitted into the mother house, was clothed and trained at Wymondham. Similarly, a thirteenth-century letter from a monk of St Albans, preserved in an abbey formulary,

---

7   See p. 100; *Mon. Ang.*, III, p. 448, no. 5; Dobson, *Durham Priory*, p. 304.
8   E.g. Robert, son of Godric, of Sudbury gave property to St Bartholomew's Priory in the same town on this condition in the late twelfth century: E. Mason, *Westminster Abbey and its People, c.1050–c.1216* (Woodbridge, 1996), p. 99. The majority of such incidences concerned larger priories, such as St Nicholas' Exeter, Brecon and Snape: e.g. *English Episcopal Acta XI: Exeter 1046–1184*, ed. F. M. Barlow (Oxford, 1996), no. 7, pp. 6–7; Cowley, *Monastic Order*, p. 41; *Catalogue of Ancient Deeds*, 6 vols (HMSO, 1916–69), II, p. 191 (A3430).
9   *Registrum Epistolarum fratris Johannis Peckham, Archiepiscopi Cantuariensis*, ed. C. T. Martin, 3 vols, RS, lxxvii (1882–5), II, no. 452, p. 581, III, nos 587, 599, pp. 810, 831–2.
10   See above, pp. 99–100.

relates how his younger brother, who had very recently taken his vows at St Albans, had now been transferred to one of the abbey's cells.[11]

Such practices might have been tolerated at sizeable daughter houses, but understandably the posting of untrained brethren to small dependencies was generally considered inappropriate. Benedict XII's constitutions for both the Benedictines and the Augustinian canons ordained that inmates were not to be sent to any non-conventual place during the time of their probation; and it was thought worthy of complaint at Norwich Cathedral Priory in 1514 that 'junior monks are sent to cells before they have been instructed in divine offices and other necessities'.[12] The rarity with which monks at cells show up in episcopal ordination records suggests that most dependencies did not ordinarily train their own inmates. Ordination lists do however show some monks passing through major orders at a daughter house. Numerous Gloucester monks were ordained subdeacons, deacons or priests while they were staying at St Guthlac's Hereford between 1346 and 1375, and the occasional ordination, mostly to deacon or priest, is recorded at several other larger dependencies.[13] Monks rarely passed through orders at St Guthlac's after 1375, however, and the large number of younger brethren sent here in the preceding years may well reflect a shortage of Gloucester monks available for service in its cells after the Black Death. It is also significant that no monk is known to have been ordained at any of the smaller Gloucester satellites.

It seems fair to conclude that many abbeys were willing to send unpriested monks to their larger dependencies when the need arose, but that in general they preferred to dispatch more mature inmates. Regardless of the spiritual dangers inherent in permitting inexperienced brethren to dwell in a small daughter house, the burden of intercessory masses to be celebrated therein generally dictated that only those who had attained the rank of priest should be sent to dependencies. Indeed, for this reason it was laid down at the re-foundation of Alcester, Cowick and Goldcliff as English cells in the mid-fifteenth century that only monks who were priests should serve in these priories.[14] Equally, although a significant number of the heads of Durham's

[11] *Registra*, II, pp. 89–90; *Mon. Ang.*, III, pp. 345–6, no. 1; *GASA*, II, pp. 373–4; R. Hill, *Ecclesiastical Letter-Books of the Thirteenth Century* (privately printed, no date), p. 102.

[12] Wilkins, *Concilia*, II, pp. 606–7, chap. 23; *The Chapters of the Augustinian Canons*, ed. H. E. Salter, C&Y Soc., xxix (1922), p. 215; *Visitations of the Diocese of Norwich AD 1492–1532*, ed. A. Jessopp, Camden Society, new series, xliii (1888), p. 74.

[13] *Registrum Johannis de Trillek, Episcopi Herefordensis, AD 1344–1361*, ed. J. H. Parry, C&Y Soc., viii (1912), pp. 430, 503–4, 514, 524, 556; *Registrum Ludowici de Charltone, Episcopi Herefordensis, AD 1361–1370*, ed. J. H. Parry, C&Y Soc., xiv (1914), pp. 77, 81, 85, 92, 98, 112, 114; *Registrum Willelmi de Courtenay, Episcopi Herefordensis, AD 1370–1375*, ed. W. W. Capes, C&Y Soc., xv (1914), pp. 42–54. Ordinations of monks at the cells of Brecon, Colne, St Nicholas' Exeter, Hurley, Leominster, St Bees and Wetheral, and at the smaller houses of Belvoir, Hatfield Peverel and Hertford, are also recorded.

[14] Worcestershire Record Office, b716.093–BA.2648/6(ii), fols 198v–199v (Alcester); Devon Record Office, W1258M, D82/28 (Cowick); *Mon. Ang.*, VI, p. 1023, no. 3 (Goldcliff).

dependencies are known to have held office in old age, Alan Piper has recently presented the prosopographical evidence for believing that 'service at the [Durham] cells . . . was not seen as particularly fitting for monks of advanced years'.[15] It would seem, then, that the very old and the very young alike were not usually considered suitable for service in a daughter house; and when Bishop Hatfield of Durham visited his cathedral priory in c.1371, he encountered outrage that 'youths not at all proven in religion are quickly sent to cells, ignorant of regular observance and that which they are bound to know, to the destruction of religion' and also that aged monks were left to die there 'in very much misery'.[16]

The anonymity of the vast majority of monks sent to dependent priories makes it difficult to draw general conclusions about them. Even at Norwich and St Albans where a great deal of biographical information about individual monks is available, only a handful of brethren serving in cells can be named. It is only for Durham that sufficient material survives to provide a statistical basis for statements concerning daughter-house monks. Names of Durham brethren staying in the priory's cells can be gleaned from references in account rolls and uniquely from letters instructing individuals to leave a particular cell, often copied into the prior of Durham's personal register. Mr Piper's forthcoming biographical register of the Durham monks will make this wealth of information readily accessible, but in the meantime we may rely on the conclusions provided in his extremely enlightening articles on the Durham dependencies.[17]

What kinds of monks populated the eight cells of Durham? Piper has found that the majority of those dwelling at St Leonard's Stamford in the fifteenth century were mature men, with between ten and twenty years of monastic experience behind them. A good number of those known at Jarrow were even older, and few Durham brethren seem to have been sent out to dependencies in the decade following their profession. More interestingly, the majority of the monks who manned the Durham cells had not studied at Durham College, Oxford. This has led Piper to talk of a 'stratification in the Durham community' in the later middle ages, with about half of its inmates attending university as preparation for holding most of the important priory offices, and the other half serving as claustral monks in the mother house and its cells. It would appear, then, that the Durham satellites were generally populated by middle-aged monks without particular distinction, although Piper is rather harsh in branding them 'failures'.[18] The limited evidence from

---

15 A. J. Piper, 'The Monks of Durham and Patterns of Activity in Old Age', in *The Church and Learning in Later Medieval Society: Essays in Honour of R. B. Dobson*, ed. C. M. Barron and J. Stratford (Donnington, 2002), pp. 51–63.

16 DCM, 2.8 Pont. 12.

17 Piper, 'Wearmouth'; Piper, 'Stamford'; Piper, *Jarrow*. This latter article contains an appendix giving all known biographical detail for those known to have been master or monk at Jarrow.

18 Piper, *Jarrow*, p. 19; Piper, 'Stamford', p. 12.

St Mary's York suggests a similar policy might have obtained there. Of the fifteen known monks at fifteenth-century Rumburgh Priory who can be traced in the York ordination records, most were sent to the Suffolk cell between five and fifteen years after their ordination as priests, but younger and older monks are also represented; and the St Mary's chronicle displays a similar pattern for the sixteen monks staying in the abbey's cells in 1293.[19] The house's chronicler also criticised Abbot John of Gilling (1303–13) because, against the customs of the abbey, 'he sent all the more senior and able monks to cells, to stay without return in his time'.[20] The monks in the four surviving Gloucester cells in 1510 and 1514, however, seem to have been among the more junior in the abbey, and it is possible that monasteries with fewer dependencies to fill were able to provide for the service of these houses without troubling the more mature brethren.[21]

It is likely that the resentment voiced against Abbot Gilling's practice of dispatching senior monks accustomed to office-holding to serve as mere claustral monks in cells would have resonated elsewhere. Prior Richard de Hoton of Durham was criticised in 1300 for sending dissident obedientiaries to daughter houses, and the St Albans chronicles portray the transfer to dependencies of men like Reimund, the abbey's prior, by Abbot William of Trumpington (1214–35), as acts of banishment.[22] The exiling of monks to the abbey's cells features heavily in the writings of Matthew Paris, suggesting that this was a common occurrence at thirteenth-century St Albans. Abbot Warin (1183–95) is accredited with the inauguration of the custom, which reached its apogee in the abbacy of John de Cella (1195–1214). Now numerous monks are said to have been sent in misery to the abbey's most remote cells 'without cause, at the judgement of the abbot and the impulse of his will, and the sly accusations of tale-bearers . . . not without bitterness of heart and scandal'. When confronted with these malpractices, de Cella is said to have swiftly banished his accusers to distant dependencies, blithely enjoining them to 'bless those who persecute you'.[23] Matters came to a head in the abbot's last hours, when a committee of senior monks, detailing the turmoil endured by the banished, particularly at the perceived infringement of their vow of stability, requested de Cella to seal a charter abolishing the practice. When the dying man, unable to speak, attempted to communicate

19 SROI, HD 1538/335/1; A Calendar of the Register of Richard Scrope Archbishop of York, 1398–1405, ed. R. N. Swanson, 2 vols, Borthwick Texts and Calendars, VIII, XI (1981–5); York, Borthwick Institute of Historical Research, Archbishops' Registers 17–24; The Register of Thomas Rotherham, Archbishop of York 1480–1500, vol. I, ed. E. E. Barker, C&Y Soc., lxix (1976), passim; C. Cross and N. Vickers (eds), Monks, Friars and Nuns in Sixteenth-Century Yorkshire, Yorkshire Archaeological Society, Record Series, CL (1991–2), pp. 67–74; St Mary's Chronicle, pp. 129–39.
20 St Mary's Chronicle, pp. 55–6.
21 Hist. et Cart. Gloucestriae, III, pp. xxxii–xxxiv, xlviii–xlix.
22 C. M. Fraser, A History of Antony Bek, Bishop of Durham 1283–1301 (Oxford, 1957), p. 130; GASA, I, pp. 257–8.
23 Matthew, V, 44.

his disapproval by signs and by turning away, his delegation, declaring 'silence signifies assent', sealed the charter anyway. Their success, however, was short-lived. Abbot John's successor, William of Trumpington, although one of those who had dubiously obtained the restraining document, soon resumed the practice of banishing monks to cells.[24]

Paris' vivid and humorous depiction of these disputes has led some historians to imagine dependencies teeming with exiled monks, simmering with discontent and prone to behavioural problems. Knowles characterised many monks in cells as '*mauvais sujets* or psychological invalids', and others have echoed the sentiment, if not the phraseology.[25] There is no doubt that monasteries often did use their cells as outlets for troublesome inmates, and numerous examples of this could be cited from chronicles, visitation records, registers and formularies. Alexander Langley, a St Albans monk who went mad through excessive study, was sent to Binham in fetters by Abbot Trumpington, whereas priors of Norwich were criticised for sending troublesome monks to cells in visitations of 1347 and 1526. Meanwhile, Archbishop Morton's visitation of St Nicholas' Exeter in June 1492 found there a rebellious Battle monk, who had previously been sent to that abbey's other cell at Brecon, and was now causing considerable disruption by breaking down doors, threatening his co-brethren and growing his hair long. And as we have seen, Colne Priory had apparently acquired the name of a prison by 1303 owing to the abbot of Abingdon's propensity for dispatching miscreants there.[26] The most famous incorrigible to be sent away to a daughter house was Roger Norris, made prior of Penwortham (1213–14 and 1218×1219–1224×1225) after a disastrous spell as abbot of Evesham in order to free the mother house from his malign presence.[27]

The advantages in using satellites as pressure valves for the mother house also commended themselves to the ecclesiastical authorities. Numerous instances of bishops sending monks and canons to perform penance in cells can be found in the printed registers. In May 1308, following his visitation of Kirkham Priory, Archbishop Greenfield of York ordered that a canon of that house should be removed to its cell of Carham as a punishment for his misdemeanours; and five years later, Greenfield issued similar mandates for two canons of Nostell to be sent to Hirst and Breedon Priories respectively.

[24] GASA, I, pp. 216, 247–9, 251–3, 255–8.

[25] Knowles, MO, p. 686.

[26] GASA, I, p. 266; C. R. Cheney, 'Norwich Cathedral Priory in the Fourteenth Century', *Bulletin of the John Rylands Library*, xx (1936), p. 106; *Norwich Visitations*, p. 197; *The Register of John Morton, Archbishop of Canterbury 1486–1500*, ed. C. Harper-Bill, 3 vols, C&Y Soc., lxxv, lxxviii, lxxxix (1987–2000), II, no. 277, p. 75; *Registrum Radulphi Baldock, Gilberti Segrave, Ricardi Newport, et Stephani Gravesend, Episcoporum Londoniensium, AD 1304–1338*, ed. R. C. Fowler, C&Y Soc., vii (1911), p. 79; see above, p. 101.

[27] *Chronicon Abbatiae de Evesham ad annum 1418*, ed. W. D. Macray, RS, xxix (1863), pp. 250–3.

Greenfield's contemporary, Walter Langton of Coventry and Lichfield, responded in the same way in December 1315 when he found three Chester monks 'whose insolence and malice have disturbed the peace and quiet of the brethren', sending one of them to the abbey's small cell on Hilbre Island.[28]

Nevertheless, monastic opinion itself seems gradually to have turned against this solution to disciplinary problems. The 1277 statutes of the Canterbury provincial chapter and those of the 1310 York chapter had both prescribed the sending of monks to dependencies as an initial disciplinary measure 'if the abbots think it useful and peaceful for their monastery', although brethren who proved incorrigible were to be removed to another full-scale monastery. But the general chapter statutes of 1343 sent out a more ambivalent, if not contradictory, message. It was first ordained that monks were not to be sent to a cell on account of their vice nor out of a prelate's malice, but a second article qualified that 'since it is better that one should perish than all', troublesome monks *should* where possible be transferred to a daughter house after three warnings. By the time of the promulgation of the chapter's 1444 statutes, however, this indecision had been resolved and only the first of these two articles was published.[29] The Benedictine chapter, therefore, no longer recommended the use of daughter houses as a punishment for difficult monks, and few if any examples of diocesan visitors sending miscreants to cells are recorded after this date; although, as the examples given above from Norwich and St Nicholas' Exeter show, this practice continued at some mother houses.

But even though cells were regularly used as dumping grounds, particularly in the thirteenth and fourteenth centuries, it would be wrong to think that abbeys were always prepared to sacrifice the religious life of their daughter houses for a quiet life at home. Two disorderly monks were recalled to Battle from St Nicholas' Exeter, c.1330, while about one hundred years later Prior Wessington wrote that he would send no monk to St Leonard's Stamford who was likely to bring shame on St Cuthbert or his monastery.[30] Equally, we should not necessarily assume that monks were in general relegated to cells irresponsibly. When in December 1306 Archbishop Greenfield asked the abbey of St Mary's York to receive the unruly Selby monk, Henry Belton, into their small cell at Rumburgh for correction, it was responded that Rumburgh was unsuitable for this undertaking. The archbishop accepted this argument and, after a short period of detention in St Mary's, Belton was transferred instead to the abbey's more sizeable dependency of St

---

[28] *The Register of William Greenfield, Lord Archbishop of York 1306–1315*, ed. W. Brown and A. H. Thompson, 5 vols, SS, cxlv, cxlix, cli–cliii (1931–40), III, no. 1427, p. 132, II, nos 1022, 1026, pp. 165–8; *The Register of Walter Langton, Bishop of Coventry and Lichfield 1296–1321*, vol. I, ed. J. B. Hughes, C&Y Soc., xci (2001), no. 809, pp. 106–7.

[29] CBM, I, pp. 76, 267–8, II, 51–2, 207.

[30] BL, Harley MS 3586, fol. 23r; Dobson, *Durham Priory*, p. 303.

Bees, whose larger community was presumably considered better equipped to monitor their guest.[31] And the perennial preference of the abbots of St Albans for Tynemouth as a destination for exiled monks was no doubt a product of its size as well as its remoteness.

Nevertheless, as long as the decision to transfer inmates to, from and between cells was the sole preserve of the superior, the temptation to banish difficult monks remained. The desire to ensure a fairer system for the manning of dependencies produced several attempts to restrict the abbot's powers in this regard, mostly imposed from outside the monastery. William of Trumpington's decision to ignore the charter forced on his predecessor at St Albans was supported by the papal legate Nicholas de Romanis, cardinal bishop of Tusculum, who himself tore up the offending document in chapter on the grounds that it contravened the monks' vow of obedience.[32] But several diocesans took a rather different view, and issued injunctions against the unilateral removal of brethren to cells. In response to an ordinance to that effect from Archbishop Hubert Walter, Abbot Reading of Ramsey's constitutions of 1205×1207 prohibited the sending of monks away from the abbey without 'common consent'. A similar injunction was issued by the bishop of Salisbury's official at Abingdon in 1245, following conventual complaints to the bishop of Salisbury, ordering that 'no monk be sent to the priory or cell of Colne for trivial matter unless the cause shall first have been known to the brothers and considered reasonable'; and episcopal legislation to the same effect was also promulgated at Westminster a few years later. The prior of St Osyth's was also required to explain his reasons for sending canons to the house's cell at Blythburgh by Bishop Baldock of London in 1308, but managed to win the concession eight years later during a vacancy of the see that the support of the bishop alone would be sufficient for this purpose if the prior and convent disagreed. And a similar agreement was made at late thirteenth-century Reading Abbey, again in response to episcopal injunctions, that the abbot would send no monk to a dependency 'without the advice of the prior and the wiser part' of the convent.[33]

These injunctions, though assisting the convent's cause, all remained vague. More precise was Bishop Woodlock of Winchester's 1314 stipulation that no inmate of Chertsey should be sent to the abbey's cell at Cardigan

---

[31] *Reg. Greenfield*, II, pp. 13–19, 21. However, even St Bees proved an inadequate home for Belton, who ran away from the cell soon after its prior had naively acquired a licence for him to take walks outside the house's precinct: ibid., II, pp. 55, 113–14, 193–4.

[32] *GASA*, I, pp. 256–7.

[33] *Cartularium Monasterii de Rameseia*, ed. W. H. Hart and P. A. Lyons, 3 vols, RS, lxxix (1884–93), II, nos 331, 328, pp. 212, 205; *Two Cartularies of Abingdon Abbey*, ed. C. F. Slade and G. Lambrick, 2 vols, OHS, new series, xxxii–xxxiii (1990–2), II, no. C7, pp. 23–4; *VCH, London*, I, pp. 448–9; *Reg. Baldock*, pp. 59–60, 62–5; *Registrum Ricardi de Swinfield, Episcopi Herefordensis, AD 1283–1317*, ed. W. W. Capes, C&Y Soc., vi (1909), p. 168.

without the consent of the house's leading obedientiaries and at least five senior claustral monks.[34] Yet more restrictive was an ordinance included in Archbishop Winchelsey's injunctions to Gloucester Abbey of July 1301. Winchelsey required firstly that no monk should be transferred to or from the abbey's cells without the advice of a committee comprising the prior, subprior, third prior, precentor and five senior claustral monks. However, he went on to stipulate that monks 'should not stay in the cells beyond a year [and] nor should they be sent again to the cells within a year of their recall'.[35] Although disorderly monks were exempted from this statute, along with those living out of the abbey for health reasons, this principle of regular rotation tended to reduce the likelihood that cells would become houses of correction. Instead, service in a cell was to be shared out evenly with personnel to be chosen by rota and not rancour.

The regular rotation of the monks and canons dwelling therein is one of the most important characteristics of dependent priories. Although the great paucity of information about the personnel staying at daughter houses (apart from those of Durham) precludes certainty, the fragments of evidence that do survive all point to the conclusion that there was a rapid turnover of inmates in all but the largest cells. We cannot be sure that Archbishop Winchelsey's ordinance for annual circulation at the Gloucester dependencies was rigidly observed, but the only surviving lists of monks at the abbey's cells, the election records of 1510 and 1514, suggest that they were followed at least in spirit. Of the eleven inmates in its satellites in 1510, only two are found in the same cell four years later. The continuing presence of John Stanford, monk of St Guthlac's Hereford, can be explained by his elevation to sub-prior of that cell; and the *stabilitas* of William Elmeley at Ewenny (Glamorgan) should perhaps be attributed to Welsh patriotism, since he was transferred permanently on his request to Abergavenny Priory in August 1516.[36]

At St Mary's York too a regular rotation of monks seems to have been the norm, since in four of the five complete fifteenth-century accounts of Rumburgh Priory, a payment was made for the *remocione* of two brethren to or from the priory. Since the Rumburgh community generally consisted of only a prior and two monks in the later middle ages, it would appear that the entire 'convent' was being regularly circulated.[37] There are also hints that the inmates of the Norwich cells were rotated in this way. Margery Kempe mentions the replacement of Norwich monks at Lynn at 'the tyme of

---

[34] *Registrum Henrici Woodlock, diocesis Wintoniensis, AD 1305–1316*, ed. A. W. Goodman, 2 vols, C&Y Soc., xix, xxx (1915–24), I, p. 534.

[35] *Hist. et Cart. Gloucestriae*, I, pp. lxxxvii–lxxxviii.

[36] Ibid., III, pp. xxxii–xxxiv, xlviii–xlix, 296–8.

[37] SROI, HD 1538/335/1, nos 13, 21–2, 34–5. More details about the service of fifteenth-century Rumburgh can be found in my 'Rumburgh Priory in the Later Middle Ages: Some New Evidence', *Proceedings of the Suffolk Institute of Archaeology*, xl (2001), pp. 8–23.

remownyng, as custom was a-mongys hem', and the Lynn and Yarmouth accounts include very regular entries for the carriage of monks to Norwich.[38] The late medieval accounts of Ramsey similarly suggest a swift turnover of monks at Modney, while in the face of complaints about lengthy stays at St Ives an abbey ordinance of 1345 established that this cell should be served by rota, with brethren staying for only seven weeks at a time.[39] At Calwich, meanwhile, it was the frequent circulation of canons that infuriated the priory's patron, Nicholas of Longford, and contributed to that house's successful bid for independence in the mid-fourteenth century.[40] The length of the average sojourn at the Durham cells was certainly short. Alan Piper has calculated that the average stay at Jarrow between 1432 and 1518 was sixteen months, and that it was also under two years at Wearmouth in the later middle ages. Similarly, it was rare for fifteenth- and sixteenth-century monks of Stamford to reside there for more than a few years at a time. Indeed, it was even the practice at Durham to compensate monks who had dwelt away from the mother house for as long as seven years with gifts of clothing.[41] From what limited evidence survives, it would therefore seem that mother houses were generally careful to restrict the length of time brethren were required to serve in their cells.

The Operation of Dependencies: Priors

A good deal more information survives about the priors of cells than the monks under their charge. Priors are named at the head of account rolls, in chronicles, legal records, reports of mother-house elections and, when instituted by the ordinary, in bishops' registers; and, for the period 1216–1377 all this information has been masterfully assembled by Professor David Smith and Mrs Vera London.[42] It is therefore possible to address questions about the kinds of monks promoted to the headship of dependencies and the duration of their rule with more confidence. All mother houses were aware of the need to exercise caution in their choice of priors. The custody of a cell often afforded much more authority and independence than was allowed to most internal obedientiaries, and it conferred responsibility over souls as well as property. The rare instances where clearly unsuitable priors were tolerated

---

38 *The Book of Margery Kempe*, ed. L. Staley, Middle English Texts Series (Kalamazoo, 1996), p. 137; NRO, DCN 2/1, 2/6.
39 BL, Add. MS 33445, fols 36r, 51v–52v; BL, Add. Ch. 33666.
40 See above, p. 108.
41 Piper, *Jarrow*, p. 19; Piper, 'Wearmouth', p. 9; Piper, 'Stamford', part ii, p. 12. In July 1310, the prior of Nostell successfully overturned Archbishop Greenfield's injunction that sojourns at the priory's cells should be restricted to one year, but this does not necessarily imply that long stays were the norm at Nostell: *Reg. Greenfield*, II, pp. 90–1.
42 *HRH*, II, esp. pp. 89–137.

either to relieve tension in the mother house (e.g. Roger Norris at Penwortham) or to prevent the erosion of the abbey's rights (e.g. William of Ledbury at Great Malvern) should not lead us to conclude that headships were distributed carelessly.[43] It would appear that the approval of the convent was as often needed for the appointment of the prior of a cell as it was for the transfer of ordinary monks. The Ramsey ordinances of 1205×1207 laid down that the prior of St Ives, along with important mother-house obedientiaries, 'should not be imposed, nor deposed, without the advice of the convent in chapter', and a near-identical injunction was issued at Evesham in 1206 for Penwortham. Moreover, at Durham, where the prior moved monks around dependencies at will, the heads of Coldingham and St Leonard's Stamford were chosen with conventual consent, while at late medieval Peterborough the warden of Oxney was the abbey's only obedientiary not selected by the abbot alone.[44] Such restraints were intended to reduce the scope for whimsical appointments, and the not infrequent remarks in monastic chronicles and visitation records about the capabilities of priors suggest that the force of 'public opinion' within the monastery worked to the same end.

The criticisms of priors emanating from the mother-house community also indicate the kinds of qualities heads of cells were expected to possess. Abbot Gilling was accused by the chronicler of St Mary's York of choosing as prior of Wetheral a monk 'who was not a man of great stature or knowledge but an effigy of a man', while Prior Cowton of Durham was criticised during a visitation of c.1332 for appointing young men to rule cells and mother-house offices.[45] The desired attributes of the head of a dependency are even more clearly detailed in a letter from a fifteenth-century prior of Durham probably to one of the Stanley family, concerning the cell of Lytham. The recipient is informed that 'my brethre and I have provid such a man to be Priour at Lethom as we suppose is full expedient and profitable to that place and acordable to the cuntree the which is a clerke and hath been in mony and most worshipfull offices with us at durham . . . I trust to gode he sall please you right wele'.[46] The ideal prior of a daughter house should therefore be mature, experienced and learned, provident and popular with his lay neighbours.

Although we cannot easily measure these last two qualities, it can be demonstrated that many priors were indeed mature, experienced and relatively well-educated men. Assuming they had passed through orders at the earliest opportunity, the average age of the later priors of St Leonard's Stamford was about forty-five and those of Jarrow about fifty; and the priors of

43 See pp. 82, 120.
44 *Cart. Rameseia*, II, no. 331, p. 213; *Chronicon Abbatiae de Evesham*, p. 206; Dobson, *Durham Priory*, p. 301n; *Visitations in the Diocese of Lincoln, 1517–31*, ed. A. H. Thompson, 3 vols, Lincoln Record Society, xxxiii, xxxv, xxxvii (1940–7), I, p. 76.
45 *St Mary's Chronicle*, p. 37; DCM, Loc. XXVII: 12.
46 DCM, Loc. IX: 10.

Rumburgh and of the five cells of Norwich were also predominantly middle-aged men.[47] For Durham, Norwich and Westminster the career progressions of monks can be traced, showing that the vast majority of priors had spent several years as obedientiaries in the mother house before they were entrusted with the rule of a cell. Not only were most priors of their dependencies mature monks with a good deal of administrative experience, but a surprising number of them were also drawn from the mother house's intellectual elite. By the fifteenth century, it was common for the priors of the cells of Durham, Norwich, St Albans and Westminster to have spent some time at university. Eleven of the last seventeen priors of St Leonard's Stamford had studied at Durham College and after 1400 seven of the eight known priors of Lynn and perhaps as many as ten of the twelve known priors of Yarmouth all held degrees.[48] Moreover, almost every recorded late medieval prior of a Norwich cell who is not known to have been at university can be connected with a surviving book. The unique list of nine volumes, belonging to the Durham monk Henry Helay, sent to St Leonard's Stamford after Helay's appointment as head of that house in March 1422 – including works of theology, devotion, hagiography, canon law and the letters of Ailred of Rievaulx – should also prevent us from underestimating the intellectual interests and capabilities of priors without university training.[49]

In judging the level of experience and learning of the priors of dependencies we must rely heavily on statistics from Durham and Norwich. Both were large and prestigious cathedral priories with notable intellectual traditions and some medium-sized abbeys might not always have been able to find experienced and educated monks to rule their cells. It does seem, however, that the headship of a daughter house was everywhere regarded as a prestigious office. Priors of cells were public figures, often placed on royal and episcopal commissions.[50] Moreover, the post-Dissolution pension lists for numerous abbeys, including Tavistock, Sherborne, Thorney, Tewkesbury and Evesham, show the heads of their cells ranked after only the abbot and

[47] Piper, 'Stamford', part ii, p. 8; Piper, *Jarrow*, p. 18; Greatrex, *BRECP*, pp. 466–576. The Rumburgh evidence, based on York ordination records and Norwich institution records is discussed in Heale, 'Rumburgh Priory'.

[48] Piper, 'Stamford', part ii, p. 9; J. G. Greatrex, 'Monk Students from Norwich Cathedral Priory at Oxford and Cambridge, c.1300–1530', *EHR*, cvi (1991), pp. 570–3; J. G. Clark, 'Intellectual Life at the Abbey of St Albans and the Nature of Monastic Learning in England, c.1350–c.1440: the Work of Thomas Walsingham in Context', unpublished Oxford D.Phil. thesis (1997), p. 65; E. H. Pearce, *The Monks of Westminster* (Cambridge, 1916); B. F. Harvey, 'The Monks of Westminster and the University of Oxford', in *The Reign of Richard II. Essays in Honour of May McKisack*, ed. F. R. H. Du Boulay and C. M. Barron (London, 1971), p. 123.

[49] For the books associated with Norwich monks, see Greatrex, *BRECP*, pp. 466–576; *Catalogi veteres librorum ecclesie cathedralis Dunelmensis*, ed. J. Raine, SS, vii (1838), p. 116.

[50] See below, pp. 169–71.

prior of the mother house and better remunerated than the rest of their colleagues.[51]

We must also consider the possibility that it might have been easier for monasteries with one or two dependencies to find suitable priors than it was for mother houses like Durham or Norwich with a large family of cells. The study of career patterns at Durham and Norwich reveals that the headship of some satellites was considered a more senior position than that of others.[52] The Norwich cells of Lynn and Yarmouth and the Durham priories of Coldingham, Finchale and Holy Island were routinely ruled by highly respected members of these communities. The Durham and Norwich monks chosen as priors of smaller daughter houses, however, were often less experienced and, judging by the other obediences they held, less able. A similar hierarchy of cells can be seen to have existed at other monasteries with families of dependencies, with less senior monks running the house's less important satellites: for example, at St Mary's York and Nostell, the seniority of the priors of St Bees, Wetheral and Breedon is evinced by the relative regularity with which they and no other rulers of cells were elected head of the mother house.[53] It was inevitable that hierarchies of this kind should develop. Of the forty-six monks of Norwich in 1492, as many as twenty-two served as priors of the cathedral's cells at some stage of their careers; and this was also true for nineteen of the forty-eight Norwich brethren of 1499. With such a high proportion of monks sharing in the rule of daughter houses, those selected to be priors could not have been taken solely from the abbey's administrative and intellectual elite.

Of the Durham cells the least prestigious seems to have been Farne Island, where a succession of relatively inexperienced masters are known to have presided. Several of these men were manifestly unsuitable for the job, and Farne appears as something of a running sore in the fifteenth-century Durham registers. Master John of Ripon was summarily dismissed from the rule of Farne in September 1407 for running-up large debts. John Harom was similarly removed in September 1443 for dilapidation, pawning the cell's silver, associating with 'ribalds' and for travelling around the mainland in rags and covered in mud; and the prior of Durham complained to John Kirke, a later master, that 'your rule and demeanour is noght religious in many poynts', including a negligent approach to the *opus dei* and frequent visits to

---

[51] *L&P*, XIV(i), nos 429, 556, pp. 172, 215, XIV(ii), no. 621, p. 226, XV, nos 49, 118, pp. 19, 37–8. For a fuller discussion of the prestige accompanying the headship of a cell, see below pp. 171–2.

[52] Piper, 'Stamford', part ii, pp. 8–9; Greatrex, *BRECP*, pp. 466–576: all the statistics relating to Norwich monks have been gleaned from this invaluable volume.

[53] *HRH*, II, pp. 86–8, 438–9; *The Register of the Priory of St Bees*, ed. J. Wilson, SS, cxxvi (1915), p. xxxv; *The Register of the Priory of Wetherhal*, ed. J. E. Prescott, Cumberland and Westmorland Antiquarian and Archaeological Society, Extra Series, I (1897), p. xxxii; R. McKinley (ed.), 'The Cartulary of Breedon Priory', unpublished Manchester MA thesis (1950), pp. xxxi–xxxiii.

the houses of women.[54] No other cell proved so troublesome to Durham, and it would seem fair to attribute many of Farne's problems to the under-qualification of some of its masters. Even monks apparently well-equipped to rule a daughter house might prove less than satisfactory. The talents of the St Albans chronicler, Roger of Wendover, did not extend to administration and he was recalled from the rule of Belvoir after Abbot Trumpington discovered him to have 'dissipated the goods of the church in heedless prodigality'.[55] Indeed there are occasional signs that the headship of a daughter house was often considered the due of a senior monk, regardless of whether he had demonstrated sufficient competence in previous offices. The St Albans monk, William Alnwick, was appointed prior of Belvoir after he had failed badly in the important abbey office of archdeacon, and it was even contemplated at Durham during the Partrike dispute that that rebellious prior of Lytham should be offered the rule of Wearmouth as compensation.[56]

Nevertheless, even when bad appointments were made, the jealously guarded abbatial right of removing subordinate priors at will ensured that unsuitable heads could always be recalled swiftly to the mother house. At the cells of Durham and Norwich, although the length of priorates varied, stints of about five years were fairly typical. Between the years 1275 and 1375, between ten and fifteen priors are recorded at the St Albans dependencies of Beadlow, Belvoir, Hertford and Wallingford, which, allowing for the imperfections of the evidence, suggests a similar turnover. In this period, however, only seven priors are known at the larger St Albans priories of Binham and Wymondham, and it may well be that the heads of more sizeable cells enjoyed longer rules. A succession of relatively short priorates over these years can also be observed at St Nicholas' Exeter, St Bees and Wetheral, whereas at Rumburgh, Brooke and Calwich heads seem often to have been changed after only a couple of years.[57] Competent heads might be left *in situ* for a considerable length of time, but the dative status of the priors of most English cells provided mother houses with a powerful weapon for controlling discipline at their satellites.

Discipline at Cells

The rudiments of the operation of the majority of cells can thus be enumerated. Firstly, most monks and canons sent to dwell in satellite priories were already priests and had therefore completed their monastic training. Secondly, although the practice of exiling troublesome brethren to cells was

54 J. Raine, *The History and Antiquities of North Durham* (London, 1852), pp. 349, 351–2, 354–5n.
55 *GASA*, I, pp. 270–1, 274–5.
56 C. E. Hodge, 'The Abbey of St Albans under John of Whethamstede', unpublished Manchester Ph.D. thesis (1933), pp. 111–12; Dobson, *Durham Priory*, p. 337.
57 *HRH*, II, pp. 89–137, 327–490.

quite widespread, and indeed at times prescribed by the Benedictine chapter and the wider ecclesiastical authorities, it should not be concluded that satellites were overwhelmed with miscreants. What evidence survives suggests it was common practice to spread the burden of service in cells among ordinary members of the community; and where it was deemed necessary to intersperse difficult brethren with these monks this seems usually to have been done responsibly. Thirdly, monks were rarely allowed to remain out of the mother house for more than a few years at a time and the personnel at most dependencies was circulated regularly. Fourthly, mother houses seem to have taken care to appoint suitable monks to the headship of their satellites, with men of experience and education favoured wherever possible. And fifthly, though priors remained longer at cells than the monks under their charge, they too were changed regularly. It could be argued therefore that disciplinary problems might in fact have been less severe in satellite priories than in small independent monasteries. The personnel of dependencies, and particularly the priors, were probably of a higher standard and their rotation would have reduced the likelihood of spiritual torpor setting in. It would thus be unfair to assume that because of their size cells inevitably suffered from low standards of observance. In other words, we must admit the possibility of living a praiseworthy life in small dependent priories before we approach the evidence for levels of discipline in these houses.

Evidence for the standards of monastic observance, though relatively plentiful, is notoriously difficult to interpret. For dependencies, it comes from three main sources: the remarks of often hostile contemporaries, the reports of episcopal visitors, and the internal records produced by mother houses in monitoring their satellites. The first of these categories is the most eye-catching and the least reliable. No medieval author wrote more about cells than Gerald of Wales and nearly all his references to them are tales of turpitude.[58] Monks sent to dependencies are said to have thrown off their religion with abandon and to have literally revelled in their independence, to the extent that 'I would rather return to my monastery than do that' became a common saying. Another monk is reported to have caused a scandal by arriving at a cell accompanied by 'non socium sed sociam'. Gerald's most shocking tale involves Great Malvern's dependency of Llandovery. When he visited Rhys ap Gruffydd there, in c.1185, Gerald reports that he found the burgesses of Llandovery castle prepared to leave 'for the sake of their wives and daughters whom these monks frequently and openly abused'. Soon afterwards, the cell was closed down by Rhys and the bishop of St Davids in response to the intolerable vice of its inhabitants. The veracity of these, like all Gerald's stories, is difficult to establish; but it is probably significant that all are based in remote parts of Wales where acceptable levels of

[58] Gerald's attacks on cells are mostly found in his *Speculum Ecclesie: Giraldi Opera*, IV, esp. pp. 29–37, 51–3, 100–4.

observance would have been particularly hard to maintain. Moreover, the majority of Gerald's tales relate to alien, not English cells, and he himself wrote that 'it is undoubtedly true that the monks sent from the kingdom of France to cells in England conduct themselves much more disgracefully and incontinently than the native English monks', because they were less well-regulated.

Gerald of Wales was not the only contemporary observer to consider cells of two or three monks a shocking abuse. The reformed monastic orders of the twelfth century renounced offshoots of this kind and St Bernard condemned those 'synagogues of Satan, the cells where three or four monks live without order or discipline'.[59] Later critics included Pierre Dubois, whose *Plea for the Recovery of the Holy Land* (1307) attacked cells for the 'lechery, drunkenness and other dishonesties' practised there and claimed that some young monks were deliberately quarrelsome in order that they might be sent to a dependency where they could live in luxury and debauchery. Guillaume de Maire, bishop of Angers, attacked cells at the Council of Vienne (1311), stating that there were committed in dependencies 'many . . . grievous sins whereof it is shameful and base to speak', and arguing that they should either be made conventual or closed down; and a century later Jean Gerson considered tiny dependencies to be urgently in need of reform.[60] But as can be easily seen from the register of Odo Rigaldi, archbishop of Rouen (1248–69), there were many more very small cells in France than in England: indeed, Rigaldi visited seventy-nine priories, many of them deserted, with a combined population of only 109 religious.[61] It is therefore dangerous to assume that attitudes towards daughter houses were identical in different countries. Moreover, it is probably significant that criticism of this kind from within the ecclesiastical establishment does not seem to have been at all common in medieval England.

Cells, however, do sometimes feature in English satirical writings of the period, usually as the scene of laxness and depravity. In the anonymous Anglo-Latin poem of the late twelfth or early thirteenth century, 'De Visitatione Abbatis', an abbot visiting his daughter house is seduced by the extravagant fares consumed therein and is thus unable to enforce his own statute against meat-eating. Another Anglo-Latin poem of a similar date,

---

[59] *Sancti Bernardi Opera*, ed. J. Leclercq, C. H. Talbot and H. Rochais, 8 vols (Rome, 1957–77), VIII, ep. 254, p. 156.

[60] These references are mostly taken from the remarkable collection of anti-monastic criticisms brought together in G. G. Coulton, *Five Centuries of Religion*, 4 vols (London, 1923–50), II, Appendices 34 and 36, esp. pp. 310, 533–5; and see also J. Avril, 'Le statut des prieurés d'après les conciles provinciaux et les statuts synodaux (fins XIIᵉ–début XIVᵉ siècles)', in *Prieurs et prieurés dans l'occident médiéval*, ed. J.-L. Lemaître, Hautes études médiévales et modernes, lx (Geneva, 1987), pp. 71–93.

[61] *The Register of Eudes of Rouen*, trans. S. M. Brown, ed. J. F. O'Sullivan, Records of Civilization, Sources and Studies, LXXII (New York, 1964); G. G. Coulton, *Five Centuries of Religion*, 4 vols (London, 1923–50), II, pp. 195–227.

'De Mauro et Zoilo', compares the inhabitants of cells with pagans for their unfaithfulness.[62] Writing in this tradition, Chaucer designated his worldly monk 'kepere of the celle', although the alternative description of Dan Piers as an 'outridere' might imply that a grange with a chapel is meant by 'celle', rather than a small dependency.[63] Moreover, it may well be that the cells and outriders found in the writings of both Chaucer and Langland serve as literary devices designed to bring the otherwise cloistered religious into view, rather than reflecting deeply held antagonisms towards dependent priories.[64] Nevertheless, it would appear that the association of cells with ill discipline was not at all uncommon in the middle ages.

The interpretative problems of visitation records are well known.[65] While bishops' injunctions are agreed to be essentially reliable gauges of the spiritual temperature of a house, they inevitably stress the community's faults to the neglect of its strengths. Individual shortcomings reported to the visitor might represent factionalism rather than vice, just as a clean bill of health might have proceeded from a conspiracy of silence. And we often cannot be sure whether the failings uncovered are a product of stringent self-scrutiny against the rigorous ideals of the Rule, or whether they exhibit the worldly indulgence of men lacking the vocation of a monk. These difficulties are in some ways magnified for very small cells, where only two or three witnesses to the levels of observance at the priory are available. Furthermore, disappointingly few visitation records survive for daughter houses, since several satellites were exempt from episcopal jurisdiction, and in many other cases dependencies were included in the mother-house visitation.

The run of sixteenth-century visitations of Norwich Cathedral Priory illustrates the shortcomings of this latter practice. Firstly, not all the monks staying in the priory's cells attended these inspections since some were needed to keep up the liturgical round in their own houses; in 1514 only the heads of the cells were present at the visitation.[66] And secondly, the affairs of the cathedral priory's satellites were clearly relegated behind those of the mother house. In 1526 and 1532, the priors of the Norwich cells were interrogated about the state of the cathedral priory, about which they knew little,

62 *The Latin Poems commonly attributed to Walter Mapes*, ed. T. Wright, Camden Society, old series, xvi (1841), pp. 184–7, 246.
63 *The Riverside Chaucer*, ed. L. D. Benson, 3rd edn (Oxford, 1987), p. 26. Or perhaps a composite picture is intended: cf. C. N. L. Brooke, 'Monk and Canon: Some Patterns in the Religious Life of the Twelfth Century', in *Monks, Hermits and the Ascetic Tradition*, ed. W. J. Sheils, SCH, XII (1985), pp. 110–12.
64 Cf. D. Pearsall, ' "If heaven be on this earth, it is in cloister or in school": the Monastic Ideal in Later Medieval English Literature', in *Pragmatic Utopias. Ideals and Communities, 1200–1630*, ed. R. Horrox and S. Rees Jones (Cambridge, 2001), pp. 11–25.
65 See Knowles, *RO*, I, pp. 83–4 for a sensitive discussion of these difficulties.
66 *Norwich Visitations*, pp. 65–71. For early fourteenth-century examples of the prior of Norwich ordering monks to stay behind in the cells during an episcopal visitation, see NRO, DCN 40/9, fols 5v, 39v.

with hardly any information sought or recounted about the condition of their own houses.[67] A similar bias is shown by two early fourteenth-century sets of articles for episcopal visitations of Durham. The first contained over one hundred questions to be asked, with only seven relating to the priory's cells; and both sets were largely concerned with the manner in which the mother house managed its dependencies and whether the heads of the cells provided satisfactory reports of their administration, rather than with the spiritual condition of the daughter houses. Even the numerous comments made about Freiston Priory during the Crowland visitations of 1434 and 1440 give very little information about discipline at the cell and focus almost entirely on the house's prior.[68]

Alongside the occasional disclosure in the records of mother-house visitations, we have a number of episcopal reports direct from cells, several dating from the late thirteenth century. In his discussion of this early set of injunctions, Knowles concluded that almost all the dependencies visited were in an unacceptable condition, and bemoaned 'the usual story . . . of irregular life at a cell'.[69] The standard of observance at several satellites inspected at this time was undoubtedly deficient. The visitations of Leominster of 1282 and 1286 uncovered a number of extremely serious faults, with senior monks on both occasions accused of incontinence with several women, including a nun and a relative. Archbishop Pecham was moved to depose the prior of Kidwelly in 1284 'because of his manifest demerits' and a prior of Brecon for incontinence, only to discover that both had been reappointed to their offices. At Ewenny in 1284, Pecham found fault with the prior's administration and the monks' public meat-eating; and Bishop Cantilupe of Hereford (1275–82) was not impressed with the monks of Bromfield, some of whom were hunters. Bishop Sutton of Lincoln's visitation of Brooke in 1298 also discovered serious problems, this time caused by an absentee and improvident prior. But these reports were not wholly bad: Bishop Giffard's inspection of St James' Bristol in May 1284 found nothing to criticise, whereas Archbishop Pecham was even led to praise the purity of religion practised at Blythburgh following his visit to that priory in June 1281.[70]

---

[67] *Norwich Visitations*, pp. 196–203, 263–5.

[68] DCM, 2.9 Pont. 4, Reg. II, fols 49v–51r; *Visitations of Religious Houses in the Diocese of Lincoln, 1420–1449*, ed. A. H. Thompson, 3 vols, Lincoln Record Society, vii, xiv, xxi (1914–29), I, pp. 34–9, II, pp. 54–60. However, Archbishop Greenfield's visitation of Nostell Priory in 1313, when he demanded the recall of the priors of Breedon and Bamburgh, indicates that the spiritual well-being of cells was not wholly ignored by diocesans inspecting the mother house: *Reg. Greenfield*, II, no. 1022, p. 165.

[69] Knowles, *RO*, I, p. 112.

[70] *Registrum Thome de Cantilupo, Episcopi Herefordensis, AD 1275–1282*, ed. R. G. Griffiths, C&Y Soc., ii (1907), pp. 265–7; *Reg. Swinfield*, pp. 149–50; *Registrum Epistolarum Peckham*, III, nos 582, 588, pp. 798–800, 810–11; *The Register of John Pecham Archbishop of Canterbury 1279–1292*, ed. F. N. Davis and D. C. Douie, 2 vols, C&Y Soc., lxiv–lxv (1908–69), I, pp. 198–9; *Reg. Trillek*, p. 237; *The Rolls and Register of Bishop Oliver Sutton 1280–1299*, ed. R. M. T. Hill, 8 vols, Lincoln Record Society,

Moreover, another batch of fifteenth- and sixteenth-century visitation records survives from cells which paints a rather more positive picture. Pilton Priory received an entirely satisfactory report from Archbishop Morton in 1492, whereas a series of three visitations of Blythburgh Priory between 1520 and 1532 found no personal shortcomings other than the excessive strictness of one the house's priors.[71] Late medieval visitations of the cells of Battle uncovered problems, but no sign of depravity. There was insufficient respect shown to the prior at St Nicholas' Exeter in 1492 and an exile from the mother house was causing serious disruption. Meanwhile at Brecon in 1401, the prior's administration was heavily criticised but no moral shortcomings were reported, and in 1504 the prior and monks declared that all was well, although the visitor's injunctions do not survive.[72] And Bishop Alnwick of Lincoln's inspection of Durham's small cell at St Leonard's Stamford in 1440 found a certain weariness in the face of perennial financial strain, but also what appears to have been a tolerable level of observance, since the only fault uncovered was the failure of the small community to rise during the night for matins.[73]

It would be reckless, however, to conclude from these relatively favourable reports that there was a significant improvement in standards of observance in cells in the later middle ages. A much more critical report was made by Bishop Hatfield following his visitation of Durham in c.1371, that 'neither discipline nor any regular correction is had in the cells'; and the condition of Breedon Priory in 1441 was also less than satisfactory, with one of the prior's companions fleeing the visitation and the other a quondam prior responsible for serious dilapidations of the house.[74] A number of other disciplinary problems at cells were also brought to the attention of the diocesan in the later middle ages, such as an incontinent prior of Carham in 1432, whereas another fifteenth-century canon of Breedon was imprisoned for his misdemeanours.[75] Moreover, the difference between the earlier and later sets of visitation records from cells may have more to do with the quality of inspection than that of the communities inspected. Professor Knowles

xxxix, xliii, xlviii, lii, lx, lxiv, lxix, lxxvi (1948–86), II, pp. 145–7; *Episcopal Registers, Diocese of Worcester: Register of Bishop Godfrey Giffard, 1268–1301*, ed. J. W. Willis Bund, 2 vols, Worcestershire Historical Society, xv (1898–1902), II, p. 234; *Blythburgh Priory Cartulary*, ed. C. Harper-Bill, 2 parts, Suffolk Records Society, Suffolk Charters, II–III (1980–1), I, no. 208, pp. 120–1.

71 *Reg. Morton*, II, no. 284, p. 78; *Norwich Visitations*, pp. 177, 216, 284–5.
72 *Reg. Morton*, II, no. 277, p. 75; *The Episcopal Registers of the Diocese of St Davids, 1397 to 1518*, ed. R. F. Isaacson, 3 vols, Cymmrodorion Record Society, vi (1917–20), I, pp. 230–4; G. Williams, *The Welsh Church from Conquest to Reformation*, 2nd edn (Cardiff, 1976), pp. 376, 397.
73 *Lincoln Visitations, 1420–1449*, III, pp. 346–7.
74 DCM, 2.8 Pont. 12; *Lincoln Visitations, 1420–1449*, II, pp. 40–3.
75 *The Register of Thomas Langley, Bishop of Durham, 1406–1437*, ed. R. L. Storey, 6 vols, SS, clxiv, clxvi, clxix–clxx, clxxvii, clxxxii (1956–70), IV, no. 996, p. 65; VCH, *Leicestershire*, II, p. 9.

believed that Morton's provincial visitation of 1492 was not very thorough, whereas many of the reports from late medieval Norwich diocese were extremely brief.[76]

The evidence from episcopal visitation records is therefore imperfect and inconclusive. While it would surely be wrong to endorse Knowles' depiction of almost inevitable irregularity, it can hardly be claimed that the surviving visitation material demonstrates much more than the inadequate diocesan supervision of many dependencies. It would appear, then, that most cells were reliant on their mother houses for regular inspection. Clearly the thoroughness with which monasteries monitored their daughter houses would have been a crucial determinant of the quality of observance maintained therein. Paradoxically, therefore, the absence of criticism of their cells in mother-house sources may be the product of deficient surveillance rather than a high standard of religion, whereas the frequent highlighting of failings at a dependency may reflect the diligence of its parent as much as the turbulence of the satellite.

The yearly audit of the cell's accounts at the mother house provided an opportunity for a spiritual check-up, but more regular contact with the monks dwelling in dependencies would have been required to prevent irregularities taking root. As we have seen, few if any daughter houses seem to have been visited by their parents as often as once a year.[77] This is not to say, however, that mother houses took little interest in the standard of observance in their cells. The itinerary of Abbot Wenlock of Westminster between 1286 and 1292 reveals numerous sojourns at Hurley and Great Malvern, although admittedly none at the abbey's smaller cell in Sudbury.[78] Several mother houses are also known to have issued legislation for their dependencies at general chapters.[79] Where abbots' registers survive, it is sometimes possible to follow the more regular forms of correspondence maintained between monastery and cell. The registers of abbots, like those of bishops, tend to become increasingly formalised with time, and some, like the sixteenth-century Gloucester volumes, contain little apart from presentations, leases and appointments to offices. One or two earlier examples, however, such as the fourteenth-century register of Battle, include letters sent to daughter houses in response to particular issues.[80] Even more informative are the small registers of the priors of Durham, unique survivals which record much of the priors' more personal correspondence that had been squeezed out of the large registers, and show them responding to the

[76] Knowles, RO, III, pp. 79–80; Norwich Visitations, passim.

[77] See above, p. 91.

[78] Documents Illustrating the Rule of Walter de Wenlock, Abbot of Westminster, 1283–1307, ed. B. F. Harvey, Camden Society, 4th series, ii (1965), pp. 34–45. It is only for these six years that sufficient information survives for a detailed itinerary of the abbot.

[79] See above, pp. 90–1.

[80] Gloucester, Dean and Chapter Library, Registers C (1500–14) and D (1514–38); BL, Harley MS 3586, esp. fols 21v–29r.

problems and needs of their cells. The care with which the abbots of St Albans monitored their dependencies can be seen from Abbot de la Mare's formulary and from the letters of Abbot Whethamstede to individual priors. Whethamstede's missives, informal in content if not in style, cover such diverse issues as discipline, the payment of taxes to the abbey, the treatment of servants and overeating.[81] Sources like these show superiors advising, reproaching and encouraging the priors of their cells in ways that are never seen in the more formal records on which we must normally rely.

What conclusions about the standards of discipline in cells can be drawn from mother-house records for the monitoring of their own dependencies? Very few injunctions from internal visitations survive and, although the St Albans chronicles sometimes report the deposition of a prior, their faults are generally described as administrative rather than moral.[82] The registers of Battle and Durham are more informative about irregularities in daughter houses. Several of the letters that abbots of Battle sent to their priors in Brecon and Exeter concern the unsatisfactory behaviour of their inmates. The priory of St Nicholas' Exeter seems to have been particularly unstable in the fourteenth century, with internal dissension, the incontinence of two of its monks and the refusal of another to obey his prior forming the subject of three missives from Battle.[83]

The fuller Durham registers contain many more indications of indiscipline, causing Professor Dobson to conclude that the Durham cells maintained a 'somewhat chequered spiritual life' and must have been a cause of despondency to the mother house.[84] As we have seen, Farne Island was the greatest culprit, with a succession of priors recalled or reproached for misbehaviour, but standards of discipline were not much higher at Lytham. Two successive priors of Lytham, who ruled the cell from 1389 to 1412, were accused of incontinence but were able to purge themselves of the charge. The belligerent George Cyther caused a commotion at Lytham in the 1430s by the 'feghtyng and strikyng of seculares' and threatening a fellow monk and the parish priest there with his knife and a stave, 'likely for to sle or mayne thaym had hit not happenet at there was mony men be syde the whech helde the foreseide dan George'. And in 1460, the prior of Durham recalled William Easby from Lytham, writing to Sir John Butler that 'ther hath been now late straunge rewle in our celle at Lethom such as I never hard of in no place belonging to us'.[85] Disciplinary problems can also be seen

---

81 CUL, MS Ee.IV.20; *Registra*, II, Appendix E, pp. 365–476. A stray letter of c.1500 in the British Library, from the prior of Belvoir to the prior of St Albans, thanking him for his advice about certain financial matters, indicates that this kind of correspondence was not one-way: BL, Royal roll 14 B.li.

82 E.g. William of Trumpington's recall of the priors of Belvoir, Wymondham and Hatfield Peverel: GASA, I, pp. 270–4.

83 BL, Harley MS 3586, fols 21v, 23r–23v.

84 Dobson, *Durham Priory*, pp. 297–8.

85 Ibid., pp. 328–9; DCM, Loc. XXV: 39, Reg. IV, fols 137v–138r.

at Holy Island where two monks were admonished for refusing to celebrate masses or sing services and two others for not showing reverence to their elderly prior.[86]

Entries like these suggest that cells were prone to irregularities, but they do not allow the quantification of faults. No doubt if more abbots' registers and visitation records were extant many more examples of laxness and corruption in daughter houses would have survived with them. But before we conclude that such failings were inevitable in small satellite priories, it should be noted that the plentiful Durham sources contain very few complaints about the monks dwelling in the priories of Jarrow, Wearmouth and St Leonard's Stamford.[87] In assessing the quality of religion in dependencies, as in all monasteries, we cannot simply recount a list of recorded abuses and extrapolate. The patchy evidence that survives does suggest the vulnerability of small cells to irregular observance and to serious moral lapses. As Dr Chibnall has observed, service in a dependent priory must have provided 'unparalleled opportunities of worldly living' for those lacking the vocation of a monk, such as one Thomas, a canon of Kirkham, who took two forged seals of that priory to its cell at Carham, before fleeing with the proceeds of his deceit.[88] How common such disciplinary problems were is very difficult to assess. Much of the material we have comes from great and stately houses like Durham, and it seems fair to conclude that if these monasteries experienced regular difficulties with their cells, then no abbey's dependencies would have been free from disciplinary problems.

However great were the spiritual dangers faced by monks staying in small cells, as we have seen measures were always available to mother houses to reduce the potential for indiscipline. The control of distant daughter houses must have presented particular problems, although abbeys could presumably rely on their cells' diocesans, inmates and lay patrons to inform them of serious difficulties. Where monasteries failed to take appropriate measures, however, the condition of cells could easily become scandalous. For this reason, laxity in a mother house spread quickly to its dependencies. Equally the development of factionalism in a monastery often resulted in the passing of disorderly or discontented monks onto its cells. It would seem fair to conclude, then, that the greatest single determinant of the quality of religious life in a dependency was the standard of religion in its mother house. But even if it was far from inevitable that service in a cell would have harmed the monks sent to stay there, it can still be argued that the potential for such trouble made the possession of daughter houses a source of weakness to their parent abbeys. It is therefore necessary to consider why mother houses were not deterred by the disciplinary dangers created by their cells.

---

[86] BL, Cotton MS Faust. A.vi, fols 8v–9r, 10r–10v.
[87] A point made by Mr Piper in his articles on these three priories.
[88] Morgan, *Bec*, p. 9; J. E. Burton, *Kirkham Priory from Foundation to Dissolution*, Borthwick Paper, no. LXXXVI (1995), pp. 19–20.

Practical Benefits of Daughter Houses

A number of practical advantages can be seen to have ensued from the possession of dependent priories. First and foremost, cells could be a source of financial profit. The potential pecuniary benefits of the possession of daughter houses have rarely been thought worth investigating. Historians have tended to assume that the cost of maintaining poor dependencies must have greatly exceeded the sums any mother house could have extracted in taxation. It must be appreciated, however, that monasteries did not in general subsidise their cells, which were expected to be entirely self-supporting units. Abbeys very rarely contributed to the endowment of their satellites, apart from some of the dependencies they themselves founded. Even for self-foundations the alienation of mother-house property could prove controversial and Matthew Paris heavily criticised Abbot Warin for endowing St Albans' dependent hospital of St Mary de Pré from abbey resources.[89] Later grants of property to cells are almost unknown. Monasteries can occasionally be found relieving their satellites of short-term financial hardship, but it seems only as a last resort. Some of the cells of Durham were among the poorest monasteries in medieval England, but incidences of the mother house supporting any of its dependencies financially are hard to find. Jarrow Priory was subsidised by several Durham obedientiaries during the years 1416–21, whereas the even more extreme step of assigning new revenues was considered necessary to arrest the alarming fall in the receipts of Wearmouth at around the same time and again to assist Jarrow in the early sixteenth century; though in the case of Wearmouth this amounted only to returning income from the priory's own parish which had been siphoned off by the mother house. However, instead of mounting a similar relief operation for the penurious cell of St Leonard's Stamford in the 1420s, first one and then both of the priory's monks were temporarily recalled to Durham, an expedient repeated at Jarrow between 1425 and 1432.[90] Durham's reluctance to subsidise its cells with mother-house income was highlighted by Bishop Kellaw in 1314; and a similar attitude can be seen at Gloucester where one of the reasons given for the closure of its priory at Ewyas Harold in 1359 was that the satellite's survival depended on regular contributions from the abbey's common fund, a state of affairs which could be tolerated no longer.[91]

It would seem therefore that the fragile revenues of cells were not ordinarily augmented by their mother houses: that is, dependencies were not in general dependants. Nevertheless, the possession of satellite priories could

---

[89] GASA, I, pp. 202, 215.
[90] Dobson, *Durham Priory*, p. 312; Piper, 'Wearmouth', pp. 6–7; Piper, *Jarrow*, p. 9; Piper, 'Stamford', part i, p. 15.
[91] DCM, Reg. II, fol. 51r; *Mon. Ang.*, III, pp. 629–30, no. 3. This attitude contrasts with the willingness of mother houses to forego the pensions owed to them by their cells when the smaller houses were experiencing financial hardship: see below, p. 275.

still prove burdensome when challenges to their status or rights necessitated action in the courts. As we have seen, disputes involving cells were far from uncommon and the protracted character of many of these must have been costly. When Abbot de la Mare was seeking to commute the customary payment of one thousand marks for papal confirmation of newly elected heads of St Albans into an annual pension, it was pleaded lest it be thought that its cells rendered the abbey wealthy, that they in fact contributed to its impoverishment 'because the abbot prosecuted and defended many times the business of his cells at his own expense'.[92] Financial records do not survive from St Albans to test this claim but it should be noted that not all the legal costs of dependencies were met by their mother houses. The Lynn accounts show that priory spending considerable sums on the defence of its own parochial rights, including payments of over £80 in 1380/1; and even the poorly endowed Hoxne Priory financed its own suit concerning presentation to the church of Denham in 1502/3.[93] Furthermore, all the cells of Norwich were required to make regular contributions towards their mother house's own legal costs. Between 1393 and 1404, the priors of Lynn paid about £80 to Norwich for its dispute with Bishop Despenser, a cause to which the cathedral priory's other cells also contributed a few pounds.[94] It would appear therefore that the defence of daughter-house rights might not have been as expensive as the St Albans plea implied, at least where relatively wealthy cells like Lynn were involved.

Equally, the sums extracted by monasteries from their dependencies could be considerable. A handful of cells served as depots, sending back the larger part of their revenues to the mother house. Nostell Priory received substantial sums from its satellite at Bamburgh and was badly hit by the loss of revenues from its Northumberland property caused by the Scottish wars from the late thirteenth century.[95] But although most daughter houses spent their income on their own needs, every priory was expected to make some financial contribution to its mother house. The most notorious exponent of daughter-house taxation was the St Albans abbot, Hugh of Eversden (1309–27), who was said to have exacted during his rule £6,000 from the abbey's cells in subsidies and to have raised a further £1,000 from selling corrodies there. Priors were browbeaten by threats of an extended visit of four or six months by the abbot and his household should they refuse to pay, provoking Prior Somerton of Binham to launch a full-scale rebellion against the abbot.[96]

---

[92] GASA, III, p. 149. De la Mare also claimed, a little dubiously, that numerous seculars from the neighbourhood of the abbey's cells came to St Albans for hospitality.

[93] NRO, DCN 2/1/5–6, 21(vii), 31; Windsor, St George's Chapel, I. C. 34.

[94] NRO, DCN 2/1/20(iii–vi), 21(i–viii) (Lynn), DCN 2/2/2 (Aldeby), DCN 2/3/11, 12, 17(i–ii) (St Leonard's Norwich). Only one account from these years survives for Yarmouth and none for Hoxne.

[95] A History of Northumberland, ed. H. H. E. Craster, 15 vols (Newcastle, 1893–1940), I, pp. 84–90.

[96] GASA, II, pp. 130–45, 178–9; see above, pp. 97–8.

These enormous sums – if they can be trusted – were quite exceptional, but most mother houses sought to siphon off at least some of their cells' wealth either by an annual pension or by extraordinary levies in response to particular needs. A number of foundation charters specified the annual sum to be paid to the mother house as a token of the priory's subjection. The priory of May in Scotland was required to pay its mother house, Reading, a considerable tribute of sixteen marks per year, but in most cases the amounts laid down were only nominal, such as the two silver marks owed by Penwortham to Evesham or the half mark payable by Snape to Colchester. The yearly pension owed to Battle by St Nicholas' Exeter was originally set at 60s., but was reduced to only 20s. in 1249 (in line with the sum paid by Brecon, Battle's other daughter house) owing to the financial strains experienced by that cell.[97] But it soon became customary for abbeys to impose new pensions on their satellites, often earmarked for a particular obedientiary or cause, which were usually far more substantial. The fifteenth- and sixteenth-century accounts of St Ives show annual payments of between £15 and £19 (about a fifth of the cell's yearly revenue) to Ramsey for the abbey's spices, as well as an annual pension of 68s. to the abbey chamberlain. Similarly, the priors of St James' Bristol and Cranborne each owed the Tewkesbury chamberlain a yearly sum of £6 13s. 4d., more than a tenth of their 1535 income.[98] Predictably, larger pensions were taken from the wealthier cells. In the second half of the fourteenth century, Yarmouth was paying £30 and Lynn about £18 a year in pensions to Norwich out of annual incomes of about £200 each.[99]

By the later middle ages, these exactions had acquired the status of custom and the failure of a cell to pay excited reprisals from its mother house. It was ordained at St Albans in 1355 that cells which had not paid their pensions within a month of the due date without reasonable cause would have to pay double, 'with no hope of remission'.[100] The imposition of new pensions, however, might provoke equally vociferous reactions from the other direction. Benedict XII's requirement that dependencies should contribute to the support of their mother houses' university students seems to have been quietly accepted, but other novelties caused more friction. During the abbacy of John de Maryns (1302–9), the priors of the St Albans cells

---

97 'Documents relating to the Priory of the Isle of May, c.1140–1313', ed. A. A. M. Duncan, *Proceedings of the Society of Antiquaries of Scotland*, xc (1956–7), p. 60; *The Lancashire Pipe Rolls and Early Lancashire Charters*, ed. W. Farrer (Liverpool, 1902), pp. 320–2; *Cartularium Monasterii Sancti Johannis Baptiste de Colecestria*, ed. S. A. Moore, 2 vols, Roxburghe Club (1897), I, pp. 168–70; *The Chronicle of Battle Abbey*, ed. E. Searle, Oxford Medieval Texts (Oxford, 1980), pp. 82–5, 88–9; BL, Cotton MS Vit. D.ix, fol. 99v.

98 BL, Add. MS 33448, fols 126v ff.; 'A Tewkesbury Compotus', ed. F. W. P. Hicks, *TBGAS*, lv (1934), p. 251; *Valor*, II, pp. 484–5. The Tewkesbury pensions are not mentioned in the *Valor*.

99 NRO, DCN 2/4/1–2, DCN 2/1/1–21.

100 GASA, II, pp. 448–9.

strongly resisted the granting of a pension of £30 for three lives to the bishops of Coventry and Lichfield because they did not want to contribute.[101] But much more troublesome were the abbey's attempts to levy new contributions from its cells towards the annual pensions granted to king and pope by Abbot de la Mare, designed to replace the enormous sums hitherto charged for the confirmation of the newly elected abbots of St Albans. The decision of Abbot de la Moote (1396–1401) to raise half of the seventy marks now due from the abbey each year from its cells was deeply unpopular. This discontent had not abated by the time John Whethamstede was elected abbot in 1420, and in the second year of his rule he settled the dispute by modifying considerably the sums demanded from the cells.[102]

But although abbeys were always eager to pass a proportion of any new burden onto their satellites, it would be wrong to conclude that mother houses put their own profit before the welfare of their dependencies. It was common practice to take into account the income of a cell before setting rates of taxation and to extract more from wealthier priories. De la Moote's pension was graduated, with Tynemouth paying £7, Wymondham £5, Binham £4, down to the 6s. 8d. expected from the abbey's poorest priory, Beadlow; and the other regular dues taken from the St Albans cells were calculated according to each priory's means.[103] Moreover, the accounts of the Norwich cells show the mother house's willingness to suspend or to reduce permanently a pension owed by one of its cells, 'because of the poverty of the benefice'. On several occasions, the priory tolerated the accumulation of substantial arrears in the payment of its poorer cells' pensions, some of which were apparently never made up.[104] Equally generous was the diminution of Yarmouth's annual payment to the Norwich cellarer from £26 13s. 4d. in the late fourteenth century to only 40s. by 1441/2, after the Yarmouth revenues had plunged over this time from £200 a year to under £100.

An awareness of what a dependency could afford can also be seen in the aids levied by mother houses to cover extraordinary costs. It was generally acknowledged that 'just as they [the cells] participate in the advantages they should also participate in the burdens' of the mother house, providing subsidies 'whenever hard business or accidental misfortunes, insupportable to the monastery, should arise'.[105] Contributions might be demanded to help meet the costs of law suits, new buildings, the graduation of scholar-monks or in response to temporary financial difficulties at the mother house. At Durham, sums were raised from its cells to subsidise Durham College (until 1381 when its endowment was considerably expanded), for Prior Wessington's building

---

101 Wilkins, Concilia, II, pp. 596–7, chap. 9; GASA, II, p. 93.
102 GASA, III, pp. 468–70; Amundesham, I, pp. 83–5. For the grateful response of the prior of Belvoir to Abbot Whethamstede's generosity in reducing his pension from 40s. to 12s. 8d., see Cambridge, Trinity College MS O.9.25, fol. 1v.
103 GASA, III, p. 468; Amundesham, II, Appendix F, pp. 307–10.
104 NRO, DCN, 2/4/1–10; see below, p. 275.
105 GASA, III, p. 469.

campaigns and to relieve the debts of the bursar's office after 1438, although
the poorest dependencies were usually exempted.[106] In the face of more
serious financial problems, a superior might decide to lighten the abbey's
burden for a time by making an extended visit to a daughter house, as did
Abbot Dumbleton of Reading to his cell of Leominster in 1364 and Abbot
Heyworth of St Albans (1401–20) for the best part of two years immediately
after his election.[107]

The possession of one or more dependencies could therefore prove useful
at times of economic strain or when unexpected outlays arose. Equally, the
imposition of annual pensions provided a steady source of income for mother
houses without seriously encumbering their cells. Some abbeys extracted
more than others from their satellites, but the pensions received from a
family of daughter houses could prove a useful and dependable source of
income. In the fifteenth century Durham extracted about £25 a year in
regular pensions from its dependencies; in the early 1300s, Gloucester was
receiving £28 a year in this way from its six daughter houses; and even before
Abbot de la Moote's new pension was imposed, the eight cells of St Albans
together provided annual subsidies of a little over £50 to the mother
house.[108] The poorest cells paid out very little and could only have been a
burden to the house that owned them. But it would appear that many satellite priories were a source of modest profit to their parents.

Cells might have proved useful to their mother houses in a number of
other ways. Although few English dependencies acted as bailiwicks, managing outlying properties belonging to their mother houses, the head of a cell
was well placed to handle any abbey business in his locality. The priors of St
Leonard's Stamford regularly served as proctors for Durham's affairs in the
south. They stood in for the prior of Durham at the Benedictine provincial
chapter meetings in Northampton several times during the fourteenth
century and can also be seen acting on Durham's behalf in disputes involving
the mother house's property in Stamford and the Midlands.[109] The priories of
Rumburgh and Breedon seem to have served a similar function for their
Yorkshire mother houses. St Mary's York muniments sent to Rumburgh for a
case involving the abbey's lands in Cambridgeshire were confiscated in 1528
at the cell's suppression; whereas the details of a 1329 quo warranto inquisition concerning Nostell Priory's Nottinghamshire property were entered
into the Breedon cartulary.[110] It was not only distant priors who could assist
in this way. In 1314 the prior of Cranborne paid suit in place of the abbot of

106 Dobson, *Durham Priory*, pp. 307–8.
107 *CPR, 1361–1364*, p. 504; GASA, III, pp. 494–5. Heyworth stayed at Binham,
Hatfield Peverel and Belvoir in succession, 'with a moderate household'.
108 Piper, *Jarrow*, p. 15; 'Early Deeds relating to St Peter's Abbey, Gloucester', ed. W. St
Clair Baddeley, *TBGAS*, xxxvii (1914), p. 222; *Amundesham*, II, Appendix F, pp.
309–10.
109 Piper, 'Stamford', part ii, p. 1; BL, Cotton MS Faust. A.vi, fols 11v–12r.
110 *Mon. Ang.*, III, pp. 613–14, no. 7; McKinley, 'Cartulary of Breedon', no. 5, pp. 4–9.

Tewkesbury for lands held from Glastonbury Abbey, while in 1486 the prior of St James' Bristol is found receiving Tewkesbury's pension from Margam Abbey on behalf of his superior.[111] Cells could prove convenient bases too. The satellites of St Leonard's Stamford and St James' Bristol were used by Durham and Tewkesbury as staging posts for journeys to London and Wales respectively, and new abbots of St Albans found Hertford Priory an ideal place to linger before making their first grand entry into the abbey as its head.[112] Evesham Abbey also benefited from the location of its cell at Penwortham in the form of salmon and herrings sent from Lancashire to the mother house by way of a pension.[113]

The possession of one or more dependencies also provided abbeys with an outlet for monks who were not prospering in the mother house. Brethren were sent out of the abbey not only for disciplinary reasons, but also because they might have preferred the smaller setting of a cell or because of sickness. The use of daughter houses as health resorts was not uncommon. Jarrow was regarded as a salubrious spot and several ailing inmates of Durham were sent there in the later middle ages. Freiston was housing sick monks in 1434 and 1519, as was Belvoir in the 1530s.[114] Urban monasteries could be unhygienic, and a papal licence was granted to a monk of Bath in 1401 to dwell in the priory's cells of Dunster or Waterford whenever sick, owing to 'the unwholesomeness of the air at Bath'![115] Another kind of monk often best dwelling away from the mother house was the quondam abbot, and some monasteries chose to use their dependencies as retirement homes for former superiors. Heads of Norwich, Nostell, Shrewsbury and Whitby are known to have spent the final years of their lives in cells, but this practice was especially common at Durham. Richard of Claxton (1286) and Geoffrey of Burdon (1321) were both granted Wearmouth Priory after resigning the headship of Durham, whereas William of Tanfield (1313) and Robert of Walworth (1394) withdrew to Jarrow, the latter after three years of retirement at Finchale.[116] Disappointed contenders for the headship of the mother house

111 VCH, Dorset, II, p. 71; BL, Harley Ch. 75. A. 29.
112 Piper, 'Stamford', part ii, p. 2; 'The Priory of Cardiff and other Possessions of the Abbey of Tewkesbury in Glamorgan: Accounts of the Ministers for the year 1449–1450', ed. W. Rees, South Wales and Monmouth Record Society, ii (1950), pp. 158–9; GASA, III, p. 492.
113 Chronicon Abbatiae de Evesham, pp. 217, 297.
114 BL, Cotton MS Faust. A.vi, fol. 16r; DCM, Reg. parv. II, fol. 17v; Piper, Jarrow, p. 20; Lincoln Visitations, 1420–1449, I, pp. 34–9; Lincoln Visitations, 1517–1531, II, pp. 108–11; Mon. Ang., III, p. 292, no. 18.
115 CPL, V, p. 414.
116 Historiae Dunelmensis Scriptores Tres, ed. J. Raine, SS, ix (1839), pp. 73, 95, 102, clxiv, clxxiv–clxxv. Prior Simon Bozoun of Norwich retired to St Leonard's Norwich for health reasons in 1352 and Prior William Melsonby of Nostell to Bamburgh Priory (with a fellow canon) in 1489, whereas both Richard Marshall of Shrewsbury and John Hexham of Whitby, former abbots of their communities, were allowed after the Dissolution to remain in the cells they had been given on their resignation:

could also be compensated with the rule of a dependency. In 1332, after Robert of Sutton's election as prior of Bath was overruled by a provision from Pope John XXII, Sutton was compensated with a grant of Dunster Priory on much more favourable terms than were usually conceded. Richard Bell of Durham was similarly given the consolation prize of the popular headship of Finchale Priory following his narrow defeat in the mother-house election of 1456.[117] Roger Norris' posting to Penwortham should also be considered in this context and not simply as another example of a bad monk exiled to a dependency.

The possibility that some monks preferred life in a small dependency must also be considered. Certain Durham brethren are known to have spent most of their careers in the priory's cells and this was probably at their own behest.[118] The possession of a remote daughter house might also have provided an opportunity for monks with eremitical leanings. There are numerous examples of twelfth-century Benedictines opting to leave their monastery for a hermitage, as the Rule had predicted they would.[119] Since a number of cells – such as Farne Island, Coquet Island, Hilbre Island, Scilly and Trokenholt – were established in specifically eremitical locations to commemorate saintly solitaries, they were ideally suited for this purpose. Of Farne, Geoffrey of Coldingham wrote in the twelfth century that 'it always contains, indeed it actually forms men of virtue, because when someone is led by the Spirit into its desert, he must expect to be tempted by the devil. Consequently he either cultivates sanctity or else he leaves this holy place'.[120] It seems likely that more monks dwelling in isolated satellites in the later middle ages wished to leave than cultivated sanctity, but there are indications that dependencies of this kind were sometimes used for monks seeking solitude. Prior Melsonby of Durham retreated as a hermit to Farne Island in 1244 where he is said to have displayed signs of sanctity, and a

---

NRO, DCN 40/10, fol. 40v; York, Borthwick Institute of Historical Research, Archbishops' Register 23, fols 127v–128r; VCH, Shropshire, II, p. 30; VCH, Yorkshire, III, p. 106. Prior Thomas Sutton of Repton also retired briefly to his house's cell at Calke in September 1486, but this move was successfully opposed by his successor and Sutton was evicted: VCH, Derbyshire, II, p. 61.

[117] The Register of Ralph de Shrewsbury, bishop of Bath and Wells, 1329–1363, ed. T. S. Holmes, 2 vols, Somerset Record Society, ix–x (1896), I, no. 486, p. 121; R. B. Dobson, 'Richard Bell, prior of Durham (1464–78) and bishop of Carlisle (1478–95)', Transactions of the Cumberland and Westmorland Antiquarian and Archaeological Society, new series, lxv (1965), pp. 182–221. Sutton was allowed to choose any number of companions for himself at Dunster and to replace them as he wished.

[118] E.g. Piper, 'Stamford', part ii, p. 12.

[119] The Rule of St Benedict in Latin and English, ed. J. McCann (London, 1952), chap. 1, pp. 14–15; J. E. Burton, 'The Eremitical Tradition and the Development of Post-Conquest Religious Life in Northern England', in Eternal Values in Medieval Life, ed. N. Crossley-Holland, Trivium, xxvi (1991), pp. 18–39.

[120] Geoffrey of Coldingham, Life of Bartholomew of Farne, in Symeonis Monachi Opera Omnia, ed. T. Arnold, 2 vols, RS, lxxv (1882–5), I, p. 312.

more famous Durham monk found the surroundings at Farne conducive to his mystical meditations in the second half of the fourteenth century.[121]

The cells of Hilbre Island and Trokenholt are both referred to as 'hermitages' in the early 1300s, and at the 1323 visitation of Chester Abbey it was ordered that another monk should be sent to Hilbre to support Brother Robert de Marketon who had unwisely vowed to become an anchorite there.[122] It should also be noted that saintly monks are sometimes found in larger, less remote dependencies. The revelation of an unnamed Binham monk, of c.1485, was entered into at least two surviving commonplace books, whereas John of Bridlington, a monk of St Mary's York who dwelt at Wetheral for at least twelve years up to his death in 1305, was given the dubious encomium 'vir sanctus sed lunaticus' by the mother-house chronicler.[123]

Rest-houses

In most cases, the uses to which dependencies could be put were circumscribed by the spiritual services owed to benefactors. But occasionally, monasteries were able to run a cell according to their own specific needs. Before the end of the fourteenth century, when Durham College was established on a firm footing, Durham used their priory in Stamford as a study house. About one in three monks, including Uthred of Boldon, were sent here to study and the youth of many of these suggests St Leonard's might have served, in the words of Dr Meryl Foster, as 'a preparatory school for would-be university monks'.[124] Much about the school at Stamford remains obscure, but it is clear that the priory was no longer being used in this way in the fifteenth century. Of more enduring value to their mother houses were those dependencies set apart as holiday homes. St Albans' priory of Redbourn, Durham's Finchale, Peterborough's Oxney and quite possibly Norwich's St Leonard's Priory (in the same city) all accommodated monks sent away from the mother house for short breaks. Each of these four cells was situated within a few miles of their mother house and all, with the exception of Finchale, were self-foundations which could be operated without the interference of an external patron.

The practice of monks taking time off from full monastic observance might appear to be contrary to the Benedictine Rule, and Knowles discussed

---

121 *Hist. Dun. Scrip. Tres*, p. 41; *The Monk of Farne*, ed. D. H. Farmer (Baltimore, 1961).
122 *The Cartulary or Register of the Abbey of St Werburgh Chester*, ed. J. Tait, 2 vols, Chetham Society, new series, lxxix, lxxxii (1920–3), II, no. 521, p. 299; *VCH, Cambridgeshire and the Isle of* Ely, II, p. 214; *VCH, Cheshire*, III, p. 138.
123 Oxford, Bodleian Library, Rawlinson MS Liturg. e.6, fols 96v–97v, Gough MS Liturg. 7, fol. 56r; *St Mary's Chronicle*, p. 131.
124 M. R. Foster, 'Durham Monks at Oxford, c.1286–1381: a House of Studies and its Inmates', *Oxoniensia*, lv (1990), pp. 99–114; Piper, 'Stamford', part ii, pp. 10–12.

monastic rest-houses in the context of the breakdown of the common life in late medieval monasteries.[125] Nevertheless, such *ludi* had become commonplace by the later middle ages and were highly valued by as prominent a Benedictine as Thomas de la Mare.[126] In adopting this practice most monasteries had no alternative but to send their inmates to abbatial manor houses: as Knowles related, Christ Church Canterbury used Caldicote in this way; Westminster, the manor of Hendon; Bardney, Suthrey; Tewkesbury, the Mythe; and Worcester, Battenhall.[127] The possession of a cell converted into a rest-house ensured that an abbey's inmates could take holidays without leaving a monastic setting, rather than utilising ordinary manors where a more secularised regime would have been inevitable. These four dependencies were therefore of some value to their mother houses and are worth examining in a little detail.

Redbourn Priory, founded soon after the discovery of the bones of St Amphibalus on its site in 1178, was used from the start as a holiday home for St Albans monks. Abbot Warin's injunctions for blood-letting and the sick (1183×1195) mention 'brethren sent to Redbourn for recreation', and the next evidence we have for the cell, a 1275 ordinance of Abbot Roger of Norton for brethren dying there, records that inmates were staying at the priory *causa solatii*.[128] Most of the later evidence for Redbourn also takes the form of abbatial constitutions governing its operation, with Abbots Richard of Wallingford, Thomas de la Mare and John Whethamstede (twice) all issuing detailed legislation for the cell; and for this reason the pattern of life at Redbourn is much better known than that of any other St Albans dependency.[129] Abbot Wallingford (1327–36) ordained that three claustral monks should stay in succession at Redbourn, along with its prior, for a month at a time. They were to observe all the canonical hours, including the night office, and to celebrate masses daily, with persistent transgressors to have their *ludi* abrogated. Abbot de la Mare (1349–96) ensured this liturgical minimum was observed by staying regularly at Redbourn and often ringing the bell for matins himself, but in 1423 Abbot Whethamstede was led to legislate against brethren *in solatii* missing matins because of 'excessive and immoderate vigils'. Whethamstede's regard for St Amphibalus caused him in 1439 to seek to impose a more stringent observance on the brethren staying at Redbourn. He first ordained that an extra monk should be maintained at

[125] Knowles, *RO*, II, pp. 245–6. Another monk-historian, however, regarded this practice more favourably: 'some such amusements were necessary . . . The monastic granges to which from time to time the religious went for a change of scene and life were most useful in this regard and enabled them [the monks sent there] to recreate their strength for another period of service': F. A. Gasquet, *English Monastic Life* (London, 1904), pp. 146–7.
[126] *GASA*, II, pp. 399–400.
[127] Knowles, *RO*, II, p. 246.
[128] *GASA*, I, pp. 211, 452–3.
[129] Ibid., II, pp. 202–5, 397–401; *Amundesham*, I, pp. 113–14, II, pp. 203–12.

the cell. As well as maintaining the canonical hours and daily masses, the community were to celebrate festivals in the same extended manner as the abbey's other dependencies, and weekly commemorations of St Amphibalus were also to be introduced. However, these innovations were strongly opposed by the St Albans convent, on the grounds that they rendered stays in the rest-house not very restful and Whethamstede was reluctantly forced to retract his reforms. Presumably the customs established by Abbot Wallingford continued to serve as the framework for observance at Redbourn until its dissolution.

It is not possible to say whether the other cells in question were used as rest-houses from their foundation. Finchale appears to have acquired this status gradually. It seems unlikely that its founder Henry du Puiset would have consented to the conversion of his monastery into a holiday home, and the obligation to keep up the suffrages for Henry's soul ensured that Finchale was never occupied solely by monks 'ad spaciandum'. The development of the prior's suite at Finchale during the first half of the fourteenth century, accompanied by the conversion of the frater into a first-floor hall at this time suggests an increasing domestication of the priory over these years.[130] In c.1330, complaints were made about the impotence of the brethren sent to Finchale, but this does not seem to refer to monks taking recreation. More revealing is a letter of 1347 for the appointment of a subprior of Finchale, licensing him to hear the confessions of 'our co-brethren . . . [who are] staying there for a time and also of those who happen to have been sent to that cell for recreation'. The two-tiered organisation of Finchale at this date is confirmed by Bishop Hatfield's complaint, during a visitation of Durham in c.1371, that there were six impotent monks only at Finchale together with a few ludentes, in contrast to the usual pre-Black Death number of thirteen monks, with two ludentes.[131] It would seem therefore that only a small proportion of the monks dwelling in fourteenth-century Finchale were on vacation, although several of the others might have been sent there in retirement; and as a result, the prior of Durham's manor of Bearpark was regularly used for monks' ludi in the fourteenth century.[132] That the balance of monks at Finchale shifted in favour of holidaying monks in the fifteenth century is indicated by a Durham ordinance of 1408. It was then laid down that four of the eight brethren dwelling at Finchale should be continually resident with the other four sent for recreation from Durham, for three weeks at a time. Of the four monks on holiday, two were to be present at all the daily services and the other two at mass and vespers only, with all four

130 C. R. Peers, 'Finchale Priory', Archaeologia Aeliana, 4th series, iv (1927), pp. 193–220; E. Impey, 'The Origins and Development of Non-Conventual Monastic Dependencies in England and Normandy, 1000–1350', 2 vols, unpublished Oxford D.Phil. thesis (1991), II, pp. 152–4.
131 DCM, Misc. ch. 2645; BL, Cotton MS Faust. A.vi, fol. 4r; DCM, 2.8 Pont. 12.
132 E.g. Raine, Priory of Finchale, p. lviii; Extracts from the Account Rolls of the Abbey of Durham, ed. J. T. Fowler, 3 vols, SS, xcix–c, ciii (1898–1901), II, pp. 390, 515.

celebrating high mass at least once a week and attending chapter and Lady mass on Sundays.[133] There were generally nine brethren (including the prior) staying at Finchale from this time until the Dissolution and so it seems likely that this arrangement obtained for the remainder of the cell's history.

It is not clear when Peterborough first established their cell at Oxney. Originally only a grange, Oxney might have begun to acquire monastic characteristics when Abbot William de Hotot retired there after his resignation in 1249. A 1292 constitution of Abbot Richard of London, copied into the Peterborough consuetudinary, provides the first sign that the manor of Oxney had been converted into a rest-house for the abbey's brethren, when the abbot ordained that the monks staying at Oxney or elsewhere *causa solatii* should continue to discharge their share of the abbey's prayers and masses.[134] The essentially monastic character of the settlement at this date is also illustrated by Abbot Godfrey of Crowland's grant of cheese, butter and milk to those 'serving God and the church of St Mary of Oxney' in May 1307.[135] It is possible to recover the basic outline of life at Oxney from the fifteenth-century Peterborough visitation records. In 1437, Richard Harlton, the abbey's prior, told Bishop Alnwick that six monks were always maintained at the cell, a number corroborated by the list of monks staying there at the time of the 1442 visitation.[136] The duration of the monks' seynies at Oxney is not given, but was apparently short. A lighter routine was expected at the cell and it was complained in both 1437 and 1518 that monks *in recreacione* were being made to rise for matins during the night rather than during the day, as was accustomed.[137] However, the abbey customary stipulated that the monks resting at Oxney should return to the mother house for certain ceremonial occasions, such as the Quinquagesima procession and absolution and mass on Maundy Thursday.[138]

[133] Raine, *Priory of Finchale*, no. 32, pp. 30–1.

[134] J. Sparke (ed.), *Historiae Anglicanae Scriptores Varii*, 2 vols (London, 1724), II, p. 128; London, Lambeth Palace MS 198b, fol. 285v.

[135] *The White Book of Peterborough. The Registers of Abbot William of Woodford, 1295–99 and Abbot Geoffrey of Crowland, 1299–1321*, ed. S. Raban, Peterborough Cathedral and Northamptonshire Record Society (2001), no. 212, pp. 218–19. The 'chapel' of Oxney was dedicated by the Archbishop of Armagh in 1315: Sparke, *Historiae Anglicanae*, II, p. 127.

[136] *Lincoln Visitations, 1420–1449*, III, pp. 273, 283–4. The Peterborough almoner, William Morton, also purchased wine for the six monks staying at Oxney in 1460: *The Book of William Morton, Almoner of Peterborough Monastery 1448–1467*, ed. W. T. Mellows, P. I. King and C. N. L. Brooke, Northamptonshire Record Society, xvi (1954), p. 139. Morton was later warden of Oxney in the early 1460s, but his jottings from this period reveal disappointingly little about the rest-house. His book does show, however, that the cell was used for a lengthy stay by the Peterborough prior each September, who entertained every abbey monk at Oxney at least once during his sojourn: ibid., pp. 150–1, 160–1, 164–5.

[137] *Lincoln Visitations, 1420–1449*, III, pp. 277, 279; *Lincoln Visitations, 1517–1531*, III, pp. 76, 79.

[138] London, Lambeth Palace MS 198, fols 115r, 140r.

Despite the large number of late medieval accounts to survive from St Leonard's Norwich, the manner in which it functioned remains difficult to recover.[139] Unique among dependencies for its extreme proximity to its mother house, the monks of St Leonard's were in constant contact with the main community. Several priors of the cell are known to have held an office in the mother house concurrently, and the surviving Norwich chapter ordinances enjoin that the prior of St Leonard's and his brethren should attend services at the cathedral priory on principal feast days.[140] That the priory might have been used in some way for the relaxation of inmates is suggested by several entries in the Norwich accounts. Many of the mother-house obedientiary rolls include the entry *apud sanctum leonardum* or occasionally *in le parlyng apud sanctum leonardum*, sometimes extended to *apud sanctum leonardum cum aliis recreacionibus* or *apud sanctum leonardum aliis quia recreacionibus*. Moreover, an entry in the precentor's account of 1394/5, records the payment of 7s. *in infirmaria camera minutorum et apud Leonardum*.[141] The St Leonard's accounts themselves provide little indication of this role, although between 1457 and 1468 they detail the sums spent *in recreacionibus confratrum*, as well as on food for the 'parlyng' from 1457 into the 1530s.[142] But although these entries are not entirely unambiguous, it seems likely that St Leonard's performed at least some of the functions of a rest-house in the later middle ages.

It can be seen from this account that rest-houses functioned to a large extent as ordinary priories, ensuring that a sufficient liturgical routine was maintained by the brethren taking their *ludi*. It would also appear that these holiday homes were closely regulated by their mother house's superiors who were zealous – sometimes over-zealous – to preserve their brethren from sloth. Not only were choir duties carefully specified, but suitable leisure pursuits were also prescribed. The taking of air was encouraged at Finchale and Redbourn, although, according to Abbot Wallingford's constitutions, 'only in nearby places removed from the public concourse' and always with the prior's consent. Abbot Whethamstede's 1439 ordinances for Redbourn warned sternly against idleness and recommended that leisure time be spent 'in reading or study', with more knowledgeable monks instructing their less learned colleagues 'whether [in] a liberal science or some other mechanical art'.[143]

Indeed, it appears that rest-homes were better equipped for study than

---

139 For a discussion of the role of this priory, see my 'Veneration and Renovation at a Small Norfolk Priory: St Leonard's, Norwich in the Later Middle Ages', *Historical Research*, lxxvi (2003), pp. 431–49.

140 Greatrex, *BRECP*, pp. 466–576; Cheney, 'Norwich Cathedral Priory', pp. 117–20.

141 E.g. NRO, DCN 1/9/37 (precentor, 1424/5), DCN 1/12/42 (communar/pittancer, 1408/9), DCN 1/9/24 (precentor, 1394/5). 'Parling', meaning speaking or conversing, presumably refers to monastic relaxation.

142 NRO, DCN 2/3/69–140.

143 Raine, *Priory of Finchale*, p. 30; GASA, II, p. 203; *Amundesham*, II, pp. 208–11.

moot daughter houses. Several abbots of St Albans donated books to Redbourn, including two surviving *Sanctilogia*, and Abbot de la Mare constructed for himself a *secretum studium* at Redbourn which might have been used by the priory's community in later years.[144] Both Finchale and St Leonard's Norwich possessed small but adequate reference libraries. Although only a few basic study books are found in the 1481 inventory of Finchale, in the 1520s there was a collection of over forty volumes there, covering theology, canon law, philosophy and medicine. The two surviving fifteenth-century inventories of St Leonard's show a stable collection of about thirty-five library books, mainly basic theology, canon law, grammar and logic, assigned the Norwich pressmark 'K'. It was also easy for resting monks to borrow books from the mother house library, and a fourteenth-century prior of Durham had to recall numerous volumes, 'especially of the decretals and the canons', which had been taken to Finchale without permission.[145]

However, despite this careful supervision and the provision of facilities for constructive leisure time, the rest-house was perhaps inevitably prone to a laxness in standards. The severity of Abbot Whethamstede's 1439 ordinances for Redbourn suggests an inappropriate degree of relaxation was being enjoyed there. Whethamstede had already been moved to legislate against late-night gatherings at Redbourn and similar drinking parties were reported at Oxney in 1437.[146] Both Abbots Wallingford and Whethamstede were also concerned about the introduction of suspicious persons into Redbourn, as well as their brethren's forays out of the cell. The holidaying monks did not spend all their spare time in study, and the inhabitants of both Finchale and Redbourn had to be warned against hunting and keeping dogs.[147] Occasional complaints were also made about excessive comfort in rest-houses, such as against the monks of Finchale who were wearing linen instead of linsey-woolsey in 1453; and payments to minstrels and actors regularly appear in the accounts of St Leonard's Norwich.[148] But it would be wrong to portray life in a monastic rest-house as always unacceptably luxuri-

---

[144] GASA, I, p. 294, II, p. 399; *Registra*, I, Appendix D, p. 458. The *Sanctilogium* of John the Englishman was given to Redbourn by Abbot de la Mare and that of Guido de Castris, abbot of St Denis, by Abbot Whethamstede: BL, Cotton MS Tib. E.i, Royal MS 5 F.x. For a discussion of books and learning at ordinary cells, see below, pp. 181–2.

[145] J. T. Fowler (ed.), 'Inventory of the Vestments, Books, etc. of the Priory of Finchale, AD 1481', *Transactions of the Architectural and Archaeological Society of Durham and Northumberland*, iv (1896), pp. 134–47; DCM, Finchale Repertory, fols 2r–3r; Sharpe, *Shorter Catalogues*, B62–3, pp. 312–21; BL, Cotton MS Faust. A.vi, fols 15v–16r.

[146] *Amundesham*, I, pp. 113–14; *Lincoln Visitations, 1420–1449*, III, pp. 273, 276.

[147] GASA, II, pp. 203–4; BL, Cotton MS Faust. A.vi. fol. 9r.

[148] VCH, *Durham*, II, p. 104; NRO, DCN 2/3. The Durham monks holidaying at Finchale also enjoyed their own chamber in the splendid domesticated range of the cell's prior, although the 1408 ordinance specified that they sleep in the dormitory with the other four monks at the priory: Peers, 'Finchale Priory', pp. 193–220; Raine, *Priory of Finchale*, no. 32, pp. 30–1.

ous. In c.1357, William of Goldsborough, prior of Finchale, reported that that house had been 'roofless' for forty years. Even more serious hardship was found at Redbourn by Abbot de la Mare. Such was the cell's poverty that its monks had been forced to beg, whereas the food sent to Redbourn from St Albans, in accordance with Abbot Wallingford's constitutions, was cold on arrival and their supplies of fuel were inadequate. The monks of Oxney were not receiving sufficient ale in 1518, and the slender income of St Leonard's Norwich cannot have permitted too many delights.[149] But despite these diffi-culties, rest-houses served a useful purpose in providing a much more fitting setting for monastic leisure than the manor houses employed by most large abbeys.

Later Acquisitions and Suppressions of Cells

That there could be definite advantages arising from the ownership of cells is also shown by the eagerness of a number of monasteries to acquire new daughter houses in the later middle ages.[150] The occasional dependency was established after 1250 by mother houses, such as the priories of Oxney (Peterborough), Modney (Ramsey) and Snaith (Selby). In an exchange of property with the French abbey of Troarn in 1262, Bruton Priory received the priory of Horsley which it continued to serve, somewhat reluctantly, as a daughter house. More unusual was the foundation of a new dependency of Hexham Priory at Ovingham by Gilbert III de Umfraville and Henry Percy, ninth earl of Northumberland in 1378. In return for the grant of the churches of Ovingham and Ilkley, Hexham was required to find three canons 'to celebrate divine services daily in the church of Ovingham for the good estate of the king, the said Gilbert and Henry during their lives, and for their souls after death, and the souls of the late king and his progenitors, and of the ancestors of the said Gilbert and Henry and others'.[151]

Although very few mother houses could hope to acquire a new foundation in this way, from the mid-fifteenth century there arose the occasional oppor-tunity to appropriate pre-existing houses as cells. Between 1449 and 1533, nine previously independent houses were converted into Benedictine or Augustinian dependencies owing to their financial collapse, whereas four former alien priories were granted to English abbeys as cells.[152] In December 1449, Ely Cathedral Priory appropriated the struggling priories of Molycourt and Spinney as satellites and in April 1466 Evesham similarly acquired

---

149 DCM, 1.9 Pont. 1b; GASA, II, pp. 397–8; *Lincoln Visitations, 1517–1531*, III, p. 80; NRO, DCN 2/3.
150 For cells founded after c.1250, see Appendix Two.
151 *History of Northumberland*, XII, pp. 51–4; CPR, *1377–1381*, p. 218.
152 See Appendix Two. For a fuller discussion of the acquisition and suppression of cells in late medieval England, see my 'Dependent Priories and the Closure of Monasteries in Late Medieval England, 1400–1535', *EHR*, cxix (2004), pp. 1–26.

Alcester Abbey, also said to be in financial ruin. Between 1460 and 1481, the indigent Augustinian priories of Chetwode, Wormegay, Great Massingham and Llanthony Prima were also converted into cells of neigh-bouring houses; and two further priories of that order, Flitcham and Stavordale, became dependent on Walsingham and Taunton respectively shortly before the Dissolution.[153] Similarly, in the early 1440s, St Albans was given the suppressed alien priory of Pembroke by Humphrey, duke of Glou-cester and Tewkesbury Abbey received Goldcliff Priory, formerly a depend-ency of Bec. Goldcliff was transferred to Eton College by Henry VI in 1451, but restored to Tewkesbury in 1462 by Edward IV; however, this grant too was reversed five years later, with Tewkesbury receiving Deerhurst Priory in return. Finally, Tavistock was given Cowick Priory, another cell of Bec that had been granted to Eton, by Edward IV in 1462.[154]

Several of these new cells had substantial endowments and were conse-quently very welcome acquisitions. The financial distress of Spinney, Alcester and Llanthony Prima must have been temporary since they were valued at £55, £102 and £112 respectively in the 1530s, whereas Cowick, Deerhurst and Pembroke were all worth over £100 in the late fifteenth- and early sixteenth-centuries.[155] Surviving accounts from Cowick and Pembroke show that Tavistock and St Albans were able to draw considerable sums from these dependencies – about £10–£20 a year from Cowick and an annual pension of £40 from Pembroke – and Tavistock was even able to increase the size of its own community after 1495 with Cowick money. It is unsurprising, therefore, that both mother houses were prepared to endure prolonged and expensive legal cases to defend their new daughter houses from alternative claimants.[156] Bruton and Taunton Priories, however, seem to have been

---

153 NRO, Reg/6/11, fols 278v–280r; Worcestershire Record Office, b.716.093–BA.2648/6(ii), fols 198v–203v; Lincolnshire Archives Office, Lincoln Episcopal Registers, Reg. XX, fols 75v–76r; NRO, Reg/6/11, fols 293r–294r, Reg/6/12, fols 221r–222r; CPR, 1476–1485, p. 284; L&P, IV(ii), no. 5219, p. 2254; VCH, Somerset, II, pp. 140–1.

154 Registra, I, pp. 41–50; CPR, 1441–1446, p. 29, 1446–1452, p. 457, 1461–1467, p. 93, 1467–1477, pp. 62, 66–7.

155 PRO, SC6/HenVIII/7288, mem. 47; Valor, III, p. 88, II, p. 431; Devon Record Office, W1258M/G4/53/1–5; Valor, II, p. 484; PRO, E315/272, fols 78r–78v.

156 DRO, W1258M/G4/53/1–5; PRO, E315/272, fols 78r–78v; DRO, W1258M/D32/26. St Albans overcame attempts to resume Pembroke by Jasper, earl of Pembroke in 1453 and by Edward IV in 1461: Registra, I, pp. 92–4, 415–18; and a lengthy legal battle was fought between Eton and Tavistock over Cowick. The priory was granted ineffectually to Eton in 1467 and the abbey's possession of Cowick was still fragile enough for Abbot Dynyngton to send Edward IV a document pleading for its retention some time between 1478 and 1483: CPR, 1467–1477, p. 63; DRO, W1258M/D82/32. A similar dispute between Eton and Tewkesbury over Deerhurst continued into the mid-1490s, when the former party was still seeking redress in the courts: Eton College Records, Coll/Est/Go.71, Coll/Est/Tay.6.

excessively eager to profit from the priories of Horsley and Stavordale and attracted complaints that they were dilapidating their cells.[157]

But if there were considerable practical advantages in the acquisition of some of these dependencies, impoverished cells, such as Molycourt and Wormegay, can have brought few such benefits. Moreover, mere pragmatism cannot explain the tenacity with which mother houses preserved even their poorest satellites throughout the medieval period. Several daughter houses were suppressed in the twelfth and thirteenth centuries, but after 1300 the closure of cells became rare.[158] A number of shadowy priories, like Coquet Island, Ratlinghope and Trokenholt, might have been suppressed in the later middle ages, but only a handful of fully established dependencies were definitely dissolved in the fourteenth and fifteenth centuries. Several of these houses, like Durham's Coldingham in Scotland and Little Malvern's Irish cell at Castleknock, were situated in enemy territory and therefore proved unsustainable. The location of Gloucester's Marcher cells of Ewyas Harold (1359) and Kilpeck (1428) was also said to have been responsible for their termination, whereas the demise of Cardiff has traditionally been attributed to a raid by Owen Glendower in 1403.[159] Similarly, Rocester Abbey's closure of its cell at Halywell was sanctioned in December 1325 on account of its situation 'in a solitary dangerous spot on the highway of Watling Street, frequented by robbers who rob the canons dwelling there and others passing along that street'.[160]

In fact, only three cells in peaceful surroundings were unquestionably dissolved in this period, namely the priories of Horsley (Bruton) and Cockerham (Leicester) in the late fourteenth century, and St Albans' satellite of Beadlow in 1428.[161] The canons of Bruton never seem to have been satisfied with their obligation to maintain two of their inmates at Horsley, no doubt because the property they had held before the exchange with Troarn had carried no such commitment. Following considerable disciplin-

---

157 *Reg. Giffard*, II, p. 216; *Three Chapters of Letters relating to the Suppression of Monasteries*, ed. T. Wright, Camden Society, old series, xxvi (1843), p. 51.

158 See Appendix Five.

159 R. B. Dobson, 'The Last English Monks on Scottish Soil: Coldingham Priory 1461–1478', *Scottish Historical Review*, xlvi (1967), pp. 1–25; A. Gwynn and R. N. Hadcock (eds), *Medieval Religious Houses: Ireland* (London, 1970), p. 105; *Mon. Ang.*, III, pp. 629–30, no. 3; *Registrum Thome Spofford, Episcopi Herefordensis AD 1422–1448*, ed. A. T. Bannister, C&Y Soc., xxiii (1919), pp. 104–6; G. Williams, 'The Church in Glamorgan from the Fourteenth Century to the Reformation', in *Glamorgan County History, III, The Middle Ages*, ed. T. B. Pugh (Cardiff, 1971), p. 149. The Irish cells of Glastonbury at Kilcommon (c.1332) and St Nicholas' Exeter at Begerin (1400) were also dissolved in the later middle ages: Gwynn and Hadcock, pp. 104, 107.

160 *CPR, 1324–1327*, p. 202.

161 The priory of Bentley may also have been discontinued by St Gregory's Canterbury in the early sixteenth century, since it was recorded as having been empty for two years in 1512 and was leased out in 1532: *VCH, Middlesex*, IV, p. 206n.

ary and financial problems at the cell during the rule of Prior William Cary, Bruton obtained permission from the Crown, as patron, to suppress the cell in the early 1370s, which seems to have been accomplished in 1380.[162] Leicester Abbey had attempted to close their cell at Cockerham in the 1360s, on the apparently accurate grounds that the donor of that manor, William of Lancaster, had not required the presence of any religious on the site. Nevertheless, there were still two canons at the house in 1381, and only in January 1400 did Leicester obtain the consent of the lady of the manor, the countess of Oxford, to withdraw its religious from Cockerham. It should also be noted that a solitary canon was maintained at the site until 1477, perhaps for convenience but perhaps also out of reluctance to abandon the site altogether.[163] Neither was the closure of Beadlow a straightforward operation. Not only did the suppression provoke opposition from within the abbey, but the inhabitants of the vill are said to have considered it to be 'a perverse and impious deed, tending directly to the extinction of devotion'.[164]

The paucity of such examples of early suppression implies a strong commitment among the mother houses of late medieval England to ensure the preservation of even the smallest of their dependencies. It is striking that so few monasteries opted to close down tiny cells, even though it would undoubtedly have been in their financial interests to do so, and even though many houses, like Leicester, were not bound by lay founders to maintain any religious presence at their satellites.[165] How can this attitude be explained? A monastery naturally felt bound to defend its endowment, which was considered to be the patrimony of its patron saint. Equally, the well-being of

---

162 *Two Cartularies of the Augustinian Priory of Bruton and the Cluniac Priory of Montacute in the Co. of Somerset*, ed. T. S. Holmes et al., Somerset Record Society, viii (1894), no. 369, p. 97; HRH, II, pp. 170–1; *A Calendar of the Register of Henry Wakefield, Bishop of Worcester 1375–1395*, ed. W. P. Marett, Worcestershire Historical Society, new series, vii (1972), no. 848, p. 162.

163 VCH, *Lancashire*, II, pp. 152–3; CClR, *1364–1368*, pp. 222–3; F. P. Mackie, 'The Clerical Population of the Province of York: An Edition of the Clerical Poll Tax Enrolments 1377–81', 2 vols, unpublished York D.Phil. thesis (1998), II, p. 52; CPR, *1399–1401*, p. 197. A similar withdrawal may well have occurred from the Tavistock cell of Scilly after the mid-fifteenth century, probably because of the insecurity of the location. Nevertheless, a single monk was apparently maintained at Scilly down to the Dissolution, again perhaps for historical reasons: *Reg. Morton*, II, no. 292, pp. 81–2; *The Itinerary of John Leland*, ed. L. Toulmin Smith, 5 vols (London, 1907–10), I, p. 318. I am very grateful to Professor Nicholas Orme for sharing his findings about the priory of Scilly with me.

164 *Amundesham*, I, pp. 29–30, 43, II, pp. 106–7. The Beadlow endowment was supposedly used for the abbey's students, but in fact most of it was diverted to Abbot Whethamstede's new office, the master of the works, to finance the upkeep of the abbey's buildings and his own anniversary: ibid., I, pp. 279–86; BL, Arundel MS 34, fols 60r–65r.

165 See above, pp. 30–4, and particularly the case of Lincoln Priory where it was demonstrated under legal challenge that St Mary's York had no obligation to maintain a small community of monks there.

benefactors' souls was understood to be dependent on the prayers supported by their gift. However, neither of these considerations would necessarily require a monastery to maintain a daughter house. The recall of their monks would not diminish the mother house's overall endowment, whereas the prayers owed to the cell's founder could be transferred, with his consent, to another institution.

Yet it is also inadequate to attribute this reluctance to dissolve daughter houses simply to a reactionary temperament. Instead it seems to have been the product of a widely held ideology that traditionally monastic sites should not be abandoned wherever possible. This ideology can also be seen in the conversion of financially collapsed houses and alien priories into cells of English monasteries in order to prevent their dissolution in the mid-fifteenth century.[166] It was Abbot John Dynyngton of Tavistock who articulated this conservative attitude most clearly in a petition to the king of 1478×1483, in favour of Cowick Priory remaining in Tavistock's possession and not being returned to Eton.[167] Dynyngton argued that 'yt myght not stonde with goddis lawe nor mannys lawe ne by gode Reason the said pryory to be commyttid to seculer use *butte oonly to be occupied and servid with Religiouse men yf eny coude be founde*' (my italics). In other words, not only should traditionally monastic property remain in the hands of monks in perpetuity, but some physical monastic presence at a traditionally cenobitic site should also be maintained if at all possible.

This was essentially the same belief that had engendered the foundation of several cells in the twelfth century, including Cranborne, Horton and Holy Island.[168] In theory, the withdrawal of monks from their cells could have been accomplished by many mother houses with little difficulty. Not only did many daughter houses have no lay patrons, but a large number of those who did seem to have had little contact them in the later middle ages.[169] It seems likely that many patrons, if pressed, would have accepted the suppression of a cell, in return for prayers at the mother house and some compensation, as did the distant 'founders' of Ewyas Harold, Kilpeck and Beadlow. But despite the lack of obstacles, such a move was apparently not even contemplated by most monasteries. Mother houses valued their daughters, above all, for their occupation of traditionally monastic sites. The locations of some priories, such as the Durham cells of Farne and Holy Islands,

---

[166] See Heale, 'Dependent Priories'. As well as the examples given above, the previously independent priories of Dodford and Guyzance were also made cells of the Premonstratensian abbeys of Halesowen and Alnwick in the fifteenth century.

[167] Devon Record Office, W1258/D82/32. Dr Chibnall dated this document to either before 1462 or shortly after Edward IV's ineffectual restitution to Eton in 1467: Morgan, *Bec*, p. 135n. However, the abbot of Tavistock refers to the ratification of Cowick's appropriation to his abbey by Sixtus IV, which was made in June 1478: DRO, W1258M/D82/25.

[168] See above, pp. 30–1, 33.

[169] See below, pp. 196–200.

were associated with saints and were thus considered especially important. But a history of monastic occupation was sufficient to mark out a site as special and requiring a continued presence. To this extent, a balance sheet of the practical advantages and disadvantages of the ownership of daughter houses – even including the threat of indiscipline and backsliding at their cells – would have seemed of little relevance to their parents. The perpetual maintenance of their dependencies was simply a religious duty and one that could not be lightly disregarded.

PART II

The Dependent Priory as Small Monastery

4

Monastic Life in Dependent Priories

Small Monasteries and Dependent Priories

In the conclusion to the second volume of his *Religious Orders in England*, Professor Knowles lamented that monastic history had inevitably to be drawn largely from the affairs of a small number of great houses. Although remarking that 'it is natural . . . to desire some knowledge of the life and social relations of a smaller house', he concluded that 'the inner life and personal activities of such places must almost always elude observation'.[1] Since nearly two-thirds of the monasteries of late medieval England enjoyed an annual income of under £200 and therefore came under the government's definition of a 'lesser monastery' in 1536, the extent of our ignorance about monastic life is obvious. Studies of particular orders, such as Professor Sir Howard Colvin's account of the Premonstratensians and the work of Dr J. C. Dickinson and Dr David Robinson on the Augustinian canons, have added significantly to our understanding of the smaller religious house.[2] Important advances in the field have come more recently from archaeology, with a growing number of small and medium-sized houses being excavated in unprecedented detail, and from the study of nunneries.[3] The work of

---

[1] Knowles, *RO*, II, p. 363.
[2] H. M. Colvin, *The White Canons in England* (Oxford, 1951); J. C. Dickinson, *The Origins of the Austin Canons and their Introduction into England* (London, 1950), as well as several articles; D. M. Robinson, *The Geography of Augustinian Settlement in Medieval England and Wales*, British Archaeological Reports, British Series, LXXX (1980).
[3] In particular, see J. P. Greene, *Norton Priory* (Cambridge, 1989); S. M. Hirst and S. M. Wright, 'Bordesley Abbey Church: A Long-Term Research Excavation', in *The Archaeology of Rural Monasteries*, ed. R. Gilchrist and H. Mytum, British Archaeological Reports, British Series, CCIII (1989), pp. 295–311; M. A. Hodder, 'Excavations at Sandwell Priory and Hall 1982–8', *South Staffordshire Archaeological and Historical Society Transactions*, xxxi (1991). Female monasticism is currently enjoying a historiographical boom. Recent studies of note for the later middle ages include J. H. Tillotson, *Marrick Priory: A Nunnery in Late Medieval Yorkshire*, Borthwick Paper, no. LXXV (1989); R. Gilchrist, *Gender and Material Culture. The Archaeology of Religious Women* (London, 1994); R. Gilchrist, *Contemplation and Action. The Other Monasticism* (London, 1995), pp. 106–56; M. Oliva, *The Convent*

Professor Roberta Gilchrist and Dr Marilyn Oliva, in particular, has revealed a great deal about the internal affairs of small nunneries, although it has also raised questions about whether conclusions reached for female monasteries can be applied to male houses of a similar size. However, it remains true that we cannot study the history of the vast majority of small monasteries in any great detail. In most cases, a fragmentary picture constructed from government records or bishops' registers, perhaps supplemented by a cartulary, is the best that can be accomplished. Historians must therefore rely largely on visitation records, legal documents and pleas of poverty; and the extremely negative picture of small monasteries found in many studies – ill-disciplined, isolated and impoverished houses, deservedly dissolved in 1536–7 – has proceeded naturally from such source material. It is only when much fuller evidence survives, either material or documentary, that this stereotype can be tested and challenged.

The survival of substantial quantities of evidence relating to English dependencies in the archives of their mother houses therefore presents a rare opportunity to study the history of a group of small monasteries in considerable detail. This material, which comes largely from the Benedictine cells, allows a much fuller examination of the everyday affairs of the monks, their relations with their secular neighbours and their economic fortunes than would be possible even for most medium-sized houses. It also raises the intriguing possibility that something may be learned about small monasteries in general from the experience of these dependencies. Historians have never before considered approaching daughter houses in this way, since they have usually regarded cells as administrative tools rather than genuine monasteries. However, as we have seen, the majority of English dependencies were founded for religious reasons and as a result they were organised in much the same way as small independent houses.

Nevertheless, we cannot apply conclusions formed for cells to other lesser monasteries without exercising considerable caution. In some respects, dependencies were clearly exceptional. Many cells housed only two or three monks and were therefore significantly smaller than most of the smallest autonomous priories, which tended to maintain communities of six to twelve monks. On the other hand, their personnel were probably of a higher calibre than many autonomous priories could have mustered, a factor that would have greatly affected their quality of religious life and financial management. Satellite priories benefited too from access to the facilities and social networks of their mother houses and were often closely regulated by their parents. There is therefore reason to believe that dependencies might have

and the Community in Late Medieval England. Female Monasteries in the Diocese of Norwich, 1350–1540 (Woodbridge, 1998); N. B. Warren, *Spiritual Economies. Female Monasticism in Later Medieval England* (Philadelphia, 2001); P. Lee, *Nunneries, Learning and Spirituality in Late Medieval English Society. The Dominican Priory of Dartford* (York, 2001).

fared rather better than small independent houses in some respects. But in other ways, the fortunes and characteristics of cells were probably determined more by their size than by their dependent status. Patterns of everyday life and the liturgical and administrative activities of the monks; the layout of their priories and the buildings in which they resided and worshipped; the services they provided for their neighbours; their interaction with lay religion; the ways in which they responded to economic difficulties, and their success in doing so; in all these areas and others the experience of dependent priories was probably not dissimilar to that of many independent small monasteries. The extent to which the evidence for cells can be considered representative will perhaps become clear only when more work has been done on the lesser religious houses of medieval England. At the very least, a detailed study of dependent priories cannot fail to pose questions and suggest future lines of enquiry for the study of the mass of small priories about which we know so little.

Numbers

A significant amount can be learned about the activities, the standard of living and the surroundings of those monks sent to dwell for a time in daughter houses. This information is of some interest not only for what it can tell us about monastic life in at least one category of small monastery, but also because very many Benedictine monks, and a good number of Augustinian canons, would have faced a stint in a cell at some time in their careers. Their pattern of life away from the mother house and their reaction to this change of circumstances is therefore an important, if neglected, facet of 'the monastic experience'. We have seen that the majority of stays in dependencies were relatively short and that some cells were earmarked as places of relaxation.[4] Another critical determinant of the conditions of life in a daughter house was the number of monks dwelling therein. The persistent legislation against the sending of solitary monks to man cells seems to have taken effect and only a few examples of inmates living alone in satellites are known after the twelfth century.[5] But whether there was a small community of five or six religious or just a remnant of two or three must have made a marked difference to the character of life in a satellite priory. Statistics for the number of monks at cells are not always easy to find, although few houses are entirely devoid of evidence: this information is laid out in Appendix Three. For a small number of cells, however, it is possible to trace in outline fluctuations in numbers over the middle ages.

Figure 4.1 shows the changes in the size of the monastic community in the twelve cells for which reasonably certain figures are known from at least

4   See above, pp. 115–24, 144–50.
5   See above, pp. 27–8, and Appendix Three.

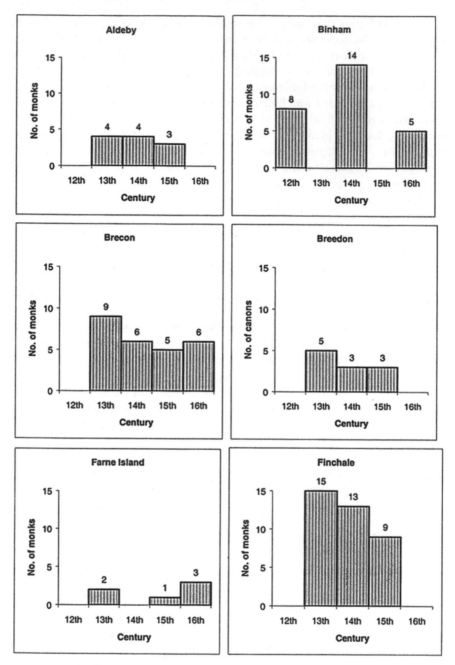

Figure 4.1: Numbers of Religious in English Cells

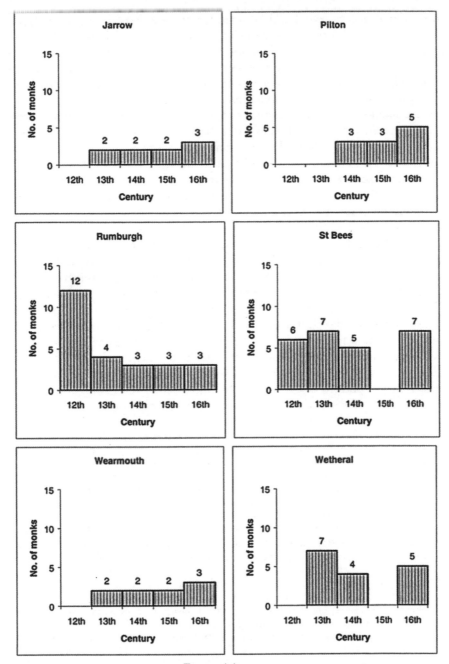

Figure 4.1: *cont.*

three different centuries. It will be seen that the numbers at some priories fell over time, whereas others remained relatively stable. Although a few cells held over six inmates in earlier times, by the late fourteenth century a community of this size was rare. The surviving evidence, though uncertain in many places, suggests that a significant number of dependencies – perhaps as many as a dozen – declined from semi-conventual establishments of eight or twelve monks to small communities of six or under in the later middle ages, as at Brecon, Binham and Rumburgh. In some cases convents diminished long before the Black Death, but the permanent contraction of mother-house communities caused by this demographic cataclysm perpetuated and exacerbated the trend.[6] Nevertheless, it is important not to overemphasise this fall in numbers: the majority of cells were founded as tiny communities and managed to live up to their low numerical standards throughout the middle ages. In a few cases, as at the small Durham cells and Pilton, numbers even rose in the sixteenth century. Some benefactors granted property to cells on the condition that extra monks would be added to their communities. The priories of Belvoir and Hertford (twelfth century), Finchale (thirteenth century), Hoxne (early fourteenth century) and Wallingford (1445) were all enlarged following such grants, Finchale from about eight monks to fifteen.[7] On several occasions, the ecclesiastical authorities tried to reverse numerical decline by ordering the mother house to restore the customary number of inmates to a priory, and in 1366 Edward III complained that only four monks were staying in Wetheral Priory, of which he was patron, when there should have been twelve;[8] but criticisms of this kind apparently made little impression on mother houses.

[6] It is only for the priory of Felixstowe that there survives reasonably good evidence to suggest that the Black Death was primarily responsible for the change from conventual priory to small cell. In 1307, we hear of a prior and thirteen monks at this house, but a community of only three was recorded in the poll tax returns of 1381 and there had probably been only a few monks when the priory was relocated in the 1360s: see below, p. 188; *Calendar of Inquisitions Post Mortem* (HMSO, 1904–), IV, p. 534; J. C. Russell, 'The Clerical Population of Medieval England', *Traditio*, ii (1944), p. 189n.

[7] J. Nichols, *The History and Antiquities of the County of Leicester*, 4 vols (London, 1795–1811), II(i), Appendix II, pp. 4–5; *Mon. Ang.*, III, pp. 299–300, nos 1–2; Raine, *Priory of Finchale*, nos 112–13, 160, pp. 103–4, 148–9; NRO, DCN 40/9, fol. 9v; *CPR, 1441–1446*, p. 362.

[8] Such complaints were made against several of the Durham cells in the fourteenth century and the priories of Ewenny (1284), Leominster (1286), Bromfield (late C13), Brecon (1401) and Freiston (1434 and 1440): *Registrum Epistolarum fratris Johannis Peckham, Archiepiscopi Cantuariensis*, ed. C. T. Martin, 3 vols, RS, lxxvii (1882–5), III, no. 582, pp. 798–800; *Registrum Ricardi de Swinfield, Episcopi Herefordensis, AD 1283–1317*, ed. W. W. Capes, C&Y Soc., vi (1909), pp. 108–11; *Registrum Johannis de Trillek, Episcopi Herefordensis, AD 1344–1361*, ed. J. H. Parry, C&Y Soc., viii (1912), p. 287; *The Episcopal Registers of the Diocese of St Davids, 1397 to 1518*, ed. R. F. Isaacson, 3 vols, Cymmrodorion Record Series, vi (1917–20), I, pp. 230–7; *Visitations of the Religious Houses in the Diocese of Lincoln, 1420–1449*, ed. A. H. Thompson, 3 vols, Lincoln Record Society, vii, xiv, xxi (1914–29), I, pp. 38–9, II, pp. 54–60; *CPR, 1364–1367*, pp. 359–60.

Whether the withdrawal of monks from daughter houses was prompted by financial difficulties or by the inability of the parent abbey to spare monks for service in its cells is difficult to say. In some cases, economic factors must have been important.[9] Nevertheless, the numerical evidence for satellite priories indicates that they consistently housed considerably fewer inmates than independent monasteries of similar means. Dr Robinson's statistics for the Austin canons shows that the majority of autonomous Augustinian communities with annual incomes of between £50 and £150 (the typical income bracket for English cells) generally numbered six to twelve inmates in the later middle ages, although the poorest priories were sometimes smaller; and lesser Premonstratensian houses were equally populous.[10] Indigent nunneries often held even larger convents. All eleven East Anglian nunneries maintained at least eight religious, even though nine had incomes of under £70 per year. Professor Gilchrist, meanwhile, has calculated that over half of all Benedictine nunneries received yearly revenues of under £5 per nun.[11] In contrast, several English cells, including Lynn, Yarmouth and Wallingford, housed only three or four monks in the later middle ages, while enjoying incomes of over £100 per year, or more than £30 per monk.

It may be, therefore, that the dwindling size of parent abbey communities often played an important part in the decline in their cells' populations. But it is difficult to escape the conclusion that mother houses sometimes allowed numbers in their cells to fall to ensure that they would not become a drain on abbey finances.[12] At the same time, there was concern that daughter houses should not become too small, and in 1513 Durham took the unusual step of assigning the revenues from eight salt-workings to Jarrow Priory in order to finance an extra monk to be maintained there and at Durham's other impecunious dependencies of Farne Island and Wearmouth.[13] Nevertheless, numbers in the wealthier cells continued to fall. By the later middle ages, the most significant numerical distinction among dependencies was between those houses with two or three brethren (always the majority) and those with four or five. By the time of the Dissolution, although Freiston, Finchale, Hurley, Leominster, St Bees and St Ives Priories might still have done, only the semi-independent cells of Colne, Dover, Great Malvern and Tynemouth definitely housed more than six inmates.

9 See below, p. 275.
10 Robinson, *Geography of Augustinian Settlement*, Appendix 20, pp. 399–403; J. A. Gribbin, *The Premonstratensian Order in Late Medieval England* (Woodbridge, 2001), pp. 54, 82.
11 Oliva, *Convent and Community*, p. 41; Gilchrist, *Gender and Material Culture*, p. 43. See also C. Cross, 'Yorkshire Nunneries in the Early Tudor Period', in *The Religious Orders in Pre-Reformation England*, ed. J. G. Clark (Woodbridge, 2002), pp. 145–54.
12 See above, p. 137, for the reluctance of mother houses to subsidise their cells.
13 Piper, *Jarrow*, p. 9.

In Transit

Therefore, by the fifteenth century, monks posted even to a wealthier daughter house would have had to adjust to life in a very small community. Those sent to a dependency carried a letter from their abbot or prior instructing the head of the cell to receive the new arrival with charity.[14] The monks also brought their own bedding and clothing, and the transportation of other belongings seems to have been common too. In a visitation in 1308, Bishop Salmon of Norwich enjoined that 'the clothes, books and other property of the monks destined for cells shall be decently and in a seemly manner transferred by road', in sacks provided by the daughter-house priors. Similarly, at St Albans in 1269, it was ordained that when any monk was sent 'from this monastery to any cell, or from a cell to the monastery, or from cell to cell, there should be transferred with him two frocks, namely one new and the other used, but whole and not damaged, and two new cowls and one used'.[15] At fifteenth-century Rumburgh, meanwhile, it was customary for new arrivals to receive a pair of shoes.[16] The travel expenses of inmates going to and from cells were sometimes met by the mother house and sometimes by the satellite. At Norwich, it was the priors of the cells who were responsible for all these costs and regular payments for 'the carriage of fellow monks' appear in their accounts. At Durham, the burden fell on whoever currently housed the monk to be transferred and this was probably the most common procedure.[17]

For those cells situated a considerable distance from their mother house, the monks' travel arrangements required some attention. Occasional complaints can be found about the inadequate provision made for brethren journeying to and from dependent priories. In c.1370 Bishop Hatfield was informed during a visitation of Durham that 'claustral monks and especially the young who are sent to cells do not receive sufficient funds for them and the men and horses going with them and to return to the house', and similar complaints had been made against Prior Fossor in the 1350s.[18] Concerns of this kind were expressed elsewhere and the fifteenth-century priors of Brecon were required to swear on taking office that they would provide 'an

---

[14] Several such letters survive in the private registers of the priors of Durham: Dobson, *Durham Priory*, p. 302.

[15] E. H. Carter (ed.), *Studies in Norwich Cathedral History* (Norwich, 1935), p. 23; Cambridge, Trinity College, MS O.9.25, fol. 13r. For examples of the transportation of priors' books to and from dependencies, see below, pp. 181–2.

[16] SROI, HD 1538/335/1, no. 11.

[17] The Norwich custom is described in an internal chapter ordinance of 1379: C. R. Cheney, 'Norwich Cathedral Priory in the Fourteenth Century', *Bulletin of the John Rylands Library*, xx (1936), p. 119; e.g. J. Raine, *The History and Antiquities of North Durham* (London, 1852), p. 79; Raine, *Priory of Finchale*, nos 35–7, pp. 32–3.

[18] DCM, 2.8 Pont. 12, 1.9 Pont. 1a.

adequate mount' for monks travelling to Battle.[19] Even when sufficient measures were taken, long journeys could still prove troublesome as one thirteenth-century monk of St Albans travelling to Tynemouth who managed to
lose his horse en route discovered, leaving him stranded, 'placed in incredi-
ble disgrace and reduced to great ignominy'.[20]

A little surprisingly, however, travel to those cells situated in the vicinity
of their parent abbeys seems also to have caused considerable difficulty. In
1319, Prior Burdon of Durham and the prior of Finchale were criticised for
not providing transport for brethren travelling to and from the nearby cell,
and only a decade or so later Durham monks were again journeying to
Finchale on foot because there were insufficient horses in the mother house
to carry them and their possessions.[21] Similar problems faced the monks of
fifteenth-century Ramsey destined for the priory of St Ives. In 1432, Bishop
Gray of Lincoln ordered that the Ramsey obedientiaries should supply
'seemly horses and riding gear and servants as befits the honesty of the monastery' for monks travelling the ten miles to St Ives and elsewhere. But seven
years later Bishop Alnwick found that horses were still not being provided
for this purpose, and as a result of this neglect there were sometimes no
monks at the cell other than the prior, cellarer and sacrist.[22] At least as prevalent among mother houses as this insouciance, though, was concern that
their brethren should not attract adverse attention in transit, and Abbot
Whethamstede went so far as to instruct Redbourn monks returning to St
Albans that 'they should turn aside as much as possible from the *via regia* and
make their journey by private paths, where they believe fewer strangers will
be met'.[23] The Benedictine general chapter also legislated in 1444 for the
conduct of monks journeying to and from cells, requiring that each carry a
portiforium so that they could say the necessary services en route.[24]

The Lifestyle of the Priors

What lifestyle would a new arrival have encountered in a cell? Very little is
known about everyday life in small monasteries, although historians have
tended to assume that it was characterised by poverty, indiscipline and
boredom. Any discussion of monastic life in dependencies must of course
distinguish between the experience of priors and that of ordinary choir

19 *Cartularium Prioratus S. Johannis Evangeliste de Brecon*, ed. R. W. Banks, *Archaeologia
    Cambrensis*, 4th series, xiii–xiv (1882–3), xiv, p. 302.
20 R. Hill, *Ecclesiastical Letter-Books of the Thirteenth Century* (privately printed, no date),
    pp. 56–7.
21 DCM, 2.9 Pont. 2, Misc. Ch. 2645.
22 *Lincoln Visitations, 1420–1449*, I, pp. 103–7, III, pp. 302–19.
23 *Amundesham*, I, p. 114.
24 CBM, II, pp. 207–8. A '*portiforium pro equitant''* is included in the fifteenth-century
    inventory of Yarmouth Priory: Sharpe, *Shorter Catalogues*, B64, p. 325.

monks. Despite the limitations imposed on many priors' financial management, the head of a cell usually controlled most of his house's day-to-day
affairs;[25] and as the abbot's deputy, he exercised authority over the monks
under his charge. However, it appears that this authority sometimes needed
bolstering by the head of the mother house. The abbots of Battle, St Albans
and St Mary's York, and quite probably several others, considered it necessary to dispatch new priors with a letter ordering the monks of their daughter
house to obey them.[26] At St Albans, Abbot de Maryns (1302–9) also issued a
chapter ordinance laying down strict penalties for disobedience against the
heads of the abbey's cells, and demanding that serious offenders should seek
a pardon from the abbot himself.[27]

In order to lead their communities more effectively, de Maryns also
instructed the heads of St Albans' cells to be present in chapter and cloister
as much as possible 'to hear confessions and to instruct their brethren
actively and by example', an injunction very similar to that issued to the
prior of Holy Island in the mid-fourteenth century.[28] The priors of daughter
houses were also expected to be present in choir for divine service: in the
mid-fourteenth century, William of Lynn, prior of Hoxne, requested that he
be recalled from his office since he was too infirm to say masses or attend
matins; and the heads of several other cells were ordered to attend services
whenever possible or rebuked for failing to do so.[29] It is characteristic that,
while the cellarer of Freiston was partially exempted from choir service, the
prior of that cell was not. Although the prior of Breedon was given permission to take three years' study leave in 1418, in general absentee heads of
cells were not tolerated.[30]

Mother houses nevertheless recognised that priory business and other
duties would sometimes take heads of houses away from their communities.
Almost no information survives about the itineraries of daughter-house
priors and so we cannot calculate what proportion of their time they spent in
their cells. There is no evidence that priors of dependencies ever sojourned
at manors belonging to the cell, although some, like the priors of Yarmouth
and Lynn, had special chambers reserved for them in the mother house.[31]
Heads of cells were summoned to their abbeys for annual general chapters
and monastic elections, and surviving accounts show priors making

25 See above, pp. 83–94.
26 BL, Harley MS 3586, fol. 13v; CUL, MS Ee.IV.20, fols 100r, 282r; York Minster
   Library, M2/6a, fols 8r–8v.
27 GASA, II, pp. 96–7.
28 Ibid., II, p. 96; DCM, Loc. XXVII: 4.
29 NRO, DCN 40/10, fol. 38r; GASA, II, pp. 96, 428; Raine, North Durham, pp. 354–5n;
   Cowley, Monastic Order, pp. 108–9.
30 Lincoln Visitations, 1420–1449, II, pp. 56–7; The Register of Bishop Philip Repingdon, ed.
   M. Archer, 3 vols, Lincoln Record Society, lvii–lviii, lxxiv (1963–82), III, no. 499, p.
   271.
31 R. Gilyard-Beer, Abbeys, 2nd edn (London, 1976), p. 39.

occasional trips to their mother house on business or for its patronal festival.[32] Small but regular amounts spent on their priors' business appear in the surviving accounts for the Norwich cells and Rumburgh Priory. The prior of Wallingford incurred more substantial costs of several pounds per year in riding with his servants to St Albans, London and elsewhere in the 1480s, and their cell's affairs also took the heads of Hertford and Snape to the capital.[33] Court cases, the supervision of estates, meetings with the ecclesiastical authorities and the purchasing of provisions all necessitated the absence of priors from their houses. At other times, heads of cells were required to attend the Benedictine chapter as proctors for their abbots, and occasionally even in their own right.[34]

There is even more evidence for the public role played by many priors. It seems that the heads of the larger dependencies were summoned to Convocation at regular intervals.[35] Furthermore, the priors of cells were commonly appointed commissioners by the Crown, the papacy and the episcopate, even though technically most should have been freed from all such duties as dative priors. Nearly 150 secular commissions to heads of Benedictine daughter houses and sixty-one ecclesiastical ones have been found in the printed public records and elsewhere, and no doubt many more were issued. Commissions to the heads of Augustinian cells were rather rarer, but the priors of Brooke and Blythburgh seem to have been regularly employed by the ecclesiastical authorities.[36] Over one hundred of the aforementioned secular commissions concerned the assessment and collection of the clerical tenth. Despite the claims for exemption from tax collection made by some

---

32 E.g. Oxford, Corpus Christi College, MS Z/2/1/1–2; NRO, DCN, 2/1–6.

33 NRO, DCN 2/1–6; SROI, HD 1538/335/1; PRO, SC6/HenVIII/3402, 1696.

34 Although the heads of independent monasteries only were normally called to the Benedictine chapter, the occasional prior of a cell was cited on account of his personal stature. John of Longney of St Guthlac's Hereford was appointed diffinitor in 1338 and preacher in 1340; Simon Southerey of Belvoir preached and was one of the electors for the following chapter's presidents in the 1390s; while John Dereham of Lynn took on the same roles in 1423. Dereham and the priors of Wallingford and St Ives were also appointed to the committee assembled to rebuff Henry V's reforming articles in 1421, after the heads of cells had exceptionally been called to that meeting of the chapter convened by the king: CBM, II, nos 150, 159, 164, 169, 171, pp. 9, 12, 93, 95, 106, 121–4, 152, 155.

35 E.g. L&P, IV(iii), no. 6047, pp. 2696–702; Registrum Roberti Mascall, Episcopi Herefordensis, AD 1404–1416, ed. J. H. Parry, C&Y Soc., xxi (1917), pp. 60–5; NRO, Reg/5/9, fols 98v–99r; The Register of Thomas Langton, Bishop of Salisbury 1485–93, ed. D. P. Wright, C&Y Soc., lxxiv (1985), no. 517, pp. 86–7.

36 E.g. Rotuli Roberti Grosseteste, Episcopi Lincolniensis, 1235–1253, ed. F. N. Davis, C&Y Soc., x (1913), p. 240; The Rolls and Register of Bishop Oliver Sutton 1280–1299, ed. R. M. T. Hill, 8 vols, Lincoln Record Society, xxxix, xliii, xlviii, lii, lx, lxiv, lxix, lxxvi (1948–86), V, p. 211; CPR, 1317–1321, p. 268; Blythburgh Priory Cartulary, ed. C. Harper-Bill, 2 parts, Suffolk Records Society, Suffolk Charters, II–III (1980–1), I, pp. 3–4.

priors, many cells were unable to escape this burden.[37] The priors of twenty-two dependencies are known to have been appointed tax collectors, including those of the tiny cells of Cardigan and Morville.

The heads of those houses situated in parts of the kingdom where larger monasteries were rare, such as the south-west, Wales and the Welsh marches, were in particular demand for this service. Among the leading monastic dignitaries of their localities, the priors of Brecon, Bromfield (Shropshire), St Nicholas' Exeter and St Guthlac's Hereford received regular commissions to collect royal taxes; and the prior of Brooke, as the only monastic superior in Rutland, was also regularly appointed. Many other superiors, especially those of the smaller cells, seem to have avoided this duty altogether, no doubt because they resembled mother-house obedientiaries more than priors. Tax collection proved an onerous task, with commissioners having to publish the grant, gather in the correct sums (though this might have been done by a deputy), issue receipts and arrange for the money to be transported to the exchequer.[38] Moreover, since the collectors were required to make up any arrears themselves they needed to discharge their duties with great thoroughness, and some priors found themselves out of pocket. Both St Guthlac's Hereford and Wymondham, the two cells most burdened by this public service, experienced severe financial problems at some time as a result.[39]

The other royal commissions issued to priors of dependencies varied greatly in their magnitude. The most laborious, though also the rarest, involved travel abroad in the king's service. Two priors of Hurley, in 1256 and 1347, took part in diplomatic missions overseas; although when Prior Dereham of Lynn was summoned to accompany Henry V to France in 1422, 'wyth gret hevynes . . . for he was a ful weyk man and a febyl of complexion', he was spared by the king's sudden death.[40] Several priors were required to help safeguard the peace or the defence of the realm, with for example the prior of Ewenny playing an important role in the loyalist resistance to Owen Glendower and the prior of Wetheral called to mobilise men to resist a possible invasion in 1525.[41] Other less dramatic commissions included the prevention of a tournament from taking place in 1252 (to the priors of St

---

[37] See above, p. 112. I have included tax collection in the secular statistics since this duty was performed for the Crown, even though the actual issuing of commissions was delegated to bishops.

[38] A. K. McHardy, 'Clerical Taxation in Fifteenth-Century England: the Clergy as Agents of the Crown', in *The Church, Politics and Patronage in the Fifteenth Century*, ed. R. B. Dobson (Gloucester, 1984), pp. 168–92. The numerous grants of exemption made to penurious houses in the later middle ages complicated the task of collection still further.

[39] *CPR, 1388–1392*, p. 403; see above, p. 81, for Wymondham.

[40] *CPR, 1247–1258*, pp. 459–60; E. H. Pearce, *The Monks of Westminster* (Cambridge, 1916), pp. 77–8; *The Book of Margery Kempe*, ed. L. Staley, Middle English Texts Series (Kalamazoo, 1996), p. 165.

[41] G. Williams, *The Welsh Church from Conquest to Reformation*, 2nd edn (Cardiff, 1976), p. 231; *L&P*, IV(i), p. 782.

Leonard's Stamford and Deeping St James) and the arrest of all men from Lübeck in Lynn in 1453 (to the prior of the cell there) after two royal ambassadors had been arrested in the German city.[42] Priors might also be called upon to preserve the Crown's financial interests, as in 1406 when the prior of Pilton was appointed a surveyor of the king's silver mines in Devon and the head of St James' Bristol was commissioned to investigate royal officers in that town and to borrow money for the king.[43] The other main category of secular commission involved the maintenance of the king's feudal rights, and priors of cells received oaths of fealty on the king's behalf or conducted inquisitions into the lands of the deceased.

The majority of these public duties, though inconvenient, would not have occupied monastic superiors for more than a few days at a time, and such appointments seem to have been rather less frequent than those for tax collection. The same can be said for ecclesiastical commissions. Many of these involved visiting religious houses and resolving disputes within the Church. A significant number of priors, particularly from the cells of St Albans, were appointed papal judges-delegate but less important appointments from Rome were more common.[44] These kinds of commissions, secular and ecclesiastical, seem to have been fairly evenly spread among the larger and medium-sized cells. Of the thirty-six houses whose priors are known to have been employed in this way, only about half a dozen were what could be called very small dependencies. Indeed, the majority of the heads of the smallest and poorest cells seem hardly to have been troubled by public duties at all, and it may be significant that when Thomas Flete was given the headship of Westminster's tiny offshoot of St Bartholomew's Sudbury for life in July 1499, this was said to be 'to grant him some rest after his strenuous labours' in the mother house.[45] Although we cannot measure the amount of time superiors of larger cells were taken away from their houses on priory business and public service, such commitments do seem to have been onerous and the lives of such men can hardly have been restful. Moreover, the frequency with which the priors of many daughter houses undertook secular and ecclesiastical public services indicates that they were considered important figures in their localities.

Indeed there are other signs that the headship of even a moderate dependency conferred some status. Priors of cells clearly held a senior position in the mother-house hierarchy, and were regularly appointed compromitters in mother-house elections.[46] Meanwhile, a few priors were

42 CPR, 1247–1258, p. 123, 1452–1461, p. 119.
43 Ibid., 1405–1408, pp. 124, 155.
44 E.g. CPL, XIII(i), pp. 32–3, I, p. 47, III, pp. 80, 117, 549; J. E. Sayers, Papal Judges Delegate in the Province of Canterbury 1198–1254 (Oxford, 1971), pp. 280–309.
45 Charters of St Bartholomew's Priory, Sudbury, ed. R. Mortimer, Suffolk Records Society, Suffolk Charters, XV (1996), no. 131, pp. 89–90.
46 A St Albans tract laid down that two of the nine compromitters for abbey elections should always be priors of cells, but in practice more than two were often appointed:

able to use their office as a springboard to positions of real influence in a way that would have been unlikely for ordinary obedientiaries. Two priors of Finchale were appointed successive bishops of Durham in the thirteenth century, whereas heads of Alvecote, St Nicholas Exeter and Holy Island were all made suffragan bishops in the sixteenth.[47] A few priors of cells also attracted sufficient attention to be selected as abbots of major monasteries other than their own. In the twelfth and early thirteenth centuries, when the election of superiors from outside one's own community was more common, priors of Freiston, Hurley, Leominster, St Ives and Stone became abbots of Thorney, Evesham, Shrewsbury, Selby and Haughmond respectively; and in the later middle ages we hear of priors of Binham (Rochester), Hertford (Whitby), Letheringham (Pentney), Wallingford (Chester) and perhaps Hoxne (Wymondham, now independent) enjoying the same career progression.[48] Even more notably, perhaps, a small number of heads succeeded in winning the affection of the king. Priors of Hurley and Cranborne were granted favours by Henry III and Edward II respectively out of royal regard, and more than one prior of Wallingford seems to have earned the good will of the monarch. Henry VI made two grants to the priory in 1445–6 'in consideration of the kindness which they have shewn the king'; and a later prior was one of the legatees of Henry VII's will.[49] It would appear, therefore, that an appointment as prior of a daughter house could substantially advance a monk's career as a result of the standing that that office conferred.

The headship of a dependency brought not only status but also certain material benefits. Every prior received a sum of money '*pro necessariis suis*', ranging from the 20s. per year given to the prior of Hoxne to as much as the four or five pounds a year received by the heads of Belvoir, Binham, Hertford

R. Vaughan, 'The Election of Abbots at St Albans in the Thirteenth and Fourteenth Centuries', *Proceedings of the Cambridge Antiquarian Society*, xlvii (1953), pp. 4–5. See above, pp. 126–7, for evidence of the high status of priors of cells from the pension lists produced as the Dissolution.

[47] *Historiae Dunelmensis Scriptores Tres*, ed. J. Raine, SS, ix (1839), pp. 45, 56; Knowles, *RO*, III, p. 494; *L&P*, IX, no. 191, p. 59, XI, no. 877, p. 350.

[48] *VCH, Cambridgeshire and the Isle of Ely*, II, p. 213; Pearce, *Monks of Westminster*, pp. 48–9; B. R. Kemp, 'The Monastic Dean of Leominster', *EHR*, lxxxiii (1968), p. 507; *CPR, 1216–1225*, p. 297, *1232–1247*, pp. 256–7; Greatrex, *BRECP*, pp. 604–5; W. Frampton Andrews, 'Sir Edward Bensted, kt', *East Hertfordshire Archaeological Society Transactions*, ii (1903), pp. 185–94; *The Register of William Bateman Bishop of Norwich, 1344–1355*, ed. P. E. Pobst, 2 vols, C&Y Soc., lxxxiv, xc (1996–2000), II, no. 1005, p. 3; BL, Stowe MS 141; S. Martin-Jones, *Wymondham and its Abbey*, 6th edn (Wymondham, 1932), p. 33. According to Blomefield, William Buckenham, the second abbot of Wymondham (1465–71), was the same man as the Norwich monk who had been prior of Yarmouth and Hoxne in the preceding two decades: F. Blomefield, *An Essay Towards a Topographical History of the County of Norfolk*, 11 vols (London, 1805–10), II, p. 519.

[49] *CPR, 1247–1258*, p. 492, *1327–1330*, pp. 376, 384, *1441–1446*, pp. 362, 449; *L&P*, III(i), no. 308, p. 142.

and St Ives.[50] It is to be assumed that the duty of entertaining important guests allowed the heads of dependencies to live a more exalted life than ordinary monks, and occasional account roll entries for minstrels and actors indicate that some had access to secular entertainment.[51] In their accommodation, too, the heads of cells often enjoyed higher standards of comfort than their brethren. It is generally thought that by the later middle ages even small religious houses afforded separate living quarters for the superior, usually in the western range of the cloister.[52] In the first decade of the fourteenth century, Abbot de Maryns of St Albans issued constitutions requiring the priors of the abbey's cells to sleep within the common dormitory, but instructing them to lie 'in their chamber or in an honest place separate from the others' at the entrance to the dorter.[53] These injunctions, however, were relaxed by Abbot de la Mare in 1351, who permitted priors to sleep in their own rooms providing at least four monks remained in the common dormitory.[54] A set of articles for a Benedictine chapter visitation, datable to the second half of the fourteenth century, also seems to allow for individual sleeping arrangements for the priors of cells, although the monks staying there were ordered to sleep together in one place.[55]

By the mid-fourteenth century, therefore, the total withdrawal of the prior of a cell from his community at night was apparently quite widely countenanced. Numerous inventories and account rolls refer to the existence of a 'prior's *camera*', in both larger cells and in small houses like St Leonard's Norwich, Rumburgh, Jarrow and Wearmouth.[56] But whether these references allude to chambers within private apartments or enclosed spaces inside or adjacent to the dormitory itself is much harder to say. Only at Yarmouth is there a clue about the position of the prior's *camera*, which is said to have been '*super dormitorium*'.[57] This probably indicates a chamber at the entrance to the dormitory, but even if it refers to a room above the dorter this still rules out a separate suite of rooms in the west range of the cloister.

---

50 NRO, DCN 2/6; PRO, E315/272, fols 71r–72r, 74r–74v; BL, Add. MSS 33448–9. The prior of Hoxne's allowance did rise to 40s. per year in the 1520s: NRO, DCN 2/6/42–5.
51 E.g. NRO, DCN 2/3/10, 29; Oxford, Corpus Christi College, MS Z/2/1/1–2.
52 J. C. Dickinson, *Monastic Life in Medieval England* (London, 1961), pp. 38–9; D. Knowles, 'The Monastic Buildings of England', in *The Historian and Character and other Essays* (Cambridge, 1964), p. 19; Gilchrist, *Contemplation and Action*, p. 132.
53 GASA, II, p. 98. The prior of Tynemouth was exempted from this decree because he already enjoyed his own quarters, parts of which, most notably the early thirteenth-century prior's chapel, still stand. An earlier abbatial injunction of 1292 countenanced but did not counsel a separate chamber within the dormitory: Cambridge, Trinity College, MS O.9.25, fols 10r–10v.
54 GASA, II, p. 428.
55 CBM, II, no. 158, p. 89.
56 NRO, DCN 2/3/66(ii); SROI, HD 1538/335/1, no. 32; Raine, *Jarrow and Monk-Wearmouth*, e.g. pp. 10, 12–13, 139, 146, 148.
57 NRO, DCN 2/4/9.

In fact, only at a small number of daughter-house sites does enough of this range survive to prove the existence of domestic accommodation there. At Binham and Ewenny the prior's quarters are usually said to have been in this position, and an impressive set of chambers and hall survive in the west range at St Nicholas' Exeter; but in each case, although it seems likely in houses of this size, we cannot be entirely sure that it was the prior and not just guests that were accommodated therein.[58] Two references to the prior of Wallingford's house confirm that this superior enjoyed his own separate apartments, and the extensive remains at Finchale and Holy Island display the spacious and comfortable quarters of their heads.[59] In neither of the two latter priories, however, was the prior's housing in the west range of the cloister and it would clearly be unwise to assume that this was the normal arrangement in daughter houses. It may be that the development of priors' lodgings in cells was stunted by the abrogated sojourns of individual heads, who lacked the time and incentive to build and adorn private apartments. No firm conclusions are yet possible, but a variety of solutions seem to have been found to the problem of the superior's accommodation in dependencies.

One final benefit enjoyed by priors of daughter houses, and by no means the least significant, was the provision made for them in death. Perhaps in part because they were accountable for the souls under their charge, deceased heads of cells were often granted generous commemoration in prayers and masses. Priors were given more lavish funerals than ordinary monks and twice as much was spent on tapers for the priors of Norwich's cells than for ordinary brethren. Burial stones, like that of marble brought from London for the late Prior Richard Lamplew of Hertford in 1489, or other monuments, such as the two *Orate* inscriptions still in the chancel of Wetheral church for sixteenth-century priors of that house, were put on display in order to encourage commemoration.[60] Moreover, a few records of special anniversaries granted to priors of cells survive. In 1264, Prior Ralph of Belvoir agreed with his convent, with the assent of the abbot of St Albans, that certain revenues should be assigned for his anniversary; and in 1328 detailed arrangements were made by another prior of Belvoir, John of

---

58 L. Butler and C. Given-Wilson, *Medieval Monasteries of Great Britain* (London, 1979), pp. 152–3; E. Fernie, 'Binham Priory', *Archaeological Journal*, 137, 1980, p. 329; D. Knowles and J. K. S. St Joseph, *Monastic Sites from the Air* (Cambridge, 1952) pp. 46–7. For a description of the survivals at St Nicholas' Priory, Exeter, see H. L. Parry and H. Brakspear (revised by J. Youings), *St Nicholas Priory Exeter* (Exeter, 1960), pp. 21–30.
59 *Mon. Ang.*, III, pp. 282–3, no. 10; *Historical Manuscripts Commission: The Duke of Rutland*, IV (1905), p. 151; C. R. Peers, 'Finchale Priory', *Archaeologia Aeliana*, 4th series, iv (1927), pp. 193–220; A. H. Thompson, *Lindisfarne Priory* (London, 1949), pp. 11–13.
60 NRO, DCN 1/4/109; PRO, SC6/HenVIII/1696. Very few monuments of this kind survive, however, despite the large number of priory churches which remain. Priors were perhaps more often buried in their cells' chapter houses than in their churches.

Kendal, for his commemoration there. In return for the gift of a chamber to the house's convent and an increase in their clothes-money, Kendal was granted on his anniversary a *placebo and dirige*, one morning mass and a special mass by every priest present in the priory or fifty psalms from those of lower rank.[61] Records of anniversaries also survive for priors of Dunster, Hurley and Wymondham in their cells, and interestingly for heads of Penwortham and Tynemouth in their mother houses.[62] The latter provision was given only to priors who had ruled their houses with outstanding success, but even if a small minority of superiors were favoured in these ways, the possibility of making a name for oneself in a daughter house was held out to all.

There are therefore several reasons to think that, in many cases, the headship of a daughter house was a position to be coveted. It is likely, though, that the rule of some cells was more prestigious and more comfortable than that of others. We have seen how an active public role was mainly the preserve of the priors of the larger dependencies, and these heads were also more likely to be promoted to a higher office than their counterparts in small cells. Naturally, the priors of wealthier houses received larger allowances and more spacious apartments, and they would probably have enjoyed greater freedom in the management of their priories too.[63] In contrast, the rule of a small, indigent daughter house could be wearisome. Prior Richard Barton of Stamford remarked during a visitation of 1440 that 'the priors of this place are so [often] removed, and have not the will to abide therein', because of the poverty of the cell; and the large number of the heads of Brooke Priory who resigned in the late thirteenth and early fourteenth century suggests that a similar attitude prevailed there at that time.[64] In particular, priors might have feared having to assume accountability for the debts accumulated at the cell during their time in office, as seems often to have been the case at late medieval Hoxne.[65] But although the headship of poor, remote daughter houses was probably never very popular, the rule of any priory with an adequate income must have been a welcome opportunity to any ambitious monk or canon.

---

61 Nichols, *History and Antiquities of Leicester*, II(i), Appendix II, p. 13; HMC: *Rutland*, IV, p. 122; Cambridge, Trinity College, MS O.9.25, fol. 15v.
62 *Two Chartularies of the Priory of St Peter at Bath*, ed. W. Hunt, Somerset Record Society, vii (1893), part ii, no. 884, p. 176; *St Mary's, Hurley, in the Middle Ages*, ed. F. Wethered (London, 1898), no. 79, p. 115; BL, Cotton Titus C.viii, fols 11v–12r; *Documents relating to the Priory of Penwortham and other Possessions in Lancashire of the Abbey of Evesham*, ed. W. A. Hulton, Chetham Society, xxx (1853), no. 26, p. 28; BL, Cotton MS Nero D.vii, fol. 51v.
63 See above, pp. 83–90.
64 *Lincoln Visitations, 1420–1449*, III, p. 347; HRH, II, pp. 349–50. Cf. the comment of one resigning prior in Brooke, who claimed he was 'neither able nor willing' to cope with the problems of ruling the cell at a time of severe financial difficulties: VCH, *Rutland*, I, p. 160.
65 See below, pp. 267–9.

The Lifestyle of the Monks and Canons

The experience of ordinary monks at cells is less well documented than that of their priors, but a good deal can still be discovered about their routine and standard of living. The most important activity of the choir monk was the constant round of divine service, but the value of the small-scale, colourless recitation possible in a house of three or four brethren has often been questioned. But despite the limitations of the *opus dei* in priories of this size, it was still supposed to be performed as fully as possible. Numerous injunctions make clear that the night office and the seven daily hours were to be said in every cell.[66] Moreover, every surviving inventory shows an adequate set of service books in the dependency, usually consisting of at least one ordinal, antiphoner, psalter, *portiforium*, legendary, missal, gradual and martyrology, almost always in good condition.[67] Nevertheless, the frequent ordinances concerning attendance at matins suggest that a lack of communal encouragement at daughter houses caused many to succumb to 'the excuses to which the sleepy are addicted'.[68] It was reported in 1440 that Prior Barton and his solitary companion at St Leonard's Stamford 'do not get up for matins by night because they are so few in number'; and the monks of Holy Island and Finchale were guilty of the same failing in the fourteenth century, as were many of the St Ives community in 1530.[69]

Cells were expected to follow broadly the liturgical rhythms of their mother houses. The calendars that survive for dependent priories, as at Deeping St James and Dunster, very largely cohere with those of their parent abbeys, with minor variations to mark the cells' own dedication and any saints of local importance.[70] The 1351 constitutions of Abbot de la Mare of

---

66   The fullest to survive are the mid-fourteenth century Durham chapter ordinances for Holy Island Priory: DCM, Loc. XXVII: 4.

67   For example, Sharpe, *Shorter Catalogues*, B62–4, B122–4, pp. 313–25, 788–97; Raine, *North Durham*, pp. 93–8, 117–18, 125–7, 347–8, 353, 357–8.

68   *The Rule of St Benedict in Latin and English*, ed, J. McCann (London, 1952), chap. 22, pp. 70–1.

69   *Lincoln Visitations, 1420–1449*, III, p. 347; DCM, 2.8 Pont. 12; *Visitations in the Diocese of Lincoln, 1517–31*, ed. A. H. Thompson, 3 vols, Lincoln Record Society, xxxiii, xxxv, xxxvii (1940–7), III, p. 93. For mother house injunctions on this subject, see GASA, II, p. 428; Amundesham, I, p. 208; DCM, Loc. XXVII: 4; BL, Cotton Faust. A.vi, fols 8r–8v.

70   F. Wormald, *English Benedictine Kalendars after AD 1100*, 2 vols, Henry Bradshaw Society, lxxvii, lxxxi (1939–46), I, pp. 129–60. Unpublished calendars also survive from St Guthlac's Hereford, St Bees and Wymondham: N. Ker and A. G. Watson, *Medieval Libraries of Great Britain: A List of Surviving Books*, 2nd edn, 2 vols (London, 1964–87), I, pp. 99–100, 169, 216. Equally, the calendar that Wormald assigned to Malmesbury might instead have come from its cell at Pilton: Wormald, *English Benedictine Kalendars*, II, pp. 75–90. Although no calendars of Thorney and Bath are extant, the character of the Deeping and Dunster versions leaves no doubt that these were mother-house schedules with occasional local variations.

St Albans, meanwhile, laid down that the abbey calendar should be followed in all of its cells in all the festivals of the year, with special commemorations for St Oswin at Tynemouth and St Mary Magdalene, the patron saint of the priory church, at Beadlow.[71] That efforts were made to add some richness to feasts of higher rank is shown by the arrangements recorded at two cells for their patronal festival. At St Leonard's Norwich, the subprior and succentor with one or more companions came up from the cathedral priory to assist in the celebration of St Leonard's day; and the prior, succentor, subsacrist and two other monks of Thorney travelled to Deeping St James on its patronal day for the same reason.[72]

What quality of liturgical observance was ordinarily possible in small daughter houses is harder to say. Benedict XII's 1339 constitutions for the Augustinian canons laid down that 'in places where there are three or more [brethren], at least one sung mass should be celebrated by them each day and the canonical hours should also be sung'; and a similar injunction was issued for the Benedictines three years earlier.[73] One of the five canons of Blythburgh, however, complained in June 1526 that the accustomed sung mass at the priory was no longer being observed, and the small independent houses of Bradwell and St Olave's also found it necessary to recite at least part of their daily round of services without music in the later middle ages.[74] Nevertheless, recent work on parochial liturgy in English towns has suggested that the range of musical activities possible in small churches has been greatly underestimated, because of the regular exchange of singers that took place in this environment.[75] It is likely that small monasteries took advantage of these opportunities whenever possible. Abbot Whethamstede's rejected constitutions for Redbourn (1439) required a more elaborate commemoration of major festivals, and ordered that two singing clerks should be hired for the purpose; and Finchale was rebuked by Bishop Hatfield of

[71] GASA, II, pp. 423–7. This injunction might have introduced a previously imperfect standardisation, since we are told that during his noviciate at Wymondham, de la Mare himself laboured 'to know both the customs of that place [Wymondham] and those of the principal monastery': ibid., II, p. 374.

[72] NRO, DCN 2/3; BL, Harley MS 3658, fols 75r–75v. The St Leonard's book-list of 1453 included 'j quaternus notatus pro festo sancti Leonardi': Sharpe, Shorter Catalogues, B63, p. 318.

[73] Chapters of the Augustinian Canons, ed. H. E. Salter, C&Y Soc., xxix (1922), p. 242; Wilkins, Concilia, II, p. 608, chap. 26.

[74] Visitations of the Diocese of Norwich AD 1492–1532, ed. A. Jessopp, Camden Society, new series, xliii (1888), pp. 216, 129–31; Lincoln Visitations, 1420–1449, I, pp. 22–3. Late thirteenth-century statutes from the diocese of Anjou required that matins and vespers should be sung in small priories on Sundays and important feast days, but apparently not at other times: J. Avril, 'Le statut des prieurés d'après les conciles provinciaux et les statuts synodaux (fins XIIe–début XIVe siècles)', in Prieurs et prieurés dans l'occident médiéval, ed. J.-L. Lemaître, Hautes études médiévales et modernes, lx (Geneva, 1987), p. 90.

[75] In particular, see C. Burgess and A. Wathey, 'Mapping the Soundscape: church music in English towns, 1450–1550', Early Music History, xix (2000), pp. 1–46.

Durham for failing to maintain the two secular priests who were supposed to help with masses and the *opus dei*.[76] The large clerical establishments at several cells, particularly those who employed chantry priests or shared their churches with parochial congregations, might also have contributed to services at these priories. We learn, for example, that the vicar of Leominster 'together with his priests' was supposed to attend the monastic choir of that church on major festivals for vespers, masses and processions, but this custom is only recorded because of the vicar's refusal to observe it in the 1390s.[77]

At some medium-sized cells, there are even signs of a more ambitious approach to the liturgy. The priory of St Guthlac in Hereford, although it housed only five monks in the early sixteenth century, nevertheless continued to appoint a precentor, surely a sign of commitment to the priory's musical activities.[78] Of even more interest are the modest Lady chapel choirs maintained at both Brecon and Wallingford in the late middle ages.[79] At Wallingford in 1484/5, this consisted of 'two boys singing daily in the chapel of the Blessed Virgin Mary for the mass of the same', at a cost of 8s., and it is unlikely that anything more than plainsong was attempted. But we cannot discount the possibility that daughter houses extended their liturgical activities to include polyphony. The extent to which London parish churches and hospitals performed composed music of this kind has recently been demonstrated, and that lesser monasteries might do the same is illustrated by Tutbury Priory's employment in the early sixteenth century of a layman 'to keep oure lady masse daily with priksong and organs and every night after evensong an antem of oure lady and odur divine servyce of festivall dais . . .'[80] The smallest cells of two or three monks cannot often have aspired to such musical sophistication, but it is not impossible that medium-sized daughter houses may have set out to mark important festivals with considerable liturgical elaboration.

The religious activity of the monks staying in cells, however, did not end with the services in choir. As the enormous necrology from Belvoir Priory illustrates, the burden of masses for deceased benefactors and monks could be considerable. Indeed in the eleventh century, Cluniac cells of only two or three monks had to be excused from the full observance of anniversaries for their fellow brethren, receiving permission to substitute almsgiving for the

---

76 *Amundesham*, II, pp. 205–6; DCM, 2.8 Pont. 12.

77 K. Wood-Legh, *Perpetual Chantries in Britain* (Cambridge, 1965), pp. 276–7; *Registrum Johannis Trefnant, Episcopi Herefordensis, AD 1389–1404*, ed. W. W. Capes, C&Y Soc., xx (1916), pp. 140–3.

78 *Hist. et Cart. Gloucestriae*, III, pp. xxxii–xxxiv, xlviii–xlix. A precentor of Blythburgh is also recorded in the late twelfth century: *Blythburgh Cartulary*, I, p. 3.

79 R. Bowers, 'The Almonry Schools of the English Monasteries c.1265–1540', in *Monasteries and Society in Medieval Britain*, ed. B. Thompson (Stamford, 1999), pp. 177–222; Oxford, Corpus Christi College, MS Z/2/1/2.

80 Burgess and Wathey, 'Mapping the Soundscape', *passim*, esp. pp. 18–19.

saying of masses.[81] It is not clear whether the inmates of daughter houses attended a daily chapter meeting: Benedict XII's 1336 constitutions for the Benedictine order decreed that daily gatherings should take place at every monastery with six or more monks and at others where this was customary, although when legislating for the Augustinians three years later houses of four or more canons were deemed an acceptable minimum for daily chapter meetings. The mid-fourteenth-century ordinances for Holy Island enjoined that a chapter should be held 'two or three times a week', and this was perhaps a more common solution.[82] Nevertheless, on balance it would seem that the burden of religious services resting on dependencies – providing it was adequately discharged – could be considerable.

Another common monastic activity was administration. It is well known that a large proportion of the inmates of great houses held offices of some kind, but the extent to which the monks of smaller monasteries did so is less certain. Dr Oliva, however, has recently shown that even small nunneries appointed obedientiaries to share in the management of the house.[83] At daughter houses, too, where numbers rose above four or five monks, administrative offices can very often be traced, although in many cases it is unclear whether or not these offices carried their own endowments. At the larger cells, numerous obediences were distributed. We hear of the subprior, cellarer, almoner, sacrist and chamberlain of Binham and the subprior, cellarer, sacrist, precentor and prior's chaplain of Wymondham in the thirteenth and fourteenth centuries when these communities numbered over a dozen monks.[84] More surprisingly, several conventual officers are recorded at medium-sized and small cells too. At various times, there was a subprior, cellarer, sacrist, almoner, infirmarer and refectorer at the priory of Belvoir. A cellarer, sacrist and almoner were appointed at Brecon, although in 1401 the prior was holding all these offices in his own hands, and a sacrist and cellarer at Wallingford in the thirteenth and fifteenth centuries respectively.[85] The priories of Freiston and St Ives, housing six or seven choir monks in the

---

81 For a discussion of the Belvoir martyrology, see below, pp. 206–8; N. Hunt, *Cluny under Saint Hugh 1049–1109* (London, 1967), p. 179.

82 Wilkins, *Concilia*, II, p. 594, chap. 6; *Chapters of the Augustinian Canons*, p. 218; DCM, Loc. XXVII: 4.

83 M. Oliva, 'Aristocracy or Meritocracy? Office-Holding Patterns in Late Medieval English Nunneries', in *Women in the Church*, ed. W. J. Sheils and D. Wood, SCH, XXVII (1990), pp. 197–208.

84 GASA, II, p. 16; *Matthaei Parisiensis, Monachi Sancti Albani, Chronica Majora*, ed. H. R. Luard, 7 vols, RS, lvii (1872–83), VI, pp. 89–91; BL, Cotton MS Claud. D.xiii, fol. 55r; GASA, II, pp. 145, 374; *Registra*, I, p. 147.

85 *Mon. Ang.*, III, pp. 291–2, no. 16; HMC: *Rutland*, IV, pp. 117, 122; Cambridge, Trinity College, MS O.9.25, fols 9v, 12v; *Registers of St Davids*, I, pp. 232–3; *Cartulary of the Medieval Archives of Christ Church*, ed. N. Denholm-Young, OHS, xcii (1931), p. 147; *Registra*, I, p. 146. Such references to obedientiaries, also found for Bromfield and Holy Island, provide further evidence that there were larger communities at several cells in the thirteenth and early fourteenth centuries than after the Black Death.

fifteenth century, both appointed a cellarer and a sacrist at this date and there was a subprior and cellarer in the slightly larger community at fifteenth-century Finchale. Even more strikingly the five monks which comprised the St Guthlac's Hereford convent in the 1510s included a subprior, sacrist and precentor, and cellarers are found at the very small priories of Calke and Llanthony Prima at around the same date.[86]

Even when monks were not appointed to specific offices, as in the smallest dependencies, there is some reason to believe that many played a part in the business affairs of the priory. The heads of cells must have needed administrative assistance from their brethren, particularly during their absences from the house. A monk of Dunster is found serving as his prior's proctor in a legal case at Wells in 1344; and the clerical duties of Thomas Wheill, one of William Partrike's brethren at Lytham, emerge from the records of Partrike's rebellion against Durham.[87] The position of prior's *socius*, nominated to scrutinise his superior's business activities on behalf of the mother house, had in fact been formalised at the Durham cells since the mid-thirteenth century. Prior Bertram of Middleton (1244–58) ordered that every prior and obedientiary of the monastery should appoint a deputy who was to be kept informed about all the receipts and expenses of their office.[88] That such expectations persisted is indicated by an order to Prior Tickhill of Finchale (1363–7), applicable also to the heads of the other Durham cells, to appoint a certain monk as his *socius*, who should monitor 'the receipts and expenses, sales and leases of lands and tithes and the proceeds of all kinds of your priory' through the issuing of indentures, which were to be brought each year to the Durham general chapter for inspection.[89] Such formal appointments might well have been made elsewhere; in the early thirteenth century, it was enjoined that every Ramsey obedientiary, almost certainly including the prior of St Ives, 'should pay out the expenses of his office and should reckon with the advice of his *socius*'.[90] In all, it seems unlikely that monks sent to dwell in small daughter houses of two or three inmates could have altogether avoided administrative duties of some kind.

86 *Lincoln Visitations, 1420–1449*, I, p. 38, II, p. 57; BL, Cotton MS Julius F.ix, fol. 1r; Raine, *Priory of Finchale*, p. xxiii; *Hist. et Cart. Gloucestriae*, III, pp. xlviii–xlix; Anon, 'Repton Charters', *Journal of the Derbyshire Archaeological and Natural History Society*, new series, vi (1932), no. 3, p. 66; *A Calendar of the Registers of the Priory of Llanthony by Gloucester 1457–1466, 1501–1525*, ed. J. Rhodes, Bristol and Gloucestershire Archaeological Society, Gloucestershire Record Series, XV (2002), no. 251, p. 103. Several other examples of daughter-house obedientiaries could be cited.

87 Greatrex, *BRECP*, p. 33; Dobson, *Durham Priory*, pp. 334–5. See above, p. 95.

88 BL, Cotton MS Faust. A.vi, fol. 61v. A similar ordinance was issued soon afterwards by Prior Hugh of Darlington (1258–73, 1286–90), with any priors concealing this information to be excommunicated: *Durham Annals and Documents of the Thirteenth Century*, ed. F. Barlow, SS, clv (1945), no. 31, pp. 102–3.

89 BL, Cotton MS Faust. A.vi, fol. 61v.

90 *Cartularium Monasterii de Rameseia*, ed. W. H. Hart and P. A. Lyons, 3 vols, RS, lxxix (1884–93), II, no. 331, p. 214.

For those monks not regularly involved in priory business, some fruitful occupation was needed when they were not in choir. The occasional reference to manual work in dependencies is found, but the most common solution proposed to this problem was study.[91] In May 1347, Bishop Bateman of Norwich required that all those monks in his cathedral priory's cells with the aptitude should occupy themselves 'in the study of holy scripture or the canons', and Abbots de Maryns, de la Mare and Whethamstede of St Albans all issued injunctions prescribing intellectual activity in the abbey's dependencies.[92] Although the quantity of study carried out in daughter houses cannot be measured, there is considerable evidence for the existence of books at even the smallest cells. Numerous codices associated with satellite priories survive, though only for three houses – Dover, Tynemouth and St Guthlac's Hereford – are more than ten extant. More importantly, thirty-seven separate book-lists from dependencies are known, the majority from the well-recorded satellites of Durham and Norwich.[93] It is undeniable that most of these lists display extremely small collections of little more than a dozen study books. On the other hand, very few give a complete record of the volumes held by the cell, the majority being either lists of books donated or transported, or inventories which included only the codices of the institution, and not those owned by individual monks.

In assessing the number of books likely to have been held at a daughter house at any one time, it is necessary to distinguish between three categories of books: those held permanently by the cell, those loaned by the mother house and those owned by the priors and monks staying at the cell. Leaving aside large semi-independent houses like Dover and Tynemouth, which can be seen to have possessed impressive libraries, from only two satellite priories is there evidence of reasonable permanent collections. The fifteenth-century pressmarks in the extant books from St Guthlac's Hereford reach number forty-five, indicating that at least this number were owned; and the two surviving inventories of St Leonard's Norwich, of 1424 and 1453, show a stable

---

[91] The fourteenth-century Monk of Farne describes his work chopping wood; and Abbot de la Mare's 1351 constitutions recommended that monks in the abbey of St Albans and its cells should engage in some 'manual work', such as writing, correcting, illuminating or binding manuscripts: D. H. Farmer (ed.), *The Monk of Farne* (Baltimore, 1961), p. 14; GASA, II, pp. 433–4. The evidence for intellectual activity at dependencies is discussed more fully in my 'Books and Learning in the Dependent Priories of the Monasteries of Medieval England', in *The Church and Learning in Later Medieval Society: Essays in Honour of R. B. Dobson*, ed. C. M. Barron and J. Stratford (Donnington, 2002), pp. 64–79.

[92] Cheney, 'Norwich Cathedral Priory', pp. 106–7; GASA, II, pp. 96, 433–4; *Amundesham*, II, pp. 210–11.

[93] Many of these lists have been published in Sharpe, *Shorter Catalogues*, and *Dover Priory*, ed. W. P. Stoneman, Corpus of British Medieval Library Catalogues, V (1999). The others, principally those of the Durham cells, will be published in that series in due course.

collection of about thirty-five volumes.[94] But although they do not seem to have possessed large numbers of their own books, there is good reason to believe that volumes belonging to the parent abbey or to individual monks were regularly transported to cells.[95]

Mr Piper has demonstrated that the books in the Durham 'Spendement' were regularly lent out in this way, and it is even possible that the Lindisfarne Gospels were held at Holy Island in the mid-fourteenth century.[96] Moreover, all the volumes in the fifteenth-century inventory of Yarmouth Priory seem from their pressmarks to have belonged to Norwich, while successive lists of Rumburgh and Holy Island show a considerable turnover of library books, suggesting that many were supplied by their mother houses.[97] Equally, there is ample evidence of monks taking their own books to daughter houses, and it is likely that such volumes would not have been entered into cells' inventories. For example, nine books belonging to Henry Helay followed him to St Leonard's Stamford in 1422 and three entries in the Norwich accounts record the transportation to and from Lynn of volumes owned by priors of that cell.[98] Where books can be shown to have been carried to a daughter house in this way, it seems likely that they were used there. There is therefore good reason to believe that monks wishing to pursue their studies in a dependency were always able to and that it was possible to generate an atmosphere of learning even in the smallest cell.

In all dependencies, and not just in those cells earmarked as rest-houses, some provision was also made for leisure. The opportunity to take short holidays was available to the inmates of the Durham satellites in the early fourteenth century, when Bishop Kellaw ordered that 'priors and wardens of such cells should provide for the monks staying in such cells transport and other necessities when they visit their friends and relatives'.[99] The main leisure activity practised within dependencies seems to have been walking.

---

94 N. R. Ker, 'The Medieval Press-Marks of St Guthlac's Priory, Hereford, and of Roche Abbey, Yorks.', *Medium Aevum*, v (1936), pp. 47–8; Sharpe, *Shorter Catalogues*, B62–3, pp. 312–21. The St Leonard's collection, all bearing a Norwich pressmark, was probably provided by the mother house for the use of its monks while on their *ludi*: see above, p. 149.

95 The regular loans of library books to their Oxford colleges by Canterbury and Durham Cathedral Priories are well known. See, for example, A. J. Piper, 'The Libraries of the Monks of Durham', in *Medieval Scribes, Manuscripts and Libraries. Essays Presented to N. R. Ker*, ed. M. B. Parkes and A. G. Watson (London, 1978), pp. 244–8; or C. de Hamel, 'The Dispersal of the Library of Christ Church, Canterbury, from the Fourteenth to the Sixteenth Century', in *Books and Collectors. Essays presented to Andrew Watson*, ed. J. P. Carley and C. G. C. Tite (London, 1997), pp. 263–79.

96 Piper, 'Libraries of Durham', pp. 236, 241–2; DCM, Holy Island Status, 1367.

97 Sharpe, *Shorter Catalogues*, B64, B122–4, pp. 321–5, 788–97; DCM, Holy Island Status, 1348, 1362, 1367, 1401, 1409, 1417, 1437, 1494, 1533.

98 *Catalogi veteres librorum ecclesie cathedralis Dunelmensis*, ed. J. Raine, SS, vii (1838), p. 116; NRO, DCN 1/9/37, 2/1/30, 32.

99 DCM, Reg. II, fol. 51r.

Brethren were sometimes sent away from urban mother houses to more rural satellites in order to take the air there; and Abbot John de la Moote (1396–1401) of St Albans' permission to the monks of the abbey to go for walks during Lent was extended to those staying in its cells.[100] There are signs, however, that the desire for entertainment in daughter houses was at times a little too strong. The regularity with which choir monks were warned in letters and injunctions not to leave the precinct for eating and drinking implies that such outings could be a serious problem in dependencies.[101] These references remind us that for all the occupations that were available even in smaller cells, there were always some who eschewed their monastic duties for other pastimes. Boredom might well have been a greater problem in small monasteries than it was in larger ones: it is probably significant that six of the seven St Albans monks who joined Bishop Despenser's crusade in 1383, 'to whom the quiet of the cloister was displeasing', were then dwelling in the abbey's cells.[102] Nevertheless, the evidence from the English dependencies suggests that the disciplinary problems often experienced in lesser houses should be attributed more to a lack of communal encouragement than to enforced inactivity.

Material Surroundings

Not only is it possible to study the pattern of life in dependencies more closely than for other monasteries of a similar size, but we can also recover something of the environment in which monks sent to cells lived and the quality of life they encountered. It has sometimes been suggested that a sojourn in a cell must have been something of an ordeal.[103] There is certainly evidence to suggest that service in satellite houses was unwelcome to some. Several letters survive in the Durham muniments from monks pleading to be allowed to return to the mother house, and the St Albans *Gesta Abbatum* vividly describes the misery of the abbey's inmates sent in exile to distant cells.[104] Indeed the St Albans' cell at Tynemouth appears to have generated particular distaste among monks used to more comfortable surroundings. One thirteenth-century inmate dwelling there states himself to have been 'pining for a long time with a sickness which I have caught from the intolerable smell of the fish, and the thick, loathsome mists, and the terrible storms

---

100 See above, p. 142; GASA, III, p. 471. The apostasy of Henry Belton from St Bees after he was allowed to take air outside its precinct provides another indication that walking was a common leisure pursuit at dependencies: see above, pp. 121–2.

101 E.g. CUL, MS Ee.IV.20, fols 88v, 91r; CBM, II, no. 177, p. 221; Cheney, 'Norwich Cathedral Priory', pp. 106–7, 117–18; GASA, II, pp. 99, 203.

102 GASA, II, p. 416.

103 Raine, *North Durham*, p. 132; Dobson, *Durham Priory*, p. 303; C. Platt, *The Abbeys and Priories of Medieval England* (London, 1984), p. 142.

104 E.g. Barlow, *Durham Annals*, nos 32–5, pp. 104–6; GASA, esp. I, pp. 247–58.

which beat fiercely upon the surrounding country'; whereas to another St Albans monk, Tynemouth was a place 'deprived of all amenity, lacking all comfort and delight', whose occupants suffered constant hoarseness and sore throats and where spring and summer never came.[105] But it would perhaps be unwise to extrapolate confidently from these examples, since most of the Durham cells were either desperately poor or placed in the most savage environments, while the correspondence of the exiled tends naturally to pathos. The situation of a daughter house was obviously a crucial factor in its inmates' quality of life. As we have seen, a significant number of cells were established in remote sites owing to their association with saints or with hermit communities. Not all such houses retained their austere character but life at those that did, like the priories of Farne Island or Hilbre Island, could be extremely uncomfortable. It also appears that service in those satellites distant from their mother house, like Tynemouth, was often unpopular. It is therefore difficult to generalise about the experience of monks sent to dwell in daughter houses, but there is good evidence that the conditions they encountered there were not in general deficient nor unduly uncomfortable.

The quantity of archaeological information available for the English dependencies is extremely variable. Several cells have been excavated, but only a handful in any detail and with modern techniques;[106] and no daughter house has been the subject of the kind of prolonged and meticulous study that has uncovered so much material at the medium-sized houses of Bordesley and Norton. As a result, to date we know very little about, for example, the phases of construction or the character of outbuildings in dependencies. On the other hand, the basic plans of many cells are known and the survival of a good number of their churches, in whole or in part, provides much useful information. The first detail to emerge about the monastic plan in daughter houses is the relatively large size of the churches even of less populous priories like Lynn and Leonard Stanley. In many cases, this stature resulted from the sharing of the priory church with a parochial congregation.[107] For those cells whose churches were not divided in this way, cruciform buildings of some size were apparently still common. The medium-sized priories of St Guthlac's Hereford and Holy Island possessed impressive churches, and the cruciform church of the smaller cell of St Leonard's Stamford was originally a remarkable 150 feet long even before its chancel was extended by another fifteen feet in the thirteenth century.[108] Equally

105 Hill, *Ecclesiastical Letter-Books*, p. 7; *A History of Northumberland*, ed. H. H. E. Craster, 15 vols (Newcastle, 1893–1940), VIII, pp. 71–3; CUL, Ee.IV.20, fols 283r–283v.

106 Most notably, R. Cramp, 'Excavations at the Saxon Monastic Sites of Wearmouth and Jarrow, co. Durham: an Interim Report', *Medieval Archaeology*, xiii (1969), pp. 21–66; S. E. West, 'The Excavation of Walton Priory', *Proceedings of the Suffolk Institute of Archaeology*, xxxiii (1975), pp. 131–52; C. M. Mahany, 'St Leonard's Priory, Stamford', *South Lincolnshire Archaeology*, i (1977), pp. 17–22.

107 For a discussion of this phenomenon, see below, pp. 208–18.

108 Thompson, *Lindisfarne Priory*, pp. 6–9; Mahany, 'St Leonard's Priory', pp. 17–22. The

strikingly, the monks of the tiny cell at Lincoln also appear to have wor-shipped in a cruciform chapel of good size, although a full-scale excavation of the site is needed to provide more concrete details.[109] The chapels of other minute dependencies may have taken the form of aisleless parallelograms, like the surviving example at Sudbury now used as a barn, but such buildings seem to have been rare. Although the high proportion of churches shared with a parish probably renders cells not entirely representative, what evi-dence survives for these priories tends to confirm the impression given by Dr Robinson's statistics that the churches of small monasteries were often built on a considerable scale.[110]

The layout of small monasteries remains a subject not fully explored, despite recent contributions of note.[111] It is generally agreed, however, that many alien priories were not arranged according to the normal claustral layout. Foreign cells like Grove, Minster Lovell, Steventon and Wilmington seem to have been designed like manor houses with chapels and with no trace of a conventual plan.[112] This secular, domestic appearance was no doubt attributable to the administrative rationale that underpinned these houses' existence and was apparently not replicated in other small religious houses. Professor Gilchrist has found that small nunneries generally followed the standard claustral plan, although she suggests that some houses might have lacked fully developed cloisters or have been physically detached from the churches in which the nuns worshipped. Less is known about small male monasteries and there has been no attempt to test Dr Dickinson's theory that smaller Augustinian priories were often arranged in a simple L-shaped block containing the chapel in one wing and the domestic buildings in the other.[113]

As far as we can tell, the majority of English cells conformed to the usual monastic plan of buildings arranged around a cloister, attached to their place of worship. In other words, there are very few signs of English satellites origi-nally set out according to the manor-house pattern found at several exca-vated alien priories or making use of a church or chapel at a little distance

remnants of the church of St Guthlac's are now under the Hereford bus station and have not yet been excavated. A seventeenth-century description of the priory church, however, described it as 'a large melancholy chapell, which being built with many descents into it from the ground, and than of a great height in the roofe, strucke the enterers with a kind of religious horrour': BL, Harley MS 6868.
109 D. Stocker, 'Recent Work at Monks' Abbey, Lincoln', *Lincolnshire History and Archaeology*, xix (1984), pp. 103–5.
110 Robinson, *Geography of Augustinian Settlement*, Appendix 19, pp. 397–8.
111 In particular, Gilchrist, *Gender and Material Culture*, pp. 92–127, and *Contemplation and Action*, pp. 115–56.
112 A. J. Taylor, 'The Alien Priory of Minster Lovell', *Oxoniensia*, ii (1937), pp. 103–17; M. Morgan (Chibnall), 'Inventories of three small Alien Priories', *Journal of British Archaeological Association*, 3rd series, iv (1939), pp. 141–9; Knowles and St Joseph, *Monastic Sites*, p. 50; Platt, *Abbeys and Priories*, pp. 28, 174–5.
113 Gilchrist, *Contemplation and Action*, pp. 119–20; Dickinson, *Monastic Life*, pp. 42–3.

from the priory. Indeed the strong evidence that many English cells were initially provided with buildings of an obviously monastic rather than secular character, unlike many of the alien priories, adds considerable weight to the contention that the majority of these houses were indeed founded to be proper monasteries in miniature and not mere bailiwicks.[114] All the larger dependencies, that is those that at times housed six or more inmates, were undoubtedly provided with the usual claustral ranges. But although we know less about the plans of the very smallest cells, documentary, archaeological or architectural evidence also survives for cloisters at several humble dependencies, including Alvecote, Dunster, Jarrow, Leonard Stanley, St Leonard's Norwich, Pilton, Rumburgh, St Leonard's Stamford, Wearmouth, Woodkirk and Yarmouth.[115]

As many as ten of the thirty cloisters whose location is known were situated to the north of the priory church. This is an almost identical percentage of northern cloisters to that found at nunneries by Professor Gilchrist, and must therefore cast doubt on her theory that this arrangement in women's monasteries should be attributed to specifically female iconography rather than to more practical considerations, such as the location of lay cemeteries or running water.[116] If the L-shaped plan obtained for any satellite priories, it can only have been for the very smallest. The buildings at Coquet Island seem to have consisted only of a chapel and a two-storey domestic range to its west, and this plan might have been adopted by other tiny satellites never intended to hold more than two or three monks.[117] It has been suggested that the priories of Cranborne, Kilpeck and Penwortham were situated a short distance from the church in which they worshipped, but only at the re-founded Felixstowe (Walton) Priory can this be shown with any certainty to have been the case (see below).[118] In most cases, it appears that even tiny

114 See above, pp. 22–55.
115 CPR, 1330–1334, p. 506; F. Hancock, Dunster Church and Priory (Taunton, 1905); Cramp, 'Excavations at Wearmouth and Jarrow', pp. 21–66; C. Swynnerton, 'The Priory of St Leonard of Stanley, co. Gloucester, in the light of recent discoveries documentary and structural', Archaeologia, 2nd series, xxi (1921), pp. 199–226; NRO, DCN 2/3/52; H. and T. Miles, 'Pilton, North Devon. Excavations within a Medieval Village', Devon Archaeological Society Proceedings, xxxiii (1975), pp. 267–95; Mon. Ang., III, pp. 615–16, no. 9; Mahany, 'St Leonard's Priory', pp. 17–22; Medieval Archaeology, ix (1965), p. 183; N. Pevsner and B. Wilson, Buildings of England: Norwich and North-East Norfolk, 2nd edn (London, 1997), pp. 504–5.
116 Gilchrist, Gender and Material Culture, pp. 128–43.
117 J. Grundy, G. McCombie, P. Ryder, H. Welfare and N. Pevsner, Buildings of England: Northumberland, 2nd edn (London, 1992), pp. 235–6.
118 A seventeenth-century plan of Cranborne shows what appear to be monastic buildings fifty feet from the church, whereas it is claimed that the priory buildings at Penwortham were about three hundred feet to the north-east of the church: Royal Commission on Historical Monuments (England): Dorset, V (London, 1975), p. 5; VCH, Lancashire, VI, p. 53. The second statement is unsubstantiated, while the Cranborne buildings shown might have been priory outbuildings. The evidence for Kilpeck is rather stronger and the priory is thought to have been 340 metres

daughter houses used churches or chapels attached to their domestic buildings.

Much about the character of the domestic buildings at dependencies remains obscure. For many sites, we must rely on fragmentary survivals and partial excavation. Only at Binham, Finchale, Holy Island and Tynemouth is there still enough above ground to reconstruct the monastic plan in some fullness, although archaeological exploration has recovered similarly detailed information from a few other cells. Moreover, at Holy Island alone can the outer court and outbuildings be traced.[119] What material evidence we have reveals miniature monasteries exhibiting the usual domestic buildings; and a similar picture emerges from the paper survey of Rumburgh Priory, which describes the claustral ranges of the cell together with a number of outbuildings.[120] No chapter house is mentioned at sixteenth-century Rumburgh, and visitation reports from the Augustinian cells of Breedon and Blythburgh reveal that these two priories were using parts of their churches for chapter meetings in the later middle ages.[121] But with the possible exception of chapter houses, it appears that most English cells were planned to look like full-scale independent monasteries on a smaller scale.

However, there are also several signs of an increasing domestication of daughter-house plans in the later middle ages as their populations began to dwindle and as standards of living began to rise outside the cloister. Indeed the sites of Finchale and Holy Island are chiefly famous for the evidence they provide for the secularisation of small monasteries. At Finchale, a sumptuous domestic range south-east of the cloister was built for the prior, which also provided facilities for those monks sent on their *ludi*. In the later middle ages, the Holy Island cloister was re-modelled around the prior's apartments in the south range, with the monastic refectory converted into his hall and a

south-east of the famous parish church of St David: R. Shoesmith (ed.), 'Excavations at Kilpeck, Herefordshire', *Transactions of the Woolhope Naturalists' Field Club*, xlvii (1992), pp. 162–209. It may well be therefore that the monks walked across the fields to this building for their services. The connection between the priory and the church of Kilpeck, however, may not be quite as secure as has always been thought. J. F. King has recently questioned the assumption that the monks were responsible for this fine Norman church by dating it to the 1120s or early 1130s, before the foundation of the monastery in 1134: J. F. King, 'The Parish Church at Kilpeck Reassessed', in *Medieval Art, Architecture and Archaeology at Hereford*, ed. D. Whitehead, British Archaeological Association Conference Transactions, XV (1995), pp. 82–93. And although the monks were initially installed in the parish church, it is not impossible that they moved at a later date to their own place of worship, as did their neighbours at Ewyas Harold. For other possible examples of detached priory buildings, see Gilchrist, *Gender and Material Culture*, pp. 119–20.

[119] There is no evidence of separate infirmary courts at daughter houses. Several of the larger cells seem to have had infirmaries of some kind, but it is likely that they were placed within the main claustral ranges as at Holy Island: Thompson, *Lindisfarne Priory*, p. 12.

[120] *Mon. Ang.*, III, pp. 615–16, no. 9.

[121] *Lincoln Visitations, 1420–1449*, II, p. 41; *Norwich Visitations*, p. 177.

bakehouse and brewhouse added to the west range.[122] A similar domestication of claustral buildings seems to have taken place at Jarrow, another
Durham cell, where the east and south ranges were apparently adapted to
resemble a secular house.[123] That other dependencies took on a more domestic appearance in the later middle ages, particularly those that experienced a
fall in numbers, is suggested by the terminology of numerous inventories. To
take a few examples, the fifteenth-century inventories of St Leonard's
Norwich mention a pantry, buttery, kitchen, hall, chambers, study and dormitory; that of Hatfield Peverel in 1536 refers to the hall, kitchen, buttery
and several chambers and parlours; and the Rumburgh paper survey describes
a hall, with a parlour and chamber at its east end, a house with a larder, an
old hall, two kitchens and seven chambers, one with a buttery attached.[124]

In most cases, these changes seem to have involved only the adaptation of
pre-existing claustral buildings to give them a more domestic character. A
much more far-reaching secularisation, however, was undertaken by the
priory of Felixstowe (or Walton) in the mid-fourteenth century. The original
priory was gravely damaged by flooding in or shortly before the summer of
1367 and two years later a papal licence was issued to Rochester to rebuild
their cell in the parish of St Mary, Walton.[125] As far as we can tell, the original priory had been laid out according to the normal claustral principles, and
it is recorded that Prior Silvester 'made a refectory and dormitory and hos-
telry' at Felixstowe in the late twelfth century.[126] By the time of the flooding,
the population of the priory had probably already fallen from the fourteen
monks recorded in the early fourteenth century to the three dwelling there
in 1381, and so large-scale monastic buildings were not needed. Instead a
domestic block with a hall and chambers was constructed, similar to those
found at alien cells like Minster Lovell and Grove.[127] No chapel was built,
with the monks using the nearby parish church of St Mary for their services.
A similar block of buildings seems to have been built for the four canons
dwelling at Ovingham, the cell of Hexham founded in 1378.[128] No doubt the
designs adopted for Ovingham and the re-founded Felixstowe were chosen
for pragmatic reasons. But the apparently widespread movement to convert
priory buildings from the traditional claustral plan to a more domestic layout

---

122 Peers, 'Finchale Priory', pp. 214–18; Thompson, *Lindisfarne Priory*, pp. 10–13;
   Knowles and St Joseph, *Monastic Sites*, pp. 40–3.
123 Cramp, 'Excavations at Wearmouth and Jarrow', pp. 54–7.
124 W. S. Bensly, 'St Leonard's Priory, Norwich', *Norfolk Archaeology*, xii (1895), pp.
   196–227; R. C. Fowler (ed.), 'Inventories of Essex Monasteries in 1536', *Transactions
   of the Essex Archaeological Society*, new series, ix (1906), pp. 395–400; *Mon. Ang.*, III,
   pp. 615–16, no. 9.
125 CPL, IV, pp. 66, 79.
126 *Registrum Roffense*, ed. J. Thorpe (London, 1769), p. 121.
127 West, 'Excavation of Walton Priory', pp. 131–41. At a later date, the monks replaced
   the original hall and extended one of the chamber blocks.
128 Pevsner et al., *Northumberland*, pp. 538–9.

could be seen as an indication of the loss of monastic character at many cells in the later middle ages.

Standards of Living

The increasing domestication of daughter houses also suggests that life in these small priories might not have been quite so uncomfortable as has sometimes been assumed, although of course the standard of living in a cell could not compare to that enjoyed in the mother house. The small size of many daughter-house communities in relation to their incomes would have permitted more spending on the provisions and amenities of individual monks than was possible in many lesser independent priories. In some dependencies, monks might have spent much of their time in the prior's quarters. Continued reference to dormitories in inventories and to repairs carried out there in account rolls, however, suggests that ordinary brethren continued to sleep in the common dorter, albeit possibly divided into cells by the fifteenth century.[129] They probably ate with the prior in the hall, however, since more than one ordinance ordered that the whole community 'should eat and drink in one place constituted for that purpose'.[130] It may well be that the redesigning of refectories into secular halls was partly a device to facilitate meat-eating in daughter houses. With the mother house community spending less time in oversized fraters and more in comfortable misericords, it would hardly be surprising if the brethren in their cells followed suit. Eating meat at Benedictine cells was strictly forbidden in a number of ordinances of the thirteenth and early fourteenth centuries, but after the toleration of meat-eating in the 1336 constitutions of Benedict XII this practice was probably as common in black monk dependencies as in other houses of the order.[131]

The quality of food available in daughter houses is harder to judge, since it is impossible to know which of the items recorded in accounts appeared on the monks' table. Small quantities of spices and wine were often purchased even by poor priories like Aldeby and Hoxne, but these might well have been reserved primarily to the prior and his guests. Complaints about the inadequate provision of food were made against the priors of St Leonard's Stamford in 1261–2 and Freiston in 1434, but do not seem to have been

---

129 References to cells in the dormitories of St Leonard's Norwich and Yarmouth are made in these priories' accounts in the mid-fifteenth century: NRO, DCN 2/3/64, DCN 2/4/6.

130 DCM, Loc. XXVII: 4; CBM, II, no. 158, p. 89; *Chapters of the Augustinian Canons*, p. 242.

131 GASA, II, pp. 304, 441; Barlow, *Durham Annals*, no. 30, pp. 99–100; *Hist. et Cart. Gloucestriae*, I, pp. 42–3; *Registrum Epistolarum Peckham*, III, no. 582, p. 799; Knowles, RO, II, pp. 4–5.

particularly common.[132] Some priors were apparently more concerned with food than others. Under Prior John Stowe of Aldeby, kitchen expenses rose between 1439 and 1442 by 50 per cent from about £10 per year to over £15 per year, with considerably more spent on spices than had previously been the case; and Prior William of Colne was commended for increasing his monks' food allowances and pittances in the late twelfth or early thirteenth century.[133] In general, the large quantities of meat and fish of several varieties purchased at those cells for which accounts survive suggest that an upper-class diet was still available to monks dwelling away from their mother houses, albeit one comparable to that of the gentry rather than the more lavish fare on offer in the great abbeys they had left behind.[134]

Another determinant of the standard of living in dependencies was the upkeep of the buildings. There are signs of the disrepair of monastic buildings at a number of cells, though it is hard to assess the scale of damage from complaints in visitation records. At Aldeby, Binham, Breedon, Brooke, Finchale, Hurley and St Ives, either the church or the monks' apartments were said at one time or other to be 'ruinous', though few details are given about the nature of the damage.[135] The most serious case seems to have been Kidwelly in the early sixteenth century, where it was necessary to sequester the priory's revenues to mend the chancel and priory house.[136] But against these examples must be placed the evidence for new building and updating in cells. Many of the claustral buildings that still stand were built or altered in the later middle ages. Aside from the later adaptations made at Finchale and Holy Island, the surviving buildings at St Nicholas' Exeter and Dunster are almost entirely of the fifteenth century, whereas the new cloister at St James' Bristol and the hall at Yarmouth were the work of the fourteenth.[137]

---

132 Barlow, *Durham Annals*, no. 57, pp. 123–4; *Lincoln Visitations, 1420–1449*, I, p. 38. For the regularity of monastic complaints about food, see C. Harper-Bill, 'The Labourer is Worthy of his Hire? – Complaints about Diet in Late Medieval English Monasteries', in *The Church in Pre-Reformation Society*, ed. C. M. Barron and C. Harper-Bill (Woodbridge, 1985), pp. 95–107.

133 NRO, DCN 2/2/13–15; *Chronicon Monasterii de Abingdon*, ed. J. Stevenson, 2 vols, RS, ii (1858), II, pp. 294–5.

134 Cf. C. Dyer, 'English Diet in the Later Middle Ages', in *Social Relations and Ideas*, ed. T. H. Aston et al. (Cambridge, 1983), pp. 191–216; C. Dyer, *Standards of Living in the Later Middle Ages* (Cambridge, 1989), pp. 55–70.

135 *Norwich Visitations*, pp. 73, 75–6, 78 (Aldeby); *Registra*, I, pp. 137–43 (Binham); *Lincoln Visitations, 1420–1449*, II, p. 41 (Breedon); *VCH, Rutland*, I, p. 160; *L&P*, X, no. 1191, p. 499 (Brooke); DCM, 1.9 Pont. 1b (Finchale); *CPR, 1399–1401*, p. 487, *1485–1494*, p. 304 (Hurley); *Lincoln Visitations, 1517–1531*, III, p. 87 (St Ives).

136 G. Williams, 'Kidwelly Priory', in *Sir Gâr: Studies in Carmarthenshire History*, ed. H. James, Carmarthenshire Antiquarian Society Monograph Series, IV (1991), pp. 199–200. It may also be that the nave of the priory/parish church was shortened at this time.

137 Youings et al., *St Nicholas Priory*, pp. 22–30; H. C. Maxwell-Lyte, *A History of Dunster and of the Families of Mohun and Luttrell*, 2 vols (London, 1909), II, p. 392; *Medieval*

This impression of the regular rebuilding and renovation of domestic buildings is reinforced by documentary sources. The accounts of the Norwich cells, for example, show the spending of considerable sums on construction projects in the fifteenth century. Lynn Priory disbursed about £100 on a 'new building' and other works between 1400 and 1403, and well over £40 on a new hall in the years 1442–8. A new dormitory was put up at Hoxne in the 1450s and a porch added to its hall soon afterwards.[138] Not every cell could afford to undertake renovations on this scale in the later middle ages. Nevertheless, alongside the favourable reports of the suppression commissioners about the condition of many small monasteries in 1536–7 and recent archaeological work at lesser houses like Bordesley and Thornholme, where the use of modern stratographical techniques has revealed far more alterations to buildings than had been imagined, the evidence for cells looks significant.[139]

There is also some reason to believe that the standard of sanitation at the majority of daughter houses was quite adequate. Excavation has discovered remarkably sophisticated water management at many monasteries, large and small alike, although it has been argued that the poorest nunneries did not achieve such high levels of hygiene.[140] That the Norwich cells considered water management a priority is indicated by the regular sums disbursed on their latrines, cisterns, aqueducts, drains and gutters in the later middle ages.[141] St Nicholas' Exeter paid 8s. per year to be connected to the conduit of the cathedral and town corporation, and the late medieval stone-lined drain of St James' Bristol has recently been located by excavation.[142] The standard of the latrines at daughter houses is harder to discover. The monks of Leominster seem to have flushed their latrines by a canalised stream running alongside their reredorter, but the facilities at St Leonard's Stamford were not quite so advanced. There the monks made do with a stone-lined cesspit, in the manner of an ordinary garderobe, which had to be dug out

Archaeology, xxxviii (1994), p. 191; Pevsner and Wilson, Norwich and North-East Norfolk, pp. 504–5.

[138] NRO, DCN, 2/1/21(v–vii), 2/1/38–44, 2/6/18, 20. For the wholly exceptional building programme at St Leonard's Norwich in the mid-fifteenth century, see below, pp. 265–6.

[139] Knowles, RO, III, pp. 314–15; Hirst and Wright, 'Bordesley Abbey Church', pp. 295–311; G. Coppack, 'Thornholme Priory: the Development of a Monastic Outer Court', in Gilchrist and Mytum, Archaeology of Rural Monasteries, pp. 185–222.

[140] E.g. C. J. Bond, 'Water Management in the Rural Monastery', in Gilchrist and Mytum, Archaeology of Rural Monasteries, pp. 83–111; J. Bond, 'Monastic Water Management in Great Britain: A Review', in Monastic Archaeology. Papers on the Study of Medieval Monasteries, ed. G. Keevill, M. Aston and T. Hall (Oxford, 2001), pp. 88–136; G. Coppack, English Heritage Book of Abbeys and Priories (London, 1990), pp. 95–8; Gilchrist, Contemplation and Action, p. 145.

[141] E.g. NRO, DCN 2/1/19, 20(ii, v), 21(v), 58, 2/2/16, 21, 2/4/10, 12–13; Windsor, St George's Chapel, I.C.14, 29.

[142] Youings et al., St Nicholas Priory, p. 12; Medieval Archaeology, xl (1996), p. 240.

regularly. More archaeological study is needed to confirm whether the Leominster or the Stamford system was more common in cells.[143]

But however comfortable the conditions in dependent priories might have been, they could not have compared to the amenities available in the mother house. As a result, a potential cause of discontent among the inmates of dependencies was always the belief that they were receiving inferior treatment to the main community. These concerns manifested themselves most obviously in contentions over the provision of pocket money and post mortem services. By the later middle ages, the payment of clothes and spice money in cells seems to have been universal, but the amounts given sometimes caused controversy. Although an episcopal visitation of Durham in the first half of the fourteenth century ordered that 'the brethren staying in cells and external places should be supplied with clothes and oblations just as is supplied to others staying in the church', it was complained in the 1350s that monks in dependencies received half as much as those at Durham. And after similar complaints in the Gloucester satellites, it was agreed in October 1317 that all dwelling in cells should be paid one silver mark per year.[144] The amounts received at daughter houses nevertheless varied according to custom and to the wealth of the house concerned; at the cells of Durham by the late fifteenth century, 32s. was given to individual monks at Farne Island each year, 44s. to those at Holy Island and Lytham, 46s. 8d. at Wearmouth, 47s. 4d. at Stamford and 49s. at Jarrow.[145] But the arguments for uniformity seem to have borne fruit elsewhere. In the 1520s, the St Albans monks at Belvoir, Binham, Hatfield Peverel, Hertford and Wallingford all received 40s. per year, although those dwelling at Pembroke were given 53s. 4d.; and in 1352 the chamberlain of Tewkesbury was paying 27s. to every monk of the abbey both in the mother house and in its cells.[146]

Even more important than money to brethren sent to daughter houses were equal rights in death. It was laid down in several ordinances of the thirteenth and early fourteenth centuries that a monk's soul should be properly provided for whether he died in the mother house or in a cell.[147] The custumary of St Mary's York ordered that any monk dying in its satellites should be commemorated in the mother house 'in everything just as if he

---

[143] D. L. Brown and D. Wilson, 'Leominster Old Priory: Recording of Standing Buildings and Excavations, 1979–80', *Archaeological Journal*, cli (1994), pp. 307–68; Mahany, 'St Leonard's Priory', pp. 17–22.

[144] DCM, 2.9 Pont. 10, 1.9 Pont. 1b; *Hist. et Cart. Gloucestriae*, I, pp. 42–3.

[145] Piper, *Jarrow*, p. 16.

[146] PRO, E315/272, fols 70r–78v; 'A Tewkesbury Compotus', ed. F. W. P. Hicks, *TBGAS*, lv (1934), p. 255.

[147] For an account of the post-mortem provision for brethren dying in dependent priories laid down in French and German customaries, see J.-L. Lemaître, 'La mort et la commémoration des défunts dans les prieurés', in *Prieurs et prieurés dans l'occident médiéval*, ed. J.-L. Lemaître, Hautes études médiévales et modernes, lx (Geneva, 1987), pp. 181–90.

had died in his own house among us'.[148] Similarly, when the communities of Gloucester and Bath laid down the services to be performed for deceased brethren it was made clear that monks dying in their cells were to be included in this provision; and in ordaining in 1274 that a daily mass should be said for all the souls of the community after Lady mass, Abbot Norton of St Albans made the same guarantee.[149] The inmates of cells were increasingly intolerant of disparity. In March 1311, the abbot and convent of Reading granted for the first time to its brethren dying at Leominster a year's corrody to finance suffrages for their souls; and an identical injunction was made by the prior and convent of Hurley two and a half years later in order to bring their practice into line with that of their mother house, Westminster.[150] But even when monks in cells were accorded the same privileges in life and death as those remaining in the mother house, service in these small offshoots was no doubt often unpopular. Nevertheless, a close examination of the life experienced in dependencies does not produce the picture of boredom and privation that we have been led to expect in lesser monasteries and in daughter houses in particular.

What this account of everyday life in cells can tell us about the experience of other lesser monasteries remains open to question. In some areas, such as the administrative roles of their monks and the generally good repair of their buildings, the evidence from dependencies accords with conclusions that have been tentatively advanced for autonomous small houses. In others, like the prominent public role of their priors, the monastic plan and the adequate standard of living, most of the surviving material comes from the middling rather than the smallest cells. In these matters, therefore, comparison should be made with priories of a similar income bracket, that is about £100 per year. In still other ways, dependencies are clearly unrepresentative, for example in their extremely small populations and their access to motherhouse libraries. Nevertheless, the impression of monastic life in a small priory that emerges from a study of satellite priories is suggestive. Our understanding of monasteries of this size is so limited and so skewed by the kinds of references to their affairs that survive that the opportunity provided by the abundant material for daughter houses is too good to miss, despite the problems it raises. Further work, both archaeological and wherever possible documentary, is needed to shed more light on the lesser religious houses of medieval England and Wales. But in the meantime, the possibility that these priories were rather more vital than has been allowed should be taken seriously.

---

148 *St Mary's Chronicle*, p. 104.
149 *Hist et Cart. Gloucestriae*, I, pp. 32–3; Hunt, *Bath Chartularies*, part ii, no. 808, p. 152; GASA, I, pp. 449–51.
150 BL, Harley MS 82, fol. 1r; Wethered, *St Mary's, Hurley*, no. 214, p. 149.

5

Dependent Priories and their Neighbours

The importance of the role played by monasteries in local society is one of the most difficult questions of monastic history. Due to deficiencies in evidence, basic issues like the economic impact of religious houses on their locality, the extent of the social services they provided or how much layfolk showed an interest in the monks' religious activities remain very hard to elucidate. Perhaps most difficult of all to establish is the degree of favour with which monasteries were viewed by their secular neighbours. This issue has appeared particularly urgent to historians of the Dissolution seeking to explain why the wholesale suppression of religious houses provoked relatively little uproar in the 1530s. It used to be fashionable to attribute the ease of the Dissolution to the unpopularity of monasticism in Tudor England, but more recent studies have argued that there was no hostility and even some support for the monastic ideal at this time.[1] But although considerable effort has been invested in stressing the popularity and vigour of parochial religion in the period preceding the Reformation, much less work has been done to locate the place of religious houses in this picture of apparent vitality and strength.[2]

The role of monasteries in local society occupies a relatively minor place in Professor Knowles' history of the religious orders, but considerable advances have been made in this subject over the past thirty years. The enormous archive at Durham allowed Professor Dobson to portray in remarkable detail the position of the late medieval priors of Durham in northern aristocratic society.[3] More recently the work of Benjamin Thompson and Marilyn Oliva has revealed much about lay attitudes to lesser houses, both

---

[1] J. J. Scarisbrick, *The Reformation and the English People* (Oxford, 1984), pp. 61–84; J. A. F. Thomson, *The Early Tudor Church and Society* (London, 1993), pp. 188–232; C. Harper-Bill, *The Pre-Reformation Church in England 1400–1530* (London, 1989), pp. 36–43.

[2] But see the essays in *The Religious Orders in Pre-Reformation England*, ed. J. G. Clark (Woodbridge, 2002), and J. G. Clark, 'Selling the Holy Places: Monastic Efforts to Win Back the People in Fifteenth-Century England', in *Social Attitudes and Political Structures in the Fifteenth Century*, ed. T. Thornton (Stroud, 2000), pp. 13–32, for some important recent contributions to this question.

[3] Dobson, *Durham Priory*, pp. 114–202.

male and female.[4] Thompson has highlighted the reliance of smaller monasteries on their patrons but has argued that there was a sizeable proletariat of religious houses whose spiritual services were of little interest to lay elites. Oliva has presented a more positive picture of nunneries by examining the responses of other social strata to religious communities. Her analysis of wills suggests that small nunneries attracted considerable support from the lesser gentry and yeoman farmers, leading her to the conclusion that the small female monasteries of East Anglia were 'an integral part of the local social landscape'.[5]

However, the view that the monasteries of pre-Reformation England, though inoffensive to their neighbours, were doing little to attract lay support remains dominant.[6] Only the austere orders and the friars were regularly remembered by testators, whereas in the foundation of chantries or in the place of burial, monasteries had been replaced by parish churches as the favoured choice of the elites in late medieval England.[7] Lesser religious houses in particular – too small to attract the attention of aristocratic benefactors, too poor to contribute much in social services or economic stimulus and apparently too weak spiritually to win the approval of the pious – are thought to have made little impression on their localities. This view, however, can be challenged. The suppression of the smaller houses seems to have provoked widespread resistance in 1536–7, and it is possible that such communities enjoyed closer relations with their neighbours than did monasteries of great size and wealth.[8] Moreover, the evidence surviving for depend-

4   B. Thompson, 'Habendum et Tenendum: Lay and Ecclesiastical Attitudes to the Property of the Church', in Religious Belief and Ecclesiastical Careers in Late Medieval England, ed. C. Harper-Bill (Woodbridge, 1991), pp. 197–238; B. Thompson, 'The Laity, the Alien Priories, and the Redistribution of Ecclesiastical Property', in England in the Fifteenth Century, ed. N. Rogers (Stamford, 1994), pp. 19–41; B. Thompson, 'Monasteries and their Patrons at Foundation and Dissolution', TRHS, 6th series, iv (1994), pp. 103–26; B. Thompson, 'Monasteries, Society and Reform in Late Medieval England', in Clark, Religious Orders, pp. 165–95; M. Oliva, The Convent and the Community in Late Medieval England. Female Monasteries in the Diocese of Norwich, 1350–1540 (Woodbridge, 1998); M. Oliva, 'Patterns of Patronage to Female Monasteries in the Late Middle Ages', in Clark, Religious Orders, pp. 155–62.
5   Oliva, Convent and Community, pp. 174–83.
6   E.g. 'Increasingly in the later Middle Ages, however, the enclosed religious orders failed to satisfy the spiritual needs and aspirations of the laity': Harper-Bill, Pre-Reformation Church, pp. 40–1.
7   Scarisbrick, Reformation and English People, pp. 5–6; C. Cross, 'Monasticism and Society in the Diocese of York, 1520–40', TRHS, 5th series, xxxviii (1988), pp. 131–45; J. Rosenthal, The Purchase of Paradise (London, 1972), pp. 82–4; N. Saul, 'The Religious Sympathies of the Gentry in Gloucestershire, 1200–1500', TBGAS, xcviii (1980), pp. 99–112.
8   Several studies have argued that the dissolution of the lesser monasteries was a relatively unimportant factor in the Pilgrimage of Grace and the Lincolnshire rising of 1536, including most recently R. W. Hoyle, The Pilgrimage of Grace and the Politics of the 1530s (Oxford, 2001), esp. pp. 46–50. But for convincing cases that the suppression of the lesser houses was a prominent grievance in these rebellions, see

ent priories, though inadequate in some respects, suggests that these houses were often an important part of the fabric of local religion and had much more to offer their lay neighbours than has usually been allowed.

Aristocratic Interest

In studying the impact of monasteries on their localities, we are faced with the obvious difficulty that rather more can be recovered about the predilections of the aristocracy than of other groups. Of the several studies which have investigated the spiritual preferences of the elites of late medieval England, all have concluded that monasteries were no longer central to their religion.[9] More recently, Benjamin Thompson's work on aristocratic attitudes towards smaller monasteries, and particularly the alien priories, has powerfully reinforced this impression. Thompson has shown how the patronage of many lesser houses in Norfolk had passed by the later middle ages into the hands of the Crown or the nobility – an 'upward-mobility of advowsons' – who often had little interest in these small foundations. With their spiritual services of no value to their current patrons and their suffrages performed primarily for the benefit of deceased benefactors, Thompson argues that 'the myriad small and poor institutions . . . were often not seen to be performing a useful contemporary function for the living'.[10] This conclusion relates only to patronal attitudes towards late medieval monasteries, and does not take into account how other sections of society might have viewed them. Nevertheless, the loss of the support of one's patron, the special protector of a monastery's interests, would have been a severe blow for any house. It is therefore necessary to ask whether Thompson's findings for Norfolk can be said to apply to English dependencies.

Thompson has suggested that smaller houses often did not even know who their patrons were by the later middle ages. This appears to have been the case at Great Massingham in January 1510, when Henry VIII granted the patronage of that cell to the Dominican nuns of Dartford, since there were doubts over whether or not the priory's advowson was attached to the nuns' manor of Massingham.[11] It is important to note, however, that many daughter houses did not have a secular patron in the first place. In the case of

C. S. L. Davies, 'The Pilgrimage of Grace Reconsidered', *Past and Present*, xli (1968), pp. 54–76 and C. Haigh, *The Last Days of the Lancashire Monasteries and the Pilgrimage of Grace*, Chetham Society, 3rd series, xvii (1969), pp. 50–85.

9   E.g. Rosenthal, *Purchase of Paradise*; M. G. Vale, *Piety, Charity and Literacy among the Yorkshire Gentry, 1370–1480*, Borthwick Paper, no. 1 (1976); Saul, 'Religious Sympathies', pp. 99–112; P. W. Fleming, 'Charity, Faith and the Gentry of Kent, 1422–1529', in *Property and Politics: Essays in Later Medieval English History*, ed. A. J. Pollard (Gloucester, 1984), pp. 36–58.

10 Thompson, 'Monasteries and their Patrons', p. 121.

11 *L&P*, I(i), no. 357(31), p. 165.

wholly self-founded cells – perhaps up to a quarter of English dependencies – the advowson belonged to the mother house and no lay intermediary existed. In several other instances, there was an episcopal patron. With this in mind, it can nevertheless be seen that a significant number of English daughter houses found their advowsons to be upwardly mobile in the later middle ages. The patronage of several cells, including Ewenny, Kidwelly and Lytham, originally held by knights, eventually passed to the Crown (in these instances all via the Duchy of Lancaster); and the advowsons of other priories, such as Deeping St James, Kilpeck and Snape had come by the four-teenth century from equally humble beginnings into the hands of peers, namely the earls of Kent, Ormond and Suffolk respectively. It is likely that in such instances, the priories concerned received less attention from their more exalted patrons than had previously been the case. However, the example of Breedon, where the mother house itself engineered the replace-ment of the resident lord of the manor as its cell's patron by Thomas, earl of Lancaster in the early fourteenth century, suggests that to dependent priories (which already had influential backing from their parents) a more distant patron might even be considered preferable.[12]

But if several cells did find their advowsons coming into the hands of remote and powerful patrons, this trend was not linear or universal. A good number of daughter houses were founded by men of the highest social stand-ing, and the patronage of some of these actually passed to families of lower rank through inheritance, enfeoffment or purchase. Wymondham Priory was founded by William d'Aubigny *pincerna*, and its advowson was in the posses-sion of the earls of Arundel for generations. Later patrons, however, were of lower rank, including the de Tateshall family and, in the mid-fifteenth century, the naturalised Danish soldier Sir Andrew Ogard. The patronage of Rumburgh Priory, founded by the first earl of Richmond, was in the hands of John de Nerford, as tenant-in-chief of the king, at his death in August 1363; and the advowson of the Berkeley foundation of Leonard Stanley passed suc-cessively to three local gentry families in the fifteenth century, the de Cauntelos, Cheddars and Wykeses.[13] The upward mobility of advowsons could also be checked by the division of a priory's patronage between coheirs, as at St Bees after the death of John de Multon, lord of Egremont in 1334.[14] In general, Thompson's findings for Norfolk carry considerable validity for English cells, but the complexity of the pattern must also be acknowledged.

Every dependent priory, with the single remarkable exception of the de Vere foundation at Colne, also faced the replacement of their founding fami-lies by newcomers. As Thompson has argued, monasteries situated at the

12 See above, pp. 71–2.
13 GASA, II, pp. 65–6; *Calendar of Inquisitions Post Mortem* (HMSO, 1904–), XI, no. 565, pp. 429–30; VCH, Gloucestershire, X, p. 260.
14 CClR, 1337–1339, pp. 366–8. The St Bees advowson was then divided into three and remained so until the priory's dissolution.

head of a lordship were more likely to retain the interest of new patrons than less accessible houses, and many English dependencies fell into this category.[15] Where new families already possessed several lordships, however, their lesser seats might become of secondary interest. The advowsons of the tiny Marcher cells of Ewyas Harold and Kilpeck both passed to non-resident lords in the fourteenth century, the de la Warrs and the Butler earls of Ormond respectively. As a result, both families took little interest in their priories and both readily consented to Gloucester Abbey's proposal to close down each house and to transfer their prayers to the mother house.[16] Some of the larger dependencies, and particularly those located at the *caput* of major baronies, were more successful in retaining the active support of successive patrons. From the limited evidence that survives, representatives of more than one patronal family are known to have been buried in the priories of Belvoir, Brecon and Dunster. Indeed, Belvoir seems to have maintained especially close ties with its new patrons, the Ros family of Helmesley, who were generous benefactors to the priory in the later middle ages.[17] It is notable, too, that Snape's and Wymondham's successful attempts to win independence from their mother houses in the fifteenth century were assisted by patrons of different lineages from the priories' founders.[18]

Nevertheless, it may well be true that only a minority of wealthier and well-situated English dependencies were able to retain the active interest of their lay patrons in the later middle ages. Instances of patrons endowing cells at this time are few. Moreover, only a handful of cells (Belvoir, Brecon, Colne, Deeping St James and Dunster) can be seen providing practical services, such as keeping genealogical records or storing arms or deeds, for their patrons.[19] Since most of these priories are known from other sources to have enjoyed particularly close relations with their patrons, the lack of other examples of this kind is probably significant. It may be that cells were unrepresentative in this respect: as we have seen, the patronage of daughter houses conferred rather fewer benefits than that of an independent monastery, since the parent abbey reserved to itself several of the traditional patronal rights.[20] However, there is also evidence to suggest that the vacuum created by an indifferent or non-existent patron was sometimes filled by others and that the opportunity to forge close relations with other local families was usually

---

[15] Thompson, 'Monasteries and their Patrons', p. 113. Several of these cells were responsible for services in castle chapels which would have helped build relations with new patronal families.

[16] See above, pp. 152, 154.

[17] *Mon. Ang.*, III, p. 291, no. 14; *Historical Manuscripts Commission: The Duke of Rutland*, IV (1905), pp. 120–1.

[18] See above, pp. 108–9, 109–10.

[19] Cambridge, Trinity College, MS O.9.25, fols 6v, 8v; BL, Add. Ch. 19868; *Cal. Inq. Post Mort.*, XV, no. 889, pp. 349–50; *Calendar of Inquisitions Miscellaneous*, 7 vols (HMSO, 1916–69), VII, no. 53, p. 39; CPR, 1281–1292, p. 24.

[20] See above, pp. 69–73.

available to religious houses. Dr Greene has described how the medium-sized Norton Priory came under the protection of the Dutton family in the later middle ages as the house's patrons, the barons of Halton, lost interest; and Professor Colvin noted a similar trend at a number of Premonstratensian houses.[21]

The evidence surviving for dependencies also affords several examples of local worthies taking a close interest in the affairs of these small houses. Professor Dobson has shown how the patronless cells of Durham came under the influence of important local families, such as the Homes (Coldingham), Hiltons (Wearmouth), Ogles (Farne and Holy Islands) and Stanleys (Lytham), who effectively sought to arrogate the vacant position of patron to themselves. Similarly, the lords of Blythburgh, although not officially the patrons of that cell, seem to have taken a particular interest in its affairs.[22] It is much easier to trace the aristocratic contacts of religious houses in the twelfth and thirteenth centuries when regular benefactions were being made; but it should not be assumed that the drying up of grants of land to monasteries in the later middle ages was necessarily a symptom of apathy towards them.

There remains the suspicion, however, that much of the attention paid by local elites to daughter houses was designed to produce some material return. By courting a cell, a benefactor might hope to curry favour with its powerful mother house. Moreover, the priors of all but the smallest dependencies had some quantity of patronage in their gift and so their favour was also worth acquiring. Several letters survive in the archives of Durham and St Albans requesting the appointment of individual monks as priors of cells or that existing heads might not be recalled. In the mid-fifteenth century, Elizabeth Lady Grey wrote to Durham asking that Dan John, a monk of their cell at Stamford, should be made prior of that house, since 'I withe othur lordes ladys and gentils in these parties haue gode love and effection' for him, and remarking that she would be 'gode and tendur lady unto that saide place' if her wishes were met; and similar letters about this Stamford monk were sent to Durham by Sir John Basing and Lord Zouche.[23] It may be that these advances were ignored, since in 1486 Prior Auckland of Durham, in refusing a similar petition from the earl of Northumberland, boasted that the heads of the cathedral priory had never yielded to such a request 'fro the fundacyon of our monastery unto this tyme'.[24] Nevertheless, petitioners to St Albans appear to have enjoyed some success in this regard;[25] and in any case the

21 J. P. Greene, *Norton Priory* (Cambridge, 1989), pp. 9–15; H. M. Colvin, *The White Canons in England* (Oxford, 1951), pp. 302–4.
22 Dobson, *Durham Priory*, pp. 304–5; *Blythburgh Priory Cartulary*, ed. C. Harper-Bill, 2 parts, Suffolk Records Society. Suffolk Charters, II–III (1980–1), I, pp. 3, 7. See above, p. 95, for the role of the Stanleys in William Partrike's attempts to win greater freedom of action from Durham.
23 DCM, Loc. XXV: 135; Piper, 'Stamford', part ii, p. 3.
24 J. Raine, *The History and Antiquities of North Durham* (London, 1852), p. 356.
25 *Registra*, II, pp. 165–6, 268–9.

strong interest shown in the choice of priors by these cells' influential neighbours is of greater interest than the outcome of their requests. More-over, as William Partrike and William of Somerton found, there were always men who could be persuaded to bypass the mother house altogether to secure the presence of a sympathetic prior in the hope of future rewards.[26]

Daughter houses not only had ecclesiastical patronage in their gift, but also secular offices. Since so many cells lacked active lay patrons in the later middle ages, either because existing 'founders' took no interest or because the advowson belonged to the mother house or some other ecclesiastical owner, the office of the priory's head steward might carry particular influ-ence. The stewardships of the larger daughter houses seem to have been highly coveted: Sir William Stonor unsuccessfully sought that office at Wallingford Priory in 1479; and Lord Dacre and the earl of Cumberland fought over several stewardships in the 1530s, including that of the priory of Wetheral.[27] A similar conclusion emerges from an examination of the lay office holders listed for numerous cells in the *Valor Ecclesiasticus*, which included fees as an allowance. Of the forty dependencies whose officers are named, thirteen employed men ranked as knights or higher as head steward. These dignitaries included the earl of Worcester at Ewenny, the earl of Derby at Penwortham and Lytham and Lord Dacre at Wetheral.[28] Fifty per cent of dependencies valued at over £100 per year in the *Valor* are shown to have been employing titled stewards, compared with 40 per cent of those worth over £50 and 13 per cent of houses assessed at under £50. It would seem therefore that it was only the smallest cells which were unable to attract aristocratic interest at this time; indeed certain tiny dependencies, including Lincoln and Middlesbrough do not seem to have employed a steward at all in the 1530s. In contrast, many medium-sized and larger dependencies seem to have retained their relevance to local elites, even if relatively few maintained close relations with lay patrons by this date. But it may well be that this interest was focused primarily on the material benefits these priories could offer rather than the spiritual services they provided.

Social Services

Another attraction of daughter houses to local worthies was their hospi-tality. Although there is considerable evidence that the religious houses of late medieval England took very seriously St Benedict's exhortation that 'all guests that come be received like Christ', there nevertheless remains a

---

[26] See above, pp. 95, 97–8.
[27] *Kingsford's Stonor Letters and Papers 1290–1483*, ed. C. Carpenter (Cambridge, 1996), part ii, no. 244, p. 82; *L&P*, VII, no. 1549, p. 576.
[28] *Valor*, II, pp. 421–2, V, pp. 305, 233. The earl of Worcester was also receiving a fee of 40s. from Brecon Priory, although his office is not named and he was not the house's steward: ibid., IV, p. 401.

question mark over the quality and quantity of hospitality that smaller monasteries could afford to give.[29] It appears, however, that even the smallest houses kept guest houses in their western claustral range or outer court and that most cells did the same is suggested by the numerous documentary references to *hospitii* in their accounts and inventories.[30] The range of their provision is harder to assess. Some of the largest cells, notably Tynemouth and Dover, suffered from excessive levels of visitors owing to their strategic locations, and the situation of a cell would have been an important factor in determining its burden of entertaining.[31] The closure of Gloucester's daughter house at Kilpeck in 1428 was attributed in part to 'the immoderate concourse of people at the table of the priory' particularly, it appears, Welshmen from across the border.[32] Peter of Blois, however, found the monks of Wallingford to be somewhat less hospitable when he sought shelter there in the late twelfth century.[33] Fortunately, and most unusually for monasteries of this size, we do not need to rely solely on anecdotal evidence for information about the standard of hospitality at daughter houses because of the survival of so many account rolls. While the figures provided by this source are fragmentary, they point to a greater quantity of entertaining in cells than might have been expected.

The exact amounts spent on hospitality cannot be gleaned from account rolls because of inadequate itemisation and the impossibility of knowing from cash accounts how much home-grown produce found its way into the guest house. But even when there are no separate sections for expenditure on visitors, as in the accounts of the Norwich cells, a close reading gives the impression that considerable sums were used for this purpose. At the wealthier priories of Lynn and Yarmouth in particular, very large amounts regularly over £100 at the former house and around £50 at the latter, were spent on food in the second half of the fourteenth century (see Table 6.7, p. 263). Most of these provisions cannot have been consumed by the three or four monks at each cell and their modest households alone, and indeed occasional references in the accounts imply that a good deal was intended '*pro hospicio*'.[34] Wine and spices for guests are also regularly recorded at Lynn and Yarmouth, often at times when the monks themselves do not appear to have been enjoying these delicacies. Similarly, the accounts of all the Norwich cells are scattered with remarks that smaller receipts than usual have ensued

29 *The Rule of St Benedict in Latin and English*, ed. J. McCann (London, 1952), pp. 118–19, chap. 53.
30 For evidence of guest houses at nunneries, see R. Gilchrist, *Contemplation and Action. The Other Monasticism* (London, 1995), pp. 132–4.
31 *A History of Northumberland*, ed. H. H. E. Craster, 15 vols (Newcastle, 1893–1940), VIII, pp. 93, 98; *CPR, 1385–1389*, p. 494, *1485–1494*, pp. 423–4.
32 *Registrum Thome Spofford, Episcopi Herefordensis, AD 1422–1448*, ed. A. T. Bannister, C&Y Soc., xxiii (1919), pp. 104–6.
33 *Mon. Ang.*, III, p. 279.
34 E.g. DCN 2/1/5–6, 20(iv–vi), 21(i), 28–31.

from a particular source of income that year owing to hospitality expenses. For much of the fifteenth century, Lynn also regularly received annual sums of several pounds and Yarmouth a little less from paying guests ('in commensalibus').[35] As their incomes declined over the fifteenth century, expenditure on victuals fell significantly at both Lynn and Yarmouth to about £30 per year, suggesting that their hospitality provision was considerably curtailed in the face of financial difficulties.[36] Although much smaller sums were apparently diverted to entertaining at the poorer cells of Aldeby and Hoxne, it would seem that in times of prosperity both Lynn and Yarmouth were spending very large amounts on this service.

A few surviving accounts from the dependencies of St Albans and the priory of St Ives provide more evidence for hospitality expenses. At first glance, these documents seem to show a remarkably large proportion of the priories' incomes being spent on the entertainment of guests. About £40 was said to have been expended on the hospitium of the priories of Binham, Hatfield Peverel, Hertford, Pembroke and Wallingford in 1525/6, out of total incomes ranging from £80 to just over £140.[37] There is a strong suspicion, however, that these sums also include the dietary expenses of the convent and its servants, since no other food costs are recorded at each cell.[38] Similarly, the St Ives accounts show the priory spending between £11 and £27 per year between 1481 and 1526 'in hospicio', out of an annual income of about £100, but these entries might also refer primarily to household expenses.[39] On the other hand, these amounts hide large quantities of food supplied from the priory's own estates and, as at Lynn and Yarmouth, the large and fluctuating sums spent on provisions at St Ives do suggest that a considerable number of guests were fed there. The cumulative evidence from surviving accounts therefore, though indirect, implies that guests were often entertained on a significant scale at the medium-sized and larger cells of late medieval England.

Evidence for the other social services provided by cells, and particularly those aimed at the poor, is scanty. The educational work of dependencies seems to have been minimal, and there is no certain evidence for schools at any daughter house except the large and semi-independent Dover.[40] This

---

35 NRO, DCN 2/1 (Lynn), 2/4 (Yarmouth).
36 See below, pp. 246–8, 262–7 for a detailed discussion of the changing incomes and expenditure of these two cells.
37 PRO, E315/272, fols 70r–78v.
38 The other surviving accounts for the daughter houses of St Albans, from Hertford and Wallingford in the late fifteenth and early sixteenth centuries, record similar sums under the heading of 'kitchen expenses' and give no indication that these provisions were for the benefit of guests: PRO, SC6/HenVIII/106, 1696, SC11/277; Oxford, Corpus Christi College, MS Z/2/1/1–2.
39 BL. Add. MS 33448, fols 126v–128r, 142v–143r, Add. MS 33449, fols 15r–16r, 20v–21v, 30v–31r, 45r–46v, 61v–63v, 100r–102r, 128r–129r, 142r–143r, 167v–168v.
40 C. R. Haines, Dover Priory (Cambridge, 1930), pp. 350–1. Blomefield and Cox asserted that the monks of Hoxne kept a school for the children of the parish and

absence should probably be attributed to the fact that cells generally had no novices to train and were therefore not geared towards educational provision, rather than to their size or income. This is not to say that daughter houses made no contribution to education in their neighbourhood – we know, for example, that in October 1387 Finchale Priory was providing the food and lodgings and funding the education of one boy 'at the grammar school in Durham or anywhere else where it might seem more expedient', and a fourteenth-century prior of Lytham is found petitioning for a place in his mother house's school for a local boy – but in general it seems that cells did not have much to offer in this regard.[41]

There is also little to suggest that the level of charity provided by dependencies was particularly high. The figures for contractual almsgiving in the *Valor Ecclesiasticus* record that only about half of the Benedictine cells for which fully itemised entries survive made doles of this kind, amounting to about 5 per cent of their income, or 3 per cent if the atypical Great Malvern is omitted from the figures.[42] The generally much poorer Augustinian cells, meanwhile, are not shown to be making any contractual almsgiving at all in the *Valor*, with the exception of Llanthony Prima which spent 6s. 8d. to this end each year on Maundy Thursday.[43] Owing to the small incomes of many daughter houses, only at the priories of Belvoir, Finchale, Hatfield Peveral, Holy Island and Penwortham were yearly sums of £5 or more expended in this way. Yet the extent to which the *Valor* gives an accurate impression of monastic charity is difficult to judge. The tax assessment excludes the monks' voluntary doles and there are signs that it does not give exhaustive details of contractual almsgiving either: Dr Oliva has found that the *Valor* omitted several obligatory doles of the nuns of East Anglia recorded elsewhere.[44] Unfortunately, the evidence from cells sheds little light on this subject partly because the *Valor* often gives insufficient information to match the alms it records with the doles specified at anniversaries we know about from other sources.

The evidence from surviving account rolls, however, does not suggest that payments to the poor consumed much daughter-house income. The isolated accounts of several priories make no mention of charitable spending, whereas those of St Ives, Wallingford and the cells of Durham and Norwich

---

supported two of the scholars, but this claim cannot be substantiated: F. Blomefield, *An Essay towards a Topographical History of the County of Norfolk*, 11 vols (London, 1805–10), III, pp. 607–10; VCH, *Suffolk*, II, p. 76. A school was granted to Brecon Priory in the twelfth century but there is no evidence that it continued to operate thereafter: Cowley, *Monastic Order*, p. 187n.

41 DCM, Register II, fol. 252r; BL, Cotton MS Faust. A.vi, fols 15r–16r.
42 As Professor Savine famously calculated, only 3 per cent of total monastic income was spent on contractual almsgiving according to the *Valor*: A. Savine, *English Monasteries on the Eve of the Dissolution*, Oxford Studies in Social and Legal History (Oxford, 1909), pp. 227–40.
43 *Valor*, II, p. 431.
44 Oliva, *Convent and Community*, p. 142.

record only a few shillings each year in almsgiving.[45] The poorest priories like Aldeby and Hoxne unsurprisingly gave very little, and the latter house was even the recipient of charity in some years. Moreover, it is noticeable that almsgiving was cut back at times of financial difficulty, and sometimes abrogated altogether, as at St Leonard's Norwich in the second half of the fifteenth century.[46] Casual doles of leftovers and other food, which would not show up in formal accounts, probably added something to these priories' provision. Daughter houses were certainly supposed to help the poor in this way, but as the complaints made at Ewenny (1284) and Redbourn (1326×1335) show, they did not always meet this requirement.[47] It is important to remember, however, that most of the surviving accounts come from smaller cells. The charitable work of 'the Poor Men's Parlour' at the larger priory of St Nicholas in Exeter, where seven paupers were fed daily before dinner and others from the priory's estates and fee afterwards, together with more general doles at Easter and on St Nicholas' day, was fondly remembered after the house's dissolution.[48] We should not therefore discount the possibility that the almsgiving of larger dependencies was more important on a local scale than the surviving records suggest.

Another area where the presence of daughter houses must have made some local impact was in the economic stimulus they provided, though again there is insufficient material to measure its extent. Every monastic institution provided employment for household servants, agricultural labourers and the building industry, although it has recently been argued that even a great ecclesiastical corporation like Durham Priory could provide 'a realistic living wage for only a relatively small number of workers', with its role in the local employment market 'far less central than might otherwise have been thought'.[49] The size of cells' households varied considerably. Leominster was maintaining thirty regular servants in the early fifteenth century while St Ives employed eighteen in the late 1400s and Brecon fifteen at the Dissolution. The smaller priory of Aldeby kept eight permanent servants in the second quarter of the fifteenth century, including a butler, cook, baker, ploughman, washerwoman and barber, and the equally modest Brooke Priory was employing eleven servants at its suppression in 1536.[50] The wages of

---

45   BL, Add. MSS 33448–9; Oxford, Corpus Christi College, MS Z/2/1/1–2; Raine, *North Durham*, pp. 82–130, 344–58; Raine, *Priory of Finchale*, pp. i–ccccxvi; NRO, DCN 2/1–6.

46   NRO, DCN 2/3/66(iv)– 139.

47   *Registrum Epistolarum fratris Johannis Peckham, Archiepiscopi Cantuariensis*, ed. C. T. Martin, 3 vols, RS, lxxvii (1882–5), III, no. 582, pp. 798–800; GASA, II, p. 203.

48   H. L. Parry and H. Brakspear (revised by J. Youings), *St Nicholas Priory Exeter* (Exeter, 1960), p. 14.

49   C. M. Newman, 'Employment on the Priory of Durham Estates, 1494–1519: the Priory as an Employer', *Northern History*, xxxvi (2000), pp. 43–58, at pp. 44, 51.

50   D. L. Brown and D. Wilson, 'Leominster Old Priory: Recording of Standing Buildings and Excavations 1979–80', *Archaeological Journal*, cli (1994), p. 362; PRO, LR6/152/1; BL, Add. MS 33448, fol. 142v; NRO, DCN 2/2/9–17; Mon. Ang., VI(i), p. 235, no. 5.

numerous short-term labourers and harvest workers also appear in nearly every cell account.

In addition, satellite priories provided an economic stimulus as consumers.[51] Accounts rarely specify the provenance of the priories' purchases, but since they consisted principally of fresh meat and fish, and cloth for clothing, they were probably made locally. The bulk of Lynn's and Yarmouth's considerable expenditures on foodstuffs took place 'in foro', whereas only occasional purchases of wine or spices at the larger dependencies seem to have come from outside their immediate neighbourhoods.[52] Several priories held annual fairs, some of which appear to have been quite large-scale affairs. The five-day fair at Nostell Priory was transferred to that house's cell of Breedon in July 1330, whereas the fair of Woodkirk Priory, another dependency of Nostell, was assessed to be bringing in annual profits of £13 6s. 8d. in 1535.[53] The wealthier houses exerted considerable influence as landlords, whereas the presence of even a small priory must have had a significant, if unquantifiable, economic effect on its immediate locality.

Monastic Prayers

Although the social and economic impact of English cells must remain vague, their most important function was always the religious services they provided. The extent to which the spiritual activities of small monasteries appealed or even seemed relevant to their lay neighbours in late medieval England has often been questioned.[54] In particular, the evidence extracted from testamentary records by several scholars has provided no basis for thinking that the suffrages of lesser religious houses were at all valued by their contemporaries. Whereas bequests to monasteries for prayers generally occur only in 10–20 per cent of wills in fifteenth-century England, smaller houses of monks and canons seem to have received very few bequests

---

[51] Cf. C. Dyer, 'The Consumer and the Market in the Later Middle Ages', EcHR, 2nd series, xlii (1989), pp. 305–27; C. Dyer, 'Trade, Towns and the Church: Ecclesiastical Consumers and the Urban Economy of the West Midlands, 1290–1540', in The Church in the Medieval Town, ed. T. R. Slater and G. Rosser (Aldershot, 1998), pp. 55–75.

[52] For example, in 1489 the prior of Hertford spent 30s. on fish at Stourbridge fair and paid 7s. 8d. for his predecessor's purchase of red wine in London: PRO, SC6/HenVII/1696.

[53] R. McKinley (ed.), 'The Cartulary of Breedon Priory', unpublished Manchester MA thesis (1950), no. 57, pp. 66–7; Valor, V, p. 64. There is no indication that the cell of St Ives played any official role in the famous fair of Ramsey Abbey there, although the monks may have helped supervise proceedings.

[54] Hence Dr Dickinson judged that 'a considerable number of small English monasteries could profitably have been closed down and their brethren and resources transferred to those large houses where alone an effective communal life could be maintained': J. C. Dickinson, Monastic Life in Medieval England (London, 1961), p. 118.

indeed.[55] Professor Claire Cross's analysis of five thousand York diocesan wills between 1520 and 1540 found that only a handful of small monasteries received more than five bequests over this period.[56] This is not a very promising picture. Moreover, only a small number of chantries are known to have been established in daughter houses in the later middle ages. A few of these, like the Bohun chantry in Hurley (1343) and the Ros chantry in Belvoir (1439), were set up by the houses' patrons;[57] and a further ten, including sizeable chantries at the smaller cells of Hatfield Peverel and St Bartholomew's Sudbury, were founded by other benefactors.[58] Of these chantries, however, only two or three were to be served by the religious themselves.

But before writing off the spiritual services of daughter houses on the evidence of wills and chantry foundations alone, it is worth recalling the limitations of these sources as indicators of lay religious preferences. Wills cannot reveal much about religious activities during one's lifetime and, as Dr Clive Burgess has demonstrated, bequests do not even comprise the totality of an individual's provision for his soul.[59] Burgess was able to point to the church-book of All Saints' Bristol to reveal a much wider range of pious donations by parishioners than would be guessed from their wills alone. Similarly, an indication of the value that could be attached to the prayers of a medium-sized daughter house is provided by the surprising levels of interest shown in the Belvoir Priory confraternity. Smaller cells did not have their own confraternities, with benefactors and supporters of these priories instead rewarded with confrater status at the mother house.[60] Indeed, the possibility

55 E.g. Oliva, *Convent and Community*, pp. 168–83; M. Bowker, *The Henrician Reformation. The Diocese of Lincoln under John Longland 1521–1547* (Cambridge, 1981), pp. 48, 148; A. D. Brown, *Popular Piety in Late Medieval England. The Diocese of Salisbury 1250–1550* (Oxford, 1995), pp. 28–32. See also the works in n. 7.

56 Cross, 'Monasticism and Society', pp. 132–3.

57 *St Mary's, Hurley, in the Middle Ages*, ed. F. T. Wethered (London, 1898), no. 382, p. 184; *Mon. Ang.*, III, p. 291.

58 These were the Greystoke chantry at Tynemouth (1315), the de Ultyng chantry at Hatfield Peverel (1317), the de Louches chantry at Wallingford (1333), the Turtle and Stone chantries at St James' Bristol (1339 and 1400), the de Harnhull chantry at Blythburgh (1345), the Thebaud chantry at Sudbury (1349), the Rendelysham chantry at Snape (1405), the Farceux chantry at Freiston (1413) and the Lessy chantry at Hurley (1489): *Mon. Ang.*, III, p. 305; *CClR, 1409–1413*, pp. 219–20; *Calendar of Charters and Rolls preserved in the Bodleian Library*, ed. W. H. Turner and H. O. Coxe (Oxford, 1878), Berks. ch. 74, p. 7; *CPR, 1338–1340*, p. 322; *The Great Red Book of Bristol*, ed. E. W. W. Veale, 5 vols, Bristol Record Society Publications, ii, iv, viii, xvi, xviii (1931–53), II, pp. 243–4; *CPR, 1343–1345*, p. 559; *Charters of St Bartholomew's Priory, Sudbury*, ed. R. Mortimer, Suffolk Records Society, Suffolk Charters, XV (1996), no. 48, p. 49; *CPR, 1405–1408*, p. 27, *1408–1413*, p. 472; *VCH, Berkshire*, II, p. 76.

59 C. Burgess, 'Late-Medieval Wills and Pious Convention: Testamentary Evidence Reconsidered', in *Profit, Piety and the Professions in Later Medieval England*, ed. M. A. Hicks (Gloucester, 1990), pp. 14–33.

60 For examples of the regular grants of confraternity at Durham to friends of its cells, see DCM, Reg. II, fols 65v, 263v, 327v, Reg. III, fols 15v, 18r, 110v. Similar grants were

of being awarded this privilege from a prominent abbey should be included among the reasons for taking an interest in a small cell. However, three medium-sized dependencies, the St Albans priories of Belvoir and Binham and Battle's cell at Brecon, are known to have had this facility in their own right.[61] The survival of the Belvoir martyrology – containing not only a necrology showing when confraters were to be commemorated but also several fourteenth- and fifteenth-century lists of those admitted to the priory confraternity – together with a handful of surviving letters of confraternity from the cell, provides an almost unique opportunity to measure the appeal of such an institution at a small monastery.[62]

The grant of confraternity at Belvoir, as elsewhere, promised the recipient a share in the spiritual benefits accruing from monastic services of all kinds. Additional details are given in two letters of confraternity of 1292 printed by the county historian John Nichols. The rector of Redmile (Leicestershire) was promised a special collect at morning mass for every day of his life, followed after his death by an anniversary consisting of a *Placebo et Dirige*, a sung requiem mass and a dole of a farthing loaf and two herrings each to twenty paupers. The grant to Lady Eustace of Fancourt was similar, consisting of a yearly mass during her lifetime replaced by a requiem mass and dole for forty paupers on the anniversary of her decease. Whether Belvoir's grants of confraternity ordinarily included almsgiving is uncertain and it may be that both these recipients were granted a fuller commemoration than usual.[63]

made by Rochester Cathedral Priory to benefactors of its cell at Felixstowe, and by Westminster Abbey for those supporting St Bartholomew's Sudbury: BL, Cotton Faust. C.v, fols 38r–38v, 64v; *Sudbury Charters*, no. 124, pp. 85–6.

61 Cambridge, Trinity College, MS O.9.25 (Belvoir); Clark, 'Selling the Holy Places', p. 28 (Binham); *Mon. Ang.*, III, p. 261; BL, Harley MS 3586, fol. 22r (Brecon). Clark-Maxwell's references to a confraternity at Hatfield Peverel, another cell of St Albans, in fact pertain to the independent small priory of Hatfield Regis: Prebendary Clark-Maxwell, 'Some Further Letters of Fraternity', *Archaeologia*, 2nd series, xxix (1929), p. 181.

62 Cambridge, Trinity College, MS O.9.25, especially fols 2r–2v, 6v, 155v–166r, 179v; J. Nichols, *The History and Antiquities of the County of Leicester*, 4 vols (London, 1795–1811), II(i), Appendix II, nos 52–3, 81, pp. 14–15, 21–2. A summary of much surviving evidence for confraternities is given in Prebendary Clark-Maxwell, 'Some Letters of Confraternity', *Archaeologia*, 2nd series, xxv (1926), pp. 19–60; Clark-Maxwell, 'Further Letters', pp. 179–216; and H. M. Colvin, *White Canons*, pp. 258–64; and see also R. N. Swanson, 'Mendicants and Confraternity in Medieval England', in Clark, *Religious Orders*, pp. 121–41 for a recent overview of the subject. For necrology, lists of entrants and letters of confraternity to survive for a single institution is extremely rare.

63 The principle that benefactors should receive a graded commemoration was apparently well established. The Beauchief obituary distinguishes between *magna* and *media commendatio*, and the Prémontré Ordinal prescribed that 'the obsequies [granted to a *confrater*] should have regard to the rank of the person commemorated . . . and the amount of prayer, in the form of masses and psalms, which is enjoined in chapter should be in proportion to the amount of alms given': Colvin, *White Canons*, pp. 257–8.

A third letter for confraternity at Belvoir, to Thomas Lord Lovell and his wife Isabella of c.1500 is rather more vague, promising 'in your life and death alike, full participation of all spiritual good works' performed in the priory and commemoration after death as a confrater according to custom.[64]

In any case, it is clear that many wished to enter the Belvoir confraternity. Twenty-six men and women were admitted between 1366 and c.1370 and a further fifty-eight in the years 1422–34. Of these eighty-four, twelve were local clergymen and a further twenty-three are specified as of gentle birth, including six members of the Ros family, the priory's patrons. The remaining entrants, often couples and as many women as men, were probably from more modest backgrounds and most seem to have come from the priory's environs judging from their surnames. The necrology itself contains hundreds of names, including apparently every deceased monk of St Albans and the most notable of mother-house benefactors. A large number of aristocratic names are entered, but still more untitled, suggesting again that the Belvoir confraternity was popular among the local elites and the priory's neighbours of less exalted rank alike. A detailed study of the names contained in the Belvoir martyrology would reveal much about the cell's network of contacts, but a more cursory survey is sufficient to demonstrate the quite unexpected level of interest in the spiritual services provided by this small and apparently insignificant priory.

Monastic–Parochial Churches

A further indication of the potential influence of dependent priories on popular religion can be seen in the close interaction of these cells with neighbouring parishioners. Late medieval monasteries are often presented as isolated and remote from everyday religion, but this interpretation appears highly questionable in the light of the fact that a large number of houses shared their churches with a parochial congregation. It has long been known that parochial altars were found in the naves of the churches of certain monasteries, particularly smaller ones, but the frequency and significance of this arrangement are only just coming to be understood.[65] It is now clear that a significant number of larger monasteries also cohabited with parochial congregations, although many succeeded in making alternative arrange-

64 Nichols, *History and Antiquities of Leicester*, II(i), Appendix II, no. 81, pp. 21–2.
65 For a bibliography of works on this subject, see my 'Monastic-Parochial Churches in Late Medieval England', in *The Late Medieval English Parish*, ed. E. Duffy and C. Burgess (forthcoming). A discussion of the sharing of churches between parishes and academic colleges can also be found in C. N. L. Brooke, 'The Churches of Medieval Cambridge', in *History, Society and the Churches. Essays in Honour of Owen Chadwick*, ed. D. Beales and G. Best (Cambridge, 1985), pp. 49–76.

ments for the parish as the inconvenience of sharing became apparent.[66] However, precise statistics for how many monasteries were tied to parishes in this way are extremely difficult to find.[67] Where all or part of a monastic church remains in parochial use today, there is evidence that it might have been shared in the middle ages, although some monastic churches were bought by parishes at the Dissolution and other previously shared buildings have fallen into desuetude since the sixteenth century. In other places there are doubts over whether the surviving building was the monastic church or not. Archaeological and architectural evidence, where forthcoming, can play a crucial part in resolving this question, but in many individual cases we must rely primarily on written documentation. For numerous small houses this is not available, but fortunately sufficient material is extant from dependent priories to produce reasonably reliable statistics.[68]

These figures are of some interest. Of the Benedictine cells that survived beyond the thirteenth century, forty-two out of seventy-four almost certainly inhabited churches used by parochial congregations, and a further four might well have done. Of the thirty Augustinian cells which meet this criterion, about fourteen appear to have occupied monastic–parochial churches. In other words, up to 62 per cent of black-monk dependencies and just under 50 per cent of Augustinian daughter houses seem to have shared their churches with parishes. Indeed, the proportion of Benedictine cells affected by this arrangement was even higher than these figures suggest. A further four black-monk houses, Colne, Cowick, Ewyas Harold and St Guthlac's Hereford, originally cohabited but subsequently moved into churches of their own. Therefore, perhaps as many as fifty out of seventy-four Benedictine cells, or 68 per cent, were affected by this phenomenon. This is a remarkably high percentage, and suggests that the sharing of churches was much more common than even modern commentators have appreciated.

The reasons why these priories did not have their own churches deserve attention. The work of John Blair, Michael Franklin and Gervase Rosser has shown how in many cases the sharing of a church between religious commu-

---

[66] See, for example, M. J. Franklin, 'The Cathedral as Parish Church: the Case of Southern England', in *Church and City 1000–1500. Essays in Honour of Christopher Brooke*, ed. D. Abulafia, M. J. Franklin and M. Rubin (Cambridge, 1992), pp. 173–98.

[67] In the late nineteenth century, J. F. Hodgson calculated that exactly 119 Benedictine monasteries and thirty-seven Augustinian houses occupied shared churches: J. F. Hodgson, 'On the Difference of Plan alleged to exist between Churches of Austin Canons and those of Monks; and the Frequency with which such Churches were Parochial', *Archaeological Journal*, xli (1884), pp. 374–414, xlii (1885), pp. 96–119, 215–46, 331–69, 440–68. Although a useful starting point, there are a number of problems with Hodgson's estimates. A tentative revision of Hodgson's list can now be found in M. Heale, 'Monastic-Parochial Churches in England and Wales, 1066–1540', *Monastic Research Bulletin*, ix (2003), pp. 1–19.

[68] This information is laid out and discussed in Appendix Four.

nity and parish stemmed from pre-Conquest arrangements.[69] This was true for a number of cells, most notably those dependencies established in former minsters, like Bromfield and Morville. In a few instances from the north of England, namely Woodkirk, Hood and Middlesbrough, a monastic church or chapel took on parochial characteristics at a later date.[70] But the decision of founders to place their new communities in existing parish churches rather than provide them with buildings of their own was the cause of the majority of cohabitations. Whether or not this represents the commitment of founders to involve monks in pastoral work is uncertain; it is perhaps more likely that it was simply a device for economy.[71]

What does emerge clearly, however, is the very large number of founders who made that choice. In fact, the great majority of cells which were not initially placed in parish churches can be assigned to one of two categories: those priories established at venerated sites, like Finchale, Redbourn or St Ives, where the church had to be on a precise spot; and cells, such as Alvecote, Richmond or St Bartholomew's Sudbury, founded by laymen of low social standing who presumably did not hold the advowson to the local parish church and therefore did not have the power to sequester it in this way. In other words, we are left with the striking conclusion that the large majority of founders of English dependencies who were able to establish a cell in a parish church decided to do so. This seems to have been just as true for later foundations like Cockerham and Ovingham as it was for earlier ones such as Belvoir or Hurley. The relatively high social status of the founders of daughter houses probably renders cells atypical amongst lesser monasteries in the proportion of communities required to cohabit with parochial congregations, since many of those establishing poor Augustinian priories or nunneries would not have owned advowsons of parish churches. Nevertheless, the extraordinary popularity of this arrangement among the founders of daughter houses strongly suggests that the placing of monastic communities in parish churches was a very common occurrence in Anglo-Norman England.

A large number of dependent priories were therefore situated in very close

---

69 E.g. J. Blair, 'St Frideswide's Monastery: Problems and Possibilities', Oxoniensia, liii (1988), pp. 221–58; Franklin, 'Cathedral as Parish Church'; G. Rosser, 'The Cure of Souls in English Towns before 1000', in Pastoral Care before the Parish, ed. J. Blair and R. Sharpe (Leicester, 1992), pp. 267–84.

70 The churches of Woodkirk and Hood were initially used by the canons only, but parishioners of each are referred to subsequently. Middlesbrough Priory's chapel, meanwhile, was raised to the status of a parish church following a dispute between Whitby Abbey and Guisborough Priory in the 1130s over parochial tithes and offerings: The Register of John le Romeyn, Lord Archbishop of York, 1286–1296, ed. W. Brown, 2 vols, SS, cxxiii, cxxviii (1913–17), I, no. 125, pp. 53–4; The Register of William Melton, Archbishop of York, 1317–1340, ed. R. M. T. Hill, D. B. Robinson and R. Brocklesby, 4 vols, C&Y Soc., lxx–lxxi, lxxvi, lxxxv (1977–97), II, nos 411, 414B, pp. 154, 157; J. E. Burton, 'Monasteries and Parish Churches in Eleventh- and Twelfth-Century Yorkshire', Northern History, xxiii (1987), p. 49.

71 See above, pp. 38–9.

proximity to a parochial congregation. It is important to ask how this propinquity affected the interaction of cells with their neighbours. Historians have been undecided over whether to represent cohabitation as a positive or negative influence on monastic–community relations. Oliva, who mistakenly claims that more nunneries in East Anglia shared churches than male houses, has presented this arrangement as a cause of harmony.[72] However, she is wrong to imply that this was a service provided to layfolk by the nuns, since in the majority of cases the churches were parochial before they were monastic. Equally, her argument that the religious facilitated parochial activities is highly contentious.[73] Several other historians, most recently Dr Katherine French, have drawn attention to the divisiveness that could result from the clash of regulars and parish over shared space and have shown how the monastic presence often hindered parochial freedom.[74] Whether concord or conflict was more prominent is clearly a vital question in evaluating the contribution of daughter houses to local religion.

The first issue to be resolved was the demarcation of space within the shared building. Both religious and parish required sufficient room for their activities and some division of the church had to be agreed in order to prevent each community disturbing the other. In the majority of cases the arrival of the religious engendered a rebuilding of the existing church on a larger scale. It is likely that the monastery or its founder financed this initial construction, although the religious seem to have devoted more attention to their own section of the building: at the shared Norman churches of Ewenny and Leonard Stanley the standard of decoration increases significantly on leaving the nave; and at Binham the final three western bays of the nave were not completed by the monks until the second quarter of the thirteenth century when Prior Richard de Parco also provided the church's magnificent west front.[75] The need for space created some of the largest and most impressive parish churches in medieval England and Wales. The only parish churches to be built with aisles in twelfth-century Norfolk were divided between monks and laity, as at Binham, Wymondham and Lynn, whereas subsequent enlargements produced such remarkable buildings as St Nicholas' Yarmouth, the biggest parish church in England with aisles wider than those of York Minster, and Leominster, with its three parallel naves.[76] Parochial

72 Oliva, *Convent and Community*, pp. 148–9.
73 'The nuns' facilitation of these [parochial] activities, indirect as it may have been, was not lost on the villagers who relied on these churches for these and other services': ibid., p. 149.
74 K. L. French, 'Competing for Space: Medieval Religious Conflict in the Monastic-Parochial Church at Dunster', *Journal of Medieval and Early Modern Studies*, xxvii (1997), pp. 215–44.
75 N. Pevsner and B. Wilson, *Buildings of England: Norwich and North-East Norfolk*, 2nd edn (London, 1997), p. 92.
76 N. Batcock, 'The Parish Church in Norfolk in the Eleventh and Twelfth Centuries', in *Minsters and Parish Churches. The Local Church in Transition 950–1200*, ed. J. Blair, Oxford University Committee for Archaeology, Monograph no. XVII (1988), pp.

alterations like these were especially common, with numerous additions of aisles (where the monastic cloister did not prevent this) and clerestories, and even the occasional western extension of the nave, as at Brecon, Freiston and Tynemouth; but many priories also opted to enlarge their portion of the church. A good number of chancels were rebuilt in the thirteenth century, as at Binham, Brecon, Breedon, Dunster and most impressively Tynemouth, according to the fashion for larger, squared-off east ends. Other houses, such as St Bees and Yarmouth, chose to add chancel aisles later, or to build new chapels or expand existing ones, like at Hurley and Brecon again. The monks of Dunster substantially rebuilt their chancel in the fifteenth century, but as numbers at many cells fell in the later middle ages, most priories seem to have been content by this date with the dimensions of their part of the building.

If the need for space does not seem to have created undue friction, nor on the whole do arrangements for the partitioning of the church. In a building where two separate communities each pursued their own particular liturgical routines, the potential for disruption and cacophony was evident. Cells seem to have been spared the problem of parochial altars in transepts or other inconvenient locations, which plagued several houses where the arrangements for sharing the church went back to pre-Conquest days.[77] In almost every case, the parish was restricted to the nave, with the religious inhabiting the chancel, transepts and sometimes the eastern part of the building's western arm. Only at Lynn does the parish seem to have encroached into the monastic portion of the building in the later middle ages. In the late fifteenth century, the Trinity Guild had its chapel on the north side of the chancel of St Margaret's church, whereas a parishioner of Lynn apparently financed the rebuilding of part of the south aisle of the chancel in 1472, again suggesting parochial use of that section of the building.[78]

At what stage these divisions were formalised and what partitions if any were initially erected is not entirely clear, although the surviving stone dividing screens at Binham and Tynemouth both date from the later twelfth century and that of Ewenny from the thirteenth. The only recorded instance of conflict between cell and parish over how their church should be divided comes from Wymondham in the mid-thirteenth century. This discord

---

179–90. Both Leominster and Yarmouth had enormous parishes and St Nicholas' Yarmouth would have been even larger had not the Black Death rendered superfluous plans for an enormous Galilee chapel: A. W. Morant, 'Notices of the Church of St Nicholas, Great Yarmouth', *Norfolk Archaeology*, vii (1872), pp. 215–48. The unusual shape of the Leominster church was dictated by the conventual buildings adjoined to the north of the nave. The parishioners therefore had to make do with their small Norman north aisle and extend their building to the south.

77 E.g. Blair, 'St Frideswide's Monastery'.

78 *The Making of King's Lynn: a Documentary Survey*, ed. D. M. Owen, British Academy Records of Social and Economic History, new series, IX (1984), pp. 27–8. For an account of parochial expansion in other shared churches, see Heale, 'Monastic-Parochial Churches'.

reached such a pitch that Pope Innocent IV was called in to adjudicate, with the parish being allocated most of the nave apart from the south aisle (which adjoined the monks' cloister) and the south-west tower, which were to belong to the priory.[79] The monks' part of Wymondham church also extended three bays into the nave and several other cells seem to have encroached one or two bays west of the crossing.[80] But the western arch of the crossing was probably the most usual dividing line between monks and parish, according the latter the entirety of the nave. This might often have necessitated that the eastern bay of the cloister aisle was screened off and allocated to the monks, as at Brecon, in order that the eastern cloister door entered into the monastic portion of the church. At Ewenny and Leonard Stanley, extra doors were added in the south wall of the south transept to overcome this problem.

There remained, however, some ambiguity over which party was responsible for the bell-tower over the crossing. By the mid-thirteenth century, it had been laid down that the belfries of ordinary parish churches were to be the responsibility of the parishioners rather than the rector.[81] In 1270, the priory and parishioners of Pilton agreed that they should jointly finance the rebuilding of the church's bell-tower and its maintenance thereafter, and a similar settlement was reached at St James' Bristol in 1374.[82] Matters at Dunster, however, proved harder to resolve. By a composition of January 1357, the monks of that cell undertook to maintain the church tower, although with a parochial contribution. In the mid-fifteenth century, however, the bell-tower was considerably enlarged by the parishioners, who thereby took control of this part of the building. Subsequently, in the course of another dispute between monks and parish in the time of Henry VII, 'to fulfil and satisfie theire croked apetites', the parishioners 'toke up the bell ropis and said that the Prior and convent there shuld have no bellis there to ryng'.[83]

[79] S. Martin-Jones, *Wymondham and its Abbey*, 6th edn (Wymondham, 1932), pp. 21–2; S. Yaxley, *Wymondham Abbey before the Dissolution: The Episcopal Visitations of 1492–1532* (Dereham, 1986), pp. 10–11.

[80] Confusion over the screening arrangements in shared churches has led some writers to equate the position of rood screens in the nave, sometimes revealed by the remnants of rood lofts or beams, with the point of division between the parochial and monastic parts of the church. Since traces of these screens can sometimes be seen as far as halfway down the nave, it has been concluded that the monks occupied the lion's share of the building: e.g. N. Pevsner, D. Veray and A. Brooks, *Buildings of England: Gloucestershire, the Cotswolds*, 3rd edn (London, 1999), pp. 444–5. For fuller discussion of screenwork in shared churches, see Heale, 'Monastic-Parochial Churches'.

[81] J. Blair, 'Clerical Communities and Parochial Space: the Planning of Urban Mother Churches in the Twelfth and Thirteenth Centuries', in Slater and Rosser, *Church in Medieval Town*, p. 284.

[82] *Registrum Malmesburiensie*, ed. J. S. Brewer and C. T. Martin, 2 vols, RS, lxxii (1879–80), II, chap. 304, pp. 171–2; W. Barrett, *The History and Antiquities of the City of Bristol* (Bristol, 1789), pp. 385–6.

[83] H. C. Maxwell-Lyte, *A History of Dunster and of the Families of Mohun and Luttrell*, 2 vols (London, 1909), II, pp. 393–5, 399–401.

As this dispute suggests, the allocation of authority within shared churches was of more importance than the mere division of space, and it was monastic attempts to maintain supremacy over the entire building that generated the most discord between the two parties. Numerous parochial challenges to monastic hegemony within shared churches have left records, involving both daughter houses and independent monasteries.[84] In each of these disputes, the lay congregation sought to win rights which other parishes had long taken for granted: the ability to hold services at their own rather than the monastic altars; their own bells to summon parishioners to mass; unrestricted access to their church; and the use of parochial offerings for the parish's own benefit. The encroachment of the religious into the nave for processions on Sundays and feast days was another potential source of dissension. Clashes over bells were particularly common, the most acrimonious incident taking place at Wymondham in 1408–9, when certain parishioners blocked up the monks' doors to the nave, attacked monastic property in the cemetery and besieged the prior in his chamber for three days as part of an ultimately successful campaign for their own belfry.[85] Disagreements over the possession or tolling of bells also played a part in priory–parish conflicts at Binham, St James' Bristol, Dunster and Leominster.[86] In every case, the priory was forced to concede the parishioners' demands, although the monks of Binham succeeded in establishing that 'the [parish] bell shall not be rung at any time to the prejudice or derogation of the office of the Sacrist of the Priory'.

Wymondham aside, the fiercest disputes involving dependencies seem to have been at Dunster and Leominster, where there were regular rifts throughout the later middle ages. Problems are recorded at Leominster from the late thirteenth century, when the monks were locking the church at night and thus preventing the parish from gaining access to the sacrament when it was needed for last rites. Bishop Cantilupe and Archbishop Pecham disagreed over the solution to this difficulty, as over so much else, but

---

84 For accounts of disputes at Daventry, St Frideswide's Oxford, Rochester and Sherborne, see M. J. Franklin, 'The Secular College as a Focus for Anglo-Norman Piety: St Augustine's, Daventry', in Blair, *Minsters and Parish Churches*, pp. 97–104; Blair, 'St Frideswide's Monastery', pp. 255–8; Franklin, 'Cathedral as Parish Church', pp. 178–82; Brown, *Popular Piety*, pp. 37–8.

85 H. Harrod, 'Some Particulars relating to the History of the Abbey Church of Wymondham in Norfolk', *Archaeologia*, xliii (1890), pp. 263–72. In the mid-fifteenth century, the Wymondham parishioners built a new west tower of a similar height to the monks' perpendicular central tower. Dominated by these two massive competing structures, the church at Wymondham expresses more clearly than any other building the rivalry between the parties in a shared church.

86 NRO, MS 9253; E. B. Burstall, 'A Monastic Agreement of the Fourteenth Century', *Norfolk Archaeology*, xxxi (1955–7), pp. 211–18 (Binham, 1432); Barrett, *History of Bristol*, pp. 385–6 (St James' Bristol, 1374). For references for the confrontations at Dunster and Leominster, see below. The Binham dispute encompassed not only parochial affairs but also tenurial grievances.

matters were eventually resolved by the construction of a chapel in the outer court of the priory which was to be open to the parish at all times.[87] Just over a century later, in 1397, another argument broke out, largely because the parish had closed off the altar of Sts Mary Magdalene, Katherine and Margaret in the nave to the monks. This was apparently a dispute over offerings, since the subprior of Leominster was accustomed to celebrate at the altar in question on the feasts of dedication of the three saints, thereby receiving the considerable oblations offered to the altar on those days.[88] The bishop judged in favour of the priory, and a similar settlement was made at Brecon shortly before 1527, when it was agreed that the monks would (presumably continue to) receive all the grain and wax and 'all other offerings that come to the rood soller within the said church' together with all oblations given in the chapel of St Laurence on St Laurence's day: a significant concession since the Brecon rood was a renowned site of pilgrimage in the later middle ages (see below).[89]

The parishioners of Dunster were rather more successful than those of Leominster and Brecon in asserting their perceived rights. The Dunster disagreements, described in detail by Sir Henry Maxwell-Lyte and recently analysed by Dr French, do not need to be re-examined in full here.[90] These clashes over offerings, the provision of wax, church maintenance, the bell-tower, processions and the vicar's stipend are most interesting, as French has noted, for the swing in the balance of power from the monks to the parish shown in the concords of January 1357 and April 1498. From having to process with the monks in an inferior position, concede many parochial oblations to them and attend high mass in the monastic church in 1357, the second settlement accorded the parishioners strict equality with the priory in processional order, the receipt of their own offerings and the granting of their own choir. This last privilege was particularly important for the parishioners, who were now given permission to divide their church into nave and chancel and to install their own high altar, thereby ending their liturgical subservience to the priory. It would appear from other evidence that the Dunster parishioners were unusual in being denied their own chancel and high altar until such a late date, and the problems experienced at this cell

[87] *Registrum Thome de Cantilupo, Episcopi Herefordensis, AD 1275–1282*, ed. R. G. Griffiths, C&Y Soc., ii (1907), pp. 46–8, 88–9; *Registrum Ricardi de Swinfield, Episcopi Herefordensis, AD 1283–1317*, ed. W. W. Capes, C&Y Soc., vi (1909), pp. 149–50; *Registrum Epistolarum Peckham*, II, no. 389, pp. 505–7. The so-called Forbury chapel at Leominster still stands.

[88] *Registrum Johannis Trefnant, Episcopi Herefordensis, AD 1389–1404*, ed. W. W. Capes, C&Y Soc., xx (1916), pp. 140–3.

[89] Mon. Ang., III, pp. 267–8. Professor Gwynn-Jones erroneously followed Theophilus Jones in stating that the offerings to the 'rood soller' were assigned to the vicar in this agreement: D. Gwynn-Jones, 'Brecon Cathedral c.1093–1537: the Church of the Holy Rood', *Brycheiniog*, xxiv (1990–2), p. 32.

[90] Maxwell-Lyte, *History of Dunster*, II, pp. 393–407; French, 'Competing for Space' pp. 215–44.

should not therefore be considered typical.[91] In most cases it would seem that the religious were prepared to compromise in order to maintain harmony with their cohabitees.

Another way in which cells in monastic–parochial churches influenced the religious lives of their lay neighbours was through their appointment of the parish priest. The *Valor Ecclesiasticus* and the surviving accounts of many cells which shared their churches reveal that their parishes were often served by stipendiary chaplains rather than perpetual vicars. As a result, the great bulk of parochial revenues, including lesser tithes and altarage dues, came into the hands of the religious.[92] The appointment of chaplains without security of tenure not only allowed the religious considerable control over parochial affairs, but it also enabled them to select their own brethren as parish priest whenever they wished. Augustinian canons served parochial altars with some regularity in the later middle ages, and although few are known to have acted as parish priests in shared churches belonging to cells it is likely that this was a relatively common scenario.[93] Moreover, a high proportion of the Benedictine monks recorded to have served parish altars in the later middle ages did so in monastic–parochial churches. Monk-priests serving such churches are recorded at Wallingford (1349–55), Snape (1378 and 1515), Penwortham (1394), Kidwelly (1404), Middlesbrough (1452 and 1459), Lynn (1458–9 and 1465–9), Binham (1481–3), Aldeby (1485–6), Pilton (1502) and Hertford (1525–6).[94] Several of these examples are known

---

91 For example, the parish's high altar at Belvoir is specifically mentioned in a (fourteenth-century?) description of the place of burial of the priory's benefactors and that of Wymondham is referred to during the early fifteenth-century dispute: *Mon. Ang.*, III, p. 289, no. 2; Harrod, 'Some Particulars', pp. 265–6. A fuller discussion of this question can again be found in Heale, 'Monastic-Parochial Churches'.

92 For a discussion of the value of this source of income to the monks, and its importance to the finances of several priories, see below, pp. 244–5.

93 This was a regular practice in the shared churches of the independent Augustinian priories of Kirkham, Cartmel, Bruton and Owston, as well as the former cell of Weybourne, in the later middle ages: J. Burton, 'Priory and Parish: Kirkham and its Parishioners 1496–7', in *Monasteries and Society in Medieval Britain*, ed. B. Thompson (Stamford, 1999), pp. 329–47, esp. pp. 335–7; CPL, IV, p. 366; VCH, *Somerset*, II, pp. 135–6; *Visitations in the Diocese of Lincoln 1517–1531*, ed. A. H. Thompson, 3 vols, Lincoln Record Society, xxxiii, xxxv, xxxvii (1940–47), III, p. 44; *Visitations of the Diocese of Norwich, 1492–1532*, ed. A. Jessopp, Camden Society, new series, xliii (1888), pp. 56–7.

94 Turner and Coxe, *Calendar of Bodleian Charters and Rolls*, Berks. ch. 95, p. 19; BL, Add. Ch. 26263; PRO, SC6/HenVIII/3402; VCH, *Lancashire*, II, p. 105n; *The Episcopal Registers of the Diocese of St Davids, 1397 to 1518*, ed. R. F. Isaacson, 3 vols, Cymmrodorion Record Society, vi (1917–20), I, p. 310; Anon., 'Ecclesiastical Middlesbrough in Medieval Times', YAJ, xviii (1905), pp. 71–2; VCH, *Yorkshire*, III, p. 105; NRO, DCN 2/1/55, 60–3; NRO, Reg/7/12, fol. 233r; CPL, XIII(i), p. 156; NRO, DCN 2/2/24; Thomson, 'Early Tudor Church', pp. 214–15 (though the evidence is misinterpreted here); PRO, E315/272, fols 77r–77v. The existence of Manuals in many of the surviving book-lists from cells which shared their churches also points to the conclusion that the religious there contributed to parochial service.

only from account rolls and many more instances would no doubt be recorded if more documents of this kind were extant. Moreover, at a few priories, such as Cardigan, Penwortham and Scilly, there are hints that monk-priests were the norm rather than the exception.[95] In contrast, very few monks or canons dwelling in cells are to be found serving parochial altars in churches separate from their own.

It is not obvious how the appointment of parochial chaplains and the regular use of monk-priests would have affected the relations between religious and parish in shared churches. It may be that some parishioners resented monastic control over their minister – although no disputes with cells over this matter are recorded – but equally it is quite possible that the frequent employment of religious to serve parishes themselves brought the two parties closer together. The numerous entries in the account rolls of Lynn and Yarmouth for the payment of preachers, presumably for the benefit of their parishioners, suggest that the presence of a monastic community on one's doorstep could confer certain benefits.[96] Although she was hardly the typical parishioner, several episodes in Margery Kempe's career reveal her particularly close relationship with the monks sharing her parish church in Lynn. On more than one occasion Kempe was taken into the 'Priowrys cloistyr' to prevent her crying from disturbing the townsfolk further, although this can hardly have helped the calm of the monastic precinct. For a time she was also 'houseled' in the prior's chapel until one of the monks objected, and the identity of future priors was of sufficient importance to her to be the subject of direct divine revelation.[97]

Another indication that lay congregations in shared churches ordinarily maintained close relations with their monastic neighbours comes from wills. The account rolls from Aldeby, Lynn and Yarmouth show regular streams of bequests to each priory, sometimes of considerable sums. In contrast, those Norwich cells which occupied their own chapels, Hoxne and St Leonard's Norwich, received very little income of this kind.[98] Moreover, several testators from the parish of Dunster, of all places, are known to have left money to their neighbouring monastery, occasionally directly to individual monks with whom they must have been well acquainted.[99] More substantially, a

95 CPL, VIII, pp. 51–2; Documents relating to the Priory of Penwortham and other Possessions in Lancashire of the Abbey of Evesham, ed. W. A. Hulton, Chetham Society, xxx (1853), no. 62, pp. 97–105; The Itinerary of John Leland, ed. L. Toulmin Smith, 5 vols (London, 1907–10), I, p. 190.
96 NRO, DCN 2/1/69ff., DCN 2/4/8ff.
97 The Book of Margery Kempe, ed. L. Staley, Middle English Texts Series (Kalamazoo, 1996), pp. 136–8, 151, 159, 164–5.
98 NRO, DCN 2/1–6; Windsor, St George's Chapel, I.C.1–39. Annual receipts from wills, though not always itemised separately, often amounted to several pounds at Lynn and Yarmouth.
99 Somerset Medieval Wills, ed. F. W. Weaver, 3 vols, Somerset Record Society, xvi, xix, xxi (1901–5), II, pp. 139, 180–1, III, pp. 13–14; F. Hancock, Dunster Church and Priory (Taunton, 1905), pp. 66–7.

study of the wills of parishioners in several shared churches in the diocese of York (though not including any English dependencies) reveals that over 50 per cent made some bequest to their neighbouring priory, a much higher proportion than applies generally.[100] It would be unwise, therefore, to take the sporadic reports of discord at Dunster, Wymondham and elsewhere to be representative of normal relations between cohabiting priories and parishes. Rather, testamentary evidence seems to indicate that the religious in shared churches were able to make a positive and valued contribution to parochial religion in late medieval England.

Saint Cults

The closeness of the ties between local parishes and those dependencies which did not share their churches is harder to elucidate. The long naves and screening arrangements of most monasteries suggest that they were intended to be open to layfolk, but it is very hard to tell how often their secular neighbours actually made use of these churches. That the women of Exeter had a close acquaintance with the priory church of St Nicholas is indicated by their fury at the removal of the house's rood screen at the Dissolution.[101] Moreover, it is clear that certain abbeys and priories attracted considerable numbers to their churches from near and sometimes far by the saint cults they sponsored. Many of the larger monasteries of medieval England housed major shrines, the popularity of which can often be measured through the records of offerings made by the faithful.[102] The degree to which smaller houses touched popular religious life in this way, however, has never been investigated. The unusually full evidence surviving for cells provides an opportunity to study this question in some detail. In a surprisingly large number of daughter houses there can be traced some cult of local, and occasionally regional, significance. Moreover, several new cults were established in the later middle ages, generally based on images in or near the priory church, which show the monks interacting with lay religion in an intimate and unexpected way.

A small number of cells were set up by mother houses specifically to occupy hallowed locations and thereby to foster saint cults.[103] Redbourn and St Ives were founded on the sites where the bodies of St Amphibalus and St

---

[100] See Heale, 'Monastic-Parochial Churches'. This figure does not include bequests for forgotten tithes.

[101] J. Youings, *The Dissolution of the Monasteries* (London, 1971), pp. 164–5.

[102] Systematic statistics for the offerings received from the shrines of English cathedrals and Westminster Abbey are given in B. J. Nilson, *Cathedral Shrines of Medieval England* (Woodbridge, 1998). See also Clark, 'Selling the Holy Places' for the attempts of larger Benedictine houses to re-invigorate their saint cults in fifteenth-century England.

[103] See above, pp. 33–4.

Ivo had been exhumed, and the Durham cells of Holy Island, Farne Island and Finchale were established at places inseparably associated with St Cuthbert and St Godric. The locations of Hoxne and St Bees Priories were also largely determined by the pre-existing cults of St Edmund and St Bega functioning there. Tynemouth, meanwhile, possessed from its foundation the important shrine of St Oswin. Evidence for the sponsoring of these cults, as well as some indication of their early impact, is provided by the *Miracula* written for Durham, St Bees, St Ives and Tynemouth.[104] These reveal a significant amount of popular support at a local level and occasional interest from much further afield. Reginald of Durham devoted nineteen chapters of his *Libellus de Admirandis Beati Cuthberti* to the saint's miracles on Farne Island, the place of his death, and there are also signs that the *tumba* of the saint at Holy Island was a site of pilgrimage in the early twelfth century.[105] Dr Tudor has suggested that the focus of St Cuthbert's cult was deliberately shifted to Durham by the mother house in c.1170, and it may well be that popular resort to both islands declined as a result. No such moves were made to divert interest in St Godric away from Finchale. The saint's tomb was placed in the chapel of St John the Baptist there, around which the new priory church was soon built.[106] The *Miracula* of St Godric, also written in the late twelfth century by Reginald of Durham, portray a cult of considerable local importance, particularly popular it seems with women and the lower sections of society.[107]

The smaller collection of miracles of St Bega, of uncertain authorship and date, reveals another cult achieving local prominence in the twelfth century. The veneration of this saint in Coupland was based on her miraculous bracelet, on which oaths were sworn in a number of surviving charters of the priory.[108] But perhaps the most impressive set of miracle stories comes from St Ives. Although the bodies of St Ivo and his companions were translated to Ramsey on their discovery in 1001×1002, a spring of water with healing

104 *Reginaldi Monachi Dunelmensis Libellus de Admirandis Beati Cuthberti*, ed. J. Raine, SS, i (1835); *Libellus de Vita et Miraculis Sancti Godrici, Heremitae de Finchale, auctore Reginaldo Monacho Dunelmensis*, ed. J. Stevenson, SS, xx (1847); *Vita et Miracula Sanctae Begae Virginis in Provincia Northanhimbrorum*, in *The Register of the Priory of St Bees*, ed. J. Wilson, SS, cxxvi (1915), pp. 497–520; Goscelin of St Bertin, *Miracula Sancti Ivonis*, in *Chronicon Abbatiae Ramseiensis*, ed. W. D. Macray, RS, lxxxiii (1886), pp. lix–lxxxiv; *Vita Oswini Regis Deirorum*, in *Miscellanea Biographica*, ed. J. Raine, SS, viii (1838), pp. 1–59.
105 E. Craster, 'The Miracles of Farne', *Archaeologia Aeliana*, 4th series, xxix (1951), pp. 93–107; A. J. Piper, 'The First Generations of Durham Monks and the Cult of St Cuthbert', in *St Cuthbert, His Cult and His Community to AD 1200*, ed. G. Bonner, D. Rollason and C. Stancliffe (Woodbridge, 1989), pp. 437–46; V. Tudor, 'The Cult of St Cuthbert in the Twelfth Century: The Evidence of Reginald of Durham', in ibid., pp. 447–67.
106 C. R. Peers, 'Finchale Priory', *Archaeologia Aeliana*, 4th series, iv (1927), p. 199.
107 The miracles of St Godric are analysed in R. C. Finucane, *Miracles and Pilgrims. Popular Beliefs in Medieval England* (London, 1977), pp. 127, 166–9.
108 *Register of St Bees*, nos 304, 474, 488, pp. 313–14, 468–9, 479–80.

qualities was found to issue forth from the site of the exhumation at Slepe (thereafter known as St Ives). Judging from the saint's *Miracula*, written by the hagiographer Goscelin of St Bertin in the 1090s, this holy spring was considerably more popular than the actual shrine of the saint at the mother house.[109] Seeking to capitalise on this perhaps unexpected development, the monks of Ramsey returned the relics of three of St Ivo's companions to the cell in the early twelfth century, 'for then the church there would both be held more distinguished and it would be visited more frequently and faith-fully by the people from all over the place for the sake of the intervention of the patron saints there'. This move seems to have paid dividends since the continuation of the *Miracula* records several more healing miracles at St Ives; and, although most of these involved local people, the mention of the spring by William of Malmesbury in the 1120s – 'pleasant to drink from and helpful for all illnesses. It is impossible to guess (much less describe on paper) the number of the crowds of people healed by St Ivo' – suggests that its fame had become widespread by this date.[110]

Another cult of considerable importance in the twelfth century was that of St Oswin, controlled by the monks of Tynemouth. The miracles of St Oswin began soon after his body was exhumed at Tynemouth in 1065 and a large number are recorded between this date and the mid-twelfth century. Even this cult, though, was primarily local in character, with most of the recorded miracles involving monks or servants of the priory or pilgrims, espe-cially humble women, from county Durham. It is much harder to judge the early popularity of the cults at Redbourn and Hoxne from which no sets of miracle stories have come down. Redbourn, comparable to St Ives in many ways, probably did not fare quite as well as the Huntingdonshire priory after the translation of St Amphibalus to St Albans. The only sign of veneration at this cell in the St Albans records is recorded after Abbot William of Trumpington (1214–35) presented two gilded shrines with relics of St Amphibalus and his companions to the cell, when miracles were said to have been performed.[111] However, the presence of the *puella Ridibowne* on the rood screen at Gateley in Norfolk, commemorating two girls said to have been healed by praying before the relics of St Amphibalus, suggests a cult of a wider appeal.[112] The cult of St Edmund at Hoxne also appears to have been substantial. Before the foundation of the priory there, it was being claimed that the chapel at Hoxne occupied the site of St Edmund's death, and by the early fourteenth century the monks there had built a second chapel nearby

[109] For an account of the cult at St Ives, see S. B. Edgington, *The Life and Miracles of St Ivo* (St Ives, 1985).
[110] *William of Malmesbury, The Deeds of the Bishops of England*, trans. D. Preest (Wood-bridge, 2002), p. 216.
[111] GASA, I, pp. 282–3.
[112] W. W. Williamson, 'Saints of Norfolk Rood-Screens and Pulpits', *Norfolk Archaeolgy*, xxxi (1955–7), p. 308.

to mark the spot where the saint's severed hand was said to have been discovered.[113]

Like the vast majority of Anglo-Norman cults, those centred on these
eight cells declined in popularity over the middle ages. Late medieval financial records survive for many of the above priories and suggest limited lay
enthusiasm for their saints by this time. The accounts of Holy Island and
Farne Island show little or no offerings made by visitors, and although the
'pyx of St Godric' at Finchale attracted donations of between 27s. and 55s. in
the 1350s, this source of income apparently produced nothing after 1364.[114]
The cult of St Edmund at Hoxne seems to have aged a little better, with a
small stream of oblations amounting perhaps to about one pound per year
continuing into the sixteenth century.[115] Popular support for the holy spring
at St Ives, however, looks to have almost entirely dried up by the time of
Archbishop Arundel's metropolitan visitation of the diocese of Lincoln in
1411. Shocked at the lack of veneration shown at St Ives, the archbishop
issued a decree that the feast of the Invention and Translation of St Ivo
should henceforward be celebrated in the archdeaconry of Huntingdon, and
also offered indulgences to any pilgrims visiting the priory. Despite these
efforts to reinvigorate the cult, no offerings to the saint are found in the priory's eleven accounts of the late fifteenth and early sixteenth centuries.[116]
The cult of St Oswin appears to have remained relatively popular in the
mid-fourteenth century, when Prior de la Mare moved the saint's shrine
away from the high altar 'so that those approaching could more quietly,
freely and spaciously continue their devotions around the Martyr', and
Thomas Walsingham records a miracle of the saint in 1384.[117] However, the
sole surviving priory account of 1525/6 shows no income from offerings to
the shrine, suggesting that the cult had withered by this date.[118]

Records do not survive to measure the appeal of the cult at Redbourn in
the later middle ages, and it is only at St Bees that a reasonable level of
support for a traditional saint can be shown to have been maintained
throughout this period. Not only does the chronicle of St Mary's York
mention several miracles at St Bees in the early fourteenth century, but the
sole extant account roll of the priory, for the year 1516/17, records the

113 M. Carey Evans, 'The Contribution to Hoxne of the Cult of St Edmund King and
   Martyr in the Middle Ages and Later', Proceedings of the Suffolk Institute of Archaeology, xxxvi (1987), pp. 182–95.
114 Raine, North Durham, pp. 82–130, 344–58; Raine, Priory of Finchale, pp. i–ccccxvi.
115 NRO, DCN 2/6; Windsor, St George's Chapel, I.C.1–39. The Hoxne accounts do
   not itemise oblations and so exact figures for this category of income cannot be
   recovered. The cult of St Robert [sic] at Hoxne, however, was assessed at 13s. 7d. in
   the Valor, a figure considerably higher than the 6½d. given for the image of St
   Leonard at Hoxne's sister house in Norwich: Valor, III, p. 285.
116 PRO, E135/18/22; BL, Add. MSS 33448–9.
117 GASA, II, pp. 379–80; Sancti Albani, Chronica Monasterii: Thomae Walsingham,
   Historia Anglicana, ed. H. T. Riley, 2 vols, RS, xxviii(i) (1863–4), II, pp. 116–17.
118 Mon. Ang., III, pp. 319–20, no. 27.

unspectacular but respectable sum of 67s. 9d. in offerings to St Bega's brace-let.[119] It appears that relic collections attracted no more support than these long-established cults by the later medieval period. Inventories of Finchale, Holy Island, St Leonard's Norwich, St Bartholomew's Sudbury and most impressively Leominster show sizeable hoards of relics, whereas the *Compendium Compertorum* notes that there were venerated relics at Wetheral and Tynemouth.[120] But there is little reason to think that such artefacts captured the popular imagination, with surviving account rolls making only very occasional references to offerings made to relics, such as the sums of up to a few shillings accounted for at Yarmouth Priory during the 1440s.[121] It may be that relics had attracted rather more interest in earlier days; those of St Olaf at St Nicholas' Exeter are said to have helped to raise sufficient income for the construction of the priory church in the early twelfth century, and were considered sufficiently important to merit a special feast of relics at the priory which was still being observed in the 1470s.[122] But it is perhaps not surprising that the relic collections of dependent priories did not win great support in later medieval England if the entry in the St Leonard's Norwich account roll of 1478/9, 'Also given to a certain woman offering relics of St Leonard and St Katherine as she claimed on oath – 2s.', represents common methods of procurement.[123]

It is well known that the later middle ages saw a decline in the popularity of many traditional saints and their relics and a concomitant rise in support for Christocentric and Marian cults and for images of saints.[124] This shift in veneration from corporeal remains to pictorial representations created an opportunity for smaller monasteries which could never compete with great

---

[119] *St Mary's Chronicle*, pp. 47, 49, 55; Cumbria Record Office, D/Lons./W/St Bees 1/1. Another earlier daughter house cult which survived into the fifteenth century was that of St Walter of Cowick, inherited by the Tavistock monks who took over the priory in 1462. Reference is made in the mid-1460s to 'the makyng and byndyng of a New box to Saynt Water' and to the payment of two men hired to serve pilgrims on St Walter's day, although no indication is given of the extent of offerings then received: N. I. Orme, 'Saint Walter of Cowick', *Analecta Bollandiana*, cviii (1990), pp. 387–93.

[120] J. T. Fowler (ed.), 'Inventory of the Vestments, Books, etc. of the Priory of Finchale, AD 1481', *Transactions of the Architectural and Archaeological Society of Durham and Northumberland*, iv (1896), pp. 139–41; DCM, Holy Island Status, e.g. 1362, 1401; W. T. Bensly, 'St Leonard's Priory, Norwich', *Norfolk Archaeology*, xii (1985), pp. 196–226; *Sudbury Charters*, no. 130, pp. 88–9; *Reg. Swinfield*, pp. 124–5; *L&P*, X, no. 364, pp. 140, 142.

[121] NRO, DCN 2/4/6–10.

[122] *The Chronicle of Battle Abbey*, ed. E. Searle, Oxford Medieval Texts (Oxford, 1980), pp. 82–3; R. Graham, 'The Benedictine Priory of St Nicholas, at Exeter', *JBAA*, new series, xxxiii (1927), p. 60.

[123] NRO, DCN 2/3/88.

[124] For discussions of this trend in later medieval England, see Finucane, *Miracles and Pilgrims*, pp. 191–202; J. Sumption, *Pilgrimage. An Image of Medieval Religion* (London, 1975), pp. 267–88.

houses in the market for saints' bodies and relics. It appears that numerous cells benefited from this change in religious tastes with images on display in their churches receiving notable levels of support from their lay neighbours. The monks of St Leonard's Stamford were receiving as much as £5 per year from the pyx of St Leonard in the late fourteenth century, although annual oblations had fallen to under a pound by the 1430s.[125] Of more enduring appeal was the image of St Bega at Rumburgh Priory. The veneration of this north-western saint in a corner of late medieval Suffolk is a most intriguing phenomenon, and it must be assumed that the cult was transplanted to Rumburgh from Cumberland, with remarkable success, by a monk of St Mary's York who had previously served at St Bees. Accounts from the priory show that the bejewelled image brought yearly offerings of two or three pounds throughout the fifteenth century, and this cult was said at the suppression of the priory in 1528 to be attracting 'moche offeryng uppon Mighelmas day of money and cheses'.[126]

Marian images were especially popular in later medieval England and it would appear that some cells were able to capitalise on this trend. We hear of statues of the Virgin at several houses, but for three in particular there is evidence of considerable popular interest.[127] John Leland noted that there was formerly 'a pilgrimage of our Lady of Hilbyri' at Hilbre Island, which was almost certainly connected with Chester's cell there. A Marian cult of considerable local prominence flourished at Pilton in the sixteenth century, receiving offerings of £10 per year in the 1530s; and in 1538 Cardigan Priory possessed a miraculous taper of Our Lady which was said to attract 'a great pilgrimage', and was 'so worshipped and kissed and used to swear in difficult matters that the profits amounted to a great sum, twenty nobles [£6 13s. 4d.] of which went as a pension to the abbot of Chertsey'.[128] Christocentric cults were also fashionable, and the several references to the Holy Rood of Brecon Priory in Welsh poetry of the fifteenth century suggest a pilgrimage venue of some importance.

These indications of saint cults of surprising vigour at a number of cells are of some interest, but it is only when a run of accounts survive that we can trace something like the full impact of monastic images on lay piety. This evidence survives for the cells of Norwich Cathedral Priory to suggest that by their cults lesser monasteries could occupy a place of real importance in the

---

[125] Piper, 'Stamford', part i, pp. 13–16.

[126] SROI, HD 1538/335/1, nos 6–7, 13, 21–2, 34–5; Mon. Ang., III, pp. 615–16, no. 9. This cult is discussed in more detail in my 'Rumburgh Priory in the Later Middle Ages: Some New Evidence', Proceedings of the Suffolk Institute of Archaeology, xl (2001), pp. 8–23.

[127] The popular Marian cult at Caversham has been excluded from this account since the Notley settlement here does not appear to have been a true cell. See above, p. 6.

[128] Leland's Itinerary, III, pp. 91–2; R. Whiting, 'Abominable Idols: Images and Image-breaking under Henry VIII', JEH, xxxiii (1982), p. 38; L&P, XIII(i), no. 634(ii), p. 235.

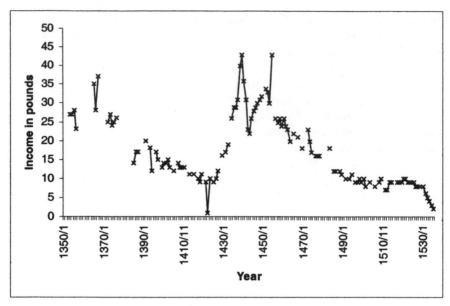

Figure 5.1: Income Received from the Image of St Leonard,
Norwich, 1350–1535

popular religion of their localities. Although the small houses of Aldeby and
Hoxne did not shelter cults of any size, the priories of Lynn, Yarmouth and
St Leonard's Norwich were major players in the religious life of their
environs. The rise of the cult of St Leonard at the priory dedicated to him in
Thorpe wood just outside Norwich, though little known, was one of the most
remarkable of its kind in fifteenth-century England.[129] The offerings received
at St Leonard's in the later middle ages are shown in Figure 5.1. As this
graph indicates, it is perhaps more accurate to talk of the renewal of the cult
in the fifteenth century, since the image of St Leonard was regularly bringing
in revenues of over £25 between the 1350s and 1370s.[130] Yearly offerings
then fell to only a few pounds by 1425/6, but most unusually a recovery then
set in. Annual receipts had risen to back over £25 by 1434/5 and reached
£42 in 1439/40. After a slight dip, oblations topped £30 every year between
1447 and 1455, reaching a maximum of £43 4d. in 1454/5, before slowly
declining to almost nothing in the 1530s. The popularity of St Leonard's as a

---

129 NRO, DCN, 2/3. See my 'Veneration and Renovation at a small Norfolk Priory: St
Leonard's, Norwich in the Later Middle Ages', *Historical Research*, lxxvi (2003), pp.
431–49, for a much fuller account of this cult.

130 The income recorded in the earliest accounts includes oblations from other images,
which are not separately itemised at this time. But since the great majority of the
cell's offerings were given to the image of St Leonard, rather than the other lesser
images venerated at the priory, when the accounts begin to give more detail in the
1370s, it seems reasonable to assume that the bulk of oblations were directed at the
cult of St Leonard in the preceding decades: NRO, DCN 2/3/1–7.

place of pilgrimage among the wealthier sections of Norfolk society is intimated in several surviving wills and by references to the cult in the Paston
Letters. Moreover, the two surviving priory inventories of 1425 and 1452
reveal valuable votive gifts left at the shrine by the earl of Suffolk, Sir John
Fastolf and Sir Andrew Ogard.[131] The sums received at this small cell for
much of the fifteenth century exceeded those offered to most of the major
cathedral shrines at this date, and suggest that the cults of smaller monasteries could be as influential as those sponsored by the greatest houses.[132]

The saint cults at Lynn and Yarmouth did not attract the same level of
offerings as that of St Leonard, but the evidence of image veneration from
these two houses is just as illuminating.[133] The images erected within the
priory churches seem to have held limited appeal, but those in chapels under
the monks' control both within and without their precincts proved far more
popular. Nevertheless, the only sum of any significance received in offerings
to images at either priory in the first half of the fifteenth century was the £10
or so collected each year from Yarmouth's chapel of St Mary of 'Arneburgh'.
But as the income of both houses began to decline significantly over the
century, a more proactive stance was taken over saint cults. In 1479–81,
offerings of a few shillings to Lynn Priory are recorded from the chapel of St
Mary 'on the bridge'. The next two priory accounts add small amounts from a
similar chapel 'on the mount'. In 1484/5, however, oblations at the latter,
presumably made to an image of the Virgin inside, brought in the substantial
sum of £20, rising to £34 by 1497/8 and stabilising at around £15 between

131 E.g. R. Hart, 'The Shrines and Pilgrimages of the County of Norfolk', *Norfolk
Archaeology*, vi (1864), pp. 277–94; *Paston Letters and Papers of the Fifteenth Century*,
ed. N. Davis, 2 vols (Oxford, 1971–6), I, nos 126, 160, pp. 217–19, 267–8; Bensly, 'St
Leonard's Priory', pp. 200–1, 214–15.
132 Nilson, *Cathedral Shrines*, pp. 147–65, 211–31. See below, pp. 265–6, for an account
of how this windfall was spent by the priors of fifteenth-century St Leonard's.
133 NRO, DCN 2/1, 2/4. Professor Robert Swanson has discussed the evidence for the
veneration of images at these priories in two articles: R. N. Swanson, 'Standards of
Livings: Parochial Revenues in Pre-Reformation England', in Harper-Bill, *Religious
Belief and Ecclesiastical Careers*, pp. 151–96; and R. N. Swanson, 'Urban Rectories and
Urban Fortunes in Late Medieval England: the Evidence from Bishop's Lynn', in
Slater and Rosser, *Church in Medieval Town*, pp. 100–30. However, Swanson treats
both as evidence for the profitability of saint cults in parish churches. Although many
parish churches did have images around which popular cults developed, the material
from Lynn and Yarmouth can only be taken as evidence for image veneration in
small monasteries. In both cases it was clearly the monks rather than the parish who
sponsored the cults, spending large sums of money on the construction of new
chapels. At times, however, there is an ambiguity in shared churches over whether
particular images or relics belonged to the monks or the parish. The aforementioned
images at Leominster and Pilton, as well as the Holy Rood of Brecon, were all housed
within the parish church, and might have been closely connected with the parishes.
In these three cases, however, the fact that the monks received the offerings from the
faithful suggests that they ultimately controlled the cults. This is clearly a grey area,
but the evidence from Lynn and Yarmouth indicates that it was not only images
within their own churches that were sponsored by the religious.

1500 and 1525, before tailing off. These sums were bolstered by offerings from a 'good cross' erected in St Margaret's cemetery in the early sixteenth century, bringing nearly £7 in 1506/7, before dropping to between 10s. and 20s. per year through the 1510s and falling off to no more than a few shillings thereafter.[134] The extent to which the monks of Lynn directed these cults or responded to popular interest is difficult to judge. Dr Eamon Duffy has concluded that the cult of saints in late medieval England was in general led by the affections of the laity and not by the institutional church, and it does appear that popular interest in Our Lady on the Mount pre-dated the monks' involvement in the cult.[135] However, the dramatic upturn in offerings to the image coincided exactly with the first signs of investment in the cult by the brethren of Lynn, who paid to lease the land where the chapel housing the image stood as well as the stipend of the chapel's warden in 1484/5. Moreover, it seems likely that the longevity of the support for this Marian image had much to do with the construction of an impressive new chapel by the monks of Lynn in 1489 at a cost of over £38, and that the enterprising approach taken by the priory to this new cult greatly increased its popularity.

At the same time that Lynn was capitalising on the chapel of St Mary on the Mount, the monks of Yarmouth were building a chapel dedicated to St John the Baptist in a corner of their cemetery to contain a new image of Henry VI. Once again, although this move was quite possibly in reaction to existing popular interest in the image, the investment of the priory in constructing the chapel and the resulting formalisation of the cult almost certainly widened its impact. This cult was a little less successful than Lynn's equivalent, and annual receipts fell from a height of £17 in 1484/5 to about £5 in 1490/1 and then to an average of only 30s. in the early sixteenth century.[136] Another up-to-date cult had been developed at Binham by the start of the sixteenth century, since the 1508 will of Richard Easingwold of Islip, Northamptonshire, requested burial 'before the holy image of maister John Shorne' in the priory.[137] Not every attempt to harness popular piety proved successful, and an image of 'Good King Henry' erected at St Leonard's Norwich at the same time as that of Yarmouth never attracted offerings of more than a few pence.[138] Nevertheless, examples like these indicate that daughter houses were responsive to the latest trends in popular piety, and actively sought, often with some success, to foster saint cults in the later middle ages. There are, moreover, several indications that cells were not

---

[134] NRO, DCN 2/1/69–91. The curious chapel of the 'Red Mount' in Lynn has survived intact.

[135] E. Duffy, *The Stripping of the Altars. Traditional Religion in England c.1400–c.1580* (Yale, 1992), p. 165.

[136] NRO, DCN, 2/4/16–21.

[137] R. M. Serjeantson and H. I. Longden, 'The Parish Churches and Religious Houses of Northamptonshire: their Dedications, Altars, Images and Lights', *Archaeological Journal*, lxx (1913), p. 264.

[138] NRO, DCN, 2/3/91–140.

alone among small monasteries in this endeavour.[139] Indeed, the evidence from English dependencies suggests that lesser religious houses were involved in popular religion through the provision of venerated shrines, relics and images on a much greater scale than has been appreciated.

Conclusion

The considerable material surviving from dependencies therefore indicates much closer ties between these small houses and their localities than many studies of monasteries have allowed. It is impossible to see these priories as isolated or irrelevant to the lives of neighbouring layfolk. Despite the apparent indifference of many patrons, there is sufficient evidence of these cells' contacts with local elites to suggest that good relations between land-owners and monks, based on mutual benefits, were normal. Although the social services provided by daughter houses do not seem to have been substantial, they probably made some impact on a local scale. The role of daughter houses in the religious lives of their neighbours emerges much more clearly from the surviving records. The wide interest in the Belvoir confraternity suggests that monastic prayers may well have been considerably more valued than the evidence of wills alone reveals. Moreover, the many monastic communities who shared their churches with parochial congregations were closely integrated with parish life, while the extent of the conflict between the two parties should not be exaggerated. Even more impressive, perhaps, is the contribution of many cells to popular piety in their localities through the saint cults they controlled.

It would however be a mistake to ignore the signs of disharmony between the religious and their neighbours. Acrimonious disputes between cells and their lay neighbours were not uncommon and numerous acts of violence were committed against satellite priories. Binham and Felixstowe were attacked during the Peasants' Revolt and many of their records destroyed.[140]

---

[139] To give just two examples of many, in c.1330, the monks of Bradwell built a chapel against their church to house a popular statue of the Virgin, while in 1351 Bishop Grandisson of Exeter condemned the canons of Frithelstock for constructing a new chapel near the priory and erecting an image of the Virgin there 'not for the devotion of faith but out of greed': E. C. Rouse, 'Bradwell Abbey and the Chapel of St Mary', *Milton Keynes Journal*, ii (1973), pp. 34–8; *The Register of John de Grandisson, Bishop of Exeter (AD 1327–1369)*, ed. F. C. Hingeston-Randolph, 3 vols (London and Exeter, 1894–9), II, pp. 1110–12. The Frithelstock episode has been discussed in N. I. Orme, 'Bishop Grandisson and Popular Religion', *Reports and Transactions of the Devonshire Association*, cxxiv (1992), pp. 107–18. I am very grateful to Professor Orme for drawing my attention to this article and for several other references to saint cults associated with small monasteries in south-west England. I intend to discuss the wider evidence for popular cults in lesser religious houses in more detail elsewhere.
[140] Burstall, 'Monastic Agreement', p. 211; K. Davison, 'History of Walton Priory', *Proceedings of the Suffolk Institute of Archaeology*, xxxiii (1975), p. 142.

The priories of Bamburgh (1371), St Bees (1372), Wymondham (1376), Wearmouth (1439) and St Ives (1450), among others, were also subjected to lay aggression during the later middle ages.[141] Similarly, in 1461, the prior of Durham was forced to write to Lord Fauconberg requesting that the master of Jarrow 'may surely ride and goo in the cuntry, whar he liketh, for the wele and profett of his place' and not be forcibly confined to his priory, after it was alleged that he was a Lancastrian supporter.[142] The monks sojourning in some distant dependencies, particularly those in Wales and Ireland, were clearly viewed as unwelcome outsiders, and at times faced considerable animosity. The Durham cell in Lytham seems to have been the least popular of all cells and endured the intermittent hostility of the Lancashire gentry throughout the later middle ages, climaxing in a series of attacks on its property by the Butlers in the 1530s.[143] However, most of the recorded disputes with neighbours were the result of contested rights, and not a symptom of the inherent unpopularity of the monks. But if such clashes should not be given undue prominence, they certainly counsel against rosy depictions of mutual admiration between monasteries and their neighbours. To claim that daughter houses were widely popular requires a certain leap of faith; their full integration into local society, and quite possibly that of many other small monasteries, is rather better attested.

[141] CPR, 1370–1374, pp. 177, 243–4, 1374–1377, p. 318; Dobson, Durham Priory, pp. 195–6; CPR, 1446–1452, pp. 378–9.
[142] Raine, Jarrow and Monk-Wearmouth, p. xxii.
[143] VCH, Lancashire, II, p. 108; Dobson, Durham Priory, p. 328; History of the Parish of Lytham in the County of Lancaster, ed. H. Fishwick, Chetham Society, new series, lx (1907), pp. 11–15.

6

The Economy of English Cells

Sources and Questions

The economic activity of dependent priories has very often been considered their primary function. Some historians have likened these small houses to granges and for others the term 'cell' has virtually become synonymous with bailiwick.[1] Both comparisons, however, are misleading as far as English cells are concerned. Although a tiny dependency might superficially resemble a grange, the purely agricultural rationale of the latter is in stark contrast to the multi-faceted life of the daughter house. The bailiwick analogy is more profitable and is particularly appropriate for the mass of tiny alien priories. The classic account of such houses remains Dr Chibnall's depiction of the cells of the Norman abbey of Bec-Hellouin.[2] From the 'priories' of Ogbourne, Steventon and Wilsford the canonical minimum of two Bec monks administered the abbey's scattered estates in southern England, sending back most of the annual profits from these lands as 'apports'. As we have seen, the circumstances of the foundation of many English dependencies indicates that the management of mother-house properties was never their principal *raison d'être*.[3] Moreover, it appears that even those cells that were initially founded by an abbey to overcome the problems of administering distant estates, such as St Nicholas' Exeter, often soon acquired a religious momentum of their own.

By the late thirteenth century, when relevant documentation first survives, very few English dependencies were sending back a sizeable apport. It would seem that several Irish cells were dispatching most of their income to their English mother houses in the later middle ages, and the complaints of hardship at Nostell after the decline in the value of Bamburgh from the late thirteenth century indicate that the mother house had profited considerably from this cell.[4] But it appears that the bulk of the revenues of the vast

---

1   E.g. B. Waites, 'The Monastic Grange as a Factor in the Settlement of North-East Yorkshire', YAJ, xl (1959–62), pp. 627–56. See above, pp. 4–5.
2   Morgan, *Bec.*
3   See above, pp. 22–55.
4   E.g. E. St John Brooks, '14th Century Monastic Estates in Meath. The Llanthony Cells of Duleek and Colp', *Journal of the Royal Society of Antiquaries of Ireland*, lxxxiii (1953), pp. 140–9; CPR, *1436–1441*, p. 190.

majority of cells was always reserved for their own use. Daughter-house patrons and bishops were wary of mother houses diverting their cells' reve- nues to their own coffers, an attitude also expressed by Bishop Hugh of Wells in relation to Breedon Priory when he required that 'all the goods of the said church should be spent at Breedon, to sustain five canons staying there, and the ministers of the church and giving hospitality'.[5] Every cell owed its mother house some kind of pension, but it is rare to find priories passing over a very large proportion of their annual revenues. In 1291, Leominster, a conventual house, was paying £240 out of its total income of £303 3s. to Reading Abbey; and in 1535 Penwortham owed its mother house, Evesham, a pension of just over £63 out of yearly receipts of about £115.[6] But in general English dependencies were financially independent and spent most of their revenues on themselves, and in this vital respect they resemble autonomous small monasteries rather than bailiwicks or the alien priories.

Because of this financial integrity, these cells can serve as examples of the economic fortunes of a group of small religious houses in medieval England. Once again, any comparison with independent priories of a similar size must take into account the unique characteristics of dependencies, such as the ready access to mother-house subsidies and the unusually small number of inmates maintained therein. In other ways, however, the experience of dependencies must have accorded closely with that of other small houses, for example in the economic circumstances they faced and how these affected monastic income. This is important, since, as a result of the survival of mother-house archives and the continued insistence of abbeys that the priors of their satellites give a regular account of their administration, a tremen- dous amount of financial documentation survives from cells, dwarfing any- thing available for independent small monasteries. Large numbers of priors' accounts pertaining to their thirteen cells remain in the voluminous archives of Norwich and Durham Cathedral Priories, and small series or individual accounts exist for at least fifteen other dependencies.[7] The only part of this

---

5   *Rotuli Hugonis de Welles, episcopi Lincolniensis A.D. MCCIX–MCCXXXV*, ed. W. P. W. Phillimore and F. N. Davis, 3 vols, C&Y Soc., i, iii–iv (1907–9), I, p. 252. For an account of lay attitudes to the income of daughter houses, see B. Thompson, 'The Statute of Carlisle, 1307, and the Alien Priories', *JEH*, xli (1990), pp. 543–83.

6   *Taxatio Ecclesiastica Angliae et Walliae auctoritate P. Nicholai IV, circa AD 1291* (HMSO, 1802), p. 173; *Valor*, V, p. 233. There is no entry for Leominster in the *Valor*. This priory was probably founded by Reading to administer its Herefordshire endowment and so its large pension might well have evolved from the annual delivery of estate profits. Penwortham, however, was established by a lay founder, Warin Bussel. Its pension apparently represents a fixed sum owed to the mother house for those lands in Lancashire that had been granted specifically to Evesham and not to its cell, which Penwortham managed on its parent's behalf: see the charters collected together in *Documents relating to the Priory of Penwortham, and other Possessions in Lancashire of the Abbey of Evesham*, ed. W. A. Hulton, Chetham Society, xxx (1853).

7   Long runs of accounts survive for the eight cells of Durham: Coldingham, Farne Island, Finchale, Holy Island, Jarrow, Lytham, St Leonard's Stamford and Wearmouth

corpus to have been used extensively by historians are the Durham rolls, many of which were printed in part or in full by James Raine father and son.[8] In contrast, the Norwich accounts have until very recently been almost ignored;[9] and for this reason this chapter will draw many of its statistics from the Norwich series. Most studies of lesser religious houses have had to rely on tiny samples of accounts or the static picture provided by the tax assessments of 1291 and 1535.[10] However, only a run of accounts can provide a nuanced picture of an institution's financial affairs or give information about fluctuations in its income or its reactions to changing economic circumstances. Accounts can also shed light on the financial strength or weakness of an institution, and therefore the large sample surviving for daughter houses provides some data for the crucial issue of the economic viability of the apparently frail small monasteries of medieval England.

(DCM, under cell name: for printed Durham accounts, see below); and the five cells of Norwich: Aldeby, Hoxne, Lynn, St Leonard's Norwich and Yarmouth (NRO, DCN, 2/1–6 and Windsor, St George's Chapel, I.C.1–39, XV.55.75–8). Single or scattered accounts are extant from numerous other priories: Binham, Belvoir, Hatfield Peverel, Hertford, Pembroke, Tynemouth and Wallingford (PRO, E315/272, fols 70r–78v); Hertford (PRO, SC6/HenVII/1696, SC11/277); Wallingford (PRO, SC6/HenVIII/106; Oxford, Corpus Christi College, MSS Z/2/1/1–2); Colne (Essex Record Office (Chelmsford), Probert MSS); Cowick (Devon Record Office, W1258M, G4/53/1–5); Dover (BL, Add. MS 25107); Felixstowe (PRO, SC6/HenVII/691); Rumburgh (SROI, HD 1538/335/1, nos 6–7, 13, 21–2, 34–5); St Bees (Cumbria Record Office, D/Lons./ W/St Bees 1/1); St Ives (BL, Add. MS 33448, fols 126v–128r, 142v–143r, Add. MS 33449, fols 15r–16r, 20v–21v, 30v–31r, 45r–46v, 61v–63v, 100r–102r, 128r–129r, 142r–143r, 167v–168v); and Snape (PRO, SC6/HenVIII/3402). It is quite possible that other accounts from cells remain, since several of the above have only recently come to light.

8   Raine, Priory of Finchale, pp. i–ccccxvi; The Correspondence, Inventories, Account Rolls and Law Proceedings of the Priory of Coldingham, ed. J. Raine, SS, xii (1841), pp. i–cvii; J. Raine, The History and Antiquities of North Durham (London, 1852), pp. 82–130, 344–58; (Rev. J.) Raine, Jarrow and Monk-Wearmouth; Dobson, Durham Priory, pp. 297–341; Piper, 'Wearmouth'; Piper, 'Stamford'; Piper, Jarrow.

9   The Norwich cell accounts are briefly described in H. W. Saunders, An Introduction to the Obedientiary and Manor Rolls of Norwich Cathedral Priory (Norwich, 1930), pp. 145–8. They have lately been trawled for biographical information by Dr Joan Greatrex, while Professor Robert Swanson has recently studied the Lynn and Yarmouth accounts to very good effect to glean information about parochial and urban revenues in late medieval England: Greatrex, BRECP, pp. 466–576; R. N. Swanson, 'Standards of Livings: Parochial Revenues in Pre-Reformation England', in Religious Belief and Ecclesiastical Careers in Late Medieval England, ed. C. Harper-Bill (Woodbridge, 1991), pp. 151–96; R. N. Swanson, 'Urban Rectories and Urban Fortunes in Late Medieval England: the Evidence from Bishop's Lynn', in The Church in the Medieval Town, ed. T. R. Slater and G. Rosser (Aldershot, 1998), pp. 100–30.

10 E.g. E. Power, Medieval English Nunneries c.1275–1535 (Cambridge, 1922), pp. 96–236, esp. pp. 97–8; J. H. Tillotson, Marrick Priory: a Nunnery in Late Medieval Yorkshire, Borthwick Paper, no. LXXV (1989); M. Oliva, The Convent and the Community in Late Medieval England. Female Monasteries in the Diocese of Norwich, 1350–1540 (Woodbridge, 1998), pp. 190–8; D. M. Robinson, The Geography of Augustinian Settlement in Medieval England and Wales, British Archaeological Reports, British Series, LXXX (1980), pp. 109–348, Appendix 18, pp. 395–6.

This evidence is not without its pitfalls. Most of the complications arising in the interpretation of medieval accounts stem from the fact that these are charge–discharge accounts and not the more familiar profit-and-loss variety. In order to demonstrate clearly who owed what to whom, certain distorting accounting techniques were employed. The sums entered under receipts or expenses often represent what should have been received and spent rather than what actually was. It is often unclear, therefore, to what extent the accounts have been fictionalised to ensure that the accountant was not unfairly burdened or let off lightly. Moreover, most of the surviving cell accounts are cash accounts only, and give no impression of the quantities of stock or produce handled. As a result, a misleading impression of changing circumstances can be created by the consumption of previously marketed produce or vice versa. One must also be wary of the sums carried over from previous years which can mask the true financial state of the priory. Finally, there always remains the possibility that a surviving account does not represent the entire income and expenditure of the institution. It may be that some of the obedientiaries known to have been appointed at English cells also accounted for some proportion of the priory's revenues, in which case the extant prior's accounts would provide only a partial picture of the house's financial affairs. But despite these caveats, there is no better guide to the economic fortunes of a religious house and the problems and opportunities it experienced.

This wealth of material can also contribute something to the growing debate about the fortunes of the small landlord in late medieval England. In contrast to the attitude of most ecclesiastical historians towards lesser monasteries, economic historians have long suggested that smaller landlords might have coped relatively well during the later middle ages, although the reasons proffered for drawing this conclusion have differed. In 1947, Professor Rodney Hilton argued that 'the small estate like that of Owston Abbey with a fairly stable rent income in cash forming the bulk of its receipts could probably weather the changing conditions of the late Middle Ages better than the large ecclesiastical corporation with its far-flung estates'. Professor Michael Poston was more pessimistic about the profitability of renting, but nevertheless believed that 'the smaller landowners may have suffered less since most of them consumed a large proportion of their produce and presumably farmed out little, if any, of their land'.[11]

Over the past generation, it has increasingly been argued that by engaging in direct farming, lesser landlords were able to ride the unpropitious economic conditions of the fifteenth century. Several studies of the fifteenth-century gentry have suggested that flexible and specialised demesne farms could often be a source of profit, although this conclusion has not been

---

[11] R. H. Hilton, *The Economic Development of some Leicestershire Estates in the 14th and 15th Centuries* (Oxford, 1947), pp. 117–18; M. M. Postan, *The Medieval Economy and Society* (Harmondsworth, 1975), p. 194.

universally accepted.[12] The importance of demesne farming to the economies of smaller ecclesiastical corporations has also been stressed.[13] For example, Dr Andrew Watkins has recently demonstrated how the medium-sized abbey of Merevale in the forest of Arden engaged in commercial grazing and some arable farming in the fifteenth century, leasing property from others and reclaiming land in order to extend its activities. However, the limited geographical range of much of this work is evident, and the concentration of nearly every study of smaller landlords – including those focused specifically on ecclesiastical institutions – on temporal sources of income to the neglect of spiritualities is a serious deficiency.

The *Valor Ecclesiasticus*

The vast majority of surviving cell accounts date from after 1370, and this source can therefore tell us very little about the financial affairs of these priories before the Black Death or the result of that demographic catastrophe on their economies. There is however considerable information about land acquisition by dependencies in the twelfth and thirteenth centuries from surviving collections of charters. The larger cells of Belvoir, Binham, Brecon, Colne, Deeping St James, Dover, St Nicholas' Exeter, Finchale, St Guthlac's Hereford, Leominster, St Bees, Stone, Tynemouth, Wetheral and Wymondham have all left their own cartularies, and in each case it would be possible to give a detailed account of the development of their

---

12 E.g. C. Dyer, 'A Small Landowner in the Fifteenth Century', *Midland History*, i (1972), pp. 1–14; C. Richmond, *John Hopton. A Fifteenth-Century Suffolk Gentleman* (Cambridge, 1981), pp. 34–8, 79–85; C. Carpenter, *Locality and Polity. A Study of Warwickshire Landed Society, 1401–1499* (Cambridge, 1992), pp. 46–7; A. Watkins, 'Landowners and their Estates in the Forest of Arden in the Fifteenth Century', *Agricultural History Review*, xlv (1997), pp. 18–33; D. Youngs, 'Estate Management, Investment and the Gentleman Landlord in Later Medieval England', *Historical Research*, lxxiii (2000), pp. 124–41. For a dissenting voice, see J. Hatcher, 'The Great Slump of the Mid-Fifteenth Century', in *Progress and Problems in Medieval England. Essays in Honour of Edward Miller*, ed. R. Britnell and J. Hatcher (Cambridge, 1996), pp. 237–72.

13 *The Sibton Abbey Estates. Select Documents 1325–1509*, ed. A. H. Denney, Suffolk Records Society, ii (1960), pp. 35–9, 141–2; S. M. Jack, 'Of Poverty and Pigstyes: the household economy of some of the smaller religious houses on the eve of the Dissolution', *Parergon*, new series, i (1983), pp. 69–91; A. Watkins, 'Merevale Abbey in the Late 1490s', *Warwickshire History*, ix (1994), pp. 87–104; A. Watkins, 'Maxstoke Priory in the Fifteenth Century: the development of an estate economy in the Forest of Arden', *Warwickshire History*, x (1996), pp. 3–18; Watkins, 'Landowners and their Estates', pp. 18–33. For the comparable position of individual obedientiaries at larger houses, see R. A. Lomas, 'The Priory of Durham and its Demesne in the Fourteenth and Fifteenth Centuries', *EcHR*, 2nd series, xxxi (1978), pp. 339–53; and R. A. Lomas, 'A Northern Farm at the End of the Middle Ages: Elvethall Manor, Durham, 1443/4–1513/14', *Northern History*, xviii (1982), pp. 26–53.

endowments.[14] Lesser cells sometimes kept their own cartularies, although their charters were more often preserved in their mother-house archives.[15] Of particular interest is the evidence from a number of small dependencies of the accumulation and consolidation of holdings in the thirteenth century. Humble priories like St Bartholomew's Sudbury and Blythburgh in Suffolk can be seen to have been heavily involved in the land market at this time, and to have extended their properties considerably through purchase. The Breedon cartulary similarly reveals the canons resuming land from their tenants in the thirteenth century, as well as consolidating their holdings through exchanges of property.[16]

Although the *Taxatio* of 1291 provides considerable information about the income of English dependencies, it is clear that the rental values given seriously underestimate the actual revenues available to individual houses, and that any comparisons with the earliest extant account rolls would be hazardous.[17] A rather more reliable tax assessment to compare with the private financial records of cells is the *Valor Ecclesiasticus* of 1535, and this is the best starting point for an analysis of the income of English dependencies.

[14] See G. R. Davis, *Medieval Cartularies of Great Britain* (London, 1958). Several of these have been edited or calendared: *Historical Manuscripts Commission: The Duke of Rutland*, IV (1905), pp. 98–173 (Belvoir); *Cartularium Prioratus S. Johannis Evangeliste de Brecon*, ed. R. W. Banks, *Archaeologia Cambrensis*, 4th series, xiii–xiv (1882–3); *Cartularium Prioratus de Colne*, ed. J. L. Fisher, Essex Archaeological Society, Occasional Publications, I (1946); 'List of Charters in the Cartulary of St Nicholas Priory, at Exeter', ed. J. Nichols, *Collectanea Topographica et Genealogica*, i (1834); Raine, *Priory of Finchale*, pp. 1–163; *The Register of St Bees*, ed. J. Wilson, SS, cxxvi (1915); 'The Stone Chartulary', ed. G. Wrottesley, *Staffordshire Historical Collections*, vi(i) (1885), pp. 1–28; and *The Register of the Priory of Wetherhal*, ed. J. E. Prescott, Cumberland and Westmorland Antiquarian and Archaeological Society, Record Series, I (1897).

[15] The Augustinian cells of Blythburgh, Breedon and Scokirk produced their own cartularies, whereas fragments of cartularies survive from Brooke, Hoxne and Rumburgh Priories, although the Hoxne manuscript is currently missing: *Blythburgh Priory Cartulary*, ed. C. Harper-Bill, 2 parts, Suffolk Records Society. Suffolk Charters, II–III (1980–1); R. McKinley (ed.), 'The Cartulary of Breedon Priory', unpublished Manchester MA thesis (1950); *The Chartulary of Tockwith alias Scokirk, a Cell to the Priory of Nostell*, ed. G. C. Ransome, in *Miscellanea III*, Yorkshire Archaeological Society, Record Series, LXXX (1931), pp. 151–206; PRO, E135/2/9; SROI, HD 1538/265/1, 1538/335/1, no. 53. Particularly full collections from mother-house archives are printed in: *A Register of the Churches of the Monastery of St Peter's Gloucester*, ed. D. Walker, in *An Ecclesiastical Miscellany*, Publications of the Bristol and Gloucestershire Archaeological Society, Records Section, XI (1976), pp. 3–61 (Ewyas Harold); Hulton, *Priory of Penwortham*; *Charters of St Bartholomew's Priory, Sudbury*, ed. R. Mortimer, Suffolk Records Society, Suffolk Charters, XV (1996). Many surviving charters of the sizeable Westminster cell of Hurley are also extant in the abbey archive and have been calendared in *St Mary's, Hurley, in the Later Middle Ages*, ed. F. T. Wethered (London, 1898) and *The Lands and Tythes of Hurley Priory, 1086–1535*, ed. F. T. Wethered (Reading, 1909).

[16] For references, see note 15.

[17] R. Graham, 'The Taxation of Pope Nicholas IV', in Graham, *English Ecclesiastical Studies* (London, 1929), pp. 271–301 is still the most useful introduction to this source, but a much-needed new edition of the *Taxatio* is currently under preparation.

It is first important, however, to recognise the limitations of this invaluable document on which historians of the monasteries of late medieval England and Wales are so reliant. There remains some disagreement about the fundamental accuracy of the *Valor*'s figures. Some scholars have endorsed the views of Professor Savine – still the only historian to make a thorough study of the *Valor* – that the tax assessment's valuations in most cases only slightly underestimated monastic incomes.[18] Others, however, have followed Professor Knowles in arguing that a comparison of the *Valor* with pre-Reformation accounts often suggests a rather larger shortfall in the former's figures, perhaps amounting to as much as 20 per cent.[19]

The survival of numerous cell accounts supplies a little more data with which to assess the *Valor*'s accuracy. Unfortunately, not every account can be compared to an entry in the survey. The *Valor* does not always provide full information about cells' possessions and income since the assessment of some dependencies, including those of Norwich, was entered imperceptibly among the mother-house properties. Moreover, the 1535 returns for some counties are no longer extant and therefore the only information available for numerous monasteries is a bald figure for net income (i.e. gross income minus certain tax deductible expenses) from an exchequer digest.[20] In a few other cases, the priory for which accounts survive was dissolved before 1535. As a result, it is only in nine instances that it is possible to compare sixteenth-century account rolls with full assessments of gross income recorded in the *Valor*, although a comparison with net income is available for another four cells (see Table 6.1). The sums in Table 6.1 seem to suggest a considerable undervaluation of cells' annual revenues in the *Valor*. As regards the nine dependencies with gross valuations, the accounts show on average an income 50 per cent higher than does the survey; and for those priories with only net totals, the figure is 55 per cent, implying a significant discrepancy even after the addition of allowances to the *Valor* figure. However, the preponderance of northern houses in our sample, which are known to have been undervalued to a much greater extent than their southern equivalents, creates a false impression. Where gross income figures are available, on average the *Valor* underestimates northern cells by 69 per cent and southern cells by only 14 per cent. Since relatively few English dependencies were situated in the north, Knowles' estimate of a 20 per cent undervaluation may well hold good for this category of monastery.

18 A. Savine, *English Monasteries on the Eve of the Dissolution*, Oxford Studies in Social and Legal History (Oxford, 1909); F. Heal, *Of Prelates and Princes* (Cambridge, 1980), pp. 54–60; J. Youings, 'The Monasteries', in *Rural Society. Landowners, Peasants and Labourers 1500–1750*, ed. C. Clay (Cambridge, 1990), p. 90. Savine found, however, that several northern monasteries were seriously undervalued in the *Valor*.

19 Knowles, *RO*, III, pp. 244–5; I. Kershaw, *Bolton Priory. The Economy of a Northern Monastery 1286–1325* (Oxford, 1973), p. 186; Robinson, *Geography of Augustinian Settlement*, pp. 144–5; Oliva, *Convent and Community*, p. 99.

20 Savine, *English Monasteries*, pp. 23–4.

Table 6.1: Comparison of Income from Accounts with the *Valor Ecclesiasticus*

Priory	Year of account	Income in account	Income in *Valor*	% difference
Farne Island	1536/7	26.1.4	12.17.7	105
Wearmouth	1533/4	50.8.4	26.18.4	88
Jarrow	1536/7	73.17.11	40.7.8	83
Holy Island	1536/7	98.1.2	60.5.0	63
Finchale	1528/9	210.10.2	146.19.2	43
St Bees	1516/17	194.6.4	149.19.7	30
St Ives	1525/6	83.14.8	67.16.8	23
St L's Stamford	1532/3	41.15.2	36.1.5	16
Belvoir	1525/6	132.14.4	129.17.6	2
Pembroke	1525/6	136.17.11	57.9.4*	136
Hatfield Peverel	1525/6	88.2.3	60.14.11*	45
Binham	1525/6	179.1.2	140.5.4*	28
Hertford	1525/6	81.18.8	74.14.3*	9

Note: * signifies net income. Sums in all the tables are rounded up to the nearest penny. The sixteenth-century accounts chosen are those closest in time to 1535.

Source: Valor; Raine, *North Durham*, pp. 127–30 (Holy Island), p. 358 (Farne Island); Raine, *Jarrow and Monk-Wearmouth*, pp. 135–6 (Jarrow), pp. 231–2 (Wearmouth); Raine, *Priory of Finchale*, pp. ccccxi–ccccxiv; Cumbria Record Office, D/Lons./W/St Bees 1/1 (St Bees); BL, Add. MS 33449, fols 167v–168v (St Ives); Piper, 'Stamford', part i, p. 14; PRO, E315/272, fols 70r–78v (Belvoir, Pembroke, Hatfield Peverel, Binham and Hertford).

One final conclusion can be drawn from these statistics. It appears that the *Valor* most seriously underestimated the income of the poorest cells, like Farne Island, Wearmouth and Jarrow. This feature was noted by Dr Sybil Jack in her important study of the records generated by the suppression of the smaller monasteries in 1536–7. Jack attributed this phenomenon to the relative importance of demesne farming to the smallest religious houses, and demonstrated that the value of this enterprise must have been far greater to these priories than the figures in the *Valor* would suggest.[21] As will appear below, the home farms of several well-recorded small cells were indeed vital to their economies, and as a result it is very likely that the poorest dependencies were in fact rather less indigent than the 1535 survey implies. This conclusion goes some way towards explaining how the 9 per cent of monasteries assessed at under £20 per year in 1535 managed to survive throughout the middle ages.

---

[21] Jack, 'Of Poverty and Pigstyes', pp. 69–91. Savine also noted that the survey's valuation of demesne land held in hand was too low, but correctly concluded that in most cases this did not greatly affect overall values since most monasteries kept only a small proportion of their land in hand by 1535: Savine, *English Monasteries*, pp. 34, 48–9, 145.

It is also important to bear in mind the dangers of assuming that the static sums given in the *Valor* necessarily represent anything like the income enjoyed by a monastery over the later middle ages. As Figure 6.1 shows, this was not the case with all of the Norwich cells. Both Lynn and Yarmouth experienced a heavy drop in revenues between the late fourteenth century and the 1530s, although this decline occurred sporadically, interspersed with spells of stability. However, the incomes of Aldeby and Hoxne, though liable to short-term fluctuations, were remarkably buoyant over the later middle ages. The receipts of St Leonard's Norwich, consisting primarily of offerings to images, oscillated throughout this period, although they had fallen permanently by the end of the fifteenth century. The accounts from St Ives also show some stability, although the priory faced a serious decline in income during the 1520s.[22] The Durham cells too received widely varying revenues, with the second half of the fourteenth century and the 1420s particularly difficult periods. But the five Durham priories shown in Table 6.1 all enjoyed greater receipts in the sixteenth century than they had done in the first years of the fifteenth.[23] These figures will be broken down and analysed in detail below, but they demonstrate clearly enough how little we can know from tax assessments alone.

Spiritual Income

We must therefore be aware of the limitations of the *Valor Ecclesiasticus* before we approach this source. For some cells without accounts, it is quite possible that the 1535 figures show a considerably underestimated income, which had in any case fallen from a significantly higher level over the previous two centuries. For others, the *Valor* figure may accurately represent the state of the house both in the 1530s and for much of its late medieval history. Nevertheless, the survey remains an indispensable tool, and is the only source of information about the income of numerous daughter houses. Fifty-two Benedictine and fourteen Augustinian cells were assessed in 1535, although for the reasons discussed above only forty-five have fully and clearly itemised entries.[24] It is possible to study the incomes of these houses in some detail, together with those of six more dependencies – Binham,

---

22 For St Ives' income, see Figure 6.3 below.
23 Raine, *Priory of Finchale*, pp. i–ccccxvi; Raine, *North Durham*, pp. 82–130, 344–58; Piper, *Jarrow*, pp. 6–12; Piper, 'Stamford', part i, pp. 12–20; Piper, 'Wearmouth', pp. 3–7.
24 There are of course no entries in the *Valor* for several previously suppressed cells. The priories of Aldeby, Bedeman's Berg, Bentley, Calke, Carham, Chetwode, Coquet Island, Deeping St James, Hilbre Island, Hood, Horton, Hoxne, Hurley, Leominster, Lynn, Marsh Barton, Morville, St Leonard's Norwich, Ovingham, Oxney, Puffin Island, Ratlinghope, St Anthony in Roseland, Scilly, Spinney, Stavordale, Trokenholt, Wormley, Yarmouth and All Saints' Fishergate, York are also omitted or not itemised separately from their mother houses, although a number of these cells were definitely functioning in 1535.

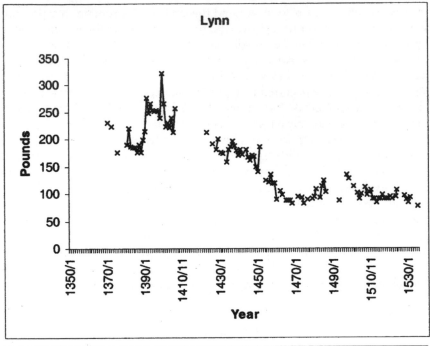

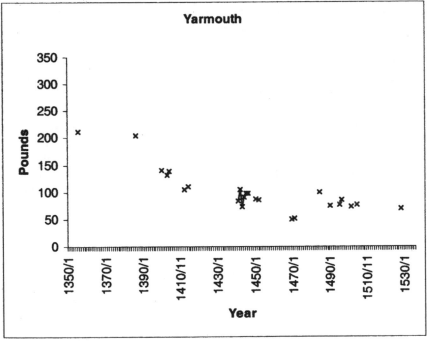

Figure 6.1: The Incomes of the Norwich Cells, 1350–1535

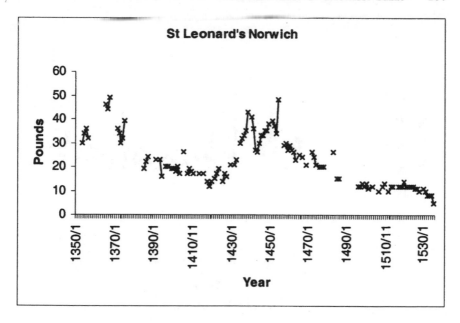

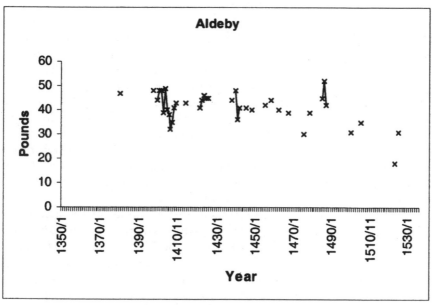

Figure 6.1: *cont.*

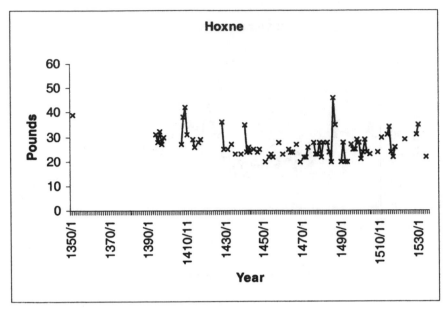

Figure 6.1:   *cont.*

Hatfield Peverel, Horton, Hurley, Ovingham and St Anthony in Roseland – whose incomes are not fully itemised in the *Valor* but can be viewed in extant ministers' accounts produced at their suppression. As Table 6.2 shows, thirty-four of these fifty-one priories had gross annual incomes of under £100 in 1535 (twenty-two of which were under £50), sixteen had receipts of £100–£200 per year and one priory, Great Malvern, drew over £200. Nearly all these daughter houses therefore qualify as 'lesser monasteries' according to the government's criteria in 1536, and a good number were among the poorest monasteries of medieval England. The cells of Augustinian canons were particularly penurious, with nine of the thirteen itemised priories valued at under £50 and four at £25 or under.

Table 6.2 also shows the importance of spiritualities in the incomes of many English dependencies in 1535. Although Savine calculated that spiritualities comprised nearly 25 per cent of the gross income of all the monasteries included in the *Valor*, this category of revenue remains seriously understudied.[25] Spiritual income was even more important to small houses, with the Augustinian canons as an order receiving 37 per cent of their income from such sources.[26] For the fifty-one English dependencies shown in Table 6.2, a remarkable 45 per cent of their income came from spiritualities. Twenty-three cells enjoyed more revenue from spiritualities than temporalities, and at five small priories – Bamburgh, Cranborne, Kidwelly, Cardigan

25   Savine, *English Monasteries*, p. 101.
26   Robinson, *Geography of Augustinian Settlement*, p. 128.

Table 6.2. Cells Fully Itemised in the *Valor* or Ministers' Accounts

Priory	Ref. in *Valor*	Gross Income	Gross Sps	Gross Temps	Sps as % of Gross Income
Great Malvern	III, 237–41	375.0.7	117.1.4	257.19.3	31
St G's, Hereford	II, 420–1	189.2.2	54.10.8	134.11.6	29
Freiston	IV, 85–7	167.8.2	83.1.6	84.6.8	50
St N's, Exeter	II, 313	161.8.1	51.9.4	109.18.9	32
Deerhurst	II, 484	158.2.7	48.10.2	109.12.5	31
St Bees	V, 11	149.9.7	70.5.0	79.4.7	47
Binham	MA	147.5.10	17.0.0	130.5.10	12
Finchale	V, 303–4	146.19.2	60.13.4	86.5.10	41
Brecon	IV, 401	134.11.4	76.5.4	58.6.0	57
Hurley	MA	133.1.2	50.9.8	82.11.6	38
Belvoir	IV, 116–17	129.17.6	69.12.8	60.4.10	54
Wetheral	V, 10	128.5.3	70.15.0	57.10.3	56
Leonard Stanley	II, 419	126.0.8	80.2.0	45.18.8	64
Bamburgh[A]	V, 64	124.15.7	108.0.0	16.15.7	87
Penwortham	V, 233	114.16.10	84.13.11	30.2.11	73
Llanthony I[A]	II, 431	112.0.5	54.3.7	57.16.10	48
Alcester	III, 88	101.14.0	73.12.9	28.1.3	72
Hatfield Peverel	MA	83.19.7	46.5.4	37.14.3	55
Ewenny	II, 421–2	78.14.0	40.2.4	38.11.8	51
Bromfield	II, 422	67.18.4	21.3.0	46.15.4	31
St Ives	IV, 272–3	67.16.8	26.13.4	41.3.4	39
Dunster	I, 220	65.7.9	34.18.8	30.9.1	52
Flitcham[A]	III, 396–7	62.16.1	14.16.8	47.19.5	24
Blythburgh[A]	III, 439	62.2.4	32.0.0	30.2.4	52
Pilton	II, 355	61.17.10	32.15.2	29.2.8	53
St J's, Bristol	II, 484–5	61.7.0	18.0.0	43.7.0	29
Holy Island	V, 304–5	60.5.0	36.3.0	24.2.0	60
Cranborne	II, 485	55.6.1	41.7.1	13.19.0	78
Lytham	V, 305	53.15.10	10.7.3	43.8.7	19
Woodkirk[A]	V, 64	49.7.2	14.17.0	34.10.2	30
Richmond	V, 10–11	45.19.3	26.8.4	19.10.11	57
Jarrow	V, 304	40.7.8	19.13.4	20.14.4	49
Ovingham[A]	MA	38.11.1	38.0.1	0.11.0	99
Snaith	V, 14	38.3.1	25.8.1	12.15.0	66
Kidwelly	IV, 412	38.0.0	31.6.8	6.13.4	82
St L's Stamford	V, 305–6	36.1.5	2.13.4	33.8.1	7
Wormegay[A]	III, 394	35.9.1	9.0.0	26.9.1	25
Alvecote	III, 74	34.8.0	3.12.0	30.16.0	10
Letheringham[A]	III, 423–4	32.13.4	23.0.0	9.13.4	70
Cardigan	IV, 393	32.0.0	25.6.8	6.13.4	79
Horton	MA	31.12.4	9.7.10	22.4.6	30

Priory	Ref. in *Valor*	Gross Income	Gross Sps	Gross Temps	Sps as % of Gross Income
Roseland[A]	MA	28.4.2	17.0.0	11.4.2	60
Wearmouth	V, 304	26.18.4	18.5.0	8.13.4	68
Lincoln	V, 10	26.1.3	7.14.5	18.6.10	30
Breedon[A]	IV, 176–7	25.8.1	17.0.0	8.8.1	67
Massingham[A]	III, 392	24.16.0	0	24.16.0	–
Middlesbrough	V, 83	21.3.8	2.8.2	18.15.6	11
Farne Island	V, 305	12.17.8	0	12.17.8	–
Scokirk[A]	V, 64	8.0.0	0	8.0.0	–
Hirst[A]	V, 64	7.11.8	0	7.11.8	–
Marsh	V, 179	6.7.2	0	6.7.2	–

Note: A signifies Augustinian house; 'MA' signifies figures from minister account: Binham (SC6/HenVIII/2623, mem. 53r), Hurley (SC6/HenVIII/107, mems 6r–7r), Hatfield Peverel (E315/397, fol. 113r), Horton (SC6/HenVIII/654, mem. 9r), Ovingham (SC6/HenVIII/7346, mem. 6r) and St Anthony in Roseland (SC6/HenVIII/597, mem. 20v).

and Ovingham – spiritual receipts comprised over 75 per cent of total annual income. Other cells, like St Leonard's Stamford or Alvecote relied almost exclusively on temporalities, whereas the tiny priories of Great Massingham, Farne Island, Marsh, Scokirk and Hirst were receiving no spiritual income at all in 1535. But on the whole, the prominence of spiritualities in their receipts is the most striking feature of the endowments of the English dependencies. Indeed it may well be that daughter houses relied more heavily on spiritual income than any other group of monasteries in medieval England.

The most important element of spiritual revenue was tithes. Table 6.3 shows that the large majority of the cells assessed in 1535 held appropriated churches and a few, like Brecon, St Guthlac's Hereford and Belvoir, also received a large number of pensions. More strikingly, it can be seen that, of the twenty-four assessed cells to draw income from between one and three churches in 1535, twenty-two received the full rectorial income from them all.[27] In the large majority of cases these appropriations had already taken place by 1291 and so there was very little scope by the later middle ages for most small cells to augment their spiritual resources by acquiring new churches *in proprios usus* without the additional, and unlikely, grant of new advowsons. In a handful of cases, a priory's patron did give an advowson to his cell for the appropriation of the church, pending episcopal consent.

[27] It is in fact likely that the totals of non-appropriated churches given in Table 6.3 are inflated, since the *Valor* does not differentiate between pensions received from churches whose advowsons were held and those received for other reasons (e.g. as a result of a composition made after a dispute over parochial revenues). A few of these non-appropriated churches may also have been chapels which could not be appropriated anyway.

Table 6.3: Numbers of Churches Appropriated by Cells in 1535

Priory	Total no. of churches possessed	No. of appropriated churches	% of churches appropriated
Freiston	6	6	100
Blythburgh^A*	5	5	100
Letheringham^A*	3	3	100
Wormegay^A*	3	3	100
Binham	2	2	100
Cranborne*	2	2	100
Finchale	2	2	100
Penwortham	2	2	100
Alvecote*	1	1	100
Bamburgh^A	1	1	100
Breedon^A*	1	1	100
Bromfield*	1?	1?	100
Flitcham^A*	1	1	100
Holy Island*	1	1	100
Horton*	1	1	100
Jarrow*	1	1	100
Middlesbrough*	1	1	100
Ovingham^A*	1	1	100
Pilton*	1	1	100
Roseland^A*	1	1	100
Snaith*	1	1	100
St Bees	1	1	100
Wearmouth*	1	1	100
Woodkirk^A*	1	1	100
Brecon	12	8	75
Alcester	4	3	75
Deerhurst	4	3	75
Ewenny*	4	3	75
Wetheral	6	4	67
Great Malvern	13	8	62
Dunster*	5	3	60
Hatfield Peverel*	5	3	60
St Ives*	5	3	60
Hurley	8	4	50
St N's Exeter	8	4	50
Cardigan*	2	1	50
Lytham*	2	1	50
Leonard Stanley	9	4	44
St G's Hereford	13	5	38
St J's Bristol*	9	3	33
Llanthony I^A	6	2	33

Priory	Total no. of churches possessed	No. of appropriated churches	% of churches appropriated
Belvoir	22	7	32
Lincoln*	4?	0	–
Farne Island*	0	0	–
Hirst^A*	0	0	–
Marsh*	0	0	–
Massingham^A*	0	0	–
Richmond*	0?	0	–
Scokirk^A*	0	0	–
St L's Stamford*	0	0	–

Note: A signifies Augustinian house; * signifies priory with gross income of under £100 in Valor or minister account.

Source: See Table 6.2. Kidwelly has been omitted from this table because the Valor gives insufficient information about its spiritual income.

William de Ros granted the advowson of Woolsthorpe to Belvoir Priory in 1308; the de Veres provided the patronage of Bentley (1320) and Wickham (1361) to their house at Colne; and Brecon (Amersham, 1348) and Wallingford (St Andrew, Chinnor, 1445) were also favoured by their patrons in this way.[28] All of these instances involved dependencies which are known to have maintained close ties with their patrons in the later middle ages due to their size or location, and few other cells could hope for such largesse. The only example of a non-patronal benefactor making the gift of a church to a dependent priory seems to be the grant to Letheringham Priory by John, duke of Norfolk and his wife of the church of Hoo in 1475, which the canons succeeded in appropriating seven years later.[29] Those cells that held unappropriated churches, and thus received only an annual pension rather than the greater tithe of the parish, may be thought to have failed to maximise their spiritual income. Most of these houses, however, were relatively prosperous and already owned several churches in proprios usus and so had less need to press for further appropriations, even if they could find a compliant diocesan.

Although most of the smaller dependencies (those valued at under £100 per year in 1535) owned only one or two churches, for many such cells this source of revenue provided a large proportion of their total income. Particularly important to those many dependencies which occupied a shared church were the revenues from their home parishes. All shared churches were appropriated to the monks dwelling therein, and since a good number of these parishes were either extremely populous or very large, they carried a

---

28 HMC: Rutland, IV, p. 166; CPR, 1317–1321, p. 437, 1361–1364, p. 121, 1348–1350, p. 39, 1441–1446, p. 362. However, it is not always clear that these appropriations ever took place, since the Valor entries for Belvoir and Brecon do not include the churches in question.

29 VCH, Suffolk, II, p. 108.

considerable tithe income. Dependencies which had grown out of minsters, like Bromfield or Leominster, or had replaced Welsh *clas* churches, like Cardiff, were centred in unusually large parishes, as were a number of northern cells like St Bees and Holy Island. Two other priories not itemised in the *Valor*, Lynn and Yarmouth, controlled parishes which comprised entire towns, and were therefore exceedingly valuable (see below). Whereas many of the larger parishes of the eleventh century subsequently splintered into more convenient (for the parishioners, if not the rectors) units, the daughter houses which were so dependent on parochial proceeds vociferously and largely successfully resisted any such change.[30] More remarkably, the *Valor* shows that in a large number of these home parishes, the religious drew the smaller as well as the greater tithes, and appointed a stipendiary chaplain (or chaplains) in place of a perpetual vicar. The value of the smaller tithes of a parish, usually comprising tithes of all produce but grain, plus personal tithes (from wages and profits) and altarage dues, was variable but could be very considerable, particularly in an urban parish. As a result, the value of their home parish to many cells was substantial. The *Valor* tells that in 1535 Bamburgh received £108 out of a total income of £124 from its huge parish, St Bees £70 out of £150, Freiston £50 out of £167, Deerhurst £37 out of £158 and Penwortham nearly £37 out of £115. Several smaller dependencies relied almost entirely on the revenues proceeding from their home parish: £36 of Holy Island's annual income of £60 came from this source, along with £33 of Pilton's £62, £20 of Cardigan's £32, £18 of Wearmouth's £27 and £16 of Jarrow's £40, whereas only 11s. out of Ovingham's total yearly proceeds of £38 11s. 1d. did not issue from the rectory there. Some cells also received large sums from other appropriated churches, such as Wetheral's Morland rectory, worth nearly £40 in 1535, but the prominence of the home parish in the income of many houses is particularly notable.

The value of spiritualities to daughter houses is therefore clear from the evidence of the *Valor*. An even more detailed examination of spiritual income can be made from the surviving cell accounts. In discussing the economic fortunes of lesser ecclesiastical landlords in later medieval England, historians have largely confined their analyses to temporalities.[31]

---

30 The continual and effective measures taken by the monks of Lynn to prevent their chapels of St Nicholas and St James in the town from acquiring parochial rights can be followed in outline in *The Making of King's Lynn: a Documentary Survey*, ed. D. M. Owen, British Academy Records of Social and Economic History, new series, IX (1984). Leominster also successfully preserved most of the dues from its huge parish: B. R. Kemp, 'Some Aspects of the *Parochia* of Leominster in the Twelfth Century', in *Minsters and Parish Churches. The Local Church in Transition 950–1200*, ed. J. Blair, Oxford University Committee for Archaeology, Monograph no. XVII (1988), pp. 83–95.

31 For a recent example of this tendency, see T. A. R. Evans and R. J. Faith, 'College Estates and University Finances 1350–1500', in *The History of the University of Oxford*, *II, Late Medieval Oxford*, ed. J. I. Catto and R. Evans (Oxford, 1992), pp. 635–707; although it is true that academic colleges relied on spiritual income much less than did cells. The only scholar to study spiritualities in detail has been Professor Swanson in

This tendency is understandable: temporal income accounted for more than half of the revenues of lesser religious houses, and in any case spiritualities were principally a land-based form of income. But although much more work is needed on the subject, spiritual receipts like tithes and parochial offerings might respond to changing economic circumstances differently from temporalities. It is therefore important to consider the ways in which the spiritual income of small monasteries was affected by the economic conditions of the later middle ages. Although it can give only a rough indication of change, a comparison between the tax assessments of 1291 and 1535 does suggest that there occurred a significant fall in the value of spiritual income over this period. In 1291, the parishes of Holy Island and Snaith were assessed at £230 15s. and £153 6s. 8d. respectively, whereas that of Breedon, although valued at only £33 6s. 8d. in 1291, was said at this time to be worth £100.[32] In 1535, however, these three rectories were assessed at £36, £25 and £17 respectively. Similarly, the spiritual income of Rumburgh Priory was said to be bringing in £60 a year in 1291, whereas the fifteenth-century accounts of the priory indicate that annual sums of around £25 were normal at that time.[33] However, it is only when a run of accounts survives that this impression of significant decline can be tested.

The Norwich cells of Lynn and Yarmouth, both urban houses, were largely dependent on their spiritualities and therefore provide important data about the changing patterns of this kind of income. As Table 6.4 shows, the bulk of the revenues of both priories came from their parishes in the form of personal tithes and compulsory parochial oblations, that is, payments for ceremonies like marriage, burial and purification, and offerings at the principal feasts of the year (as opposed to voluntary oblations to shrines and images). The livelihood of both priories was therefore based on the possession of what ordinarily would have been a perpetual vicar's share of the parochial income. Professor Swanson has charted in detail the fluctuations of these sources of income, and so figures from certain decades only are shown in Table 6.4.[34] At Lynn it can be seen that tithe income almost halved between the 1400s and 1430s and then dropped by a further 60 per cent or so between that decade and the 1460s before stabilising thereafter. The decline in compulsory oblations to the parish church and its chapels of St Nicholas and St James was almost as sharp between the 1400s and 1460s, although this source of revenue showed some recovery in the final years of the century before tailing off after 1500. The very strong dependence of the cell on its

---

his articles on Lynn and Yarmouth (see n. 9) and his 'Episcopal Income from Spiritualities in the Diocese of Exeter in the Early Sixteenth Century', *JEH*, xxxix (1988), pp. 520–30.

[32] J. R. H. Moorman, *Church Life in England in the Thirteenth Century* (Cambridge, 1955), p. 136; McKinley, 'Cartulary of Breedon', p. xxi.

[33] See my 'Rumburgh Priory in the Later Middle Ages: Some New Evidence', *Proceedings of the Suffolk Institute of Archaeology*, xl (2001), pp. 10–11.

[34] Swanson, 'Standards of Livings', pp. 165–70; Swanson, 'Urban Rectories', pp. 109–21.

Table 6.4: The Spiritualities of Lynn and Yarmouth Priories, 1370–1529

Lynn	1370–9	1400–9	1430–9	1460–9	1490–9	1520–9
Tithes	86.14.9*	111.2.9*	59.2.1	22.5.2	22.14.3	25.3.11
Compulsory Obls	99.19.5	100.19.2	68.7.2	35.6.2	41.2.5	21.17.6
Voluntary Obls	–	–	1.9.7	0.17.2	21.3.6	13.2.11
Wills & Morts	–	–	11.18.5	2.4.6	1.7.1	3.0.2
Private Masses	–	–	4.19.9	3.6.0	2.4.4	2.0.0
Total Spirits	**187.7.8**	**212.1.11**	**145.17.0**	**63.9.0**	**88.11.7**	**65.4.6**
Total Income	**209.8.11**	**235.18.10**	**180.7.11**	**92.7.0**	**116.18.9**	**95.16.10**

Yarmouth	1380–9	1400–9	1440–9	1460–9	1490–9	1520–9
Tithes	43.9.2	27.8.0	22.1.11	13.11.6	17.19.1	No info.
Compulsory Obls	75.13.8	52.6.8	36.3.2	21.1.4	22.13.2	
Voluntary Obls	25.5.8	21.9.9	10.11.7	2.14.5	12.2.1	
'Christ's Part'	6.15.2	9.2.2	5.5.0	1.5.2	6.3.9	
Wills & Morts	–	5.10.1	2.1.0	1.13.4	1.4.6	
Masses	–	–	4.11.9	2.12.6	3.0.10	
Total Spirits	**173.9.0**	**115.16.8**	**80.14.7**	**42.18.3**	**63.3.5**	
Total Income	**205.6.2**	**136.19.3**	**91.3.3**	**49.5.2**	**78.13.2**	

Note: * includes wills.

Source: NRO, DCN 2/1, 2/4; Windsor, St George's Chapel, XV.55.75–8.

spiritual income, although less marked after 1500, is also manifest and it was only a temporary upturn in offerings to images in the late fifteenth century that halted the trend of decline. As Swanson has noted, this fall in income must surely be connected to a fall in the prosperity of the town of Lynn over the fifteenth century, although other factors like non-payment of tithes should also be taken into account, and it suggests a rough chronology for that decline. The town is thought to have fallen in population from c.6,400 in the 1370s to c.4,500 in the 1520s, while Lynn's trade in woollen cloth, fish and wine all contracted over the fifteenth century.[35] Personal tithes would have been heavily affected by both of these developments and paro-chial offerings, though less badly hit, clearly also suffered from the decline in the town's wealth and population.

A similar pattern can be traced at Yarmouth. In this town too there was a serious fall in ordinary parochial income over the later middle ages, miti-gated only by occasional and temporary swells of voluntary offerings, causing a dramatic decline in the priory's total revenue. At Yarmouth, however, the

---

[35] D. M. Palliser, 'Urban Decay Revisited', in *Towns and Townspeople in the Fifteenth Century*, ed. J. A. F. Thomson (Gloucester, 1988), p. 9; E. Carus-Wilson, 'The Medieval Trade of the Ports of the Wash', *Medieval Archaeology*, vi–vii (1962–3), pp. 182–201.

greatest loss of income came in the last years of the fourteenth century, fitting well Dr Saul's thesis of an earlier decline at this coastal town than elsewhere as a result of a major contraction in the town's shipping and herring industries; although it is noticeable that the fall in the priory's cash income from fish tithes ('Christ's part') did not follow this chronology.[36] As at Lynn, the nadir at Yarmouth came during the 1460s, after which some small recovery set in.[37] The only element of spiritual income which does not seem to have been closely linked to the economic prosperity of the priory's environs was offerings to images. Both Lynn and Yarmouth were fortunate in the popularity of their saint cults in the later middle ages and their sister house, St Leonard's Norwich, received the greater part of its income from this volatile source over the same period.[38]

The endowments of the Durham cells of Jarrow and Wearmouth were also based on spiritualities, and especially the tithes of their large parishes.[39] Both cells appointed a secular chaplain, but Durham reserved to itself the greater tithes of Jarrow parish, except for those of the townships of Jarrow and Hedworth, and a portion of those belonging to the parish of Wearmouth. A significant part of Jarrow's revenue came from the tithes of fishing at South Shields: in the early fifteenth century about half of its cash income was provided by these tithes and the gradual decline of this source of revenue from £20 per year in the late fourteenth century to a little more than £10 by 1479/80 had a significant impact on the priory's economy.[40] The altarage received by Jarrow was never large, but the 'Lenten cess' (payments made in Lent by penitents) fell over the later middle ages, standing at about £10 in 1345/6 and dropping to only £5 or £6 per year after the second quarter of the fifteenth century. Wearmouth suffered a short-term financial crisis in the early 1400s when its revenue from tithes and oblations fell from £20–£25, out of a total annual income of about £40, to under £15; as a result, Durham had to provide the cell with the remainder of its parochial income for a time to aid its recovery. Tithe income might also be affected by changes in the use of land. For those small monasteries which received most of their income from greater tithes, like Holy Island, a switch from arable to pastoral farming

---

[36] A. Saul, 'English Towns in the Late Middle Ages: the Case of Great Yarmouth', *Journal of Medieval History*, viii (1982), pp. 75–88.

[37] Cf. Hatcher, 'Great Slump', pp. 237–72.

[38] See above, pp. 223–7. Over 80 per cent of the St Leonard's income came from such offerings during most of its later history.

[39] Raine, *Jarrow and Monk-Wearmouth*; Piper, *Jarrow*, pp. 6–12; Piper, 'Wearmouth', pp. 3–7.

[40] Dr Richard Lomas, pointing to an increase in the number of tenants and the rents they paid over this period, has suggested that the fishing industry at South Shields expanded during the fifteenth century: R. Lomas, *North-East England in the Middle Ages* (Edinburgh, 1992), pp. 197–8. It is possible that increased consumption of fish tithes by the monks of Jarrow was at least partially responsible for the decline in cash income received from this source recorded in the accounts. I am grateful to Dr John Lee for this reference.

as occurred in north Northumbria in the later middle ages proved seriously damaging.[41]

The figures for tithe receipts given in cell accounts must be treated with some caution: with the exception of personal tithes, they generally represent sales of tithe produce, and a fall in their value may simply be the result of increased household consumption of this produce. Nevertheless, it would appear that income from both tithes and compulsory offerings often declined steeply in the later middle ages as a result of falling population and wealth.[42] Whereas a priory with a substantial landed endowment could attempt to buck economic trends by struggling to maintain high rents or switching to a different form of land exploitation, a monastery reliant on spiritualites was largely dependent on factors outside its control. Admittedly, tithes could be and often were farmed out in the later middle ages to provide a more stable income, but such farms were usually short-term and were therefore heavily affected by market conditions. Although the responsiveness of different categories of spiritual income to movements in population, wealth, prices or wages remains seriously understudied, it may be therefore that monasteries heavily reliant on this form of income suffered more acutely than those more dependent on land. The only form of spiritual income which sometimes rose significantly over the later middle ages was the receipts from shrines and images. But as the highly changeable income at St Leonard's Norwich shows, over-reliance on such an unpredictable source of revenue was hazardous.

Rents and Farms

The prominence of spiritual income in the endowments of daughter houses and many other lesser monasteries, therefore, might well have presented severe financial problems during the difficult conditions of the late fourteenth and fifteenth centuries. Although their annual incomes might have recovered slightly by the 1530s, it appears likely that priories shown to have been heavily dependent on spiritualities in the *Valor* would have enjoyed higher revenues in earlier years. But temporalities always remained the more important source of income for most lesser houses, and for twenty-eight of the fifty-one cells shown in Table 6.2, temporal income amounted to over half their annual receipts. According to the *Valor*, this income came principally from rents and farms, and surviving priors' accounts add considerably to the information given in the 1535 survey. Unfortunately, the accounts of the

41 Lomas, *North-East England*, pp. 59–61, 137; A. J. Pollard, 'The North-Eastern Economy and the Agrarian Crisis of 1438–1440', *Northern History*, xxv (1989), pp. 88–105; Dobson, *Durham Priory*, pp. 250–96.
42 For a similar conclusion, see Lomas, *North-East England*, p. 137. The large number of disputes between cells and vicars over parochial revenues in the later middle ages may well be an indication of insecurity about falling spiritual income.

Norwich dependencies give no entry for arrears (in the modern sense) and therefore do not show what proportion of these priories' rents and farms were actually collected. They do, however, record when properties stood vacant. Lynn seems to have faced increasing difficulty in finding tenants for its town property during the second half of the fifteenth and the early sixteenth century, while St Leonard's struggled to fill its tenements in nearby Pockthorpe from the 1430s to the mid-1490s.[43] There is little sign, however, that expectations were adjusted downwards at any of the Norwich cells during the later middle ages and the valuations given for rents and farms at each priory were relatively stable throughout this period.

The cells of Durham seem to have been less resilient. Jarrow's rental fell from about £4 in the 1410s to only £1 7s. 8d. by the end of the century, and that of Wearmouth from £4 10s. in the 1340s to a little over £1 in the early 1400s. St Leonard's Stamford also saw its rent income decline seriously over the later middle ages, from over £50 in 1380/1 to £34 in 1532/3.[44] Holy Island's rents fell over the fourteenth century, but stabilised thereafter, although the farm of its manor at Fenham did not change in value from the time it was first demised, in 1398/9, through to the Dissolution.[45] Moreover, the build-up of arrears, particularly during the early fifteenth century, must have created financial problems for these priories in the short term. St Ives, meanwhile, was forced to write off over £10 from its annual rental of c.£40 in the early 1520s, after years of rent arrears, and saw the farm of its manor of Wicken fall in value from £12 per year to £9 between 1519 and 1523.[46]

The evidence from these accounts points to a significant fall in rents and farms over the later middle ages, although for a good number of smaller cells this decline did not create serious long-term difficulties because this source of income was relatively unimportant to them. The larger dependencies, however, usually received a much higher income from rents and farms. With the exception of the priories of Freiston and Breedon, these cells possessed relatively compact estates of the kind Professor Hilton thought reasonably profitable in the later middle ages.[47] Unfortunately, few accounts survive for wealthier cells and so it is difficult to know whether or not their incomes declined seriously over the later middle ages. The one larger dependency with a long series of surviving accounts is Finchale, and its average receipts from rents and farms over selected decades are shown in Table 6.5. It can be seen that Finchale's rents and farms did not decline over the later middle ages, but actually rose. Since rents generally comprised the single most important source of income at the cell, its total income remained remarkably buoyant throughout the period in sharp contrast to that of Lynn and

[43] NRO, DCN 2/1/62–82, 2/3/49–97.
[44] Piper, *Jarrow*, pp. 8–9; Piper, 'Wearmouth', pp. 5–6; Piper, 'Stamford', part i, pp. 13–15.
[45] Raine, *North Durham*, pp. 82–130.
[46] BL, Add. MSS 33448–9.
[47] See above, p. 232; *Valor*, IV, 85–7, 176–7.

Table 6.5: Rents and Farms of Finchale Priory, 1370–1529

	1370–9	1400–9	1430–9	1460–9	1490–9	1520–9
Yokefleet rents	22.16.4	25.7.5	25.7.3	25.7.3	25.7.3	25.7.3
Rents of waters	34.11.1	41.1.8	41.7.4	39.10.8	33.0.0	39.14.5
Wingate	3.9.3*	7.6.8	9.16.8	6.16.2*	12.10.0	12.10.0
Haswell	1.6.8*	4.13.4	6.10.4	5.3.8*	7.6.8	7.6.8
Softley	4.14.2	6.4.2	6.4.2	6.4.2	6.4.2	11.10.0
Redmershill	1.18.9	2.6.8	2.6.8	2.6.8	1	1
Middleham	2.13.4	3.13.4	3.0.0	3.0.0	2.2.4	3.0.0
Crook fishery	2.5.7	1.6.8	1.5.2	1.11.0	1.13.4	1.13.4
Other rents	0.9.6	3.6.8	0.2.9	–	9.14.4	6.13.4
Total rents	**74.5.1**	**95.6.7**	**96.0.4**	**89.19.8**	**103.3.11**	**107.15.1**
Arrears/decay	1.8.0	22.12.7	27.9.11	14.8.11	13.6.7	6.13.6
Total income	**205.4.11**	**192.4.4**	**183.2.1**	**203.7.10**	**203.1.11**	**209.4.7**

Notes: * signifies manor in hand for some of the decade; 1 signifies lands exchanged for 'other rents'. All properties are manors, unless otherwise stated, except Middleham which was glebe land.
Source: Raine, Priory of Finchale, pp. i–ccccxvi.

Yarmouth. The figures given under 'Total rents' need to be treated with a little care, since they represent sums expected rather than actually received. In every decade shown there were some arrears, waste and decay of rent which prevented the priory from collecting all that it was due, and this must be subtracted from total rents to arrive at the figure actually collected.[48] The heavy arrears of the 1400s and 1430s – although not all arrears of rents – must have brought the priory into some financial difficulty. Nevertheless, Finchale was not forced to lower its expectations and succeeded not only in preserving its long-term income from rents throughout the fifteenth century, but even in raising certain farms when conditions improved towards the end of the century. It may be, however, that inflation was responsible for much of this increase, and it must also be appreciated that the increase in the priory's rental was partly achieved by farming out properties which had previously been held in hand. It would be mistaken, therefore, to infer from the bald figures that Finchale enjoyed financial stability in the later middle ages. Nevertheless, the cell does seem to have coped with the economic downturn relatively successfully. It is very difficult to know whether the experience of Finchale was typical for cells of its size. Other dependencies might have suffered more heavily than Finchale from declining rents and circumstances

[48] In fact, this calculation cannot be made with precision since the sum entered under arrears, waste or decay in the accounts includes payments not received from the farm of the priory's mills and of tithes, which are not included in the table. Therefore the amounts given above do not represent arrears of rents and farms alone, which were rather smaller over any given decade.

must have varied according to the location of the priory. But the evidence of its accounts suggests that cells dependent on rents and farms, despite facing considerable difficulties in finding tenants who could afford to pay for much of the fifteenth century, might have fared rather better than those houses like Lynn and Yarmouth whose economies were based principally on tithes and offerings.

Direct Farming

Rent was not the only form of temporal income received by daughter houses. Every cell owning a manor was paid some level of curial income, and this source is probably underestimated in the *Valor*. Both the priories of Aldeby and Hoxne regularly received over £1 a year from their courts, which proved an important addition to their small endowments. Woodkirk Priory, meanwhile, was said in 1535 to be enjoying an income of £13 6s. 8d., out of total receipts of just under £50, from its fair. Industrial income also formed a significant portion of the revenues of a number of priories. Several cells drew sizeable sums from the fishing industry. The importance of fishing tithes to Yarmouth and Jarrow and of the waters belonging to Holy Island have already been seen. Jarrow and Wearmouth also drew annual sums of up to a few pounds from their fisheries, and Wetheral's fishery at 'le Baye' was being farmed for £8 per year in 1535.[49] Both Holy Island and Farne Island, meanwhile, were actively involved in sea fishing, maintaining boats for their own catches or for hire.[50] Similarly, in the sixteenth century Jarrow regularly received over £17 per year from eight salterns on the Tyne, granted by its mother house, Durham, in 1513; and Finchale drew a sizeable income from coal mining over the later middle ages.[51] However, the most significant source of temporal income other than rents came from the monks' own agricultural activity, which represented 13 per cent of cells' total temporalities in the *Valor*.

Historians are becoming increasingly aware of the importance of direct farming to smaller landlords in the later middle ages, when the great landlords moved over to renting. The evidence for dependent priories reinforces this picture. The *Valor* and the surviving cell accounts indicate that the majority of daughter houses maintained at least a modest home farm. Despite its limitations, the 1535 survey nevertheless contains much useful material about the lands managed directly by cells. From Table 6.6, it can be seen that only thirteen of the forty-nine cells for which information survives seem

---

49 This fishery was valued at £10 in the priory's post-dissolution minister account: PRO, SC6/HenVIII/7357, mem. 20r.
50 Raine, *North Durham*, pp. 82–130, 344–58.
51 Piper, *Jarrow*, p. 9; Raine, *Priory of Finchale*, pp. i–ccccxvi; Dobson, *Durham Priory*, p. 279.

to have been without lands they farmed themselves at this date. The value of
these demesne farms varied considerably from 10s. up to over £20, and so did
their importance to the priories concerned. Dr Jack detected that priories
valued at under £100 a year in the *Valor* drew a much larger proportion of
their total income from their direct farming activity than those with
£100–£200 a year, and the same conclusion can be drawn from Dr Robinson's statistics for the Augustinian canons.[52] This tendency is confirmed by
the *Valor* entries for dependencies, as shown in Table 6.6. For those cells
valued at under £100 per year, their demesne land held in hand formed 22
per cent of their total assessed temporal income, whereas for those worth
over £100, such lands contributed only 8 per cent of temporalities. When we
consider that demesne land was seriously undervalued in 1535, the importance of direct farming to many small dependencies becomes clear.

Only occasionally does the *Valor* give more than the briefest of entries for
demesne lands, and because most daughter houses were spared in the first
wave of suppressions of 1536–7 very few paper surveys – which describe
monastic demesnes in some detail – were produced for cells. Moreover, there
is an almost complete absence of manorial accounts for the demesnes of
cells. As a result much basic information about demesnes, such as acreages,
the importance of arable, pasture, meadow or woodland, quantities of crops
sown and their yields and the numbers of livestock maintained is not available for most dependencies. The many surviving priors' accounts from cells
can shed light on demesne farming only indirectly. The central problem
with these accounts is that they give little or no indication of the amount of
produce consumed by the monastic household. In rare cases, for example
when expenditure on meat and grain rises dramatically after an estate is
leased, some impression of the quantities delivered to the monks for
consumption can be gained; but usually we have only the sums of money
received from sales of produce. Since few daughter houses farmed principally
for the market in the later middle ages, with houses instead often selling only
surplus production (see below), this is a serious weakness in the sources.
Nevertheless, the critical importance of demesne farming to many small cells
emerges clearly from surviving accounts, and certain aspects of this activity
can be traced.

We are not entirely ignorant about the size and make-up of cells' demesne
land held in hand. For a small number of dependencies, the *Valor* or records
produced at the Dissolution give useful information about these farms. The
Valor and the ministers' accounts often record the location of the house's
demesne, indicating that most cells held no more than one estate in hand,
almost always situated on their doorstep: that is, a home farm. Alcester
Priory seems to have held land directly in both Alcester and Pebworth
(Gloucestershire), but might have been unique among dependencies in this
by the 1530s. The valuation of some demesnes, however, suggests consider-

52 Robinson, *Geography of Augustinian Settlement*, p. 298.

Table 6.6: Value of Demesne in Hand in the 1530s

Priory	Demesne in hand (value)	Gross temporal income	Demesne as % of total temporalities
Hurley	21.10.0	82.11.6	26
Great Malvern	21.6.8	257.19.3	8
Jarrow*	19.6.8	20.14.4	93
Flitcham[A]*	18.13.3	47.19.5	39
Alvecote*	18.6.0	30.16.0	59
Freiston	16.0.4	84.6.8	19
St Bees	15.0.0	79.4.7	19
Brooke[A]*	13.16.8	46.18.10	29
Alcester	11.3.4	28.1.3	40
Ewenny*	11.0.0	38.11.8	29
Lincoln*	10.0.0	18.6.10	55
Massingham[A]*	9.6.8?	24.16.0	38
Hatfield Peverel*	8.10.0	37.14.3	23
Lytham*	8.8.0	43.8.7	19
Scokirk[A]*	8.0.0	8.0.0	100
Wearmouth*	7.6.8	8.13.4	84
Richmond*	6.13.11	19.10.11	34
Woodkirk[A]*	6.13.8	34.10.2	19
Wetheral	6.13.4	57.10.3	12
Llanthony I[A]	5.17.3	57.16.10	10
Leonard Stanley	5.6.8	45.18.8	12
St J's, Bristol*	5.0.6	43.7.0	12
Deerhurst	4.9.8	109.12.5	4
Wormegay[A]*	4.0.0?	26.9.1	15
St L's Stamford*	3.18.4	33.8.1	12
Bromfield*	3.13.4	46.16.2	8
Dunster*	3.10.6	30.9.1	11
Belvoir	3.6.8	60.4.10	5
Holy Island*	3.2.0	24.2.0	13
Breedon[A]*	2.18.9	8.8.1	35
Finchale	2.0.0	86.5.10	2
Hirst[A]*	2.0.0	7.11.8	26
Middlesbrough*	1.10.0	18.15.6	8
Cranborne*	1.1.8	13.19.0	8
St G's, Hereford	0.13.4	134.11.6	0.5
Bamburgh[A]	0.10.0	16.15.7	3
Binham	0?	130.5.9	–
Blythburgh[A]*	0	30.2.4	–
Cardigan*	0	6.13.4	–
Farne Island*	0	12.17.8	–
Horton*	0	22.4.6	–

Priory	Demesne in hand (value)	Gross temporal income	Demesne as % of total temporalities
Letheringham[A]*	0	9.13.4	–
Marsh*	0	6.7.2	–
Ovingham[A]*	0	0.11.0	–
Penwortham	0	30.2.11	–
Pilton*	0	29.2.8	–
Snaith*	0	12.15.0	–
St Ives*	0	41.3.4	–
St N's, Exeter	0	109.18.9	–

Note: A signifies Augustinian house; * signifies gross annual income of under £100.

Source: See Table 6.2. The figures for Brooke Priory, not itemised in the *Valor*, come from the Brief Certificate made at the suppression of the priory: *Mon. Ang.*, VI(i), p. 235, no. 5. Insufficient information survives in the *Valor* entries for Brecon and Kidwelly, whereas St Anthony in Roseland is omitted because it is not clear from the surviving minister account whether the priory's demesne land had been farmed since the house's suppression.

able properties held in hand. For the cells of Tewkesbury and for Llanthony Prima, the *Valor* also gives details of acreages directly farmed. Cranborne's demesne land, valued at 21s. 8d., consisted of a modest sixty-five acres of arable and pasture; that of Deerhurst, said to be worth £4 9s. 8d., was composed of seventy acres of arable, nine of pasture and five and a half acres of meadow; and the demesne farmed directly by St James' Bristol, assessed at £2 13s. 6d., was made up of 153 acres of arable and forty-eight of pasture. The land held in hand by Llanthony Prima, meanwhile, was valued at £5 17s. 3d. and consisted of twenty-six acres of meadow, 245 of pasture in the Black Mountains and 167 acres of other land. As these figures suggest, any attempt to estimate acreages from valuations alone would be hazardous, but demesnes valued at more than a few pounds in the *Valor* must have been sizeable. The ministers' accounts very occasionally provide further details to bolster this conclusion. The home farm of Middlesbrough, assessed at only 30s. in 1535, had been demised for nearly £4 by 1539/40 and is shown to have consisted of seven closes of one hundred acres, seventy-eight of which were arable, twelve pasture and ten unspecified.[53]

Most informative of all are the paper surveys surviving for the dependencies of St Mary's York. Both Wetheral and Richmond held about one hundred acres in hand at their dissolution, but the small priories of Lincoln and Rumburgh are shown to have kept more substantial home farms.[54] That of Lincoln (relatively highly valued in 1535) consisted of five small closes of pasture, one meadow of thirty acres, thirteen acres of marshland (with a

---

53 PRO, SC6/HenVIII/4624, mem. 11r.
54 *Mon. Ang.*, III, p. 599, no. 44, pp. 606–8, no. 11, pp. 615–16, no. 9, pp. 618–19, no. 7.

fishery) and well over one hundred acres of arable land and nearly fifty of pasture mostly in the common fields. The Rumburgh demesne was even larger, containing nearly three hundred acres of enclosed land and sixty acres of woodland all in the manor of Rumburgh itself. The St Bees farm, valued at £15 in the *Valor*, and so among the largest maintained by a cell in 1535, was most impressive of all. Made up of compact enclosures, it comprised about 350 acres in all, including the thirty acres of Salter Grange, two sheep-gates, seventy acres of woodland and at least seventy-three acres of arable land.[55] Much of this land must have been pasture, however, since the surviving priory account of 1516/17 records that the monks owned 220 cattle and over one thousand sheep.[56]

A little more information about the scope of the agricultural enterprises of English cells is contained in inventories. It has been calculated that Jarrow cultivated a little under two hundred acres of arable land during the fourteenth century, although this had fallen to only ninety acres by the end of the fifteenth as the priory switched its interest over to pastoral farming.[57] In the late fourteenth century, the small cell of St Bartholomew in Sudbury was sowing eighty-six acres with wheat, barley, peas and oats and keeping a small number of animals, including ten hives of bees.[58] In general, surviving inventories provide rather more information about numbers of livestock than sown acreages. The totals recorded are often modest and do not approach the numbers found at St Bees. Jarrow kept two to four hundred sheep during much of the fifteenth century, whereas at its suppression Brooke Priory is said to have had three hundred sheep and thirty cattle in Leighfield forest.[59] A smaller enterprise is found at Rumburgh where the monks held a stock of about fifty cattle, along with twenty sheep, thirty-four pigs and eighty-six poultry in 1439. Wearmouth's stock was of a similar magnitude, and an inventory made at Hatfield Peverel in 1536 shows eighty-seven sheep and a few cattle and swine.[60]

These figures would suggest that smaller cells were not ordinarily engaged in farming for the market, but were primarily interested in providing for their own household. However, the evidence from priors' accounts shows that a number of dependencies regularly raised significant sums from the sale of surplus grain, stock or wool or the by-products of their farming.[61] As Figure

---

55 PRO, E315/399, fols 53r–54r.
56 Cumbria Record Office, D/Lons./W/St Bees 1/1.
57 Piper, *Jarrow*, p. 10.
58 *Sudbury Charters*, no. 130, pp. 88–9.
59 Piper, *Jarrow*, pp. 10–12; *Mon. Ang.*, VI(i), p. 235, no. 5.
60 SROI, HD1538/335/1, nos 6–7; Piper, 'Wearmouth', pp. 4–5; R. C. Fowler (ed.), 'Inventories in Essex Monasteries in 1536', *Transactions of the Essex Archaeological Society*, new series, ix (1906), pp. 395–400.
61 In some cases, the accounts fail to distinguish between sales of the priory's own produce and the sale of tithes, which complicates any assessment of the scope of the cells' own enterprises; but most accounts do make this distinction.

6.2 shows, sales of produce formed a particularly important part of the income of the small rural Norwich cells of Aldeby and Hoxne. Before c.1500, Aldeby regularly received over £20 a year, or about half of its annual income, from the sale of corn (mostly barley and barley malt) and, to a lesser extent, stock; and small sales of wool and animal skins sometimes added a little extra revenue. Hoxne rarely marketed so much, but nevertheless often drew sums of up to £10 from the sale of wheat, barley, oats, stock and dairy produce at nearby Yaxley, Denham or Hoxne itself.[62] Indeed the fluidity of Hoxne's sales, both in terms of quantity and kinds of produce, suggests that the cell's marketing policy might have been dictated by the relative prices of its various produce in any given year as well as the quality of harvests. The higher, more stable revenues of Aldeby, however, suggest a deliberate policy of commercial farming and the success of this venture throughout the fifteenth century did much to keep the cell's income stable (see Figure 6.2).

Another dependency that seems to have farmed for the market in the fifteenth and early sixteenth centuries was St Ives (see Figure 6.3). Between 1480/1 and 1516/17, before its manor of Wicken was farmed out, the priory received variable but substantial sums of up to £60 from the sale of corn, stock, wool and legumes. These totals include tithe produce received, but the priory accounts also record large quantities of grain diverted to hospitality and therefore not sold. A smaller level of sales from the priory home farm continued after the leasing of its manor of Wicken, although the apparent upturn in 1525/6 was the result of the monks' keeping in hand and selling that year tithes normally farmed out, rather than increased sales of their own produce. Several other cells for which accounts survive can be seen receiving useful sums from the sale of their own produce, which formed a vital component of their small annual income. In the fifteenth century, Jarrow regularly drew £10 a year from the sale of wool and stock, and the six surviving accounts from Rumburgh show annual receipts of £5–£10 from corn, stock, hides and skins, wool and dairy produce sold. For both priories, these proceeds represented a significant proportion of their total incomes of about £50 per year.[63]

Furthermore, in 1497/8, Felixstowe received over £13 – 40 per cent of its revenue that year – from the sale of wheat and a little barley; and individual sixteenth-century accounts from Snape (for half the year) and Belvoir show sums of about £10 ensuing from the marketing of grain and wool. Meanwhile, the larger-scale pastoral farming practised at St Bees yielded an income of over £43 in 1516/17, mostly from sales of wool and hides to wholesalers.[64] Together with the evidence from the Valor and the suppres-

---

62 The manor of Yaxley and the rectory of Denham were held by Hoxne Priory, so it seems likely that the monks made most of their sales to their own tenants. No information survives about where produce was marketed at Aldeby, but it is probable that this cell also sold its produce locally.

63 Piper, Jarrow, pp. 10–12; SROI, HD 1538/335/1, nos 6–7, 13, 21–2, 34–5.

64 PRO, SC6/HenVII/691, SC6/HenVIII/3402, E315/272, fols 74r–74v; Cumbria Record Office, D/Lons./W/St Bees 1/1.

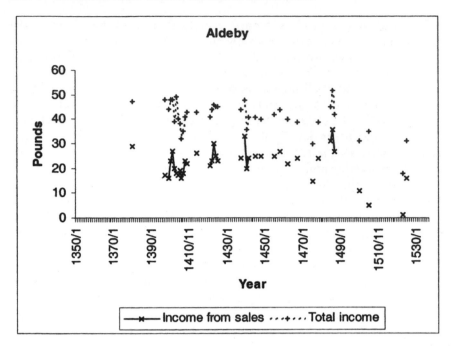

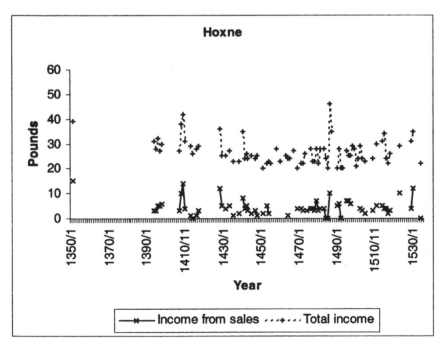

Figure 6.2: The Sale of Agricultural Produce at Aldeby and Hoxne, 1350–1535

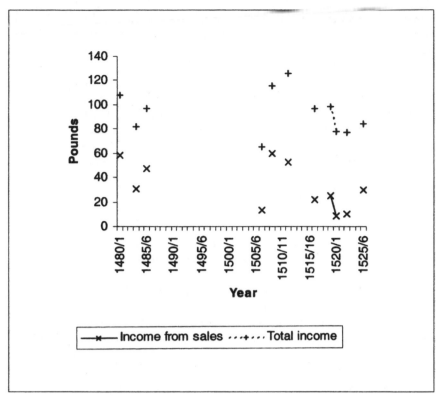

Figure 6.3: The Sale of Agricultural Produce at St Ives, 1480–1526

sion records, these accounts clearly show how common direct farming was among dependencies. The accounts, however, provide a much clearer indication than the *Valor* of the true value of this activity to many cells. For most of the priories for which accounts survive, the sale of their own surplus produce was a very important source of revenue as well as vital for their own provisioning. At Aldeby, St Ives and St Bees, and perhaps Belvoir, Felixstowe and Snape too, there is also evidence of production for the market, albeit on a relatively small scale. Several cells continued with grain production despite the slump in prices throughout much of the fifteenth century, and the stability of Aldeby's income from this source suggests such an enterprise could be profitable.

Yet for the majority of cells which marketed only surplus production, the earning of a profit was not their intention. Such priories often spent more on demesne farming than they recovered in cash from the sale of produce, but at the same time they released themselves from the need to spend large sums on food for their household and its guests. For many cells, it was probably their need for a regular supply of provisions that led them to keep up their home farms throughout the later middle ages. As a result, even though they bought and sold a certain amount of food and drink, many smaller dependencies were to a large degree insulated from the vagaries of the market. As Professor Postan noted, this must have been of real assistance during the worst depressions of the fifteenth century. Yet very few daughter houses, whatever their size, were prepared to keep any more of their possessions in hand throughout the later middle ages beyond their compact home farms. As we have seen, of the cells fully itemised in the *Valor* only Alcester was directly farming a second estate in 1535, although St Ives continued to hold its manor of Wicken in hand until c.1517. Holy Island leased out its manor of Fenham permanently in 1398/9 and Finchale demised all its demesnes over the second half of the fourteenth century for good, apart from a brief experiment of direct farming at Wingate between 1445 and 1459. Hoxne leased its sole manor (Yaxley) throughout the later middle ages, and so, it appears, did Lynn (Havelose) and Yarmouth (Thurlton) although the priory accounts are not entirely clear in this regard.[65] There is, moreover, no sign that any cell sought to benefit from the economic upturn of the 1500s by bringing more land under direct cultivation, as some religious houses are known to have done.[66]

It can be seen, therefore, that these small monasteries were no more prepared to engage in direct farming on a considerable scale than were the great ecclesiastical landlords of late medieval England. As several recent studies have shown, it was compact, specialised farms that were most likely to succeed in the adverse conditions of the later middle ages, and daughter houses, like many small landowners, were careful not to overreach themselves. At the same time, many cells were renting property from others in order to consolidate their holdings still further: Lynn Priory, for example, was spending about £4 a year on rents for much of the later middle ages. This policy, cautious yet not submitting to the convenience of wholesale leasing – a luxury, in any case, few small cells could afford since the rent charged would have had to allow for the lessee's own profit – seems to have served many daughter houses relatively well over the later middle ages.

Having analysed all the major forms of income received by dependencies in the later middle ages, it is possible to draw some general conclusions about their changing revenues over this period. Most cells enjoyed three main sources of income: spiritualities, rents and farms and the proceeds of their own direct farming activity. In general, priories worth over £100 per year were more reliant on rents, and cells worth under £100 per year on direct farming, with each group unusually dependent on spiritual income. Rents often declined over this period and were very difficult to collect in times of hardship; but in the longer term they seem to have provided a relatively reliable source of income. The profits of direct farming varied considerably, according to yields, prices and household requirements, and the decline in

---

[65] Raine, 'North Durham', pp. 114–130; Raine, *Priory of Finchale*, pp. xciii, ccxliv–cclxxvii; NRO, DCN 2/1, 2/4, 2/6.
[66] Youings, 'Monasteries', in Clay, *Rural Society*, pp. 76–80.

grain and wool prices in the fifteenth century must have taken its toll. Demesne farming was not profitable enough to encourage cells to embark on large-scale commercial enterprises, and the leasing of estates became more common over the last one hundred and fifty years of these priories' existence. Nevertheless, almost every daughter house found it prudent to maintain a home farm of some size in the fifteenth and early sixteenth centuries, and the buoyancy of Aldeby's income over this period suggests that the compact and small-scale farms of cells could produce some dividend. Spiritual income, however, appears to have been particularly badly affected by the economic and demographic downturn of the fifteenth century. And since so many small monasteries depended heavily on tithes and offerings, it may well be that lesser ecclesiastical landlords experienced a greater decline in revenues over the later middle ages than many small secular landlords.

Expenditure

If it is right to discern some decline in the income of most small monasteries between the later fourteenth century and the Dissolution, it is natural to ask whether this brought about serious financial problems. Many priories had slender incomes, and even a slight decline in their receipts might have led to insolvency. Although few religious houses faced economic collapse during the later middle ages, it is significant that several small priories were closed down or otherwise converted into cells in order to ensure their survival during the depression of the mid-fifteenth century.[67] Many ecclesiastical historians have highlighted the financial straits of lesser monasteries. Older works by Snape and Power are permeated by this assumption, and although Professor Knowles suggested that many small houses were in fairly good financial health in the 1530s, the extreme poverty of lesser monasteries has remained a commonplace in many works. More recently, Professor Butler has characterised post-Conquest nunneries as 'poorly endowed and lurching from one financial crisis to another, perhaps also beset by scandal'; whereas talking about the resilience of sixteenth-century monasteries, Professor Hoyle has concluded that 'it is hard to see a future for the poorer English monasteries; at a time of static rents there can be little doubt that mid-Tudor inflation would, in time, have destroyed them'.[68]

[67] Seventeen of the twenty-two denizen religious houses definitely closed or converted into cells in the fifteenth century, ostensibly for reasons of economic collapse, met their fate between the years 1444 and 1484 when economic conditions were at their worst: see my 'Dependent Priories and the Closure of Monasteries in Late Medieval England, 1400–1535, *EHR*, cxix (2004), pp. 1–26; cf. Hatcher, 'Great Slump', pp. 237–72.

[68] R. H. Snape, *English Monastic Finances in the Later Middle Ages* (Cambridge, 1926); Power, *English Medieval Nunneries*; Knowles, *RO*, III, pp. 69–70, 307; L. Butler, 'The Archaeology of Rural Monasteries in England and Wales', in *The Archaeology of Rural*

This view inevitably results from an over-reliance on visitation records and monastic claims of poverty, which are the only kinds of evidence to exist for the finances of many small houses. Episcopal visitations certainly highlight numerous examples of poor administration, ruinous buildings and economic distress, but one shocking report tends to overshadow three good ones; and, as we have seen, the buildings of daughter houses do not seem to have been in a particularly bad state in the later middle ages.[69] Claims of poverty, moreover, may represent special pleading in the face of tax demands, or simply the insecurity of an institution managing to survive on meagre and declining resources but fearful for the future.[70] It is much safer, therefore, to rely on financial records where these are available. For most monasteries, however, we must make do with tax assessments which give information about income alone and not expenditure and so do not allow any conclusions about the sufficiency of a monastery's resources. A number of recent studies of small nunneries, based it must be said on extremely slender collections of accounts, have argued that such houses often managed their modest resources successfully.[71] A much fuller picture can be produced for daughter houses. The many extant accounts reveal cells' outgoings and show whether priories were able to react to changing incomes with any success, or whether they were indeed crippled by falling revenues in the later middle ages.

The main fields of expenditure by daughter houses were provisions, wages, agricultural costs, taxation, and repairs or building. An itemisation of the expenses of the Norwich cells in selected years under these headings is given in Table 6.7.[72] The amount spent on food varied enormously between cells and over time. Lynn and Yarmouth produced very little of their own provisions and received mostly personal tithes rather than those of agricultural produce. They were therefore forced to spend heavily on meat, fish and corn. About a quarter of the annual expenditure of Aldeby and Hoxne was on food supplies, and both seem to have provided for many of their own needs. St Leonard's Norwich spent remarkably small sums on food over the fifteenth and sixteenth centuries, and must either have been virtually self-sufficient (which seems unlikely considering the priory's tiny endowment and the absence of agricultural expenses) or to have had provisions delivered from

---

Monasteries, ed. R. Gilchrist and H. Mytum, British Archaeological Reports, British Series, CCIII (1989), p. 3; R. W. Hoyle, 'The Origins of the Dissolution of the Monasteries', Historical Journal, xxxviii (1995), p. 276.

69 See above, pp. 190–2.

70 Even wealthy houses like Durham felt this insecurity during the fifteenth century: Dobson, Durham Priory, pp. 250–1.

71 Tillotson, Marrick Priory; J. Mountain, 'Nunnery Finances in the Early Fifteenth Century', in Monastic Studies II: The Continuity of Tradition, ed. J. Loades (Bangor, 1991), pp. 263–72; Oliva, Convent and Community, pp. 90–8.

72 The accounts do not always provide enough information to assign every act of spending neatly to one of these five categories, but the figures given are largely accurate.

Table 6.7: Expenditure of the Norwich Cells, 1355–1526

Lynn	1372/3	1400/1	1423/4	1450/1	1474/5	1498/9	1524/5
Provisions	95.2.3	117.7.9	83.17.0	64.4.8	32.13.4	34.0.0	37.2.4
Wages	32.3.0	30.7.6	35.15.8	37.8.3	28.10.0	27.8.5	30.17.4
Agriculture	–	–	–	–	–	–	–
Taxation	29.2.3	31.4.11	18.7.0	15.11.9	16.17.3	4.0.8	11.16.9
Reps/building	5.13.3	83.9.11	13.2.0	5.11.9	18.12.6	8.3.0	–
Other Exps	45.11.9	43.19.3	52.17.8	34.19.9	24.3.2	14.9.4	13.10.9
Total Exps	**208.2.6**	**305.10.4**	**203.19.4**	**157.16.4**	**120.6.3**	**88.11.5**	**92.17.2**
Total Income	**222.9.3**	**265.19.9**	**211.17.5**	**141.13.9**	**82.10.8**	**128.7.2**	**107.2.3**

Yarmouth	1355/6	1400/1		1450/1	1471/2	1501/2
Provisions	103.10.8	68.19.0		35.9.11	24.0.6	41.15.4
Wages	15.6.6	16.12.9		18.10.5	12.13.6	12.7.8
Agriculture	–	–		–	–	–
Taxation	41.7.5	48.0.9		10.5.9	8.11.6	8.12.8
Reps/building	–	1.3.4		5.13.9	5.18.11	9.18.2
Other Exps	32.9.2	13.6.7		15.19.4	8.1.7	14.2.10
Total Exps	**192.13.9**	**148.2.5**		**85.19.2**	**59.6.0**	**86.16.8**
Total Income	**212.2.6**	**140.11.9**		**86.11.8**	**50.17.8**	**71.17.2**

St Leonard's	1375/6	1400/1	1425/6	1449/50	1474/5	1500/1	1525/6
Provisions	5.18.4	4.13.4	1.11.10	3.0.0	1.19.1	2.0.2	2.4.3
Wages	4.8.7	3.2.3	3.17.4	6.3.2	5.1.10	3.18.4	3.2.0
Agriculture	5.6.8	–	–	–	–	–	–
Taxation	7.12.2	7.4.7	5.18.7	9.12.0	5.17.9	5.14.6	4.10.6
Reps/building	10.1.5	1.12.5	1.11.6	13.17.2	5.2.9	0.4.11	0.4.2
Other Exps	6.3.4	3.10.5	2.6.9	3.15.10	2.10.9	1.12.0	0.16.9
Total Exps	**40.0.6**	**20.3.0**	**15.6.0**	**36.8.2**	**20.13.0**	**13.9.11**	**10.17.8**
Total Income	**39.7.3**	**18.2.2**	**14.4.2**	**38.8.3**	**21.1.4**	**12.6.10**	**11.16.1**

Aldeby	1380/1	1399/00	1425/6	1448/9	1475/6	1500/1	1525/6
Provisions	11.11.9	12.19.2	10.0.2	8.14.2	8.19.4	10.13.4	8.17.0
Wages	10.3.0	10.8.3	13.10.4	11.1.7	6.14.4	16.0.1*	6.12.4
Agriculture	15.11.2	11.7.11	8.3.10	7.2.10	5.3.3	–	2.0.0
Taxation	5.0.0	6.4.0	6.4.0	5.5.6	7.4.11	7.10.1	7.0.3
Reps/building	–	0.11.4	6.6.4	2.13.3	2.19.1	9.16.4	15.2.4
Other Exps	4.15.5	1.12.6	3.5.2	5.15.5	10.12.4	1.19.3	5.6.3
Total Exps	**47.1.4**	**43.3.2**	**47.9.10**	**40.12.9**	**41.13.3**	**45.19.1**	**44.18.2**
Total Income	**46.18.5**	**43.19.3**	**44.14.9**	**40.8.10**	**29.17.7**	**31.4.3**	**31.6.5**

Hoxne	1351/2	1398/9	1428/9	1451/2	1476/7	1500/1	1523/4
Provisions	9.4.7	2.16.0	9.18.5	5.0.5	7.0.10	14.14.6	10.0.9
Wages	3.1.0	5.9.0	5.0.8	5.16.8	5.11.7	6.8.4	7.15.4
Agriculture	3.8.5	0.19.0	6.12.9	1.4.3	2.12.6	1.18.7	2.9.9
Taxation	9.1.9	9.12.1	1.19.8	0.17.10	0.3.0	0.4.6	1.6.5
Reps/building	10.18.6	–	2.0.2	0.8.0	1.8.5	2.0.0	10.5.2
Other Exps	5.12.3	6.8.11	6.19.4	5.14.6	8.8.5	15.12.9	5.2.11
Total Exps	**41.6.6**	**25.5.0**	**32.11.0**	**19.1.8**	**25.4.9**	**40.18.8**	**37.10.4**
Total Income	**38.16.10**	**30.0.11**	**35.15.9**	**19.14.11**	**28.6.4**	**20.17.2**	**29.6.2**

Note: * includes agricultural expenses. Selected years are those closest in time to 1350, 1375, 1400, 1425 and so on, where a suitable candidate survives.

the cathedral priory just over the Wensum.[73] Wages proved an important expense for all the Norwich dependencies, and consumed up to a quarter of the total expenditure of the smaller priories.[74] Agricultural expenses were naturally highest at Aldeby and Hoxne, and provide a rough indication of the commitment of these cells to direct farming. Taxation for all the Norwich cells was principally paid to the mother house although the Crown regularly levied sums of several pounds from the wealthier priories. Repairs and building, both within and without their precincts, was the most variable form of expenditure and, as an extraordinary expense, is in some ways the best measure of the financial health of these priories. A cell which could not even afford to pay for the regular upkeep of its buildings was clearly struggling. Equally, since there is no sign of the Norwich cells building recklessly, an increase in expenditure on building work is often a sign of prosperity (see below).

The Norwich accounts also give an impression of how the cathedral priory's cells reacted to declining incomes. Firstly, the priors of Aldeby, Hoxne, Lynn and Yarmouth began to account for their receipts and expenses in much greater detail than before during the first half of the fifteenth century.[75] And secondly, significant economies were made. At Aldeby, overall expenditure remained fairly stable, even when income dropped, but there were cutbacks in the wage bill and in agricultural costs. Similarly, when Hoxne was forced to reduce its expenditure in the mid-fifteenth century, this was achieved mainly by cuts in food and agricultural spending.

[73] In the fourteenth century, the food and drink of Redbourn Priory were delivered daily from St Albans: see above, p. 150.
[74] This heading generally comprises only the wages of household servants and not hired workers (which are usually entered under agricultural or building expenses in the accounts). Also included here are the stipends of the parochial chaplains, which were important costs at Lynn and Yarmouth where several priests were employed.
[75] This switch to more detailed accounting took place at Hoxne during the first decade of the fifteenth century, at Aldeby in 1423–4, at Lynn in 1436–7 and at Yarmouth at some time between 1413 and 1441: NRO, DCN 2/6/6, 2/2/9, 2/1/32, 2/4/6.

Even more drastic economies were needed at Lynn and Yarmouth. At both, savings were made in three areas: wages, pensions to the mother house and food. The amounts spent on the stipends and liveries of their *famuli* were cut gradually at Lynn from £19 10s. in 1372/3 to only £7 in 1498/9, whereas at Yarmouth this cost fell from about £10 in 1400/1 to under £7 in 1471/2. But these savings, though they might well have involved a significant reduction in their household staff, were insignificant in comparison to the priories' fall in revenue. Much more money was salvaged from the payments both cells made to Norwich. In 1400/1, Lynn had paid over £41 to the mother house in pensions, gifts and a contribution of over £8 for legal costs; but after its annual pensions had been reduced from over £18 to 66s. 8d., total payments to Norwich in 1498/9 were only £4. Yarmouth saw a similar cut in its yearly deliveries to the cathedral priory, from £44 in 1400/1 to only £6 in 1471/2. But the greatest economies were made on provisions. At Lynn, this expense fell from £117 in 1400/1 to £64 in 1450/1, and to only £32 in 1474/5, and the decline at Yarmouth was equally precipitate. Since there is no sign of a reduction in the size of the community at either priory over this period, it is likely that these large savings manifested themselves primarily in severely abrogated hospitality.[76]

The accounts for the cell of St Leonard Norwich are in some ways of even greater interest because they show how a small priory might react to an unexpected windfall. The remarkable popularity of the monks' image of St Leonard in the mid-fifteenth century increased the cell's annual receipts from £14 in 1425/6 to between £30 and £50 over the period 1434–59.[77] Table 6.7 gives a rough indication of how this extra income was used. Rather than raise food expenses to the levels of the fourteenth century, the amount spent on household servants was modestly increased, significantly more money was siphoned off by the mother house, and most importantly, a much greater sum was spent on building and repairs. The boost to this latter form of expenditure is shown in Figure 6.4.

Between 1433 and 1476, the priory spent well over £300 on additions and improvements to their chapel, claustral buildings, outbuildings, tenements, vestments and books. The monks' first major project was the construction of four new tenements in Pockthorpe in 1436/7, at a cost of over £23, in response to the cell's recent difficulties in finding tenants for its existing properties there. Over the following years, a systematic programme of build-

---

[76] See above, pp. 201–2. Quantities of wheat and malt given in the Lynn accounts show that this fall in expenditure was not principally the result of changes in prices. In the late fourteenth century, Lynn was usually buying between sixty and one hundred quarters of wheat and between 150 and two hundred quarters of malt per year; but by the mid-fifteenth century these quantities had fallen to about twenty-five quarters of wheat and fifty quarters of malt.

[77] See above, pp. 224–5, and my 'Veneration and Renovation at a small Norfolk Priory: St Leonard's, Norwich in the Later Middle Ages', *Historical Research*, lxxvi (2003), pp. 431–49.

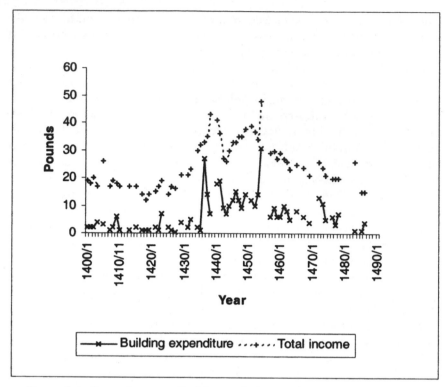

Figure 6.4: Expenditure on Building at St Leonard's Norwich in the C15

ing and repairs was carried out. Amongst other things, several of the domestic buildings of the priory were re-roofed, re-glazed and their walls and ceilings wainscoted. In the main chapel, new floor-tiles, stalls and a new reredos were provided, the great *tabula* at the altar of St Leonard renovated and a number of windows reglazed. Two new cisterns were built, the priory's well repaired and several service books rebound. A new house was built next to the chapel and the walls enclosing the precinct and the priory's woodland much repaired. To some extent, this extensive scheme of renovation probably constituted necessary repairs which had previously been unaffordable. But a good deal of this work represents investment (generally by improving existing properties rather than acquiring new ones) and, in particular, adornment. It is clear from the St Leonard's accounts that building work and large-scale repairs were considered extraordinary expenditure, and that so great a proportion of the offerings received in the mid-fifteenth century were put towards this cause suggests that the monks regarded the proceeds from their image as an extraordinary and fleeting receipt: it was easier not to increase substantially the size and fare of one's household when such an action might have to be reversed at any moment. For the other Norwich cells, a regular stream of minor repairs was financed within their ordinary income, but any larger projects, such as the construction of a new building and the 'great gutter' at Lynn in 1400–1, which cost the priory £75, had to be paid for by credit.

Debt

In general, it can be seen from the Norwich cells' accounts that priors sought wherever possible to adapt their expenditure to any changes in the income they received. Nevertheless, it is equally clear that these priories, in the language of medieval accounts, ordinarily ran a 'surplus': that is, they were normally in debt.[78] Historians used to be censorious about monastic indebtedness, but it has long been recognised that the existence of debt is in itself no indication of financial hardship. Ecclesiastical institutions as diverse as Canterbury Cathedral Priory, Bolton Priory and Exeter College, Oxford seem to have relied almost constantly on credit in both good times and bad.[79] It has also been pointed out that a large surplus on an account might often result from the accumulation of several years of small deficits rather than a financial crisis.[80]

The vast majority of the Norwich cell accounts show that the priory concerned, having carried over its surplus or arrears from the previous account, was in debt at the end of the financial year. Of the 105 years for which we can discern the year's final balance at Hoxne, the priory's expenses exceeded its receipts in ninety-one of them. At Lynn, the ratio of indebted years to non-indebted years was 116:10 and at Yarmouth 39:2, whereas Aldeby was in debt in every one of the fifty-two years for which evidence survives. St Leonard's Norwich, with a ratio of 108:43, was the only Norwich cell not to be indebted throughout virtually the entire later middle ages.[81] How heavy was this burden? Precisely at what proportion of a priory's annual income indebtedness becomes serious is not clear, but it has been suggested that only when debts exceeded that year's receipts was there cause for major concern.[82] Indeed the Norwich cell accounts make clear that a moderate level of indebtedness, maintained over a number of years, was of little concern to most priors. Until the mid-fifteenth century, the heads of Lynn happily tolerated a debt of £50 or £60, although when the sums owed rose above this

---

[78] The use of the term 'surplus' to mean what we would call a deficit is one of several potential confusions arising from the study of medieval accounts.

[79] R. A. L. Smith, *Canterbury Cathedral Priory* (Cambridge, 1969), p. 52; M. Mate, 'The Indebtedness of Canterbury Cathedral Priory 1215–95', *EcHR*, 2nd series, xxvi (1973), pp. 183–97; Kershaw, *Bolton Priory*, pp. 168–78; A. F. Butcher, 'The Economy of Exeter College, 1400–1500', *Oxoniensia*, xliv (1979), pp. 38–54.

[80] F. R. H. Du Boulay, 'A Rentier Economy in the Later Middle Ages: the Archbishopric of Canterbury', *EcHR*, 2nd series, xvi (1963–4), pp. 436–7.

[81] Since each year's 'surplus' or 'arrears' (that year's excess of receipts over expenditure) was usually carried over, figures for outstanding debts can be seen for several more years than we have account rolls.

[82] Knowles, *RO*, III, pp. 252–5, 314.

figure (between a third and a quarter of total income), some efforts were made to reduce them by economising.[83] The failure of daughter houses to save for times of difficulty or establish a reserve fund also suggests a readiness to live off credit. The size of the surplus at Lynn exceeded the priory's total income on only five occasions, all during the troubled 1460s when the cell's receipts reached their lowest point. This level of indebtedness is not recorded in any of the Yarmouth accounts, and in only seven accounts from Hoxne (6 per cent) and eleven from St Leonard's Norwich (7 per cent). Aldeby, however, owed more than it levied in ten of its extant accounts, or 29 per cent of the total. But even these figures cannot be taken entirely at face value. When debts rose to what was considered to be an unmanageable level at the Norwich cells, they were often written off before a new prior took office. A surplus of almost £100 had to be condoned at Lynn at the end of the 1460s, whereas significant sums were cleared with some regularity at late medieval Hoxne and Yarmouth.[84] This practice could conceal the accumulation of a cell's indebtedness, as a stream of priors overspent for several years and were then recalled before the surplus became unmanageable, as seems to have been the case at Hoxne in the fifteenth and early sixteenth centuries. For this reason, any assessment of a monastery's economic health from the surplus or arrears of an isolated account is clearly hazardous.

The best measure of the success with which a priory was able to live within its income is therefore the amount by which expenditure exceeded or fell short of receipts in individual years (see Figure 6.5). These graphs confirm the conclusion that the Norwich cells ordinarily adjusted expenditure to income with some success. In very few years did expenses heavily outweigh receipts, and it is noticeable that several instances of serious overspending, including at Lynn in 1391/2, at St Leonard's during the late 1430s and at Hoxne in the late 1480s, occurred at times of rising income: evidently this represents an increased confidence in their financial situation, rather than hardship. Conversely, the apparent reluctance of priors to overspend heavily at other times might suggest that extraordinary expenditure, such as investment and repairs, was not easily affordable. However, it is only when expenses exceeded receipts by more than a few pounds over a period of several successive years that a priory was obviously experiencing difficulty in making ends meet. In such circumstances, surpluses mounted quickly, as

---

83 DCN 2/1. Moreover, Prior Zouche of Wallingford, with an annual income of under £150 at his disposal, was able to pay off £70 of his predecessor's debts over a single year in 1481/2, and only three years later the priory was in the black: Oxford, Corpus Christi College, MS Z/2/1/1–2.

84 E.g. NRO, DCN 2/1/63–4, 2/4/7–9, 14–15, 20, 2/6/9, 17–18, 29–30; Windsor, St George's Chapel, I.C.31–2, 35. In such cases, the outgoing prior and sometimes his predecessor would forego the sums they were owed from underwriting the cell's debts during their time of office. The mother house might also write off unpaid pensions due from the cell, but in general does not seem to have contributed any of its regular income to assist a dependency.

occurred at Hoxne between c.1485 and c.1515, Aldeby in the 1520s and St Leonard's for much of the period 1490–1535.

It is also possible to discern from these graphs whether periods of insolvency were the product of falling incomes or excessive expenditure. The difficulties at Lynn in the 1460s and St Leonard's between 1490 and 1535 were evidently caused by falls in receipts; whereas the financial plight at Aldeby in the 1520s was instead apparently the work of an improvident prior, Edmund Norwich.[85] But in all, the Norwich cell accounts display little recklessness, and little evidence of serious hardship. This impression is probably slightly false, since as we have seen these accounts do not show arrears in payments to the cells, which would have caused considerable short-term discomfort. Nevertheless, the two larger Norwich cells, Lynn and Yarmouth, seem to have adapted remarkably successfully to their declining incomes and encountered few discernible financial problems of any magnitude during the later middle ages.[86] Undoubtedly Aldeby, despite its relative stability of income, experienced the greatest difficulties, regularly maintaining a large surplus. The greatest problem faced by very small cells was in recovering from financial hardship when it arose, and it was only the regular clearing of debts that prevented surpluses mounting up to impossible proportions. It must therefore be concluded that, although their receipts ordinarily covered their expenses, priories of the size of Aldeby and Hoxne had little or no response to occasional crises, whether natural, structural or caused by bad management.

The long-term viability of very small houses like these therefore must have depended on external assistance in times of difficulty. For independent small monasteries, apart from occasional benefactions, help could perhaps have come from the diocesan or otherwise only from creditors prepared to wait for the repayment of their loans or even to cancel them altogether if necessary.[87] In June 1532, Blythburgh Priory was indebted by £30, £10 of which was owed to the bishop of Norwich.[88] Much remains obscure about the attitudes of those lending money to religious houses. It has been suggested that some loans to monks were effectively bank deposits with very

---

85 No complaints are made against this monk's management of Aldeby in the episcopal visitations of 1526 and 1532, suggesting that his rule improved after the final Aldeby account of 1525/6. The cell, however, seems to have been experiencing financial difficulties in 1514, when it was complained that its buildings were in poor repair and that it had debts of £10: *Visitations of the Diocese of Norwich, AD 1492–1532*, ed. A. Jessopp, Camden Society, new series, xliii (1888), pp. 65–79, 196–206, 262–70.

86 For several examples of aristocratic landowners of various incomes succeeding in adjusting their expenditure in the face of falling revenues in the later middle ages, see C. Dyer, *Standards of Living in the Later Middle Ages. Social Change in England c.1200–1520* (Cambridge, 1989), pp. 95–9, 108.

87 See Tillotson, *Marrick Priory*, pp. 12–13 for examples of poor nunneries relying on regular charity from friends and neighbours to make ends meet.

88 *Norwich Visitations*, pp. 284–5. Professor Harper-Bill has suggested that this debt represents unpaid first fruits: *Blythburgh Cartulary*, I, p. 4.

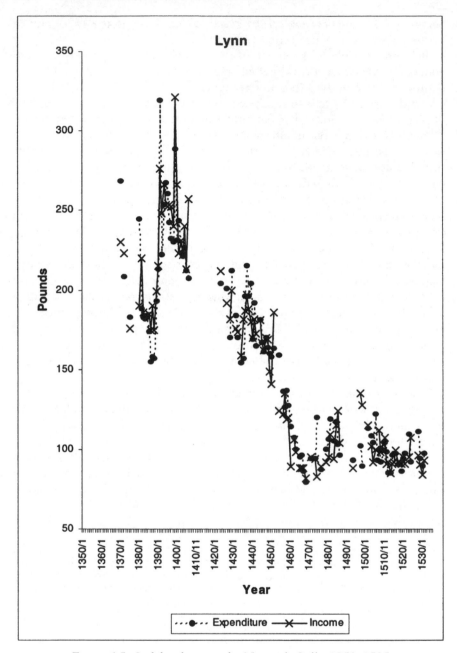

Figure 6.5: Indebtedness at the Norwich Cells, 1350–1535

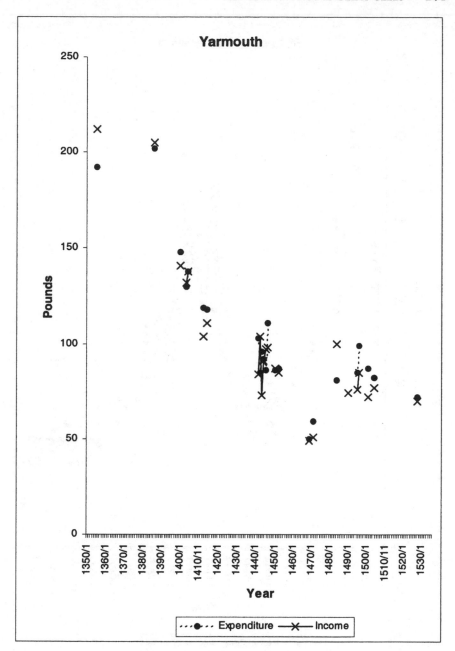

Figure 6.5: *cont.*

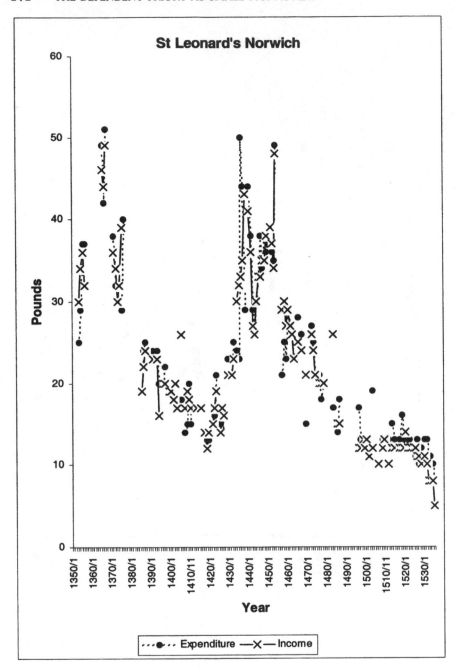

Figure 6.5: *cont.*

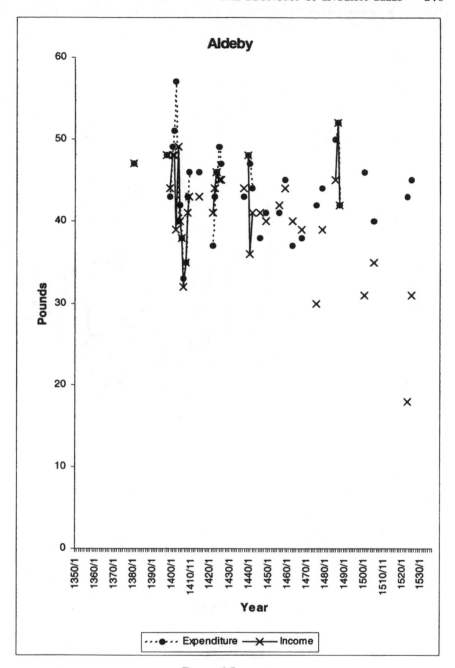

Figure 6.5: *cont.*

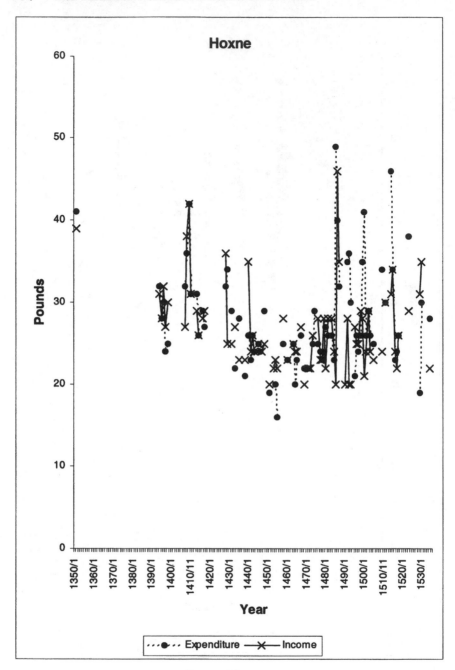

Figure 6.5: *cont.*

little pressure exerted for repayment, or that the monks' friends might have lent to them in times of need.[89] Where a priory could benefit from a succession of friendly, relaxed creditors, even a large surplus need not be considered particularly problematic. Moreover, the surviving accounts from several cells indicate that a large part of their surpluses was in fact arrears in the monks' own payments to servants, workmen, rentiers or those to whom they owed pensions.[90] Several years of non-payment could probably have been tolerated by such 'creditors' in the expectation of further business or perhaps some compensation.

Dependent priories were, of course, particularly fortunate in that any shortfalls in one year's income could often be made up by withholding part or all of the pensions owed to their mother house. This was certainly often the case at the Norwich cells. Of the £35 owed by Lynn in the year 1479/80, £27 10s. was due to the prior of Norwich, and 14s. 4d. each to the cathedral priory's chamberlain and pittancer in unpaid pensions.[91] Similarly, Aldeby's surplus of nearly £16 in December 1399 was all owed to the mother house, though much of it was apparently a loan from the Norwich convent.[92] The possibility of such support, either by allowing arrears of pensions to accumulate or by condoning or by advancing loans, was of tremendous benefit to daughter houses. In more extreme cases, mother houses could assist their satellites even more directly. In the first half of the fifteenth century, Durham temporarily recalled the monks from St Leonard's Stamford (1424–6) and Jarrow (1425–32) in order to clear large debts at both cells. The monks at Farne Island, meanwhile, were domiciled at Holy Island from 1438 to 1440, because of the non-payment of their pension from the mayor and citizens of Newcastle upon Tyne on which they were heavily dependent.[93] Such instances were extremely rare. Alternatively, a mother house might reduce the number of religious at a cell, at least temporarily, in response to continuing financial difficulties; although in general the numbers in dependent priories do not seem to have fallen by much over the later middle ages.[94]

These options were not available to small independent monasteries. Many lesser priories, and particularly nunneries, housed considerably larger communities than English cells in the later middle ages and would therefore have struggled to cut back their outgoings at times of falling income. On the other hand, it should be noted that many of the cells for which a run of financial

[89] Mate, 'Indebtedness of Canterbury Cathedral Priory', p. 191; Knowles, RO, III, p. 254; Kershaw, Bolton Priory, pp. 175–8.
[90] E.g. SROI, HD 1538/335/1, nos 6–7, 13, 21–2, 34–5; Piper, 'Stamford', part i, p. 14.
[91] NRO, DCN 2/1/69.
[92] NRO, DCN 2/23. Colne Priory is also recorded requesting loans from its mother house, Abingdon, in the mid-thirteenth century in order to purchase property: R. Hill, Ecclesiastical Letter-Books of the Thirteenth Century (privately printed, no date), pp. 70–1, 73–4.
[93] Piper, 'Stamford', part i, p. 15; Piper, Jarrow, p. 9; Raine, North Durham, p. 351.
[94] See Appendix Four.

records survive were tiny, with incomes of £50 a year or under. As far as we can tell, even dependencies of this size were ordinarily able to weather the storms of the later middle ages, with some assistance from their mother houses. Their annual incomes were in fact larger than the *Valor Ecclesiasticus* implies, and their recourse to direct farming, sometimes on a substantial scale, helped them to cope with the difficult economic conditions of the day. As a result, these cells' receipts do not seem to have declined seriously over the later middle ages unless they were heavily dependent on spiritualities. Their debts were sometimes heavy, but this did not necessarily create problems and in most years their income more or less covered their expenditure. Independent houses of this size must have found life much harder, and their ability to cope with extraordinary expenditure and sudden falls in receipts probably depended on their success in finding generous creditors. Yet the level of indebtedness even of these priories was generally within manageable proportions in 1536.[95] What remains unclear is the extent to which lesser monasteries were forced to reduce numbers in order to overcome financial difficulties. The sources reveal the economies made, but the spiritual costs which may have accompanied them are incalculable.

Although they were atypical in certain respects, the example of daughter houses reveals much about the pressures facing small monasteries in the later middle ages and the ways in which they could face up to them. Their study also illustrates the need to distinguish carefully between categories of lesser monasteries. Historians have often described any religious house ranking below the well-recorded elite of Benedictine abbeys and cathedral priories as 'smaller' and the result has been a confusing array of characteristics and generalisations applied to the lesser religious house. Houses like Merevale or Bolton, which avoided suppression in 1536–7 with annual incomes of over £200, need to be distinguished carefully from very small priories with incomes of £50 or £100. The Finchale accounts suggest that the larger cells did not face collapse during this period, but even when the income of wealthier priories did drop substantially, as at Lynn and Yarmouth, adjustment to new economic realities could be achieved. These conclusions chime with the picture of generally well-stocked, well-maintained priories clear from high levels of debt given by the Brief Certificates of the commissioners for the suppression of the lesser monasteries in 1536–7.[96] The evidence for dependencies also casts some light on the experience of smaller landlords in general in the late medieval period, and in particular the long-standing home farms of several cells suggest the importance of their agricultural activity to this group. Further studies of the economies of small monasteries are needed, but the many surviving accounts from cells give some indication of why and how the vast majority of religious houses of this size were able to survive the depression of the later middle ages.

[95] Knowles, *RO*, III, pp. 253–5.
[96] Ibid., III, pp. 511–15.

Epilogue:
The Dissolution of English Cells

Although the dissolution of the alien priories has understandably attracted far more attention, the manner in which English cells were suppressed was also highly unusual. This peculiar course of dissolution has never before been traced, and the main source of information for the suppression of daughter houses remains the statistics assembled in Knowles and Hadcock's *Medieval Religious Houses: England and Wales*. These figures present an intriguing picture. Of the sixty-eight Benedictine and twenty-three Augustinian cells which are said to have survived into the sixteenth century, nine are listed as dissolved before 1536, thirteen in 1536, eight in 1537, twenty-two in 1538, thirty in 1539 and seven in 1540, with two others closed at some indefinite time between 1536 and 1540. A comparison of the years of dissolution given for satellite priories with those of their mother houses also indicates that half of these cells (forty-five) survived to be terminated with their parents, whereas the same number were closed early. The final cell, Letheringham Priory, provides a unique example of a dependency that was dissolved several years after its mother house.[1]

These figures, however, are not wholly reliable. They include a number of tiny priories which had probably disappeared before the sixteenth century, and many dates have been taken straight from the notoriously inconsistent *Victoria County History*.[2] Although for a significant minority of English cells, ironically including those of Norwich and Durham Cathedral Priories, it is very difficult to locate the date of suppression, it can be seen that the statistics given by Knowles and Hadcock over-estimate the number of daughter houses dissolved at the same time as their parents. Indeed, it would appear that only somewhere between twenty and thirty-seven cells were dissolved at the same time as their mother houses, out of eighty-seven dependent priories surviving beyond 1500. This early closure of so many dependencies needs to be explained, particularly in the light of the exemption of cells from the Act

---

[1] Letheringham's dependence to St Peter and St Paul's Ipswich seems to have always been limited, since the daughter house enjoyed the right to elect its own perpetual priors: see above, p. 84.

[2] There is considerable doubt as to whether the cells of Coquet Island, Hood, Ratlinghope, Scilly and All Saints' Fishergate, York, none of which appear in the *Valor* as priories, survived into the sixteenth century. Hackness certainly did not: A. H. Thompson, 'The Monastic Settlement at Hackness and its relation to the Abbey of Whitby', *YAJ*, xxvii (1924), pp. 388–405. Amended dates for the suppression of the English dependencies are given in Appendix Five.

of Dissolution of 1536. Broadly speaking, these premature suppressions fall
into three categories: those dependencies dissolved by Wolsey, those
suppressed by the Crown between 1536 and 1540 independently of their
parent abbeys, and those wound up and leased out by their mother houses
themselves. As this classification suggests, the story of the dissolution of
English dependencies is a complex one, but it is also of some interest, particularly for what it reveals about attitudes towards cells and the experience of
several great Benedictine and Augustinian monasteries during the troubled
years of 1536–40.

Among the twenty-nine houses suppressed by Wolsey between 1524 and
1529 for his twin educational establishments at Oxford and Ipswich were
three daughter houses.[3] It is perhaps surprising that Wolsey looked to
dependencies for the endowment of his colleges rather than to relatively
defenceless autonomous houses, and that he was prepared and able to strip
assets from some of the greatest monasteries in the land illustrates again the
power he exerted over the English Church in the 1520s. The dissolution of
Wallingford was in fact relatively easy, since the priory was already under
Wolsey's direct jurisdiction as abbot of St Albans *in commendam*. The confiscation of both Felixstowe and Rumburgh, however, was opposed by their
mother houses, albeit fruitlessly. Abbot Whalley of St Mary's York wrote to
Wolsey eleven days after the suppression of Rumburgh, offering a donation
of three hundred marks to Ipswich College in return for the restoration of his
abbey's cell, said to have been worth just £30 per year; and the prior of Rochester was still hoping for the return of his house's property in Felixstowe in
April 1532.[4] St Osyth's Abbey seems to have been more successful in resisting Wolsey, since its cell at Blythburgh survived despite having its suppression authorised by Clement VII in 1528.[5]

The quasi-autonomous priory of Dover surrendered in November 1535,
apparently under some pressure, shortly after the royal visitors had allegedly
found serious failings there.[6] More cells were to follow in 1536, following the
passage of the Act of Dissolution in March or April. Although this statute
asserted that 'every suche Celle shalbe and remayne ondissolvyd in the same
Estate Qualytye and Condycyon as yf this acte had never be made', the terms
by which it defined a cell made many dependencies vulnerable. Only those

3   The best account of Wolsey's suppressions remains Knowles, *RO*, III, pp. 161–4 and
     Appendix II, p. 470. There is very little on this aspect of the Cardinal's career in
     P. Gwyn, *The King's Cardinal. The Rise and Fall of Thomas Wolsey* (London, 1990).
     The priory of Snape, formerly a daughter house of Colchester, was also dissolved by
     Wolsey.
4   *L&P*, IV(ii), no. 4762, p. 2064, V, no. 963, p. 452. Judging from the priory's late
     fifteenth-century accounts, Rumburgh was probably worth a little more than £30 per
     year: SROI, HD 1538/335/1, nos 34–5.
5   *Blythburgh Priory Cartulary*, ed. C. Harper-Bill, 2 parts, Suffolk Records Society,
     Suffolk Charters, II–III (1980–1), I, p. 4.
6   *L&P*, IX, nos 669, 717, 756, 816, 829, pp. 226, 241, 257, 273, 278.

priories whose heads were unable to plead at law in their own names and were removable at the will of their superior were to be exempt.[7] As we have seen, although few priors of cells were perpetual, the right to sue or be sued seems to have been enjoyed at times by the priors of a good number of dependencies.[8] Other criteria might also be employed in assessing the status of a priory. In March 1538, Richard Rich undertook to suppress Binham, 'which pretends to be a cell of St Albans, but has fines levied and leases made, not naming the abbot of St Albans'.[9] It is clear, moreover, that the procedures utilised in 1536–7 to determine whether a priory should be exempted as a cell were extremely rigorous. Presumably the suppression commissioners could have used the *Valor Ecclesiasticus* to learn which priories were daughter houses, but instead every monastery valued at under £200 in that survey was revisited. On the commissioners' arrival, the head of the house was to declare the priory's status and was then bound to appear before the Chancellor and Council of the Augmentations within a fortnight.[10] An even more detailed examination into the status of Kidwelly Priory, 'whiche is pretendid and supposid to be a Cell to the monasterye of Shirbourne', is recorded to have taken place at Sherborne in December 1536, when the heads of both abbey and cell were required to hand over all the priory's records to the commissioners for inspection at the Augmentations.[11]

With such close scrutiny, it is not surprising that a small number of cells were dissolved in 1536 and early 1537. There has been some confusion over which daughter houses were closed with the lesser monasteries, but the receivers' accounts, pension lists, leases and other records produced at this stage of the dissolution process leave little room for doubt. Knowles and Hadcock name twenty cells dissolved in 1536 or early 1537, but only eight of these can be authenticated.[12] To these eight priories of Blythburgh, Brooke, Colne, St Nicholas' Exeter, Hurley, Letheringham, Ovingham and Wormegay should be added Brecon and Pilton; and Llanthony Secunda's wealthy Irish cells of Colp and Duleek were also dissolved at this time. The suppression of Brecon has always been assigned to 1538, but the 1536/7 receiver's account for the suppressed monasteries of Wales dates its closure to 12 August 1536.[13] The dissolution of Pilton can also be safely placed in 1536

7   *Statutes of the Realm*, 10 vols (HMSO, 1810–24), III, pp. 575–8.
8   See above, pp. 85–6.
9   *L&P*, XIII(i), no. 625, p. 232.
10 E.g. ibid., X, no. 1191, pp. 495–500, for the cells of Alcester, Alvecote, Breedon and St Ives.
11 PRO, E135/2/53.
12 The priories of Alcester, Alvecote, Bamburgh, Hatfield Peverel, Holy Island, Jarrow, Middlesbrough, Modney and Wearmouth were almost certainly dissolved later, whereas Bedeman's Berg and All Saints' Fishergate, York, were probably closed some years before. No reliable date for the suppression of Puffin Island has been found. See Appendix Five for supporting references.
13 PRO, LR6/152/1. Knowles and Hadcock placed Brecon's dissolution in 1538 and this date was followed by D. Walker, 'Brecon Priory in the Middle Ages', in *Links with the*

from the evidence of a pension of 1536/7, a lease of December 1536 and a surviving minister account of 1537/8 all pertaining to the cell.[14] It would also appear that Colp and Duleek had been suppressed by March 1537, when the prior of Llanthony Secunda unsuccessfully requested permission to dissolve its cell of Llanthony Prima to make up for the loss of the mother house's Irish revenues.[15]

The suppression of Ovingham and Wormegay at this time took place because their mother houses, Hexham and Pentney Priories, themselves came under the terms of the 1536 Act;[16] and if the cell of Puffin Island was still functioning by this date it too would have been dissolved with its mother house, Penmon, in 1537. The closure of Letheringham at this juncture is also readily explicable since its mother house, the priory of St Peter and St Paul's Ipswich, had already been suppressed by Wolsey, incongruously without its cell. Colne Priory had been virtually independent of Abingdon since 1311, whereas the large measure of autonomy enjoyed by Hurley must also have attracted the attention of the suppression commissioners. The early dissolution of Blythburgh, Brecon, St Nicholas' Exeter and Pilton might perhaps have resulted from the attention of unusually sceptical commissioners, since all four houses possessed rights which could have brought into question their status as cells according to the Act of Dissolution's definition.[17] But most controversial of all was the suppression of Brooke Priory in the summer of 1536. A cell of Kenilworth Abbey, and not known to have enjoyed any of the privileges of a 'semi-conventual' cell,[18] its premature closure was engineered by a rebellious prior, Roger Harwell, who claimed the cell was independent. Harwell had been resisting the authority of Kenilworth for more than a year, with the support of local gentlemen. Abbot Walle claimed that Harwell had decided to surrender the priory to the royal commissioners because 'he had not such profitable and commodyous pencyon assigned and made sure unto him during his life as he and his coun-

---

Past: Swansea and Brecon Historical Essays, ed. O. W. Jones and D. Walker (Llandybie, 1974), p. 56; and G. Williams, The Welsh Church from Conquest to Reformation, 2nd edn (Cardiff, 1976), p. 561. Further evidence for the closure of the cell in 1536 comes from the inclusion of Prior Robert Holden in a printed pensions list of 1536/7 and the minister account for the priory from 1536/7: L&P, XIII(i), no. 1520, p. 575; PRO, SC6/HenVIII/4843, mem. 1r.

14   See Appendix Five.

15   L&P, XII(i), no. 569, p. 264. Cf. ibid., XII(ii), nos 1288, 1310, pp. 450, 458–66.

16   The role played by the Master of Ovingham in the resistance of the canons of Hexham to the suppression of their priory is well-known. When the suppression commissioners attempted to enter the Hexham precinct, they were repelled by the canons, with the Master, brandishing 'a bowe bentt with arrowes' calling down 'We be xxti brethern in this hous, and we shall dye all, or yt shall ye have this hous': The Priory of Hexham, ed. J. Raine, SS, 2 vols, xliv, xlvi (1863–4), I, no. 96, pp. cxxvii–cxxx.

17   See above, pp. 84–6. Alternatively, their dissolution might have resulted from pressure exerted on their mother houses, Battle and Malmesbury.

18   See above, pp. 83–90.

sels wold and could devyse and aske'; and it is indeed unlikely that Harwell would have been rewarded at the mother house as handsomely as the pension of £10 per year he received from the Crown.[19] Although Walle wrote to Cromwell in June 1536 to assert Kenilworth's genuine claims and reminding him of the abbey's willingness to lease the cell to one of Cromwell's friends, the vicegerent revealingly preferred to proceed with the outright suppression of Brooke. By early August, this had been achieved and the property granted away.[20]

Nevertheless, only a handful of dependencies had been suppressed by late summer 1537, when the closure of the lesser monasteries under the 1536 statute was completed. Many more were to be shut down independently from their mother houses in the coming months. What brought this about? The majority of these early closures were undoubtedly the product of government pressure. Indeed the constant harrying of mother houses for their cells was one of the main ways in which the great Benedictine monasteries felt their dependence on Cromwell in the years between 1536 and their own downfall.[21] In a few cases daughter houses were dissolved outright, regardless of their status as cells, with the property passing to the Crown. In others an abbey was persuaded to farm out their satellite to a government servant or friend, often at a discounted rate but at least to the profit of the monastery. Most of the cells dissolved independently by the Crown between late 1537 and 1539 were larger dependencies, such as Binham (by May 1538), St Bees (by June 1538), Wetheral (October 1538) and Tynemouth (January 1539). Rich's letter about Binham of March 1538, written shortly before the house's closure, suggests that such suppressions were justified by impugning the cell's dependent status. At Binham, Hatfield Peverel (suppressed by December 1537) and St Bees, only the priors were granted pensions, presumably because the monks were allowed the option of returning to their mother house and were therefore considered to be in the same bracket as the 1536–7 dispossessed. However, at the quasi-independent Tynemouth and – harder to explain – Wetheral, the monks received pensions too.[22]

---

[19] The priors of the comparable Augustinian cells of Blythburgh and Letheringham received pensions of only £6 and £5 respectively the following year: L&P, XIII(i), no. 1520, pp. 576–7.

[20] Ibid. VII, no. 749, p. 280, X, nos 444, 1151, pp. 180, 483, XI, no. 519(13), p. 209; Mon. Ang., VI(i), p. 234.

[21] Another source of pressure exerted on larger houses in these years was forcible exchanges which were very much to the benefit of the Crown, a subject deserving more research. In the summer of 1536, Westminster Abbey was compelled to purchase back its recently dissolved priory of Hurley in return for the prime Middlesex manors of La Neyte, Teddington, Hyde and Eyebury, Covent Garden and lands in Westminster, Charing Cross, St Martin in the Fields and East Greenwich, along with the rectory of Teddington and the advowson of Chelsea: Mon. Ang., III, pp. 436–9, no. 15; Westminster Abbey Muniments, 32340.

[22] L&P, XIII(i), no. 1520, p. 583 (Hatfield Peverel), XIV(i), no. 1355, pp. 596 (Binham), 599 (Wetheral), 601 (Tynemouth and St Bees).

Much more frequent than this pattern of suppression and confiscation between 1537 and 1539, however, was the leasing of daughter houses. From as early as March 1536, when Anthony Budgegood requested the lease of one of the Gloucestershire cells, petitions for the grant of dependencies were made to Cromwell.[23] Such requests were also made by Richard Zouche for the priory of Stavordale in his patronage, and by Richard Southwell for Spinney, on behalf of Edward Bestney of Soham, a regular correspondant of the vicegerent. Sir William Kingston, meanwhile, appealed straight to the abbot of Tewkesbury for one of his monastery's dependencies.[24] Cromwell was himself active in writing to the heads of mother houses to request the farm of a cell for an associate, and replies to Cromwell's entreaties concern-ing eight different daughter houses survive amongst his papers.[25] On at least one occasion, moreover, the king himself wrote to an abbey ordering the leasing of its cell.[26] Unsurprisingly Henry's demand was met with prompti-tude, but Cromwell's requests were not always received so passively. In several cases, the heads of the importuned monastery sought to evade or at least delay the farming of their dependency, and this tactic seems to have proved successful in preserving Alcester, Richmond and Woodkirk until the dissolution of their mother houses. Persistent government demands, however, were difficult to resist indefinitely and at least twenty-three daugh-ter houses were leased to laymen between 1536 and 1539.[27] The best source for the farming of cells are the ministers' accounts which often record the date and terms on which the property had been demised to the current occu-pier. A few leases are preserved among the 'conventual leases' in the Public Record Office and others are occasionally mentioned when a former cell was re-leased or sold. In one or two instances, the farming of a dependency is known only from mother-house records, or can be inferred only from infor-mation provided at its suppression. Hitherto unremarked, the leasing out of cells before the suppression of their mother houses was evidently a common occurrence in the late 1530s.

Many of the known lessees were royal servants and so the inference must be that they were granted the cell as a result of pressure from above. Crom-well and the king were not the only suitors; Rich's request of Penwortham

23 Ibid., X, no. 567, p. 222.
24 Ibid., X, nos 390, 507, pp. 156, 203; V, no. 1737, p. 722. Kingston's efforts were assigned to 1532 in the calendar, but a date of 1536 or later is much more likely.
25 Ibid., X, no. 444, p. 180 (Brooke), no. 1206, p. 505 (Hoxne), XII(i), no. 620, p. 280 (Alcester), XIII(ii), no. 746, p. 288 (Richmond), no. 1265, p. 521 (Woodkirk), XIV(i), no. 54, p. 23 (Freiston), no. 334, p. 130 (Bamburgh), no. 591, p. 231 (Lincoln). A request for 'the late priory of Aldeby' was also made in April 1539 after Norwich Cathedral Priory had been converted into a secular cathedral: ibid., XIV(i), no. 779, p. 374.
26 For the Gloucester cell of Leonard Stanley, 11 June 1538: VCH, Gloucestershire, II, p. 73.
27 See Appendix Five. Evidence for the farming of cells is scattered and it is likely that further leases will come to light in the future.

for Sir John Fleetwood was eventually acceded to by Evesham in February 1539, and Thorney leased its cell at Deeping St James to the duke of Norfolk's mistress, Elizabeth Holland, in May of the same year.[28] Where they are known, the sums received were variable. Sir William Kingston paid only £20 per year to Gloucester for Leonard Stanley, valued at £126 in 1535; Gloucester also received only £20 10s. per year for Ewenny (£78 in 1535) and Selby only £8 for Snaith (£38). On the other hand, Evesham was paid £99 5s. 3d. per year for Penwortham (£114), and Durham received £48 19s. 6d. for Lytham (£53) and an even more generous £40 7s. 8d. for Jarrow, exactly the amount recorded in the *Valor* for the cell.[29] This diversity is difficult to explain. But one factor in the setting of rents might have been the degree of duress involved in the transaction. Leonard Stanley was demised to Kingston by order of the king, who seems to have insisted on favourable terms. Equally, it is possible that the Durham leases of Lytham to Thomas Dannet (1536×1539) and Jarrow to Richard Bellasis (April 1539) were made at the initiative of the cathedral priory itself; although Bellasis as a member of the Council of the North and brother of Anthony Bellasis, servant of Cromwell, was a likely beneficiary of government largesse.[30] Leasing a priory themselves would have ensured that the satellite's property remained in the hands of the mother house and that an adequate rent would be received. It may well be that a number of abbeys leased their cells, as they are known to have leased other properties, in order to win friends and pre-empt government interference.[31] After their suppression, leases by Plympton and Nostell Priories of their cells of Marsh Barton and Scokirk were overturned, whereas a suitor to Cromwell complained in August 1539 that Repton Priory had pre-dated a lease of their cell of Calke made shortly before the mother house's suppression in order to frustrate him.[32]

Even more intriguing are the terms of the lease of Ewenny to Sir Edward Carne on 28 February 1537, for ninety-nine years.[33] Carne's rent of £20 10s. seems meagre, but he also undertook to pay an annual salary of £6 13s. 4d. to Edmund Wotton, the 'former prior' of the cell for the rest of his life, and 66s. 8d. each to two monks staying at Ewenny for the same duration. On top of this, Carne was to pay for the food, drink and board of the three religious while he dwelt at Ewenny, or to provide an allowance for them if he chose to

---

28 *L&P*, XI, no. 25, p. 14; PRO, SC6/HenVIII/4047, mems 45r–45v; *Mon. Ang.*, IV, p. 171, no. 8.
29 PRO, E303/4, Gloucestershire no. 4, SC6/HenVIII/1248, mem. 16v, E303/25, Yorkshire no. 915; *L&P*, XVIII(i), no. 100(18), p. 66; *Mon. Ang.*, IV, p. 283, no. 5; PRO, SC6/HenVIII/708, mem. 4r. An earlier lease of Leonard Stanley set the rent at £36 13s. 4d., but this seems to have been revised: VCH *Gloucestershire*, II, p. 73.
30 R. R. Reid, *The King's Council in the North* (London, 1921), pp. 151–2.
31 E.g. G. W. O. Woodward, *The Dissolution of the Monasteries* (London, 1966), pp. 109–10.
32 *L&P*, XIV(ii), nos 47, 558, pp. 14, 195–6, XV, no. 1032, p. 559; PRO, SC6/HenVIII/4579, mem. 1r.
33 PRO, SC6/HenVIII/1248, mem. 16v.

live elsewhere. It was also agreed that on the death or recall of Wotton, Carne should support at Ewenny a prior and one monk at the same rate. How can this most unusual agreement be explained? The closest parallel to this lease seems to come from the Nottinghamshire nunnery of Wallingwells, brought to wider attention by Professor Scarisbrick.[34] In June 1537, the nuns agreed to lease all their possessions to the Yorkshire gentleman, Richard Oglethorpe, for twenty-one years, who would allow them to continue to use the conventual buildings and provide them with food, fuel and servants. Scarisbrick convincingly interpreted this agreement as an attempt to forestall the suppression of the priory by a kind of feoffment to use: since the 1536–7 dissolution had proceeded by the confiscation of the regulars' property, a monastery with no legal title to any possessions would theoretically be secure.[35] It must be questioned whether Edward Carne, a senior diplomat, would have collaborated in such a plan, but it is at least possible that Carne's religious convictions, which caused him to die an exile in Rome after Elizabeth's accession, overcame his political loyalties. Another peculiar transaction was Durham's lease of its cell at Holy Island to that house's prior, Thomas Sparke, suffragan bishop of Berwick in c.1537, which might also have been an attempt to shield the priory from confiscation.[36] And perhaps a similar motive was behind the rent-free lease of Middlesbrough Priory, on 1 January 1539, to four men during the lifetime of John Hexham, the retired abbot of Whitby who had been granted the cell on his resignation.[37] These leases remain shadowy dealings, but there is good reason for thinking that some mother houses took measures to try to ensure that their vulnerable dependencies would not be prised from their grasp during the uncertain and difficult years after 1536.

By whatever means, a significant number of daughter houses survived to be suppressed with their parents. The exact number of survivors is difficult to compute, and clear evidence for dissolution at this late stage can be found for only a small number of cells. For rather more dependencies, only the negative evidence that no indication of an earlier closure is to hand can be cited in support of their inclusion in this category of suppressions. Therefore any number between twenty and thirty-seven cells might have been closed with their mother house (as well as the leased but occupied or partly occupied priories of Ewenny, Holy Island, Middlesbrough and Morville). In a small

---

34 J. J. Scarisbrick, *The Reformation and the English People* (Oxford, 1984), pp. 75–7; *Mon. Ang.*, IV, pp. 298–9.
35 In the event, the religious of both Wallingwells and Ewenny were eventually expelled in December 1539 and January 1540 respectively, at a very late stage in the Dissolution process.
36 J. Raine, *The History and Antiquities of North Durham* (London, 1852), p. 133.
37 *L&P*, XVIII(i), no. 982, p. 553, XIII(i), no. 1113, p. 407. One other cell was leased to a former abbot of the mother house, but without any signs of subterfuge: Abbot Richard Marshall of Shrewsbury, on his resignation from that office, was given the cell of Morville, but this grant was made as early as 1529: *VCH, Shropshire*, II, p. 30.

number of cases, a daughter house is explicitly stated to have been suppressed with its parent. The suppression documents for the Augustinian priories of West Acre, Llanthony Secunda and Walsingham in 1538 all indicate that the houses' cells of Great Massingham, Llanthony Prima and Flitcham respectively were closed down at the same time.[38] Another indication that a cell might have been dissolved at the same time as its mother house is the appearance of the dependency's prior in the abbey's pension list. Such lists, however, still leave considerable room for doubt. Among the Tewkesbury pensioners of 12 January 1540 are the priors of St James' Bristol and Cranborne, even though these cells were both leased in January of the previous year.[39] Some lists refer to the 'late prior' of a cell, which may indicate that the priory was closed months ago or merely days. Moreover, several pension lists give no information about the holders of monastic offices and therefore provide no clue about the fate of the monastery's daughter houses. As well as those of St James' Bristol and Cranborne, the current (as opposed to 'late') priors of Cowick, Deerhurst, Dunster, Hilbre Island, Horton, Kidwelly and Oxney are recorded in their mother houses' pension lists.[40]

In a few cases, some other evidence that the cell was suppressed with its parent can be found. In a letter of July 1541 it is said that Belvoir came into the king's hands with the dissolution of St Albans; and a similar reference to Leominster passing to the Crown by the attainder of the abbot of Reading is found in the appointment of Thomas Vachell as overseer of the possessions of the abbey and cell in February 1540.[41] A commission to suppress Cardigan issued on 26 June 1538, a week after the dissolution of its parent, Bisham (formerly Chertsey) Abbey, indicates that this cell endured even a few days beyond its mother house. Otherwise, it is very difficult to establish with any certainty that a daughter house survived till the end. But as the preceding account has demonstrated, any cell which did achieve that feat was fortunate. Right to the last, monasteries came under pressure to give up their cells. Just two weeks before its own surrender, St Mary's York was forced after a lengthy struggle to lease out its priory at Lincoln.[42] The last days and months of numerous mother houses were spent desperately trying to preserve

---

38 *L&P*, XIII(i), nos 85, 482, pp. 28–9, 176, XIII(ii), no. 31, p. 11.
39 Ibid., XV, no. 49, p. 19; PRO, SC6/HenVIII/1260, mems 37v, 47v–48r. One explanation for this apparent discrepancy is that the monks of Bristol and Cranborne remained *in situ* after the farming-out of their priories. This is not impossible, but the lessees of these houses, Sir Anthony Kingston and Thomas Derby, were both prominent royal servants and would hardly have colluded with any arrangement designed to frustrate the Crown. Alternatively, and more probably, the terminology of the pension list may be misleading.
40 *L&P*, XIV(i), no. 148, pp. 54–5 (Bath), no. 429, p. 172 (Tavistock), no. 556, p. 215 (Sherborne), XIV(ii), no. 602, pp. 212–13 (Peterborough), XV, no. 49, p. 19 (Tewkesbury), no. 87, p. 29 (Chester).
41 Ibid., XVI, no. 1056(78), pp. 505–6, XV, no. 282(115), p. 116.
42 Ibid., XIV(i), nos 415, 591, 963, pp. 168, 231, 447, XIV(ii), no. 522, p. 183; PRO, SC6/HenVIII/4595, mem. 40v.

their dependencies from closure. Despite their shortcomings, and the mis-givings of many historians, these small priories were highly valued and seen to be performing a useful function to the very end.

Conclusions

In seeking to summarise the place of dependent priories in the monastic firmament, and in the medieval Church in general, both positive and nega-tive factors must be taken into consideration. Traditionally, historians have accentuated the problems associated with small daughter houses. It cannot be doubted that the practice of sending out groups of two or three religious to dwell away from their community, sometimes in remote locations, had serious disciplinary and psychological repercussions. A sojourn in a cell unquestionably provided 'unparalleled opportunities of worldly living',[43] and attempts to regulate distant daughter houses, though sincere, can never have been entirely successful. The constitutional ambiguity of dependent priories placed a particular strain on the parties involved. The energies of mother and daughter houses were too often directed towards struggles with alterna-tive jurisdictions, rather than to the provision of a high level of observance at the satellite. Numerous disputes with the diocesans and patrons of their cells are recorded, but most alarming to parent abbeys was the prospect of their own personnel rebelling or seeking unacceptable levels of autonomy. The sense of anxiety, and even weariness, over its dependencies that pervades the most compelling account of a family of cells so far written may well reflect the experience of a number of mother houses.[44]

And yet to dismiss dependent priories as serving 'no religious purpose whatever' and a prominent cause of 'spiritual decay' is to misunderstand the rationale behind these foundations.[45] In general, they were established by lay founders or by their own mother houses for spiritual purposes, and indeed purposes which retained much of their relevance throughout the middle ages. Like other monasteries, dependent priories were established above all to provide prayer for their benefactors. In the late eleventh and twelfth centuries they offered a relatively cheap and convenient template for the foundation of a religious house, which proved especially popular for men and women of limited means as well as those seeking to put down roots in dis-puted territory. In many other instances, cells were conceived as mechanisms for the fitting service of venerated sites, allowing the mother house to super-vise and commemorate locations of particular historical significance and sanctity. The very presence of a cenobitic community was sufficient to confer sacred status on a site, and in time the maintenance of their cells itself

---

[43] Morgan, Bec, p. 9.
[44] Dobson, Durham Priory, pp. 297–341.
[45] Knowles, MO, p. 136.

came to be considered a religious duty by mother houses. Meanwhile, the suffrages for the founders and benefactors of these satellite priories could not be neglected, even after the original patron's line had long been extinguished. Although a lack of patronal interest might seem to bring into question the usefulness of many cells, it would appear from the popularity of at least some daughter-house confraternities that the prayers of the religious did not lose all significance in the later middle ages.

Despite their shortcomings, it is therefore clear that the dependent priories of English monasteries were first and foremost religious houses, and not the barely monastic tools of administration they are often depicted to be. In consequence, the experience of these well-documented priories can shed some light on the obscure history of the many small religious houses of medieval England. Of course, the significance of cells does not lie merely in their possible resemblance to other small monasteries: they were an important phenomenon in their own right, as the sheer number of these foundations shows. Furthermore, as we have seen, there are considerable difficulties in drawing direct parallels between dependent and independent houses. In many ways, their access to the networks and facilities of their wealthy parents render daughter houses unrepresentative of small monasteries in general. Nevertheless, cells were characterised as much by their size as by their subject status. If the possibility of mother-house assistance enabled them to navigate the storms of the fifteenth-century economy with more confidence than most, the financial difficulties they faced were no different from those encountered by other houses of their size. Similarly, daughter houses were by no means unique in occupying churches shared with parochial congregations or in seeking to influence local religion through popular saint cults. The well-documented experience of cells can therefore reveal much about the interaction of small monastery and lay religion. The everyday life and environs of dependent priories, which emerges in rather more detail than can be recovered for small independent houses, can also be used – with caution – to understand more about the experience of those dwelling in lesser monasteries. Even where the analogy is imperfect, it may be that we can still learn more about small religious houses from studying cells than we can from other means. In particular, the information readily available from dependencies can be used to highlight potentially fruitful areas of research into lesser monasteries and to provide a framework for the scattered and often decontextualised fragments of evidence surviving for priories of this size. A great deal more remains to be learned about small religious houses, from both documentary and material sources, but if this study does anything to persuade scholars that research of this kind will be a worthwhile and profitable enterprise, it will have served its purpose.

A second consequence of the overtly monastic character of the majority of cells can also be seen. As genuine religious houses the presence of these 143 or so priories served to widen considerably the monastic impact on medieval England and Wales. In short, a great many localities had a monastery in their midst than would otherwise have been the case. If it be concluded that there were already too many religious houses, consuming too much wealth, in medieval Britain, then this might be considered an unwelcome outcome. But as a more positive evaluation of the contribution of monasticism to late medieval religion and society starts to take root, the potential advantages of the further dissemination of religious houses seem more tangible.[46] It would appear from the evidence of probate records that monasteries were more likely to receive bequests from their immediate neighbours than from anyone else, suggesting that the presence of a religious house in the locality was often appreciated.[47] Although cells do not appear to have made a substantial charitable and educational impact, their contribution to the spiritual life of their environs, particularly through their confraternities and saint cults, cannot be questioned. The numerous networks of dependencies might also serve as arteries carrying the lifeblood of monastic culture throughout the kingdom. Architectural styles, such as the famous early appearance of bar tracery at Binham in the 1240s, were transmitted. Liturgical fashions were disseminated, and local saint cults such as that of St Bega translated from their place of origin to distant parts of the country. Manuscripts and learning were also passed on, and Dr Clark's recent study of St Albans has demonstrated clearly how the studies pursued at that abbey's cells derived from and complemented those undertaken at the mother house.[48] Daughter houses were not simply outlets for the unsatisfactory elements of monastic life; their life and observance also reflected its strengths and diversity. Despite their evident weaknesses, they served the religious needs of the time. And for that reason alone, dependent priories deserve a more sympathetic hearing than they have been given.

[46] For a forceful re-assessment of the place of monasteries in late medieval England, see J. G. Clark, 'The Religious Orders in Pre-Reformation England', in Clark, *The Religious Orders in Pre-Reformation England* (Woodbridge, 2002), pp. 3–33.

[47] M. Oliva, 'Patterns of Patronage to Female Monasteries in the Late Middle Ages', in Clark, *Religious Orders*, pp. 155–62; C. Cross, 'Monasticism and Society in the Diocese of York, 1520–40', *TRHS*, 5th series, xxxviii (1988), pp. 131–45. Also see above, pp. 217–18, for the regularity with which parishioners remembered the religious sharing their churches in their wills.

[48] J. G. Clark, 'Intellectual Life at the Abbey of St Albans and the Nature of Monastic Learning in England c.1350–c.1440: the Work of Thomas Walsingham in Context', unpublished Oxford D.Phil. thesis (1997).

Appendix One:
The Foundation of English Cells,
c.1017–c.1250

Priory	Date	Founder	Mother House
1. St Ives	c.1017	Mother	Ramsey
2. Belvoir	1076×1088	Robert de Tosny	St Albans
3. St Leonard's Stamford	+ 1083×1146[1]	Mother	Durham
4. Holy Island	+1083×1172[2]	Mother	Durham
5. Jarrow	+1083 (late C12?)[3]	Mother	Durham
6. Wearmouth	+1083 (late C12?)[4]	Mother	Durham
7. Great Malvern	1085	Bishop Wulfstan/Mother	Westminster
8. Hurley	−1087	Geoffrey I de Mandeville	Westminster
9. St Nicholas' Exeter	1087	Mother	Battle
10. Wallingford	c.1087×1089	Geoffrey the Chamberlain[5]	St Albans
11. Tynemouth	−1089	Earl Robert de Mowbray	St Albans
12. Dunster	+1090	William I de Mohun	Bath
13. Binham	−1093	Peter de Valognes	St Albans
14. Hertford	−1093	Ralph de Limesy	St Albans
15. Westbury-upon-Trym	c.1093	Bishop Wulfstan/Mother	Worcester
16. St Leonard's Norwich	c.1095	Bishop Herbert de Losinga/ Mother	Norwich
17. Odense (Denmark)	1095×1096	King Eric the Good of Denmark	Evesham
18. All Saints' Fishergate	−1100[6]	William II	Whitby
19. Hackness	c.1100[7]	William de Percy/Mother	Whitby

A signifies Augustinian house. All dates as in Knowles and Hadcock (K&H) and other *Medieval Religious Houses* volumes unless otherwise indicated. Several of these amendments are taken from Brooke and Smith, 'Addenda'. The date of first foundation is given for St Guthlac's Hereford, Ewenny and Cardigan, but not for Tynemouth which was probably never a true cell of Durham. All the dates given represent the foundation of the priory *as a cell*, and not necessarily as a religious house.

1 St Leonard's Stamford. K&H: +1083. See Piper, 'Stamford', part i, pp. 5–7 ('Addenda', p. 9).
2 Holy Island. K&H: 1083. See Piper, 'First Generations of Durham Monks', p. 444n.
3 Jarrow. K&H: 1083. See Piper, *Jarrow*, pp. 4–5 ('Addenda', p. 7).
4 Wearmouth. K&H: 1083. See Piper, 'Wearmouth', p. 2.
5 Wallingford. K&H: Robert d'Oyley or Geoffrey the Chamberlain. For the strong evidence in favour of the latter, see Keats-Rohan, 'Devolution of Honour of Wallingford', p. 312.
6 All Saints' Fishergate. K&H: +1087. See Burton, *Monastic Order in Yorkshire*, p. xvii ('Addenda', p. 11).
7 Hackness. K&H: c.1095. See Burton, *Monastic Order in Yorkshire*, pp. xvii, 37–8 ('Addenda', p. 6).

Priory	Date	Founder	Mother House
20. Richmond	c.1100[8]	Wymar the Steward	St Mary's York
21. St Guthlac's Hereford	1100×1101[9]	Hugh de Lacy	Gloucester
22. Aldeby	c.1100×1119	Agnes de Beaupré	Norwich
23. Lynn	c.1100×c.1150[10]	Bishop Herbert de Losinga/ Mother	Norwich
24. Ewyas Harold	+1100	Harold of Ewyas	Gloucester
25. Hatfield Peverel	+1100	William Peverel	St Albans
26. Pheleley	+1100?	Henry I/Mother?	Eynsham
27. Yarmouth	+c.1101[11]	Bishop Herbert de Losinga/ Mother	Norwich
28. Cranborne	1102	Mother	Tewkesbury
29. Penwortham	1104×1122	Warin Bussel	Evesham
30. Felixstowe	c.1105	Roger Bigod	Rochester
31. Cardiff	−1106?	Robert fitz Hamo	Tewkesbury
32. Wetheral	1106×1112[12]	Ranulf le Meschin	St Mary's York
33. Colne	−1107	Aubrey I de Vere	Abingdon
34. Wymondham	−1107	William d'Aubigny *Pincerna*	St Albans
35. Brecon	c.1110	Bernard of Newmarch	Battle
36. Carmarthen	c.1110	Henry I/Mother?	Battle
37. Llandovery	c.1110	Richard fitz Pons	Great Malvern
38. Cardigan	c.1110×1115	Gilbert fitz Richard	Gloucester
39. Scilly	−1114	Henry I/Mother?	Tavistock
40. Lamanna	−1114	Ancestor of Hastulf de Soleigny/ Mother	Glastonbury
41. Kidwelly	1114	Bishop Roger of Salisbury/ Mother	Sherborne
42. Edwardstone	1114×1115	Hubert de Montchesney	Abingdon
43. St Bart.'s Sudbury	−1116[13]	Wulfric the Moneyer	Westminster
44. Bassaleg	1116	Robert of Hay	Glastonbury
45. Llanbadarn-Fawr	1116×1117	Gilbert fitz Richard	Gloucester
46. Bolton/Embsay[A]	1120×1121	William le Meschin and Cecily de Rumilly	Huntingdon
47. Middlesbrough	c.1120×1130	Robert I de Brus	Whitby
48. St Bees	+1120	William le Meschin	St Mary's York
49. Scokirk[A]	−1121[14]	Geoffrey fitz Pain or Everard	Nostell

[8] Richmond. K&H: 1100×1137. See Burton, *Monastic Order in Yorkshire*, p. xvii ('Addenda', p. 9).

[9] St Guthlac's Hereford. K&H: c.1101. See *HRH*, I, p. 91 ('Addenda', p. 7).

[10] Lynn. K&H: c.1100. The first certain evidence of a cell at Lynn, as opposed to the presence of an individual monk-priest there, comes in a charter of Bishop William Turbe of 1146×c.1150: *Norwich Charters*, I, no. 124, pp. 70–1.

[11] Yarmouth. K&H: −1101. The first reference to a priory at Yarmouth comes only in 1253: *Norwich Charters*, I, no. 215, p. 126.

[12] Wetheral. K&H: c.1106. See Burton, *Monastic Order in Yorkshire*, p. 43 ('Addenda', p. 10).

[13] St Bart.'s Sudbury. K&H: c.1115. See *Sudbury Charters*, p. 1 ('Addenda', p. 9).

[14] Scokirk. K&H: 1100×1135. Henry I's confirmation charter to Nostell Priory, dated to before 1121 by Burton, includes the chapel of All Saints here: *Early Yorkshire Charters*, III, no. 1428, pp. 129–36; Burton, *Monastic Order in Yorkshire*, p. 73n ('Addenda', p. 17). Nicholl places the foundation before 1114, and also assigns it to

Priory	Date	Founder	Mother House
50. Woodkirk[A]	–1121×1127[15]	Ralph de Lisle	Nostell
51. Hirst[A]	1121×1129[16]	Nigel d'Aubigny	Nostell
52. Breedon[A]	–1122	Robert de Ferrers	Nostell
53. Horton	1122×1139	Bishop Roger of Salisbury/ Mother	Sherborne
54. Coquet Island	–1125	Mother	Tynemouth
55. Calwich[A]	1125×1130[17]	Nicholas of Gresley	Kenilworth
56. Hoxne	1130	Maurice of Windsor	Norwich
57. Ewenny	–1131[18]	William of London	Gloucester
58. Carham[A]	+1131	Mother	Kirkham
59. Kilpeck	1134	Hugh fitz William of Kilpeck	Gloucester
60. Blythburgh[A]	–1135	Mother?	St Osyth's
61. Brinkburn[A]	–1135	William Bertram	Pentney
62. Lincoln	c.1135?	Mother	St Mary's York
63. Wickham Skeith	+1135	Robert de Sakeville	Colchester
64. Bradwell	–1136[19]	Meinfelin of Wolverton	Luffield
65. Dover	1136	Henry I/Mother	Christ Church Canterbury
66. Llanthony Secunda[A]	1136	Milo of Gloucester	Llanthony Prima
67. Rumburgh	+1136[20]	Alan III, 1st earl of Richmond	St Mary's York
68. St James' Bristol	c.1137	Earl Robert of Gloucester	Tewkesbury
69. Hilbre Island	1137×1140[21]	Mother	Chester
70. Morville	1138	Bishop Robert de Béthune	Shrewsbury
71. Stone[A]	1138×1147[22]	Robert II of Stafford	Kenilworth

Everard, rather than Geoffrey fitz Pain, on the strength of a confirmation which refers to 'a certain chapel in the wood of Tocwic with all the lands and things which pertain to the fee of Everard who gave them to the chapel': Nicholl, *Thurstan, Archbishop of York*, p. 130.

15 Woodkirk. K&H: –1135. The 'chapel' of Woodkirk had been granted to Nostell by the time of Henry I's confirmation charter of 1121×1127: *Early Yorkshire Charters*, III, no. 1428, pp. 129–36. K&H attribute the foundation to William, earl of Warenne and others, though Henry I's charter records that the chapel was given to Nostell by Ralph de Lisle and his son, William; Warenne's role was probably just to confirm this grant as de Lisle's overlord.

16 Hirst. K&H: –1135. See *Honour of Mowbray*, no. 15, pp. 17–18.

17 Calwich. K&H: –1148. See VCH, *Staffordshire*, III, p. 237; *English Episcopal Acta III*, p. 36; *English Episcopal Acta XIV*, p. 47.

18 Ewenny. K&H: –1141, by Maurice of London. It is likely that the first founder of Ewenny was William of London, who died in 1131: Conway Davies, 'Ewenny Priory', pp. 120–2; Cowley, *Monastic Order*, pp. 15–16.

19 Bradwell. K&H: –1136×1144. See *Foundation of Walden Monastery*, pp. 10–11, based on the assertion that William, first prior of Bradwell, assumed this office before becoming prior of Walden ('Addenda', p. 4).

20 Rumburgh. K&H: 1135, by Stephen, count of Brittany. See Oxford, Bodleian Library, Top. MS Suffolk, d.15, fols 35r–35v.

21 Hilbre Island. K&H: +1093. Chester did not acquire Hilbre Island until 1137×1140: Burne, *Monks of Chester*, pp. 7–8; *Chester Cartulary*, II, no. 504, pp. 289–90.

22 Stone. K&H: c.1135, by Enisan de Walton. Walton sold the church of Stone to Geoffrey de Clinton, for the latter's foundation of Kenilworth, and a late medieval

Priory	Date	Founder	Mother House
72. Coldingham (Scotland)	–1139	Mother?	Durham
73. Deeping St James	1139	Baldwin fitz Gilbert	Thorney
74. Leominster	1139[23]	Mother?	Reading
75. Beadlow	1140×1146	Robert d'Aubigny	St Albans
76. Freiston	1141×1142[24]	Alan de Craon	Crowland
77. Marsh Barton[A]	1142	Alice, daughter of Sheriff Baldwin	Plympton
78. Hood[A]	1145	Mother?	Newburgh
79. Leonard Stanley	1146	Roger III of Berkeley/Mother	Gloucester
80. St Helen's Derby[A]	c.1146	Mother?	Darley
81. Little Malvern	–1150?[25]	Bishop Simon of Worcester/ Mother	Worcester
82. Rhynd (Scotland)	– c.1150	David I of Scotland	Reading
83. May (Scotland)	–1153	David I of Scotland	Reading
84. Brooke[A]	–1153	Hugh de Ferrers	Kenilworth
85. Dale[A]	1153×1158	Serlo de Grendon	Calke
86. Trokenholt	1154×1169	Bishop Nigel of Ely/Mother	Thorney
87. Bromfield	1155	Henry II/Mother	Gloucester
88. Bedeman's Berg	c.1155[26]	Henry II	Colchester
89. Snape	c.1155	William Martel	Colchester
90. Felley[A]	1156[27]	Ralph Brito of Annesley	Worksop
91. Alvecote	1159	William Burdet	Great Malvern
92. Denney	c.1160	Robert the Chamberlain	Ely
93. Canonsleigh[A]	c.1161	Walter de Clavile	Plympton
94. Sheringham[A]	1164	Mother?	Notley
95. Ranton[A]	–1166	Robert fitz Noel	Haughmond

foundation narrative of Stone names Walton as the priory's founder. However, as Dickinson and Franklin have argued, the true founder of Stone appears to be Robert II of Stafford, whose charter endowing the priory can be dated to 1138×1147: 'Staffordshire Chartulary', II(i), pp. 201–4; Mon. Ang., VI, pp. 230–1, no. 2; VCH, Staffordshire, III, pp. 240–1; English Episcopal Acta XIV, nos 37–8, pp. 35–7.

[23] Leominster. K&H: +1123. See Kemp, 'Monastic Dean', pp. 505–15 ('Addenda', p. 7).

[24] Freiston. K&H: +1114. Alan de Craon's foundation charter is wrongly placed under 1114 in Pseudo-Ingulph. However, this charter states that his grant was made to Abbot Geoffrey (1138×1139–1142) after the liberation of King Stephen (1141): Fulman, Rerum Anglicarum Scriptorum Veterum, I, pp. 113–14, 124–5; Mon. Ang., IV, p. 125, no. 1.

[25] Little Malvern. K&H: 1171. Although the annals of Worcester date the foundation of the cell to 1171, the charter of Bishop Simon of Worcester of c.1149×50 for the establishment of a priory at Little Malvern suggests otherwise: Annales Monastici, IV, p. 382; Worcester Cartulary, no. 61a, p. 37. It is not obvious how this contradiction should be resolved.

[26] Bedeman's Berg. K&H: –1135. Originally the hermitage of Robert de Sakeville, Bedeman's Berg was converted into a cell by Henry II: Cartularium de Colecestria, I, pp. 38–9.

[27] Felley. K&H: 1152. Ralph Brito of Annesley granted the church of Felley, where there was a hermit community, to Worksop in 1151, but it was apparently only in 1156 that he founded a priory on the site: VCH, Nottinghamshire, II, p. 109; Binns, Dedications of Monastic Houses, p. 133.

Priory	Date	Founder	Mother House
96. Bentley[A]	1171?	Archbishop of Canterbury?[28]	St Greg.'s Cant.
97. Calke[A]	1172	Mother/Matilda, countess of Chester?	Repton
98. Redbourn	+1178	Mother	St Albans
99. Nendrum (Ireland)	c.1179	John de Courcy	St Bees
100. Duleek[A] (Ireland)	c.1180	Hugh de Lacy	Llanthony Secunda
101. Baxterwood[A]	+1180	Henry du Puiset	Guisborough
102. Begerin (Ireland)	1181	Sons of Robert fitz Godebert	St Nich.'s Exeter
103. Colp[A] (Ireland)	c.1182	Hugh de Lacy/Mother	Llanthony Prima
104. Castleknock (Ireland)	c.1185	Hugh Tyrrell	Little Malvern
105. Pilton	–1187[29]	Mother?	Malmesbury
106. Mountjoy	+1189	William de Gynes	Wymondham
107. Lytham	1191×1194	Richard fitz Roger of Woodplumpton	Durham
108. Farne Island	c.1193	Mother	Durham
109. Finchale	1196	Henry du Puiset	Durham
110. Weybourne[A]	+1199	Ralph Mainwaring	West Acre
111. Letheringham[A]	–1200	William de Bovile	St Peter & St Paul's, Ipswich
112. Kilcommon (Ireland)	c.1200	Philip of Worcester	Glastonbury
113. Kilrush[A] (Ireland)	c.1201	William Marshall	Cartmel
114. Ardaneer (Ireland)	c.1202	William de Burgo	Glastonbury
115. Cockerham[A]	1207×1208	Gilbert, son of Roger fitz Reinfrid and wife, Heloise	Leicester
116. Ratlinghope[A]	–1209	Mother?	Wigmore
117. Bamburgh[A]	c.1221[30]	Mother	Nostell
118. Alberbury[A]	c.1221×1226	Fulk fitz Warin	Lilleshall
119. Mobberley[A]	1228×1240	Gilbert de Barton	Rocester

[28] Bentley. K&H: Ranulph de Glanville in 1171. There is no reliable evidence connecting Glanville with the priory, whereas an early sixteenth-century court roll asserts that this priory was established by an archbishop of Canterbury. Since Bentley was in Harrow, a peculiar of the archbishop, this seems a plausible claim: *VCH, Middlesex*, IV, p. 206.

[29] Pilton. K&H: C12. Although the precise foundation date of Pilton Priory remains unknown, the cell was definitely in existence by 1187: *HRH*, I, p. 95.

[30] Bamburgh. K&H: 1121 & c.1228. Henry I's grant of Bamburgh to Nostell makes no mention of the foundation of a cell there, and there is no evidence of any Nostell presence at Bamburgh prior to c.1221 when the Yorkshire priory was finally able to take possession of the parish church there: *History of Northumberland*, I, pp. 73–94; *CPL, 1198–1304*, p. 82. Knowles and Hadcock suggest a small cell was maintained from the early twelfth century at the church of St Oswald in Bamburgh, but this seems unlikely since all the profits of the parish were attached to St Aidan's. It has even been suggested recently that there was no separate church of St Oswald at all, but a single church with a joint dedication: *English Episcopal Acta XXIV*, no. 113, pp. 96–7.

Priory	Date	Founder	Mother House
120. Puffin Island[A]	1237×1414	Mother?	Penmon
121. Halywell[A]	1240×1270	Robert de Cotes and Richard Fiton	Rocester
122. Warkworth	−1241×1249	Bishop Nicholas Farnham	Durham
123. Wormley[A]	−c.1260	Mother?	Holy Sepulchre Thetford[31]
124. St Anthony in Roseland[A]	−1288	Mother?	Plympton

[31] Wormley. K&H: Waltham. The attribution of the cell of St Laurence Wormley to Waltham was made by Salter, presumably on the grounds that Waltham held considerable property in that vill, including the parish church: *Chapters of the Augustinian Canons*, p. 275n. However, this priory, which appears in lists of Augustinian houses compiled in the late thirteenth, the mid-fourteenth and the early sixteenth centuries, was undoubtedly a dependency of the canons of the Holy Sepulchre, Thetford: see *Visitations of the Diocese of Norwich*, p. 32; *L&P*, XIII(ii), no. 784, p. 281.

Appendix Two:
Later Foundations/Acquisitions Of English Cells, c.1250–1533

Priory	Date	Founder	Mother House
1. Horsley[A]	1262	Henry III?	Bruton
2. Modney	–1291	Mother	Ramsey
3. Oxney	–1292[1]	Mother	Peterborough
4. Snaith	–1310[2]	Mother	Selby
5. Marsh (Tickhill)[3]	–1360	Mother?	Humberston
6. Ovingham[A]	1378	Gilbert III de Umfraville and earl of Northumberland	Hexham
7. Goldcliff	1442	Henry VI/executors of Isabel, countess of Warwick	Tewkesbury
8. Molycourt	1449[4]	Bishop Walter Lyhert/Mother	Ely
9. Spinney	1449	Bishop Walter Lyhert/Mother	Ely
10. Chetwode[A]	1460	Mother?	Notley
11. Cowick	1462–3[5]	Edward IV	Tavistock
12. Alcester	1466	Bishop John Carpenter/Mother	Evesham
13. Deerhurst	1467	Edward IV	Tewkesbury
14. Wormegay[A]	1468	Earl of Northumberland/ Mother?	Pentney

A signifies Augustinian house. All dates from Knowles and Hadcock (K&H) unless otherwise indicated.

[1] Oxney. K&H: –1272. This date comes from Tanner and cannot be verified. The first known reference to the use of Oxney as a rest-house comes in a constitution of Abbot Richard of London of 1292: London, Lambeth Palace MS 198b, fol. 285v.

[2] Snaith. K&H: 1310. It appears from Archbishop Greenfield's confirmation of the way in which Selby served the churches of Snaith and Adlingfleet and the chapel of Selby in 1310 that two monks of that abbey were already accustomed to dwell at Snaith: *Reg. Greenfield*, II, no. 875, pp. 81–2.

[3] Marsh. K&H: listed as a hospital, annexed to Humberston in the fourteenth century. There are references to two priors in the 1360s, including a Robert of Humberston, and the house was treated as a cell at the Dissolution: *HRH*, II, p. 131; *L&P*, X, no. 1238, pp. 575–7, XIII(ii), no. 460, p. 180.

[4] Molycourt. K&H: 1446. Although Henry VI granted licence to the prior and convent of Molycourt to grant their property to the prior and convent of Ely in mortmain on 7 August 1446, Bishop Lyhert of Norwich did not enact the union until 4 December 1449: *CPR, 1441–1446*, p. 456; NRO, Reg/6/11, fols 278v–280r.

[5] Cowick. K&H: +1464. The letters patent granting Cowick to Tavistock were issued 12 November 1462: *CPR, 1461–1467*, p. 222. It is not known when this grant was confirmed by the bishop of Exeter, but the first Tavistock monks did not arrive at Cowick until 10 April 1463: Yeo, *Monks of Cowick*, p. 22.

Priory	Date	Founder	Mother House
15. Pembroke	c.1471[6]	Mother	St Albans
16. Great Massingham[A]	1476	Bishop James Goldwell	West Acre
17. Llanthony Prima[A]	1481	Edward IV	Llanthony Secunda
18. Flitcham[A]	1528[7]	Cardinal Wolsey	Walsingham
19. Stavordale[A]	1533	Mother	Taunton

[6] Pembroke. K&H: 1443. Pembroke Priory was granted to St Albans by Humphrey duke of Gloucester in August 1443: *Registra*, I, pp. 41–50. However, Duke Humphrey's schedule for 'the charges and observances appointed to be perpetually boren by thabbot and convent of the monastery of St Alban' make clear that the services to be said for Humphrey's soul as a result of this grant were to be performed at St Albans and not at Pembroke itself: Vickers, *Humphrey Duke of Gloucester*, pp. 439–41. As a result, the abbey does not seem initially to have sent any monks to Wales and no prior of Pembroke is named at the St Albans elections of 1452 and 1465: *Registra*, I, pp. 11–13, II, pp. 27–8. The first reference to such an office comes in January 1471, and the cell of St Albans at Pembroke probably dates from this time: ibid., II, pp. 96–7.

[7] Flitcham. K&H: +1216. Although Cox believed that Flitcham was a cell of Walsingham from an early date, there seem to have been no firm ties between the two priories before Wolsey annexed Flitcham to Walsingham in 1528: *VCH, Norfolk*, II, pp. 380–1; Dickinson, *Shrine of Walsingham*, pp. 48–9.

Appendix Three:
Numbers of Religious in English Cells

Priory	Number of Religious
Alcester	founded for 3 (1466); 3 (1498)
Aldeby	**4 (Knowles & Hadcock)**; to be 4 (1256); 5 down to 4* (1308); at least 3 (1319); 3 (1481)
Alvecote	founded for at least 4* (1159); 4 (*C16– Leland*)
Bamburgh^A	**6–7 (K&H)**; 2 (1371); 4 (*1534– Russell*)
Beadlow	**4–5 (K&H)**; *4 or 5 (C12– VCH)*; 4 (1428)
Bedeman's Berg	founded for 2 (c.1155); *1 (1530s– Leland)*
Belvoir	**4 (K&H)**; founded for 4* (late C11); 6 (1377); 7 (1381); 5 (1525–6); not > 4 or 5 (1530s); *3–4 (1538– VCH)*
Binham	founded for not <8* (–1093); 14 (1320); 13 (1377); 11 (1381); 5 (1525/6); 4 (1534); 6 (1539)
Blythburgh^A	**6 (K&H)**; 7 (1407); 4 (1427); 4 (1473); 4 (1520); 5 (1526); 4 (1530s)
Brecon	*founded for 6 (c.1110– K&H)*; 9 (c.1283); 6 (1377); 5, when should be 9 (1401); 6 (1435); 5 (1504); 6 (1529); 6 (1534)
Breedon^A	**6 (K&H)**; 5 (c.1220); 3 (1377); 3 (1441)
St James' Bristol	founded for 12* (c.1137); *3 (1540– VCH)*
Bromfield	*12 (before 1325– VCH)*; 3 (1510×1514)
Brooke^A	**3 (K&H)**; 3 (1305); 3 (–1535)
Calke^A	**2–3 (K&H)**
Calwich^A	**4 (K&H)**; 4 (C14)
Cardiff	**5 (K&H)**
Cardigan	said to be 2 or 3 customarily (1428); *2 (1530s– Leland)*
Carham^A	**2–3 (K&H)**; *2 (1530s– Leland)*
Chetwode^A	**2 (K&H)**; 2 (1524)
Cockerham^A	3–4 (early C13); 2 (1381)
Coldingham	to be 31 (c.1235); 7 (1304); 3–4 (said to be down from 24) (1379); 2 (1438); 4 (1446)
Colne	6 up to 12* (1100×1117); 11 (1534)
Coquet Island	2 (2nd half of C14); 2 (1442)
Cowick	founded for 3 (1462); 2–4 (1460s–1490s)
Cranborne	**3 (K&H)**; 3 at foundation (1102); *3 (1530s– Leland)*; *3 (1540– VCH)*
Deerhurst	founded for 5 (1467); *3 (1540– VCH)*
Dover	13 (1136); *12 (C13– Moorman)*; 14 (1511); 13 (1534); 13 (1535)
Dunster	**3–4 (Greatrex)**; to be 5 (1330); 5 (1447); 4 (1495)
Ewenny	re-founded for 12* (1141); 3 (1510×1514); 3 (1534)

Priory	Number of Religious
Ewyas Harold	to be at least 2 (1196); >2 (late C13); said to be for 2 or 3 (1359)
St Nichs' Exeter	**6 (K&H)**; 6 (1459); 6 (1492)
Farne Island	**2 (K&H)**; 2 (mid-C13); 1 (c.1332); 1 (1449); 2 up to 3 (1513)
Felixstowe	**2 or 3 (Greatrex)**; 14 (1307); 3 (1381); 3 (1528)
Felley[A]	**5–6 (K&H)**
Finchale	**9 (K&H)**; 10 up to 15 (1278); 9 *(1317– Raine)*; 13 (1350s); 7 (1379); 6 (1381); 9 (1408); 9 (1449); 8 (1464); *13 (1530s– Leland)*
Flitcham[A]	4 (1528); 4 (1532)
Freiston	*founded for 13 (1141×1142– K&H)*; 7 (1377); 7, when should be 9 (1434); 8, when should be 10 (1440)
Goldcliff	founded for 3 (1442)
Great Malvern	**26 (K&H)**; 30 (early C12); 26 *(c.1300– Snape)*; 12 (1349); 14 (1382); 15 (1381); 15 (1397); 12 (1540)
Gt Massingham[A]	**2 (K&H)**; 2 (1520)
Hatfield Peverel	4 (1381); 4 (1525–6)
St G.'s Hereford	**not >5 (K&H)**; 6 (1510×1514)
Hertford	founded for 6*, soon raised to 7* (late C11); 4 (1525–6)
Hilbre Island	**1–2 (K&H)**; 2 (C16– VCH)
Hirst[A]	1 (K&H – after C14); 1 (1121×1129); 2 (1138×1148); 1 (1472)
Holy Island	6 *(1343– Raine)*; 5 (1379); 3 (early C15); 2 (1449); 4 (1464)
Hood[A]	1 (1332)
Horsley[A]	**2 (K&H)**; 2 (1262)
Horton	**4–5 (K&H)**; 3 or 4 (1310)
Hoxne	**7 or 8 (K&H; Greatrex)**; 2 up to 3* (early C14); 2 (C14)
Hurley	*founded for 13 (–1087– K&H)*; 15* (1300); 8 *(1536– Westlake)*
Jarrow	2 (mid-C13); 1 (c.1371); said to be customarily 2 (1394); 2 (1449); 2 up to 3 (1513)
Kidwelly	**3 (K&H)**; 3 (1310); 2 (1534)
Leominster	6 (1277); 8 (1283); <customary 12* (1286); 11 (1340); 10 (1379)
Leonard Stanley	at least 5 (1230s); 3 (1510×1514); *3 (1535– VCH)*
Letheringham[A]	**4–5 (K&H/VCH)**
Lincoln	**2–3 (K&H)**; 3 (1258); 2 (c.1293); 3 (1531)
Llanthony Prima[A]	5 (1481); 5 (1534); 5 (1539)
Lynn	**4 (K&H)**; to be 4 (1256); 4 (early C15); 4 (1426)
Lytham	**2–3 (K&H)**; 2 (mid-C13); 3 up to 4 (C14); 2, but should be 3 (1350s); 1 (c.1371); 2 (1381)
Marsh Barton[A]	**3–4 (K&H)**; 2 (1492)
May	*founded for 10 (–1153– Cowan and Easson)*; to be 13 (1166×1171)
Middlesbrough	**2–3 (K&H)**; 2 (1452); 2 (1521)
Modney	**1–2 (K&H)**; 2? (mid-C14); 2 (1530)
Molycourt	**1–2 (K&H)**
Morville	**3 at most (K&H)**; 1? (1372); *1 (1518–21– VCH)*
St L.'s Norwich	**7 or 8 (K&H; Greatrex)**; 4? (C14); *at least 5 (1514– VCH)*

Priory	Number of Religious
Ovingham[A]	4 (1378); 3 (1381); 4 (1530s– Leland)
Oxney	2 (K&H); 6 (1437); 6 (1442)
Pembroke	4–5 (K&H); 3 (1525–6)
Penwortham	founded for 3 (1104×1122); 2 (c.1330); 2 (1381); at least 2 (1418)
Pilton	3 (1381); 2? (1442); 3 (1492); 5 (1527); 3 (1534)
Ratlinghope[A]	3 (K&H)
Redbourn	4 (K&H); 4 (early C14); 4 (mid-C14); to be 5 (1439)
Richmond	9–10 (K&H); 2 (1258); 2 (c.1293); 2 (1379–81)
Rumburgh	founded for 12* (c.1136); 4 (1258); 2 (c.1293); 3 (1379–81); 3 (C15); 3 (1528)
St Anthony in Roseland[A]	2 (K&H); 2 (1492); 2 (1530s– Leland)
St Bees	founded for 6* (+1120); 7 (1258); 8 (c.1293); 4 (1379); 5 (1381); 7 (1516–17)
St Ives	to be full convent (late C12); 9 (1439); 3–4 (1439– VCH); 9 (1530)
Scilly	2 (K&H); at least 3 (1161×1184); 2 (1346)
Scokirk[A]	1–2 (K&H)
Sheringham[A]	3 (K&H)
Snaith	founded for 2 (1310); 2 (c.1382); 1 or 2 (1381); 2 (1535)
Snape	founded for 12* (c.1155– K&H)
Spinney	3–4 (Greatrex); 4 (1453)
St L.'s Stamford	2–5 (C13– Foster); >2 (mid-C13); 1 (1350s); 2 (1377); 3 (1381); 2 (1440); 2 (1449)
Stavordale[A]	6 (1533– Russell)
Stone[A]	c.13 (K&H)
St B.'s Sudbury	1–2 (K&H); at least 2 (1189×1190); 3 (early C13)
Trokenholt	to be 2 or 3, as before (1293×1305)
Tynemouth	30 (1090– K&H); 18 (1379); 16 (1381); 16 (1536); 19 (1539)
Wallingford	5–6 at most (K&H); 5 (1481–2); 4 (1484–5); 4 (1525–6); 4 (1528)
Warkworth	2 (K&H); founded for 2 (C13)
Wearmouth	3–4 (K&H); 2 (mid-C13); 1 (1350s); 1 (c.1371); 2 (1379–81); 3 (c.1430); 2 (1449); 2 (1464); 2 up to 3 (1513)
Wetheral	9 (K&H); founded for 12* (1106×1112– VCH); 7 (1258); 7 (c.1293); 4, when should be 12 (1366); 4 (1379–81); 5 (1539– VCH)
Weybourne[A]	7 (Robinson)
Woodkirk[A]	3–4 (K&H)
Wormegay[A]	2 (1532)
Wymondham	founded for 20 (–1107– VCH); 36 (1260– Snape); 20 (–1399); 14 (1381); 16 (1382); 16 (1423); 15 (1447)
Yarmouth	to be 4 (1256); 3 up to 4* (1308)
Fishergate York	not >3–4 (K&H)

Only British cells which survived into the thirteenth century and beyond are shown above. Numbers are only given for priories during their lifetime as a cell of an English house. Entries in italics signify information taken from another source without verification; unsupported statements by antiquaries are not included. Entries in bold signify general estimates given by secondary authorities. A signifies Augustinian house; * signifies that the number of religious at a priory has been recorded without any indication of whether or not this total includes the prior. The numbers given do not include this notional prior, and therefore several of the entries marked with a * may well be one short. No data or estimates are known to survive for the cells of Alberbury, Bassaleg, Bentley, Canonsleigh, Deeping St James, Halywell, Kilpeck, Lamanna, Llanthony Secunda, Marsh, Mobberley, Puffin Island, Ranton and Wormley.

Appendix Four:
Dependent Priories and Shared Churches

1. Benedictine cells

Shared Church	Church of own	Chapel of own[1]
1. Aldeby*[2]	1. Alcester	1. Bedeman's Berg
2. Belvoir[3]	2. Alvecote	2. Coquet Island
3. Binham*[4]	3. Beadlow	3. Farne Island
4. Brecon*[5]	4. Colne (C12)[6]	4. Hilbre Island
5. St James' Bristol*[7]	5. Cowick (C12)[8]	5. Hoxne
6. Bromfield*[9]	6. Dover	6. Lincoln
7. Cardiff[10]	7. Ewyas Harold (C12)[11]	7. Marsh
8. Cardigan*[12]	8. St Nicholas' Exeter	8. St Leonard's Norwich
9. Cranborne*[13]	9. Finchale	9. Oxney
10. Deeping St James*[14]	10. Great Malvern*[15]	10. Redbourn

Only British priories surviving beyond 1300, when sufficient information survives to judge the status of the priory church, are included.
* signifies that the monastic church remains in use today in some form. (C12) signifies that the priory only acquired its own church at some date in the twelfth century after its foundation, and originally shared a parish church.

[1] It is not uncommon to find places of worship described as both churches and chapels. Those buildings referred to at least intermittently as chapels have been included under this heading, since even occasional use of this term implies that the place of worship was not parochial.

[2] Aldeby. The dedication of both the priory and parish church to the Virgin and the constant references in the priory accounts to repairs to the chancel of their church but not to the nave provide good evidence that the church was shared.

[3] Belvoir. A (fourteenth-century?) description of the burial place of benefactors in the priory church also mentions a burial by 'the high altar of the parish church of Belvoir': *Mon. Ang.*, III, p. 289, no. 2.

[4] Binham. Burstall, 'Monastic Agreement'.

[5] Brecon. *Mon. Ang.*, III, pp. 267–8, no. 12.

[6] Colne. *Cartularium de Colne*, nos. 1, 23, pp. 1–2, 13–14.

[7] St James' Bristol. Barrett, *History and Antiquities of Bristol*, pp. 385–6.

[8] Cowick. Yeo, *Monks of Cowick*, pp. 9–11.

[9] Bromfield. The remains of Charles Foxe's mansion built over the chancel of Bromfield parish church indicate that the building had been shared: Cranage, *Architectural Account*, p. 71.

[10] Cardiff. Rees, 'Priory of Cardiff', pp. 148–9.

[11] Ewyas Harold. Walker, *Register of the Churches*, nos 99–100, p. 39.

[12] Cardigan. Evidence from dedications and contiguous monastic remains.

[13] Cranborne. Evidence from dedications.

[14] Deeping St James. Several references to the 'parish church of St James, Deeping' survive: e.g. *CClR, 1500–1509*, no. 770 (vii), p. 292.

Footnote 15 appears on the following page

Shared Church	Church of own	Chapel of own
11. Deerhurst*[16]	11. St G.'s Hereford (C12)[17]	11. Richmond
12. Dunster*[18]	12. Holy Island	12. Trokenholt
13. Ewenny*[19]	13. Molycourt	
14. Felixstowe*[20]	14. St Ives	
15. Freiston*[21]	15. St Leonard's Stamford	
16. Goldcliff[22]	16. St Bart.'s Sudbury	
17. Hatfield Peverel*[23]		
18. Hertford[24]		
19. Horton*[25]		
20. Hurley*[26]		
21. Jarrow*[27]		
22. Kidwelly*[28]		
23. Leominster*[29]		
24. Leonard Stanley*[30]		
25. Lynn*[31]		
26. Lytham[32]		
27. Middlesbrough[33]		
28. Morville*[34]		
29. Pembroke*[35]		
30. Penwortham*[36]		

[15] Great Malvern. The priory church was bought by the town's parishioners to replace their own smaller church in the 1540s: this example illustrates the dangers of equating surviving priory churches with buildings shared with a parish.

[16] Deerhurst. VCH, Gloucestershire, VIII, pp. 34–49.

[17] St Guthlac's Hereford. Leland's Itinerary, II, p. 66; English Episcopal Acta VII, nos 19, 21, pp. 19–21.

[18] Dunster. French, 'Competing for Space'.

[19] Ewenny. Turbervill, Ewenny Priory, pp. 2, 5.

[20] Felixstowe: Although the earlier arrangements of the monks are not clear, they unquestionably shared the parish church of St Mary, Walton, after the house was relocated in the mid-fourteenth century: West, 'Excavation of Walton Priory'.

[21] Freiston. Visitations of Religious Houses, 1420–49, I, p. 38n.

[22] Goldcliff. Williams, 'Goldcliff Priory', p. 37.

[23] Hatfield Peverel. RCHME: Essex, II, pp. 122–6.

[24] Hertford. A thirteenth-century vicar was presented to the 'church of St Mary of the Monks of Hertford': Rotuli Gravesend, p. 176.

[25] Horton. RCHME: Dorset, V, pp. 34–5.

[26] Hurley. VCH, Berkshire, III, pp. 152–60.

[27] Jarrow. Piper, Jarrow, p. 6.

[28] Kidwelly. Leland's Itinerary, III, p. 51.

[29] Leominster. Reg. Cantilupo, pp. 46–8; Leland's Itinerary, IV, p. 166.

[30] Leonard's Stanley. Middleton, 'Stanley St Leonards', pp. 122–3.

[31] Lynn. Owen, Making of King's Lynn, no. 151, pp. 146–7.

[32] Lytham. VCH, Lancashire, VII, pp. 216–17.

[33] Middlesbrough. The priory church was made parochial in the 1130s after a tithe dispute with Guisborough Priory: Burton, 'Monasteries and Parish Churches', p. 49.

[34] Morville. VCH, Shropshire, II, p. 29.

[35] Pembroke. Freeman, 'Collegiate Church of Arundel', p. 253.

[36] Penwortham. Hulton believed the surviving parish church was not used by the monks,

Shared Church	Church of own	Chapel of own
31. Pilton*[37]		
32. Rumburgh*[38]		
33. St Bees*[39]		
34. Scilly[40]		
35. Snaith*[41]		
36. Tynemouth[42]		
37. Wallingford[43]		
38. Wearmouth*[44]		
39. Wetheral*[45]		
40. Wymondham*[46]		
41. Yarmouth*[47]		
42. Fishergate York[48]		
43. Kilpeck?[49]		
44. Modney?		
45. Snape?		
46. Spinney?		

but the editors of Dugdale disagreed: Hulton, *Priory of Penwortham*, p. xxxv; *Mon. Ang.* III, p. 418. Leland's comment that 'Penwardine is a paroch chirch and celle to Eovesham Abbay', and the dedication of both churches to St Mary seem to settle the matter: *Leland's Itinerary*, IV, p. 9.

[37] Pilton. *Registrum Malmesburiense*, II, cap. 304, pp. 171–2.

[38] Rumburgh. The priory paper survey indicates that the parish shared the monastic church, although the commissioners doubted, incorrectly, that Rumburgh church had parochial status. *Mon. Ang.*, III, pp. 615–16, no. 9; *Register of William Bateman*, II, p. 146.

[39] St Bees. *Register of St Bees*, p. iv.

[40] Scilly. I am grateful to Professor Nicholas Orme for information about the status of Scilly.

[41] Snaith. BL, Cotton MS Vit. E.xvi, fols 133v–135r.

[42] Tynemouth. The 1247 agreement between St Albans and the bishop of Durham permitted the bishop to make visitations 'in that part of the church of Tynemouth in which services are celebrated for the parishioners': GASA, I, pp. 390–1.

[43] Wallingford. The monks of St Albans were placed in the existing church of Holy Trinity, and a parish church of that dedication existed in Wallingford. It therefore seems likely that the monks shared their church: GASA, I, p. 56; Coxe and Turner, *Calendar of Bodleian Charters*, Berks. ch. 66, p. 18.

[44] Wearmouth. Raine, *Jarrow and Monk-Wearmouth*, p. xxv.

[45] Wetheral. There has been some uncertainty over whether the existing parish church was also used by the monks of Wetheral, but the inscriptions in the chancel soliciting prayer for two priors of Wetheral, and the dedication of both parish and priory church to the Holy Trinity, suggest that this was the case: *Register of Priory of Wetherhal*, p. xxxv.

[46] Wymondham. Harrod, 'Some Particulars'.

[47] Yarmouth. Thurlow, 'Great Yarmouth Priory and Parish Church', p. 14.

[48] All Saints' Fishergate. There are several references to the parish church of All Saints' Fishergate in the later middle ages: D. Palliser, 'Union of Parishes', pp. 88, 95.

[49] Kilpeck. See chapter 4, n. 118, for a discussion of the status of Kilpeck church.

2. Augustinian cells

Shared Church	Church of own	Chapel of own
1. Bamburgh*[50]	1. Blythburgh (C12?)[51]	1. Bentley
2. Breedon*[52]	2. Brooke	2. Halywell
3. Carham*[53]	3. Calke	3. Hirst
4. Chetwode*[54]	4. Calwich	4. Marsh Barton
5. Cockerham*[55]	5. Flitcham	5. Puffin Island
6. Hood[56]	6. Great Massingham	6. Scokirk
7. Horsley*[57]	7. Llanthony Prima	7. Wormley
8. Letheringham*[58]	8. Stavordale	
9. Ovingham*[59]	9. Wormegay	
10. St Anthony in Roseland*[60]		
11. Sheringham*[61]		
12. Weybourne*[62]		
13. Woodkirk*[63]		
14. Ratlinghope?*[64]		

[50] Bamburgh. It is sometimes stated that the canons were placed in a church dedicated to St Oswald, rather than the parish church of St Aidan. However, the sizeable chancel (equipped with crypt) of St Aidan's and a grant of property in Bamburgh to 'the canons . . . serving in the church of St Aidan of Bamburgh' suggests cohabitation: BL, Cotton MS Vesp. E.xix, fol. 120v.

[51] Blythburgh. Although the parish and priory church were undoubtedly separate in the later middle ages, Professor Harper-Bill has suggested that the canons' church of St Mary was initially a minster church: *Blythburgh Cartulary*, I, pp. 1–2.

[52] Breedon. *Archaeological Journal*, lxxi (1914), pp. 394–7.

[53] Carham. Hodgson records that the foundations of the priory buildings near to the present parish church were exposed in the mid-nineteenth century: Hodgson, 'On the Difference of Plan', p. 101.

[54] Chetwode. It is usually stated that the parish moved into the priory church, which it still uses, in c.1480. Even if the cohabitation of the building only began at this date, the church was nevertheless shared for most of the priory's existence as a cell: RCHME: *Buckinghamshire*, II, p. 85.

[55] Cockerham. VCH, *Lancashire*, II, pp. 152–3.

[56] Hood. Although not a parish church at its foundation, the parishioners of the church or chapel of Hood were ordered to attend the visitation of Archbishop Melton in November 1332: *Reg. Melton*, II, no. 411, p. 154.

[57] Horsley. The replacement of the prior of Horsley by a secular vicar there at the suppression of the priory implies that canons and parish had shared a single building: CPR, *1370–1374*, p. 126.

[58] Letheringham. Hodgson, 'On the Difference of Plan', p. 105.

[59] Ovingham. Hodgson, 'On the Difference of Plan', p. 106.

[60] St Anthony in Roseland. Trinick, *St Anthony's Church*.

[61] Sheringham. Hodgson, 'On the Difference of Plan', p. 107.

[62] Weybourne. Fairweather, 'Priory of Weybourne'.

[63] Woodkirk. Although described as the chapel of St Mary, and situated in the parish of West Ardesley on the foundation of the house, it would appear to have become parochial by the late thirteenth century: *Reg. le Romeyn*, I, no. 125, pp. 53–4; Borthwick Institute, Prob. Reg. 1, fol. 37v.

[64] Ratlinghope. The surviving parish church and the priory were both dedicated to St Margaret. The present structure is modern and no remains of the priory are known on the site.

Appendix Five:
The Dissolution of English Cells

1. Cells dissolved or becoming independent before the sixteenth century

Priory	Date of Dissolution
1. Westbury-upon-Trym	by 1112
2. Carmarthen	c.1125
3. Llanbadarn-Fawr	1136
4. Pheleley	c.1145
5. St Helen's Derby[A]	c.1160
6. Edwardstone	c.1160
7. Wickham Skeith	c.1164
8. Denney	by 1169
9. Odense (Denmark)	after 1174[1]
10. Bradwell	c.1180×1184[2]
11. Dale[A]	c.1184
12. Llandovery	c.1185
13. *Brinkburn*[A]	*before 1188*
14. Bolton[A]	1194×1195
15. Baxterwood[A]	1196
16. Mountjoy	after 1199
17. *Hackness*	*C12*[3]
18. Rhynd (Scotland)	C12
19. *Ardaneer (Ireland)*	*1205*
20. Llanthony Secunda[A]	1205
21. Alberbury[A]	c.1230
22. Lamanna	1239
23. Ranton[A]	1246×1247
24. Bassaleg	by 1252

A signifies Augustinian house. These dates are taken from Knowles and Hadcock (K&H) unless otherwise stated in a footnote. For those cells closed after 1535, the precise dates of suppression are justified, and any differences with the entries in Knowles and Hadcock indicated. Italicised entries indicate a significant measure of uncertainty. All references are to L&P, unless otherwise specified.

[1] Odense. Knowles, MO, p. 164.
[2] Bradwell. *Luffield Charters*, II, no. 546, pp. 272–3.
[3] Hackness. K&H: 1539. Hamilton Thompson has argued that if there was ever a cell at Hackness, it had been abandoned by the time Henry I's charter requesting a monastic presence there was copied into the Whitby cartulary, since this version of the deed makes no reference to the maintenance of monks at Hackness: *Whitby Cartulary*, I, no. 190, pp. 155–7; Thompson, 'Monastic Settlement at Hackness', p. 404.

Priory	Date of Dissolution
25. *Mobberley*[A]	*c.1259/1260*[4]
26. Felley[A]	1260
27. Stone[A]	1260[5]
28. Canonsleigh[A]	before 1285
29. May (Scotland)	c.1296×1298
30. Nendrum (Ireland)	before 1298
31. *Little Malvern*	*before late C13*[6]
32. Weybourne[A]	1314
33. Halywell[A]	1325
34. *Kilcommon (Ireland)*	*c.1332*
35. *Sheringham*[A]	*before 1345*
36. Calwich[A]	1349
37. Ewyas Harold	1359
38. Horsley[A]	1380
39. *Kilrush (Ireland)*	*C14*[7]
40. *Trokenholt*	*C14*
41. *Warkworth*	*C14*[8]
42. *All Saints' Fishergate , York*	*C14*[9]
43. *Ratlinghope*[A]	*C14*[10]
44. Begerin (Ireland)	1400
45. *Cockerham*[A]	*c.1400*[11]
46. *Cardiff*	*1403*[12]
47. Beadlow	1428[13]

4 Mobberley. K&H: ? Dunn, 'Priory of Mobberley', pp. 83–4.
5 Stone. K&H: +1260. See above, pp. 106–7.
6 Little Malvern. K&H: c.1537. See above, p. 104.
7 Kilrush. Gwynn & Hadcock: –1540. It appears that individual canons were sent to Ireland as proctors of Kilrush in the later middle ages: Dickinson, *Priory of Cartmel*, pp. 23–4.
8 Warkworth. K&H: C15. The priory is not mentioned in the 1379–81 poll tax records: Mackie, 'Clerical Population'.
9 All Saints' Fishergate, York. K&H: 1536. The priory is not mentioned in the tax records of 1379–81 and 1535: Mackie, 'Clerical Population', I, p. 103; *Valor*. In July 1384 it was stated that there had been no Whitby monks at the cell for the last twenty years, and there is no evidence that they were ever reinstalled: *CClR, 1381–1385*, p. 458.
10 Ratlinghope. K&H: 1538. There is no evidence of a monastic presence at this cell after 1291: *VCH, Shropshire*, II, p. 80.
11 Cockerham. K&H: 1477. Although a single canon seems to have remained at Cockerham until this date, the cell here was probably disbanded in the early fifteenth century: see above, p. 153.
12 Cardiff. K&H: 1403. Although the closure of Cardiff has traditionally been attributed to its sacking by Owen Glendower, there is no evidence for the occupation of this cell during the fourteenth century and so it might have been abandoned much earlier than 1403: Rees, 'Priory of Cardiff', p. 151.
13 Beadlow. K&H: 1435. Amundesham places the dissolution of the priory under 1435, but a contemporary St Albans chronicler dates its suppression to 1428. The Beadlow monks were certainly withdrawn in 1428 and Amundesham incorrectly assigns Abbot Whethamstede's petition to Martin V (1417–31) to 1435. Amundesham also refers to

48. Kilpeck	1428
49. Snape	1444
50. Wymondham	1449
51. Goldcliff	c.1455[14]
52. Coldingham (Scotland)	1479
53. Castleknock (Ireland)	before 1485
54. *Coquet Island*	C15[15]
55. Hood[A]	C15
56. *Scilly*	C15[16]

2. Cells dissolved, 1500–35

Priory	Date of Dissolution
1. *Bentley*[A]	*1510*[17]
2. Wallingford	14 January 1528 × 28 March 1528[18]
3. Felixstowe	9 September 1528[19]
4. Rumburgh	11 September 1528[20]
5. Dover	16 November 1535[21]
6. *Bedeman's Berg*	*before 1535*[22]
7. Chetwode[A]	*before 1535*[23]

a second supplication made to Eugenius IV (1431–7), who might perhaps have confirmed the cell's suppression in 1435 thus formally completing the process of dissolution: *Amundesham*, I, pp. 29–30, 43, 105–12.

[14] Goldcliff. K&H: 1450. The priory was granted to Eton College on 2 April 1451. However, the Eton rent rolls and Goldcliff court rolls indicate that Tewkesbury Abbey continued to hold Goldcliff until at least 1455: CPR, *1446–1452*, p. 457; Eton College Records, vol. 64.

[15] Coquet Island. K&H: 1539. The cell is not mentioned in 1535, and the last known reference to it is in 1442: K&H, p. 63.

[16] Scilly. K&H: 1538. Not mentioned in 1535 nor in the Tavistock pension list, 3 March 1539, although the prior of Cowick appears in both: XIV(i), no. 429, p. 172. The last certain reference to the priory comes in 1452, and there seems to have been only one monk at the cell in later decades: Devon Record Office, W1258 M/E35; *Reg. Morton*, II, no. 292, pp. 81–2; *Leland's Itinerary*, I, p. 318. I am very grateful to Professor Nicholas Orme for sharing his findings for Scilly Priory with me.

[17] Bentley. K&H: 1532. The cell was said to have been unoccupied for two years in 1512, which may mark the closure of the priory: VCH, *Middlesex*, IV, p. 206n.

[18] Wallingford. K&H: 1525–8. The priory was said to have been surrendered by Prior Geoffrey, 19 April 1525: IV(i), no. 1137, p. 502 (entered as 1524, but under 1525 in the calendar). However, not only does an account of the prior from 1525/6 survive (PRO, E315/272, fol. 73r), but a letter of 14 January 1528 requested the bells of the priory for the town of Basingstoke, since it was rumoured that Wolsey intended to suppress Wallingford: IV(ii), no. 3806, p. 1695. A post-dissolution inquest into priory's Oxfordshire property took place on 28 March 1528 (PRO, C/142/76/31).

[19] Felixstowe: IV(ii), no. 4755, pp. 2062–3.

[20] Rumburgh: IV(ii), no. 4755, p. 2063.

[21] Dover: IX, no. 816, p. 273.

[22] Bedeman's Berg. K&H: 1536. The priory is not mentioned in 1535 and the last indication that the cell was still in situ comes from the presence of its prior at a Colchester election of 1523: VCH, *Essex*, II, p. 94.

Footnote 23 appears on the following page

3. Cells dissolved independently of mother house, 1536–40

Priory	Date of Dissolution
1. Hurley	by 1 June 1536[24]
2. Colne	c.10 June 1536[25]
3. Brooke[A]	by 17 June 1536[26]
4. Brecon	12 August 1536[27]
5. Pilton	before 4 December 1536[28]
6. St Nicholas' Exeter	1536[29]
7. Letheringham[A]	8 February 1537[30]
8. Blythburgh[A]	12 February 1537[31]
9. Duleek[A] (Ireland)	before 4 March 1537[32]
10. Colp[A] (Ireland)	before 4 March 1537[33]
11. Redbourn	after March 1537[34]
12. Hatfield Peverel	c.16 December 1537[35]

[23] Chetwode. K&H: 1535? The minister's account for Notley records that the abbey leased out the manor of Chetwode, 'once called le priory de C.' on 24 February 1528: PRO, SC6/HenVIII/237, mem. 9v. However, the prior of Chetwode was summoned to Convocation in 1529, although this may have been a mistake: IV(iii), no. 6047, p. 2698. The Notley entry in the *Valor* mentions the 'rectory of Chitwood' but not the priory: *Valor*, IV, p. 233.

[24] Hurley. Westminster Abbey exchanged property for the suppressed priory's endowment on this date: Westlake, *Westminster Abbey*, I, p. 202.

[25] Colne. Fowler, 'Inventories of Essex Monasteries', pp. 330–5.

[26] Brooke. K&H: 1535–6. On 17 June 1536, the abbot of Kenilworth wrote to Cromwell asking for his support against the prior of Brooke, who had given up the house to the Crown: X, no. 1151, p. 483.

[27] Brecon. K&H: May 1538. The receiver's account of dissolved Welsh monasteries, 1535/6, dates the cell's suppression to 12 August 1536: PRO, LR6/152/1. Prior Robert Holden was entered in a list of pensions granted to ex-superiors, 1536/7, and Brecon's post-dissolution minister account for 1535/6 is also extant: XIII(i), no. 1520, p. 575; PRO, SC6/HenVIII/4843.

[28] Pilton. K&H: December 1539. A pension was granted to Prior John Rosse some time during the year 1536/7, and the priory leased to Richard Duke on 4 December 1536: XIII(i), no. 1520, pp. 576, 578. The first minister account for the priory appears in 1537/8, with Richard Duke named as the farmer of the 'former priory': PRO, SC6/HenVIII/594. The priory was also entered in a list of monasteries lately suppressed, made in February 1538: XIII(ii), no. 1195, p. 502.

[29] St Nicholas' Exeter. A pension was granted to Prior William Collumpton during 1536/7: XIII(i), no. 1520, p. 575.

[30] Letheringham. XII(i), no. 510, p. 239; cf. XII(i), no. 359, p. 158.

[31] Blythburgh. XII(i), no. 510, p. 239.

[32] Duleek. Gwynn & Hadcock: 1537. XI(i), no. 569, p. 264.

[33] Colp. Gwynn & Hadcock: –1540. Colp seems to have been suppressed together with Duleek: XII(ii), nos 1288, 1310(1–2), pp. 450, 461, 464–6.

[34] Redbourn. K&H: 1535. A certificate of this date includes: 'Note that heads of houses at Hertford, Redbourne and Hitchin have been sent to the Chancellor of Augmentations': PRO, SP5/1, fols 38r–43r.

[35] Hatfield Peverel. K&H: 1536. The suppression commissioners made an inventory of the priory, 8 June 1536: Fowler, 'Inventories of Essex Monasteries', pp. 395–400.

Priory	Date of Dissolution
13. *Hertford*	*by 9 February 1538*[36]
14. Binham	29 March × 20 May 1538[37]
15. St Bees	by 3 June 1538[38]
16. Wetheral	20 October 1538[39]
17. Tynemouth	12 January 1539[40]
18. Great Malvern	by 12 January 1540[41]
19. Alcester	before 27 January 1540[42]

4. Cells leased out before mother house dissolution, 1536–39

Priory	Date of Dissolution
1. St Bartholomew's Sudbury	leased 22 February 1536[43]
2. Ewenny	leased 28 February 1537[44]
3. Hoxne	leased c.1 April 1538[45]
4. Alvecote	leased 16 June 1538[46]
5. Leonard Stanley	leased 18 July 1538[47]
6. Bromfield	leased 1 August 1538[48]

However, the priory does not seem to have been suppressed at this time since Robert Blakeney was now prior, and a pension was granted to Prior Richard Stevenage of Hatfield Peverel on 16 December 1537: XIII(i), no. 1520, p. 583.

[36] Hertford. The priory was granted to Sir Anthony Denny and Joan Champernown on 9 February 1538. However, Reddan argued that the prior of Hertford's Amwell tithe suit of July 1539 implies that Hertford was dissolved with St Albans: *VCH, Herts*, IV, p. 420.

[37] Binham. K&H: 1539. The priory was entered in a list of monasteries lately suppressed, made in February 1538: XIII(ii), no. 1195, p. 502. However, Rich wrote on 29 March 1538 that he intended to suppress the priory: XIII(i), no. 625, p. 232. Prior Thomas Williams was granted a pension of £4, 20 May 1538: XIV(i), no. 1355, p. 596.

[38] St Bees. Prior Robert Paddy was granted a pension, 3 June 1538: XIV(i), no. 1355, p. 601. St Mary's York apparently remained in possession of the priory, since its property was leased by the abbey the following year: XXI(ii), no. 774, p. 439.

[39] Wetheral. XIII(ii), no. 657, pp. 251–2.

[40] Tynemouth. XIV(i), no. 59, p. 26.

[41] Great Malvern. K&H: 1539–40. Pensions were granted to the prior and eleven monks, 12 January 1540: XV, no. 51, p. 20.

[42] Alcester. K&H: 1536. A letter of the abbot of Evesham of 10 March 1537 indicates that the priory was not yet dissolved: XII(i), no. 620, p. 280. The pension list of Evesham, of 27 January 1540, includes £20 for Christopher Bradweye, 'cellarer, sometime prior of Alcester': XV, no. 118, p. 38. However, the minister account of Evesham, 1539/40, itemised the priory fully, which might indicate that Alcester was not leased out at this time: PRO, SC6/HenVIII/4047.

[43] St Bartholomew's Sudbury. K&H: 1538. *Sudbury Charters*, pp. 4–5.

[44] Ewenny. K&H: January 1540. PRO, SC6/HenVIII/1248, mem. 16v.

[45] Hoxne. XIII(i), no. 652, p. 251; cf. X, no. 1206, p. 505.

[46] Alvecote. K&H: 1536. PRO, SC6/HenVIII/7445, mem. 49r.

[47] Leonard Stanley. *VCH, Gloucestershire*, II, p. 73; PRO, E303/4, Gloucestershire no. 4.

[48] Bromfield. K&H: January 1540. XVI, no. 1500, p. 718; PRO, SC6/HenVIII/1248, mem. 16r.

Priory	Date of Dissolution
7. Calke[A]	leased before 25 October 1538[49]
8. Snaith	leased 20 December 1538[50]
9. *Marsh Barton*[A]	*leased 1539*[51]
10. *Scokirk*[A]	*leased 1539*[52]
11. Middlesbrough	leased c.1 January 1539[53]
12. Cranborne	leased 6 January 1539[54]
13. Spinney	leased 12 January 1539[55]
14. Breedon	leased 12 January 1539[56]
15. Woodkirk	leased 12 January 1539[57]
16. St James' Bristol	leased 26 January 1539[58]
17. Freiston	leased 27 January 1539[59]
18. Penwortham	leased 20 February 1539[60]
19. Jarrow	leased 11 April 1539[61]
20. Deeping St James	leased 20 May 1539[62]
21. Lincoln	leased c.14 November 1539[63]
22. *St Ives*	*leased by 22 November 1539*[64]
23. *Modney*	*leased by 22 November 1539*[65]

[49] Calke. K&H: 1538. XIV(ii), no. 47, p. 14. Calke's mother house, Repton, was suppressed on this date.
[50] Snaith. K&H: December 1539. PRO, E303/6, Yorkshire bundle 915.
[51] Marsh Barton. K&H: 1539. XV, no. 1032, p. 559. The date, rather than the lease, is uncertain.
[52] Scokirk. K&H: 1539. XIV(ii), no. 558, pp. 195–6. The date, rather than the lease, is uncertain.
[53] Middlesbrough. K&H: 1537. XVIII(i), no. 982, p. 553; cf. XIII(i), no. 1113, p. 407.
[54] Cranborne. K&H: January 1540. PRO, SC6/HenVIII/1260, mems 47v–48r. However, the pension list of Tewkesbury, 12 January 1540, included the 'prior of Cranborne': XV, no. 49, p. 19.
[55] Spinney. K&H: 1538. PRO, E315/98, fols 1v–3r.
[56] Breedon. Brown, *Robert Ferrar*, p. 65.
[57] Woodkirk. Brown, *Robert Ferrar*, p. 65.
[58] St James' Bristol. K&H: January 1540. PRO, E303/4, Gloucestershire no. 4. However, the pension list of Tewkesbury, 12 January 1540, included the 'prior of St James' Bristol': XV, no. 49, p. 19.
[59] Freiston. K&H: December 1539. PRO, SC6/HenVIII/2020, mem. 108r.
[60] Penwortham. K&H: +1535. XVIII(i), no. 100(18), p. 66; PRO, SC6/HenVIII/4047, mems 45r–45v. But cf. XIV(i), no. 1161, p. 520.
[61] Jarrow. K&H: 1536. PRO, SC6/HenVIII/708, mem. 4r.
[62] Deeping St James. K&H: December 1539. *Mon. Ang.*, IV, p. 171, no. 8.
[63] Lincoln. K&H: November 1539. XIV(ii), no. 522, p. 183.
[64] St Ives. K&H: November 1539. The Ramsey minister account of 1540/1 noted that the cell and much of its property had been leased to Lord Audley: PRO, SC6/HenVIII/7287, mems 65r–65v. The date of this lease is not recorded, but since the Ramsey pension list of 22 November 1539 included the 'late prior of St Ives', it may well have been made before the abbey's suppression: XIV(ii), no. 565, p. 197.
[65] Modney. K&H: 1536. Like St Ives, Modney had been farmed by 1540/1, but the prior receives no mention in the Ramsey pension list: PRO, SC6/HenVIII/7287, mem. 93r; XIV(ii), no. 565, p. 197. The cell was definitely in existence in 1536 (VCH, *Norfolk*, II, p. 349), and so may have been leased in the interim.

Priory	Date of Dissolution
24. Holy Island	leased before 30 December 1539[66]
25. Lytham	leased 1536×1539[67]
26. *St Guthlac's Hereford*	*leased 1536×1539[68]*

5. Cells dissolved with mother house, 1536–40

Priory	Date of Dissolution
1. Marsh (Tickhill)	1536–1537[69]
2. Wormegay[A]	16 February 1537[70]
3. *Wormley[A]*	*16 February 1537[71]*
4. *Puffin Island[A]*	*25 February × 13 June 1537[72]*
5. Ovingham[A]	26 February 1537[73]
6. Great Massingham[A]	15 January 1538[74]
7. Llanthony Prima[A]	10 March 1538[75]
8. Cardigan	c.26 June 1538[76]
9. Flitcham[A]	4 August 1538[77]
10. Dunster	27 January 1539[78]
11. *Stavordale[A]*	*12 February 1539[79]*
12. St Anthony in Roseland[A]	1 March 1539[80]
13. Cowick	3 March 1539[81]

[66] Holy Island. K&H: 1537. Raine, *North Durham*, p. 133.

[67] Lytham. K&H: +1535. Durham minister's account of 1540/1 records that the cell was farmed to Thomas Dannet by the prior and convent of Durham, but gives no date for this lease: PRO, SC6/HenVIII/708, mems 7r–7v.

[68] St Guthlac's Hereford. K&H: 1538. A list of Gloucester Abbey debtors in an Augmentations Office book includes £50 of farm rent due for St Guthlac's, from John ap Rees: Savine, *English Monasteries*, p. 215.

[69] Marsh. K&H: –1536. Suppressed with Humberston in 1536–7: XIII(ii), no. 1195, p. 502, XIII(i), no. 1520, p. 581.

[70] Wormegay. Presumably suppressed with Pentney on 16 February 1537: XII(i), no. 510, p. 239.

[71] Wormley. K&H: c.1510? In existence in c.1510, and although the *Valor* records no Thetford property in Wormley, the canons certainly continued to hold the chapel of St Laurence there down to the Dissolution: *Chapters of the Augustinian Canons*, p. 274; *Valor*, III, pp. 312–13; XIII(ii), no. 784, p. 281, XII(i), no. 510, p. 239.

[72] Puffin Island. K&H: 1536? Suppressed with Penmon, if not before: XII(i), no. 507, pp. 237–8, XII(ii), no. 191(14), p. 80.

[73] Ovingham. Presumably suppressed with Hexham: XII(i), no. 546, p. 256.

[74] Great Massingham. XIII(i), no. 85, pp. 28–9.

[75] Llanthony Prima. K&H: 1539. XIII(i), no. 482, p. 176.

[76] Cardigan. XIII(i), no. 1260, p. 464.

[77] Flitcham. XIII(ii), no. 31, p. 11.

[78] Dunster. XIV(i), no. 148, pp. 54–5.

[79] Stavordale. May well have been suppressed with Taunton: XIV(i), no. 276, p. 107.

[80] St Anthony in Roseland. K&H: 1538. The cell was leased on 29 October 1539, and so had probably survived to be suppressed with Plympton: XV, no. 1032, p. 562, XIV(i), no. 414, p. 168.

[81] Cowick. K&H: 1538. XIV(i), no. 429, p. 172.

Priory	Date of Dissolution
14. Horton	18 March 1539[82]
15. Kidwelly	18 March 1539[83]
16. Aldeby	6 April 1539[84]
17. *Lynn*	*6 April 1539[85]*
18. *St Leonard's Norwich*	*6 April 1539[86]*
19. *Yarmouth*	*6 April 1539[87]*
20. Leominster	17 × 19 September 1539[88]
21. *Molycourt*	*18 November 1539[89]*
22. *Bamburgh*A	*20 November 1539[90]*
23. *Hirst*A	*20 November 1539[91]*
24. Oxney	29 November 1539[92]
25. Richmond	29 November 1539[93]
26. Belvoir	5 December 1539[94]
27. *Pembroke*	*5 December 1539[95]*
28. *Carham*A	*8 December 1539[96]*
29. *Farne Island*	*30 December 1539[97]*
30. *Finchale*	*30 December 1539[98]*
31. *St Leonard's Stamford*	*30 December 1539[99]*

[82]   Horton. XIV(i), no. 556, p. 215.
[83]   Kidwelly. XIV(i), no. 556, p. 215.
[84]   Aldeby. K&H: 1538. XIV(i), no. 779, p. 374.
[85]   Lynn. No evidence of an earlier suppression, and no Norwich pension list is known.
[86]   St Leonard's Norwich. As above.
[87]   Yarmouth. As above.
[88]   Leominster. XV, no. 282(115), p. 116.
[89]   Molycourt. Ely was granted the cell on 10 September 1541, which suggests that Molycourt had not already been leased out like Spinney: XVI, no. 1226(12), pp. 575–6.
[90]   Bamburgh. K&H: c.1537. In February 1539, Prior Ferrar of Nostell granted the proctorship of the cell to Cromwell's nominee for life. It would appear that this grant was to a fellow canon of Nostell, rather than to a layman, and that the priory was still occupied at this time: XIV(i), no. 334, p. 130. It probably survived to be suppressed with Nostell in November 1539, therefore: XIV(ii), no. 557, p. 195.
[91]   Hirst. K&H: 1539? The cell was in operation in 1535, but no evidence about its suppression is known: *Valor*, V, p. 64.
[92]   Oxney: K&H: 1538. XIV(ii), no. 602, pp. 212–13.
[93]   Richmond: The priory was leased to Sir Roger Cholmeley, sergeant-at-law, 18 June 1540, suggesting that it had survived until the dissolution of its mother house: XVI, no. 1500, p. 720.
[94]   Belvoir. XVI, no. 1056(78), pp. 505–6.
[95]   Pembroke. The St Albans pension list of December 1539 gave no obedientiaries' titles: *Deputy Keeper's Eighth Report*, App. II, p. 39.
[96]   Carham. The cell was still in existence in May 1538, and probably survived to be suppressed with Kirkham: XIII(i), no. 1253, pp. 461–2, XIII(ii), no. 1009, p. 431.
[97]   Farne Island. K&H: 1538. No obedientiaries' titles are given in the Durham pension list of 30 December 1539: XIV(ii), no. 603, p. 213.
[98]   Finchale. K&H: 1538. As above. The priory was not farmed out in 1540/1: PRO, SC6/HenVIII/708, mem. 2r.
[99]   St Leonard's Stamford. K&H: 1538. As above. The priory had been leased to the

Priory	Date of Dissolution
32. *Wearmouth*	*30 December 1539*[100]
33. Deerhurst	12 January 1540[101]
34. Hilbre Island	20 January 1540[102]
35. Morville	24 January 1540[103]

duke of Suffolk by the time of the Durham minister account of 1540/1, however: PRO, SC6/HenVIII/708, mems 7v–8r.

[100] Wearmouth. K&H: 1536. As above. The priory was leased to Thomas Whitehead of Wearmouth, 18 May 1541: PRO, SC6/HenVIII/708, mem. 5r.

[101] Deerhurst. XV, no. 49, p. 19.

[102] Hilbre Island. K&H: –1539. XV no. 87, p. 29; *VCH, Cheshire*, III, p. 144.

[103] Morville. The cell was apparently surrendered with its mother house: *VCH, Shropshire*, II, p. 30. Although Abbot Marshall of Shrewsbury had dwelt here since 1529, this cannot be considered a lease.

Select Bibliography

Manuscripts

Cambridge, Trinity College
MS O.9.25   Belvoir Priory martyrology, C13–14

Cambridge, University Library
Add. MS 3020–1   Red book of Thorney, C14
Add. MS 3824   Tanner's Collections for Cambridge
EDC 1/B/15   Molycourt Priory charters
Ee. IV. 20   St Albans Abbey formulary, C14

Carlisle, Cumbria Record Office
D/Lons./W/St Bees 1/1   St Bees Priory account, 1516/17

Chelmsford, Essex Record Office
Probert MSS   Colne Priory accounts

Durham, Dean and Chapter Muniments
Finchale Repertory   Finchale Priory charters etc.
Loc. III: 46   Holy Island Priory, C15
Loc. IX: 10   Lytham Priory, C15
Loc. XXV: 39   Lytham Priory, C15
Loc. XXV: 135   St Leonard's Priory, Stamford, C15
Loc. XXVII   Durham Priory visitations
Loc. XXVII: 4   Holy Island Priory ordinances, mid-C14
Misc. Ch. 2645   Durham Priory visitation, c.1330
Misc. Ch. 4087   Holy Island Priory, 1376?
Misc. Ch. 7288   Durham Priory visitation, c.1329
Pontificalia (esp. 19, 28, 29)   Durham Priory visitations
Registrum II   Durham Priory register, 1312–1401
Registrum III   Durham Priory register, 1401–44
Registrum IV   Durham Priory register, 1444–86
Registrum V   Durham Priory register, 1486–1538
Registrum Parvum II   Durham Prior's register, 1407–45
Registrum Parvum III   Durham Prior's register, 1446–81
Registrum Parvum IV   Durham Prior's register, 1481–1519

Eton College
Coll/Est/Dun.1   Dunster Priory, early C15
Coll/Est/Go.71   Deerhurst Priory, 1496
Coll/Est/Tay.6   Deerhurst Priory, 1495–6
ECR 49/150   Cowick Priory, 1463
ECR 64   Goldcliff Priory documents

Exeter, Devon Record Office
W1258M/D82/1–32   Cowick Priory documents
W1258M/G4/53/1–5   Cowick Priory accounts, C15–16

Gloucester, Dean and Chapter Library
Register A   Gloucester Abbey cartulary, C14
Register C   Gloucester Abbey, 1500–14
Register D   Gloucester Abbey, 1514–28
Register E   Gloucester Abbey, 1528–38

Hereford, Herefordshire Record Office
BH 53/1   Rental of St Guthlac's Priory, Hereford,
                                    C15–16

Ipswich, Suffolk Record Office
HD 1538/265/1   Hoxne Priory cartulary, C14
HD 1538/335/1   Rumburgh Priory miscellany

Leeds, West Yorkshire Archives
NP/C1   Nostell Priory Act Book

London, British Library
Add. Chs 1340, 1347   Ewenny Priory leases, C16
Add. Ch. 19868   Brecon Priory, 1514
Add. Ch. 26263   Snape Priory, 1378
Add. Ch. 33666   St Ives Priory, 1345
Add. MS 15667   Malmesbury Abbey cartulary, C13
Add. MS 25107   Dover Priory account, 1530–1
Add. MS 33445   Ramsey Abbey accounts
Add. MSS 33448–9   Ramsey Abbey & St Ives Priory accounts
Add. MS 36872   Felley Priory cartulary, C16
Add. MS 47677   Kenilworth Priory cartulary, C16
Arundel MS 34   St Albans Abbey register, C16
Cotton MS Claud. D.xiii   Binham Priory cartulary, C14
Cotton MS Domit. A.iii   Leominster Priory cartulary, C13
Cotton MS Faust. A.iii   Westminster Abbey cartulary, C13–14
Cotton MS Faust. A.vi   Durham small register, c.1322–1406
Cotton MS Faust. C.v   Rochester Priory register, 1382–1417
Cotton MS Julius F.ix,   St Ives Priory, C15
Cotton MS Nero D.vii   *Liber Benefactorum* of St Albans Abbey
Cotton MS Tib. E.i   Redbourn Priory *Sanctilogium*
Cotton MS Tib. E.vi   St Albans Abbey register, c.1302–9
Cotton MS Titus C.viii   Wymondham Priory cartulary, C13
Cotton MS Titus C.ix   Evesham Abbey register, C15
Cotton MS Vesp. E.xix   Nostell Priory, C13
Cotton MS Vit. D.ix   St Nicholas' Priory, Exeter, cartulary,
                                   C13–14
Cotton MS Vit. E.xvi   Selby Abbey register, 1368–1407

Harley Ch. 75 A. 29	St James' Priory, Bristol, 1406
Harley MS 82	Reading Abbey register fragment, C14
Harley MS 602	Memorandum book of St Albans Abbey, C14–15
Harley MS 3586	Battle Abbey register, c.1351–1424
Harley MS 3658	Deeping St James Priory cartulary, C14
Harley MS 3763	Evesham Abbey register, C14
Harley MS 6868	St Guthlac's Priory, Hereford
Harley MS 6976	Brecon Priory cartulary, extracts
Lansdowne MS 375	St Albans Abbey, almoner's register, C14–15
Royal MS 5 F.x	Redbourn Priory *Sanctilogium*
Royal Roll 14 B.li	Belvoir Priory, late C15
Stowe MS 141	Wallingford Priory, C16

London, Lambeth Palace Library

MSS 198–198b	Peterborough Abbey consuetudinary
MS 448	*Chronica et Memoranda Eliensia*

London, Public Record Office

C142/76–77	Cardinal's Bundles
DL27/107	Ewenny Priory, 1338
DL42/8	Selby Abbey register, C14
E135/2/49	Lynn and Yarmouth Priories, c.1400
E135/2/53	Kidwelly Priory, 1536
E135/15/16	Snape Priory, 1413
E135/18/22	St Ives Priory, 1411
E135/19/67	Snape Priory, 1399
E179/35/16	Belvoir Priory, 1381
E303	Conventual Leases
E315/98	Leases of former monastic property
E315/272	St Albans Abbey documents
E315/397, 401–2	Surveys and rentals (post-dissolution)
LR6/152/1	Receiver's account of Welsh monasteries, 1536/7 (Brecon Priory)
SC6/HenVII/691	Felixstowe Priory account, 1497/8
SC6/HenVII/1696	Hertford Priory account, 1488/9
SC6/HenVIII	Ministers' Accounts (post-dissolution)
SC6/HenVIII/106	Wallingford Priory account, 1521/2
SC6/HenVIII/3402	Snape Priory account, 1515
SC11/277	Hertford Priory account, 1497/8
SP5	Suppression Papers

London, Westminster Abbey Muniments

WAM, Book i, Liber Niger	Westminster Abbey register, C15
WAM, Book xi, Westminster Domesday	Westminster Abbey register, C14
WAM 22929–22951	Great Malvern Priory documents

WAM 32340   Hurley Priory, 1536
WAM 32627–32664   Great Malvern Priory documents

Norwich, Norfolk Record Office
DCN 1/9/24   Norwich precentor's account, 1394/5
DCN 1/9/37   Norwich precentor's account, 1424/5
DCN 1/12/42   Norwich communar/pittancer's account,
                            1408/9
DCN 1/13   Norwich Priory *Status Obedientiarorum*
                            1363–1534
DCN 2/1/1–91   Lynn Priory accounts, 1370–1536
DCN 2/2/1–30   Aldeby Priory accounts, 1380–1526
DCN 2/3/1–139   St Leonard's Priory, Norwich, accounts,
                            1348–1536
DCN 2/4/1–21   Yarmouth Priory accounts, 1355–1529
DCN 2/6/1–45   Hoxne Priory accounts, 1394–1535
DCN 3/3   Yarmouth Priory inventory, c.1480
DCN 29/1   Rental of Lynn Priory, C16
DCN 35/7   St Leonard's Priory, Norwich, 1456
DCN 40/9   Norwich Priory, Register IX, early C14
DCN 40/10   Norwich Priory, Register X, C14
DCN 42/1/5   Visitation of Norwich Priory, 1304
DCN 44/1/17   Aldeby Priory lease, 1399
DCN 44/42/19   Lynn Priory lease, 1480
DCN 46/76/37   Lynn Priory lease, 1374
DCN 92/2   Visitation of Norwich Priory, 1319
Hare MS 2   Ramsey Abbey register, C15
MS 9253   Binham Priory, 1432
Reg/2/4   Register of Bishop Bateman, 1344–55
Reg/3/6   Register of Bishop Despenser, 1370–1406
Reg/4/8   Register of Bishop Wakeryng, 1416–25
Reg/5/9   Register of Bishop Alnwick, 1426–36
Reg/6/11   Register of Bishop Lyhert, 1446–72
Reg/7/12   Register of Bishop Goldwell, 1472–99

Oxford, Balliol College
MS 271   St Guthlac's, Hereford, cartulary, C14

Oxford, Bodleian Library
Gough MS Liturg. 7   Binham Priory, c.1485
Rawlinson MS, Liturg. e.6   Binham Priory, c.1485
Tanner MS 342   Norwich Priory register fragment, C14
Top. MS Suffolk d.15   St Michael's, South Elmham, charters
                            (Rumburgh Priory)

Oxford, Corpus Christi College
MSS Z/2/1/1–2   Wallingford Priory accounts, 1481–5

Windsor, St George's Chapel
I.C.1–39   Hoxne Priory accounts, early C14–1535
XV.55.75–8   Yarmouth Priory accounts, 1403–97

Worcester, Worcestershire Record Office
b716093–BA.2648/6(ii–iii)   Register of Bishop Carpenter, 1444–76

York, Borthwick Institute of Historical Research
Archbishops' Registers 17–24   Registers of Archbishops Bowet, Kempe,
                                     William Booth, Neville, Laurence Booth
                                     and Rotherham of York, 1407–1500
CP F.167   Prior of Lytham v. Abbot and Convent of
                                     Vale Royal, over Kirkham church, 1428–9

York, Minster Library
M2/6a   St Mary's York register, 1507–14

Primary Sources

Public Records
Calendar Inquisitionum Post Mortem sive Escaetarum, ed. J. Caley and J. Bayley, 4
    vols (HMSO, 1806–28)
Calendar of Charter Rolls, 6 vols (HMSO, 1903–27)
Calendar of Close Rolls, HMSO (1892–1963)
'Calendar of Deeds of Surrender', ed. J. Hunter, *Eighth Report of the Deputy Keeper
    of the Public Records* (London, 1847), Appendix II, pp. 1–51
*Calendar of Documents relating to Scotland preserved in Her Majesty's Public Record
    Office*, ed. J. Bain, 4 vols (HMSO, 1881–8)
Calendar of Fine Rolls (HMSO, 1911–63)
Calendar of Inquisitions Miscellaneous, 7 vols (HMSO, 1916–69)
Calendar of Inquisitions Post Mortem (HMSO, London, 1904–)
Calendar of Patent Rolls (HMSO, 1891–1916)
Calendar of the Letters and Papers, foreign and domestic, of the Reign of Henry
    VIII, ed. J. Brewer, J. Gairdner and R. H. Brodie, 22 vols (HMSO, 1864–1932)
Catalogue of Ancient Deeds, 6 vols (HMSO, 1916–69)
Domesday Book, ed. A. Farley and H. Ellis, 4 vols (HMSO, 1783–1816)
Foedera, Conventiones, Litterae . . ., ed. T. Rymer, 20 vols (London, 1704–35)
Proceedings and Ordinances of the Privy Council of England, ed. N. H. Nicolas, 7
    vols (HMSO, 1834–7)
Regesta Regum Anglo Normannorum 1066–1154, ed. H. W. C. Davis, C. Johnson,
    H. A. Cronne and R. H. C. Davis, 4 vols (Oxford, 1913–69)
Statutes of the Realm, 10 vols (HMSO, 1810–24)
Taxatio Ecclesiastica Angliae et Walliae auctoritate P. Nicholai IV, circa A.D. 1291
    (HMSO, 1802)
Valor Ecclesiasticus temp. Henrici VIII auctoritate regia institutus, ed. J. Caley and
    J. Hunter, 6 vols (HMSO, 1810–34)

Ecclesiastical Records

Accounts Rendered by Papal Collectors in England 1317–1378, ed. W. E. Lunt and E. B. Graves (Philadelphia, 1968)

Bath and Wells, The Register of Ralph de Shrewsbury, Bishop of, 1329–1363, ed. T. S. Holmes, 2 vols, Somerset Record Society, ix–x (1896)

Calendar of Entries in the Papal Registers relating to Great Britain and Ireland: Papal Letters, 1198–1492, 19 vols (London, 1893–1998)

Calendar of Entries in the Papal Registers relating to Great Britain and Ireland: Petitions to the Pope, I, 1342–1419 (London, 1896)

Canterbury, The Register of Henry Chichele, Archbishop of, 1414–1443, ed. E. F. Jacob and H. C. Johnson, 4 vols, C&Y Soc., xlv, xlii, xlvi–xlvii (1938–47)

Canterbury, The Register of John Morton, Archbishop of, 1486–1500, ed. C. Harper-Bill, 3 vols, C&Y Soc., lxxv, lxxviii, lxxxix (1987–2000)

Canterbury, The Register of John Pecham Archbishop of, 1279–1292, ed. F. N. Davis and D. C. Douie, 2 vols, C&Y Soc., lxiv–lxv (1908–69)

Cantuariensis, Registrum Epistolarum fratris Johannis Peckham, Archiepiscopi, ed. C. T. Martin, 3 vols, RS, lxxvii (1882–5)

Cantuariensis, Registrum Roberti Winchelsey, Archiepiscopi, AD 1294–1313, ed. R. Graham, C&Y Soc., 2 vols, li–lii (1952–6)

Carlisle, The Register of John de Halton, Bishop of, AD 1292–1324, ed. W. N. Thompson, 2 vols, C&Y Soc., xii–xiii (1913)

Chapters of the Augustinian Canons, ed. H. E. Salter, C&Y Soc., xxix (1922)

Chapters of the English Black Monks, Documents Illustrating the Activities of the General and Provincial, 1215–1540, ed. W. A. Pantin, 3 vols, Camden Society, 3rd series, xlv, xlvii, liv (1931–7)

Clementis Papae V, Regestum, 9 vols in 7 (Rome 1885–7)

Concilia Magnae Brittaniae et Hiberniae, AD 446–1716, ed. D. Wilkins, 4 vols (London, 1737)

Corpus Iuris Canonici, ed. E. Friedburg, 2 vols (Leipzig, 1879–81)

Councils and Synods with other Documents Relating to the English Church, ed. D. Whitelock et al., 2 vols in 4 parts (Oxford, 1964–81)

Coventry and Lichfield, The Register of Walter Langton, Bishop of, 1296–1321, vol. I, ed. J. B. Hughes, C&York Soc., xci (2001)

Durham Episcopal Charters 1071–1152, ed. H. S. Offler, SS, clxxix (1968)

Durham, The Register of Thomas Langley, Bishop of, 1406–1437, ed. R. L. Storey, 6 vols, SS, clxiv, clxvi, clxix–clxx, clxxvii, clxxxii (1956–70)

English Episcopal Acta II: Canterbury 1162–90, ed. C. R. Cheney and B. A. R. Jones (Oxford, 1986)

English Episcopal Acta III: Canterbury 1193–1205, ed. C. R. Cheney and E. John (Oxford, 1986)

English Episcopal Acta VI: Norwich 1070–1214, ed. C. Harper-Bill (Oxford, 1990)

English Episcopal Acta VII: Hereford 1079–1234, ed. J. Barrow (Oxford, 1993)

English Episcopal Acta XI: Exeter 1046–1184, ed. F. M. Barlow (Oxford, 1996)

English Episcopal Acta XIV: Coventry and Lichfield 1072–1159, ed. M. J. Franklin (Oxford, 1997)

English Episcopal Acta XXIV: Durham 1153–1195, ed. M. G. Snape (Oxford, 2002)

Exeter, The Register of Edmund Lacy, Bishop of, 1420–1455: Registrum Commune, ed. G. R. Dunstan, 5 vols, C&Y Soc., lx–lxiii, lxvi (1963–72)

Exeter, The Register of John de Grandisson, Bishop of, (AD 1327–1369), ed. F. C. Hingeston-Randolph, 3 vols (London and Exeter, 1894–9)

Exeter, The Register of Walter Bronescombe, Bishop of, 1258–1280, ed. O. F. Robinson, vol. I, C&Y Soc., lxxxii (1995)

Herefordensis, Registrum Johannis de Trillek, Episcopi, AD 1344–1361, ed. J. H. Parry, C&Y Soc., viii (1912)

Herefordensis, Registrum Johannis Trefnant, Episcopi, AD 1389–1404, ed. W. W. Capes, C&Y Soc., xx (1916)

Herefordensis, Registrum Ludowici de Charltone, Episcopi, AD 1361–1370, ed. J. H. Parry, C&Y Soc., xiv (1914)

Herefordensis, Registrum Ricardi de Swinfield, Episcopi, AD 1283–1317, ed. W. W. Capes, C&Y Soc., vi (1909)

Herefordensis, Registrum Roberti Mascall, Episcopi, AD 1404–1416, ed. J. H. Parry, C&Y Soc., xxi (1917)

Herefordensis, Registrum Thome de Cantilupo, Episcopi, AD 1275–1282, ed. R. G. Griffiths, C&Y Soc., ii (1907)

Herefordensis, Registrum Thome de Charlton, Episcopi, AD 1327–1344, ed. W. W. Capes, C&Y Soc., ix (1913)

Herefordensis, Registrum Thome Spofford, Episcopi, AD 1422–1448, ed. A. T. Bannister, C&Y Soc., xxiii (1919)

Herefordensis, Registrum Willelmi de Courtenay, Episcopi, AD 1370–1375, ed. W. W. Capes, C&Y Soc., xv (1914)

Lichfield, Magnum Registrum Album, ed. H. E. Savage, Staffordshire Historical Collections (1924)

[Lincoln, of] The Register of Bishop Philip Repingdon, ed. M. Archer, 3 vols, Lincoln Record Society, lvii–lviii, lxxiv (1963–82)

[Lincoln, of] The Rolls and Register of Bishop Oliver Sutton, 1280–1299, ed. R. M. T. Hill, 8 vols, Lincoln Record Society, xxxix, xliii, xlviii, lii, lx, lxiv, lxix, lxxvi (1948–86)

Lincolniensis, Diocesis, Rotuli Ricardi Gravesend, 1258–1279, ed. F. N. Davis, C. W. Foster and A. H. Thompson, C&Y Soc., xxxi (1925)

Lincolniensis, Rotuli Hugonis de Welles, episcopi, A.D. MCCIX–MCCXXXV, ed. W. P. W. Phillimore and F. N. Davis, 3 vols, C&Y Soc., i, iii–iv (1907–9)

Lincolniensis, Rotuli Roberti Grosseteste, episcopi, 1235–1253, ed. F. N. Davis, C&Y Soc., x (1913)

Londoniensis, Diocesis, Registrum Simonis de Sudbiria, AD 1362–1375, ed. R. C. Fowler, 2 vols, C&Y Soc., xxxiv, xxxviii (1927–38)

Londoniensium, Registrum Radulphi Baldock, Gilberti Segrave, Ricardi Newport, et Stephani Gravesend, Episcoporum, AD 1304–1338, ed. R. C. Fowler, C&Y Soc., vii (1911)

Norwich, The Register of William Bateman, Bishop of, 1344–1355, ed. P. E. Pobst, 2 vols, C&Y Soc., lxxxiv, xc (1996–2000)

Original Papal Documents in England and Wales from the Accession of Pope Innocent III to the Death of Pope Benedict XI (1198–1304), ed. J. E. Sayers (Oxford, 1999)

Papsturkunden in England, ed. W. Holtzmann, 3 vols (Berlin, 1930–52)

Rouen, Eudes of, The Register of, trans. S. M. Brown, ed. J. F. O'Sullivan, Records of Civilization, Sources and Studies, LXXII (New York, 1964)

Roffensis, Diocesis, Registrum Hamonis Hethe, AD 1319–1352, ed. C. Johnson, 2 vols, C&Y Soc., xlviii (1948)
Rule of St Benedict in Latin and English, The, ed. J. McCann (London, 1952)
St Davids, the Diocese of, The Episcopal Registers of, 1397 to 1518, ed. R. F. Isaacson, 3 vols, Cymmrodorion Record Series, vi (1917–20)
Salisbury, The Register of Thomas Langton, Bishop of, 1485–93, ed. D. P. Wright, C&Y Soc., lxxiv (1985)
Saresbiriensis, Diocesis, Registrum Simonis de Gandavo, AD 1297–1315, ed. C. T. Flower and M. C. B. Dawes, 2 vols, C&Y Soc., xl–xli (1934)
Visitations in the Diocese of Lincoln 1517–1531, ed. A. H. Thompson, 3 vols, Lincoln Record Society, xxxiii, xxxv, xxxvii (1940–7)
Visitations of Religious Houses in the Diocese of Lincoln, 1420–1449, ed. A. H. Thompson, 3 vols, Lincoln Record Society, vii, xiv, xxi (1914–29)
Visitations of the Diocese of Norwich AD 1492–1532, ed. A. Jessopp, Camden Society, new series, xliii (1888)
Wintoniensis, diocesis, Registrum Henrici Woodlock, AD 1305–1316, ed. A. W. Goodman, 2 vols, C&Y Soc., xix, xxx (1915–24)
Worcester, A Calendar of the Register of Henry Wakefield, Bishop of, 1375–1395, ed. W. P. Marett, Worcestershire Historical Society, new series, vii (1972)
Worcester, Episcopal Registers, Diocese of: Register of Bishop Godfrey Giffard, 1268–1301, ed. J. W. Willis Bund, 2 vols, Worcestershire Historical Society, xv (1898–1902)
York, A Calendar of the Register of Richard Scrope, Archbishop of, 1398–1405, ed. R. N. Swanson, 2 vols, Borthwick Texts and Calendars, VIII, XI (1981–5)
York, The Register of John le Romeyn, Lord Archbishop of, 1286–1296, ed. W. Brown, 2 vols, SS, cxxiii, cxxviii (1913–17)
York, The Register of Thomas Rotherham, Archbishop of, 1480–1500, vol. I, ed. E. E. Barker, C&Y Soc., lxix (1976)
York, The Register of William Greenfield, Lord Archbishop of, 1306–1315, ed. W. Brown and A. H. Thompson, 5 vols, SS, cxlv, cxlix, cli–cliii (1931–40)
York, The Register of William Melton, Archbishop of, 1317–1340, ed. R. M. T. Hill, D. B. Robinson and R. Brocklesby, 4 vols, C&Y Soc., lxx–lxxi, lxxvi, lxxxv (1977–97)

Cartularies and Collections of Charters

Abingdon Abbey, Two Cartularies of, ed. C. F. Slade and G. Lambrick, 2 vols, OHS, new series, xxxii–xxxiii (1990–2)
Bath, the Priory of St Peter at, Two Chartularies of, ed. W. Hunt, Somerset Record Society, vii (1893)
Blythburgh Priory Cartulary, ed. C. Harper-Bill, 2 parts, Suffolk Records Society, Suffolk Charters, II–III (1980–1)
Brecon, Prioratus S. Johannis Evangeliste de, Cartularium, ed. R. W. Banks, Archaeologia Cambrensis, 4th series, xiii, pp. 275–320, xiv, pp. 18–48, 137–68, 221–36, 274–311 (1882–3)
Brinkburn Priory, The Cartulary of, ed. W. Page, SS, xc (1893)
Bruton, Two Cartularies of the Augustinian Priory of, and the Cluniac Priory of Montacute in the Co. of Somerset, ed. T. S. Holmes et al., Somerset Record Society, viii (1894)
Calendar of Ancient Deeds, 6 vols (HMSO, 1890–1915)

Calendar of Charters and Rolls preserved in the Bodleian Library, ed. W. H. Turner and H. O. Coxe (Oxford, 1878)

Canonsleigh Abbey, The Cartulary of, A Calendar, ed. V. C. M. London, Devon and Cornwall Record Society, new series, viii (1965)

Chertsey Abbey Cartularies, ed. M. S. Giuseppe and H. Jenkinson, 2 vols, Surrey Record Society, xii (1933–63)

Chester, the Abbey of St Werburgh, The Cartulary or Register of, ed. J. Tait, 2 vols, Chetham Society, new series, lxxix, lxxxii (1920–3)

Christ Church, Cartulary of the Medieval Archives of, ed. N. Denholm Young, OHS, xcii (1931)

Colecestria, Monasterii Sancti Johannis Baptiste de, Cartularium, ed. S. A. Moore, 2 vols, Roxburghe Club (1897)

Colne, Prioratus de, Cartularium, ed. J. L. Fisher, Essex Archaeological Society, Occasional Publications, I (1946)

Darley Abbey, The Cartulary of, ed. R. R. Darlington, 2 vols (Kendal, 1945)

Derbyshire Charters, Descriptive Catalogue of, ed. I. H. Jeayes (London, 1906)

Dodwell, B. (ed.), 'Some Charters Relating to the Honour of Bacton', in *A Medieval Miscellany for Doris Mary Stenton*, ed. P. M. Barnes and C. F. Slade, PRS, new series, xxxvi (1960), pp. 149–66

Early Yorkshire Charters, ed. W. Farrer and C. T. Clay, 12 vols in 10, Yorkshire Archaeological Society, Record Series, Extra Series, I–X (1914–65)

'Exeter, St Nicholas, at, List of Charters in the Cartulary of', ed. J. Nichols, *Collectanea Topographica et Genealogica*, i (1834), pp. 60–5, 184–9, 250–4, 374–88

Eynsham, the Abbey of, The Cartulary of, ed. H. E. Salter, 2 vols, OHS, xlix, li (1907–8)

Finberg, H. P. R. (ed.), 'Some Early Tavistock Charters', *EHR*, lxii (1947), pp. 352–77

Glastonbury, The Great Cartulary of, ed. A. Watkin, 3 vols, Somerset Record Society, lix, lxiii–lxiv (1944–50)

Gloucester, St Peter's, A Register of the Churches of the Monastery of, ed. D. Walker, in *An Ecclesiastical Miscellany*, Publications of the Bristol and Gloucestershire Archaeological Society, Record Section, XI (1976), pp. 3–61

'Gloucester, St Peter's Abbey, Early Deeds relating to', ed. W. St Clair Baddeley, TBGAS, 2 parts, xxxvii (1914), pp. 221–34, xxxviii (1915), pp. 19–68

Gloucester, St Peter's Abbey, The Original Acta of, c.1122 to 1263, ed. R. B. Patterson, Publications of the Bristol and Gloucestershire Archaeological Society, Gloucestershire Record Series, XI (1998)

Gloucestriae, Monasterii Sancti Petri, Historia et Cartularium, ed. W. H. Hart, 3 vols, RS, xxxiii (1863–7)

Haughmond Abbey, The Cartulary of, ed. U. Rees (Cardiff, 1985)

Lancashire Pipe Rolls, The, and Early Lancashire Charters, ed. W. Farrer (Liverpool, 1902)

Llanthony Prima and Secunda, The Irish Cartularies of, ed. E. St John Brooks, Irish Manuscripts Commission (Dublin, 1953)

Luffield Priory Charters, ed. G. R. Elvey, 2 vols, Northamptonshire Record Society, xxii, xxvi (1968–73)

Malmesburiense, Registrum, ed. J. S. Brewer and C. T. Martin, 2 vols, RS, lxxii (1879–80)

Mowbray, Charters of the Honour of, 1107–1191, ed. D. E. Greenway, British Academy Records of Social and Economic History, new series, I (London, 1972)

Norwich Cathedral Priory, The Charters of, ed. B. Dodwell, 2 vols, PRS, new series, xl, xlvi (1965–80)

Norwich Cathedral Priory, The First Register of, ed. H. W. Saunders, Norfolk Record Society, xi (1939)

Rameseia, Monasterii de, Cartularium, ed. W. H. Hart and P. A. Lyons, 3 vols, RS, lxxix (1884–93)

Reading Abbey Cartularies, ed. B. R. Kemp, 2 vols, Camden Society, 4th series, xxxi, xxxiii (1986–7)

Roffense, Registrum, ed. J. Thorpe (London, 1769)

'Ronton Priory, The Chartulary of', ed. G. Wrottesley, *Staffordshire Historical Collections*, iv(i) (1883)

Round, J. H. (ed.), *Historical Manuscripts Commission: The Duke of Rutland*, IV (1905), pp. 98–173 (Belvoir Priory cartulary)

St Bees, The Register of the Priory of, ed. J. Wilson, SS, cxxvi (1915)

St Benet Holme, The Register of, 1020–1210, ed. J. R. West, 2 vols, Norfolk Record Society, ii–iii (1932)

St John Brooks, E. (ed.), 'Unpublished Charters relating to Ireland, 1177–82, from the Archives of the City of Exeter', *Proceedings of the Royal Irish Academy*, xliii (1936), pp. 313–66

Shrewsbury Abbey, The Cartulary of, ed. U. Rees, 2 vols (Aberystwyth, 1975)

'Staffordshire Chartulary, The, series I–II', ed. G. Wrottesley, *Staffordshire Historical Collections*, ii(i) (1881), pp. 178–276

'Stone Chartulary, The', ed. G. Wrottesley, *Staffordshire Historical Collections*, vi(i) (1885), pp. 1–28

Sudbury, St Bartholomew's Priory, Charters of, ed. R. Mortimer, Suffolk Records Society, Suffolk Charters, XV (1996)

Tockwith, The Chartulary of, alias Scokirk, a Cell to the Priory of Nostell, ed. G. C. Ransome, in Miscellanea III, Yorkshire Archaeological Society, Record Series, LXXX (1931), pp. 151–206

Westminster Abbey Charters 1066–c.1214, ed. E. Mason, London Record Society, xxv (1988)

Wetherhal, The Register of the Priory of, ed. J. E. Prescott, Cumberland and Westmorland Antiquarian and Archaeological Society, Extra Series, I (1897)

Whiteby, Cartularium Abbathiae de, ed. J. C. Atkinson, 2 vols, SS, lxix, lxxii (1878–9)

Worcester Cathedral Priory, The Cartulary of, ed. R. R. Darlington, PRS, new series, xxxviii (1962–3)

Chronicles, Annals and Hagiography

Abingdon, Chronicon Monasterii de, ed. J. Stevenson, 2 vols, RS, ii (1858)

Adami de Domerham: Historie de Rebus Glastoniensis, ed. T. Hearne, 2 vols (Oxford, 1727)

Adomnán of Iona, Life of St Columba, ed. R. Sharpe (London, 1995)

Annales Monastici, ed. H. R. Luard, 5 vols, RS, xxxvi (1864–9)

Battle Abbey, The Chronicle of, ed. E. Searle, Oxford Medieval Texts (Oxford, 1980)

Candidus, Hugh, The Peterborough Chronicle of, ed. C. Mellows and W. T. Mellows (Peterborough, 1941)

Dunelmensis, Historiae, Scriptores Tres, ed. J. Raine, SS, ix (1839)

Evesham, Abbatiae de, Chronicon, ad annum 1418, ed. W. D. Macray, RS, xxix (1863)

Fulman, W. (ed), *Rerum Anglicarum Scriptorum Veterum*, Tom. I (Oxford, 1684)

Geoffrey of Coldingham, Life of Bartholomew of Farne, in *Symeonis Monachi Opera Omnia*, ed. T. Arnold, 2 vols, RS, lxxv (1882–5), I, pp. 295–325

Gervase of Canterbury, The Historical Works of, ed. W. Stubbs, 2 vols, RS, lxxiii (1879–80)

Giraldi Cambrensis Opera, ed. J. S. Brewer, J. F. Dimock and G. P. Warner, 8 vols, RS, xxi (1861–91)

Glastonbury Abbey, The Chronicle of: An Edition, Translation and Study of John of Glastonbury's Cronica sive Antiquitates Glastoniensis Ecclesie, ed. J. P. Carley, 2nd edn (Woodbridge, 1985)

Goscelin of St Bertin, Miracula Sancti Ivonis, in *Chronicon Abbatiae Ramseiensis*, ed. W. D. Macray, RS, lxxxiii (1886), pp. lix–lxxxiv

Liber Eliensis, ed. E. O. Blake, Camden Society, 3rd series, xcii (1962)

Liebermann, F. (ed.), *Ungedruckte Anglo-Normannische Geschichtesquellen* (Strasbourg, 1879)

Matthaei Parisiensis, Monachi Sancti Albani, Chronica Majora, ed. H. R. Luard, 7 vols, RS, lvii (1872–83)

Oswini Regis Deirorum, Vita, in *Miscellanea Biographica*, ed. J. Raine, SS, viii (1838), pp. 1–59

Ramseiensis, Chronicon Abbatiae, ed. W. D. Macray, RS, lxxxiii (1886)

Reginaldi Monachi Dunelmensis Libellus de Admirandis Beati Cuthberti, ed. J. Raine, SS, i (1835)

Reginaldo Monacho Dunelmensis, auctore, Libellus de Vita et Miraculis Sancti Godrici, Heremitae de Finchale, ed. J. Stevenson, SS, xx (1847)

Sanctae Begae Virginis, Vita et Miracula, in Provincia Northanhimbrorum, in *The Register of the Priory of St Bees*, ed. J. Wilson, SS, cxxvi (1915), pp. 497–520

Sancti Albani, Chronica Monasterii: Annales Mon. Sancti Albani a Johanne Amundesham, monacho (1421–1440), ed. H. T. Riley, 2 vols, RS, xxviii(v) (1870–1)

Sancti Albani, Chronica Monasterii: Gesta Abbatum Mon. Sancti Albani, ed. H. T. Riley, 3 vols, RS, xxviii(iv) (1867–9)

Sancti Albani, Chronica Monasterii: Registra quorundam Abbatum Mon. Sancti Albani, qui saeculo xvme floruere, ed. H. T. Riley, 2 vols, RS, xxviii(vi) (1872–3)

Sancti Albani, Chronica Monasterii: Thomae Walsingham, Historia Anglicana, ed. H. T. Riley, 2 vols, RS, xxviii(i) (1863–4)

Sparke, J. (ed.), *Historiae Anglicanae Scriptores Varii*, 2 vols (London, 1724)

Stone, John, *The Chronicle of, monk of Christ Church 1415–1471*, ed. W. G. Searle, Cambridge Antiquarian Society, Octavo Series, XXXIV (1902)

Symeonis Monachi Opera Omnia, ed. T. Arnold, 2 vols, RS, lxxv (1882–5)

Walden Monastery, The Book of the Foundation of, ed. D. Greenway and L. Watkiss, Oxford Medieval Texts (Oxford, 1999)

William of Malmesbury, The Deeds of the Bishops of England, trans. D. Preest (Woodbridge, 2002)

William of Malmesbury, The Vita Wulfstani of, ed. R. R. Darlington, Camden Society, 3rd series, xl (1928)

William of Malmesbury's De Antiquitate Glastonie Ecclesie, an Edition, Translation and Study of, The Early History of Glastonbury, ed. J. Scott (Woodbridge, 1981)

York, St Mary's Abbey, The Chronicle of, ed. H. H. E. Craster and M. E. Thornton, SS, cxlviii (1934)

Collected Primary Sources and Other Printed Sources

Aethelwulf, De Abbatibus, ed. A. Campbell (Oxford, 1967)

Becket, Thomas, Archbishop of Canterbury, Materials for the History of, ed. J. C. Robertson and J. B. Sheppard, 7 vols, RS, lxvii (1875–85)

Bernardi, Sancti, Opera, ed. J. Leclercq, C. H. Talbot and H Rochais, 8 vols (Rome, 1957–77)

Book of Margery Kempe, ed. L. Staley, Middle English Texts Series (Kalamazoo, 1996)

Bracton, De Legibus et Consuetudinibus Angliae, ed. G. E. Woodbine, 4 vols (New Haven, 1915–42)

Bristol, The Great Red Book of, ed. E. W. W. Veale, 5 vols, Bristol Record Society Publications, ii, iv, viii, xvi, xviii (1931–53)

Canterbury College Oxford, Documents and History, ed. W. A. Pantin, 4 vols, OHS, new series, vi–viii, xxx (1947–85)

'Cardiff, The Priory of, and other Possessions of the Abbey of Tewkesbury in Glamorgan: Accounts of the Ministers for the Year 1449–1450', ed. W. Rees, *South Wales and Monmouth Record Society*, ii (1950), pp. 129–88

Catalogi veteres librorum ecclesie cathedralis Dunelmensis, ed. J. Raine, SS, vii (1838)

Chaucer, The Riverside, ed. L. D. Benson, 3rd edn (Oxford, 1987)

Coldingham, the Priory of, The Correspondence, Inventories, Account Rolls and Law Proceedings of, ed. J. Raine, SS, xii (1841)

Corpus Consuetudinum Monasticarum, I, ed. K. Hallinger (Siegburg, 1963)

Dover Priory, ed. W. P. Stoneman, Corpus of British Medieval Library Catalogues, V (London, 1999)

Dugdale, W., Monasticon Anglicanum, ed. J. Caley, H. Ellis and B. Bandinel, 6 vols (London, 1817–30)

Dunelmensis, Prioratus, Feodarium, ed. W. Greenwell, SS, lviii (1872)

Durham Annals and Documents of the Thirteenth Century, ed. F. Barlow, SS, clv (1945)

Durham, the Abbey of, Extracts from the Account Rolls of, ed. J. T. Fowler, 3 vols, SS, xcix–c, ciii (1898–1901)

English Benedictine Libraries: The Shorter Catalogues, ed. R. Sharpe, J. P. Carley, R. M. Thomson and A. G. Watson, Corpus of British Medieval Library Catalogues, IV (1996)

Final Concords of the County of Lancaster, 1196–1307, ed. W. Farrer, Lancashire and Cheshire Record Society, xxxix (1899)

'Finchale, the Priory of, Inventory of the Vestments, Books, etc of, AD 1481', ed. J. T. Fowler, *Transactions of the Architectural and Archaeological Society of Durham and Northumberland*, iv (1896), pp. 134–47

Finchale, the Priory of, The Charters of Endowment, Inventories, and Account Rolls of, ed. J. Raine, SS, vi (1837)

Gilbert Foliot, The Letters and Charters of, ed. A. Morey and C. N. L. Brooke (Cambridge, 1967)

Hexham, The Priory of, ed. J. Raine, SS, 2 vols, xliv, xlvi (1863–4)

Historiae Dunelmensis Scriptores Tres, ed. J. Raine, SS, ix (1839)

Hurley, St Mary's, in the Middle Ages, ed. F. T. Wethered (London, 1898)

'Inventories of Essex Monasteries in 1536', ed. R. C. Fowler, *Transactions of Essex Archaeological Society*, new series, ix (1906), pp. 280–92, 330–47, 380–400

Jarrow and Monk-Wearmouth, the Benedictine Houses or Cells of, The Inventories and Account Rolls of, in the County of Durham, ed. Revd J. Raine, SS, xxix (1854)

King's Lynn, The Making of: a Documentary Survey, ed. D. M. Owen, British Academy Records of Social and Economic History, new series, IX (1984)

King's Lynn, The Red Register of, ed. H. Ingleby, 2 vols (King's Lynn, 1922)

Leland, John, Collectanea de Rebus Brittanicis, ed. T. Hearne, 6 vols (London, 1770)

Leland, John, The Itinerary of, ed. L. Toulmin Smith, 5 vols (London, 1907–10)

Literae Cantuariensis, ed. J. B. Sheppard, 3 vols, RS, lxxxv (1887–9)

Llanthony by Gloucester, A Calendar of the Registers of the Priory of, 1457–1466, 1501–1525, ed. J. Rhodes, Bristol and Gloucestershire Archaeological Society, Gloucestershire Record Series, XV (2002)

Lytham, The History of the Parish of, in co. of Lancashire, ed. H. Fishwick, Chetham Society, new series, lx (1907)

Mapes, Walter, The Latin Poems commonly attributed to, ed. T. Wright, Camden Society, old series, xvi (1841)

'May, the Priory of the Isle of, Documents relating to, c.1140–1313', ed. A. A. M. Duncan, *Proceedings of the Antiquaries of Scotland*, xc (1956–7), pp. 52–80

Morton, William, The Book of, Almoner of Peterborough Monastery 1448–1467, ed. W. T. Mellows, P. I. King and C. N. L. Brooke, Northamptonshire Record Society, xvi (1954)

Paston Letters and Papers of the Fifteenth Century, ed. N. Davis, 2 vols (Oxford, 1971–6)

Penwortham, Priory of, Documents relating to the, and other Possessions in Lancashire of the Abbey of Evesham, ed. W. A. Hulton, Chetham Society, xxx (1853)

Peterborough, The White Book of. The Registers of Abbot William of Woodford, 1295–99 and Abbot Geoffrey of Crowland, 1299–1321, ed. S. Raban, Peterborough Cathedral and Northamptonshire Record Society (2001)

Salisbury, John of, The Letters of, ed. W. J. Millor, H. E. Butler and C. N. L. Brooke, 2 vols (London and Oxford, 1955–79)

St Albans Wills 1471–1500, ed. S. Flood, Hertfordshire Records Publications, ix (1993)

Select Cases in the Court of King's Bench, ed. G. O. Sayles, 3 vols, Selden Society, lv, lvii–lviii (1936–9)

Sibton Abbey Estates, The. Select Documents 1325–1509, ed. A. H. Denney, Suffolk Records Society, ii (1960)

Somerset Medieval Wills, ed. F. W. Weaver, 3 vols, Somerset Record Society, xvi, xix, xxi (1901–5)

Stonor Letters and Papers, Kingsford's, 1290–1483, ed. C. Carpenter (Cambridge, 1996)

'Tewkesbury Compotus, A', ed. F. W. P. Hicks, *TBGAS*, lv (1934), pp. 249–55

Warner, G. (ed.), *The Guthlac Roll*, Roxburghe Club (1928)

Wenlock, Walter de, Abbot of Westminster, *Documents Illustrating the Rule of, 1283–1307*, ed. B. F. Harvey, Camden Society, 4th series, ii (1965)

Worcestre, William, *Itineraries*, ed. J. H. Harvey, Oxford Medieval Texts (Oxford, 1969)

Wright, T. (ed.), *Three Chapters of Letters relating to the Suppression of Monasteries*, Camden Society, old series, xxvi (1843)

Secondary Works

Anon, 'Ecclesiastical Middlesbrough in Medieval Times', *YAJ*, xviii (1905), pp. 68–73

Atherton, I., Fernie, E., Harper-Bill, C. and Smith, H. (eds), *Norwich Cathedral: Church, City and Diocese, 1096–1996* (London, 1996)

Avril, J., 'Le statut des prieurés d'après les conciles provinciaux et les statuts synodaux (fins XIIᵉ–début XIVᵉ siècles)', in *Prieurs et prieurés dans l'occident médiéval*, ed. J.-L. Lemaître, Hautes études médiévales et modernes, lx (Geneva, 1987)

Bannister, A. T., *The History of Ewyas Harold: its Castle, Priory and Church* (Hereford, 1902)

———, 'A Note on an Obscure Episode in the History of St Guthlac's Priory, Hereford', *Transactions of the Woolhope Naturalists' Field Club*, xx (1908), pp. 20–4

Barlow, F. M., *The English Church 1066–1154* (London, 1979)

———, 'William I's Relations with Cluny', *JEH*, xxxii (1981), pp. 131–41

Barrett, W., *The History and Antiquities of the City of Bristol* (Bristol, 1789)

Barrow, G. W. S., 'Scottish Rulers and the Religious Orders 1070–1153', *TRHS*, 5th series, iii (1953), pp. 77–100

Baskerville, G., *English Monks and the Suppression of the Monasteries* (London, 1937)

Batcock, N., 'The Parish Church in Norfolk in the Eleventh and Twelfth Centuries', in *Minsters and Parish Churches. The Local Church in Transition 950–1200*, ed. J. Blair, Oxford University Committee for Archaeology, Monograph no. XVII (1988), pp. 179–90

Beeching, H. C. and James, M. R., 'The Library of the Cathedral Church of Norwich', *Norfolk Archaeology*, xix (1917), pp. 67–116

Bensly, W. T., 'St Leonard's Priory, Norwich', *Norfolk Archaeology*, xii (1895), pp. 190–228

Bethell, D., 'The Foundation of Fountains Abbey and the State of St Mary's York in 1132', *JEH*, xvii (1966), pp. 11–27

Binns, A., *Dedications of Monastic Houses in England and Wales 1066–1216* (Woodbridge, 1989)

Blair, J., 'Secular Minster Churches in Domesday Book', in *Domesday Book: A Reassessment*, ed. P. Sawyer (London, 1985), pp. 104–42

——, 'Introduction: from Minster to Parish Church' in Minsters and Parish Churches. The Local Church in Transition 950–1200, ed. J. Blair, Oxford University Committee for Archaeology, Monograph no. XVII (1988), pp. 1–19

——, 'St Frideswide's Monastery: Problems and Possibilities', Oxoniensia, liii (1988), pp. 221–58

——, 'Clerical Communities and Parochial Space: the Planning of Urban Mother Churches in the Twelfth and Thirteenth Centuries', in The Church in the Medieval Town, ed. T. R. Slater and G. Rosser (Aldershot, 1998), pp. 272–94

Blair, J. and Sharpe, R. (eds), Pastoral Care before the Parish (Leicester, 1992)

Blair, J. and Steane, J. M., 'Investigations at Cogges, Oxfordshire, 1976–81: The Priory and Parish Church', Oxoniensia, xlvii (1982), pp. 37–125

Blomefield, F., An Essay towards a Topographical History of the County of Norfolk, 11 vols (London, 1805–10)

Bond, C. J., 'Water Management in the Rural Monastery', in The Archaeology of Rural Monasteries, ed. R. Gilchrist and H. Mytum, British Archaeological Reports, British Series, CCIII (1989), pp. 83–111

——, 'Monastic Water Management in Great Britain: A Review', in Monastic Archaeology. Papers on the Study of Medieval Monasteries, ed. G. Keevill, M. Aston and T. Hall (Oxford, 2001), pp. 88–136

Bond, F., Screens and Galleries in English Churches (Oxford, 1908)

Bond, F. B., 'Medieval Screens and Rood-Lofts', Transactions of the St Paul's Ecclesiological Society, v (1905), pp. 197–220

Bonner, G., Rollason, D. and Stancliffe, C. (eds), St Cuthbert, His Cult and His Community to AD 1200 (Woodbridge, 1989)

Bowers, R., 'The Almonry Schools of the English Monasteries c.1265–1540', in Monasteries and Society in Medieval Britain, ed. B. Thompson (Stamford, 1999), pp. 177–222

Bowker, M., The Henrician Reformation. The Diocese of Lincoln under John Longland 1521–1547 (Cambridge, 1981)

Brett, M., The English Church under Henry I (Oxford, 1975)

Bridbury, A. L., 'The Farming out of Manors', EcHR, 2nd series, xxxi (1978), pp. 503–20

Brooke, C. N. L., 'The Missionary at Home: the Church in the Towns, 1000–1250', in The Mission of the Church and the Propagation of the Faith, ed. G. J. Cuming, SCH, VI (1970), pp. 59–83

——, 'The Churches of Medieval Cambridge', in History, Society and the Churches. Essays in Honour of Owen Chadwick, ed. D. Beales and G. Best (Cambridge, 1985), pp. 49–76

——, 'Monks and Canon: Some Patterns in the Religious Life of the Twelfth Century', in Monks, Hermits and the Ascetic Tradition, ed. W. J. Sheils, SCH, XII (1985), pp. 109–29

——, 'St Peter of Gloucester and St Cadog of Llancafarn', in Brooke, The Church and the Welsh Border in the Central Middle Ages (Bury St Edmunds, 1986), pp. 50–94

Brooke, C. N. L., Lovatt, R., Luscombe, D. and Sillem, A., David Knowles Remembered (Cambridge, 1991)

Brooke, C. N. L. and Smith, D. M., 'Addenda and Corrigenda to David Knowles and R. Neville Hadcock, Medieval Religious Houses, England and Wales, 2nd edn, Harlow: Longman Group Ltd, 1971', in *Monastic Research Bulletin*, vi (2000), pp. 1–37

Brown, A. D., *Popular Piety in Late Medieval England. The Diocese of Salisbury 1250–1550* (Oxford, 1995)

Brown, A. J., *Robert Ferrar: Yorkshire monk, Reformation bishop, and martyr in Wales (c.1500–1555)* (London, 1997)

Brown, D. L. and Wilson, D., 'Leominster Old Priory: Recording of Standing Buildings and Excavations 1979–80', *Archaeological Journal*, cli (1994), pp. 307–68

Bryant, J., 'Architectural Recording at St James' Priory, Bristol', *Bristol and Avon Archaeology*, xi (1993), pp. 18–34

Burgess, C., 'Late-Medieval Wills and Pious Convention: Testamentary Evidence Reconsidered', in *Profit, Piety and the Professions in Later Medieval England*, ed. M. A. Hicks (Gloucester, 1990), pp. 14–33

Burgess, C., and Wathey, A., 'Mapping the Soundscape: church music in English towns, 1450–1550', *Early Music History*, xix (2000), pp. 1–46

Burne, R. V. H., *The Monks of Chester: The History of St Werbergh's Abbey* (London, 1962)

Burrows, T., 'The Geography of Monastic Property in Medieval England: a case study of Nostell and Bridlington Priories (Yorks)', *YAJ*, lvii (1985), pp. 79–86

Burstall, E. B., 'A Monastic Agreement of the Fourteenth Century', *Norfolk Archaeology*, xxxi (1955–7), pp. 211–18

Burton, J. E., 'Monasteries and Parish Churches in Eleventh- and Twelfth-Century Yorkshire', *Northern History*, xxiii (1987), pp. 39–50

———, 'The Eremitical Tradition and the Development of Post-Conquest Religious Life in Northern England', in *Eternal Values in Medieval Life*, ed. N. Crossley-Holland, *Trivium*, xxvi (1991), pp. 18–39

———, 'The Monastic Revival in Yorkshire: Whitby and St Mary's York', in *Anglo-Norman Durham 1093–1193*, ed. D. Rollason, M. Harvey and M. Prestwich (Woodbridge, 1994), pp. 41–52

———, *Monastic and Religious Orders in Britain 1000–1300* (Cambridge, 1994)

———, *Kirkham Priory from Foundation to Dissolution*, Borthwick Paper, No. LXXXVI (1995)

———, *The Monastic Order in Yorkshire, 1069–1215* (Cambridge, 1999)

———, 'Priory and Parish: Kirkham and its Parishioners 1496–7', in *Monasteries and Society in Medieval Britain*, ed. B. Thompson (Stamford, 1999), pp. 329–47

Butcher, A. F., 'The Economy of Exeter College, 1400–1500', *Oxoniensia*, xliv (1979), pp. 38–54

Butler, C., *Benedictine Monachism. Studies in Benedictine Life and Rule* (London, 1919)

Butler, Lawrence, 'Post-Conquest Development of the Church', in *St Mary's Church, Deerhurst, Gloucestershire: Fieldwork, Excavations and Structural Analysis, 1971–1984*, ed. P. Rahtz and L. Watts (Woodbridge, 1997), pp. 183–7

Butler, Lionel, 'The Archaeology of Rural Monasteries in England and Wales', in *The Archaeology of Rural Monasteries*, ed. R. Gilchrist and H. Mytum, British Archaeological Reports, British Series, CCIII (1989)

Butler, Lionel and Given-Wilson, C., *Medieval Monasteries of Great Britain* (London, 1979)

Cambridge, E, 'The Early Church in County Durham. A Reassessment', JBAA, cxxxvii (1984), pp. 65–85

Carey Evans, M., 'The Contribution of Hoxne to the Cult of St Edmund King and Martyr in the Middle Ages and Later', Proceedings of the Suffolk Institute of Archaeology, xxxvi (1987), pp. 182–95

Carley, J. P., Glastonbury Abbey: the Holy House at the Head of the Moors Adventurous, 2nd edn (Glastonbury, 1996)

Carpenter, C., Locality and Polity. A Study of Warwickshire Landed Society, 1401–1499 (Cambridge, 1992)

Carter, E. H. (ed.), Studies in Norwich Cathedral History (Norwich, 1935)

Carus-Wilson, E., 'The Medieval Trade of the Ports of the Wash', Medieval Archaeology, vi–vii (1962–3), pp. 182–201

Cattermole, P. and Cotton, S., 'Medieval Parish Church Building in Norfolk', Norfolk Archaeology, xxxviii (1983), pp. 235–79

Cheney, C. R., 'Norwich Cathedral Priory in the Fourteenth Century', Bulletin of the John Rylands Library, xx (1936), pp. 93–120

Chew, H. M., The English Ecclesiastical Tenants-in-Chief and Knight Service (Oxford, 1932)

Chibnall, M., 'Inventories of three small Alien Priories', JBAA, 3rd series, iv (1939), pp. 141–9 (as M. Morgan)

——, 'The Abbey of Bec-Hellouin and its English Priories', JBAA, 3rd series, v (1940), pp. 33–62 (as M. Morgan)

——, 'The Suppression of the Alien Priories', History, xxvi (1941), pp. 204–12 (as M. Morgan)

——, The English Lands of the Abbey of Bec (Oxford, 1946) (as M. Morgan)

——, 'History of the Priory of St Neots', Proceedings of the Cambridgeshire Antiquarian Society, lix (1966), pp. 67–74

——, 'Monks and Pastoral Work: A Problem in Anglo-Norman History', JEH, xviii (1967), pp. 165–72

——, 'Monastic Foundations in England and Normandy, 1066–1189', in England and Normandy in the Middle Ages, ed. D. Bates and A. Curry (London, 1994), pp. 37–49

——, 'Le problème des réseaux monastiques en Angleterre', in Chibnall, Piety, Power and History in Medieval England and Normandy (Aldershot, 2000), V, pp. 341–52

Churchill, I. J., Canterbury Administration, 2 vols (London, 1933)

Clark, A., 'The Return to the Monasteries', in Monks of England. The Benedictines in England from Augustine to the Present Day, ed. D. Rees (London, 1997), pp. 213–34

Clark, J. G., 'Selling the Holy Places: Monastic Efforts to Win Back the People in Fifteenth-Century England', in Social Attitudes and Political Structures in the Fifteenth Century, ed. T. Thornton (Stroud, 2000), pp. 13–32

——, 'The Religious Orders in Pre-Reformation England', in Clark (ed.), The Religious Orders in Pre-Reformation England (Woodbridge, 2002), pp. 3–33

Clark-Maxwell, Prebendary, 'Some Letters of Confraternity', Archaeologia, 2nd series, xxv (1926), pp. 19–60

——, 'Some Further Letters of Fraternity', Archaeologia, 2nd series, xxix (1929), pp. 179–216

Collinson, P., Ramsay, N. and Sparks, M. (eds), *A History of Canterbury Cathedral* (Oxford, 1995)

Colvin, H. M., *The White Canons in England* (Oxford, 1951)

Constable, G., *Monastic Tithes from their Origins to the Twelfth Century* (Cambridge, 1964)

——, *Cluniac Studies* (London, 1980)

——, 'Monasteries, Rural Churches and the Cura Animarum in the Early Middle Ages', *Settimane di studio del centro Italiano di studi sull'alto medioevo*, xxviii (1982), pp. 349–89

Coppack, G., *English Heritage Book of Abbeys and Priories* (London, 1990)

——, 'Thornholme Priory: the Development of a Monastic Outer Court', in *The Archaeology of Rural Monasteries*, ed. R. Gilchrist and H. Mytum, British Archaeological Reports, British Series, CCIII (1989), pp. 185–222

Coulton, G. G., *Five Centuries of Religion*, 4 vols (London, 1923–50)

Cowan, I. B. and Easson, D. E. (eds), *Medieval Religious Houses: Scotland*, 2nd edn (London, 1976)

Cowdrey, H. E. J., *The Cluniacs and the Gregorian Reform* (Oxford, 1970)

Cowley, F. G., *The Monastic Order in South Wales 1066–1349* (Cardiff, 1977)

Cownie, E., 'Gloucester Abbey, 1066–1135: an Illustration of Religious Patronage in Anglo-Norman England', in *England and Normandy in the Middle Ages*, ed. D. Bates and A. Curry (London, 1994), pp. 143–58

——, 'The Normans as Patrons of English Religious Houses, 1066–1135', ANS, XVIII (1995), pp. 47–62

——, *Religious Patronage in Anglo-Norman England 1066–1135* (London, 1998)

Cramp, R., 'Excavations at the Saxon Monastic Sites of Wearmouth and Jarrow, co. Durham: an Interim Report', *Medieval Archaeology*, xiii (1969), pp. 21–66

Cranage, D. H. S., *An Architectural Account of the Churches of Shropshire*, 2 vols (Wellington, 1901)

Craster, H. H. E. (ed.), *A History of Northumberland*, 15 vols (Newcastle, 1893–1940)

——, 'The Miracles of Farne', *Archaeologia Aeliana*, 4th series, xxix (1951), pp. 93–107

——, 'The Patrimony of St Cuthbert', *EHR*, lxix (1954), pp. 177–99

Cross, C., 'Monasticism and Society in the Diocese of York 1520–1540', *TRHS*, 5th series, xxxviii (1988), pp. 131–45

——, 'Yorkshire Nunneries in the Early Tudor Period', in *The Religious Orders in Pre-Reformation England*, ed. J. G. Clark (Woodbridge, 2002), pp. 145–54

Cross, C. and Vickers, N. (eds), *Monks, Friars and Nuns in Sixteenth-Century Yorkshire*, Yorkshire Archaeological Society, Record Series, CL (1991–2)

Davies, C. S. L., 'The Pilgrimage of Grace Reconsidered', *Past and Present*, xli (1968), pp. 54–76

Davies, J. Conway, 'Ewenny Priory: Some Recently Found Records', *National Library of Wales Journal*, iii (1943–4), pp. 107–37

Davis, G. R. C., *Medieval Cartularies of Great Britain* (London, 1958)

Davison, K., 'History of Walton Priory', *Proceedings of the Suffolk Institute of Archaeology*, xxxiii (1975), pp. 141–9

Dawtry, A., 'The Last Bulwark of Anglo-Saxon Monasticism', in *Religion and National Identity*, ed. S. Mews, SCH, XVIII (1982), pp. 87–98

de Gray Birch, W. (ed.), 'Original Documents Relating to Bristol and the Neighbourhood', *JBAA*, xxxi (1875), pp. 289–305

——, *Catalogue of Seals in the Department of Manuscripts, British Museum*, 6 vols (London, 1887–1900)

de Hamel, C., 'The Dispersal of the Library of Christ Church, Canterbury, from the Fourteenth to the Sixteenth Century', in *Books and Collectors. Essays presented to Andrew Watson*, ed. J. P. Carley and C. G. C. Tite (London, 1997), pp. 263–79

Denton, J. H., *English Royal Free Chapels 1100–1300. A Constitutional Study* (Manchester, 1970)

Dickinson, J. C., *The Origins of the Austin Canons and their Introduction into England* (London, 1950)

——, 'Early Suppression of English Houses of Austin Canons', in *Medieval Studies presented to Rose Graham*, ed. V. Ruffer and A. J. Taylor (Oxford, 1950), pp. 54–77

——, *The Shrine of Our Lady of Walsingham* (Cambridge, 1956)

——, *Monastic Life in Medieval England* (London, 1961)

——, 'The Buildings of the English Austin Canons after the Dissolution of the Monasteries', *JBAA*, 3rd series, xxxi (1968), pp. 60–75

——, *The Priory of Cartmel* (Milnthorpe, 1991)

Dobson, R. B., 'Richard Bell, prior of Durham (1464–78) and bishop of Carlisle (1478–95)', *Transactions of the Cumberland and Westmorland Antiquarian and Archaeological Society*, new series, lxv (1965), pp. 182–221

——, 'The Last English Monks on Scottish Soil: Coldingham Priory 1461–78', *Scottish Historical Review*, xlvi (1967), pp. 1–25

——, *Durham Priory 1400–1450* (Cambridge, 1973)

——, 'The Religious Orders 1370–1540', in *The History of the University of Oxford, II, Late Medieval Oxford*, ed. J. I. Catto and R. Evans (Oxford, 1992), pp. 539–80

——, 'The Monks of Canterbury in the Later Middle Ages, 1220–1540', in *A History of Canterbury Cathedral*, ed. P. Collinson, N. Ramsay and M. Sparks (Oxford, 1995), pp. 69–153

Dodwell, B., 'The Monastic Community', in *Norwich Cathedral: Church, City and Diocese, 1096–1996*, ed. I. Atherton, E. Fernie, C. Harper-Bill and H. Smith (London, 1996), pp. 231–54

Douie, D. L., *Archbishop Pecham* (Oxford, 1952)

Doyle, A. I., 'The Printed Books of the Last Monks of Durham', *The Library*, 6th series, x (1988), pp. 203–19

Du Boulay, F. R. H., 'A Rentier Economy in the Later Middle Ages: the Archbishopric of Canterbury', *EcHR*, 2nd series, xvi (1963–4), pp. 427–38

Duffy, E., *The Stripping of the Altars. Traditional Religion in England c.1400–c.1580* (Yale, 1992)

Dunn, F. I., 'The Priory of Mobberley and its Charters', *Cheshire History*, viii (1981), pp. 73–88

Dyer, C., 'A Small Landowner in the Fifteenth Century', *Midland History*, i (1972), pp. 1–14

——, 'English Diet in the Later Middle Ages', in *Social Relations and Ideas*, ed. T. H. Aston et al. (Cambridge, 1983), pp. 191–216

————, *Standards of Living in the Later Middle Ages. Social Change in England c.1200–1520* (Cambridge, 1989)

————, 'The Consumer and the Market in the Later Middle Ages', *EcHR*, 2nd series, xlii (1989), pp. 305–27

————, 'Trade, Towns and the Church: Ecclesiastical Consumers and the Urban Economy of the West Midlands, 1290–1540', in *The Church in the Medieval Town*, ed. T. R. Slater and G. Rosser (Aldershot, 1998), pp. 55–75

Edgington, S. B., *The Life and Miracles of St Ivo* (St Ives, 1985)

Elkins, S. K., *Holy Women of Twelfth-Century England* (North Carolina, 1988)

Emden, A. B. (ed.), *A Biographical Register of the University of Oxford to AD 1500*, 3 vols (Oxford, 1957–9)

————, *A Biographical Register of the University of Cambridge to AD 1500* (Cambridge, 1963)

————, *A Biographical Register of the University of Oxford AD 1501–1540* (Oxford, 1974)

Evans, J., *Monastic Life at Cluny 910–1157* (Oxford, 1931)

Evans, T. A. R. and Faith, R. J., 'College Estates and University Finances 1350–1500', in *The History of the University of Oxford, II, Late Medieval Oxford*, ed. J. I. Catto and R. Evans (Oxford, 1992), pp. 635–707

Fairweather, F. H., 'The Augustinian Priory of Weybourne, Norfolk', *Norfolk Archaeology*, xxiv (1932), pp. 201–28

————, 'Colne Priory, Essex, and the Burials of the Earls of Oxford', *Archaeologia*, 2nd series, xxxvii (1938), pp. 275–95

Farmer, D. H. (ed.), *The Monk of Farne* (Baltimore, 1961)

Fernie, E., 'Binham Priory', *Archaeological Journal*, cxxxvii (1980), p. 329

Finberg, H. P. R., *Tavistock Abbey: A Study in the Social and Economic History of Devon*, 2nd edn (New York, 1969)

Finucane, R. C., *Miracles and Pilgrims. Popular Beliefs in Medieval England* (London, 1977)

Fleming, P. W., 'Charity, Faith and the Gentry of Kent, 1422–1529', in *Property and Politics: Essays in Later Medieval English History*, ed. A. J. Pollard (Gloucester 1984), pp. 36–58

Foot, S., 'Anglo-Saxon Minsters: a review of terminology', in *Pastoral Care before the Parish*, ed. J. Blair and R. Sharpe (Leicester, 1992), pp. 212–25

Fortescue, M., *The History of Calwich Abbey* (London, 1914)

Foster, M. R., 'Durham Monks at Oxford c.1286–1381: a House of Studies and its Inmates', *Oxoniensia*, lv (1990), pp. 99–114

Fowler, J., *Mediaeval Sherborne* (Dorchester, 1951)

Frampton Andrews, W., 'Sir Edward Bensted, kt', *East Hertfordshire Archaeological Society Transactions*, ii (1903), pp. 185–94

France, C. A. J., 'English Influence on Danish Monasticism', *Downside Review*, lxxviii (1960), pp. 181–91

Franklin, M. J., 'The Secular College as a Focus for Anglo-Norman Piety: St Augustine's, Daventry', in *Minsters and Parish Churches. The Local Church in Transition 950–1200*, ed. J. Blair, Oxford University Committee for Archaeology, Monograph no. XVII (1988), pp. 97–104

————, 'The Cathedral as Parish Church: the Case of Southern England', in *Church and City 1000–1500. Essays in Honour of Christopher Brooke*, ed. D. Abulafia, M. Franklin and M. Rubin (Cambridge, 1992), pp. 173–98

Fraser, C. M., *A History of Antony Bek, Bishop of Durham 1283–1301* (Oxford, 1957)

Freeman, E. A., 'The Case of the Collegiate Church of Arundel', *Archaeological Journal*, xxxvii (1880), pp. 244–70

French, K. L., 'Competing for Space: Medieval Religious Conflict in the Monastic-Parochial Church at Dunster', *Journal of Medieval and Early Modern Studies*, xxvii (1997), pp. 215–44

Galbraith, V. H., 'Monastic Foundation Charters of the Eleventh and Twelfth Centuries', *Cambridge Historical Journal*, iv (1934), pp. 205–22

———, 'Osbert, Dean of Lewes', *EHR*, lxix (1954), pp. 289–302

Gasquet, F. A., *English Monastic Life* (London, 1904)

Gaussin, P-R., *L'Europe des ordres et des congrégations*, CERCOM (St Etienne, 1984)

Gilchrist, R., *Gender and Material Culture. The Archaeology of Religious Women* (London, 1994)

———, *Contemplation and Action. The Other Monasticism* (London, 1995)

Gilchrist, R. and Mytum, H. (eds), *The Archaeology of Rural Monasteries*, British Archaeological Reports, British Series, CCIII (1989)

Gilyard-Beer, R., *Abbeys*, 2nd edn (London, 1976)

Golding, B., 'The Coming of the Cluniacs', *ANS*, III (1980), pp. 65–77

———, 'Anglo-Norman Knightly Burials', in *The Ideals and Practice of Medieval Knighthood*, ed. C. Harper-Bill and R. Harvey (Woodbridge, 1986), pp. 35–48

———, 'Gerald of Wales and the Monks', in *Thirteenth Century England*, V, ed. P. R. Coss and S. D. Lloyd (Woodbridge, 1995), pp. 53–64

Gomme, A., Jenner, M. and Little, B., *Bristol: an Architectural History* (London, 1979)

Graham, R., 'The Benedictine Priory of St Nicholas, at Exeter', *JBAA*, new series, xxxiii (1927), pp. 58–69

———, 'Four Alien Priories in Monmouthshire', *JBAA*, new series, xxxv (1929), pp. 102–21

———, *English Ecclesiastical Studies* (London, 1929)

Graham, R. and Clapham, A., 'Alberbury Priory', *Transactions of the Shropshire Archaeological Society*, 4th series, xi (1927–8), pp. 257–303

Greatrex, J. G., 'Monk Students from Norwich Cathedral Priory at Oxford and Cambridge, c.1300–1530', *EHR*, cvi (1991), pp. 555–83

———, 'The English Cathedral Priories and the Pursuit of Learning in the Later Middle Ages', *JEH*, xlv (1994), pp. 396–411

——— (ed.), *Biographical Register of the English Cathedral Priories of the Province of Canterbury, c.1066–1540* (Oxford, 1997)

Green, J. A., *The Aristocracy of Norman England* (Cambridge, 1997)

Greene, J. P., *Norton Priory* (Cambridge, 1989)

Greenwell, W. and Blair, C. H., 'Durham Seals: Catalogue of Seals at Durham', *Archaeologia Aeliana*, 3rd series, vii–xvii (1911–20)

Gribbin, J. A., *The Premonstratensian Order in Late Medieval England* (Woodbridge, 2001)

Gwyn, P., *The King's Cardinal. The Rise and Fall of Thomas Wolsey* (London, 1990)

Gwynn, A. and Hadcock, R. N. (eds), *Medieval Religious Houses: Ireland* (London, 1970)

Gwynn-Jones, D., 'Brecon Cathedral c.1093–1537: the Church of the Holy Rood', *Brycheiniog*, xxiv (1990–2), pp. 23–37

Haigh, C., *The Last Days of the Lancashire Monasteries and the Pilgrimage of Grace*, Chetham Society, 3rd series, xvii (1969)

Haigh, C. and Loades, D., 'The Fortunes of the Shrine of St Mary of Caversham', *Oxoniensia*, xlvi (1981), pp. 62–72

Haines, C. R., *Dover Priory* (Cambridge, 1930)

Hancock, F., *Dunster Church and Priory* (Taunton, 1905)

Hare, J. N., 'The Monks as Landlords: The Leasing of Monastic Demesnes in Southern England', in *The Church in Pre-Reformation Society*, ed. C. M. Barron and C. Harper-Bill (Woodbridge, 1985), pp. 82–94

Harper, J., *The Forms and Orders of Western Liturgy from the Tenth to the Eighteenth Century* (Oxford, 1991)

Harper-Bill, C., 'The Piety of the Anglo-Norman Knightly Class', *ANS*, II (1979), pp. 63–77

———, 'Bishop William Turbe and the Diocese of Norwich, 1146–1174', *ANS*, VII (1984), pp. 142–60

———, 'The Labourer is Worthy of his Hire? – Complaints about Diet in Late Medieval English Monasteries', in *The Church in Pre-Reformation Society*, ed. C. M. Barron and C. Harper-Bill (Woodbridge, 1985), pp. 95–107

———, 'The Struggle for Benefices in Twelfth-Century East Anglia', *ANS*, XI (1988), pp. 113–32

———, *The Pre-Reformation Church in England 1400–1530* (London, 1989)

Harrod, H., 'Some Particulars relating to the History of the Abbey Church of Wymondham in Norfolk', *Archaeologia*, xliii (1890), pp. 263–72

Hart, R., 'The Shrines and Pilgrimages of the County of Norfolk', *Norfolk Archaeology*, vi (1864), pp. 277–94

Hartridge, R. A. R., *A History of Vicarages in the Middle Ages* (Cambridge, 1930)

Harvey, B. F., 'The Monks of Westminster and the University of Oxford', in *The Reign of Richard II. Essays in Honour of May McKisack*, ed. F. R. H. Du Boulay and C. M. Barron (London, 1971), pp. 108–30

———, *Westminster Abbey and its Estates in the Middle Ages* (Oxford, 1977)

———, *Living and Dying in England 1100–1540: The Monastic Experience* (Oxford, 1993)

Harvey, S. P. J., 'The Extent and Profitability of Demesne Agriculture in England in the Later Eleventh Century', in *Social Relations and Ideas: Essays in Honour of R. H. Hilton*, ed. T. H. Aston et al. (Cambridge, 1983), pp. 45–72

Hatcher, J., 'The Great Slump of the Mid-Fifteenth Century', in *Progress and Problems in Medieval England. Essays in Honour of Edward Miller*, ed. R. Britnell and J. Hatcher (Cambridge, 1996), pp. 237–72

Hay, D., 'The Dissolution of the Monasteries in the Diocese of Durham', *Archaeologia Aeliana*, 4th series, xv (1938), pp. 69–114

Heal, F., *Of Prelates and Princes* (Cambridge, 1980)

Heale, M. R. V., 'Rumburgh Priory in the Later Middle Ages: Some New Evidence', *Proceedings of the Suffolk Institute of Archaeology*, xl (2001), pp. 8–23

———, 'Books and Learning in the Dependent Priories of the Monasteries of Medieval England', in *The Church and Learning in Later Medieval Society:*

Essays in Honour of R. B. Dobson, ed. C. M. Barron and J. Stratford (Donnington, 2002), pp. 64–79

――――, 'Veneration and Renovation at a small Norfolk Priory: St Leonard's, Norwich in the Later Middle Ages', *Historical Research*, lxxvi (2003), pp. 431–49

――――, 'Monastic-Parochial Churches in England and Wales, 1066–1540', *Monastic Research Bulletin*, ix (2003), pp. 1–19

――――, 'Dependent Priories and the Closure of Monasteries in Late Medieval England, 1400–1535', *EHR*, cxix (2004), pp. 1–26

――――, 'Monastic-Parochial Churches in Late Medieval England', in *The Late Medieval English Parish*, ed. E. Duffy and C. Burgess (forthcoming)

Henderson, C., *The Cornish Church Guide and Parochial History of Cornwall* (Truro, 1925)

Herbert, J., 'The Transformation of Hermitages into Augustinian Priories in Twelfth-Century England', in *Monks, Hermits and the Ascetic Tradition*, ed. W. J. Sheils, SCH, XXII (1985), pp. 131–45

Herbert, M., *Iona, Kells, and Derry. The History and Hagiography of the Monastic Familia of Columba* (Oxford, 1988)

Hill, J. W. F., *Medieval Lincoln* (Cambridge, 1948)

――――, *Tudor and Stuart Lincoln* (Cambridge, 1956)

Hill, R., *Ecclesiastical Letter-Books of the Thirteenth Century* (privately printed, no date)

――――, 'Bishop Sutton and the Institution of Heads of Religious Houses in the Diocese of Lincoln', *EHR*, lviii (1943), pp. 201–9

Hilton, R. H., *The Economic Development of some Leicestershire Estates in the 14th and 15th Centuries* (Oxford, 1947)

Hirst, S. M. and Wright, S. M., 'Bordesley Abbey Church: A Long-Term Research Excavation', in *The Archaeology of Rural Monasteries*, ed. R. Gilchrist and H. Mytum, British Archaeological Reports, British Series, CCIII (1989), pp. 295–311

Hodder, M. A., 'Excavations at Sandwell Priory and Hall 1982–8', *South Staffordshire Archaeological and Historical Society Transactions*, xxxi (1991)

Hodgson, J. F., 'On the Difference of Plan alleged to exist between Churches of Austin Canons and those of Monks; and the Frequency with which such Churches were Parochial', *Archaeological Journal*, xli (1884), pp. 374–414, xlii (1885), pp. 96–119, 215–46, 331–69, 440–68

Hoyle, R. W., 'The Origins of the Dissolution of the Monasteries', *Historical Journal*, xxxviii (1995), pp. 275–305

――――, *The Pilgrimage of Grace and the Politics of the 1530s* (Oxford, 2001)

Hunt, N., *Cluny under Saint Hugh 1049–1109* (London, 1967)

Jack, S., 'The Last Days of the Smaller Monasteries in England', *JEH*, xxi (1970), pp. 97–124

――――, 'Of Poverty and Pigstyes: the household economy of some of the smaller religious houses on the eve of the dissolution', *Parergon*, new series, i (1983), pp. 69–91

Jones, R., 'Excavations at St James' Priory, Bristol 1988–89', *Bristol and Avon Archaeology*, viii (1989), pp. 2–7

Keats-Rohan, K. S. B., 'The Devolution of the Honour of Wallingford, 1066–1148', *Oxoniensia*, liv (1989), pp. 311–18

Kemp, B. R., 'The Churches of Berkeley Hernesse', *TBGAS*, lxxxvii (1968), pp. 96–110

——, 'The Monastic Dean of Leominster', *EHR*, lxxxiii (1968), pp. 505–15

——, 'Monastic Possession of Parish Churches in England in the Twelfth Century', *JEH*, xxxi (1980), pp. 133–60

——, 'Some Aspects of the Parochia of Leominster in the Twelfth Century', in *Minsters and Parish Churches. The Local Church in Transition 950–1200*, ed. J. Blair, Oxford University Committee for Archaeology, Monograph no. XVII (1988), pp. 83–95

Ker, N. R., 'The Medieval Pressmarks of St Guthlac's Priory, Hereford, and of Roche Abbey, Yorks.', *Medium Aevum*, v (1936), pp. 47–8

——, *Medieval Libraries of Great Britain*, 2nd edn (London, 1964); *Supplement*, ed. A. G. Watson (London, 1987)

Kerr, B., *Religious Life for Women c.1100–c.1350: Fontevraud in England* (Oxford, 1999)

Kershaw, I., *Bolton Priory. The Economy of a Northern Monastery 1286–1325* (Oxford, 1973)

King, E., *Peterborough Abbey 1086–1310: A Study in the Land Market* (Cambridge, 1973)

King, J. F., 'The Parish Church at Kilpeck Reassessed', in *Medieval Art, Architecture and Archaeology at Hereford*, ed. D. Whitehead, British Archaeological Association Conference Transactions, XV (1995), pp. 82–93

Knowles, D., *The Religious Orders in England*, 3 vols (Cambridge, 1948–59)

——, 'The Case of St Albans Abbey in 1490', *JEH*, iii (1952), pp. 144–58

——, *The Monastic Order in England: A History of its Development from the Times of St Dunstan to the Fourth Lateran Council, 940–1216*, 2nd edn (Cambridge, 1963)

——, Review of Matthew, *Norman Monasteries*, in *JEH*, xiv (1963), pp. 93–4

——, *The Historian and Character and Other Essays* (Cambridge, 1964)

——, *From Pachomius to Ignatius. A Study in the Constitutional History of the Religious Orders* (Oxford, 1966)

Knowles, D. and St Joseph, J. K. S., *Monastic Sites from the Air* (Cambridge, 1952)

Knowles, D. and Hadcock, R. N. (eds), *Medieval Religious Houses: England and Wales*, 2nd edn (London, 1971)

Knowles, D., Brooke, C. N. L. and London, V. C. M. (eds), *The Heads of Religious Houses: England and Wales 940–1216*, 2nd edn (Cambridge, 2001)

Ladeuze, P., *Etude sur le cénobitisme Pakhomien pendant le ive siècle et la première moitié du ve* (Louvain, 1898)

Lambrick, G., 'Abingdon Abbey Administration', *JEH*, xvii (1966), pp. 159–83

Langston, J. N., 'Priors of Lanthony by Gloucester', *TBGAS*, lxiii (1942)

Lee, P., *Nunneries, Learning and Spirituality in Late Medieval English Society. The Dominican Priory of Dartford* (York, 2001)

Lemaître, J-L., 'La mort et la commémoration des défunts dans les prieurés', in *Prieurs et prieurés dans l'occident médiéval*, ed. J.-L. Lemaître, Hautes études médiévales et modernes, lx (Geneva, 1987), pp. 181–90

Lennard, R. V., *Rural England 1086–1135: A Study of Social and Agrarian Conditions* (Oxford, 1959)

Logan, F. D., *Runaway Religious in Medieval England, c.1240–1540* (Cambridge, 1996)

Lomas, R. A., 'The Priory of Durham and its Demesne in the Fourteenth and Fifteenth Centuries', *EcHR*, 2nd series, xxxi (1978), pp. 339–53

———, 'A Northern Farm at the End of the Middle Ages: Elvethall Manor, Durham, 1443/4–1513/14', *Northern History*, xviii (1982), pp. 26–53

———, *North-East England in the Middle Ages* (Edinburgh, 1992)

Mackean, W. H., *Christian Monasticism in Egypt to the Close of the Fourth Century* (London, 1920)

Mahany, C. M., 'St Leonard's Priory, Stamford', *South Lincolnshire Archaeology*, i (1977), pp. 17–22

Malden, H. E., 'The Possession of Cardigan Priory by Chertsey Abbey (a study in some medieval forgeries)', *TRHS*, 3rd series, v (1911), pp. 141–56

Mann, J., *Chaucer and Medieval Estates Satire* (Cambridge, 1973)

Martin-Jones, S., *Wymondham and its Abbey*, 6th edn (Wymondham, 1932)

Martindale, J., 'Monasteries and Castles: the Priories of Saint-Florent de Saumur in England after 1066', in *England in the Eleventh Century*, ed. C. Hicks (Stamford, 1992), pp. 135–56

Mason, E., *Westminster Abbey and its People, c.1050–c.1216* (Woodbridge, 1996)

Mate, M., 'The Indebtedness of Canterbury Cathedral Priory 1215–95', *EcHR*, 2nd series, xxvi (1973), pp. 183–97

Matthew, D., *The Norman Monasteries and their English Possessions* (Oxford, 1962)

Maxwell-Lyte, H. C., *A History of Dunster and of the Families of Mohun and Luttrell*, 2 vols (London, 1909)

McHardy, A. K., 'Clerical Taxation in Fifteenth-Century England: the Clergy as Agents of the Crown', in *The Church, Politics and Patronage in the Fifteenth Century*, ed. R. B. Dobson (Gloucester, 1984), pp. 168–92

McIntire W. T., 'A Note on Grey Abbey and other Religious Foundations on Strangford Lough affiliated to the Abbeys of Cumberland', *Transactions of the Cumberland and Westmorland Antiquarian and Archaeological Society*, new series, xli (1941), pp. 161–73

Middleton, J. H., 'Stanley St Leonards: The College of Canons and the Collegiate Church', *TBGAS*, v (1880–1), pp. 119–32

Middleton-Stewart, J., 'The Provision of Books for Church Use in the Deanery of Dunwich, 1370–1547', *Proceedings of the Suffolk Institute of Archaeology*, xxxviii (1996), pp. 149–63

Miles, H. and T., 'Pilton, North Devon. Excavations within a Medieval Village', *Devon Archaeological Society Proceedings*, xxxiii (1975), pp. 267–95

Miller, E., 'England in the Twelfth and Thirteenth Centuries: An Economic Contrast', *EcHR*, 2nd series, xxiv (1971), pp. 1–14

——— (ed.), *The Agrarian History of England and Wales, III, 1348–1500* (Cambridge, 1991)

Moir, A., *Bromfield Priory and Church* (Chester, 1947)

Moorman, J. R. H., *Church Life in England in the Thirteenth Century* (Cambridge, 1945)

Morant, A. W., 'Notices of the Church of St Nicholas, Great Yarmouth', *Norfolk Archaeology*, vii (1872), pp. 215–48

Morey, A., *David Knowles. A Memoir* (London, 1979)

Morey, A., and Brooke, C. N. L., *Gilbert Foliot and his Letters* (Cambridge, 1965)

Morris, R., *Churches in the Landscape* (London, 1989)

Mountain, J., 'Nunnery Finances in the Early Fifteenth Century', in *Monastic Studies II: The Continuity of Tradition*, ed. J. Loades (Bangor, 1991), pp. 263–72

New, C. W., *History of the Alien Priories in England to the Confiscation of Henry V* (Chicago, 1916)

Newcome, P., *The History of the Abbey of St Albans* (London, 1795)

Newman, C. M., 'Employment on the Priory of Durham Estates, 1494–1519: the Priory as an Employer', *Northern History*, xxxvi (2000), pp. 43–58

Nichols, J., *The History and Antiquities of the County of Leicester*, 4 vols (London, 1795–1811)

Nilson, B. J., *Cathedral Shrines of Medieval England* (Woodbridge, 1998)

Oliva, M., 'Aristocracy or Meritocracy? Office-Holding Patterns in Late Medieval English Nunneries', in *Women in the Church*, ed. W. H. Sheils and D. Wood, SCH, XXVI (1990), pp. 197–208

——, *The Convent and the Community in Late Medieval England. Female Monasteries in the Diocese of Norwich, 1350–1540* (Woodbridge, 1998)

——, 'Patterns of Patronage to Female Monasteries in the Late Middle Ages', in *The Religious Orders in Pre-Reformation England*, ed. J. G. Clark (Woodbridge, 2002), pp. 155–62

Oliver, G., *Monasticon Diocesis Exoniensis* (Exeter, 1846)

Olson, L., *Early Monasteries in Cornwall* (Woodbridge, 1989)

Orme, N. I., 'Saint Walter of Cowick', *Analecta Bollandiana*, cviii (1990), pp. 387–93

——, 'Bishop Grandisson and Popular Religion', *Reports and Transactions of the Devonshire Association*, cxxiv (1992), pp. 107–18

Owen, D. M., 'Bishop's Lynn: the First Century of a New Town?', ANS, II (1979), pp. 141–53

Padel, O. J., 'Glastonbury's Cornish Connections', in *The Archaeology and History of Glastonbury Abbey*, ed. L. Abrams and J. P. Carley (Woodbridge, 1991), pp. 245–56

Page, F. M., *The Estates of Crowland Abbey: A Study in Manorial Organisation* (Cambridge, 1934)

Palliser, D. M., 'The Unions of Parishes at York, 1547–1586', YAJ, xlvi (1974), pp. 87–102

——, 'Urban Decay Revisited', in *Towns and Townspeople in the Fifteenth Century*, ed. J. A. F. Thomson (Gloucester, 1988), pp. 1–21

Pantin, W. A., 'English Monastic Letter-Books', in *Historical Essays in Honour of James Tait*, ed. J. G. Edwards, V. H. Galbraith and E. F. Jacob (Manchester, 1933), pp. 201–22

——, 'The Monk-Solitary of Farne, a Fourteenth-Century Mystic', EHR, lix (1944), pp. 162–86

Parker. V., *The Making of King's Lynn* (London, 1971)

Parry, H. L. and Brakspear, H., *St Nicholas Priory, Exeter*, revised by J. Youings (Exeter, 1960)

Pearce, E. H., *The Monks of Westminster* (Cambridge, 1916)

Pearsall, D., ' "If heaven be on this earth, it is in cloister or in school": the Monastic Ideal in Later Medieval English Literature', in *Pragmatic Utopias*.

Ideals and Communities, 1200–1630, ed. R. Horrox and S. Rees Jones (Cambridge, 2001), pp. 11–25

Peers, C. R., 'Finchale Priory', *Archaeologia Aeliana*, 4th series, iv (1927), pp. 193–220

Pevsner, N. et al., *The Buildings of England* (Harmondsworth, 1951–)

Picken, W. M. M., 'Light on Lamanna', *Devon and Cornwall Notes and Queries*, xxxv (1985), pp. 281–5

Piper, A. J., 'The Durham Monks at Wearmouth', *Wearmouth Historical Pamphlet*, no. ix (1973)

——, 'The Libraries of the Monks of Durham', in *Medieval Scribes, Manuscripts and Libraries. Essays Presented to N. R. Ker*, ed. M. B. Parkes and A. G. Watson (London, 1978), pp. 213–49

——, 'St Leonard's Priory, Stamford', *The Stamford Historian*, 2 parts, no. v (1980), pp. 5–25, no. vi, 1982, pp. 1–23

——, *The Durham Monks at Jarrow*, Jarrow Lecture (1986)

——, 'The First Generations of Durham Monks and the Cult of St Cuthbert', in *St Cuthbert, His Cult and His Community to AD 1200*, ed. G. Bonner, D. Rollason and C. Stancliffe (Woodbridge, 1989), pp. 437–46

——, 'The Monks of Durham and Patterns of Activity in Old Age', in *The Church and Learning in Later Medieval Society: Essays in Honour of R. B. Dobson*, ed. C. M. Barron and J. Stratford (Donnington, 2002), pp. 51–63

Platt, C., *The Monastic Grange in Medieval England* (London, 1969)

——, *The Abbeys and Priories of Medieval England* (London, 1984)

Pollard, A. J., 'Estate Management in the Later Middle Ages: The Talbots and Whitchurch, 1383–1525', *EcHR*, 2nd series, xxv (1972), pp. 553–66

——, 'The North-Eastern Economy and the Agrarian Crisis of 1438–1440', *Northern History*, xxv (1989), pp. 88–105

Postan, M. M., *The Medieval Economy and Society* (Harmondsworth, 1975)

——, 'A Note on the Farming Out of Manors', *EcHR*, 2nd series, xxxi (1978), pp. 521–5

Potter, J., 'The Benefactors of Bec and the Politics of Priories', ANS, XXI (1999), pp. 175–92

Power, E., *Medieval English Nunneries c.1275 to 1535* (Cambridge, 1922)

Prescott, J. E., 'Notes on the Manuscript Register of Wetherhal, recently restored to the Dean and Chapter of Carlisle', *Transactions of the Cumberland and Westmorland Antiquarian and Archaeological Society*, xv (1899), pp. 285–7

Raban, S., *The Estates of Thorney and Crowland: A Study in Medieval Monastic Land Tenure*, University of Cambridge Department of Land Economy, Occasional Paper no. VII (1977)

——, *Mortmain Legislation and the English Church 1279–1500* (Cambridge, 1982)

Raine, J., *The History and Antiquities of North Durham* (London, 1852)

Reid, R. R., *The King's Council in the North* (London, 1921)

Richmond, C., *John Hopton. A Fifteenth-Century Suffolk Gentleman* (Cambridge, 1981)

Robinson, D. M., *The Geography of Augustinian Settlement in Medieval England and Wales*, British Archaeological Reports, British Series, LXXX (1980)

Robinson, J. A., *Gilbert Crispin Abbot of Westminster: A Study of the Abbey under Norman Rule* (Cambridge, 1911)

Rollason, D., 'Symeon of Durham and the Community of Durham in the Eleventh Century', in *England in the Eleventh Century*, ed. C. Hicks (Stamford, 1992), pp. 183–98

————, 'Monasteries and Society in Early Medieval Northumbria', in *Monasteries and Society in Medieval Britain*, ed. B. Thompson (Stamford, 1999), pp. 59–74

Rollason, D., Harvey, M. and Prestwich, M. (eds), *Anglo-Norman Durham 1093–1193* (Woodbridge, 1994)

Rosenthal, J. T., *The Purchase of Paradise* (London, 1972)

Rosser, G., 'The Cure of Souls in English Towns before 1000', in *Pastoral Care before the Parish*, ed. J. Blair and R. Sharpe (Leicester, 1992), pp. 267–84

Rouse, E. C., 'Bradwell Abbey and the Chapel of St Mary', *Milton Keynes Journal*, ii (1973), pp. 34–8

Royal Commission on Historical Monuments (England): Essex, II (London, 1921)

Royal Commission on Historical Monuments (England): Dorset, V (London, 1975)

Russell, J. C., 'The Clerical Population of Medieval England', *Traditio*, ii (1944), pp. 177–212

Ryan, J., *Irish Monasticism. Origins and Early Development* (Dublin, 1931)

St John Brooks, E., '14th Century Monastic Estates in Meath. The Llanthony Cells of Duleek and Colp', *Journal of the Royal Society of Antiquaries of Ireland*, lxxxiii (1953), pp. 140–9

————, 'Irish Daughter Houses of Glastonbury', *Proceedings of the Royal Irish Academy*, lvi (1953–4), pp. 287–95

St John Hope, W., 'Quire Screens in English Churches, with special reference to the Twelfth-Century Quire Screen formerly in the Cathedral Church of Ely', *Archaeologia*, 2nd series, xviii (1917), pp. 43–110

Saltman, A., *Theobald Archbishop of Canterbury* (London, 1956)

Saltmarsh, J., 'A College Home-Farm in the Fifteenth Century', *Economic History*, iii (1936), pp. 155–72

Saul, A., 'English Towns in the Late Middle Ages: the Case of Great Yarmouth', *Journal of Medieval History*, viii (1982), pp. 75–88

Saul, N., 'The Religious Sympathies of the Gentry in Gloucestershire, 1200–1500', *TBGAS*, xcviii (1980), pp. 99–112

Saunders, H. W., *An Introduction to the Obedientiary and Manor Rolls of Norwich Cathedral Priory* (Norwich, 1930)

Savine, A., *English Monasteries on the Eve of the Dissolution*, Oxford Studies in Social and Legal History (Oxford, 1909)

Sayers, J. E., 'Papal Privileges for St Albans Abbey and its Dependencies', in *The Study of Medieval Records: Essays in Honour of Kathleen Major*, ed. D. A. Bullough and R. L. Storey (Oxford, 1971), pp. 57–84

————, *Papal Judges Delegate in the Province of Canterbury 1198–1254* (Oxford, 1971)

Scarisbrick, J. J., *The Reformation and the English People* (Oxford, 1984)

Serjeantson, R. M., and Longden, H. I., 'The Parish Churches and Religious Houses of Northamptonshire: their Dedications, Altars, Images and Lights', *Archaeological Journal*, lxx (1913), pp. 217–452

Shinners, J. R., 'The Veneration of Saints at Norwich Cathedral in the Fourteenth Century', *Norfolk Archaeology*, xl (1987–9), pp. 133–44

Shoesmith, R., 'St Guthlac's Priory, Hereford', *Transactions of the Woolhope Naturalists' Field Club*, xliv (1984), pp. 321–57

——— (ed.), 'Excavations at Kilpeck, Herefordshire', *Transactions of the Woolhope Naturalists' Field Club*, xlvii (1992), pp. 162–209

Smith, D. M. and London, V. C. M. (eds), *The Heads of Religious Houses. England and Wales, II, 1216–1377* (Cambridge, 2001)

Smith, R. A. L., *Canterbury Cathedral Priory* (Cambridge, 1969)

Snape, R. H., *English Monastic Finances in the Later Middle Ages* (Cambridge, 1926)

Stenton, F. M., 'Medeshamstede and its Colonies', in *Historical Essays in Honour of James Tait*, ed. J. G. Edwards, V. H. Galbraith and E. F. Jacob (Manchester, 1933), pp. 313–26

———, *Anglo-Saxon England*, 3rd edn (Oxford, 1971)

Stocker, D., 'Recent Work at Monks' Abbey, Lincoln', *Lincolnshire History and Archaeology*, xix (1984), pp. 103–5

Storey, R. L., (ed.), 'Clergy and Common Law in the reign of Henry IV' in *Medieval Legal Records*, ed. R. F. Hunnisett and J. B. Post (London, 1978), pp. 342–408

———, 'Papal Provisions to English Monasteries', *Nottingham Medieval Studies*, xxxv (1991), pp. 77–91

Styles, D., 'The Early History of Alcester Abbey', *Transactions of the Birmingham Archaeological Society*, lxiv (1941–2), pp. 20–38

Sumption, J., *Pilgrimage. An Image of Medieval Religion* (London, 1975)

Swanson, R. N., 'Episcopal Income from Spiritualities in the Diocese of Exeter in the Early Sixteenth Century', *JEH*, xxxix (1988), pp. 520–30

———, 'Standards of Livings: Parochial Revenues in Pre-Reformation England', in *Religious Belief and Ecclesiastical Careers in Late Medieval England*, ed. C. Harper-Bill (Woodbridge, 1991), pp. 151–96

———, 'Urban Rectories and Urban Fortunes in Late Medieval England: the Evidence from Bishop's Lynn', in *The Church in the Medieval Town*, ed. T. R. Slater and G. Rosser (Aldershot, 1998), pp. 100–30

———, 'Mendicants and Confraternity in Medieval England', in *The Religious Orders in Pre-Reformation England*, ed. J. G. Clark (Woodbridge, 2002), pp. 121–41

Swynnerton, C., 'The Priory of St Leonard of Stanley, co. Gloucester, in the light of recent discoveries documentary and structural', *Archaeologia*, 2nd series, xxi (1921), pp. 199–226

Tanner, N. P., *The Church in Late Medieval Norwich*, Pontifical Institute of Medieval Studies, Studies and Texts LXVI (Toronto, 1984)

Tanner, T., *Notitia Monastica*, ed. J. Nasmith, 2nd edn (Cambridge, 1787)

Taylor, A. J., 'The Alien Priory of Minster Lovell', *Oxoniensia*, ii (1937), pp. 103–17

Taylor, P., 'The Early St Albans Endowment and its Chroniclers', *Historical Research*, lxviii (1995), pp. 119–42

Thacker, A., 'Monks, Preaching and Pastoral Care in early Anglo-Saxon England', in *Pastoral Care before the Parish*, ed. J. Blair and R. Sharpe (Leicester, 1992), pp. 137–70

Thomas, C., 'Cellular Meanings, Monastic Beginnings', *Emania*, xiii (1995), pp. 51–68

Thompson, A. H., 'The Monastic Settlement at Hackness and its relation to the Abbey of Whitby', *YAJ*, xxvii (1924), pp. 388–405

———, *History and Architectural Description of the Priory of St Mary, Bolton-in-Wharfedale*, Thoresby Society, xxx (1928)

———, *Lindisfarne Priory* (London, 1949)

Thompson, B. J., 'The Statute of Carlisle, 1307, and the Alien Priories', *JEH*, xli (1990), pp. 543–83

———, 'From "Alms" to "Spiritual Services": the Function and Status of Monastic Property in Medieval England', in *Monastic Studies II: The Continuity of Tradition*, ed. J. Loades (Bangor, 1991), pp. 227–61

———, 'Habendum et Tenendum: Lay and Ecclesiastical Attitudes to the Property of the Church', in *Religious Belief and Ecclesiastical Careers in Late Medieval England*, ed. C. Harper-Bill (Woodbridge, 1991), pp. 197–238

———, 'Free Alms Tenure in the Twelfth Century', *ANS*, XVI (1993), pp. 221–43

———, 'Monasteries and their Patrons at Foundation and Dissolution', *TRHS*, 6th series, iv (1994), pp. 103–26

———, 'The Laity, the Alien Priories, and the Redistribution of Ecclesiastical Property', in *England in the Fifteenth Century*, ed. N. Rogers (Stamford, 1994), pp. 19–41

———, 'Monasteries, Society and Reform in Late Medieval England', in *The Religious Orders in Pre-Reformation England*, ed. J. G. Clark (Woodbridge, 2002), pp. 165–95

Thompson, M. W., 'Associated Monasteries and Castles in the Middle Ages: A Tentative List', *Archaeological Journal*, cxliii (1986), pp. 305–21

Thompson, S. P., *Women Religious: The Founding of English Nunneries after the Norman Conquest* (Oxford, 1991)

Thomson, J. A. F., *The Early Tudor Church and Society* (London, 1993)

Thurlby, M., 'The Romanesque Priory Church of St Michael at Ewenny', *Journal of the Society of Architectural Historians*, xlvii (1988), pp. 281–94

———, 'The West Front of Binham Priory, Norfolk, and the Beginnings of Bar Tracery in England', in *England in the Thirteenth Century*, ed. W. M. Ormrod (Stamford, 1991), pp. 155–65

Thurlow, G., *Great Yarmouth Priory and Parish Church* (Great Yarmouth, 1961)

Tillotson, J. H., *Marrick Priory: A Nunnery in Late Medieval Yorkshire*, Borthwick Paper, no. LXXV (1989)

Todd, J. M., 'St Bega: Cult, Fact and Legend', *Transactions of the Cumberland and Westmorland Antiquarian and Archaeological Society*, new series, lxxx (1980), pp. 23–35

Trinick, G. E. M., *St Anthony's Church, St Anthony-in-Roseland, Cornwall* (Churches Conservation Trust, 1999)

Tudor, V. M., 'St Godric of Finchale and St Bartholomew of Farne', in *Benedict's Disciples*, ed. D. H. Farmer (Leominster, 1980), pp. 195–211

———, 'The Cult of St Cuthbert in the Twelfth Century: The Evidence of Reginald of Durham', in *St Cuthbert, His Cult and His Community to AD 1200*, ed. G. Bonner, D. Rollason and C. Stancliffe (Woodbridge, 1989), pp. 447–67

Turbervill, J. P., *Ewenny Priory: Monastery and Fortress* (London, 1901)

Vale, M. G., *Piety, Charity and Literacy among the Yorkshire Gentry, 1370–1480*, Borthwick Paper, no. I (1976)

Vallance, A., *Greater English Church Screens* (London, 1947)

Vaughan, R., 'The Election of Abbots at St Albans in the Thirteenth and Fourteenth Centuries', *Proceedings of the Cambridge Antiquarian Society*, xlvii (1953), pp. 1–12

Vickers, K. H., *Humphrey Duke of Gloucester* (London 1907)

Victoria History of the Counties of England, ed. W. H. Page (Oxford and London, 1900–)

Waites, B., 'The Monastic Settlement of North-East Yorkshire', *YAJ*, xl (1959–62), pp. 478–95

——, 'The Monastic Grange as a Factor in the Settlement of North-East Yorkshire', *YAJ*, xl (1959–62), pp. 627–56

Walker, D., 'Brecon Priory in the Middle Ages', in *Links with the Past: Swansea and Brecon Historical Essays*, ed. O. W. Jones and D. Walker (Llandybie, 1974), pp. 37–66

Warren, N. B., *Spiritual Economies. Female Monasticism in Later Medieval England* (Philadelphia, 2001)

Watkins, A., 'Merevale Abbey in the Late 1490s', *Warwickshire History*, ix (1994), pp. 87–104

——, 'Maxstoke Priory in the Fifteenth Century: the development of an estate economy in the Forest of Arden', *Warwickshire History*, x (1996), pp. 3–18

——, 'Landowners and their Estates in the Forest of Arden in the Fifteenth Century', *Agricultural History Review*, xlv (1997), pp. 18–33

Webb, D., *Pilgrimage in Medieval England* (London, 2000)

Welch, C. E., 'An Early Charter of Ewenny Priory', *National Library of Wales Journal*, x (1957–8), pp. 415–16

West, S. E., 'The Excavation of Walton Priory', *Proceedings of the Suffolk Institute of Archaeology*, xxxiii (1975), pp. 131–52

Westlake, H. F., *Westminster Abbey. The Church, Convent, Cathedral and College of St Peter, Westminster*, 2 vols (London, 1923)

Wethered, F. T. (ed.), *The Lands and Tythes of Hurley Priory, 1086–1535* (Reading, 1909)

Whiting, R., 'Abominable Idols: Images and Image-breaking under Henry VIII', *JEH*, xxxiii (1982), pp. 30–47

Williams, D. H., 'Goldcliff Priory', *The Monmouthshire Antiquary*, iii (1970–1), pp. 37–54

——, *Catalogue of Seals in the National Museum of Wales*, 2 vols (Cardiff, 1993–8)

Williams, G., 'The Church in Glamorgan from the Fourteenth Century to the Reformation', in *Glamorgan County History, III, The Middle Ages*, ed. T. B. Pugh (Cardiff, 1971), pp. 135–66

——, *The Welsh Church from Conquest to Reformation*, 2nd edn (Cardiff, 1976)

——, 'Kidwelly Priory', in *Sir Gâr: Studies in Carmarthenshire History*, ed. H. James, Carmarthenshire Antiquarian Society Monograph Series, IV (1991), pp. 189–204

Williams, W., 'St Benedict of Aniane', *Downside Review*, new series, xxxv (1936), pp. 357–74

Williamson, W. W., 'Saints of Norfolk Rood-Screens and Pulpits', *Norfolk Archaeology*, xxxi (1955–7), pp. 299–346

Wilson, J., 'The Foundation of the Austin Priories of Nostell and Scone', *Scottish Historical Review*, vii (1910), pp. 141–59

Wood, S., *English Monasteries and their Patrons in the Thirteenth Century* (Oxford, 1955)

Wood-Legh, K., *Perpetual Chantries in Britain* (Cambridge, 1965)

Woodward, G. W. O., *The Dissolution of the Monasteries* (London, 1966)

Wormald, F., *English Benedictine Kalendars after AD 1100*, 2 vols, Henry Bradshaw Society, lxxvii, lxxxi (1939–46)

——, 'The Sherborne "Chartulary" ', in *Fritz Saxl 1890–1948: A Volume of Memorial Essays from his friends in England*, ed. D. J. Gordon (London, 1957), pp. 101–19

Yaxley, S., *Wymondham Abbey before the Dissolution: The Episcopal Visitations of 1492–1532* (Dereham, 1986)

Yeo, G., *The Monks of Cowick* (Exeter, 1987)

Youings, J., *The Dissolution of the Monasteries* (London, 1971)

——, 'The Monasteries', in *Rural Society: Landowners, Peasants and Labourers 1500–1750*, ed. C. Clay (Cambridge, 1990), pp. 71–120

Youngs, D., 'Estate Management, Investment and the Gentleman Landlord in Later Medieval England', *Historical Research*, lxxiii (2000), pp. 124–41

Zeepvat, R. J., 'Excavations at the Site of St Mary's Priory and St John's Church, Hertford', *Hertfordshire Archaeology*, xii (1994–6), pp. 41–76

Unpublished Theses

Clark, J. G., 'Intellectual Life at the Abbey of St Albans and the Nature of Monastic Learning in England c.1350–c.1440: the Work of Thomas Walsingham in Context', Oxford D.Phil. (1997)

Hodge, C. E., 'The Abbey of St Albans under John of Whethamstede', Manchester Ph.D. (1933)

Impey, E., 'The Origins and Development of Non-Conventual Monastic Dependencies in England and Normandy, 1000–1350', 2 vols, Oxford D.Phil. (1991)

Luxford, J., 'The Patronage of Benedictine Art and Architecture in the West of England during the Later Middle Ages (1300–1540)', Cambridge Ph.D. (2002)

Mackie, F. P., 'The Clerical Population of the Province of York: An Edition of the Clerical Poll Tax Enrolments 1377–81', 2 vols, York D.Phil. (1998)

McKinley, R., 'The Cartulary of Breedon Priory', Manchester MA (1950)

Selway, K. E., 'The Role of Eton College and King's College, Cambridge in the Polity of the Lancastrian Monarchy', Oxford D.Phil. (1993)

Still, M. A., 'The Abbey of St Albans in the First Half of the Fourteenth Century', Leeds Ph.D. (1997)

Index

NB. Page numbers in bold type refer to entries in tables or appendices.

Other Volumes in
Studies in the History of Medieval Religion